THE SCIENCE AND ARCHAEOLOGY OF MATERIALS

The Science and Archaeology of Materials is set to become the definitive work in the archaeology of material. Henderson's highly illustrated work is an accessible textbook which will be essential reading for all practical archaeologists and students.

With clear sections on a wide range of materials including pottery, glass, metals and stone, this work examines the very foundations of archaeological study. *The Science and Archaeology of Materials* provides a clear and up-to-date description of how these materials were exploited, modified and manufactured in prehistoric and historic periods. The wide range of case studies provide chronological and geographical examples of how scientific and archaeological aspects can and do interact. The following case studies are included:

- Roman pale green and highly decorated glass
- seventeenth-century glass in Britain and Europe
- the effect of the introduction of the wheel on pottery technology
- the technology of celadon ceramics
- early copper metallurgy in the Middle East
- chemical analysis and lead isotope analysis of British Bronzes
- early copper alloy metallurgy in Thailand
- the chemical analysis of obsidian and its distribution
- the origin of the Stonehenge Bluestones.

This book shows how archaeology and science interact in different ways. Modern scientific techniques have provided data which, when set within a fully integrated archaeological context, have the potential of contributing to mainstream archaeology. This holistic approach generates a range of connections between archaeological and scientific research, which benefits both areas and will enrich archaeological study in the future.

Julian Henderson is Professor of Archaeological Science at the University of Nottingham.

THE SCIENCE AND ARCHAEOLOGY OF MATERIALS

An investigation of inorganic materials

Julian Henderson

London and New York

First published 2000 by Routledge
11 New Fetter Lane, London EC4P 4EE

Simultaneously published in the USA and Canada
by Routledge
29 West 35th Street, New York, NY 10001

Routledge is an imprint of the Taylor & Francis Group

Typeset in Garamond by Florence Production Ltd, Stoodleigh, Devon
Printed and bound in Great Britain by Bell & Bain Ltd, Glasgow

British Library Cataloguing in Publication Data
A catalogue record for this book is available from the British Library

Library of Congress Cataloging in Publication Data
Henderson, Julian, 1953–
The science and archaeology of materials : an investigation of inorganic materials / Julian
Henderson.
p. cm.
Includes bibliographical references and index.
ISBN 0–415–19933–6   ISBN 0–415–19933–4 (pbk.)
1. Archaeological chemistry—Methodology.   2. Archaeology—Methodology.   3. Inorganic
compounds.   4. Ceramics—Analysis.   5. Metal-work—Analysis.   6. Stone implements—
Analysis.   I. Title.

CC79.C5 H46 2000 930.1′028–dc21
00–030830

ISBN 0–415–19933–6 (hbk)
ISBN 0–415–19934–4 (pbk)

For Yvette and Charlotte

CONTENTS

FIGURES AND TABLES

Figures

Tables

PREFACE

A primary source of information used by archaeologists to understand past societies is the material culture (i.e. artefacts in the broadest sense) that survives. A starting point for the study of material culture in archaeology is the investigation of the *chaine operatoire* or life cycle of the surviving artefacts from the procurement and processing of the raw materials, through the fabrication and decoration of the artefacts, to their distribution, use, reuse and discard.

In the study of the surviving material culture, the physical sciences have a major contribution to make. This contribution can usefully be divided into two stages. The first stage consists of the *reconstruction* of the production technology, trade and exchange, and function in use associated with the artefacts. The subsequent second stage is then concerned with the *interpretation* of the *chaine operatoire* thus reconstructed, in order to obtain a better understanding of the people associated with the artefacts. This interpretation involves attempting to answer questions relating to how a new technology was discovered and why it was adopted at a particular time and place; and why a particular production technology, mode of production (i.e. household, workshop or factory), pattern of trade and exchange, and function in use were chosen.

The effective study of the *chaine operatoire* of past material cultures requires a holistic approach, taking account of the fact that the production, distribution and use associated with a particular artefact type are firmly embedded within the wider environmental, technological, economic, social, political and ideo-logical contexts and practices. Thus, one needs to consider, first, how these contexts impinge on (i.e. both constrain and drive) production, distribution and use and, conversely, how these latter impact back on the contexts. Second, one needs to consider the interdependency between these different stages in the *chaine operatoire*.

The current textbook strongly advocates such a holistic approach. Starting with a summary of the methods of analysis, there then follow four chapters considering the principal inorganic material types (i.e. glass, ceramics, metals and stone) exploited in antiquity. The particular strength of these chapters is that, following a description of the procurement and processing of raw materials and the fabrication of artefacts, each presents a series of carefully selected and in-depth case studies. These case studies span the investigation of the reasons for technological innovation, choice and change, as well as distribution (i.e. provenance) studies in which emphasis is put on the role of trade and exchange in helping to bring about technological, economic, social, political and ideological change. In addition, the degree of craft specialisation, the scale of production and the way in which production was organised are considered. The importance, in the study of technological innovation, of taking into account, first, the contact between different technologies and, second, thesocial and cultural as well as the more practical uses of the resulting material or artefact, is also emphasised. Finally, the crucial role played in such studies of combining field survey for raw material sources and the excavation of production sites with laboratory analyses of raw materials and industrial debris as well as finished artefacts is highlighted.

No previous textbook covering the scientific examination of archaeological materials has ever taken this holistic approach. Bowman (1991) in *Science and the Past* and Lambert (1997) in *Traces of the Past* provide comprehensive overviews of the subject. However, having been written as much for a general, as for an academic audience, neither include in-depth case studies in which *interpretation*, rather than just *reconstruction*, is fully considered. Pollard and Heron (1996) in *Archaeological Chemistry* provide an extremely valuable review of the basic science underlying selected topics relating to the scientific investigation of archaeological materials. However, again, the case studies presented fail to take fully into account the fact that production and distribution are firmly embedded within the wider environmental, technological, economic, social, political and ideological contexts and practices.

Thus, the present book represents an extremely valuable addition to archaeological science literature, both for the teaching of undergraduates and for postgraduates considering topics for MSc and PhD research. By combining interpretation with reconstruction, *The Science and Archaeology of Materials* should contribute towards achieving what must be seen as the final goal of materials studies which is 'not to describe microscale prehistoric *activities*, but to understand microscale social *processes*' (Dobres and Hoffman 1994: 213). Further, this book should help to bring nearer the time when the scientific examination of archaeological materials is not taught as a separate topic but is included within standard period and regional archaeological courses, with the results of such studies being incorporated into the associated archaeological textbooks.

Michael Tite
Oxford

References

Bowman, S.G.E. (ed.) (1991) *Science and the Past*, London: British Museum Publications.

Dobres, M.-A. and Hoffman, C.R. (1994) 'Social agency and the dynamics of prehistoric technology', *Journal of Archaeological Method and Theory*, 1: 211–58.

Lambert, J.B. (1997) *Traces of the Past*, Reading, MA: Addison-Wesley.

Pollard, M. and Heron, C. (1996) *Archaeological Chemistry*, Cambridge: The Royal Society of Chemistry.

ACKNOWLEDGEMENTS

In writing this book a variety of people have helped by reading through whole chapters and parts of chapters, and providing me with helpful comments. In this respect I am especially grateful to the following for reading through and commenting on sections of the book: Carol Allen (Chapter 4), Ron Firman (Chapter 6), Gavin Kinsley (Chapter 4), David Knight (Chapter 4), Matthew Ponting (Chapter 5) and Yvette Sablerolles (Chapter 3).

I am very grateful to Sabrina Rastelli who was very helpful in supplying me with her translations of Chinese reports on celadon production. I am also grateful to the following with whom I have discussed various aspects of the book at different times: James Allen, Robert H. Brill, Keith Challis, Chris Cumberpatch, Peter Crewe, Sheila Elsdon, Hamish Forbes, Ian Freestone, Mark Pearce, St John Simpson and Roger Wilson. I am also happy to record my thanks to the Director General of Antiquities and Museums for Syria, Sultan Moheisin for a licence to excavate in al-Raqqa, Syria and to those, too numerous to mention, who have taken part in the al-Raqqa Ancient Industry Project and have provided some of the 'raw materials' for this book. I am grateful to David Taylor for completing a number of illustrations and to Martin Lloyd-Ashton for taking some of the photographs.

Over the years I have benefited enormously from discussions with the late Martyn Jope, with Michael Tite and with Stanley Warren who have, together, shaped my approach(es) to science and archaeology. I am grateful to the following for permission to reproduce photographs/figures or versions of figures which appear in this book: David Peacock and Pearson Education Ltd (Figure 1.1); John Collis (Figure 1.2); Perkin Elmer (Figure 2.1); The British Museum (Figures 3.7, 3.29, 3.31, 4.12, 5.23, 5.24, 5.25, 5.34, 5.35 and 6.2); Yael Goren-Rosen (Figure 3.16); Maria Mendera (Fig. 3.17); The Society for Post-Medieval Archaeology (Figure 3.18); Joan Oates and the Macdonald Institute, University of Cambridge (Figure 3.27); Michael Tite (*Archaeometry*) (Figure 3.32); Gladys Weinberg and the University of Missouri Press (3.34); Yvette Sablerolles (Figure 3.37); Roger Wilson (Figures 4.5 and 4.6); Barry Evison for the opportunity to photograph him at work (Figures 4.2a, 4.2b, 4.7, 4.8 and 4.9); English Heritage, National Monuments record (Figure 4.11: 5, 6, and 7); Nigel Wood (Figure 4.15); David Knight (Figure 4.18), Sheila Elson (Figure 4.19); Elaine Morris (Figures 4.20, 4.21, 4.22 and 4.23); The Prehistoric Society (Figures 4.23, 6.5, 6.6 and 6.7); Alan Vince (Figures 4.24, 4.25, 4.26, 4.27 and 4.28); Yani Petsopoulos and the Alexandria Press (Figures 4.41, 4.42 and 4.48); Matthew Ponting (Figures 5.2, 5.8 and 5.9); David Jenkins and Andy Lewis (Figure 5.4); Keith Challis (Figures 5.11 and 5.12); Sariel Shalev and Peter Northover (Figure 5.19); Russell Adams (Figure 5.20); Andreas Hauptmann (Figure 5.21); The Ban Chiang Project, University of Pennsylvania Press and Joyce White (Figure 5.28); The MIT Press (Figure 5.29); Peter Crew (Figures 5.30, 5.31, 5.32); Dr Cosigny (Figures 6.3 and 6.4); Colin Renfrew and Thames and Hudson (Figure 6.6), Routledge (Figure 6.8); Academic Press Ltd (Figures 6.9 and 6.10).

1

INTRODUCTION

This book deals with ancient (inorganic) materials in a range of ways. In writing this book my aim was to relate as closely as possible scientific aspects of materials to archaeological aspects of their study in an attempt to fill a 'gap' in the literature. It is a foregone conclusion that a poorly conducted scientific enquiry generates second rate or inconsequential results, just as a poorly structured set of archaeological research objectives can also lead to ill-considered or inconsequential conclusions, so obviously both should be conducted at a high standard. This distinction between the scientific and archaeological aspects of archaeological science *ought* to be a false one: ideally they should form a seamless continuum in which both contribute in meaningful ways, but this is rarely the case.

A chapter on the principal techniques of chemical analysis is provided, which focuses especially on those mentioned in the rest of the book (Chapter 2). The remainder of the book is structured so that each chapter includes a definition of the materials considered (glass, pottery, metal and stone), followed by the ways in which the materials are obtained from the environment, how they may be refined, and, in the case of ceramics, glass and metals, how they were transformed by heat in kilns and furnaces. A range of specific examples of raw material sources/quarries/mines and the basic reasons why the materials were transformed by heat are discussed. The structures of the installations in which these transformations occurred, the kilns and furnaces, are also discussed; the fuel necessary, the gaseous atmosphere produced and the resulting effect on the materials is described.

The initial sections of each chapter are intended to provide the 'bare bones' for later sections in each chapter. They are not intended to be exhaustive; a book could easily be written about (almost) any single aspect considered – and it should be noted that only *inorganic* materials are dealt with here. Nevertheless, the intention is to provide a rounded picture, and within the scope of the book the evidence for the impact of industries on the environment is also considered such as pollution and the impact on vegetation as a result of obtaining fuel by clearance or woodland management (for example).

Although some aspects of archaeology are touched on in initial parts of each chapter, a fuller integration of scientific investigations with the archaeology of production sites and beyond is presented in the second part of each chapter in the form of a series of case studies. Each case study, which builds on the information presented in the first parts of the chapter, provides a different set of links between archaeology and science, depending on the material concerned and the social, economic or political spheres in which the industries were pursued. A different set of case studies could easily have been chosen and somewhat different forms of integration between archaeology and science might have been achieved. However, the examples that have been chosen are intended to highlight quite specific relationships between the industries concerned and the context in which the materials were produced.

The discussion of each case is also, in part, dependent on the breadth and depth of the investigations which have been carried out in each area of study. Scientific investigation of early Islamic glass production relies on excavations of an industrial complex in Syria which revealed a glass workshop with furnaces; scientific analysis of glass from the site attempts to investigate 'workshop' assemblages of glass addressing the problems and limitations of proof of potential recycling as opposed to evidence of local production among such assemblages. In the case studies of pottery, the manufacture of Chinese celadon ware has been chosen because of the comprehensive survival and excavation of pottery kilns and associated complete working areas, coupled with the scientific characterisation of the pottery produced and other ceramics used in the manufacturing process. In total contrast, the characterisation of early medieval pottery in England has been selected even though it might be assumed that there would be little mileage in attempting such a characterisation. Early medieval pottery fabric is often described as 'unpromising' from a petrological point of view. Nevertheless, not only is it possible to show how the image of 'household' production for the immediate demands of the local community had to be revised following this work, it also serves to highlight the ways in which pottery distributions changed with the emergence of urban life later in the first millennium. In addition, a post-processual interpretation of characterised early medieval pottery is presented. The example of early (Bronze Age) copper exploitation in Jordan has been selected because it provides a perfect example of where archaeological excavation of early copper mines and processing areas has been investigated and linked to the scientific investigation of the emergence of the earliest copper metallurgy in the world. The introduction of iron for the first time is used as a means of discussing the complexities of technological innovation before focusing on a case study of an exemplary excavation of an iron production site and experimental work which is based on some of the archaeological findings. In the section on stone, the continuing debate over the transportation of the Bluestones to Stonehenge hinges on the interpretation of some thought-provoking geological, landscape and scientific research (Chapter 6).

Each case study therefore provides an opportunity to examine different relationships between archaeology and science which, in some cases, go well beyond a functional interpretation of various material uses. The use of scientific techniques cannot always provide the answers to questions about how materials were produced and used. Much depends on the political, religious, economic and social environments in which the artisans worked. These parameters would clearly have affected the procedures used in ancient production processes. There is every reason to suspect that 'ancient chemists' existed, who studied the properties of the materials they made and that those properties were affected by a change in the raw materials they used. Raw materials would have been recognised by their physical characteristics (colour and perhaps hardness or fracture characteristics). Again, when reading this, there is the danger that one is drawn into an assumption that stone with better fracture characteristics was quarried at the 'expense' of a nearby stone type shown to have poorer fracture characteristics – but, in the case of polished stone axes, this is clearly shown not to be the case. Over and above the study of the use of stone of particular tensile strengths for the manufacture of Neolithic stone axes, the results have shown that some stone of inferior fracture characteristics was distributed over the widest zone. This is a good example of how easy it might be to make false assumptions about the use of raw materials in the past based solely on their material properties and to ignore aspects of human behaviour which determine their use and which are not obviously connected to positivism. The perception of raw material characteristics and the potential importance of the locations where they were quarried can therefore play an important part in raw material selection. The Chinese even distinguished between 'lovely metal' (bronze) and 'ugly metal' (iron) which may have determined the uses to which they were put.

Although 'ancient chemists' would not have been aware of specific chemical impurities which might have affected the behaviour of materials at high temperatures, such impurities may have affected the colour of the material. By working a particular material over generations there is every reason to accept the hypothesis that artisans would have been able to locate the same material and prepare it in the same way each time so as to recreate, and predict, the same working properties. Ancient technologists, if not able to 'dissect' a material into its chemical/mineralogical components would have had a highly developed sense of sight (colour changes, material transformation), smell (a particular gaseous atmosphere or even of a raw material), feel (the coarseness of a material) and taste.

Museum collections used to be displayed in a way which tended to split materials into categories; this categorisation would, in some cases, be related to the ways in which materials were stored and there-fore documented in the museum. In writing this book one of the areas which has been highlighted is not so much the differences between different production industries, but the areas of overlap between them. Ancient high-temperature industries (pyro-technology) have a range of characteristics in common. The consideration of using specific bricks to withstand the temperatures of smelting metals or melting glass in furnaces, or firing pottery in a kiln will had areas in common; the use of specific types of fuel at different times in a firing cycle was knowledge which would be unlikely to have remained 'tied' to a specific industry; the sources of silica to temper pottery, provide a 'flux' for metal-smelting and to make glass are liable to have been a common resource; the exploitation of minerals to produce metal, colour glass and colour glazes is yet another example of where there *may* have been overlaps in the exploitation of raw materials. These are just a few examples of where communication between groups of artisans may have led to cooperation and articulation with specific routes of trade or exchange. However, at the same time there is also a potential tension in which such cooperation may *not* have occurred. A range of social, political and ritual factors may have determined tight norms which affected the development of industries in which technological aspects of particular specialisations may *not* have been shared. There is also the possibility that some aspects of industries may well have overlapped with areas of domestic life and therefore have been perceived as 'less different', without the application of strict social constrictions.

Clearly it is possible to be positivist in each case and accept Auguste Compte's form of empiricism, but in so doing the affects of strict social norms on the development of technologies, for example, are ignored. Why, for example, was a glassy substance made and incorporated in faience long before glass was made separately and made into objects? The temperatures necessary for melting glass had been achieved in the manufacture of copper alloys thousands of years before. Lemonnier (1993: 3–4) notes that

> Ideas about technical elements, actors, processes and results have thus to be compatible with, as well as part of other broader social relations and logic that appear to influence and shape the representations directly involved in a human group's technology and, therefore, in the production of artefacts and in technical actions themselves.

Archaeological and archaeological–science investigations can begin to answer some of these questions, but another important source of information comes from the historical evidence. If texts are available, they can be used to augment the scientific findings – or should the problems be tackled in the reverse order? As in all of the case studies reported in this book, one of the primary areas which one is attempting to contribute to is a definition of the niche, or role, that the industry and its products played in society; the social and economic systems of Anglo-Saxon and early medieval Europe were worlds apart from those of Ottoman Turkey, so there would have been both similarities and significant differences in ways in which the organisation and function of the pottery-making industries articulated with society.

Clearly the social and economic context in which production occurred will have affected the degrees of industrial specialisation, discussed in detail by a range of authors, but perhaps the first comprehensive consideration was Peacock's (1982) study of specialised production, particularly the Roman pottery industry, based not only on the intensity and scale of production, but also on the degree of participation by elites or the government (see Figure 1.1). This is obviously a model which was designed to

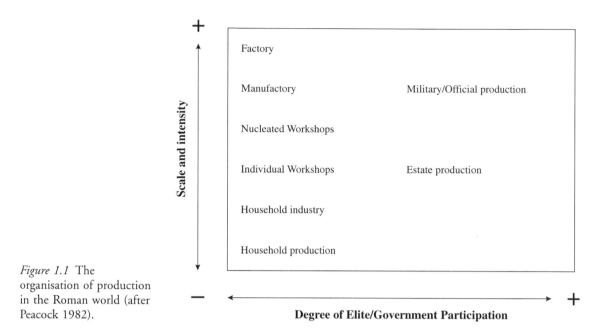

Figure 1.1 The organisation of production in the Roman world (after Peacock 1982).

apply to the 'regimented' Roman society; it does however draw together several important *interrelated* factors. This model of production went beyond that of van der Leeuw (1977) in which intensity and scale were perceived as being inseparable. The location of industries and its relationship to the structure/development of society, including the centralisation of industries (see Figure 1.2) has also been addressed by a range of researchers (Collis 1984; Costin 1991; Henderson 1991) and they have stressed the importance of location of industries in the landscape.

The research concerned directly with the chemical characterisation and analytical investigation of raw materials, products and by-products linked to a high-temperature industry can be summarised. Figure 1.3 provides a summary of the stages at which archaeological materials can be investigated scientifically, including the important selection of materials from different types of archaeological context. Scientific analysis can be considered as a basis of the scientific investigation of excavated remains of industries and should also fall within the broader consideration of ancient production in which the *form* of the industry is considered. An attempt to chemically characterise raw materials should be made. Often this can present practical

problems. Sampling of metal ore lodes, for example, can be difficult because they are chemically and structurally heterogeneous (Ericson *et al.* 1982; Craddock 1989: 195). If the ancient mining site can be located, analysis of any by-products of purification processes should be attempted. Secondly, analysis of artefacts from a production site, such as crucibles, furnace linings, slags and moulds, should be carefully planned, paying attention to the archaeological contexts which produce them and where they slot in to the interrelated procedures for which there is evidence (Craddock 1989: 198ff.). The scientific investigation of the evidence for an industry must also include a physico-chemical investigation of the structures connected to the industry (such as kilns and furnaces), the physical distribution of chemically-defined raw materials, by-products and products within the site in order to attempt to define all areas of industrial activity, the chronology of production and its possible phases; and also the relationship of style to the technology and typology of the artefacts concerned.

An attempt to assess the scale of the industry is also important, since this is involved in a full definition of the organisation of the industry at the site and its relationship to other industries on the same

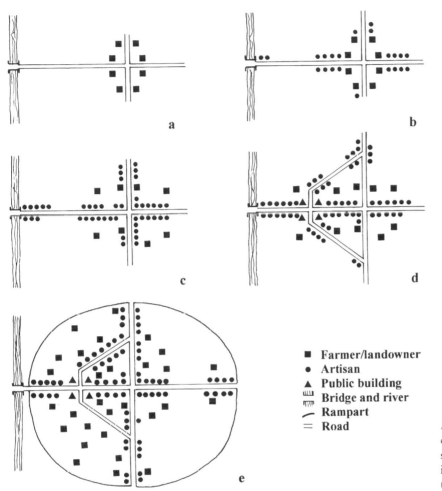

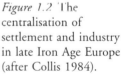

■ Farmer/landowner
● Artisan
▲ Public building
▥ Bridge and river
⌒ Rampart
= Road

Figure 1.2 The centralisation of settlement and industry in late Iron Age Europe (after Collis 1984).

site and at other sites. More broadly, the industry should be considered in terms of its role in the settlement, whether its function can be considered to have a high status, producing prestige artefacts, or a relatively low status, producing utilitarian artefacts, and whether production achieves its importance from its rarity in a regional or territorial setting. Linked to these considerations are the value of the material and the degrees of specialisation and/or standardisation achieved within both local and regional settings. In addition, there is the interpretation of the distribution patterns of chemically characterised products. Does the distribution provide evidence for an interaction zone, and does it reflect the existence of tribal or other political boundaries?

Behind the archaeological evidence for the crafts and industries are the people who actually carried out the hard work. Artisans tend to be mainly tied to the processes involved in production; the other components of the system are distribution and consumption. Various authors have considered artisans from the perspectives of their roles and status in society (Forbes 1971: 66–8). For example, in Iron Age Europe artisans have been discussed in terms of the structure of the society in which they operated, including the patron–client relationship, and the type of artefacts they made (Scott 1978: 224, n.10; Alexander 1981: 65; Champion 1985). Historical evidence of the relative status of artisans in early Christian Irish society at least 800 years later has even

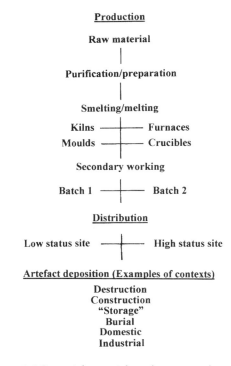

Production

Raw material

Purification/preparation

Smelting/melting

Kilns ———|——— Furnaces
Moulds ———|——— Crucibles

Secondary working

Batch 1 ———|——— Batch 2

Distribution

Low status site ———|——— High status site

Artefact deposition (Examples of contexts)

Destruction
Construction
"Storage"
Burial
Domestic
Industrial

Figure 1.3 Potential materials and processes that can be investigated scientifically. Site types and archaeological context types should determine the sampling strategy.

been compared to later Iron Age European artisans (Gosden 1985: 481; Hingley 1997: 12) in which little distinction is made between artisans involved in making high status and low status objects. In any case it would be a coincidence if the relative value (Henderson 1991: 110) or status of products (in whatever way they are measured) had remained the same over a period of more than 800 years, especially when it is difficult to show direct similarities between excavated archaeological sites, including evidence for production, in early Christian Ireland and later Iron Age Europe. In addition, the possibility that artisans of low status made objects which were associated with high status individuals cannot be ruled out. Such societal considerations must have applied to any production sphere.

Costin (1991: 9) has produced a useful set of interrelated parameters which apply to the ways in which production was organised (see Figure 1.4). These, too, allow us to think about production in a

more inclusive way than just by using a purely technological approach. Within this consideration of the organisation of production and the role of artisans is something that occupies archaeologists' pens to a high level: what do we mean by more or less specialised? Without getting too deeply involved, specialisation of production infers that a technological development has occurred against a background of a less specialised technology. For example, Rice (1981) has listed some of the characteristics which she considers to be relevant to the definition of a (more) specialised Central American ceramic industry:

1. a greater exploitation of specific raw materials (clays, tempers) allied with increased standardisation of paste composition;
2. a more conservative use of accepted conventions as to form and decoration ('increased standardisation');
3. a wider distribution of increasingly standardised products;
4. greater skill in production technology.

These characteristics form a useful range which can be generally applied to the definition of industrial specialisation. One consideration which must form part of any incipient specialisation is the appropriate context in which innovation occurred (Renfrew 1978). The conditions in which experimentation occurred, as opposed to a conservative use of accepted technological conventions, are likely to have varied, but are a critical component in any change in the established routines developed.

This book provides a wide range of examples of the ways in which ancient materials have been processed by man. It is hoped that it will highlight some of the approaches that researchers have taken to the study of ancient materials and stimulate scientists, archaeologists and archaeological-scientists to pursue research in this enormous area. One of the aims of this book is to show just how misplaced the following statement by Dunnell (1993: 165) is: 'Archaeometric contributions too are no longer confined to arcane appendices. While its visibility and context may have grown, it is not clear that the field has matured in any significant way'.

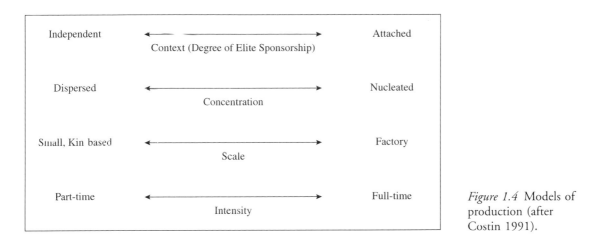

Figure 1.4 Models of production (after Costin 1991).

References

Alexander, J.A. (1981) 'The coming of Iron-Using to Britain' in H. Haefner (ed.), *Frühes Eisen in Europa, Festschrift Walter Guyan*, 57–67, Schaffhausen: Symposiums des Comité pour la Sidérurgie ancienne de l'UISPP Meili.

Champion, T.C. (1985) 'Written sources and the study of the European Iron Age' in T.C. Champion and J.V.S. Megaw (eds), *Settlement and Society, aspects of West European prehistory in the first millennium B.C.*, Leicester: Leicester University Press, pp. 9–22.

Collis, J.R. (1984) *Oppida, earliest towns north of the Alps*, Sheffield: Department of Archaeology and Prehistory.

Costin, C. (1991) 'Issues in defining documenting, and explaining the organization of production' in M.B. Schiffer (ed.), *Archaeological Method and Theory 3*, Tucson: University of Arizona Press, pp. 1–56.

Craddock, P. (1989) 'The scientific investigation of early mining and metallurgy' in J. Henderson (ed.), *Scientific analysis in archaeology, and its interpretation*, Oxford University Committee for Archaeology Monographs No. 19 and University of Los Angeles Institute of Archaeology Research Tools 5: 178–210.

Dunnell, R.C. (1993) 'Comments and reviews', *Archaeomaterials* 7, 1: 161–5.

Ericson, J.E., Pandolfi, L. and Patterson, C. (1982) 'Pyrotechnology of copper extraction: Methods of detection and implications', in T.E. Wertime and S.F. Wertime (eds), *Early Pyrotechnology, the evolution of the first fire-using industries*, Washington, DC: Smithsonian Institution Press, pp. 193–204.

Forbes, R.J. (1971 [1964]) *Studies in Ancient Technology*, volume VIII, Leiden: Brill.

Gosden, C. (1985) 'Gifts and kin in Early Iron Age Europe', *Man* 20: 475–93.

Henderson, J. (1991) 'Industrial specialization in late Iron Age Britain and Europe', *Archaeological Journal* 148: 104–48.

Hingley, R. (1997) 'Iron, ironworking and regeneration: a study of the symbolic meaning of metalworking in Iron Age Britain', in A. Gwilt and C. Haselgrove (eds), *Reconstructing Iron Age Societies*, Oxford: Oxbow Books, pp. 9–18.

Lemonnier, P. (1993) (ed.) *Technological Choices Transformation in Material Cultures since the Neolithic*, London and New York: Routledge.

Peacock, D.P.S. (1982) *Pottery in the Roman world: an ethnoarchaeological approach*, London: Longman.

Renfrew, C. (1978) 'The anatomy of innovation' in D. Green, C. Haselgrove and M. Spriggs (eds), *Social Organisation and Settlement: contributions from Anthropology, Archaeology and Geography, Part I*, British Archaeological Reports, International Series 47, Oxford: British Archaeological Reports, pp. 87–117.

Rice, P.M. (1981) 'Evolution of specialised pottery production: a trial model', *Current Anthropology* 22, 3: 219–40.

Scott, B.G. (1978) 'Iron "slave-collars" from Lagore Crannog, Co. Westmeath', *Proceedings of the Royal Irish Academy* 78C: 213–30.

van der Leeuw, S. (1977) 'Towards a study of the economics of pottery making' in B.L. van Beek, R.W. Brant and W. Groenman-van Waateringe (eds), *Ex Horreo*, Amsterdam: University of Amsterdam Press, pp. 68–76.

2

TECHNIQUES OF SCIENTIFIC ANALYSIS

2.1 Introduction

Early analytical work of archaeological materials began in Renaissance Italy and by the eighteenth century, King George III's assay master, Mr Alchorn, analysed Irish Bronze Age swords. Martin Klaproth, a famous chemist, published chemical analyses of Roman glass and bronze mirrors (Klaproth 1798). Other eminent scientists, such as Michael Faraday (1791–1867) and Humphrey Davy (1778–1829) were also involved in early analytical work on archaeological materials. Davy chemically analysed 'Egyptian blue' and an opaque red vitreous material labelled red enamel. However, even into the early 1970s there was concern over the level of accuracy achieved and that inadequate sampling procedures had been used (Organ 1971). There can be no doubt that those involved in archaeological science research have now addressed these concerns in detail, even though the level achieved and the degree of integration between science and archaeology is apparently unacceptable for some (Dunnell 1993).

Michael Tite's book, *Methods of Physical Examination in Archaeology* (1972), provides an excellent description of analytical techniques used in archaeology up to that time; Mark Pollard and Carl Heron's *Archaeological Chemistry* (1996), provides a clear and more up-to-date account of analytical techniques used in the investigation of archaeological materials.

This chapter is only concerned with the techniques which are relevant to the rest of the book.

Hence, a description of the techniques used in the investigation of organic analysis has been deliberately omitted. The early techniques used for the analysis of archaeological materials involved destruction of the artefact or, at least, the removal of samples.

Since *spectrometry* forms the basis of most analytical techniques to be described it must first be defined. Spectrometry is a form of measurement in which an exciting radiation (for example X-rays, gamma rays) is directed at a sample (whether in solid or liquid form) and the interaction generates wavelengths of energy which are characteristic of the material. If the exciting radiation is of a sufficient energy, such as X-rays or gamma rays, ionisations characteristic of the atoms of the material will occur, which, in turn, will yield particles characteristic of the material. In the case of X-ray spectrometry the result of bombarding with primary X-rays a sample of lead-rich soda-lime silica glass, for example, is to produce secondary X-rays of sodium, calcium, silicon and lead (among others). As a result of using spectrometry a spectrum of energy of the characteristic particles (each of which has its characteristic energies) is produced. If light or infrared or ultraviolet radiation is used, the interaction results in the absorption of a proportion of the spectrum of the exciting radiation and a reflection of the balance of the wavelengths. Both the absorption and reflection of proportions of the wavelengths are characteristic of the material; with light the characteristic is the observed colour.

2.2 Destructive techniques

One of the first techniques that was used for the analysis of archaeological materials to any extent was *arc emission spectrometry* (AES). AES was introduced in the 1920s (Ahrens 1954), and continued to be used until *c.* 1970 (Britton and Richards 1969), when more accurate, automated and less destructive techniques were introduced. AES involved using a powdered sample. A graphite electrode was positioned so that an arc occurred between electrode and sample causing the sample to be volatilised and to emit light. The elements present emitted wavelengths which were recorded on a photographic plate. The relative intensities of each line recorded on the photographic plate was measured and could be related to the relative concentrations in the sample; the results were semi-quantitative (*not* quantitative), but did, for example, provide a basis for chemically classifying Egyptian glass (Farnsworth and Ritchie 1938). An early investigation of Roman lead-rich glazes using this analytical technique was carried out by the late E.M. Jope (Jope 1950). Some of the earliest work on the sourcing of obsidian was also carried out using AES (Cann and Renfrew 1964; Renfrew, Dixon and Cann 1966). This analytical technique was time-consuming and destructive. As a result, a relatively small number of analyses were carried out on the materials concerned. In spite of this, some excellent results from obsidian analysis were obtained (see Section 6.6).

A more advanced wet chemical analytical technique is *atomic absorption spectroscopy* (AAS). This technique gradually replaced AES, to the extent that by the early 1970s it had almost totally taken its place. The technique involves very similar principles to those of arc emission spectroscopy (AES). However AAS involves the use of a flame to atomise the sample. The sample (of *c.* 10–20 mg) is dissolved in solution first. The solution is then injected into flames; the kind of gas being burnt depends on the element being analysed. The basis of the technique is that wavelengths of light produced when a particular chemical element is vaporised in the flame are absorbed, and others emitted. It is the absorption of the light wavelengths that is measured. At the same time a hollow cathode lamp shines through the flame onto a slit and a monochromator. The light from the lamp is dispersed into its constituent wavelengths; the wavelength dispersed into the detector depends on the element being analysed. The detector is a photomultiplier which converts light intensity into

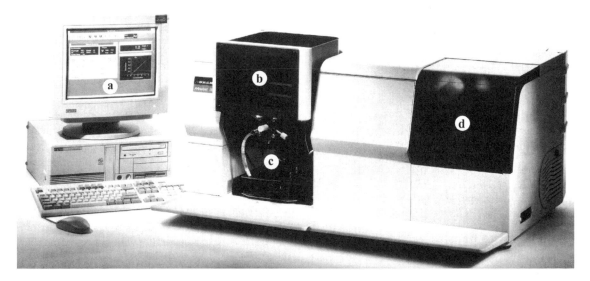

Figure 2.1 An atomic absorption spectrometry system; (a) computer for data processing; (b) flame behind screen; (c) nebuliser; (d) lamp turret. To the left of (d) is the monochromator.

an electrical signal. The difference between the signal with the lamp alone and with the sample added provides a measure of the concentration of the element present. The older instruments produced a graphical printout as a series of peaks above a background energy level; the energy that was absorbed was displayed as a peak. As with AES, atomic absorption spectrometry records the elements present, each with its own characteristic wavelength, usually one at a time, wavelength by wavelength. The spectrometer is set up so that each element can be measured in turn; a number of sub-samples of the sample solution need to be prepared.

AAS is a quantitative technique. By making up a range of solutions for each element, each containing a different concentration of that element, and analysing each in turn the relationship between peak height above background and the concentration of the element present can be achieved. When a sample with an unknown level of that element is analysed its concentration can be plotted on the calibration curve. Detection levels can be achieved of between about 1 and 100 ppm, though this depends on the element sought, the element absorption line concerned and the conditions of analysis. With the introduction of the graphite furnace, the flame no longer plays a part in AAS: the sample solution is injected into a chamber which is heated in a controlled way. This computer automation has provided a much faster processing time for the analysis. As with all analytical techniques AAS is not always plain sailing. For example, the results can suffer from interference between two or more elements if they occur in the sample together and solutions have to be made up in order to assess the extent to which the quantitative results are effected (Hughes *et al*. 1976; Hatcher *et al*. 1995). This has been one of the principal techniques used for the bulk analysis of ancient inorganic materials and has contributed in a significant way. A majority of studies using AAS have focused on the investigation of ancient pottery and metal.

Some fifteen years ago *inductively-coupled plasma emission spectroscopy* (ICPS) was added to the range of analytical techniques in use. This technique is also destructive and, like AES and AAS involves dissolving the sample. Instead of the flame used in

AAS, providing a temperature of *c*. 2000 °C, ICPS atomises the sample at temperatures above 8000 °C in a plasma torch in which argon can be combusted (Heyworth *et al*. 1991). The sample is injected into the flame which then breaks up into its constituent parts. Since the temperatures involved are more than double those used in AAS, this should in theory allow for the determination of the constituents at lower levels and reduce the amount of interference between them. The other advantage of the technique, which had originally been used for research in the geological sciences, was its speed. After calibrating the system, the technique allows the operator to analyse twenty elements simultaneously; normally a single computer-controlled detector can perform the analysis of tens of elements while the sample is being aspirated (Thompson and Walsh 1989).

Inductively-coupled plasma mass spectrometry (ICP-MS) offers the opportunity of both chemically analysing samples and at the same time determining the relative concentrations of isotopes present such as the ratios of lead isotopes (as in lead isotope analysis: see Section 5.9.4). A more recent development is *the addition of laser ablation* to the ICP-MS system. This technique allows us to analyse in quite specific locations on a solid sample. In some ways it is therefore similar to electron microprobe analysis, but it is more sensitive than the latter. A laser beam produces a crater of about 50 μm deep because it vaporises the volume of sample being analysed. One result is that the analysis at that location cannot be repeated (Jarvis *et al*. 1992). This is a powerful microanalytical technique which is increasingly being used in the analysis of archaeological materials. Mallory-Greenough *et al*. (1999) have shown that laser ablation microprobe inductively coupled mass spectrometry is more effective at fingerprinting basalts than conventional electron microprobe analysis.

X-ray diffraction spectrometry (XRD)

This technique can be used to identify crystalline materials unambiguously, or as an assessment of the degree of crystallinity. Whereas the chemical analysis of a material, if destructive, dissolves the material's structure, XRD is a way of identifying the crystals present in stone, metals, ceramics, opaque glasses and opaque glazes. The technique involves firing radiation of a particular wavelength (monochromatic) at the crystalline material which is mounted at a specific angle to the incoming energy. The interaction of the radiation with the crystal(s) produces an X-ray pattern characteristic of the structure of the crystal. Crystals are composed of lattices built up in a regular pattern; their size and spacing is characteristic of the crystal species. The technique produces spectra which sometimes include several peaks for a single crystal. Thus, while it is possible to determine the chemical composition of calcium antimonate, for example, it is only with X-ray diffraction that it is possible to distinguish between two forms of calcium antimonate, $Ca_2Sb_2O_7$ and $Ca_2Sb_2O_6$. In some cases, different species of crystals are formed at different temperatures, so it is important to determine what species are present in order to determine what temperatures were involved. For example, α-quartz is the normal form of silica which occurs in nature. When it is heated to 573±5 °C it is converted to β-quartz. At c. 867 °C β-quartz is converted into another form of silica, tridymite; at 1250 °C cristobalite is formed. These reactions can be slow, a feature which may be of interest to the archaeological-scientist because it shows that the material was held at the temperature before the transformations occurred. In any case since all three crystal types have the same chemical composition   silica — we can only identify the species involved by using X-ray diffraction.

The instrumentation originally involved a camera which took photographs of the patterns of d-spacings created by using this technique; more recently, fully automated equipment has made it possible to use a thin slurry of the material deposited on a slide. The resulting radiation is measured and the spectra fed electronically into a computer which has a library of crystal d-spacings, making it possible to match the unknown pattern to those stored in the computer. In addition it is possible to carry out quantitative assessments of the relative proportions of different crystal species in the sample by examining the relative intensities of the peak heights; this would need to be carried out on several sub-samples of the material being analysed in order to produce a representative picture. Thin-section petrology is a more effective means of carrying out such quantitative work.

Some of the earliest work on the crystalline nature of Egyptian blue was carried out using X-ray diffraction (Jope and Huse 1942). X-ray diffraction was used to investigate heat-treated chert by Weymouth and Mandeville (1975) in order to examine structural changes and the ways they may cause increased ease of chipping. Purdy and Brooks (1971) had already observed a decrease in tensile strength as a result of heating the chert to a minimum of 400 °C. Weymouth and Mandeville showed that, due to a broadening of the X-ray lines in most cases, the crystalline structure of the chert had changed. Physically this infers that there is a decrease in the distance, on average, over which crystals maintain exact three-dimensional periodicity. This could either be due to a decrease in the size of crystals present, caused by the chert breaking up or developing micro-cracks, or alternatively to an effective spread of inter-atomic distances caused by non-uniform local strain. These individual or summed effects are due to micro-cracks or local strains which break up the crystals. X-ray diffraction can therefore offer a physical reason for the reduced tensile strength and increased ease of chipping of chert heated to between 400 °C and 800 °C.

Thin-section petrology

This technique is applied to samples of pottery and other ceramic materials (crucibles, bricks, stone, slags). It should be borne in mind that it can contribute a part of the full description of fabric analysis which should include the arrangement, size, shape, frequency and composition of the material. Sections of pot are cut off the ceramic, mounted on a glass slide and then polished down to c. 30μm in thickness. The sections are then examined with a petrographic microscope. The fundamental principle behind the technique is that the interaction of polarised light with the thin section of the crystals contained in the material being examined produces characteristic colours. The sample is fixed in a horizontal plane and can be examined by rotating it through 360 degrees. The microscope has a polariser which produces polarised light in a single plane and this passes through the sample. A second polarising filter (the analyser) permits the passage of light vibrating in a plane which is perpendicular to the polariser ('east–west' as opposed to 'north–south'). Images of minerals are formed on the back lens of the objective with convergent illumination. Various optical orientations of minerals in the samples can be examined; petrographic microscopes include other ways of modifying light transmission so that it interacts with the sample in different ways with the aim of aiding identification. An iris diaphragm and a condenser between sample stage and polariser can be adjusted to concentrate the illumination. An auxiliary Amici-Bertrand lens and various accessory plates (quartz wedge, gypsum and mica plates) all help in the identification of the crystal minerals and their orientations: the light patterns produced, often in different colours, are called *interference* figures. The use of polarised light allows the analyst to identify the *anisotropic* minerals present. These minerals have physical properties which vary in different directions, as opposed to *isotropic* minerals which have the same optical properties in all directions. Anisotropic crystals split a beam of light into two beams according to their inherent vibration directions which have different velocities (a 'fast' and a 'slow' beam). *Birefringence* is a characteristic seen under the polarising microscope which is caused by this physical property of anisotropic crystals, producing characteristic colours – it is the same effect as can sometimes be seen in car windscreens. The colours observed for the mineral crystals are basically due to the differences between the largest and the smallest *refractive indices*. The refractive index is a measure of the refraction of light as it passes through the crystal, a ratio of the velocity of light in air to its velocity in the mineral. Those minerals with low birefringence appear pale yellow or grey under crossed nicols, those with slightly higher birefringence appear blue or red and those with still greater birefringence appear to be a 'high order white' – an opalescent colour. Of course in plain polarised light, minerals which contain sufficient levels of colorants, such as iron and chromium will appear brown, green, pink or light blue: these colours are caused by *pleochrism* resulting from the way in which light is altered as it passes through the crystalline lattices (atomic arrangements) of mineral crystals.

When combined with the colour of the crystal which is observed when viewed with ordinary transmitted light, there are two ways of characterising the crystals which both separately and together provide a way of identifying the crystals. Petrology would follow from a simple visual examination of freshly broken sherds; the simplest form of fabric analysis. Although the technique sounds relatively easy, and it is certainly one of the cheaper ways of examining ceramics (Peacock 1977), as with any technique of scientific analysis there are complexities which can only be mastered with practice; a novice might feel s/he has found something new and exciting from the examination of a small number of samples, which experienced workers would classify as 'normal'. The common rock-forming minerals can be identified fairly easily by an experienced analyst and manuals which list optical properties of minerals (Kerr 1977) provide a means of identifying them. However, Whitbread (1995: 366–7) makes the point that even with such a manual, which might give the impression that the process of identifying minerals and fabrics is objective, several relatively large well-formed examples of minerals in specific orientations are needed. The successful identification of plagioclase feldspar, for example, requires at least twelve examples for which the maximum angle of extinction needs to be determined aligned within narrow angles of orientation. For thin sections of pottery this is not always possible; even the identification of small isolated fragments of rock-forming minerals may present problems. Of course there are many examples of very successful studies of archaeological ceramics using thin-section petrology, so even though there are examples where these problems of subjectivity have clearly been overcome there are inherent philosophical and practical problems of how exactly pottery fabrics are described (Whitbread 1995: 366ff.).

The combination of thin-section petrology and X-ray diffraction spectrometry is a very powerful one: together they provide identifications of the crystals and a means of measuring the distribution of each crystal type through materials. Quantitative petrology is carried out by counting the relative proportion of crystal species in a field of view. Although it has been suggested that the use of such a technique can be an objective and precise way of characterising the microstructure of ceramics (Rice 1987: 309), there are exceptions to this (Whitbread 1995: 367).

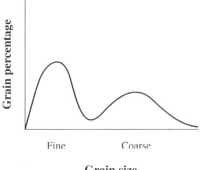

Figure 2.2 Relative grain size versus percentage of grains in a fine and coarse ceramic.

Where exotic minerals which can characterise ceramics are absent, counting the relative size and occurrence of the 'grains' (crystals) in the sample can be an alternative means of characterising the material (see Figure 2.2).

The largest number of projects using thin-section petrology have focused especially on pottery (see, for example, Sections 4.4.3 and 4.5). However, other materials have been examined using the technique. In flint, the identity of micro-organisms can be used to relate the flint sample to its source. Stone, used for polished stone axes, can be sourced geologically and has also been characterised petrologically (see Sections 6.3 and 6.8).

Neutron activation analysis (NAA)

Glascock (1992: 12) has listed the following features of NAA which makes it a technique which potentially has a lot to offer archaeologists: '(a) high sensitivity, precision and accuracy for many trace elements; (b) small sample sizes (50–200 mg); (c) relative insensitivity to the major matrix constituents; (d) the fact that it is a fully instrumental technique capable of measuring 30 to 35 elements, simultaneously; and (e) the fact that it is easily adapted to automation.' Because the technique is a sensitive one and can therefore detect elements at trace levels, some of those detected may not necessarily be attributable to the use of a particular raw material. This is one reason for using multivariate statistics, though explanations other than technological ones should never be ignored (Bishop 1992: 169). In order to carry out NAA it is necessary to have access to an atomic pile. The samples in capsules, which are often in powder form, are irradiated in an atomic pile for a defined period of time. This causes the samples to become radioactive and to decay according to their half-lives. The radiation of the elements with short half-lives obviously decays fastest. The decay is monitored in a special counter, the number of counts being directly related to the concentration of the element in the material being analysed. The longer-lived elements are counted next. The gamma radiation which is produced from the decay of the material is also directly related to the activity of the atomic flux at the time of radiation. It is essential that a standard material is included among the samples being irradiated so that a measure of the reaction to the flux can be made. Normally the standard will be made of a similar material to that being analysed.

As the sample decays, the results will be displayed as a spectrum of wavelength against peak intensity. As with various forms of spectroscopy, it is not always possible to produce 'clean' peaks because some peaks interfere with each other. Thus, as with spectrometry, it may be necessary to strip out interfering peaks.

The technique does not have to be destructive, the sample size being determined by the size of the pots into which the artefacts are placed for irradiation. When carried out successfully NAA can provide analyses of materials down to the parts per million level. The technique has been used especially for the analysis of ceramics, where the full range of trace elements detected have been analysed further using multivariate statistics (for example, Evans 1989). Much of the pottery work has been focused on the relationships between chemical characterisation, distribution patterns, the clays, other raw materials used and the location of kiln sites.

Lead isotope analysis

Lead occurs as a mixture of primordial lead, which was created when the earth formed and of radiogenic lead which has been produced as a result of the radioactive decay of uranium and thorium. Primordial lead consists of four types, which are labelled according to their different atomic masses: lead-204, lead-206, lead-207 and lead-208. Lead-204 is the only type which has *not* been formed as a result of radioactive decay and a constant amount of it remains in the earth's crust. The other forms of lead (isotopes) are continuously being added to via a decay chain by the radioactive decay of uranium-238, uranium-235 and thorium-232. As with carbon-14 dating, which relies on a comparison of the relative amounts of stable isotopes of carbon with the amount of radioactive carbon-14 in a sample, the principle of lead isotope determination also relies on the relative amounts of stable and radiogenic lead to characterise the lead-containing deposit.

Since lead occurs in a range of ancient materials, lead isotope analysis can be used in a range of archaeological and technological contexts. It can be applied to a range of materials, such as lead, silver, copper alloys, copper, pigments, glass, glazes and bones.

Lead can either occur as part of an ore mineral body such as galena (see Section 5.2), or at much lower levels in other minerals. One important assumption of the process of lead isotope analysis is that, even if the lead may be present at varying concentrations in an ore body, as long as it has been formed under the same conditions and undergone the same geological processes, the ratios between the lead isotopes present will be the same (Gulson 1986). Another important characteristic of lead is that it does not fractionate (i.e. it does not separate into its isotopes). This means that if an ore contains both lead and copper, the lead isotope ratios in one metal will also be represented in the other (Pernicka 1992). As Rohl and Needham (1998: 4) point out, if a lead-containing ore body has 'undergone a post-depositional geochemical process (e.g. remobilisation) [it] may not be very well mixed and this heterogeneity can produce a large range of lead isotope ratios, even within a single mineral type'. Since the aim of lead isotope analysis is to characterise the metal by the ratios of the lead isotopes present, this effect would clearly produce problems which would also be present in artefacts made using that lead source. Another possible complicating factor is that deposits of lead ore with very different formation times, leading to different lead isotope ratios, may be laid down very closely together. Those conducting field surveys should therefore have a detailed understanding of the geological history of the deposits being sampled. Pernicka (1993) has also noted that some ore bodies, such as copper deposits, containing low lead concentrations, can contain a range of lead isotope compositions. In this case the spread of lead isotope ratios is due to the uranium present continuing to decay after the copper ore has been formed. Although discussions of the validity of the interpretations of lead isotope analysis applied to archaeology have been extensive and lively, there is one principle that most research groups involved agree on: that twenty samples from an ore deposit is sufficient to characterise it (Reedy and Reedy 1992; Sayre *et al.* 1992; Gale and Stos-Gale 1992).

Where lead isotope analysis has been applied to metal objects a major consideration may be that the lead isotope signature will be altered in some way by the heat-treatment of the metal, and indeed as a result of corroding while buried in the ground. However, as mentioned above, lead does not fractionate – this applies generally both under high-temperature conditions and as a result of corrosion. Budd *et al.* (1995) have discussed possible fractionation during metal-smelting when large losses of lead can occur due to non-equilibrium evaporation. Subsequent research appears to show that the low vapour pressures of lead and lead oxide during *bronze casting* lead to very low losses.

The same principles of lead isotope determinations can be applied to the occurrence of lead isotopes in the full range of materials in which they occur. However, some of these materials, such as metal and glass, can be mixed as part of recycling or as a result of deliberately alloying two (or more) metals which may contain lead from more than one origin (e.g. alloying lead with bronze). Both of these processes will mix the characteristic lead isotope ratios of the lead sources involved, potentially making it impossible to disentangle the isotopic signatures.

2.3 Non-destructive and micro-destructive techniques

The principles of X-ray fluorescence spectrometry (XRF) form the basis for microanalysis in the context of electron probe microanalysis and spectrometers attached to scanning electron microscopes. The principles of XRF will therefore be described first.

X-ray fluorescence analysis can be a totally non-destructive technique. It is a surface technique of spectroscopic analysis which relies on the interaction of primary X-rays with the sample generating, among other particles, a range of secondary X-rays which have energies characteristic of each of the elements in the sample (Jenkins 1974; 1988). It produces a spectrum of energies in the same way that AES does. The primary energy source can be a radioactive material which will generate gamma rays; when fired at the sample in a solid geometry the interaction of the gamma rays with the sample will generate secondary X-rays. A much more common source of X-rays is an X-ray tube which, when configured within a commercially produced system, will be located in a stable position allowing the same analytical geometry to be repeated each time (the same analytical geometry is important if quantitative analysis is attempted).

The primary X-rays interact with each of the elements in the sample surface. During this process, secondary X-rays are emitted at the take-off angle, escaping from the sample at the same angle at which the primary X-rays were fired at the sample. A variety of energy transitions occur between inner atomic electron shells in each atom of the elements, and these lead to the generation of the secondary X-rays. The secondary X-rays hit a detector (typically silicon drifted with lithium) with an analogue-to-digital converter attached to it, which converts the pulses of discrete secondary X-ray energies into electrical pulses at the different energies which are determined by the atomic weight of the element concerned (see Figure 2.3 for a diagrammatic arrangement of a typical energy-dispersive XRF system). The electron pulses are then fed into a multi-channel analyser which displays the maxima in the spectrum of X-ray energies as a series of peaks above the background. The peaks are a gaussian shape because the process by which the peaks are formed is one dependent on counting probability whereby the maximum number of events which fall at the exact centre of the peak produce the maximum peak height. The 'tails' of the peak are due to a smaller number of events at energies above and below the peak centroid.

The depth to which the primary X-rays penetrate the sample is mainly dependent on the energy of the

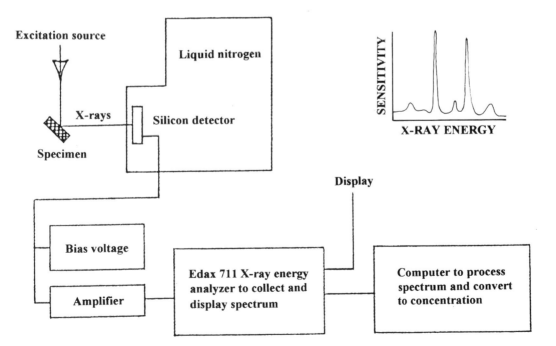

Figure 2.3 Diagrammatic representation of an X-ray fluorescence system.

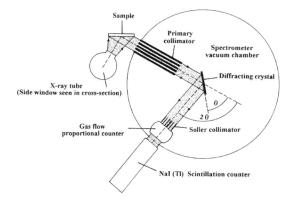

Figure 2.4 A diagrammatic representation of a wavelength-dispersive (WD) spectrometer as found in WD-XRF. The same spectrometer is used in electron microprobe, although electrons are the exciting energy instead of X-rays.

primary X-rays, the angle at which the X-rays are fired at the sample and the matrix composition of the sample. For a material which contains a relatively high proportion of heavy elements, such as lead, with an atomic number of 82, secondary X-rays which derive from it for a relatively light element also in the material, such as potassium, will be derived from a shallower maximum depth than a material which on average has a lighter matrix. The greatest depth from which elemental X-rays are derived is therefore an important consideration because it partly determines the sensitivity of each element to X-rays and therefore the number of X-ray photons that are detected per unit time. If the count rate is low, the length of the count time in order to produce acceptable counting statistics needs to be increased.

There are two principal types of X-ray fluorescence: *energy-dispersive* and *wavelength-dispersive spectrometry* (Potts *et al.* 1985). Energy-dispersive spectrometry operates by collecting data from the detector, separating it according to its energy and displaying it in spectral form. Wavelength-dispersive spectrometry, on the other hand, relies on a different means of operation. In this case the spectrometer relies on the presence of crystals causing a secondary X-ray to be diffracted at a particular angle, according to its atomic number, the secondary X-ray being

detected electronically. The dispersion of the secondary X-ray is greater than with energy-dispersive X-ray spectrometry which makes it possible to separate the X-ray peaks more completely and, in general, also makes it possible to detect elements at lower levels (see Figure 2.4). Wavelength-dispersive spectrometry is normally slower simply because the spectrometer angle needs to be changed, and also, from time to time, the crystals in the spectrometer, depending on what elements are sought.

Typically wavelength-dispersive X-ray spectrometry is used to analyse material that has been powdered and made into a silicon borate glass bead. The bead is cast so that its lower surface is flat and of the appropriate diameter for the beam of primary X-rays used for its analysis. Energy-dispersive spectrometry, on the other hand, can more readily be used as a totally non-destructive technique and is therefore more appropriate to a museum environment. However, if the sample has an irregular surface and/or is weathered/depleted in any way it is impossible to produce a quantitative result. The obvious use for energy-dispersive analysis in a museum is to provide an initial identification of a material, though it must never be forgotten that the technique only provides an analysis of the surface. The depth to which the exciting energy (X-ray or gamma ray) penetrates the sample is dependent on, in the case of an X-ray tube, the voltage used and also the matrix composition of the material: for a 'light' matrix the depth from which the heaviest secondary X-ray may escape is c. 40 microns, for the analysis of materials with 'heavy' matrices the maximum depth is more typically c. 15 microns.

The successful quantification of the results from XRF depends on a number of factors. An ideal sample is one which is polished flat and compositionally homogeneous. The factors which effect the analysis include X-ray tube voltage, the composition of the anode which is used in the X-ray tube, the geometry of the analytical system, the use of a collimator, the roughness of the sample surface, the extent of interference between elements on the X-ray spectrum, whether the X-ray emission peaks are successfully deconvoluted and the composition of the sample being analysed (a greater absorption of light elements, such as sodium or magnesia occurs in a matrix which consists of a heavier average Z [atomic number], such as one rich in lead, than in one which has a lighter average Z). In addition, the use of a reliable set of standards of known composition is absolutely essential, as it is for almost any analytical technique. Obtaining a *reliable* set of standards can be difficult and is one way of checking the quality of the analyses. Finally, the kind of quantification program employed can affect the results. In the case of XRF, the use of fundamental parameters or influence coefficients techniques can have an important impact on the results produced.

Electron probe microanalysis (EPMA)

A micro-destructive technique which produces high quality results is electron microprobe. This followed on from the milliprobe (Hall *et al.* 1973) and its early use in analysis (Brill and Moll 1963), becoming commonly used especially for research in mineral sciences in the 1970s (Reed 1996). As the technique suggests micro-samples as small as 0.5 mm can be mounted and analysed. The technique involves the use of a micro-beam of electrons which are focused on the sample surface using electrostatic lenses. The electrons themselves are generated using an electron gun (in Figure 2.4 the electron gun is vertical on the left-hand side of the machine). The interaction of the electrons with the sample generates secondary X-rays which are characteristic of the chemical elements in the material. This technique provides an analysis of a shallower layer of material than XRF (3–5 microns compared to *c.* 30–50 microns), but by sampling and preparing the sample carefully the quality of the results when compared to open geometry energy-dispersive X-ray analysis are far higher. The samples are normally embedded in epoxy resin and polished flat so that the geometry of the analysis is repeated exactly each time. In the process of doing this any weathered material can be removed.

The electron beam can be focused or defocused depending on the intended area of analysis; it may also be essential to defocus the beam in order to minimise or eradicate the possibility of volatilising the sample surface, causing elements like sodium to be boiled off (Potts *et al.* 1985; Henderson 1988). In practice, the minimum diameter of a focused electron beam during the analysis of a metal or a ceramic is 1 micron on the sample surface, which spreads out in the metal itself to *c.* 2 microns; for glass the beam needs to be deliberately defocused to *c.* 80 microns.

The electron probe was introduced in *c.* 1975 primarily as a tool used by geologists. As a result some of the early machines used were ideal for the analysis of silicates, especially for the chemical analysis of individual crystals in ceramic materials. Apart from being micro-destructive, one of the other advantages of the technique is that it is possible to locate the electron beam precisely on the area of the sample to be analysed with the use of a microscope attached to the system; if compositional heterogeneity is suspected, an energy-dispersive detector attached to the system can be used to carry out qualitative point analyses before the quantitative analyses are performed. A scanner attached to the machine can also provide image of the sample. It would be possible to quantify the energy-dispersive results from the system but the levels of precision and detection achieved with the probe are of a far higher quality (Dunham and Wilkinson 1978; Henderson 1988; Veritá *et al.* 1994). This is also true when the results from an energy-dispersive spectrometer attached to a scanning electron microscope and those from a wavelength-dispersive system in an electron microprobe are compared.

This technique is a quantitative one and, given the small beam size, it is normal to analyse 3 to 5 spots of a homogeneous material like glass, and average the results. Before chemical analysis is attempted the system must be calibrated with the use of standards for the major elements being analysed, in order to reproduce the matrix conditions of differential absorption of secondary X-rays. Geological standards may be used for pure elements occurring at minor or trace levels in the sample. As with any analytical technique, the cross-analysis of a multielement standard which was not used in calibrating the system and of proven reliability at the start and end of the analysis, will provide two things: the determination of relative analytical accuracy and a means of monitoring any drift in the system.

Scanning electron microscopy

As mentioned above scanning electron microscopy (SEM) can be used for microanalysis, and it is possible

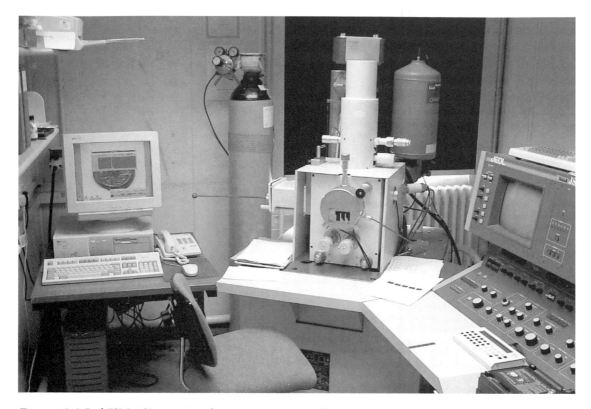

Figure 2.5 A Jeol JSM 845 scanning electron microscope with an energy-dispersive spectrometer.

to attach both energy-dispersive and wavelength-dispersive spectrometers to the instrument. However, the quality of the analyses will not be as high as for a dedicated electron microprobe because in the context of SEM it is not possible to reproduce the same analytical geometry as for a microprobe. Indeed the systems should not be confused – they are different and should be referred to as electron microprobe and analytical SEM respectively.

SEM is primarily used for imaging structurally or compositionally heterogeneous materials (Tite *et al.* 1982). The systems are often fitted with an energy-dispersive spectrometer, a secondary electron detector and a back-scattered electron detector (see Figure 2.5). The secondary electron detector provides images of the surface texture of materials whereas the use of a back-scattered detector mainly provides images of variations in composition.

The source of energy for SEM is an electron gun. Instead of the electrons being focused at a point, as in the electron microprobe, they are focused on a particular plane. They are also scanned across the material using scanning coils to build up an image of their interaction with the material. Because back-scattered electrons travel in almost straight lines and the detector is located to one side of a specimen, a shadowing effect is produced. A secondary electron image is dependent on the angle between the beam and the specimen surface (see Figure 2.6). Differences in grey level are, as a result, a reflection of the angle of the surface to the detector: the roughness of the surface and the shape of the sample can be seen clearly on the surface of the glass in Figure 2.6, including characteristic conchoidal fractures. Back-scattered electron images, on the other hand, provide pictures of compositional heterogeneity by recording the number of back-scattered electrons from the sample, giving a measure of the relative average atomic number in the area being analysed (see Figure 2.7). The secondary electron images therefore provide highly magnified images of

Figure 2.6 A secondary electron micrograph of the surface of a Bronze Age glass bead (fourteenth century BC) from Wilsford in Wiltshirc, UK (× 1000).

the surface textures of materials, whereas back-scattered electron images are built up from variations in composition (Reed 1996: 77). The two techniques can also be used in conjunction with each other: if a small area of decoration has been applied to a metal surface which is of a different composition from the body of the artefact, SEM will provide evidence for both the way in which the decoration has been attached and also how the materials used are different.

Whereas with an electron microprobe an initial examination of a thin section of a pottery sample can provide an unambiguous identification of the crystal which can then be pinpointed and analysed chemically, an electronmicrograph can provide clear images of how a particular compositional family of crystals (e.g. alkaline feldspars) might vary in composition and texture within the same sample or between samples from different sources. In a review paper, Freestone and Middleton (1987) have discussed the role of the analytical SEM specifically for the analysis of minerals in archaeological ceramics. In addition, of course, an SEM can be used to show great compositional contrasts between crystals and the matrix material they are sitting in, between layered materials and between depleted/corroded surfaces and the parent material. By examining cross-sections through materials it is possible to relate structural corrosion to changes in chemical composition which can, in turn, be recorded photographically.

For successful imaging using a back-scattered detector it is appropriate to use a sample that has been mounted and polished flat in the same way the sample was prepared using the electron microprobe. This procedure is of course inappropriate if the sample is being examined for its surface texture, in which case it should be carefully attached to a stub within the SEM and can be rotated to examine different areas of interest.

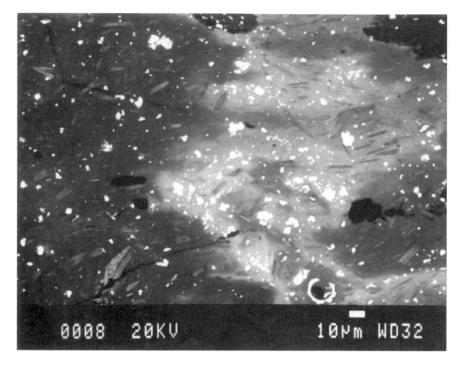

Figure 2.7 A back-scattered electron micrograph of a sample of early Christian (sixth–tenth century) opaque green glass showing white lead-tin oxide crystals in a cloud of (pale grey) high lead glass (on the right). The darker areas of the sample contain lower lead oxide levels and both areas contain elongated pale grey soda-lime-silica crystals.

In order to examine materials like metals which conduct electrons, the sample can be attached to the stub within the system. If the material is glass, glaze or obsidian (for example) and does not conduct electrons, then it needs to be coated in order to prevent distortion and deflection of the electron beam; this is also true for electron microprobe analysis. The sample size that can be examined under SEM is determined by the size of the sample chamber. Since samples are examined under vacuum, open geometry (as with XRF spectrometry) is not possible. A range of SEM systems are manufactured and relatively large objects can be accommodated, of up to *c.* 5 cm × 3 cm in dimension.

Particle-induced X-ray emission (PIXE)

The features that characterise PIXE are the cost and size of the instrument. The analytical technique requires a tandem van der Graaf accelerator in order to generate particles which are accelerated at high speeds towards the sample where they collide and penetrate the sample, still at great speeds. A particle accelerator can cost up to £500,000. The sample can be the same size and prepared in the same way as for SEM

and EPMA. It should be presented to the beam in a fixed geometry. The system can be operated in both an open geometry and by using a sample chamber, so the sample size can, theoretically, be infinite. With an open geometry system it is also possible to analyse materials containing light elements by placing the sample in a bath of helium in order to prevent the light secondary X-rays produced from being absorbed in the air before being detected (Jaksic *et al.* 1992).

Analytically, the most significant difference from EPMA is that the backgrounds produced by PIXE are a factor of 10 lower (see Figure 2.8). This is because the particles bombarding the sample enter it at such a great speed that less scattering of the particles occurs than when electrons or X-rays are used as the primary exciting energy. The net result is that the background of the X-ray spectrum is significantly lower, allowing far lower concentration of components to be detected. Some PIXE systems are fitted with scanning coils so that the distribution of elements on the surface of the material can be mapped, including at very low concentrations. The same detector system and multi-channel analyser is often used as with EPMA and SEM systems: a

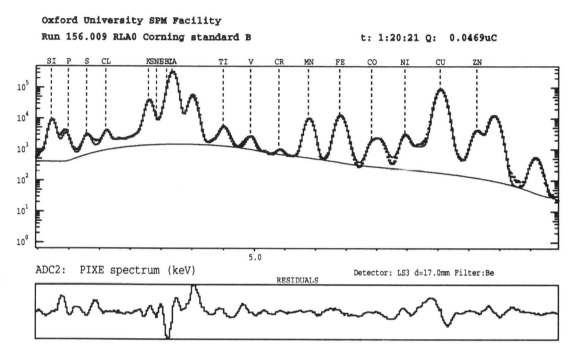

Figure 2.8 An example of the X-ray spectrum of the Corning B glass standard produced using a scanning proton microprobe. A variety of X-ray peaks are labelled: silicon, phosphorus, sulphur, chlorine, potassium, calcium, titanium, vanadium, chromium, manganese, iron, cobalt, nickel, copper zinc; all are Kα peaks.

lithium-drifted silicon detector for energy-dispersive fluorescence.

The depth of analysis during PIXE is of the same order as with stand-alone ED-XRF analysis, and, as with XRF, is dependent on the system's voltage, in the case of PIXE typically 1.5 MeV or 2 MeV. The depth of penetration by the analysing beam can be up to 50 microns in a material with a light matrix and only *c.* 15 microns in a heavy matrix. If the substance being analysed contains crystals which are 10 microns below the surface there is no way, at present, of separating the contribution made by the crystal to the analysis from that made by the matrix of the material: this is where SEM and EPMA systems are more appropriate analytical techniques in the analysis of crystalline materials.

In addition to being able to detect elements at very low concentrations, by using PIXE it is also possible to map elemental distributions through the thickness of a sample by analysing its surface. This technique is known as Rutherford back-scattering and relies on back-scattering of the protons from crystallites or other particles within the sample being analysed.

References

Ahrens, L.H. (1954) *Quantitative Spectrochemical Analysis of Silicates*, London: Pergamon Press.

Bishop, R.L. (1992) 'Comments on Section II: Variation', in H. Neff (ed.), *Chemical Characterization of Ceramic Pastes in Archaeology*, Monographs in World Archaeology No. 7, Madison: Prehistory Press, pp. 167–70.

Brill, R.H. and Moll, S. (1963) 'The electron-beam probe microanalysis of ancient glass', in *Recent Advances in Conservation*, Rome: International Institute of Conservation, pp. 147–9.

Britton, D. and Richards, E.E. (1969) 'Optical emission spectroscopy and the study of metallurgy in the European bronze age', in D. Brothwell and E. Higgs (eds) *Science in Archaeology*, London: Thames and Hudson, pp. 603–13.

Budd, P., Pollard, A.M., Scaife, B. and Thomas, R.G. (1995) 'The possible fractionation of lead isotopes in ancient metallurgical processes', *Archaeometry* 37: 143–50.

Cann, J.R. and Renfrew, C. (1964) 'The characterization of obsidian and its application to the Mediterranean region', *Proceedings of the Prehistoric Society* 30: 111–33.

Dunham, A.C. and Wilkinson, F.C.F. (1978) 'Accuracy, precision and detection limits of energy-dispersive electron microprobe analyses of silicates', *X-ray Spectrometry*, 7: 50–6.

Dunnell, R.C. (1993) 'Comments and Reviews', *Archaeomaterials* 7, 1: 161–5.

Evans, J. (1989) 'Neutron activation analysis and Romano-British pottery studies', Chapter 6 in J. Henderson (ed.), *Scientific Analysis in Archaeology, and its Interpretation*, Oxford: Oxford University Committee for Archaeology, Monograph No. 19 and UCLA Institute of Archaeology, Archaeological Research Tools 5.

Farnsworth, M. and Ritchie, P.D. (1938) 'Spectrographic studies on ancient glass. Egyptian glass mainly of the 18th Dynasty, with special reference to its cobalt content', *Technical Studies in the Field of the Fine Arts* 6, 3: 155–73.

Freestone, I.C. and Middleton, A.P. (1987) 'Mineralogical applications of the analytical SEM in archaeology', *Mineralogical Magazine* 51: 21–31.

Gale, N.H. and Stos-Gale, Z.A. (1992) 'Lead isotope studies in the Aegean (The British Academy Project)', in A.M. Pollard (ed.), *New Developments in Archaeological Science*, Proceedings of the British Academy 77, Oxford: Oxford University Press, pp. 63–108.

Glascock, M.D. (1992) 'Characterizaton of Archaeological Ceramics at MURR by Neutron Activation Analysis and Multivariate Statistics' in H. Neff (ed.), *Chemical Characterization of Ceramic Pastes in Archaeology*, Monographs in World Archaeology No. 7, Madison: Prehistory Press, pp. 11–26.

Gulson, B.L. (1986) *Lead Isotopes in Mineral Exploration*, Amsterdam: Elsevier.

Hall, E.T, Schweitzer, F. and Toller, P.A. (1973) 'X-ray fluorescence analysis of museum objects: a new instrument', *Archaeometry* 15: 53–78.

Hatcher, H., Tite, M.S. and Walsh, J.N. (1995) 'A comparison of inductively-coupled plasma emission spectrometry and atomic absorption spectrometry analysis on standard reference silicate materials and ceramics', *Archaeometry* 37: 83–94.

Henderson, J. (1988) 'Electron probe microanalyses of mixed-alkali glasses', *Archaeometry* 30 (1): 77–91.

Heyworth, M.P., Hunter, J.R., Warren, S.E. and Walsh, J.N. (1991) 'ICPS and glass: the multi-element approach', in M.J. Hughes, M.R. Cowell and D.R. Hook (eds), *Neutron Activation and Plasma Emission Spectrometric Analyses in Archaeology. Techniques and Applications*, British Museum Occasional Paper 82, London: British Museum Press, pp. 143–54.

Hughes, M.J., Cowell, M.R. and Craddock, P.T. (1976) 'Atomic absorption techniques in archaeology', *Archaeometry* 18: 19–37.

Jaksic, M., Grime, G., Watt, F. and Henderson, J. (1992) 'Quantitative PIXE analysis using a scanning proton probe', *Nuclear Instruments and Methods in Physics Research* B54: 491–8.

Jarvis, K.E., Gray, A.L. and Houk, R.S. (1992) *Handbook of Inductively Coupled Plasma Mass Spectrometry*, Glasgow: Blackie.

Jenkins, R. (1974) *An introduction to X-ray Spectrometry*, Chichester: John Wiley.

—— (1988) *X-ray fluorescence spectrometry*, Chichester: Wiley-Interscience.

Jope, E.M. (1950) 'Roman lead-glazed pottery in Britain' *The Archaeological Newsletter* 2: 199.

Jope, E.M. and Huse, G. (1942) 'Examination of "Egyptian blue" by X-ray powder Photography', *Nature* 146: 26.

Kerr, P.F. (1977) *Optical Mineralogy*, 4th edn, New York: McGraw-Hill.

Klaproth, M.H. (1798) *Memoires de l'academie royale des sciences et belle-lettres*, Berlin. Classe de philosophie experimentale.

Mallory-Greenough, L.M., Greenough, J.D., Dobosi, G. and Owen, J.V. (1999) 'Fingerprinting ancient Egyptian quarries: preliminary results using laser ablation microprobe inductively coupled plasma-mass spectrometry', *Archaeometry* 41, 2: 227–38.

Organ, R.M. (1971) 'The value of analyses of archaeological objects', *Archaeometry* 13, 1: 27–8.

Peacock, D.P.S. (1977) 'Ceramics in Roman and Medieval Archaeology', in D.P.S. Peacock (ed.), *Pottery and Early Commerce: Characterisation and Trade in Roman and Later Ceramics*, London: Academic Press, pp. 147–62.

Pernicka, E. (1992) 'Evaluating lead isotope data: comments on Sayre *et al.* "Statistical evaluation of the presently accumulated lead isotope data from Anatolia and surrounding regions": III', *Archaeometry* 34, 2: 322–6.

—— (1993) 'Evaluating lead isotope data: Further observations – Comments III', *Archaeometry* 35, 2: 259–62.

Pollard, A.M. and Heron, C. (1996) *Archaeological Chemistry*, Cambridge: The Royal Society of Chemistry.

Potts, P.J., Webb, P.C. and Watson, J.S. (1985) 'Energy-dispersive X-ray fluorescence analysis of silicate rocks: comparisons with wavelength-dispersive performance', *Analyst* 110: 507–13.

Purdy, B.A. and Brooks, H.K. (1971) 'Thermal alteration of silica minerals: an archaeological approach' *Science* 173: 322–5.

Reed, S.J.B. (1996) *Electron Microprobe Analysis and Scanning Electron Microscopy in Geology*, Cambridge: Cambridge University Press.

Reedy, T.J. and Reedy, C.L. (1992) 'Evaluating lead isotope data: comments on Sayre *et al.* "Statistical evaluation of the presently accumulated lead isotope data from Anatolia and surrounding regions": IV', *Archaeometry* 34, 2: 327–9.

Renfrew, C., Dixon, J.E. and Cann, J.R. (1966) 'Obsidian and early cultural context in the Near East', *Proceedings of the Prehistoric Society* 32: 30–72.

Rice, P.M. (1987) *Pottery Analysis: A Source Book*, Chicago: The University of Chicago Press.

Rohl, B. and Needham, S. (1998) *The circulation of metal in the British Bronze Age: the application of lead isotope analysis*, British Museum Occasional Paper, number 102, London: The British Museum.

Sayre, E.V., Yener, K.A., Joel, E.C. and Barnes, I.L. (1992) 'Statistical evaluation of the presently accumulated lead isotope data from Anatolia and surrounding regions', *Archaeometry* 34, 1: 73–105.

Thompson, M. and Walsh, J.N. (1989) *A Handbook of ICP Spectrometry*, Glasgow: Blackie.

Tite, M.S. (1972) *Methods of Physical Examination in Archaeology*, London: Seminar Press.

Tite, M.S., Freestone, I.C., Meeks, N.D. and Bimson, M. (1982) 'The use of scanning-electron microscopy in the technological examination of ancient ceramics', in J.S. Olin and A.D. Franklin (eds), *Archaeological Ceramics*, Washington, DC: Smithsonian Institution Press, pp. 109–20.

Veritá, M., Basso, R., Wypyski, M.T. and Koestler, R.J. (1994) 'X-ray microanalysis of ancient glassy materials: a comparative study of wavelength-dispersive and energy-dispersive techniques' *Archaeometry* 36: 241–52.

Weymouth, J.W. and Mandeville, M. (1975) 'An X-ray diffraction study of heat-treated chert and its archaeological implications', *Archaeometry* 17, 1: 61–8.

Whitbread, I.K. (1995) *Greek Transport Amphorae: A Petrological and Archaeological Study*, Fitch Laboratory Occasional Paper 4, Athens: The British School at Athens.

3

GLASS

3.1 Glass as a material

Glass can be classified as a ceramic. It is an amorphous solid; it lacks the long-range order which characterises crystalline materials like metals, so there is no regularity in the arrangement of its molecular constituents on a scale larger than a few times the size of these groups (Doremus 1994: 1). This means that its constituents (largely oxides) are only arranged in a regular way in small areas, as revealed by early work by Zachariasen (1932). A solid is a rigid material and does not flow when it is subjected to moderate forces. Although Jones (1956: 1) defines glass as 'an inorganic product of fusion which has been cooled to a rigid condition without crystallisation', Doremus (1994: 1) states that glasses can be prepared without cooling from the liquid state. Nevertheless ancient glasses all fall into the definition proposed by Jones, and to avoid crystallisation of the glass would have been very important to ancient glass-workers, just as it is today. Glass is also a supercooled liquid. This means that when soda-lime-silica glass is made it is cooled from temperatures above 1100 °C to a temperature at which the rate of cooling must be controlled carefully (the transition temperature, Tg). If the melt is allowed to cool too slowly a silicate can be produced which consists of a series of crystals (following the cooling curve A-B-C-D in Figure 3.1); by cooling the glass at an appropriate rate this can be avoided, and a glass which contains no crystals is formed (cooling curve A-B-E-G1 in Figure 3.1). It can be seen in Figure

3.1 that the rate at which the temperature falls between Tg and T is especially critical and is reflected in the volume of silicate material produced.

As the temperature falls an abrupt change of *volume* occurs at the glass transition (or transformation) temperature (Tg) which is equal to the coefficient of volume expansion. At around the same temperature, the heat capacity and the electrical conductivity also change abruptly, though the viscosity does not change (Doremus 1994: 113). The significance of the transition temperature is that it

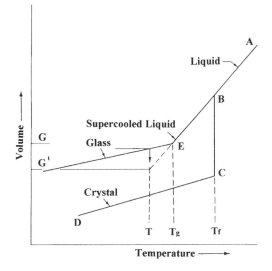

Figure 3.1 Cooling curve for glass, showing the reduction in volume as the temperature falls and the point at which glass, as opposed to silicate crystals, is formed.

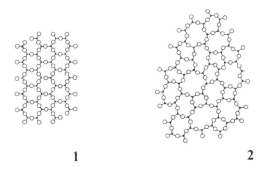

Figure 3.2 Two-dimensional representations of (1) a hypothetical crystalline compound A_2O_3; (2) the glassy form of the same compound as in (1) (after Zachariasan 1932).

appears to be the point at which a slowing down of the rearrangements in the glass structure occurs.

The chemical constituents in the glass, the oxides, are arranged in an open network (Figure 3.2-2); in a soda-lime-silica glass, the glass used for the longest period in the ancient world, the oxides in the network are sodium oxide (Na_2O), calcium oxide (CaO) and silica (SiO_2). In structural terms glasses can be defined by the relationships between network-formers and network-modifiers. Network-formers, such as silica which forms SiO_4 tetrahedra, provide a high proportion of the basic network of silicate glasses. Not all corners of the molecules are covalently shared which leaves 'holes' in the silicate network (Jones 1971: 19). These can be seen as available spaces into which network modifiers can fit (Figure 3.2(2)); Figure 3.2(1) shows a two-dimensional representation of an imaginary *crystalline* (non-glassy) compound A_2O_3. Examples of glass modifiers are singly charged ions such as Na^+ and K^+ and alkaline-earth ions such as Mg^{2+} and Ca^{2+}. There is a wide range of combinations of these network subunits which produces a correspondingly wide range of compositions. Recent work on glass structure by Wright *et al.* (1991) has recognised glass as forming four types of structural arrangements.

In ancient glasses there are impurities associated with the raw materials used, such as elements metabolised by plants in the plant-ash source of alkali used, minerals in the sand used and magnesia in a dolomitic source of limestone used. Compounds

were added deliberately in order to bring about changes in the appearance of the glass: colorants (e.g. cobalt oxide – CoO), crystalline opacifiers which make the glass opaque (e.g. tin oxide SnO_2), clarifiers which remove colour from the glass (e.g. manganese oxide, MnO), and fining agents which help to remove gas bubbles from the glass-melt (e.g. antimony trioxide, Sb_2O_3). Even though ancient glass-makers will not have identified these oxides as individual chemical compounds, and often they would be added as a component of a material, trial and error would have determined how to use the compounds to colour, opacify or clarify glass.

Early glass-makers must have passed through a period of technological experimentation and innovation both in selection of appropriate raw materials and in discovery of the properties that the different raw materials imparted to the glasses. In some cases the addition of a small quantity of a compound which was designed to modify the appearance of the glass would also change the working properties of the glass – a separate very important consideration when making a complex glass vessel or object.

3.2 The raw materials of ancient glass production

3.2.1 The alkalis

It is generally agreed that the principal source of alkali used to make glasses of the second millennium BC was ashes of the plants of the genus *Salicornia* or *Salsola,* both of which grow in the deserts found in Egypt and the Middle East (see Figure 3.3) or in maritime environments. The compositional characteristics of these halophytic plants – high soda with relatively high impurity levels of magnesia and potassium oxide – is carried through into the glass made from it. Analytical and experimental work by Brill (1970a) has shown that samples of *keli*, the ash of the *chinan* plant which grows in the Syrian desert is characterised by high soda levels (28%), relatively low potassium oxide (5.5%), high calcium oxide (21.1%) and low magnesia (0.5%) (Brill 1970a: Table 2). Other analyses of soda-rich plant ashes contained considerably higher magnesia levels accompanying the soda.

Figure 3.3 Soda-rich desert plants such as this provided the principal source of alkali for Mesopotamian, ancient Egyptian and much later Islamic glass.

A different alkali would have been used for the manufacture of later soda glasses. From *c*. 800 BC the chemical composition of soda-lime glasses changed from that of a glass which contained a high magnesia impurity to that of one which contained a low magnesia impurity; these have been referred to as high magnesia glasses (HMG) and low magnesia glasses (LMG) respectively (Sayre and Smith 1967: 285, 287). Accompanying the elevated levels of magnesia in the HMGs are correlated elevated levels of potassium oxide; in LMGs low potassium oxide impurities accompany the low magnesia levels. The most likely source of the soda alkali used to produce LMGs in Hellenistic and Roman glasses is an evaporite mineral which occurs at Wadi el-Natrun in Egypt (Forbes 1957: 142). The mineral itself has a variable composition of 22.4–75% sodium carbonate, 5–32.4% sodium bicarbonate and contains impurities of 2.2–26.8% sodium chloride and 2.3–29.9% sodium sulphate (Turner 1956b: Table IV). Twelve samples of natron taken from Wadi el-Natrun

when chemically analysed revealed its true crystalline identity to be trona, a sodium sesquicarbonate, $Na_2CO_3.NaHCO_3.2H_2O$ (R.H. Brill, personal communication). Trona also occurs in the Beheira province of Lower Egypt, a source which was certainly worked in antiquity. During New Kingdom Egypt (eighteenth century BC), however, it is claimed that ready-made glass was imported from the Middle East (Oppenheim 1973) and in any case the predominant source of alkali to make Eighteenth Dynasty glass was plant ash. There is, however, a hint that a small number of LMGs were produced before 800 BC (Shortland and Tite 2000; Henderson 2000). It is worth noting that trona was not only used for glass production (Turner 1956a) but also as a source of soap.

3.2.2 Silica sources

Silica in glass-making is provided by sand or quartz pebbles. Locating sand does not obviously pose a problem, but to locate sources which have low mineral impurities, such as iron-bearing minerals, is more difficult. Iron impurities in sand produce the common greenish colour often observed in glass. The kinds of impurities which are found in sand are: feldspars, either plagioclase or alkali, which account for some of the aluminia, calcium and sodium, or aluminium, sodium and potassium respectively in the final glass (Matson 1951: 84); titinite or sphene ($CaO.TiO_2.SiO_2$) which can potentially introduce impurities of chromium oxide and titanium oxide; chromite ($FeO.Cr_2O_3$) which can introduce iron; and chromium and epidote ($Ca_2(Al,Fe)3SiO_4$) which can introduce aluminia and iron. Both titinite and epidote are calcium-bearing minerals which can introduce small quantities of calcium to the glass (Goerk 1977: 48; Highley 1977: 9). Lucas (1948) among others has noted the presence of shell fragments in sand which could potentially provide a major source of calcium in a glass batch. At the fourth-century Jalame glass factory in Palestine, a history of the coastal landscape was studied in order to assess the possible sources of sand that led to the impurities detected in the glasses excavated from the site. Though no direct evidence for glass-*making* was found, it was suggested that a local sand source was used, perhaps to make glass at a site nearby (see Section 3.10.3). Turner (1956a: 281–2, Table III) studied the mineralogical composition of sand from Tell el-Amarna, from the Theban shore of the river Nile opposite Luxor and from the Belus river by Haifa in Syria. All the samples contained variable levels of quartz (the silica source), calcite (a calcium source), feldspars, pyroxenes and illmenite; with the sand from Thebes alone also containing mud and mica. The sand from Tell el-Amarna contained between 50% and 55% quartz, 30% and 33% calcite, 5% feldspars, 5% pyroxenes and 1% illmenite, and can thus be considered a relatively 'clean' sand. If a purer, mineral, source of silica was used, such as quartz (often in the form of river pebbles) much lower levels of impurities (such as iron) would accompany it and would find their way into the glass-melt.

3.2.3 The use of lead

From the Eighteenth Dynasty (1550–1307 BC) lead was used in Egyptian glasses, specifically for decorative opaque yellow glasses which were normally applied to core-formed vessels (in the form of lead antimonate, $Pb_2Sb_2O_7$). The presence of lead was detected by Turner and Rooksby in glass from Thebes dated 1450–1425 BC (1959: Table 1B) and confirmed by Sayre (1964). Lead has also been detected in faience (Kaczmarczyk and Hedges 1983). The earliest dated red glasses which contain relatively high lead levels are from Hasanlu (Brill 1970: 120) and Nimrud of the eighth–seventh centuries BC (Turner 1954b: 455). The earliest historical reference to lead can be found in the Mesopotamian texts dated to *c.* seventh century BC, but thought to have originally derived from a twelfth century BC source (Brill 1970a: 121). If lead is present in glass it occurs as an oxide; though there is no actual archaeological evidence on an ancient production site for lead being used as a primary raw material, it must have been added at some point in the production cycle and converted into an oxide. High lead opaque red glasses were introduced in the eighth century BC, at about the same time as the change from high magnesia to low magnesia soda-lime glasses took place, and lead oxide continued to be used in opaque glasses (Hughes 1972; Henderson and Warren 1981). Otherwise translucent high lead glasses are unusual until *c.* ninth–tenth centuries AD when they were used in the manufacture of beads and rings (Henderson and Warren 1986; Bayley 1990), and somewhat later in the manufacture of generally prestigious yellow, emerald green and opaque red medieval vessel glasses (Wedepohl *et al.* 1995). In 1670 Ravenscroft patented the use of lead for the manufacture of 'flint' glass in London, 1984).

A useful historical reference to the use of lead in glass production, which would be of relevance to the introduction of lead to glass during any period, is a twelfth–thirteenth-century AD text by Heraclius who describes the introduction of lead into the glass-melt:

Take good and shining lead and put it in a new jar and burn it in the fire until it is reduced to powder . . . Afterwards take sand and mix it well with that powder, so that two parts may be of lead and the third of sand, and put it in an earthenware vase. Then do as before directed for making glass, and put that earthen vase into the furnace and keep stirring it until it is converted into glass.

(Merrifield 1849, 216)

Another writer, Antonio Neri, in his *Dell'Arte Vetraria* (1612, Book 6) mentions that calcined (i.e. oxidised) lead should be used, because otherwise the lead will sink through the bottom of the pot.

Even if the details of these descriptions of the use of lead in glass production are somewhat different from earlier procedures, the principles of the use of lead in glass will be the same. Certainly the percentage of lead which will end up in the glass as described by Heraclius would be somewhat higher than the levels of *c.* 10–30% lead oxide found in second- and first-millennia BC glasses.

The determination of the lead isotope signatures in ancient glasses has produced information on the association between samples of the same and of different ages which is clearly of interest (Brill 1970: 151–4). Obviously a glass factory can use lead from a range of different sources during the time that it is in operation, so it would be unexpected to find that *all* glass made during a specific period had the same lead isotope signature; there is also the possibility that lead-containing glasses were recycled. Nevertheless the association or dissociation of the lead isotope signatures for ancient glasses contributes to the overall technological picture for them. Work by Brill and co-workers using lead isotope analysis (Brill *et al.* 1993) has shown that characteristic sources of lead (galena) were used for Eighteenth Dynasty Egyptian glasses which presumably existed somewhere in the Eastern Desert, or possibly along the coast of the Arabian Peninsula (Brill *et al.* 1993: 59). Brill *et al.* (1993: 60) suggested that it is possible to infer that some Egyptian lead-rich glasses have isotope signatures that are so similar that the same lead source must have been used. (However see Section 5.9.4.3 for a discussion of the potentially complex range of relationships between isotope signatures and chemical compositions.) For other Egyptian glasses the variation in the isotope signatures suggested to them that lead from the same *mining region* was used. Glasses from Nuzi, Tell al-Rimah, Hasanlu and Nimrud ranging in date from fifteenth century BC to second century BC also group

together. These are yellow and red opaque glasses, and it is considered that the lead derived not necessarily from the same mines, but from a localised mining region (Brill 1970: 152; Brill *et al.* 1973: 79; Brill *et al.* 1993: 61). It is striking, although not unexpected, that in this case the geological type of lead which was formed under the conditions which produced this lead isotope signature was evidently used over a very long period of time, and this is where the determination of the variation of lead isotope signatures for individual lead sources becomes so important. The determination of lead isotope ratios for glasses dating to between the late centuries BC and early first millennium AD showed a spread of data. This has been interpreted as the use of a multiplicity of lead sources and a degree of glass recycling (Brill *et al.* 1973). Indeed recycling is something which is crucial to the interpretation of lead isotope work, since different lead isotope signatures will be mixed and can totally confuse the issue (see Section 5.9.4.1).

When lead isotope determinations were carried out for material from factories, it was found that opaque yellow and red glasses from the third-century BC site of a Hellenistic glass factory on Rhodes did not have the same isotopic composition (Perrot and Weinberg 1968; Weinberg 1969; 1983). Brill (1970: 153) found wide variations, even among the isotope determinations of only three glasses. An additional important consideration would be to relate the lead isotope signatures in the glass to different site phases and/or production phases: it is possible that the changes in lead sources occurred fairly frequently, and it might be possible to monitor this by determining lead isotope signatures from stratified lead-rich glasses deriving from such a factory.

3.2.4 Calcium

Soda-lime glasses typically contain calcium oxide levels of *c.* 6.5–9.0%, a level frequently found in soda-lime glasses into the first millennium AD (Turner 1956b: 45; Turner 1956c; Henderson 1985: 277; 1995c). When lead oxide is present the calcium oxide level may be reduced because the lead oxide tends to be added directly to the basic soda glass. Calcium oxide is essential in glass as a network stabiliser; without it a soda-silica glass would tend to dissolve easily in water. In a discussion of the description of glass production in the ancient Mesopotamian texts, the production of *zukû*, which was almost certainly a glass, does not mention a separate substance like calcium being added to the glass-melt (Brill 1970a: 109). However, Pliny (N.H. XXXVI, 66) refers to the use of 'shells' as a glass-maker's raw material, and the obvious source would be beach sand. An alternative source of calcium used in Egyptian glass might be dolomite; however only rarely is the calcium oxide to magnesia ratio close to unity, so the use of dolomite or dolomitic sandstone is unlikely to have been common (Matson 1951), though examples can be cited occasionally (Henkes and Henderson 1998). Indeed an almost invariable positive correlation between potassium oxide and magnesia, rather than calcium oxide and magnesia shows that, in general, the magnesia would have been introduced with the potassium (both probable impurities in the alkali used) rather than as part of a dolomitic source of calcium. The surprising feature of Egyptian (and other ancient) soda-lime-silica glasses is that the calcium oxide level is consistently between *c.* 6.5% and 9%. Had the sand sources which were rich in shell fragments been used would we expect this repeatable and consistent level of calcium oxide to enter the glass-melt?

The suggestion has been made that the proportion of shell fragments is always the same in a sand source, resulting in a repeatable glass composition (Brill 1970a: 109). It is however much more likely that, as with ancient metallurgy, where consistent proportions of mineral-bearing ores would have been purified and melted, the different constituents of the sand were separated, perhaps by using a centrifugal device, so that the shell fragments could be used as a calcium source, and that they would have been added in measured quantities to the glass batch.

3.2.5 Glass coloration

The parameters which effect the coloration of glass are complex. Although the oxides of transition metal ions, such as cobalt and copper for example, can, under the right circumstances, produce the familiar deep blue and turquoise blue colours, respectively, a range of other factors play an important part (Pollard and Heron 1996: 168). Glass colour is dependent on the glass absorbing parts of the visible wavelengths of light through interaction with colorant oxides in the glass and the reflection of the balance of light wavelengths; it is the reflected light wavelengths that we observe as colour (Doremus 1994: 306). The range of factors is as follows:

(i) Preparation of the glass batch

The quality of glass produced can be affected directly by preparation of the raw materials. The preparation and use of fine particles (Stoch *et al.* 1978) of colorant materials ensures that they are dispersed in the glass-melt completely, so as to produce a homogeneous glass colour. The use of high (1400 °C) temperatures in the glass furnace is also an important factor, in that it affects the proper dispersal of the batch ingredients, including colorants.

(ii) The occurrence of transition metal ions

The most powerful transition metal colorant is cobalt; its linear absorption coefficient in glass, at its maximum value, is at least a factor of five greater than other transition metal ions (Bamford 1977: 42). This means that considerably less cobalt is necessary to produce a certain colour intensity than other transition metal ions; in a soda-lime-silica glass a typical level of cobalt oxide, which can produce a deep blue colour, may be as low as 0.05%.

(iii) Crystalline opacifiers

These may have been added to the glass or developed out of the glass by heat-treatment; crystalline impurities may also have been present which would have added to deliberate opacification (Biek and Bayley 1979), or caused partial opacification themselves. Relict silica crystals which have not completely dissolved in the glass-melt is an example of this. The 'striking' of crystals out of the glass-melt (i.e. the reheating of glass at an appropriate temperature), can be essential to the development of crystals in the glass in order to produce opaque colours. Another kind of opacification can be caused deliberately by masses of gas bubbles.

(iv) The chemical environment

The gross composition of the glass within which the colorant materials act (Bamford 1977) can have an important effect. If, for example, the same amount of potassium oxide in a glass replaces sodium oxide the colour of the glass will appear darker. This is because greater light absorption occurs in the presence of a heavier alkali.

In more scientific terms, a consideration of the atomic structure in silicate glasses (and glazes) reveals just how important (and complex) the chemical environment of transition metal ions such as cobalt, copper and iron can be. When a transition metal assumes an ionic state, the ligand (the ions surrounding the colorant) depends on both the field strength and negative charge (provided by the oxygen). In transition metals, one of the energy shells (in this case the 3d sub-shell) is only partly filled with electrons and it is this which produces some of the colouring characteristics. When coordinated with other ions, such as Si^{4+}, the energy levels of the d electrons in transition metals are split (distorted) by the electric field produced by the coordinating ions. This splitting is sensitive to the arrangement of surrounding ions (the chemical environment): the result determines the glass colour. The theory of these effects is called the 'ligand field' theory. When higher energy level orbits in the colouring ions are unoccupied, the electrons in lower energy level orbits absorb different wavelengths of light quanta in order to move up to the higher energy level. It is this last energy transition that causes the glass or glaze to appear to be a particular colour.

(v) The gaseous atmosphere of the furnace

When glass is melted (Sellner *et al.* 1979; Newton 1978; Biek and Bayley 1979; Henderson 1985; Brill 1988: 272) different gaseous atmospheres may prevail (at different times in the heating cycle). If, for example, in a copper-containing glass the atmosphere is predominantly oxidising, then a turquoise blue colour can result, if it is predominantly reducing (and the glass is heat-treated) then an opaque red colour can result.

(vi) The heating cycle, and the maximum temperatures achieved

The length of time that the melt is allowed to remain at particular temperatures may determine the extent to which a fuel is burnt up, which in turn will contribute to the gaseous atmosphere in the furnace. The maximum temperature to which a melt is heated is also critical. Newton and Davison (1989: 61) claim that ancient glass-makers had difficulty reaching temperatures above 1000 °C, but this cannot be the case, since 1100–1400 °C would have been necessary for an efficient melt for soda-lime glasses (Cable 1998). Addition of cullet to the glass batch may reduce the overall melting temperature (as indeed does the addition of lead oxide), but it is clear that temperatures above 1100 °C were attained by those involved in the glass industry – and for that matter in other ancient high-temperature industries.

3.2.5.1 Cobalt blue glass

The ultimate source of cobalt blue coloration in ancient glasses, as opposed to the blue green colour produced by (oxidised) copper or the pale blue colour produced by (reduced) iron, is cobalt-bearing minerals. Cobalt is commonly found in ancient rock mineralisations in association with other minerals, such as copper, which can potentially provide a means of characterising the cobalt ore. Trianite is a copper-bearing cobalt ore ($2Co_2O.CuO.6H_2O$); cobaltite contains cobalt in association with sulphur and arsenic and sometimes a trace of zinc (CoAsS); skutterudite contains cobalt in association with nickel, iron and arsenic (($(Co,Ni,Fe)As_3$)). Combinations of other trace elements may also be associated with cobalt-bearing minerals and may be detected in ancient blue glass. These include lead and antimony, nickel, manganese and zinc, and bismuth and iron.

The use of cobalt in ancient Egyptian glasses has produced an interesting discussion in the literature. Farnsworth and Ritchie (1938: 159) chemically analysed a series of cobalt blue Eighteenth Dynasty glasses using arc-induced emission spectroscopy and attributed the colour to the presence of cobalt and copper modified by manganese in the glass; they explicitly stated that they regarded the presence of cobalt as being a deliberate addition (Farnsworth and Ritchie 1938: 160). They even went as far as suggesting that Egyptian sources of alum which contain traces of cobalt might have been used as the source of the cobalt-bearing mineral used. Garner (1956a; 1956b) also suggested that a cobalt-bearing ore was used for the coloration of Egyptian glass and Lucas

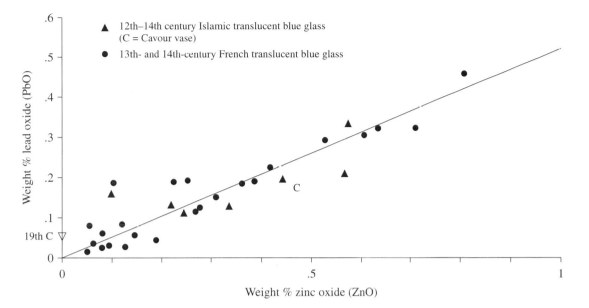

Figure 3.4 Weight % lead oxide versus weight % zinc oxide in twelfth to fourteenth-century Islamic glass (triangles) and European High Medieval blue glasses (circles). The clear positive correlation found in all the glasses suggests that the same or very similar cobalt source was used to make Islamic and European medieval glass.

(1934: 218) was more specific in suggesting a Persian source of cobalt. In another context Sayre (1964: 7–8) has made a distinction between cobalt used in 'western' Roman glasses and those found in Mesopotamia and south-western Iran on the basis of the manganese contents and the associated impurities of iron, nickel, copper, tin and lead oxides. The presence of manganese is said to be an indication of the use of ores characterised by manganese, as opposed to those characterised by the presence of arsenical ores of the Middle East (Young 1956). Kaczmarczyk and Hedges (1983: 46) have discovered that cobalt is associated with manganese, zinc, nickel and aluminia in New Kingdom cobalt blue faience and other cobalt blue objects, which contain abnormally high aluminia concentrations. Building on the work by Farnsworth and Ritchie (1938), Kaczmaczyck (1987) suggested that the source of alum mentioned by them with a significant cobalt impurity was used for Egyptian New Kingdom glass coloration. If this suggestion is taken at face value, then the relative levels of impurities in the final glasses are inconsistent with the suggestion (Lilyquist and Brill 1993: nn. 78, 94). Nevertheless the pres-

ence of aluminia at factors of five or six times higher than found in non-cobalt New Kingdom glasses needs to be explained. The most likely interpretation would seem to be that the cobalt-bearing alum was used but that the alum was modified in some way before use. An alternative explanation would be that a sand source which contained unusually high levels of aluminia was used only to make cobalt blue glasses, but this is very unlikely. Later, in the medieval period in Europe, a cobalt-bearing mineral called zaffre (or Damascus pigment) was roasted to remove any sulphur or arsenic before use.

Chemical analyses of Iron Age European blue glasses have revealed that the source of cobalt changed *c.* second century BC from an antimony-rich source to a manganese-rich source, which is no coincidence given the important changes in the industrial and social centralisation which occurred at that time (Henderson 1991c). It is therefore also possible to relate the use of different cobalt sources to the production of different Iron Age glass bead types and at the same time indirectly produce a date for cobalt blue beads using especially the relative levels of iron and cobalt (Henderson 1991c: 128,

Figures 6–8). For Roman cobalt blue glasses it has been found that a cobalt source rich in manganese (Henderson 1990: 287–8) was used. A sub-grouping of higher lead-containing blue Roman enamels was found which might suggest that a lead- and manganese-rich cobalt source was used to make them.

Work by Gratuze *et al.* (1995) on the chemical analysis of medieval blue glass in Europe has also shown that there were discrete chronological changes in the use of cobalt sources according to a range of impurities such as lead and zinc. These same impurities have been detected in Islamic glasses dating from the twelfth to fourteenth centuries, and indeed their occurrence is clearly correlated positively (see Figure 3.4) inferring that the same or a very similar geological cobalt source was used to colour the glass. This work in the sourcing of cobalt-rich colorants

used in ancient glasses is still in its infancy, but, nevertheless it has already been possible to suggest that a cobalt-rich colorant was exported from the Islamic world to High Medieval western Europe to be used as a colorant in a glass of an entirely different basic chemical composition (Henderson 1998b).

3.2.5.2 Translucent turquoise blue and red glasses; opaque red glass

The two ionic states of copper produce two correspondingly different colours in ancient glasses: a turquoise blue colour when the cupric (Cu^{2+}) ion is present (Brill 1970a: 120) and a bright sealing-wax red or a dull brown red colour when the cuprous (Cu^+) ion is present (Hughes 1972; Freestone 1987; Guido *et al.* 1984). Weyl (1951: 164–5) notes that the 'green' colour is only produced in the presence of lead oxide in the glass, although several examples

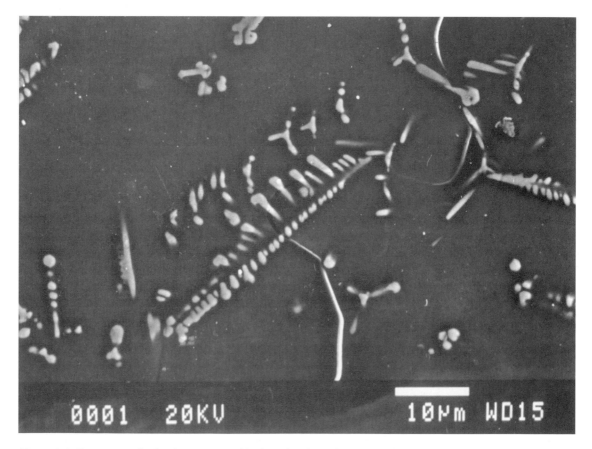

Figure 3.5 Cuprous oxide dendrites responsible for a bright sealing-wax red colour in glass and enamels.

of copper-green (translucent turquoise-green) glasses with no detectable lead have been found. After brass was introduced, copper and zinc are often found to be associated with copper in ancient turquoise glasses, where scrap brass has been used.

When crystalline forms of copper are produced in reddish glasses, the presence of lead oxide in the glass at 1% or more greatly facilitates the precipitation of the crystals out of the glass-melt. 'Striking' the copper or cuprous oxide crystals out of solution is essential to the development of the colour. This involves heat-treating (reheating) the glasses at temperatures at which the crystals can form. All Egyptian opaque red glasses which pre-date the ninth century BC contain lead levels of less than 3% oxide; after this date the lead oxide levels generally rise and a brighter (sealing-wax) red glass colour can be produced (Freestone 1987) with the development of branching dendritic cuprous oxide crystals in the glass (see Figure 3.5). The lead levels in ancient opaque red glasses rose to c. 3% between the ninth and sixth centuries BC. When low levels of lead oxide are present there can be a problem of dissolving the copper in the glass. Replication of opaque red glasses has shown that this can be overcome by introducing between 1.4% and 2.3% iron oxide in the glass (Guido et al. 1984), and this also provides the appropriate reducing environment for the precipitation of crystals of cuprous oxide or metallic copper.

Chemical analysis of opaque sealing-wax red glass used in the European later Iron Age as enamels have produced some interesting distinctions between the enamels used and (presumably) manufactured in western and eastern Britain after the second century BC (Henderson in press c) suggesting that different workshop zones existed in which somewhat different recipes were employed for making opaque red glasses used as enamels. The variation in the levels of lead and copper oxides used to make these enamels suggests that the difficult manufacturing procedures employed to make the bright sealing-wax red enamel was tightly controlled (see Henderson 1989: Figure 2.6). If the relative levels of lead and copper are plotted against each other for enamels used in the decoration of metalwork in hoards from Hertford Heath (Hertfordshire), Polden Hills (Somerset) and Seven Sisters (Glamorganshire), three sub-groupings are formed with an increasing level of lead oxide in enamels as one moves from east to west from Hertford Heath to Seven Sisters; all of these hoards are from the first half of the first century AD. It is perhaps no coincidence that the western hoards are close to a source of lead in the Mendip Hills (Henderson 1989: 47–9).

In addition to the patterns detected for sealing-wax red enamel, a duller red colour generally containing lower lead and copper levels was introduced by the Romans in the first century AD and used for the manufacture of tesserae and enamels (Hughes 1972; Henderson 1989: 48; Henderson 1991a). Figure 3.6 shows the fine parallel lines of the opacifying cuprous oxide crystals in a glass tessera; clearly this arrangement of crystals is related to the manufacturing technique used to make the tessera. The sealing-wax red enamel continued to be used in the 'Celtic' tradition of Ireland: for example, it was used for embedding translucent blue glass in the decoration of the Sutton Hoo treasure (Bimson 1983).

In the case of translucent red enamels the particles used were of a copper-rich composition, and are known as 'copper-ruby' glasses (Weyl 1951: 428–9; Biek and Bailey 1979). In 1857 Faraday recognised that 'gold ruby' glasses were produced by finely-divided gold particles; the gold is dissolved in the glass as an ion and if the glass is cooled rapidly it is retained in this state. Kunkel (1679) wrote a treatise on the manufacture of gold ruby glasses by the use of a pigment known as Purple of Cassius which consisted of colloidal gold and stannic oxide; these glasses were not dichroic.

The physical explanation for the colour of gold ruby glasses is as follows: the glass is reheated to an intermediate temperature region and nucleation of gold particles takes place. The growth of the particles takes place by diffusion of gold atoms or ions to the particles. The ruby colour is due to light being absorbed at a particular wavelength (0.53 μm) (Doremus 1994: 315). This absorption band comes from the spherical geometry of the particles and the particular optical properties of the gold. The particle size involved is c. 200–400 Å; the size of the gold particles influences the colour produced (the absorption),

Figure 3.6 Bands of cuprous oxide crystals in a sample of the dull reddish brown opaque colour found in Roman glass tesserae.

compared to crystallites of between *c.* 1 μm and 10μm in opaque glasses.

3.2.5.3 Iron-green and purple glasses

One of the principal colorant impurities in sand is iron. This can produce a range of colours in translucent glasses, depending on the furnace conditions used when the glass was made (Sellner *et al.* 1979), ranging from pale blue, brown, to yellowish green and dark olive. Iron oxide is invariably present in early glasses, and can be used deliberately to produce a translucent dark brown colour, but generally it occurs only as an impurity which is eclipsed by the addition of colorants like cobalt and copper to the glass-melt. The common iron-green glass of later periods is produced by a mixture of ferrous (Fe^{2+}) and ferric (Fe^{3+}) ions in the glass-melt (Weyl

1951: 91; Bamford 1982: 6). Although later (medieval) 'forest' glasses often contained manganese and iron together, which were introduced as impurities in the wood ash used as an alkali (Newton 1978: 60), the combination produced a range of glass colours. Earlier glasses were coloured more 'deliberately' by the probable use of minute quantities of manganese-bearing minerals such as pyrolucite (MnO_2). The chemical composition of translucent purple Egyptian Eighteenth Dynasty glasses shows an elevated manganese oxide level, apparently with few other accompanying impurities, so this infers that a relatively pure mineral source of colorant, like pyrolucite, was used. The purple colour would be produced by the trivalent Mn^{3+} ion in the glass (Weyl 1937: 118). The same deliberate use of manganese oxide has also been detected in Iron Age and Roman translucent glasses, and in these instances the deliberate use of a manganese-rich colorant is not in question either.

3.2.5.4 Opaque white, turquoise and yellow glasses

Opacity in ancient glasses is due to the presence of dispersed crystals in a translucent glass matrix. Opaque red glasses have already been discussed; other early opacifiers in white, turquoise, blue and yellow glasses all contain compounds based on antimony (Turner and Rooksby 1959; 1961; 1963; Rooksby 1962; Henderson 1985). It is the density of crystals which renders the glass opaque to wavelengths of light.

Opaque white glass, which was often used as trailed-on decoration (see Figure 3.7), contains masses of white calcium antimonate crystals which cause the light to be reflected and refracted from the glass and hence cause opacity (see Figure 3.8). Calcium antimonate ($Ca_2Sb_2O_7$ or $Ca_2Sb_2O_6$) does not occur naturally as a mineral, so the antimony added to the glass would react with the calcium in the glass to produce crystals (Turner and Rooksby 1961: 3). In order to produce an opaque turquoise glass colour antimony is added to a translucent turquoise glass instead of a weakly-tinted glass.

Before the second century BC opaque yellow glasses were coloured and opacified by the presence of lead antimonate crystals (Rooksby 1962: 23). A lead antimonate occurs naturally as Bindheimite ($Pb_2(Sb,Bi)_2O_6(O,OH)$), so an impurity of bismuth in ancient lead antimonate opacified glasses *might* show that this mineral had been used as an opacifier.

Figure 3.7 Two Eighteenth Dynasty Egyptian core-formed unguent vessels. The vessel on the left is decorated with opaque turquoise festoons and is thought to date to 1390–1352 BC; the vessel on the right with opaque yellow and white festoons is thought to date to 1390–1336 BC © The British Museum.

Figure 3.8 Back-scattered scanning electron micrograph of calcium antimonate crystals in a colourless glass matrix.

In the process of heat-treating lead-containing batches, a reaction between lead and antimony would also produce opaque yellow lead pyroantimonate $Pb_2Sb_2O_7$ which would remain incompletely dissolved in the glass under oxidising conditions; in this case the shapes of the lead antimonate crystals would reflect the heat treatment that the glass batch had been subjected to.

Another class of opacifiers is tin compounds. There is no evidence that tin-based glass opacifiers were used in ancient glasses until after the second century BC, and the earliest appear to have been produced and used in Europe (Werner and Bimson 1967; Henderson and Warren 1983; Henderson 1985). White opacity can be caused by the presence of tin oxide crystals (see Figure 3.9), which can be added to the translucent glass directly, as the mineral cassiterite. Opaque yellow glass, often of a somewhat

paler yellow colour than that produced by lead antimonate, can be produced by lead stannate crystals. By heat-treating the glass to produce the yellow crystals, other crystals, often of a soda-lime-silica composition, can develop in the glass. These soda-lime crystals provide us with information about the conditions in which the opacifying crystals developed. Lead-rich glass, including yellow glass opacified with lead stannate crystals, is more mobile than low lead glass. Figure 3.10 shows an electron micrograph of a section through a small fragment of early Christian Irish crucible in which glass opacified with lead stannate was worked and possibly made (Henderson and Ivens 1992). Layers of high lead glass appear white. The remains of the crucible fabric is on the left-hand side of the image (the 'dark' base of the crucible) fragment: it can seen clearly that the lead-rich yellow glass has infiltrated the crucible fabric comprehensively.

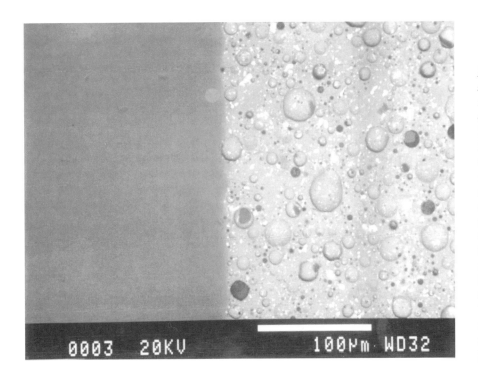

Figure 3.9 Back-scattered electron micrograph of tin oxide crystals in an Islamic (twelfth–fourteenth century) opaque white enamel. In this case the opacifying crystals are accompanied by masses of gas bubbles. Tin oxide opacifiers were first introduced in the second century BC. To the left of the opaque area is a colourless zone of glass.

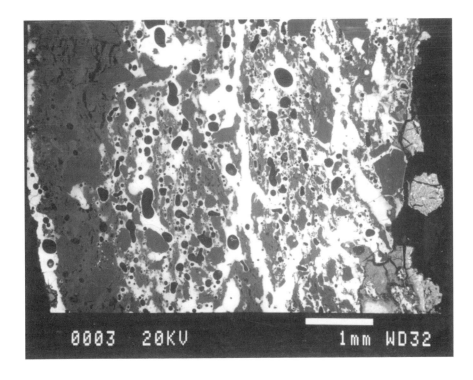

Figure 3.10 A back-scattered scanning electron micrograph of a section through the base of an early Christian (sixth–tenth century AD) crucible from Dunmisk, Co. Tyrone, Northern Ireland in which opaque lead-tin oxide glass has been worked/made.

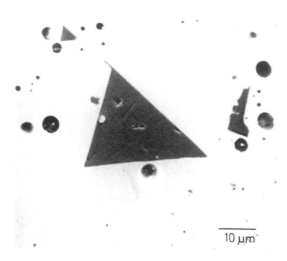

10 μm

Figure 3.11 A back-scattered scanning electron micrograph of cubic calcium fluoride crystals in a sixteenth-century Chinese enamel. This opacifier was first used in China and caused the glass to be an opaque white colour.

3.2.5.5 Other opacifiers

Opacifiers used in seventeenth-century glass include lead arsenate crystals which cause a somewhat 'milky' colour in glass. The opacifier was probably first introduced by Venetian glass-workers. Calcium phosphate can also act as an opacifier as indeed can sodium phosphate (Turner and Rooksby 1961: 2; Turner and Rooksby 1963: 306; Werner and Bimson 1963: 303; Besborodov 1975: 73). Calcium fluoride was used especially by the Chinese – see Figure 3.11 (Henderson *et al.* 1989). Incompletely dissolved raw materials (like silica) or partial devitrification of the glass can also cause opacity. Crystalline soda-lime-silicates which may be produced by incomplete vitrification of the glass, or formed out of solution when the glass was being worked, will have the same effect. Masses of air bubbles will reduce the transmission of light through the glass as well.

3.2.5.6 Glass decolorisers

The use of a silica sand source with an iron impurity generally produces a pale green glass under predominantly oxidising conditions. Two substances were used by ancient glass-workers to produce perfectly or near-perfectly colourless glasses. The first

was antimony trioxide which produces a water-clear glass. The second is manganese oxide which also produces a colourless glass, but which can be less effective as a decoloriser than antimony (Sayre and Smith 1961; Henderson 1985). The use of manganese oxide as a decoloriser can occasionally produce a very faint purple tinge and antimony trioxide a faint yellowish tinge. The use of antimony between the sixth and second centuries BC in the Middle East and Classical worlds provides a means of characterising the glasses made at that time (Sayre and Smith 1961); manganese oxide was introduced in the second century BC, even though antimony oxide was still available and sometimes used (Sayre and Smith 1963, Sayre 1964).

3.3 Glass-making/fritting

The basic procedures of glass-making can involve five main steps: (1) the selection and preparation of raw materials; (2) *making* the glass involving fritting the raw materials; (3) mixing the 'batch' and *melting* the glass; (4) *working* the glass to form the glass objects; and (5) annealing the objects.

The raw materials used are described in detail in Section 3.2. The most enduring ancient glass chemical composition was soda-lime-silica (see Section 3.6). The alkali (soda), a silica source and a lime-rich raw material are heated together initially to form a 'frit', a semi-fused granular material. True frit is defined as the semi-fused primary raw materials of glass-making (Henderson 1995: 99), in which the formation of glass has been arrested; it occurs at relatively low temperatures (see Figure 3.12). The term frit is often still misapplied to other archaeological materials, especially if the material looks granular. The hot frit may be thrown into cold water where it breaks apart. This procedure may be repeated several times. The main reason for fritting glass raw materials is in order to remove any impurities, especially gases which are derived from the breakdown of carbonates (releasing carbon dioxide) and sulphates/sulphides (releasing sulphur dioxide or trioxide); another reason is to reduce the number of gas bubbles in the glass-melt. There is scant archaeological evidence for fritting. It may have been carried out in 'open' containers such as trays in fritting ovens (see Figure 3.13) at temperatures of *c.* 700–800 °C (Turner 1954a;

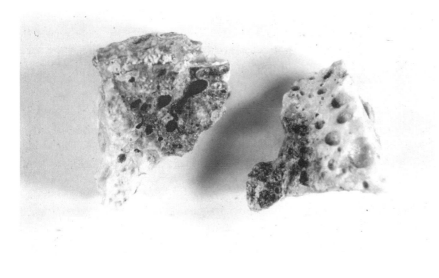

Figure 3.12 Two samples of heterogeneous over-heated frit from al-Raqqa, northern Syria, eighth–ninth century AD.

1956a); this was certainly the case in the sixteenth century. In nineteenth-century Murano, the historical glass-making centre in the Venetian Lagoon, the fritting process was carried out in a 'calcar', a shelf of refractory material in the oven onto which the raw materials were poured and raked in order to mix them (Moretti 1983: 181).

The ground-up frit is often mixed with scrap glass which has the effect of reducing the overall melting

Figure 3.13 A fritting oven. Note the tray containing lumps of frit close to the stoke hole (from Georgius Agricola's, De re Metallica, 1556).

temperature of the glass batch. Depending on the furnace type used, the melting of the glass batch was normally carried out in crucibles. The process was carried out in furnaces at temperatures of *at least c.* 1100 °C. Turner (1956a) was of the opinion that a *wood-fired* furnace would not have achieved temperatures above 1200 °C. Temperatures of 1270 °C had certainly been reached at the seventh–eighth-century site on the Venetian island of Torcello. Cable (1998: 319) considers that temperatures of at least 1350 °C must have been used to achieve a successful melt, especially those with high lime contents. There is every reason to expect this to have been the case using charcoal as the fuel and a forced draught system, although equally this would have been possible with a wood-fired furnace. Glass colorants, clarifiers and opacifying agents can be added to the initial glass batch, or at a later stage once the glass has melted fully to achieve greater control (Henderson 1985). Some opaque glass colours are produced as a result of heat-treating the glass, others may develop as a result of a (deliberate) change in the furnace atmosphere (see Section 3.2.5.4).

3.4 Glass furnaces

3.4.1 Interpreting the evidence
A range of ancient glass furnace types have been found. It is easy to be proscriptive and suggest that

the forms of ancient glass furnaces varied little and that they developed in predictable ways through time and space. There are two potential problems that archaeologists can have when excavating putative glass furnaces. The first is actually being certain that the structure was used for glass production, the second is the high degree of inference that must be used in order to 'reconstruct' furnaces from what generally consists of no more than foundation courses of bricks; this last point is equally applicable to kilns and metal-smelting furnaces. The potential problem of being sure that an excavated structure was used as a glass furnace derives from the fact that, for a range of possible reasons of deposition, there may be little clearly associated debris from the glass production process. Clearly glass artisans would not have waded in vitreous debris lying on their workshop floor and left it for archaeologists to make a clear association of the debris with the use of the industrial structures; they would have worked in a clean environment. If debris from glass production was *re-deposited* on the glass workshop floor once it had gone out of use, it is secondary evidence but does provide us with some evidence of what industrial activities were being pursued in the vicinity. One of the only sure ways to prove that a glass furnace has been found is the discovery of glass dribbles/spills inside and around the furnace, as distinct from glassy (fuel-ash) slags that can derive from any high-temperature industry by alkali-rich fuel-ash combining with silica in bricks (Biek and Bayley 1979). Spills of true glass often occur when large volumes of glass are heated and the furnace has been (re-)used over a long period – and perhaps gone out of use as a result. Needless to say, glass can be distinguished from fuel-ash slag by its chemical composition. If a sufficient proportion of the original furnace structure does survive, its function, based on its shape, may be inferred by a process of elimination. Nevertheless, in their discussion of glass-melting crucibles used for the production of glass ingots from Qantir-Piramesses, Egypt, Rehren and Pusch (1997) remind us that 'a good deal of luck' is necessary in unearthing key pieces which fit into a particular industrial process.

3.4.2 The earliest furnaces

The earliest site where the evidence for a possible glass furnace has been found is at Tell el-Amarna in Egypt. This was found among the remains of a New Kingdom, Eighteenth Dynasty industrial estate in this dynastic capital of Akhenaten (1353–1337 BC). Because the evidence is important, it will be discussed in detail; many features of interpretation are common to the remains of other industrial structures for pottery and metal production. The first putative glass furnace discovered and published by Flinders Petrie (1894: 26) was described as a 'brickwork furnace in a glazing factory' which immediately raises the question as to whether the industrial remains actually related to the production of faience rather than glass (Shortland and Tite 1998). Petrie's excavations, and subsequent excavations by Nicholson (1995) have also produced the evidence of glass-working in the form of spills of glass, vessel and rod fragments and drips of glass adhering to cylindrical ceramic vessel fragments. Although the evidence for the *working* of glass in fourteenth-century BC Egypt is indisputable, there is currently no published primary archaeological evidence for the elusive process of *making* glass from raw materials there. The remains of the larger structures discovered by Nicholson at Tell el-Amarna which had internal diameters of *c*. 1.5 m had fused clay (known locally as *khorfush*) adhering to their inner faces and were associated with a large amount of fused clay in the vicinity. This has been interpreted as a sacrificial rendering (Jackson *et al.* 1998: 13), a layer of clay which was applied to some ancient furnaces in order to protect the surfaces of bricks from the high temperatures achieved. Although this shows that the temperatures employed in the structures were high enough to melt the clay it does not, by itself, prove that glass was made or even melted in the structures; fully-fused glass adhering to the inner face would have helped to prove it. By establishing the temperatures at which the clay became vitrified in the furnaces (by re-firing a small amount), an estimate of the maximum temperatures attained would be provided. It is noted that there is no evidence for the use of a forced draught system (Jackson *et al.* 1998: 15), and it has been suggested that the temperatures achieved for 'manufacturing' glass would not have been high enough. However, there is no particular reason why the remaining fragmentary structures should provide the evidence for a forced draught system and one would be lucky to find clay tuyères (a clay cylindrical object inserted into a furnace (wall) into which a bellows nozzle would fit).

However the associated debris from glass-working, moulds for the production of faience objects and unfired sherds of pottery, at least shows that, among other activities, glass was being worked in the vicinity. Add to this the find of 'ceramic vessel' fragments whose profile fitted exactly that of blue glass ingots found in the Ulu Burun shipwreck near Kaş off the coast of Turkey, and the evidence for glass-working becomes solid. Of course there is every likelihood that glass was fused from primary raw materials, and scientific investigations by Shortland and Tite (2000) help to bolster the case for the Egyptian manufacture of (cobalt blue) glass from primary raw materials, in that most glass of that time found in Mesopotamia suggests that at least one raw material used to make it was different. There has been considerable discussion of whether glass was imported from the Middle East to be worked in Egypt, based on textual evidence (Oppenheim 1973; Newton 1980: 176; Newton and Davison 1989: 107). Indeed Newton (1980: 176) claims that 'the Egyptians could only melt other people's glass', so even though the archaeological evidence is not conclusive, analytical work suggests otherwise.

It is suggested that two other smaller circular structures were used for pottery and faience/pottery respectively (Nicholson 1995), but equally there is the possibility that the larger structures were the remains of pottery kilns. Excavations at Amarna have revealed some very interesting industrial structures but the archaeological evidence found, to date, does not prove one way or the other whether glass was made from primary raw materials there. In any case the initial process of glass-making (fritting) occurs at considerably lower temperatures than those employed for heating up the glass batch in pots; perhaps one of two smaller structures at Amarna was a fritting oven. Glass can be made using a single melt as experimental archaeology (using ashed Welsh seaweed and Amarna sand) has shown (Jackson *et al.* 1998). However, this does not prove that glass was made without fritting the raw materials first.

Indeed, if the larger structures represent the remains of glass furnaces, they *may* have been the foundation courses for the 'southern' type of glass

Figure 3.14 The 'southern' three-chambered furnace consisting of the firing chamber at the bottom, the melting chamber in the middle with 'pots' containing glass and the annealing chamber at the top (from Georgius Agricola, *De re Metallica*, 1556).

furnace (Charleston 1978) which consisted of three chambers superimposed one above the other in the shape of a bee-hive. On the other hand, the two-chambered furnace reconstructed at Amarna by Jackson *et al.* (1998: 15–16) may be the correct interpretation, but there is no definitive way of knowing. If a three-chambered furnace, the lower chamber would have been used for burning fuel which would have been divided from the middle chamber by a floor with a central hole in it through which the heat rose (see Figure 3.14). The pots/crucibles containing the glass batch, and subsequently the hot liquid glass, were placed on the floor of the middle chamber.

The 'roof' of the middle chamber acted as a floor for the top chamber in which vessels were allowed to cool slowly (annealed). A two-chambered furnace would lack the annealing chamber.

3.4.3 Roman furnaces

The archaeological evidence for glass furnaces between fourteenth-century BC Tell al-Amarna and the Roman period is sparse. Although evidence for glass-working has survived, such as in eleventh–ninth century BC contexts at Frattesina in northern Italy (Bietti-Sestieri 1981; Brill 1992; Henderson and Ponting 1999) and in Hellenistic contexts on Rhodes (Weinberg 1969), for example, it is difficult to point to the remains of glass furnaces for this period. However, it is surely only a matter of time before furnaces (which produced some very high quality glass) from this long period are discovered. In the Roman period, in Britain for example, Price (1998: 333–5) has noted the small (0.9 m diameter) furnaces with keyhole-shaped plans have been found

at Mancetter and Leicester. A rectangular structure from Caistor by Norwich (Artis 1828: 4–5; Atkinson 1932) appears to have been larger but, like those at Mancetter and Leicester, probably held one pot. The remains of another Roman glass furnace found at Wilderspool is also difficult to interpret (May 1904). Fragments of a Roman tank furnace (a basic reconstruction of such a furnace is provided in Figure 3.16) have been found in London (Shepherd and Heyworth 1991), and more recently a massive dump of Roman glass waste has also been found there (John Shepherd, personal communication). As far as it is possible to infer, in most cases these tank furnaces would have produced a large volume of raw glass, perhaps resulting from a single melting event (see Section 3.12.3.1). At Autun in France, excavations have revealed the plan of a tank furnace measuring 1.9×0.88 m with an apsidal end (Rebourg 1989).

In Cologne, Germany first-century Roman circular and rectangular structures have been found

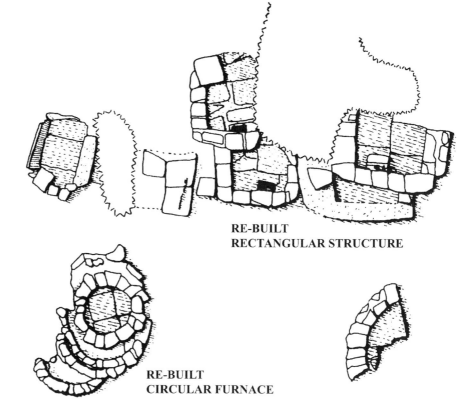

RE-BUILT RECTANGULAR STRUCTURE

Figure 3.15 Plan of the site at Eigelstein near Cologne showing plans of Roman circular furnaces and rectangular structures re-built several times, used for glass production.

RE-BUILT CIRCULAR FURNACE

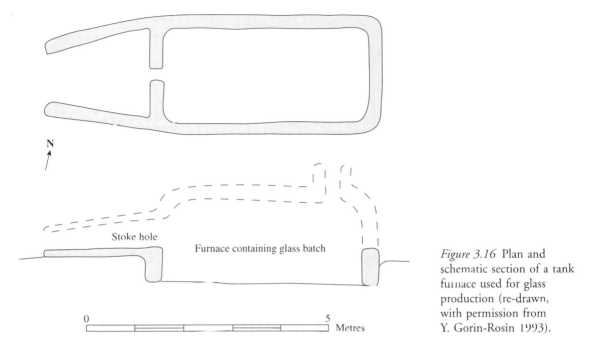

N

Stoke hole

Furnace containing glass batch

0   5
|_|_|_|_|_|_|_|_|_|_| Metres

Figure 3.16 Plan and schematic section of a tank furnace used for glass production (re-drawn, with permission from Y. Gorin-Rosin 1993).

(Doppelfeld 1965: 11; Fremersdorf 1965: 24; Seibel 1998: 43–44). The excavation plan (Figure 3.15) reveals that one small glass furnace was re-built three times, nearly in the same location. This furnace is of a comparable size to those discussed by Price (1998), though a segment of a second circular structure nearby has twice the diameter. More intriguing still is the presence of nearby rectangular structures, which appear to show two phases of construction. There is the likelihood here that the different shapes of structures related to different parts of the glass production process: fritting, glass-melting and perhaps annealing. At least one of the circular structures was probably used for melting the glass; the rectangular structures may have been used for fritting, or possibly annealing. A series of small Roman furnace structures have also been found during excavations at Kaiseraugst, Augst, Switzerland. The seven structures found were circular or oval in plan and ranged in length between *c*. 0.7 m to 1.5 m (Tomasevic 1977: 243). Associated pottery suggests that they were used in the second and third centuries AD. Similar small furnaces used in glass production have been found at Avènches, Switzerland (Morel *et al.* 1992). Many of these circular structures may well have been three-chambered

glass furnaces, though without better preservation it is difficult to be sure.

Twentieth-century excavations of a Punic glass furnace at Carthage were so poorly recorded that they will not be mentioned further (Gauckler 1915: 10). Extensive excavations have been carried out of a fourth-century AD glass factory at Jalame (Weinberg 1988), near where, according to the Roman historian Pliny (23–79 AD), glass-making was first discovered at the mouth of the river Belus in the Levant (now called the river Naaman). Here traders in natural soda are said to have supported their cauldrons which were being used to prepare a meal with blocks of natural soda. These were said to have reacted with the sand to form glass. Although a possible event, given present evidence it is more likely that glass was first made elsewhere in the Levant (see Section 3.9).

The excavations at Jalame are important because the entire workshop and all the glass found have been fully published. The excavations revealed somewhat ambiguous structural evidence for a furnace with the discovery of a firing trench. In the comprehensive scientific report (Brill 1988) indicated that glass was worked but not made on the site (Section 3.10.3).

3.4.4 Early medieval, Islamic and other 'southern' glass furnaces

The quality of evidence for glass furnaces in the early medieval period (seventh–eighth centuries) on the island of Torcello in the Venetian Lagoon is high. Excavations revealed a glass-house (Tabaczynska 1965; Gasparetto 1965; Leciejewicz *et al.* 1963–4; 1969–70; 1977) with clear evidence for functionally discrete structures which can be related to different glass-making/production processes. A circular central furnace was assumed to be for glass fusion; a rectangular structure for annealing; and another rectangular structure was interpreted as having been used for glass fusion. A fourth structure, with a poorly defined plan, was interpreted as for the preparation of frit. These suggested interpretations are sensible given the relative size and positions of the structures; again it was impossible to be certain what exact form the furnaces found at this important site would have taken in three dimensions.

In Israel the impressive remains of sixteen early Byzantine tank furnaces at Hadera (Gorin-Rosen 1993) is a reflection of the massive scale of production of raw glass (see Figure 3.16). Gorin-Rosen estimates that between eight and ten tons of glass were produced each time the furnace was fired; perhaps ingots were also produced (Foy and Jézégou 1998: 124). After the furnace was used it was destroyed. The famous slab of glass at Bet She'arim, also in Israel, is likely to be the remains of such a single chamber tank furnace (Brill 1965a: 261–2). Slightly later, in an eighth– ninth-century phase at al-Raqqa in Syria, massive fragments of tank furnaces have been found there (Section 3.12.3.1) reminding us that it is likely that, in many cases, they were used only once. During their fieldwork in western India in the late 1980s Jan Kock and Torben Sode discovered that fritting was carried out first and that the glass was *still* being melted in tank furnaces (Kock and Sode 1999). In an early phase of the al-Raqqa, Syria, glass workshop, the excavations revealed the remains of three-chambered glass furnaces with the lowest courses of the upper chamber (a clay dome) still *in situ* (Henderson 1999b) – see Section 3.12.2. Excavations of an eighth–ninth-century glass furnace at Glastonbury, Somerset, revealed a long structure with an oval plan (Charleston 1978: 22); Bayley (in press) provides a detailed consideration of the evidence found.

Investigation in eleventh–twelfth-century Corinth revealed remains to which it was less easy to ascribe a function (Davison 1940; Whitehouse 1991).

Excavations of other medieval glass furnaces have sometimes revealed a better degree of preservation. At Cadrix, France, a stoke hole and the base of the middle chamber of a presumed three-chambered furnace survived (Foy 1989). The textual evidence for the industry together with the location and form of medieval glass furnaces in southern France were considered in detail, together with the products and their chemical compositions. In this study Foy (1989) has significantly advanced our understanding of European medieval glass production by examining the evidence in the context of an impressive regional research programme.

So far we have considered glass furnaces which have circular plans and tank glass furnaces which have rectangular plans. Although a distinction has been made between 'northern' and 'southern' furnace types, having two and three chambers superimposed upon each other respectively (Charleston 1978), most excavations have not revealed a means of reconstructing the furnaces, and assumptions normally have to be made about the original shapes of the furnaces. Indeed the distinctions which have been made between northern and southern furnace types should not be dogmatically applied to glass-house excavations since predetermined expectations can sometimes shape the methodology and progress of excavations. The reconstruction of furnaces and their functions within workshops is of course dictated by the known processes of glass-making and working which are documented and are carried out today. Sometimes inspired reconstructions result: see Figure 3.17 (Mendera 1991). It is however very difficult to ascertain precisely what function each structure had in the excavated glass-workshops (Foy 1989: 147; Henderson 1999b). However, in the case of the al-Raqqa glass-workshop, while the southern furnaces discovered fit the suggested pattern, there is also another strand of evidence which can be introduced in the interpretation of the excavated structures. This is the survival of a ninth-century Syriac text, currently housed in the British Museum (Dillon 1907: 122–4) which is discussed more fully in Section 3.12.3.2. Where available, historical evidence for the existence of hierarchies of artisans, guild structures and/or the

Figure 3.17 A reconstruction of the glass workshop at Germagnana, northern Italy of twelfth–thirteenth century AD date (after Mendera 1991).

(centralised) control over production processes can all contribute to the interpretation of archaeological evidence. The evidence of excavated industrial remains can also generate models for production, including artisan interaction and, when combined with the results of scientific investigations, putative cross-fertilisation between industries.

3.4.5 'Northern' and later types of glass furnaces

The 'northern' type of glass furnace, as defined by Charleston (1978), was basically a tunnel-shaped structure with a firing trench along the middle and *sieges* (shelves) at either side on which the glass pots containing the glass-melt were located. A medieval example was found at Blunden's Wood, Hambledon, Surrey (Wood 1965) of a probable fourteenth century date. Others of a similar plan (and section) have been found elsewhere in Europe, such as the fifteenth-century example at Eichsfeld, Germany (Lappe and Möbes 1984). The early fifteenth-century manuscript depicting Sir John Mandeville's *Travels*, also in the forest tradition, shows a furnace with an *oval* plan and domed roof. It has a stoke hole

below, two glory holes containing glass pots on the upper level and an annealing oven at the 'back' of the furnace. It is difficult to tell whether there was a separate fire pit for the annealing oven. The furnace depicted is therefore different from the typical northern furnace. This reminds us that it is difficult to apply hard and fast rules to a 'typology' of glass furnaces; many of the ancient glass furnace remains which have been discovered have their own characteristics which distinguish them from others. Nevertheless a text entitled *De re Metallica*, written by a German monk Georgius Agricola (1556) provides an excellent series of illustrations and a description of the processes of glass production (see Figures 3.13 and 3.14). The production processes are relevant to a consideration of almost any other period of glass production. In these texts the working furnace (*clibanus operis*) (Figure 3.14) is distinguished from the fritting oven (Figure 3.13); he even suggests that the working furnace can be used for fritting overnight, when not being used for the principal purpose for which it was designed. A second beehive form of furnace, which lacks the annealing chamber, is also described. Agricola describes a third

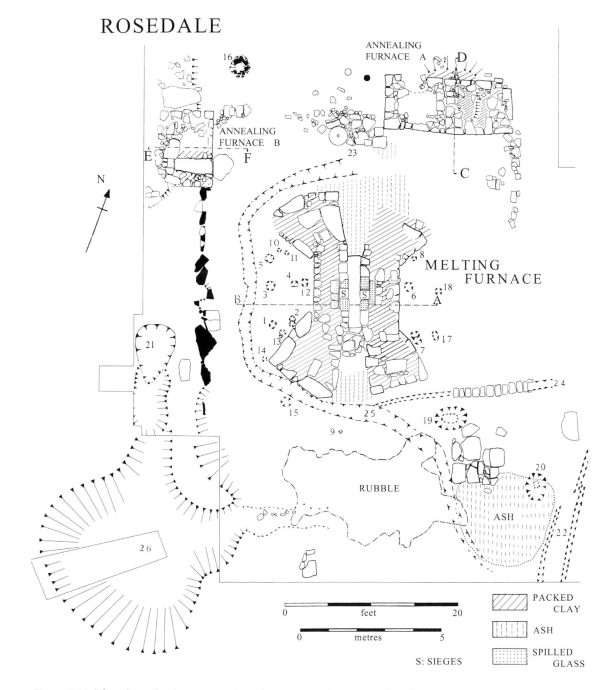

Figure 3.18 The plan of a late sixteenth–early seventeenth-century glass furnace and associated structures at Rosedale, north Yorkshire (after Crossley and Aberg 1972).

separate structure, the annealing furnace (*lehr*), which has a rectangular plan with a vaulted roof. Vessels are placed in 'oblong receptacles' before being annealed. In Damascus today, vessels are placed in small carts which are then set in a lehr which extends across the back of the furnace. As new carts are added the earlier ones are displaced, the vessels becoming increasingly cooler the further along the lehr they are pushed. The receptacles in Agricola's description may however simply be to make it easier to remove the batches of cool glass vessels. Agricola's text also reminds us that the 'southern' form of glass furnace continued to be used into the sixteenth century and was used for the manufacture of world-famous Venetian glassware. In spite of this the 'northern' furnace type was preferred north of the Alps.

Among the best excavated and published examples of the 'northern' furnace type are the post medieval examples from Hutton and especially Rosedale, north Yorkshire, England (Crossley and Aberg 1972): see Figure 3.18. Not only did excavations of the late sixteenth-century Rosedale furnace reveal solid evidence for the use of the northern furnace type with room for two pots at any given time, but they also showed that the process of annealing occurred in separate annealing ovens. In addition, Crossley and Aaberg uncovered 'wings' (extensions) on the four corners of the furnace, a technological development which is thought to have been introduced by immigrant glass-workers from Lorraine (Crossley 1990: 229). Although the wings may have been used for annealing glass vessels, the construction of separate (rectangular) annealing ovens suggests that the wings may have been used for fritting or as 'pot ovens' (Crossley 1990: 230). After 1615 James I decreed that coal should be used instead of wood as the principal fuel in glass furnaces. The furnace at Kimmeridge which also encompassed wings was fired with coal (Crossley 1987). Excavations at Bolsterstone, south Yorkshire have revealed an early eighteenth-century glass furnace which still incorporated the principal features of *sieges* for placing the pots on. However a new feature was the insertion of below-ground flues drawing on an air supply from outside (Ashurst 1992). Fragments of large almost completely enclosed crucibles, known as 'closed crucibles', with domed tops and an opening which fitted into the glory hole, found at Bolsterstone (Ashurst 1992: 37–8) represent the earliest evidence for their use (Crossley 1990: 236). They were introduced because the coal particles and sulphurous fumes had a detrimental effect on the quality of the glass produced when open crucibles were used. The below-ground flue system was incorporated in the later English invention of the imposing glass cones still surviving at, for example, Catcliffe, Yorkshire and near Stourbridge in the West Midlands.

3.5 Glass-working

The first step in the production of a glass vessel is the gathering of a *gob* of hot glass from a crucible or other container. The glowing glass would then be blown into the desired vessel shape (see Figure 3.19); small collars of glass (moils) which are attached to the blowing iron once the blown vessel has been removed are often the only archaeological evidence that glass-blowing has occurred. The blown vessel could subsequently be worked in various ways. It may have been blown into a mould such as that shown in Figure 3.20, so that the glass picks up the decoration on the inside of the mould (see Figure 3.21). Although these moulds can be ceramic, Folsach and Whitehouse (1993) describe three Islamic glass moulds made out of metal. The vessel may have been subsequently re-inflated, producing what is known as an optically-blown vessel. By transferring the base of the glass vessel onto the end of a metal rod known as a *pontil* (see Figure 3.22) it allowed the glass-worker to then work the vessel rim with a range of metal and wooden tools (see Figure 3.23). If modern craft glass-workers need to cool down *a particular area* of the glass vessel they roll it in damp newspaper; undoubtedly ancient glass-workers would have used an equivalent material, such as wet leather. Pieces of carved wood in the shape of a bowl (with a handle extension) could be used for shaping the glass vessel. During the process of forming the vessel it may have been re-inserted into the glass furnace several times in order to soften it so that the glass vessel could continue to be worked. The glass vessel would then be placed in an annealing oven which, in ancient glass furnaces might either form an

Figure 3.19 Glass blowing in a contemporary glass workshop in Damascus, Syria.

Figure 3.20 A ribbed glass mould, Matlock, Derbyshire.

'extension' of the furnace (as a separate chamber next to, or superimposed on, the others: see Figure 3.14) or be a separate low-temperature structure (see Figure 3.18). In the annealing oven the glass vessels are allowed to cool down slowly so that the stresses that may be built up during vessel production are released.

3.6 The chemical compositions of ancient glasses

In the 1950s and 1960s the chemical analysis of ancient glass was in its infancy. Turner assembled some of the few analyses that had been carried out, and produced some very informative papers which showed some of the potential (Turner 1956a, b), but these relied on mixtures of other peoples' analyses using various wet chemical techniques and some of the samples analysed had a relatively insecure provenance. Turner contributed to ancient glass studies, especially in relation to the possible identification of the raw materials used to make glass (Turner 1956a). Caley's book, *Analysis of Ancient Glasses 1790–1957* (1962) recorded the existence of the analyses of ancient glasses, but made few attempts to identify

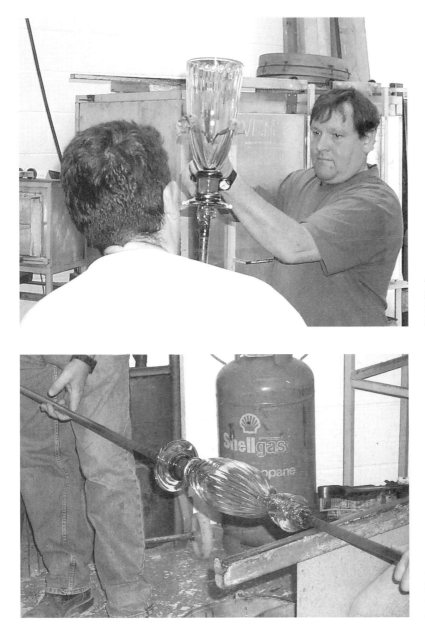

Figure 3.21 A mould-blown glass vessel produced using the mould in Figure 3.20, Matlock, Derbyshire.

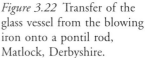

Figure 3.22 Transfer of the glass vessel from the blowing iron onto a pontil rod, Matlock, Derbyshire.

clear trends in the data. In any case, given the range of laboratories involved and the time scale over which the analyses had been carried out, the potential sources of unquantifiable error were wide indeed, making it difficult to compare results in a way which could provide coherent compositional trends. Forbes (1957) did, however, note chronological changes in the use of glass raw materials.

It was not until the early 1960s, when E.V. Sayre first published the results of his analytical investigations of ancient glass with R.W. Smith, that the potential range of technological information which could be gleaned from analyses was fully realised. Over and above the compositional types that Turner had enumerated, Sayre and Smith's paper published in the journal *Science* (Sayre and Smith 1961), based

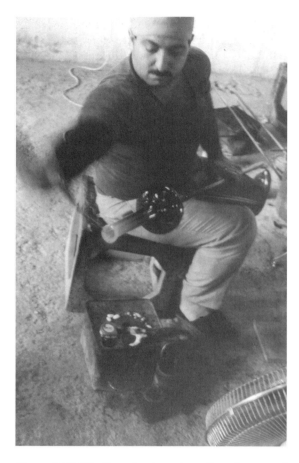

Figure 3.23 Working the hot rim of a glass vessel attached to the pontil rod in Damascus, Syria.

on neutron activation analyses of groups of glass samples, showed definable compositional groupings which could be correlated to both geographical and chronological criteria. The compositional types were based on the occurrence in ancient glasses of five element oxides: those of manganese, antimony, lead, magnesia and potassium. The first two of these were used in a discriminatory way in their role as decolorants, lead oxide was used as a major component, magnesia and potassium oxide as impurities in the alkalis used.

The glass types which Sayre and Smith defined are found at different times: high magnesia soda-lime glasses between *c*. 1500 and 800 BC; low magnesia soda-lime glasses between *c*. 800 BC and

1000 AD; high antimony soda-lime glasses between *c*. 600 BC and 200 BC; Islamic high lead glasses between *c*. 1000 and 1400 AD and Islamic high magnesia between *c*. 840 and 1400 AD. The time ranges associated with these compositions are rather approximate, but are in general still perfectly valid.

Sayre's papers, particularly those published in 1964, 1965 and 1974 (solely authored by Sayre) and those published in 1963 and 1967 (with R.W. Smith) built on the results discussed in his 1961 paper. These papers dealt with discrete groupings of glasses, which reflected specific aspects of ancient glass technology, and considered broader trends. In spite of criticism from Ankner (1965), the compositional groupings that Sayre and Smith defined have stood the test of time. Sayre (1965, 145–6) also noted that ancient soda-lime glasses can be divided into those which contain either high or low magnesia levels (HMG and LMG respectively); Turner (1956b: 176–7) had noted that magnesia was an important constituent of ancient glasses but not that it occurred in quite different compositional families of glass which could be linked to both time, and less easily, place of production. It was found that a correlation between potassium and magnesia oxides in ancient glasses reflected the exploitation of mineral (low magnesia) or plant-ash (high magnesia) sources of alkali in ancient glasses. Within the HMG compositional group Sayre (1965: 146–7) noted very close similarities in the standard deviation ranges of a number of non-colorant oxides in second-millennium BC Egyptian, Mycenean– Minoan and Sumerian–Elamite glasses, underlining the innate conservatism of glass technology at that time (with a potential inference that there were either a small number of glass production centres or that a larger number used the same or similar raw materials). Sayre and Smith's 1967 paper emphasised even more firmly how conservative ancient glass-making traditions must have been (for the glasses that have survived), with quite specific compositional characteristics recurring in glasses over broad time periods.

Ancient glasses of other compositions can now be added to the five compositional types that Sayre and Smith defined in 1961. The first is a low magnesia, high potassium oxide glass (LMHK) which occurs between *c.* 1150 and 700 BC in Europe (Henderson 1988; Brill 1992; Hartmann *et al.* 1997); this was an unexpected discovery which clearly reflected innovation with new raw materials at an early time in the prehistory of Europe. A second compositional type is high potassium (and high barium) oxide glasses of the Chinese Han Dynasty (206 BC–221 AD in the east (Meiguang *et al.* 1987; Jiazhi and Xianqiu 1987), a Chinese invention. Third, high aluminia glasses from first-millennium AD India (Brill 1987) again reflect the use of new raw materials. Fourth, lead oxide-silica glasses from *c.* tenth–fourteenth century AD are the earliest example of the use of a high level of lead oxide as a glass former; some lead oxide levels are as high as 65% (Henderson and Warren 1986; Wedepohl *et al.* 1995). 'Potash' glasses of the high medieval period (Cox *et al.* 1979) frequently, though not exclusively (Cox and Gillies 1986) used for the production of medieval church and cathedral windows and vessel glass in the west were not included in the initial study by Sayre and Smith. A range of post-medieval glasses of mixed-alkali, low alkali–high calcium and soda-lime-silica compositions have been identified (Mortimer 1995; Henderson 1998a) (see Section 3.13.4). There are no doubt other glass compositional types yet to be discovered which will also be characteristic of their time of production.

Occasionally glass compositions can be characteristic of their *place* of production, as is apparently the case for glass found in large quantities at Frattesina in northern Italy of *c.* eleventh–ninth century BC date (Bietti-Sestieri 1980; Henderson 1988b) of a mixed-alkali composition. Generally, though, it can be difficult to be confident that the glass found at a factory site is characteristic to that site.

3.7 The working properties of soda-lime-silica glass

Alkalis flux silica (sand or quartz), lowering the melting temperature of pure silica from 1710 °C to a minimum liquidus temperature (the absolute melting temperature of the glass above which nuclei and crystals cannot form) at the ternary eutectic of 725 °C for a composition of 21.9% soda, 5% calcium oxide and 73.1% silica (Morey 1964: Figure 20, Tables 13, 33). The eutectic mixture is one which has the lowest freezing point of all possible mixtures of sodium, calcium and silicon oxides. Most ancient translucent glasses are soda-lime-silica in composition, but generally contain lower levels of soda and silica than in the ternary eutectic (see below). The liquidus temperature for a soda-lime-silica glass containing 18.8% soda, 7% calcium oxide and 74.2% silica is 867 °C which rises to 1060 °C for a glass containing 17.6% soda, 15% calcium oxide and 64.7% silica (Morey 1964). The former composition is closest to that for second- and first-millennia BC glasses.

A closer comparison is provided by the work of Brill (1988) for low magnesia soda-lime glass of fourth century AD date: the basic composition is similar to other, earlier, soda-lime glasses, with some important differences in impurity patterns. Brill showed that for a typical soda-lime glass of 68–73% silica, *c.* 14–17.4% soda and *c.* 7.4–10% calcium oxide ('lime') the liquidus temperature was *c.* 700 °C, the softening temperature was *c.* 1000 °C and the marvering and gathering temperatures were *c.* 1000–1100 °C (see Figure 3.24). The glass would therefore have had a relatively short working time. Opaque glasses used in the decoration of glass vessels often contained high lead oxide levels and would therefore have had a much longer working time *and* a lower softening temperature of *c.* 750 °C, depending on the level of lead oxide involved. Opaque lead-rich glasses were also used as enamels and with their relatively high lead levels it was possible to soften them without distorting the metal being enamelled; the same would have been true of the high lead opaque white glass used for decorating the Portland vase (Bimson and Freestone 1983). The opaque white glasses used for decorative trailing on Egyptian vessels, on the other hand, would have been more difficult to work because they contained little or no detectable levels of lead oxide. These glasses would have been applied as opaque rods to the surface of the core-formed vessels (Gudenrath in Tait 1991), which would have been continuously reheated in order to soften them. This, in turn, could have led to distortions of the patterns, but the most difficult part

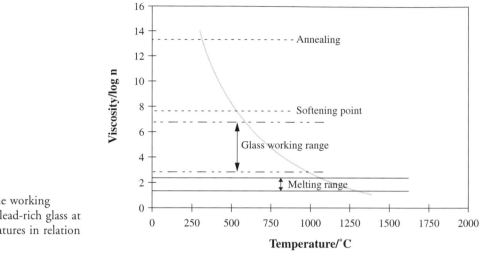

Figure 3.24 The working properties of a lead-rich glass at various temperatures in relation to its viscosity.

of the operation would have been to avoid distorting the glass vessel while at the same time keeping the rod of decorative glass sufficiently soft to work. The complete decorated core-formed vessels very rarely display any signs that the artisan who made them had problems decorating them.

3.8 Ritual aspects

Apart from these practical considerations the ritual and ethnographic aspects of glass production are just as important, if rather more difficult to assemble. Information provided by the translations of cuneiform tablets, where processes of glass production are described, can be relevant and useful to the reconstruction of ancient procedures. Arguably the most significant texts that have survived were found in the Palace of Asurbanipal, King of Assyria (664–27 BC) at Kuyunjik (Nineveh), Mesopotamia which are thought to describe much earlier procedures as well as those carried out in the seventh century BC (Oppenheim *et al.* 1970). The texts also describe ritual aspects of glass production including a reverence for the materials (Peltenburg 1971) where solids are transformed into a glowing liquid and, on cooling, back to a translucent 'solid'. The glassmaking locality was placed under the protection of the gods, sacrifices were made to Kubu-deities and

the glass was melted when the moon was in the right quarter, on a propitious day of the month (Oppenheim *et al.* 1970: 33). Clearly evidence for these rituals is (normally) absent from excavated sites.

3.9 The origins of glass and its early production in the Mediterranean and Mesopotamia

3.9.1 Introduction
Ancient glass made during the second millennium BC was some of the first to have been made in the world in any quantity. Although small objects of glass, particularly beads, were made in the third millennium BC, it was not until the second millennium BC that glass started to be mass-produced. The manufacture of core-formed glass vessels in Egypt during the New Kingdom Eighteenth Dynasty (*c.* mid-fourteenth century) is an example of mass-production; by that period the glass was of a high quality, involving the use of a wide range of translucent and opaque colours in the manufacture of often highly decorated core-formed vessels (see Figure 3.7) such as small containers/phials serving as unguent flasks. The precise locations of the glassmaking centres, where the glass was fused from primary raw materials, in the Middle East and Egypt

are yet to be found. The most recent excavations at Tell el-Amarna in Egypt (Nicholson 1995) have revealed evidence of high-temperature industries involving vitreous materials, but direct evidence for the manufacture of glass involving fritting is yet to be identified (see Sections 3.3 and 3.4.2)

3.9.2 The origins of glass: fuel-ash slags, glazed stones and faience

In considering the origins of glass production it is worth being aware that it must have shared many features of pyrotechnology which are found in metal production, for example the use of specific fuels which provided a predictable source of heat could have been used in glass production. The charcoals produced from different species of plants yield heat which can vary in calorific value according to the species involved. There is every reason to suspect that ancient glass-makers were well aware of this. Another possible area of shared information would be the construction of kilns and furnaces using bricks having the specific characteristics which enabled them to be heated to relatively high temperatures (perhaps as high as 1400 °C). Indeed such a high-temperature environment could potentially lead to the manufacture of a glassy material adventitiously and this would probably have been how glass was first observed before being manufactured deliberately. The glassy material is known as a fuel-ash slag (Biek and Bayley 1979; Henderson *et al.* 1987) and can even form when a wheat field is burnt. Its formation requires an association of a silica-rich material with a plant ash. In the context of metal production, silica in crucibles or in furnace walls fuse with alkaline plant ashes in the environment which may be present when burnt wood is used as fuel. Thus in the manufacture of copper and copper alloys the fuel-ash slag is often a red colour because the copper present may be reduced, producing a reddish cuprous oxide or metallic copper colorant; in appearance it

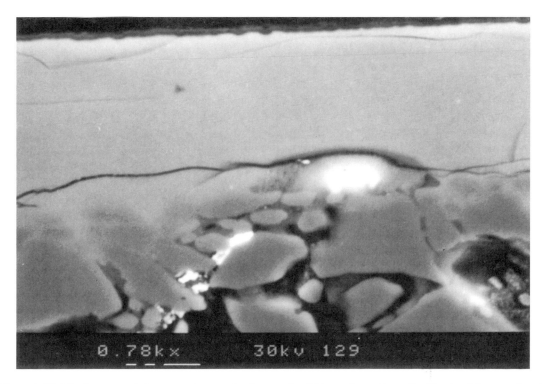

Figure 3.25 A back-scattered electron micrograph of a sample of faience from Cova d'es Carritx, Menorca showing dark grey silica crystals in the lower half with a surface glassy layer. The bright inclusions just under the glassy surface are rich in lead, phosphorus and calcium. Elsewhere in the sample copper chloride and zinc were detected.

can sometimes be confused with opaque red enamel. Thus a glassy material would have been observable during the early stages of metal production, but to prove that the sight of a glazed surface is what caused or inspired an artisan to make glass and form it into artefacts is impossible. Even if copper did occur as the principal colorant in early glasses, this is not a priori evidence for a link between the two technologies. Peltenburg (1987: 20–2) has stressed the paucity of solid evidence for the link. Hodges (1970: 62ff.) also notes the very early glazing of stones by heating a copper ore on the powdered surface of talc.

Faience is also vitreous. It can be made by cementation, efforescence (Tite *et al.* 1983; 1987), and a third, the direct application of a glaze (i.e. preformed glass) to a core made from crushed quartz. Faience is essentially the combination of a vitreous component and quartz sand or crushed quartz, sometimes with mineralogical impurities. Recent investigations of Balearic faience have also revealed that the presence of impurities of a mineralogical origin (see Figure 3.25), such as antimony, is more widespread than realised to date. These impurities are thought to be characteristic of the copper sources which were used for colouring the turquoise vitreous phase in the faience (Henderson 1999c).

Since faience was manufactured and used from the fifth millennium BC, this is liable to have influenced the deliberate production of glass in the third millennium BC (Brill 1963). Stone and Thomas (1956: 37) stated that 'the techniques involved in the development of faience were strictly antecedent to the subsequent development of true glass' and Vandiver (1983: A-136) has pointed out that the technique of faience production which involved the direct application of glaze must have foreshadowed glass manufacture. So, although faience production is a strong contender in contributing to the development of the first glass manufacture, perhaps in northern Syria, we have yet to discover a suitable workshop where both of these technologies occurred together.

McGovern *et al.* (1991) have published a useful discussion of the chemical analysis of siliceous materials ('frit' and glass) from Dinkha Tepe, northwestern Iran, dating to the early part of the second millennium BC. The results for three blue glasses presented in their paper would seem to suggest that the samples analysed were somewhat weathered, with soda levels of between 1.7% and 9.6%, and an elevated silica level in one sample of 79.1% (ibid.: Table 2a, comparison of samples g, h and i). Even though weathered, it is possible to suggest that the glasses were originally of the typical soda-lime-silica chemical composition with elevated levels of magnesia and potassium oxides; relatively high relic levels of magnesia, for example, which is less susceptible to weathering than soda, have survived in the remaining silicate network. The existence of these early second-millennium BC glasses, probably of the high magnesia soda-lime type, suggests we should look to an even earlier period in order to identify the primary experimental phase in the production of the first glasses. Moorey (1985; 1994: 190) has noted the existence of isolated glass beads in Lower Mesopotamia and Egypt dating as early as *c.* 2500 BC, but is adamant that no well-dated glass vessels dating to before 1500 BC have been found in Egypt or the Middle East (Moorey 1994: 190). Beck's original (1934) claim that *regular* glass production originated in the Middle East rather than Egypt has withstood the test of time. Recent analyses of the vitreous component of faience found in Kerma, Sudan dating to *c.* 2000 BC however clearly show that it is *not* of the expected soda-lime-silica composition (Hatcher *et al.*, forthcoming). Kerma faience might be regarded as rather 'late' in the sequence of faience development, so we might have expected the vitreous component to be of a soda-lime-silica composition. Since this is not the case, its unexpected composition may reflect the existence of an early independent development of a vitreous industry in the region, that the silicate industry used local raw materials or that faience technology is far more complex than we are currently aware of. The origins of glass and its possible connection with faience production still needs to be re-examined closely.

3.9.3 Chemical characteristics of early glass in the Mediterranean and Mesopotamia

Few chemical analyses of second-millennium BC glass have been carried out, some of which are yet to be published. Analytical investigations of early glasses dating to between *c.* 1900 and 1550 BC from Deir ʿAin ʿAbata, Jordan (Henderson, in preparation) and nineteenth- or eighteenth-century BC Tel Dan, Israel (Ilan *et al.* 1993), have shown that HMG was certainly in use at this very early time in the history of glass technology. The data for Deir ʿAin ʿAbata glass does, however, also include possible variations from this expected result, but the nature of the archaeological deposit does not exclude a later date. The limited compositional variation so far detected can partly be attributed to the range of glass colours used rather than the principal raw materials. Chemical analyses of glass that have been carried out include some from Nuzi, Iraq (Vandiver 1982; 1983) of a probable fourteenth century date (Moorey 1985: 224–9) and an interim report on glass from the Ulu Burun shipwreck (Brill in Bass 1986: 282, n. 55). Pollard and Moorey (1982) have published a study of Middle Assyrian siliceous materials from Tell al-Rimah, Iraq which includes the results for potassium oxide level levels in one glaze and five glass samples (ibid.: Appendix, samples 1 and 9–13); some of the potassium oxides are relatively low and, in spite of the absence of results for magnesia oxide, it possible to suggest that some of the samples may be of a low magnesia soda-lime composition since levels of

potassium and magnesia oxides are invariably correlated in ancient glasses. An alternative explanation is that the glazes analysed are weathered. McGovern's (1987) discussion of silicate industries from the Baqʿah valley and Beth Shan in Palestine dating to between *c.* 1550 and 1050 BC suggests that the weathered samples may originally have used soda as the principal alkali in the production of 'fritted' materials. Here the authors refer to frit as 'a sintered, polycrystalline body with no glaze coating' (Vandiver 1982) and the material is therefore not the same as a true glass frit. The use of an analytical scanning electron microscope in this study would have provided the evidence necessary to define the materials more closely and to have separated weathered from unweathered vitreous components (where present). McGovern's other findings were that a range of colorants and opacifiers were used: manganese for purple and 'brown', a combination of copper, manganese and cobalt producing grey or 'black' (presumably very deep translucent) colours, copper for green, cobalt for blue, calcium antimonate for white, lead antimonate for yellow, ferric oxide for red (McGovern 1987: 95–100). Chemical analyses of contemporary

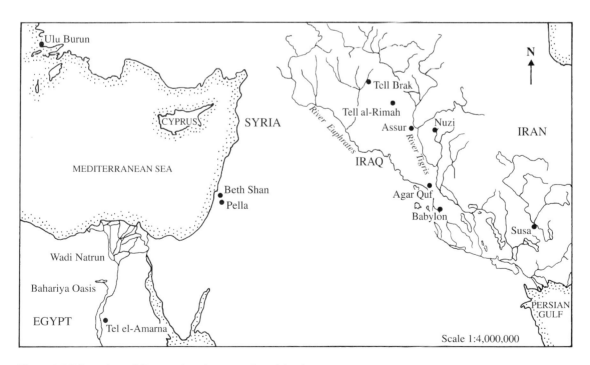

Figure 3.26 Location of Bronze Age sites mentioned in the text.

glasses show that both differences and similarities existed though the combination of 'excessive' levels of copper, manganese and cobalt to produce very deep translucent colours have not been found in contemporary glasses. For the location of sites discussed see Figure 3.26.

Early chemical analyses of Eighteenth Dynasty Egyptian glasses from Tell el-Amarna have been collected and summarised by Turner (1954: Table I). Brill and Wypyski's analyses using atomic absorption analysis and energy-dispersive X-ray fluorescence analysis (Lilyquist and Brill 1993) have provided us with very interesting data for Egyptian glasses dating to between the sixteenth and fourteenth centuries BC and as far back as Hatshepsut (1479–57 BC). Four groups of glasses were analysed. Three of them, pre-Malkata, Malkata and Amarna glasses were Egyptian and a fourth, from Nuzi, Mesopotamian. All three of the Egyptian glass groups were found to be of a soda-lime-silica with high magnesia oxide (MgO) contents. This type of soda-lime high magnesia glass (HMG) was originally defined in the seminal works of Turner (1956c) and Sayre and Smith (1961; 1967). This basic composition is suggestive of the use of crushed quartz (not sand) as the silica source and a maritime or desert plant ash as the alkali source (see Section 3.6 above). Although there was little variation in the magnesia levels, the potassium oxide levels varied widely; levels in Egyptian cobalt blue glasses in particular were found to be lower than in non-cobalt blue glasses from Egypt and Nuzi suggesting that a different base glass was used (Shortland and Tite 2000). The use of a cobalt source high in aluminium (a cobalt alum) probably located in Egypt has been inferred from the chemical analyses of cobalt blue Egyptian Eighteenth Dynasty glasses; the cobalt source used apparently introduced a relatively high level of aluminium oxide which has *only* been found in cobalt blue high magnesia glasses (Farnsworth and Ritchie 1938; Kaczmarczyk and Hedges 1983; Kazmarzyck 1987; Lilyquist and Brill 1993, nn. 78, 94; Henderson 2000). It is rare to be able to characterise colorant sources to this extent (see Section 3.2.5.1 for more examples). The other colorants used in second-millennium BC glasses include cupric oxide to make a copper green (turquoise) colour, manganese oxide to produce a translucent purple colour and a reduced

(ferrous) iron to produce a translucent brown colour. Calcium antimonate is used for opaque white glass, which is also combined with copper, manganese or cobalt to produce their respective opaque colours; lead antimonate is the principal opaque yellow glass colorant. A reduced copper (cuprous oxide/metallic copper) was used to make opaque brownish-red glass which is used for decoration. The primary raw materials used in these glasses however conform to the standard chemical composition for Eighteenth Dynasty Egyptian glasses.

Another interesting result from Lilyquist and Brill's work was that a distinct compositional *similarity* was found between most of the (non-blue) Nuzi (Mesopotamia) and Egyptian glasses. The only difference which does separate them compositionally is the lower soda levels found in some of the Nuzi glasses, but this does not (yet) constitute a means of discriminating compositionally between contemporary Egyptian and Mesopotamian glasses. So using these analyses alone it is not possible to state that there were separate production centres in fourteenth-century BC Egypt and Mesopotamia; even if Egyptian sources of cobalt were used it does not necessarily follow that the glass was also made there since it would have been possible to export cobalt-rich colorants to Mesopotamian production centres.

The discussion so far provides a clear picture of a relatively well-established glass technology which used a relatively narrow range of raw materials as reflected in the glass chemical compositions. However, the analysis of glass beads from Pella in Jordan as well as beads and vessels (such as those shown in Figure 3.27), other objects, including an ingot, from Tell Brak in Syria (Oates *et al.* 1997: 85–6), provide evidence for a degree of compositional variation which at the very least indicates a wider variation in the chemical composition of alkali source(s) used (Shortland and Tite 2000). Indeed the glasses from Pella, Tell Brak and Crete which contain magnesia levels of less than 1%, as opposed to levels of more than 3%, suggest that a mineral source of alkali was in use, rather than a plant ash (see Figure 3.28). It is known that an entirely new mixed-alkali chemical composition of glass was introduced in the late second millennium BC in Europe and the northern Mediterranean (Henderson 1988a; 1988b), but the assumption up to now has been that the same

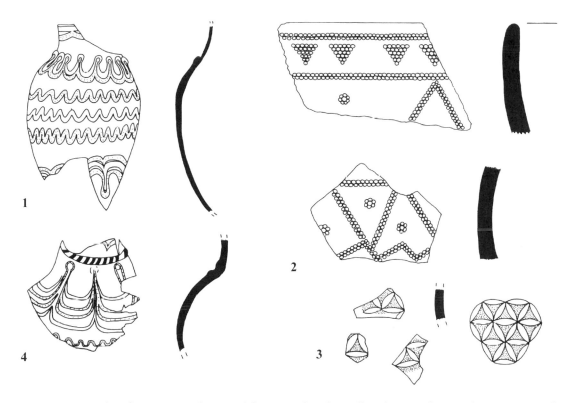

Figure 3.27 Examples of Bronze Age glass vessel fragments found at Tell Brak, Syria, fourteenth century BC (after Oates *et al.* 1998).

basic high magnesia soda-lime glass was made from a quartz sand and a halophytic plant ash before this time. The data plotted in Figure 3.28 clearly shows that the situation is, in fact, somewhat more complex than this. Even from one site, Pella in Jordan, six of the earlier glass samples (late fifteenth–fourteenth century BC) contain between 3.7% and 4.8% magnesia, with a seventh translucent green glass containing 1.4% magnesia. The more recent glass from Pella (thirteenth–twelfth century BC) contain between 0.6% and 2.0% magnesia, and none of these glasses contain the magnesia levels typical of HMG such as found in and most of the earlier Pella glasses (unpublished data produced by the author). The very unusual group of LMGs from Pella (Figure 3.28) includes two cobalt blue samples with high aluminia levels; these contain *c.* 2.0% magnesia. The remaining four glasses are all an apparent 'black' colour, in fact a deep brown colour. They contain between 0.6% and 0.8% magnesia and contain low

potassium oxide levels. Another very unusual feature of these glasses is that they contain very low calcium oxide levels – *c.* 1%. The earlier (fifteenth–fourteenth centuries BC) glasses are all HMG, apart from one (with 1.4% magnesia) and two contain low calcium oxide levels at 4.1%, some 2% lower than might be expected. These results from Pella underline the complexity of the vitreous industries in this period of their development.

Chemical analyses have been carried out on 28 samples of glass beads, vessels, 'raw glass' and an ingot from Tell Brak, northern Syria (Brill and Shirahata 1997; Henderson 1997; in preparation). Almost all date to *c.* 1300 BC apart from an opaque blue ingot of probable fifteenth century BC date and a glass bowl with opaque yellow and white decoration of probable fourteenth century BC date. The analyses clearly show that while almost all samples contain at least 2.6% magnesia there are two samples which, like four of the Pella glasses, contain less than

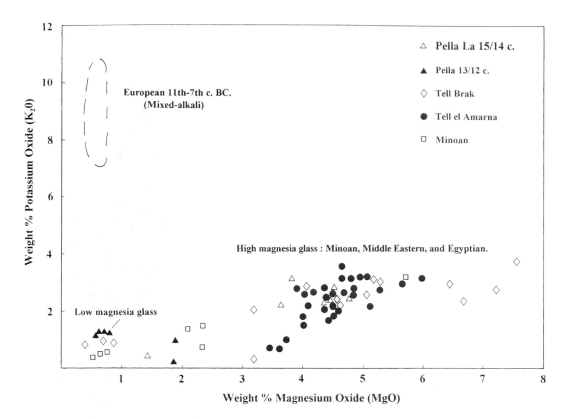

Figure 3.28 Weight % potassium oxide versus weight % magnesia in Bronze Age glass from various Bronze Age sites in the Mediterranean. Note the contrasting characteristics of (some) Bronze Age European glass.

1% magnesia. One is an opaque white decorative glass of early fourteenth century BC date, the other a green glaze. Out of seven Minoan glasses analysed (unpublished data produced by the author) three also fall into the low magnesia group, three contain between 2.1 and 2.3% magnesia and a single sample contains 5.7% magnesia (Figure 3.28). This scatter of data from the four locations in the Mediterranean clearly shows a wider compositional variation than the data published for Egyptian and Middle Eastern glass by Lilyquist and Brill (1993).

There appear to be at least two separable glass technologies identifiable: the first consists of low magnesia soda-lime glass (LMG) which contains less than 1% magnesia and correspondingly low potassium oxide levels at below 1.5%. It is likely that for these a mineral, such as natron, was used for the alkali. The glasses of this type are Mesopotamian and

Minoan as well as cobalt blue glasses from Egypt (Shortland and Tite 2000). The balance of the Egyptian glasses are of the second compositional type, high magnesia soda-lime glass (HMG). Some of the Egyptian glass from Amarna also contains very high magnesia levels, up to 6%, but these are comparable and even lower than some of the magnesia levels found in the approximately contemporary Tell Brak, Syria, glasses whose contents range up to 7.6%, so there is no apparent distinction between Mesopotamian and Egyptian HMGs.

It is clear that even in this relatively early period of glass production the situation is rather more complex than has been suspected and it is worth considering possible production models for glasses made in Mesopotamia. McGovern *et al.* (1991: 401) have suggested that between *c.* 1500 and 1200 BC in Mesopotamia the same basic raw materials were used in the manufacture of glass, but that the apparently more localised use of colorants may indicate that there were separate local industries at the time. As will become apparent below, even this model for glass production may be oversimplifying the evidence. Overall, however, it can be stated that the glass industry was sophisticated and of a high standard by the fourteenth century BC.

3.9.4 The archaeological inference

The archaeological inference that can be drawn from the existence of these two technologies in the fourteenth century BC is that two production systems must have been employed. Natron, the mineral alkali used to manufacture LMG, is likely to have derived from Wadi el-Natrun in Egypt where a deposit of this evaporite is to be found (Turner 1954a; 1956c; Henderson 1985: 272–3). Other sources of a suitable soda-rich mineral with the same specific impurity pattern are difficult to suggest. One possible implication is that these examples of LMG were made in Egypt because the soda source is there, but like most fourteenth-century BC Middle Eastern glasses, most Egyptian glasses of the period are of the HMG composition and would *not* have been made with natron but with plant ash (Lilyquist and Brill 1993). Whatever the answer is, and we still do not have evidence of where these different glasses were fused, the finding from Tell Brak shows that two different recipes were used in the manufacture of fourteenth-century BC glass found in the Middle East. Unpublished analyses of glasses from Minoan Crete, the four thirteenth–twelfth-century BC glass bead or bead fragments discussed above from Pella, Jordan (Henderson, in preparation), show that low magnesia soda-lime glasses were in use there as well. The fact that the glaze sample from Tell Brak is also of a LMG composition serves to add a further fascinating complication. Figure 3.28 shows how the levels of magnesia and potassium oxides in Tell el-Amarna glasses exhibit limited compositional variability and all apparently fall into the high magnesia (soda-lime) technology. Glasses from Tell Brak and Pella on the other hand are both high (HMG) and low magnesia (LMG) soda-lime glasses, and three of the Minoan glasses are LMG. The values of magnesia and potassium oxide in glasses from Nuzi (Vandiver

1983: Table 1) place them with the HMG group. Figure 3.28 even provides possible evidence for a mixing of low and high magnesia glasses: the six plotted points which fall between HMGs and LMGs (a late fifteenth–early fourteenth-century glass from Pella, two thirteenth–twelfth-century BC glasses from Pella and three Minoan glasses) contain between 1.5 and 2.3% magnesia. The LMGs contain a maximum level of 0.9% magnesia, and HMGs contain a minimum magnesia level of 2.9%. If a glass containing 4% MgO was mixed with one containing 0.5% MgO the resulting glass would contain 2.25% MgO, which, as we can see, would fall in the intermediate grouping. Although this suggested recycling of glass is impossible to prove absolutely, there is clear evidence here that more than a simple high magnesia glass was used in Mesopotamia in the fifteenth to twelfth centuries BC. At present the evidence suggests that, apart from some cobalt blue glasses, high magnesia glasses were used in Egypt in the fourteenth century BC.

McGovern *et al.*'s (1991: 401) suggestion that a number of production centres existed in the Middle East at which glass of slightly different compositions was made according to the colorants used needs to be examined more closely with the findings from Tell Brak in mind. If colorants were added at a number of sites, then logically we could suggest that the actual fusion of glass from raw materials occurred at a more restricted number of specialised sites and that ingots of colourless or faintly-tinted glasses were traded or exchanged with the former site types where the colorants were added. In addition, we could suggest there may have been sites where the glass was only worked and not modified (with the addition of a colorant) or made by fusing raw materials.

With the results from Tell Brak in mind we can note several things. First, with the existence of two available glass types the exchange networks (for raw materials) would have been wider than with one. Second, if a colorant was added at a number of sites we would expect to find the use of colourless or faintly-tinted glass ingots, but this appears not to be the case (Moorey 1994: 202); and third we need to explain the existence of coloured ingots such as those from Tell Brak itself (Barag 1985). Moorey (1994: 201–2) suggests that in the second half of the second millennium BC there were glass production centres in northern Mesopotamia and in Khuzistan (Susiana) and perhaps in Babylonia. The evidence from Assur (Iraq), Aqar Quf (Iraq), Nuzi (Iraq) and Susa (Iran) indicates that glass workshops operated within the orbit of major royal or temple building enterprises and, it is suggested (ibid.), served local needs. Moorey (ibid.: 202) also suggests that Syria had its own very active glass industries. With no primary evidence for a glass-working industry at Tell Brak we have to consider the industrial environment in which the glass ingots and lumps of raw glass were found. Given the range of other industries at the site, the presence of raw glass and glass ingots could suggest that glass-working occurred there in the late fourteenth century BC. In addition, it is possible that the site was involved in redistributing ingots and lumps of raw glass as part of a trade network.

Here we are reminded that the manufacture and coloration of glass was a secretive process in past societies and that ritual played an important part (Oppenheim *et al.* 1970: 32–3). Secrecy and ritual would have led to there being restricted communication of technological information about glass-making (including the construction of glass furnaces and the manufacture of crucibles from the appropriate clays). This, in turn, may have led to the development of sites which specialised in different aspects of the glass industry: fusing glass and producing ingots, adding colorants to glass, manufacturing glass objects and sites involved in the trade/exchange or redistribution of glass ingots and objects. With the available evidence of the existence of and trade in coloured ingots, such as the contemporary 'hoard' of cobalt blue glass ingots from the Ulu Burun shipwreck near Kaş, off the coast of Turkey (Bass 1986: 282, n. 55; Bass 1987: 716–18), it is possible that certain sites specialised in the production of ingots for trade; given the high level of control over the inclusion of very low levels of cobalt oxide in blue glasses, the production of the glass may have been perceived as especially difficult. This may therefore be one reason why cobalt blue glass ingots have been found: a very restricted number of production centres were involved in making cobalt blue glass.

The most economic production procedure would have been to centralise all aspects of production so that the initial fusion of the glass (fritting), addition of the colorant/opacifier and the forming of ingots for use on glass-working sites occurred on the same site. The actual *working* of glass (as opposed to *making* it) did, apparently, occur on sites which specialised in making glass artefacts, witness the trade in glass ingots. The occurrence of sites where slightly different colorant materials were used to make the objects may simply result from melting down glass ingots which have been produced using slightly different colorant raw materials. However, much more detailed analytical work needs to be carried out before we can become more confident of this production model.

In total contrast to the soda-lime technology of the mid- to late second millennium BC in the Middle East and Egypt, by the eleventh century BC a mixed-alkali glass (Figure 3.28) with a low calcium oxide content (LMHK = low magnesia, high potassium) was being used and possibly manufactured in the northern Mediterranean at Frattesina in the valley of the river Po (Bietti-Sestieri 1977; 1980; 1981; Henderson 1988b; Brill 1992). No contemporary glass of this composition has yet been published which has been found in contexts in the Middle East or Egypt, and indeed the distribution of this glass seems to be in the trans-Alpine 'Urnfield' area to the north (Henderson 1988b; Hartmann *et al.* 1997). We can therefore suggest that the existence of the glass industry at Frattesina occupied a socio-economic vacuum caused by the general collapse of circum-Mediterranean civilisations around the twelfth–eleventh centuries BC.

3.10 Roman glass production: refined specialisation or mass-production

3.10.1 Introduction

The investigation of Roman glass as a material has been approached from two ends of a technological spectrum. At one end of the spectrum is highly refined *tours de force* glass vessels which display a consummate mastery over the conditions of production, but these are only occasionally found. At the other end of the spectrum is mass-produced greenish glass destined to be blown into vessel forms found throughout the Roman Empire. The evidence for the production of vessels made as *tours de force* pieces comes from a study of the vessels themselves; evidence of mass-production is, in addition, provided by the excavated remains of glass factories. Both areas of investigation have provided some exciting information about the technologies of glass production, but only rarely have the investigations been linked to the social and economic contexts in which the vessels were used or manufactured. A high social or economic value can be attributed to some of the glass vessels, such as the Portland vase or the Lycurgus cup, where the finished article was probably used for display, and an increasing amount of work has been done in the investigation of potential links between vessel types and archaeological context (Cool and Price 1995; Baxter *et al.* 1995). It is, nevertheless, of importance to describe some of the significant results of the scientific studies of Roman glasses.

3.10.2 Specialised technology of the Portland vase and Lycurgus cup

One of the vessels which has received most attention over the years is the Portland vase (Figure 3.29), thought to have been made in Rome between 30 BC and 20 BC or a little later (Painter and Whitehouse 1990a: 122–5). This blown vessel has a body of translucent cobalt blue glass, with a casing of opaque white glass. The white glass has been carved with scenes from classical mythology. Volume 32 of the *Journal of Glass Studies* has been devoted to the historical, iconographic and technological study of the vessel. The scientific investigation of this vessel (Bimson and Freestone 1983) has shown that the translucent blue glass was composed of the expected soda-lime-silica glass with low magnesia and with a typical alumina level (2.6%) for glass of the type; the glass was coloured by cobalt oxide. The opaque white glass was opacified and coloured using calcium antimonate (see Section 3.2.5.4), the most frequently used opacifier in the Roman period (Henderson 1991a). The white glass also contained 12.0% of lead oxide: this would have made it softer and therefore easier to cut. The cobalt used as a colorant would originally have been introduced as a mineral-rich material (see Section 3.2.5.1) and was probably associated with copper, iron and perhaps manganese

Figure 3.29 The Portland vase © The British Museum.

oxide (Bimson and Freestone 1983: Table 1). When compared with the cobalt blue colorants used in opaque blue enamels, it is evident that this combination of 'impurities' is common in Roman blue glasses/enamels (Henderson 1991a: Table I), so no unique cobalt source was exploited to make the Portland vase.

Indeed we should ask the question: why should special raw materials be exploited when those which have been tried and tested can be relied upon to produce the desired results? The answer, of course, is that technological refinement does not necessarily depend on the use of special raw materials, but in this case on an understanding of the working properties of the glasses used. In the case of the Portland vase two different types of glass were used: their viscosities, their working ranges, their melting and softening temperatures and their relative coefficients of expansion and contraction would not necessarily have been recognised separately, but all would have played their parts in determining the behaviour of the glasses used. The lead-rich white glass would remain softer at lower temperatures and for longer than the cobalt blue glass which could be worked for a shorter period, and at higher temperatures. The relative coefficients of expansion for the blue and white glasses obviously worked, with the white glass having been added as a layer contracting slightly less and more slowly than the blue glass: i.e. the white glass 'fits' the blue glass well.

We can place the use of Roman lead-rich opaque white glass in a somewhat broader context. Analysis of a series of polychrome cameo and mosaic vessels of second century BC to first–second century AD date has shown that the lead-rich opaque white glass has been used for the manufacture of a range of bowl and flask forms that were in use at the same time as the Portland vase (Grose 1989). For the mainly later (first century AD) mass-produced ribbed bowls the lead oxide is no longer present (Henderson 1996a). The lead oxide used in the Portland vase (see Figure 3.30) has undoubtedly been used because the glass made from it was softer and could be cut more easily. However it would seem that the lead-rich glass may not have been

specially selected for its properties of expansion and contraction – because this same glass was used in a range of other decorative contexts, such as in mosaic glasses where these properties were less significant to the finished vessel form: it is more likely that a lead-rich opaque white glass was used as a general stock of decorative glass at the time. A study of Roman enamels has also revealed that, in spite of the use of enamels in the production of brooches in a range of metal alloys, the composition of the enamel does not necessarily vary according to the metal composition used; one might expect it to vary according to the relative expansion and contraction of the two materials (Bateson and Hedges 1975: 186). The presence of lead in the enamel would however have wetted the metal surfaces (ibid.: 185). The Portland vase is, without question, a prestigious product involving specialised skill in its manufacture. It has been suggested that it might have been a gift to honour Augustus Caesar and made to celebrate the birth of Rome from the ashes of Troy (Painter and Whitehouse 1990b: 136). It is however interesting to note that the actual raw materials used were not unusual for the time.

The Lycurgus cup (Figure 3.31) is unusual and technologically specialised in another way. It is a late

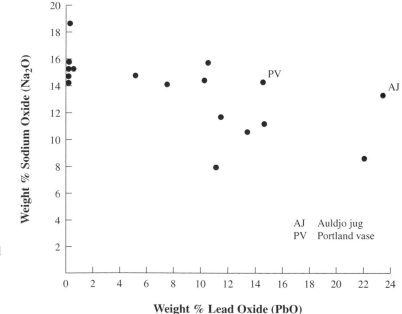

Figure 3.30 Weight % lead oxide versus weight % soda in opaque white cameo glasses including the Portland vase and the Auldjo jug; the cluster of low lead oxide/high soda compositions are for Roman enamels.

AJ　Auldjo jug
PV　Portland vase

Weight % Lead Oxide (PbO)

Weight % Sodium Oxide (Na$_2$O)

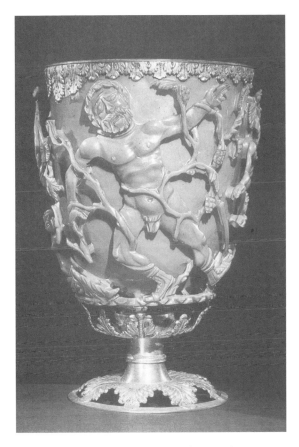

Figure 3.31 The Lycurgus cup © The British Museum.

been carried out by Brill (1965b) and by Barber and Freestone (1990). The chemical composition of the body of the glass itself is the expected soda-lime-silica, the common Roman composition. The colour of the glass is due to the presence of 300 ppm of silver and 40 ppm of gold. These particles were precipitated as colloids and form a silver-gold alloy. When viewed in reflected light the minute metallic particles are just coarse enough to reflect enough of the light without eliminating the transmission. In transmitted light the fine particles scatter the blue end of the spectrum more effectively than the red end, resulting in red transmission, and this is the colour observed. Since it is impossible that the Roman artisans managed to add these incredibly low levels of silver and gold to the volume of the glass used to make the vessel deliberately, the levels were probably added at higher levels to a glass-melt and increasingly diluted by adding more glass.

In contrast to the Portland vase, the production of this somewhat smaller vessel *did* involve the use of relatively unusual raw materials when seen in the context of Roman glass and other vitreous materials, and the technique used to produce the dispersion of minute particles in the glass is still unknown. A number of dichroic Roman enamels have been found (Henderson 1990: 291–3; Henderson 1991a: 72, 75), though the reason why they were used as an

Roman cage cup which has been cut and ground from a blown blank and has a frieze showing scenes from the myths of King Lycurgus (Tatton-Brown 1991: 92). It is characterised by being *dichroic*, that is it has different colours when viewed with transmitted and reflected light: wine red with transmitted light and 'pea' green with reflected light. This is an effect that can only be produced with glass, because of its transparent/translucent qualities. It is due to the presence of masses of minute particles in the translucent body of the glass (Figure 3.32): these are far smaller than the crystallites which cause opacity in most Roman glasses and enamels (see Figure 3.8). Indeed, the particles of this size (*c.* 70 manometers) are invisible under the scanning electron microscope and a transmission electron microscope needs to be used instead. Scientific study of the Lycurgus cup has

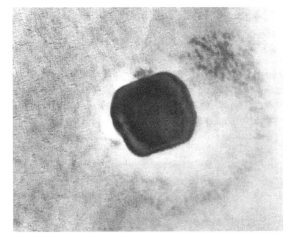

Figure 3.32 Minute particles of silver-gold alloy in the Lycurgus cup (after Barber and Freestone 1990).

enamel may have been so as to resemble a ruby or tourmaline.

3.10.3 Mass-produced greenish Roman glass

During the period that the Roman empire dominated a vast area stretching from India to northern England there was a high demand for vessel glass, especially in urban and military contexts. As for any period of glass production, the industrial evidence for the manufacture of many tons of blue green glass every year is surprisingly sparse. A survey of the evidence of the glass industry in Roman Britain reveals a relatively low distribution of the evidence (Shepherd and Heyworth 1991; Price 1998).

However, in Palestine the thorough excavation and recording of a glass-house at Jalame about 10 km south-east of Haifa (Figure 3.33) has revealed some of the complexity of a late fourth-century glass-house (Weinberg 1988). Excavations of the 'country house' at Jalame revealed a range of buildings of different functions belonging to four periods dating to between *c.* 75 and *c.* the early fifth century. Foundations of wine and olive presses belonged to the period immediately before the evidence for glass production (*c.* 275–350); glass production is attested in the succeeding period (351–83). Dating was achieved by using the association of coins and lamps in archaeological contexts; the occurrence of coins formed two maxima of dates at 337 and 375, the site being abandoned *c.* 425. In addition to the furnace, four superimposed glass-working floors were found as well as a huge amount of dumped debris. Each of the main products of late Roman fine pottery tablewares was found: African Red Slip ware, late Roman C ware and Cypriote Red Slip ware. The amount found was very large for a small site – though no explanation for this is offered in the report.

The remains of a structure thought to have been a glass furnace would probably have been a single melting chamber with a firing chamber attached (Weinberg 1988: 28–33) (see Figure 3.34): Weinberg 1988: plate 3–2C). The room in which the furnace was located, comprising a rectangular foundation, covered an area of 2.4 × 3.6 m (on average): a probable tank furnace (see Section 3.4). Relatively small amounts of blue green glass were thought to have been melted in rectangular shaped limestone vessels (ibid.: 31); no crucibles were found. However, recent finds of glass-melting furnaces in Palestine at Hadera have revealed fifth–sixth-century (Byzantine) furnaces with a similar plan where it is thought that the glass was melted in one process in a closed furnace without the need of crucibles or other containers (Gorin-Rosen 1993) and this may be the way in which the Jalame furnace was operated. In Brill's (1988) comprehensive scientific investigation of the Jalame glass and related finds he regards the use of limestone vessels for melting glass as conjectural (1988: 257, 288). Although the discovery of tank furnaces elsewhere appears to have provided a possible answer to the problem of a lack of refractory vessels at Jalame, there is a further important consideration which makes the lack of crucibles which are large enough to hold a glass-melt somewhat more problematical. At Jalame it is clear from the moils discovered that glass-blowing was an important activity; on the other hand the tank furnaces found elsewhere in the Levant were apparently mainly for producing blocks of glass for export (perhaps to a nearby glass-blowing workshop). At Jalame crucibles must have been necessary to allow the gathering of glass on a blowing iron.

The technological characteristics of the glass discussed in the Jalame report are: proportion and size of fragments, quality of material (bubbles, seed), the extent of weathering, production methods and geographical distribution of the vessel types (parallels). The range of glass vessel fragments excavated from

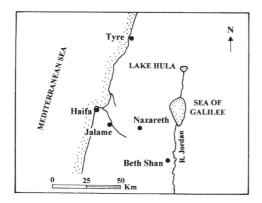

Figure 3.33 Location map for Jalame.

Figure 3.34 The Jalame glass furnace: cross-section (bottom) and reconstruction (top).

Jalame included bowls with a variety of rim forms: flaring, out-folded, incurving, double folded, over-hanging and tooled-out folded. Decoration on the vessel bodies included applied horizontal trails and horizontal ribbing. Other vessel forms consisted of cups, goblets, beakers, jugs, bottles, jars and lamps, many of which also displayed a range of decorative techniques. There are 519 individual catalogue entries, the highest proportion of the fragments described being of a translucent greenish hue (bluish-green, green and yellowish-green) with a smaller pro-portion being brown, olive green, colourless and purple (Weinburg 1988: 38).

It is very difficult to know precisely what range of glass vessels were actually created on the site of an ancient glass factory. Any or all of the broken glass frag-ments recovered during excavations *could* have been brought to the site for recycling as scrap glass (*cullet*), especially if the glass being manufactured there was all of a similar blue-green colour. If present, highly coloured glasses may have been separated from the rest since, if used in a sufficiently high proportion in the glass-melt, they could modify the final colour of the glass when melted with the rest of the scrap glass. The excavation provided ample evidence for breaking up and re-melting of imported glass chunks which were

then mixed with scrap vessel fragments from the Jalame factory itself; many of the latter resulted from poor annealing. There would be some slight problem in distinguishing Jalame glass from that imported to the site. However, in Chapter 4 (Weinberg 1988). Gladys Weinberg and Sidney Goldstein consider that there was a considerable amount of specialisation in the vessel shapes which they consider to have been made at Jalame, making it easier to identify 'locally made vessels'. In Chapter 3 of the report Weinberg makes the point that the volume of glass found far exceeds that from a glass factory of any ancient period (that was true at the time of the report, but is no longer the case); glass was evidently *obtained* cheaply. The excavated area of the glass dump alone was 150 sq m.

A thorough scientific investigation of the Jalame glass was carried out by Brill, Schreurs and Wosinski. To take a purist's view it is impossible to know what proportion of the fragments analysed was the result of glass-working on the site. There was no evidence that glass was fused from primary raw materials at Jalame (fritted), but we can be sure that glass was both melted and blown there because of the copious evidence of melted dribbles and blobs and also of glass lid moils and pontil knock-offs.

What we can expect to find in the excavations of a glass factory is material that has been dumped near the site of the furnace. There is no particular reason why waste glass would be found on the work-shop floor because glass-workers operate in a clean environment. A lot depends on the circumstances under which the workshop is deserted. Excavations can also reveal the (partially) destroyed remains of glass furnaces and associated installations. Occasion-ally closely stratified deposits of debris can be related to production phases and technological activities on the site. In general, however, this is being over opti-mistic; in any case how is it possible to recognise a deposit which reflects the full range of industrial activities of a glass factory without actually witness-ing the glass artisans deal with each variation in the raw materials used and their involvement in each technique of production? All we can expect to achieve is a statement of what we *detect* has happened at a glass workshop based on a carefully balanced consideration of the available archaeological and scientific evidence (see Sections 3.4.1 and 3.4.2).

3.10.4 *Scientific investigations*

The scientific investigations of the Jalame glass by Brill and co-workers (Brill 1988) showed that, somewhat predictably, the glass being worked and blown there was of the soda-lime-silica chemical composition with low levels of magnesia and potassium oxides, the type referred to by Sayre and Smith (1967) as a low magnesia (soda-lime-silica) glass, or LMG. Brill (1988: 260) suggests that sand from the Belus river was used for making the glass found at Jalame, though the glass was not apparently fused from raw materials there. The mouth of the Na'aman river, known as the Belus river in antiquity, is mentioned by Pliny (AD 77) as the place where glass-making was discovered:

> The river is muddy and flows in a deep channel, revealing its sands only when the tide ebbs. For it is only until they have been tossed by the waves and cleansed by impurities that they glisten. Moreover, it is only at that moment, when they are thought to be affected by the sharp, astringent properties of the brine, that they become fit for use. The beach stretches for not more than half a mile, and yet for many centuries the production of glass depended on this area alone. There is a story that once a ship belonging to some traders in natural soda (natron, an Egyptian product) put in here and that they scattered along the shore to prepare a meal. Since, however, no stones suitable for supporting their cauldrons were forthcoming, they rested them on lumps of soda from their cargo. When these became heated and completely mingled with the sand on the beach a strange translucent liquid flowed forth in streams; and this, it is said, was the origin of glass.
>
> (Engle 1973)

It is suggested by Brill (1988) that other than sand the other two principal raw materials used to make the glass worked at Jalame were shell fragments in the sand, providing the calcium oxide, and the mineral source of soda, natron, for the alkali. Two tables of results provide an interesting insight into different compositions of manganese-rich glasses (ibid.: Tables 9–3 and 9–4 with 12 analyses in total) and glasses in which the manganese was considered to have been introduced as an impurity (ibid.: Table 9–2 with 14 analyses in total). Sayre and Smith (1963) were the first to consider what might be the difference between the deliberate and accidental use of manganese in glass as a decolorant. The manganese used at Jalame appears to have been added deliberately to colour some of the glass a purple colour and impurities of iron, copper, vanadium, nickel and barium are considered to have been associated with the manganese-rich raw material used.

One of the possible outcomes of scientifically investigating an ancient glass-making site is that the products and by-products may turn out to be chemically characteristic of the site; glass recycling could however be expected to bedevil such attempts because the compositional features which could characterise individual melts would be lost in re-melting and mixing the glass. Surprisingly Brill (1988: 262) claims that the Jalame glasses *can* be compositionally distinguished using major, minor and some trace components from 'all other sizeable bodies of analyses completed' which included the few 'known' factories and outputs from the limited regions which are listed. Even the chemical analyses of glass fragments from Kafr Yasif, another glass-making site some 25 km away from Jalame are claimed to 'differ sufficiently (especially in their $Na_2O:CaO$ relationships) to distinguish the two' (ibid.: 264). No date is given for the Kafr Yasif site, so it is difficult to know whether we are making an all-important comparison between contemporary factories or whether we could explain the differences partly as a result of different dates of operation. Nevertheless, as Brill notes, one might expect that the two Roman glass-making sites would have used the same raw materials, so to be able to distinguish the compositions of the glass from the two sites is surprising and it is important to publish the figures for this distinction in full.

Streamers of yellowish or amber glass running through the Jalame green glass were found, by electron paramagnetic resonance, to be due to a ferro-sulphide colorant. Brill (1988) provides an essential and interesting discussion about how the furnace atmosphere determined the glass colour; experiments with fragments of Jalame purple and green scrap glasses showed how all the colours could be achieved by changing the gaseous atmosphere alone. Viscosity–temperature relationships for soda-lime glasses are discussed in detail and the development of strain in the glass (see Section 3.7 above).

Mass-production of greenish glass also occurred at the western end of the Roman Empire as mentioned above. A comparison between the levels of sodium and potassium oxides in greenish glasses from first–second century Silchester, southern England, and those from Jalame (Figure 3.35) reveals a general distinction between the two times and areas and gives partial support for the compositional distinction between Roman glasses observed by Brill. The distinction based on this plot is not sufficient to be able to claim that all vessels analysed from the respective areas and times can be distinguished using their chemical compositions (i.e. *chemically fingerprinted*), because there are overlaps in the points plotted. Indeed since the data for Figure 3.35 are taken from the geographical and temporal extremities of the Roman Empire, if there was no visible distinction between the data it would be time to pack up and go home. As for the Jalame glass, even in the first century the same combination of raw materials (sand containing shell fragments, and natron) is assumed to have been used, so there is no particular reason why we might expect to observe this partial distinction in the soda and potassium oxide levels. Nevertheless, some slight difference in the technological procedures employed has led to

slight corresponding differences in these impurities and recycling of the glass may have reduced the soda levels by the fourth century. By using multivariate statistics for a much larger data set of Roman glass (Heyworth *et al.* 1989; Heyworth 1991) it has been possible to distinguish between what constitute the results of two contemporary, slightly different, late Roman batch compositions from Winchester, but these, like many other chemical analyses cannot be tied directly to the scant evidence for production sites.

3.11 Early medieval glass in Europe: the continuation of a Roman tradition?

3.11.1 Introduction

One of the reasons for studying ancient technology is the possibility of detecting the effects of changes in society and in the (rest of the) economy on characteristics of production and the way it is organised. An example of this is a study of the way in which glass technology (as reflected in its chemical composition) changed once the Roman Empire had collapsed: can one detect a level of continuity or was there a re-birth and a phase of innovation? One can certainly demonstrate that Roman glass vessel forms continued to be manufactured in post-Roman contexts, but at the same time, a range of new vessel forms were manufactured. Related to this is whether

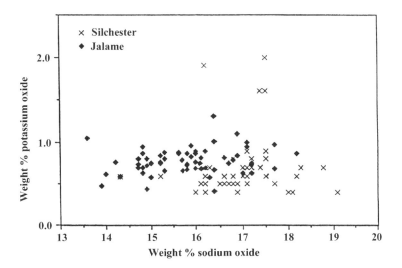

Figure 3.35 Weight % soda versus weight % potassium oxide in Roman glasses from Jalame (fourth century AD) and Silchester (first century AD).

any discernible change in the raw materials used to make glass in the second half of the first millennium AD can be detected.

In the absence of scientifically excavated early medieval production sites with furnaces in northern and western Europe, a potentially informative way of investigating the subject of technological continuity or change is through the scientific analysis of glass. When considering this theme, ideally it would be appropriate to focus on the relationship between glass compositions and changes in vessel form, through phases of continuity and modification in form, from the late fourth century to the end of the millennium. However, at present, only fragments of this analytical investigation have been carried out. Work has so far included research into early medieval glass beads which provides supporting evidence for the fragmentary work on vessel glass. This work has shown that a standard 'Roman' low magnesia soda-lime glass was in use for translucent glasses such as those found in fourth-century glass from Jalame (see Section 3.10.4). Freestone *et al.* (1999), however, have suggested that there were some exceptions to the standard 'Roman' LMGs in the early Anglo-Saxon period with the use of plant ashes as alkali

Figure 3.36 Location map of the principal early medieval glass sites mentioned in the text.

sources. Figure 3.36 shows the location of the sites discussed in this section.

The results presented here are a start at addressing this research issue. Starting with a sequence of glass vessels of late fourth to late fifth/early sixth century dates from the site of Gennep in the Netherlands (Sablerolles 1992; 1993) an interesting series of observations can be made (Henderson and Sablerolles in preparation). A range of glass vessel forms from the site were sampled and analysed (see, for example, Figure 3.37). In addition to glasses which contained no unusual impurities for a low magnesia soda-lime glass of the Roman type, the results included glasses with low impurity levels of copper, tin, antimony and lead oxides. Low levels of these four oxides normally occurred together in the glasses analysed, though occasionally lead and copper were found without tin and antimony oxides. Fifteen second-rate plain blue-green glass hemispherical cups and bowls with knocked-off rims dating to between *c.* AD 375 and 450, full of bubbles and impurities, were found to contain highly variable and very low (*c.* 0.1%) levels of these chemical impurities; in two samples none could be detected at all. Lead oxide was more consistently present, while at higher levels, the balance of impurities (when they occurred) were cupric oxide and, less commonly, antimony and tin oxides.

The chemical analysis of contemporary 'Helle' bowls and cups with pinched ribs, when compared to the group of late Roman bowls with knocked-off rims were found to be relatively free of impurities and none contained the maximum levels of lead oxide (1.7%) detected in the analyses of the plain cups and bowls.

The remaining glass samples included three Kempston cones, all dating to *c.* fifth century and which contained distinctively higher impurity levels than the Roman glasses. In contrast, the chemical analysis of contemporary cones with vertical and diagonal ribbed moulding (see Figure 3.37) has revealed consistently lower and non-detectable impurity levels. This compositional contrast infers that the two vessel types were manufactured in different traditions; the compositional differences between the Kempston cones and the Roman vessels certainly indicates this. A series of six contemporary

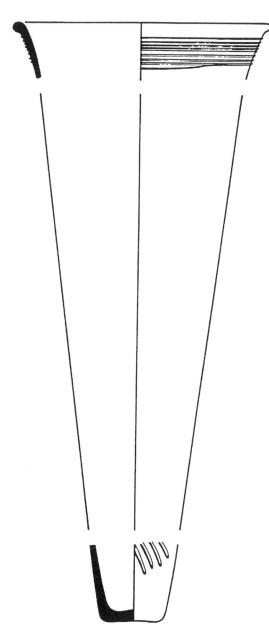

Figure 3.37 An optic-blown cone beaker from Gennep, the Netherlands, second half of the fifth century (reproduced by kind permission of Yvette Sablerolles).

translucent green bowls with tubular rims and vertically looped decoration were found to be almost impurity-free. These last have forms which are more akin to the Roman vessels with knocked-off rims – and appear to have been made with raw materials which have similarly low heavy metal impurity levels, hinting at a form of technological continuity. Chemical analysis of vessels decorated with opaque white trails considered to be products of workshops in the valley of the river Meuse, and in the Rhineland and Gaul, have revealed consistent but low heavy metal impurity levels in the Rhenish and Gaulish products and low or non-detectable levels in the Meuse products, so the latter would appear to have used somewhat different raw materials.

Thus it appears to be possible to distinguish between Roman glasses (in which one can include thousands of compositionally similar glasses with very low or non-detectable heavy metal impurity levels) and later products, and also between products manufactured contemporaneously according to the detection of heavy metal impurities. This provides a basis for testing further the chemical analysis of hypothesised workshop products.

Thus, during this important 'transitional' period in western Europe, it is possible to observe continuity with, and change from, the glass vessels made by the Romans. While the fifth-century glasses analysed are of a similar gross composition to that of the Romans, a soda-lime-silica composition with low magnesia levels (LMG), some already contain the heavy metal impurities typical of later early medieval glasses, but at markedly lower levels than found in eighth century and later glass (of the Scandinavian Viking Age, the Dutch late Merovingian–Carolingian period (Henderson 1999d: 294) and the Irish early Christian period).

It can be difficult to compare the analytical data obtained from the scientific analysis of highly decorated polychrome glass beads with vessel glass because many of the colours used were produced deliberately by the addition of mineral-rich colorants and opacifiers (Henderson 1999a; in press a); in some cases potentially discriminatory element oxides in the base glasses can be masked by the deliberate addition of the colorants. For example antimony trioxide can act as a glass clarifier (see Section 3.2.5.6 above) and can also form part of complex opacifying crystals (such as lead antimonate: see Section 3.2.5.4 above). As has been mentioned, and will become clear, antimony trioxide is one of the oxides which appears to characterise some post-Roman faintly-tinted glasses and is rarely found in Roman blue green glasses (Velde and Hochuli-Gysel 1996: 189). In order to investigate post-Roman bead technology a selection of glass beads from an Anglo-Saxon (fifth–sixth century) cemetery at Apple Down, near Chichester was analysed (Henderson 1990a). The range of bright glass colours used for making and decorating the beads was found to have been due to the use of deliberately added colorants and opacifiers. The chemical analysis of the translucent colours, including a single translucent green bead in which one might expect to detect impurities associated with the basic raw materials used, did not reveal any impurities other than those which could be explained as being introduced with the colorants used (ibid.: 158, Table 2.1). Although it is difficult to draw a conclusion about differences in the impurity levels in these beads from those detected in vessel glass, it nevertheless reminds us that bead technology *may* have used slightly different source(s) of raw glass or raw materials.

As part of the analytical study of glasses from early medieval Europe, analyses of faintly-tinted vessel glass from the sixth–seventh-century site of Dankirke in western Jutland were carried out. Again, some of the glass vessels analysed contained trace levels of lead, tin, antimony and copper in translucent pale green and brown glasses, indicating that a similar stock of glass was used as in some earlier (Gennep) and later glasses.

An analytical study of glass from a slightly later site of seventh–eighth century date at Fishergate, York (Rogers 1993), revealed that there were significant analytical differences from Roman glasses found in Britain of first–fourth century date (Jackson 1996; 1992). The compositional differences are principally due to impurity levels of the oxides of magnesia, and lead in the glasses.

Many of the analyses of glass from the eighth-century sites of Dorestad and Wijnaldum in the Netherlands (vessel glass) (Henderson 1995), Ribe in Denmark (vessel glass, beads and industrial debris, including tesserae, monochrome, bichrome and *millefiori* rods, blocks of glass, glass from crucibles – see case study below), Åhus in Sweden (vessel glass, beads and a similar range of industrial debris to Ribe) (Callmer and Henderson 1991), and Hamwic in England (vessel glass) (Heyworth 1991; Hunter and Heyworth

1998), have revealed the presence of impurities of the oxides of lead, antimony, tin and copper at levels which are distinctive and were present in the basic glass-melt (Henderson 1993). Scientific investigations of eighth- to tenth-century glass, from Borg in Norway (Henderson and Holand 1992) and ninth–eleventh-century glass from Lurk Lane, Beverley, England (Henderson 1991b; 1993) also revealed the presence of these impurities in some blue green and faintly-tinted glasses. That the four impurities formed part of the basic glass-melt (however they were introduced) can be stated with some confidence because the glass colours which contain these impurities include faintly tinted blue-green, so they cannot be attributed to the use of additives such as opacifiers or colorants. More glass samples derive from early Christian Ireland (Henderson 1988; in press a). These samples were mainly taken from glass beads and date to between the sixth and the tenth centuries (mostly probably eighth–tenth centuries) and almost all display the same impurity patterns as for the other early medieval glasses discussed. The early Christian glasses analysed were decorated and undecorated beads, monochrome, bichrome and millefiori rods, glass studs and glass-working crucibles (see Figure 3.10).

In sum, the base glasses which were made from *c.* fifth century AD and were made and/or used until *c.* ninth–tenth centuries in northern and western Europe are often characterised by increasingly higher levels of antimony, tin, lead and copper oxide impurities. It is very difficult to be certain how these impurities were introduced into the glasses. One possible source of the antimony might be recycled Roman glass tesserae. However, the association of antimony with copper and lead in the glasses suggests that, if glass tesserae did form one source, there must also have been an additional source of impurities – unless only opaque green tesserae with these oxides present were specially selected, which seems very unlikely. The presence of lead, tin and copper in the glasses might conceivably mean that crucibles which had been used for working metals of this composition was then re-used for melting glass. This is not an entirely convincing explanation either, but there is little else that can be suggested.

These findings are in contrast to the view presented by Sanderson *et al.* (1984) and Velde

(1990: 116) who claimed that, on the basis of their data, or data available to them, little or no distinction could be made between Roman and early medieval glasses. They suggest that Roman glass was melted down and recycled to make a range of distinctive early medieval vessel forms. Sanderson *et al.* did, however, suggest that a different sand source may have been used to make early medieval rather than Roman glasses, though Jackson (1996: 294) has pointed out that the different titanium and iron oxide levels which distinguish the two groups (Sanderson *et al.* 1984: Figure 1) may have been formed as a result of cullet re-use; it is however difficult to suggest how elevated titania levels would have occurred in ancient glass unless a sand source with titanium-bearing minerals had been used consistently. The most likely general interpretation for these patterns is that glass *was* fused from primary raw materials in early medieval Europe, and that perhaps some increase in volume was achieved by the inclusion of waste glass (including some Roman), such as glass mosaic tesserae (Henderson and Holand 1992). The suggestion that a metalworking crucible was used for melting glass which made a contribution to the heavy metal impurity remains a possibility, especially at sites such as Maastricht in the Netherlands (Sablerolles *et al.* 1997) where metal- and glass-working occurred on the same site – although among the small number of glass bearing crucibles that have been found no such candidates in which it might be possible to detect this scientifically have presented themselves.

3.11.2 Glass production at Ribe, Jutland

Ribe is located on the west coast of Denmark (see Figure 3.36). The town itself has grown up around the river Ribe which has afforded it docking facilities for small boats. Excavations have produced evidence for a range of industries, including glass production, during a time of early Viking occupation (Näsman 1979; Frandsen and Jensen 1987; Bencard and Jorgensen 1990; Bencard 1990). The evidence suggests that there were four principal phases of activity in the first millennium at Ribe: phase 1, a series of parallel ditches (plots of land) and ploughing which was sealed by a layer of sand;

phase 1A, walls and parallel ditches – the ditches are thought to have marked the position of stalls for craftsmen, being the foundations of a market place; phase 2, a phase when the land was sealed by a layer of cattle dung; phase 3, intensive industrial activity within the established land plots which probably took place on a seasonal basis, indicated by alternating humic layers and sand. In several instances hearths associated with workshop waste products were found, particularly for the production of glass beads and bronze jewellery. One example is a location where four hearths associated with a glass bead-maker were almost exactly superimposed on each other; another example consists of four superimposed hearths associated with the production of copper alloy 'tortoise' brooches. Lines of post holes were found in this phase as well which have been interpreted as fences. The workshop layers respected the ditch divisions. Phase 4 was a period at the end of the first millennium when there were sparse signs of cultural activity with a dearth of finds; the archaeology consisted of a series of pits cutting the earlier layers.

These phases have been dated by the use of dendrochronology, the incidence of sceattas of the Wodan monster type and the occurrence of firmly dated tortoise brooches such as the 'berdel' type in the upper layers of phase 3, now proven to be contemporary with the sceattas. This combination of dating techniques places phase 1 in the early eighth century; phase 2 *c.* 720 and phase 3 *c.* 730–60.

During phase 3 excavations, a series of closely stratified mounds consisting of interleaved bands of ash with other industrial deposits and sand have been revealed. There is evidence for iron-smelting and smithing, copper alloy-working in the manufacture of moulded 'berdel' brooches, pottery manufacture, amber-working and glass-working. There is a possibility that sceattas of the Wodan monster type were produced at Ribe which could imply a royal presence; certainly the construction of the massive Kanhave canal on Samsö suggests an abiding force that was able to control such building operations. Even if the industries were carried out on a seasonal basis, the scale of the debris from the industries suggests that the activity was intensive, that it is unlikely that the artisans were involved in non-industrial activities whilst there and that perhaps a putative royal presence in some way influenced the organisation of industrial activities, if only by providing the conditions where the industries could operate effectively.

The evidence for the glass industry is on a massive scale – a complete range of by-products for the manufacture of the beads was found (Bencard *et al.* 1979; Callmer 1988). This consisted of fragmented glass vessels, glass cakes, glass tesserae, glass cables and millefiori rods (both in fully-manufactured and partly-manufactured states), malformed and fully-formed beads, a small number of crucible fragments with opaque yellow glass adhering and dribbles and blobs of glass. A wide range of glass bead types were found decorated in a number of ways. Two of the more intricately decorated bead types are those decorated with bichrome cables and the so-called millefiori beads. Bichrome cables are sometimes mistakenly labelled *reticella* rods – a term better reserved for the seventeenth-century Venetian glass industry from which it is derived. One of the interesting aspects the character of the bead production industry at Ribe is that bichrome cables (for example) were made there. The evidence includes single thin strips of glass, partly wound cables and partially melted cables. In addition, the colours

of the large number of loose cables match those which are found on beads. The cables were formed from glass using a range of colour combinations: translucent blue and opaque white glass, translucent blue, opaque white and opaque red glass and translucent blue and opaque yellow glass. The millefiori beads were made from similar colour combinations, such as opaque red, opaque yellow and translucent blue.

Some of the bead types seem to have been made at Ribe for consumption both within and outside Ribe. One such is a translucent blue barrel-shaped bead with inlaid and marvered opaque white and opaque red wavy bands around its circumference (Callmer 1977; 1988; Bencard *et al.* 1979; Gam 1990: Figure 3g). An example of an imported type is the so-called 'wasp' bead, a deep translucent brown barrel-shaped bead with applied opaque yellow bands around its ends and around its middle.

3.11.3 Scientific investigations

The chemical composition of the translucent glass from Ribe has already been referred to as being distinctive to the period – a (low magnesia) soda-lime-silica glass with many examples characterised by impurities of the oxides of lead, tin, antimony and

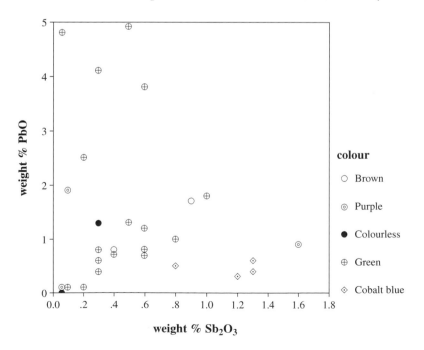

Figure 3.38 Weight % antimony trioxide versus weight % lead oxide in translucent brown, purple, colourless, green and cobalt blue glass from Ribe, Jutland.

copper in translucent green and blue glasses – but at higher levels than detected in the earlier Gennep glasses, for example. This work has shown that glass with these heavy metal impurities was found in glass vessel fragments, monochrome rods, bichrome cables, millefiori cables, *some* tesserae, glass cakes, formed and partly-formed glass beads and glass blobs and dribbles. The levels of antimony trioxide in translucent green glass (vessel fragments, monochrome rods, raw glass and the by-products of bead production) are mainly below 1%. Antimony trioxide levels in translucent blue glass forming the same artefact types as well as in translucent blue millefiori rods and bichrome cables are mainly above 1%. With a few exceptions most of the translucent glasses contain below 1% lead oxide. The compositional distinction between the impurity levels in translucent blue and green glasses may be a reflection of the consistent use of an antimony-rich cobalt source to colour the glass (which would have been added to the existing impurity level in the glass), or that a base glass with a higher antimony impurity was used. The fact that glasses from both Ribe and Åhus in Skania, Sweden, of the same colours used to make different artefacts have virtually the same impurity levels, including an apparent positive correlation of antimony trioxide and lead oxide (see Figure 3.38), shows that the same source(s) of glass were involved. If only blue glasses from both sites are selected, there is a remarkably consistent correlation between the occurrence of manganese and iron oxides in all the blue glasses analysed including raw glass, millefiori rods and beads, confirming again the inference that the glass was made using a very similar if not identical technology (Callmer and Henderson 1991: 149, Figure 11).

The fact that such a wide range of artefact types from two different sites were made with translucent blue and green colours of essentially the same basic glass, one which is somewhat different from a 'Roman' composition, is convincing evidence that the glass was manufactured using the same early medieval technology. At present we do not have the archaeological evidence available to suggest where this glass was fused using primary raw materials, so we cannot suggest how many production centres were involved. As mentioned above (Section 3.6), the likely raw materials involved would have been sand (for silica), shell fragments (for the 'lime' source) and a mineral source of the alkali soda, such as natron.

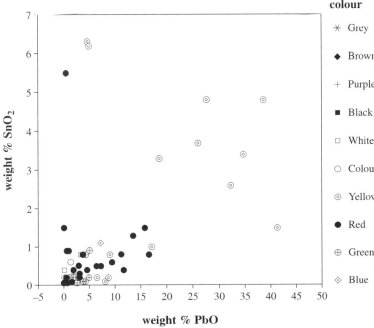

Figure 3.39 Weight % lead oxide versus weight % stannous oxide in a range of opaque (white, yellow and red) and translucent glass colours from Ribe, Jutland.

The opaque glasses used for making the beads provide us with a somewhat different level of inference. By using a combination of electron probe microanalysis and scanning electron microscopy it has been possible to establish that a lead stannate opacifier was used for the opaque yellow glasses, calcium antimonate for most of the white glasses, with a smaller proportion of tin oxide occurring in the balance of the opaque white glasses. As can be seen in Figure 3.39 the opaque yellow glasses fall into two compositional types: those which contain high and low lead oxide levels. This pattern has been detected in somewhat earlier yellow glass from Germany, so the yellow glass used for bead-making at Ribe may represent a technological continuity of this sixth–seventh-century glass. Opaque green, blue, blue-green and opaque grey-blue glasses were all opacified with calcium antimonate.

If the chemical compositions of the opaque glass tesserae found at Ribe are compared with the compositions of Roman opaque enamels (Bateson and Hedges 1975; Henderson 1991a), they are so close in composition to Ribe examples that we can state that they are almost certainly recycled Roman tesserae that have been removed from ransacked Roman (or

relatively newly built Byzantine) structures – and they do not, apparently, contain the chemical fingerprint found in the rest of the early medieval compositions found at Ribe. The white tesserae from Ribe, are opacified exclusively with calcium antimonate just as was found to be the case with Roman tesserae and have impurity patterns which set them apart from the rest of the white glass from Ribe: relatively high magnesia and low potassium oxide levels (see Figure 3.40) as opposed to more typical low levels of both. The other Ribe glass (apart from red) has consistently low levels of both magnesia and potassium oxides. The only alternative explanation possible for the compositional match between Roman tesserae and opaque white glass from Ribe found as tesserae and as parts of other artefacts is that exactly the same technological procedures, including the use of the same raw materials, were used to make them in the post-Roman world. This explanation is considerably less likely than import and re-use of 'Roman' tesserae.

The chemical composition of opaque reddish-brown glasses, frequently used in forming bi- and polychrome cables and millefiori rods is also characteristically Roman rather than early medieval. The

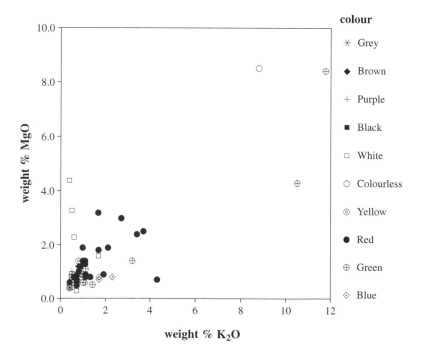

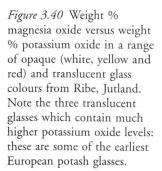

Figure 3.40 Weight % magnesia oxide versus weight % potassium oxide in a range of opaque (white, yellow and red) and translucent glass colours from Ribe, Jutland. Note the three translucent glasses which contain much higher potassium oxide levels: these are some of the earliest European potash glasses.

reddish-brown colour of glass was produced by a relatively low percentage of cuprous oxide crystals associated with elevated levels of lead and iron oxides. The iron oxide would have probably acted as an internal reducing agent and helped to retain the copper oxide present in a reduced state (Section 3.2.5.2). These red glasses are also mainly characterised by a positive correlation between tin and lead oxides (see Figure 3.39), suggesting a consistent use of the same copper-rich colorant. The relatively low levels of cuprous and lead oxides combined with relatively high levels of magnesia and potassium oxide (for a soda-lime glass) in many, as well as high iron oxide levels, clearly links them with the chemical analyses of Roman reddish brown enamels that have been published (Bateson and Hedges 1975; Henderson 1991a), so again we can suggest that a Roman glass tradition was used. Thus the scientific investigation of the glass used for making beads at Ribe clearly shows that characteristically early medieval glasses were used together with glass produced in the Roman tradition some of which was recycled.

3.11.4 The archaeological inference

The excavations at Ribe have *not* revealed the presence of a furnace structure for making beads there. Experimental archaeology has helped not only to interpret how some of the industrial debris found fitted into the techniques used, but also has provided evidence that it was possible to produce beads with only a hearth (Gam 1990; 1993) – though this does not prove that it actually happened that way. One primary factor is that the temperatures required to heat up and work the Ribe composition of soda-lime-silica glass so that it became sufficiently fluid to work would have been variable depending on the process involved: *c.* 950 °C for drawing canes, *c.* 1000 °C or less for mould pressing and drawing threads (i.e. much thinner, initially than canes) and *c.* 1000–1100 °C for marvering and gathering. These figures are based on a table published by Brill (1988, Table 9–12) for soda-lime glass of a closely similar composition to that used at Ribe. His table is partly based on scientific viscosity measurements for the glass (Holscher 1968; Hutchins and Harrington 1966).

Temperatures above about 900 °C are not achievable in the hearth used in the experiments conducted by Gam (1993), so since soda-lime glass was used for the manufacture of Ribe beads it *is most likely* that a furnace structure of some kind would have been necessary for glass-working at Ribe, but is yet to be found. Some of the modern glasses used by Gam are of a high lead oxide composition which would have a softening temperature of *c.* 200–300 °C lower than for soda-lime glasses which were used to make the Ribe beads. The other significant difference in the working properties of high lead glass as used in Gam's experiments and the soda-lime glass used at Ribe is that the former allows the glass to be worked for longer (i.e. it has a longer working period). This would certainly have made it easier to shape the glass into beads in a hearth and to reheat partly-made beads in order to continue working the glass.

The evidence for glass bead production at Ribe is comprehensive, and the material has yet to be published in full. Excavations at a contemporary Viking site, at Åhus in Skania, southern Sweden, has revealed a similar range of evidence for glass bead production (Callmer 1977; 1988; Callmer and Henderson 1991) and it is evidence that the two sites formed part of a trading system with the Baltic and the North Sea. Indeed Ribe is contemporary with a range of other important *emporia* in the North Sea region, such as Dorestad in the Netherlands (Van Es and Verwers 1980), Quentovic in northern France, and Hamwic (Saxon Southampton) in southern England (Morton 1992; Welch 1992; Hodges and Whitehouse 1983; Hunter and Heyworth 1988). The sites are linked by a series of artefact distributions such as sceattas, and querns made from a volcanic stone found in the Eifel, ancient mountains in Germany.

Like Ribe, other contemporary trading tended to be involved in a range of production industries. At Hamwic evidence was found for the working of iron, copper alloy, lead, bone, antler, wood, leather, textile manufacture and possibly glass (Morton 1992: 55–7; Welch 1992: 118). However, no evidence has been found at Hamwic or on the other *emporia* for glass bead production; it was evidently a specialisation which was restricted to certain sites such as

Ribe and Åhus. Since many of the raw materials used for bead production at Ribe were imported *secondary* ones (i.e. imported blocks of glass, glass tesserae, broken vessel fragments), the knowledge of glass-making from *primary* raw materials (fritting) and the proximity of raw material sources (suitable sand and alkali) was not something that determined the location of the industry. Instead, one might suggest that the putative royal presence at Ribe for some reason attracted the glass artisans to the growing centre on a seasonal basis, and undoubtedly the presence of workers in copper alloys and iron with the potential for sharing fuels and perhaps ceramic materials for constructing furnaces and crucibles may have attracted them.

The extent to which an industrial environment was built up in this way would partly be determined by whether each production activity was traditionally viewed by the artisans as separate 'entities' with associated separate lines of raw material supply or whether knowledge and raw materials were shared. It is almost inevitable that the knowledge of pyro-technology would have been shared and the principal link between glass-working and the other high-temperature industries would have been shared fuel supplies. As we have seen some of the temperatures for glass-working would have been as high as *c.* 1000–1100 °C, so it is likely that some form of furnace would in fact have been necessary to heat up the glass: 800–900 °C can be achieved in bonfires, but it becomes impossible to achieve temperatures above 1000 °C without a small furnace with a forced draught system. This in turn has important implications for the amount and kind of fuel used for glass-working. The density of charcoal provided by carbonising different tree species varies and this has a direct bearing on the calorific value of heat provided when the fuel is burnt. Thus some charcoals will provide intense heat for a short time at high temperatures and other charcoals prolonged heat at lower temperatures: both may have been necessary in fuelling a furnace for heating up glass as part of the bead production at Ribe. Minimum temperatures of *c.* 1100 °C would have been necessary for smelting iron at Ribe, so we can suggest that a fuel supply could have been shared between the glass- and iron-producing industries.

In sum, the evidence for the manufacture of glass beads at Ribe provides us with a good example of the way in which the location of a high-temperature industry in the Viking world had links with other sites and probably other industries there. The supply of raw glass and other materials benefited from the trade system which linked Ribe to other contemporary Viking sites like Åhus in southern Sweden and with other early medieval *emporia* like Dorestad in the Netherlands, and Hamwic in southern England (in a North Sea zone). Scientific analysis of the glass from Ribe indicates that some of it had a distinctive combination of impurities only found in early medieval glass, with some of the rest, especially the glass tesserae, being of a characteristically 'Roman' composition. This has interesting implications in terms of the ultimate source of the glass, there being no evidence for the manufacture of glass from raw materials at Ribe. From a more local perspective, a putative royal presence at Ribe may have attracted glass artisans to the site on the river bank, and equally other artisans involved in other high-temperature industries may have benefited from sharing fuel and ceramic materials.

3.12 The rise of the 'Abbasids and glass production in early Islamic Syria

3.12.1 Introduction

With the rise of Islam in the seventh century AD and the successes of the Islamic armies over vast tracks of land, cities were created with industrial areas which specialised in production using distinctive materials. With the growth of Islamic cities like Damascus and Fustat (modern Cairo), the growth of industries grew apace. What today forms the country of Syria was especially important during the Umayyad caliphate, with Damascus being a primary centre. From here in the early eighth century successful raids were launched eastwards into Transoxiana and Sind on the west coast of India. Visigothic Spain fell to Islam in 711, though the Islamic sieges of Constantinople in 673–8 and 716–17 were unsuccessful. During the time of the Umayyad caliphate (661–750) the Islamic Empire started to acquire the secular as well as the religious trappings of a great power.

From 750 the ʿAbbasids became the dominant caliphate in the Islamic world and the centre of power shifted to Baghdad in Iraq; later geographers placed Baghdad at the hub of the universe. However, one of the most famous caliphs of Baghdad, Harun ar-Rashid, moved temporarily westwards, to al-Raqqa, where his central administration was located between the years 796 and 808.

The city of al-Raqqa in northern central Syria is located close to the junction of the river Euphrates and its tributary the Balikh (see Figure 3.41). The origin of the settlement of al-Raqqa was in the third century BC when Seleucus I Nikator (301–281 BC) founded the Hellenistic city of Nikephorion, later enlarged probably by Seleucos II Kallinikos (246–26 BC) and named Kallinikos/Callinicum after him. It was destroyed by the Sasanid Khusraw I Anushirwan in AD 542, and re-built by the Emperor Justinian (AD 527–65) as part of the fortification programme of the Byzantine border along the Euphrates (Al-Khalaf and Kohlmeyer 1985).

The classical city was conquered in AD 639/AH 18 or AD 640/AH 19 by the Muslim army under ʾIyad b. Ghanm. It was an important centre in the Umayyad period (c. mid-eighth century) as a protec-tive garrison against the Byzantine armies and became known as al-Raqqa. Until the twelfth century AD a bishop resided in al-Raqqa and four monas-teries were attested to have been located there (Meinecke 1991).

During the time when the ʿAbbasid caliph Harun ar-Rashid resided in al-Raqqa between AD 796/AH 175 and AD 808/AH 187 he built a new city (ar-Rafika [translated as the companion]) next to al-Raqqa, some 20 palatial complexes and an indus-trial complex of some 3 km in length (Salibi 1954–5; Heusch and Meinecke 1989; Meinecke 1994). During this period it was the capital of the ʿAbbasid Empire.

3.12.2 Glass production at al-Raqqa on the Euphrates: the industrial context

Excavations of the palace complexes and other early Islamic structures under the directorship of the late Professor Dr Michael Meinecke occurred between 1982 and 1993, and latterly under the directorship of the author as the al-Raqqa Ancient Industry Project.

In a suburb of al-Raqqa called Mishlab a series of small tells forming a 3 km strip reflect the existence of an Islamic industrial complex in which each tell is apparently related to the manufacture of one or more materials, including glass, unglazed pottery, glazed pottery and iron. The tells are all threatened by the construction of this al-Raqqa suburb, so archaeological investigations can certainly be consid-ered as rescue excavations. Michael Meinecke's initial excavations of one such tell, the 'Black Tell' (Tell Aswad), produced evidence for ʿAbbasid pottery production (Watson, in press). Subsequently excava-tions have revealed a minimum number of three kilns in an area 40 metres to the west. In addition exca-vations on other sites have revealed further evidence for glass and pottery production dating to both ʿAbbasid and Ayyubid caliphates.

3.12.3 The glass tell, Tell Zujaj

The tell of c. 20 m × 15 m in area had been truncated before excavations commenced. The evidence re-moved in c. 1988 apparently included that for the manufacture of pottery of probable eleventh century (Fatmid/Seljuq) date (Dr Kohlmeyer, personal com-munication). This did not affect the interpretation

Figure 3.41 The location of al-Raqqa in Syria.

of evidence for glass production, as it was of a later date. The only remaining archaeological feature which was of an eleventh century date, a pit, produced evidence for sugar production (Henderson 1996b).

Excavation has revealed that there were at least three principal phases of activity on the site: the late phase, which consists mainly of massive dumps of industrial debris from glass production, a floor and a robbed furnace pit; the middle phase, which includes a complete glass workshop with two floor levels belonging to sub-phases of its use; and the early phase consisting of the remains of a hypocaust within which the glass workshop had been constructed. Only the middle and late phases, which produced evidence for glass production, will be discussed here.

3.12.3.1 The late workshop phase

The structural evidence from this phase was somewhat patchy because the tell stratigraphy was partially disturbed at the surface. The phase included a partly-destroyed plaster floor in the south-east corner of the site with the foundations of two small vitrified structures at its northern end which may have functioned as fritting ovens. In the same phase a robbed pit, which was pear-shaped in plan, had a fill of charcoal, soot, burnt bone and many glass fragments (some melted) can be interpreted as the remains of the lowest (firing) chamber of a glass furnace. The elongation at one end can be interpreted as the remains of the stoke hole creating a pear-shape similar to Roman glass furnaces (discussed in Section 3.4.3). The superstructure of the furnace was apparently destroyed prior to the truncation of the tell and it is likely that its remains were dumped in a series of pits which were cut into the central, western and northern parts of the site.

The pits found in the central, western and northern parts of the site were largely full of the debris of the glass industry including destroyed furnace bricks which had been subjected to such intense heat that they had completely melted, turned black and started to flow, as well as tons of other evidence of the glass industry. The balance of evidence consisted of evidence for casting glass into blocks of at least three different sizes: 5 sq cm, 3 sq cm and 1.5 sq cm (tesserae), glass vessel fragments, the evidence for

glass-blowing (moils: the knock-offs from blowing irons), dribbles of glass, the very important discovery of glass frit, which is evidence for the manufacture of glass from primary raw materials, and a range of fuel-ash slags which result from the fusion of silica in bricks with alkaline ash in the environment (Biek and Bayley 1979; Henderson *et al.* 1987). The discovery of frit is rare. A fuller consideration of the formation of frit is given below. Most of the bricks appear to be the remains of tank furnace floors; hot fluid glass had dribbled between the bricks and interacted with them (Henderson 1999b). It is therefore likely that the 'raw' glass was made in the tank furnace and reheated inside the furnace represented by a pear-shaped plan which was probably of the three-chambered bee-hive ('southern') construction. The hot fluid glass would have been gathered from the crucibles placed in the furnace through a glory hole so as to blow the glass, or to cast it into blocks. No such access to hot glass is afforded by a tank furnace.

3.12.3.2 The glass workshop

Excavations of the middle phase revealed the remains of an almost complete glass workshop in which all of the industrial installations have been fully excavated (see Figure 3.42). These consisted of furnaces of the same kind in the north-west, north-east and south-east corners of the room with the possible foundation of a fourth in the south-west corner of the room (see Figures 3.43 and 3.14); the remains of a possible truncated fifth furnace was located centrally in the southern wall. The first one excavated was in the south-east corner of the glass workshop; it survived to a height of 1.3 m. The top chamber, which was represented by the lowest part of the curving clay dome would have been used for annealing glass vessels, the middle chamber for melting the glass in a crucible and the bottom chamber would have been a firing chamber from which the heat rose to melt the glass. A semi-circular chamber was built on the back of the furnace which would probably have been used for annealing glass vessels.

A second well-preserved furnace of the same kind was found in the north-east corner and, as for the first furnace, a smaller installation which was probably used for annealing glass vessels had been built

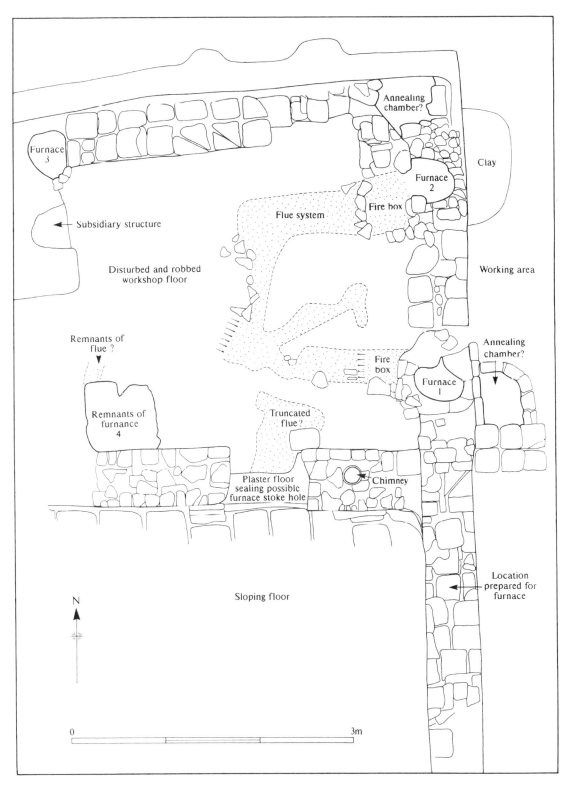

Furnace
3

Annealing
chamber?

Clay

Subsidiary structure

Furnace
2

Fire box

Flue system

Disturbed and robbed
workshop floor

Working area

Remnants of
flue ?

Fire
box

Annealing
chamber?

Remnants of
furnance
4

Furnace
1

Truncated
flue ?

Plaster floor
sealing possible
furnace stoke hole

Chimney

N

Location
prepared for
furnace

Sloping floor

0   3m

Figure 3.42 Plan of glass workshop discovered at al-Raqqa, Syria, late eighth–early ninth century.

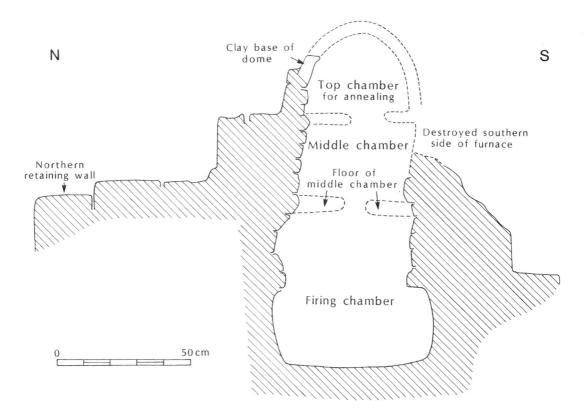

Figure 3.43 Cross-section of furnace 2 (of the 'southern' type), al-Raqqa, Syria.

against it. This chamber was built at the side of the middle chamber rather than behind the furnace (see Figure 3.42). The third furnace, again of the same type and same dimensions as the first, was excavated in the north-west corner of the room. The foundation courses of a fourth furnace were discovered in the south-west corner of the workshop. The three most complete furnaces were built on or against a wall and faced inwards. Their front faces had been largely destroyed so that the structures when first excavated were visible in longitudinal section. The furnaces were constructed out of bricks luted with clay and all of them had a fill of soot, charcoal, bone fragments, ash and fragments of highly baked clay, the latter perhaps originally forming part of the clay dome that covered the top furnace chamber; two contained glass fragments. The stoke holes of furnaces one, two and three had an arch constructed of baked clay which were found *in situ*.

As at Tell el-Amarna (Sections 3.4.1 and 3.4.2), it is necessary to question closely the possible use(s) to which these structures were put. Given that the only high-temperature industry for which there was any evidence from this phase derived from the glass industry, and that no other ancient production industry involved the use of such furnace structures, they are clearly glass furnaces. The late phase industrial dumps contained a small number of kiln bars, but no such evidence was derived from the glass workshop. No metalliferous slags or evidence for metal-smelting/ working were discovered in either phase.

The furnaces themselves were rather small with an internal diameter of *c.* 75 cm and would probably have held one pot. If four furnaces were being worked at the same time, it would not only have been possible to work quite a large amount of glass, it would also have been possible to control carefully the processes of production of each glass batch, especially the raw materials and furnace atmospheres used; this would have been especially useful if four different glass colours were being melted. The furnaces appear to be the bee-hive type of furnace that has been described in a ninth century Syriac manuscript in the British Museum (Dillon 1907: 122–4; Charleston 1978: 10; Newton and Davison 1989: 111).

The most recent translation of the relevant passage reads:

> The furnace of the glass-makers should have six compartments, of which three are disposed in storeys one above the other . . . the lower compartment should be deep, in it is the fire; that of the middle storey has an opening in front of the central chambers, these last should be equal, disposed on the sides and not in the centre, so that fire from below may rise towards the central region where the glass is and heat and melt the materials. The upper compartment, which is vaulted, is arranged so as uniformly to roof over the middle storey; it is used to cool the vessels after their manufacture . . .

Although the mention of six chambers does not, at first glance, agree with the archaeological evidence, there is, nevertheless, a clear relationship between the text and the excavated evidence with the three chambers being 'disposed in storeys one above the other'. The mention of the extra three chambers may be a reference to extra annealing chambers built against, or separated from, the main glass furnace such as the 'extra' chambers which have been found at al-Raqqa.

Other structural remains in the workshop include the remains of a stoke hole of another furnace in a central position of the southern wall of the room, truncated by the insertion of a later floor, a structure with a chimney connected to it using the southern 'wall' of the workshop and an extension of the eastern wall of the workshop to the south (see Figure 3.42). The latter had two locations which were equidistant from the two furnaces which were constructed on that wall to the north. The locations can be interpreted as places where two further furnaces were to be built, but this did not happen.

The floor of the glass workshop had been robbed and trampled during a later use; the pottery found in the disturbed layer was of 'Abbasid date. The remnants of the disturbed floor sealed a system of channels with a distinctive black fill and constructed out of clay; they led into the firing chambers of the glass furnaces in the north-eastern and south-eastern corners (Figure 3.42). Another channel which led into the base of a truncated furnace located centrally in the southern wall of the workshop had been blocked off indicating that there was at least one sub-phase in the use of the workshop. The channels were constructed out of the same clay that had been used to lute the bricks used for constructing the glass furnaces. Although there is no published parallel for the use of these channels with square sections in a glass workshop, they can be interpreted as forming a centralised flue system for the furnaces, originating at the western side of the glass workshop. Unfortunately the western part of the heating system had been destroyed. The use of the flues would have allowed the furnaces to be retained at temperatures of perhaps as high as c. 1000 °C. A bellows emplacement had survived just in front of the fire box of the south-eastern furnace. These would have been used to raise the working temperatures to above 1000 °C in the furnaces when needed. The northern retaining wall, which had originally been built for the earlier hypocaust, survived to a maximum height of c. 2 m. Clay was packed against its outer (northern) face which was thicker at the points where furnaces were constructed on its inside. The wall was constructed of two skins of bricks, with a rubble in-fill.

Below the layer containing the channels was a series of *pilae* which originally formed part of the hypocaust in which the workshop had been constructed. The re-use of a hypocaust system for industrial purposes can be paralleled elsewhere in the early Islamic period, such as at Medinet el-Fahr to the north of al-Raqqa, where an iron foundry was inserted into a previous hypocaust building (Professor C.-P. Hasse, personal communication).

3.12.4 Dating of the site
The pottery from the site, much of which is glazed, is all consistent with an early Islamic date for the late phase ('Abbasid); no recognisably later pottery was recovered from the phase. A single sherd of

Samarra lustre ware was found in the disturbed top surface layer. The chronology attributed to this ware can now be considered to extend back to as early as 820 (Dr D. Kennett, personal communication), and in any case there is now possible evidence for production of such wares in al-Raqqa itself. Excavations of the 'Black Tell' c. 1 km to the east (Miglus 1999), a tell which consists of the evidence for the manufacture of ʿAbbasid pottery, produced a very similar range of wares to those found at the glass tell, including the characteristic ʿAbbasid yellow-splashed wares (Watson, 1999). There was nothing in the pottery in the late phase which suggested a date later than the ʿAbbasid caliphate and in all likelihood the site was in use for the short period when Harun ar-Rashid resided in al-Raqqa. The middle phase, the primary fill of the glass workshop, also produced glazed ʿAbbasid pottery, but there was a much higher proportion of unglazed, including stamp-decorated, plain wares (see Section 4.3.4). As for the black fill of the hypocaust on which the floor of the glass workshop had been constructed, it represents debris from its last use and contained plain ʿAbbasid wares and a complete ʿAbbasid lamp, so it is clear that all three phases are of an ʿAbbasid date. Analysis of some of c. 600 copper alloy coins from the site by Dr Stephan Heidemann (Heidemann 1993) has provided a *terminus post quem* of 804 AD for the material dumped in the glass workshop. This is the earliest possible date for the fill, and suggests that the workshop was constructed and in use earlier than this date. The deposition of coins in such quantities, especially copper-based ones, suggests that they were no longer of any value, and that coins minted for Harun's sons replaced them. It is therefore reasonable to suggest that the coins were deposited at around the period when Harun moved to Baghdad in 808, or perhaps ten to fifteen years later. It is almost certain that the glass workshop and the dumps which sealed it were in use during the time that Harun ar-Rashid resided in al-Raqqa. The exact total length of time that the site was in use for during the early, middle and late phases is yet to be determined, but a short chronology of c. 30 years is considered to be most likely.

3.12.5 Other evidence for the glass industry

The industrial evidence found at the glass tell (Tell Zujaj) is almost entirely related to the manufacture of glass; much of the evidence was found in the industrial dumps belonging to the late phase, and a smaller amount was found in the middle phase, both in the furnaces and on the disturbed glass workshop floor. Evidence for the glass industry shows that both *glass-working* and *glass-making* were carried out on the site. The evidence for glass-working consisted of hundreds of ʿAbbasid glass vessel fragments, distorted glass vessel fragments, pulls of glass, rods of glass, dribbles and drops of glass and large lumps of raw glass mainly in translucent green, purple, colourless, brown and blue glass, with a smaller amount of red glass. Glass moils of two sizes (the knock-offs from the glass-blowing iron) were found and fragments of crucibles were found, with two coming from the disturbed workshop floor. The ceramic finds other than pottery and crucibles consisted of a large number of melted furnace bricks some of which had fused together at high temperatures (c. 1200 °C). These were found in the late phase, and are the destroyed bases and sides of tank furnaces (see Section 3.4.4) and probably also the remains of beehive shaped furnaces.

By far the largest *weight* of glass-bearing artefacts found was the broken trays which had been used for casting blocks of glass; the glass still adhered to many of these tray fragments (see Figure 3.44). At least three different sizes of glass blocks were being manufactured. The smallest size (c. 1.5 cm square) would have been suitable for use in glass tesserae mosaics. The larger blocks (3 cm and 5 cm square) may have been intended to serve as flooring materials. Just such a floor, completely made from polished glass blocks, was discovered during the excavations of palace B in al-Raqqa by Nassib Salibi (Salibi 1954–5; Ruprechtsberger 1993: 518).

The evidence for glass-making consisted of lumps of material that is probably over-cooked glass frit. The term frit is often mis-used in archaeological contexts: its definition is a material which derives from the partial fusion of the primary raw materials of glass production. At al-Raqqa the frit is a grey material full of trapped gas bubbles (see Figure 3.12).

Figure 3.44 Glass blocks in situ on the remains of the tray on which they were cast (the block is 15 cm long).

It is partly vitrified and rather brittle. In the process of fritting the aim is to avoid the full fusion of raw materials and the end result is a greyish granular material of a sugary consistency. The material from al-Raqqa has apparently been over-heated so that its constituents have started to fuse together (i.e. the process was allowed to go too far). It is only because the frit has been over-heated that it has survived at all, and this may be one reason why none has been reported before from site excavations of glass-working or making sites. The scientific examination of the frit (see below) allows one to be more confident that its identification as frit is correct. In addition to the frit some distorted trays were found which may have been used to carry out the fritting process. One interpretation of the presence of the frit, is that it represents the poorly-fused remains of the primary raw materials which were trapped in a 'cool spot' in a tank furnace.

3.12.6 Scientific investigations of the glass and allied materials

The chemical and structural analysis of glass, frit and associated debris from an Islamic glass workshop had not been carried out before. The principal aims of this investigation were (1) to determine the chemical compositions of representative glasses from the workshop and compare them with samples from the palace complexes; (2) to infer the raw materials used from these chemical compositions, including colorants; (3) to investigate the compositional (and structural) relationships between the various classes of industrial debris; (4) to investigate the relationships between glass compositions and artefact types made from them; (5) to investigate any correlations between glass composition, the archaeological phases of the glass factory and glass recovered from other sites in al-Raqqa; (6) to compare the compositional characteristics of the 'Abbasid glass from al-Raqqa, both with contemporary glass from other sites in the Islamic world, and with earlier and later Islamic glass; (7) to relate the raw materials used for the production of glass to those used in other pyrotechnologies, such as with the materials used for the construction of glass furnaces and pottery kilns and with glazes.

A discussion of the interpretation of the chemical analyses and compositional groupings has been published elsewhere (Henderson 1995; 1996b), together with a discussion of the principal raw materials used for making the glass and some discussion of the compositional characteristics of the debris, so only the principal characteristics of the compositional groupings will be summarised here. In addition, the relationships between chemical composition, glass artefact type and date/site phase will be discussed. The broader aims of the analytical project (especially items 6 and 7 above) will be addressed when more chemical analyses have been carried out on material from al-Raqqa and beyond.

Chemical analysis of 50 samples will be discussed here. These consisted of 10 samples of cast glass or glass from casting surfaces, 7 samples of raw glass, 15 samples of vessels, 1 sample from a knock-off pontil glass, 1 sample of glass from a furnace base and 1 sample of frit from Tell Zujaj. For comparison, samples of 7 window panes from the 'Abbasid Palace complexes at al-Raqqa were analysed, 4 samples of window fragments from Qasr al-Banât, the Ayyubid 'princess's palace' in al-Raqqa and fragments from a single vessel from that site. Three samples of vessel glass from the palace complexes were also analysed, including 2 from an important complete glass horn which had a translucent blue green body and translucent honey-coloured decoration. Chemical analyses of the materials associated with glass production (fuel-ash slags, slags resulting from melted bricks and other vitreous slags) were carried out, but will not be discussed here.

This investigation has produced a range of interesting results which are both complex and intriguing and reveal the need for further analytical work. All of the glass analysed (except a single window fragment from Qasr al-Banât) was found to be of a soda-lime composition. The totally unexpected feature of the data, however, was the very significant variation in the levels of impurities in the glasses analysed, something which has never been found in the investigation of an ancient glass factory before. The

technique of analysis used was electron probe micro-analysis (Henderson 1988), a micro-destructive technique which involved removal of samples of up to 1 mm in size.

The largest number of samples fall into a single compositional grouping (type 1 in Figure 3.45). It is a soda-lime glass which is characterised by containing relatively low levels of alumina and high magnesia and would probably have been manufactured using a combination of quartz and the halophytic ashes of desert plants, which still grow close to the glass tell today. The composition was typical of Islamic glass analyses that have already been published (Sayre and Smith 1961; Brill 1970a; 1970b; Henderson and Allan 1990; Henderson 1995b; 1998b; Freestone and Gorin-Rosen 1999). The glasses of this composition published up to now have mainly been of a twelfth–fourteenth century date; these results from al-Raqqa confirmed that the composition was used in Syria in the late eighth–early ninth century.

The second group, if it could be defined as such (labelled, for convenience, as type 2 in Figure 3.45), was mainly made up of highly coloured glasses (such as brown, deep yellow green and emerald green) and contained higher alumina and lower magnesia levels than type 1. It is possible that this composition resulted from mixing types 1 and 3. The presence of elevated impurity levels of titanium oxide and phosphorus pentoxide, apparently associated with high manganese and iron oxides in type 2 glasses, suggests that colorant materials were added to the mixed glass batch. Two other points plotted in Figure 3.45, for samples which contained even higher alumina levels than in the other 'type 2' samples, may have interacted with a ceramic (such as the wall of a glass-melting crucible) to the extent that alumina migrated into the glass. One of the samples of glass which contained more than 4% alumina was attached to a furnace base, and this would certainly have been enriched in this way.

The third group (type 3 in Figure 3.45) is a low magnesia soda-lime glass. It is similar to glass of 'Roman' type. Because it contains relatively high alumina levels it can be inferred that sand was used as the silica source; the low magnesia levels on the other hand suggest the use of a mineral source of

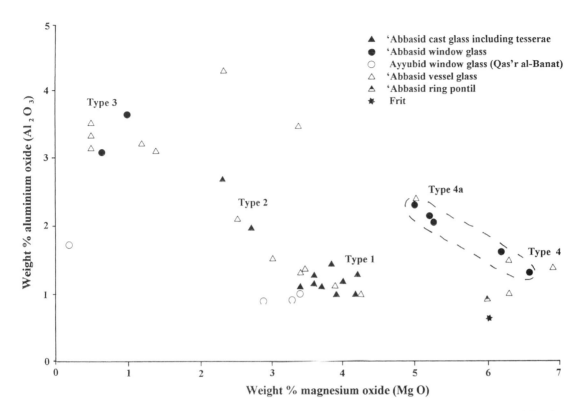

Figure 3.45 Weight % magnesia versus weight % aluminia in Islamic ('Abbasid and Ayyubid) glass and frit from al-Raqqa, Syria according to artefact type.

alkali, like natron. The glass contains lower soda and generally higher aluminia than found in Roman glasses; Roman glasses *normally* contain *c.* 2.5% aluminia (as detected in the fourth-century Roman samples from Jalame: see Figure 3.46), whereas the al-Raqqa glasses contain between 3 and 4% aluminia (see Figures 3.45 and 3.46). It should be stressed that the range of levels of aluminia plotted in fourth-century Roman glass from Jalame has also been found in thousands of other Roman glasses and so would be distinct from the al-Raqqa type 3 glasses; the aluminia levels plotted for another Levantine site, Rakit, which was contemporary with Jalame contained generally higher levels. These are exceptional among Roman glasses and are included here in order to illustrate that although al-Raqqa type 3 glass can be considered to be an Islamic version of Roman glass, and that some samples contain the highest aluminia levels, a small number of Roman

glasses do contain levels which approach those found in al-Raqqa type 3 glasses (Henderson in press d). So although al-Raqqa type 3 has characteristics in common with Roman glasses it can be regarded as an Islamic form of that glass made using raw materials akin to those used by the Romans.

The fourth group (type 4 in Figure 3.45) is another sub-type of soda-lime-silica glass, but with characteristically high magnesia levels and aluminia levels comparable with those in type 1. The elevated magnesia levels (compared with type 1) are probably due to the use of a different (sub-)species of halophytic plant to produce the alkali. A small cluster of four analyses with higher aluminia (greater than 2%) and lower, but still relatively high (compared with type 4), magnesia levels are regarded as a sub-grouping (type 4a in Figure 3.45) and conceivably represented a variation in the technique of raw material preparation.

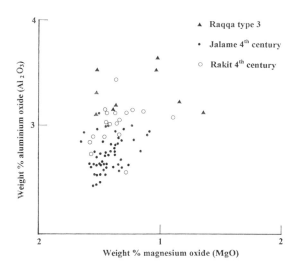

Figure 3.46 Weight % magnesia versus weight % aluminia in al-Raqqa type 3 glass compared with late Roman (fourth century) glass from Jalame and Rakit, Palestine.

If the compositional data is examined according to whether it relates to cast blocks of glass, window glass or vessel glass (Figure 3.45), some interesting correlations are evident. It is clear that almost all the cast glass is of type 1, with two points falling into type 2 (which in any case is a possible mixture of type 1 and 3). It is equally clear that *none* of the window glass analysed falls into type 1: it is either of type 3 or type 4, or falls into group 4a.

The almost perfect negative correlation of points which join the points for 'Abbasid window glass of types 4 and 4a underlines the compositional relationship between window glass in group 4 and subgroup 4a, suggesting that the same technology was involved and that more chemical analyses could link the groupings. The other two plotted points for 'Abbasid window glass fall into type 3. Therefore both high and low magnesia glasses were used for the manufacture of the window glasses found in the western palace and the eastern [palatial] complex at al-Raqqa. Types 3, 4 and 4a were used to make the western palace windows, whereas only types 4 and 4a were used for window glass found in the eastern complex. Using this data set it is clear that different glass recipes were used for the manufacture of windows and for casting glass into blocks, including

tesserae: only a plant-ash soda-lime glass for the cast glass and both a mineral-based and plant-ash alkali for the windows. It is also significant that the only analyses of glass vessels from the western palace which have been analysed are of type 3: these are a thinly-blown beaker with applied blue trail around the rim (the body was analysed) and two samples of a translucent blue glass horn with applied translucent brown decoration. The sample is far too small to suggest that these data have a chronological significance, but the results are technologically significant.

It is possible that the window glass that was made from a mineral-based alkali (type 3) found in the west palace was made in al-Raqqa; the plant-ash based glass of type 4 which was used to make window glass for both the eastern complex and the west palace is of the same composition as the frit found at Tell Zujaj (the glass tell), so this strongly suggests that the window glass of type 4 composition was made in al-Raqqa. It would, after all, have been normal to have made the window glasses 'to order', and presumably in an industrial complex close to where the palaces were being built.

Because the glassy phase of the frit (see below) is of a type 4 composition it may be regarded as a *workshop composition* – something which can only rarely be suggested with any confidence, the reason being that frit is only rarely found or recognised. The same combination of raw materials may have been used at other Islamic workshops, but we can still suggest from these data, that glass vessels and some window glass were made using type 4 composition at al-Raqqa in the industrial complex. In contrast, we see from Figure 3.45 that 'Abbasid vessel glass fragments, including fragments of bowls, a jug handle, beakers, phials/flasks, bottles, a ring pontil of type 4 (showing that this kind of glass was definitely made and blown into vessels at al-Raqqa) and deformed undiagnostic vessel fragments, fall into all the major groupings represented; in this instance it is apparent that the working properties of these different glass compositions had little bearing on the vessel forms made from them.

The small number of samples of window glass of Ayyubid date from Qas'r al-Banât which were analysed have distinctively different compositions from the 'Abbasid window glass: the Ayyubid glass is either of type 1 (similar to the cast glass) which continued to be used in the eleventh century or, in one case of a lead oxide-silica composition (containing 0.9% total alkali, 30.5% silica, 66.1% lead oxide, 0.2% magnesia and 1.7% aluminia). This lead rich glass is similar to some contemporary glaze compositions. Ayyubid window glass was therefore made with an entirely different technology from that used in the earlier 'Abbasid palaces and illustrates that glass of type 1 continued in use in al-Raqqa. The lead oxide-silica window glass is a bright emerald green colour which is caused by cupric oxide in a lead-rich environment. This is, to the author's knowledge, the first reported incidence of lead-glass used as a window pane in the Islamic world.

The bivariate plot of weight % magnesia *vs.* weight % aluminia for glasses from 'early' contexts of the glass tell and from palace contexts has been drawn in order to investigate whether there may be any chronological relationships to the use of glass types. The trampled remains of the workshop floor, the earliest context with glass in the workshop, produced 'plant-ash' glass (type 1) and mineral-based alkali glass (type 3) compositions: this context therefore produced the earliest type 1 glass from the site, which is likely to be early ninth century in date.

Glass found in the furnaces, the first fill following the abandonment of the workshop, includes glass of the two plant-ash groupings (types 1 and 4) as well as type 3, the low magnesia glass made from a mineral-based alkali. The same inference can be drawn as for the glass found on the trampled workshop floor: the production of type 3 (a variant of an existing 'Roman' technology) is probably relatively early in the sequence because it has been found in the early ninth-century palaces and in contexts which date immediately *after* the abandonment of the glass workshop. This adds to the impression that we are dealing with a short chronology for all three phases of the glass tell.

If it is argued that the use of the western palace dates to Harun ar-Rashid (796–808), then glass from inside the furnace and from the trampled workshop floor of the same compositions *could* also be of a similar date. Indeed the frit analysed (see below), which derives from the late phase of the site in layers which seal the workshop, fall into the same grouping as the windows (made using plant ash) from both

the eastern complex and western palace. Since the frit derived from the 'late' phase on the site, and glass of that composition was probably used to make window glass for the 'early' west palace and eastern complex, this also argues for a short chronology for the excavated remains of glass production on the site, lying within the period when Harun ar-Rashid resided in al-Raqqa and perhaps up to ten to fifteen years later.

The fact that none of the glass of type 2 has been found in an 'early' context up to now provides tentative indirect evidence that, for some reason, glasses of types 1 and 3 were mixed at a 'later' date (i.e. perhaps only five years later). Certainly some of the glasses which fall into this group contain magnesia and aluminia levels which are intermediate between groups 1 and 3. Another characteristic of the glasses is that they are generally highly coloured.

It is possible that the production of glass could have continued later (post-808) at the glass tell – but why? With the move of Harun al-Rashid to Baghdad in 808 the demand for glass would have dropped off dramatically, so although it is not unreasonable to suggest that the industry continued, that the palaces continued in use and that the towns of al-Raqqa and al-Rafica still functioned, there is no direct archaeological evidence for this. If occupation and industrial production continued, it is likely to have gone into a rapid decline rather than to have tailed off gradually, since Harun had moved to Baghdad together with his armies and administrative structures.

Until now there has been little published evidence for the dated use of the type 1 (plant-ash glass) earlier than 845. The published evidence for its use is after 845 and is in the form of the chemical analyses of dated Egyptian glass weights: see Figure 3.47 (Matson 1948; Sayre 1965; Gratuze and Barandon 1990). Any published chemical analyses of glasses of seventh century date from the Levant (Dussart 1995; Fischer and McCray 1999) have demonstrated the persistence of 'Roman' low magnesia glass made from a mineral (natron) source of alkali – and in Israel this continued to be used, even in later centuries (Fischer and McCray 1999). Even though desert plants suitable for use as an alkali source were available in Egypt – in addition to the mineral source of

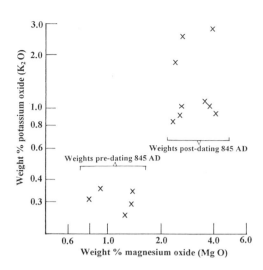

Figure 3.47 Weight % magnesia versus weight % potassium oxide in Islamic Egyptian glass weights; those predating 845 AD relate to al-Raqqa type 3 and those post-dating 845 AD to al-Raqqa type 1.

alkali found at Wadi al Natrun (see Section 3.2.1), plant ashes were apparently not used in Egypt until 845. It would have been more economical to have used the locally available alkali – plant ash – in Egypt before *c.* 845, but currently there is no published evidence for it.

It follows therefore that, the plant-ash glasses (types 1, 4 and 4a) from al-Raqqa which pre-date 845 by up to 40 years suggest that one of the industrial locations where the transition from the mineral-based alkali to the plant ash-based alkali in glass-making occurred was in al-Raqqa itself. It is also worth considering the possibility that the alkali change occurred on a regional basis, so that the change may have occurred at rather different times in different places, even though the alkali raw material – desert plant ashes – would have been easily available. Perhaps difficulty in obtaining natron through the traditionally established routes triggered the use of halophytic plants instead. The inference that experimentation with new raw materials occurred in al-Raqqa is not entirely unexpected since it was the capital of the 'Abbasid caliphate at the time. This technological transition is especially interesting because it occurs at almost exactly the same time in the west (Henderson

1993; Wedepohl 1997). However, in the west, the change would have been to tree ashes rather than to maritime or desert plant ashes (Turner 1956a; Brill 1970a; Besborodov 1975; Henderson 1988; see Section 3.2.1).

3.12.7 Scientific analysis of the frit

Frit is a material which is produced at the end of the first stage of glass production. It results from the primary raw materials being heated together at a relatively low temperature of *c.* 700–800 °C; this initiates a solid state reaction between the silica and the alkali, but no more (see Section 3.3). The aim is to avoid complete fusion and to drive off any gaseous oxides from the breakdown of impurities such as sulphates and carbonates in the glass batch (i.e. to produce sulphur dioxide and carbon dioxide). The process of fritting is carried out in trays in specifically designed fritting ovens in which frit was raked from time to time. It must be carried out several times; the hot frit being thrown into cold water (quenched) between each fritting operation. If necessary the granular material is crushed in order to increase the surface area to volume ratio of the particles and to aid their fusion when the batch is later heated to above *c.* 1100–1200 °C to make glass. The result of a successful fritting operation should be a granular sugary material. The overall reason for fritting is to eventually produce a good quality glass by removing impurities (especially gaseous).

Several blocks of a semi-vitrified grey material, which were suspected as being over-cooked frit, were excavated from the late phase at Tell Zujaj, al-Raqqa (see Figure 3.12). One was sampled and subjected to chemical and structural analysis. As mentioned above, the matrix of the frit was found to have the composition of al-Raqqa type 4 glass (see Figure 3.45). The other feature of the material which shows that it is indeed a frit, is the occurrence of crystals of relic high-temperature minerals such as alkaline feldspar and of quartz with slightly rounded profiles. This shows that some glass had already formed, with the smaller silica grains having reacted completely, and that some of the larger silica grains were just starting to react. The fact that the silica crystals have rounded profiles indicates that the temperature involved was insufficiently high to dissolve completely the larger crystals of silica in the glassy phase, but was just high enough to start the melting process. This reaction would be dependent on the chemical composition of the glassy matrix, the size of the reacting particles and the temperatures involved. The production of this over-cooked frit would have been at a temperature which was slightly above that at which fritting would have normally occurred (i.e. it has gone too far) so one result was to produce a glassy phase. Another sign that *relatively* low temperatures were involved (perhaps around 800–900 °C) is the survival of the alkaline feldspar crystals – though this would need to be confirmed with re-firing experiments.

The presence of small particles of bone in the frit, some of which had already dissolved and others which were in the process of breaking-up and dissolving (Figure 3.48) suggests that bone was added as a calcium source to the material before the frit was chilled. The pale compositional lines seen in Figure 3.48 are due to variations in the silica to calcium ratio and also reflect the high degree of compositional heterogeneity in the frit (Henderson 1995a). Since quartz was used as a silica source, crushed bone would have been a good alternative source of calcium to the shell fragments in sand, normally assumed to introduce calcium in soda-lime glass.

This picture is therefore entirely consistent with the material being an over-heated frit which has been discarded. As mentioned above, another possible interpretation is that a one-stage glass production process in a tank furnace occurred at al-Raqqa, and that the least successful (partly-fused) areas of the melt were removed. Frit is rarely, if ever, found or recognised on ancient glass producing sites.

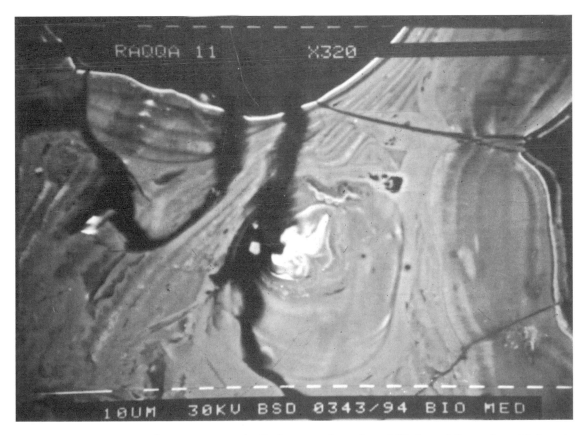

Figure 3.48 Back-scattered electron micrograph of a fragment of over-heated frit from al-Raqqa (late eighth–early ninth century) showing compositional variations determined by relative calcium and silicon oxide levels. The large white particle in the centre is bone.

3.12.8 Summary

In the excavations of the 'glass tell' some of the best preserved three-chambered glass furnaces yet discovered in the ancient world have been found, together with comprehensive evidence for the manufacture (glass-working and glass-making) at the site. The workshop was located within one room of a pre-existing hypocaust. Located at the centre of the Islamic world, evidence has been found for technological innovation with glass. Scientific analyses have strengthened these findings and provided evidence that a major technological innovation may have occurred at al-Raqqa, introducing a glass composition which was to last relatively unchanged for about 600 years and which was used throughout the Islamic world. Because the glass industry formed part of an industrial complex, the artisans would probably have benefited by sharing technological knowledge; the production of bricks of sufficient refractory quality was probably shared between the pottery and glass-making industries. Indeed it is also interesting to speculate about the relative status of the artisans who worked in such environments, and whether their status was in any way tied to the value of the materials and objects that they were making.

It is only with the discovery, excavation and scientific investigation of other Islamic glass workshops that it will be possible to make direct comparisons with other production centres such as those which are attested to have existed in Damascus, Aleppo and Fustat. Such a comparison will allow one to suggest how important the manufacture of glass was to the city of al-Raqqa and ultimately to the rest of the Islamic world.

3.13 Seventeenth-century glass production in Europe

3.13.1 Introduction

The study of glass from the medieval and post-medieval periods contrasts with earlier material in the west because it is possible to include historical evidence in the interpretation of its use and distribution. Although archaeological excavations of the remains of post-medieval and medieval buildings can produce deposits of pottery and glass, it does not necessarily follow that these can be tied easily to the use of the buildings concerned. Indeed, in the excavations of medieval Southampton, Brown (1997) has shown that historical evidence for the location of prestigious houses is not always reflected in the distribution of archaeological material. There can be many complex reasons for this, one being that material from elsewhere, not associated with the use of a prestigious house, may be dumped in its remains. It is, nevertheless, worth pursuing the potential links between historical evidence such as probate inventories for identifiable properties, the identity of the owner and the excavated ceramics and glass from that property (Henderson 1998a). This may provide a social context for the glass.

One of the other advantages of working with glass from the seventeenth century is that documentary evidence can also sometimes provide evidence of trade links which are reflected in the archaeological assemblages. In such historical periods it is also possible to refer to port records in which the relative costs of glass of different origins is listed. Even if that changed once traded 'inland' from the port, the economic value listed is nevertheless excellent data with which to compare other characteristics of the glass, such as the suggested origin of the glass and its chemical composition (a reflection of the raw materials used of varying purity or rarity). Such correlations can be linked directly with their actual social value, however that may be estimated.

3.13.2 The production and use of sixteenth–seventeenth-century glass goblets and beakers in Britain

Many of the post-medieval beakers excavated from Britain are faintly tinted with brown, grey or green colours; the vessels are considered to have been used for beer drinking and generally to have had a lower social value than goblets which would have been used for wine drinking. One further means of distinguishing between goblets and beakers is that most colourless goblets are rather finely made and may be elaborately decorated. Additionally, like some of the ('second-rate') beakers, some goblets may be faintly tinted with brown, green and grey, in which case they are invariably of a plainer design than the colourless

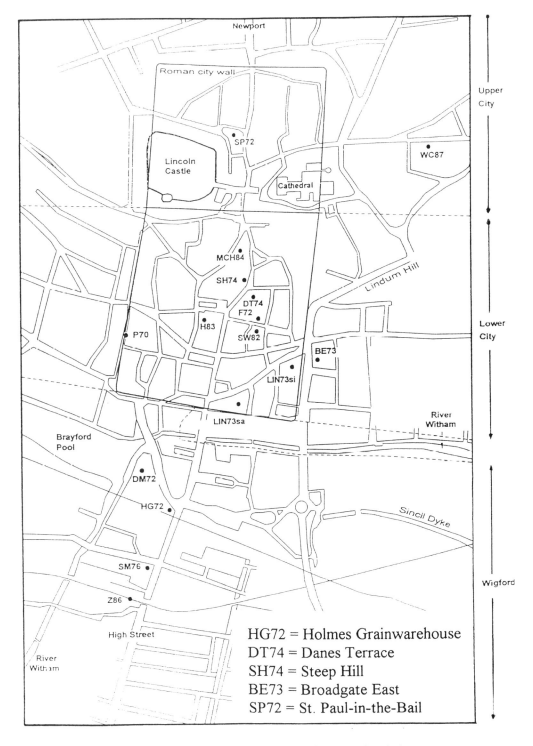

Figure 3.49 Location of sites excavated in Lincoln which produced post-medieval glass.

goblets inferring that they may have had a lower social and economic value.

Given the complex interrelations brought about by a fully developed market economy and its associated trade network in seventeenth-century Europe, one might have predicted that the trade in broken glass vessels (cullet) and ingots (Rednap and Freestone 1995) would have led to large-scale recycling, mixing and homogenisation of scrap glass produced in different parts of Europe. In addition variability in the compositions of plant ashes used as alkali sources (Besborodov 1975; Sanderson and Hunter 1981; Henderson 1988) might be expected to make it difficult if not impossible to identify groupings of glass compositions characteristic of production zones. It could also be difficult to distinguish compositionally between faintly tinted and colourless glasses.

By chemically analysing fragments of goblets and beakers from Lincoln and London using electron probe microanalysis (Henderson 1988a) an attempt was made to establish whether suggested origins of the vessels based on their forms and colour could be related to their chemical compositions. The suggested origins of the glass in Italy, the Low Countries, southern and northern England, were initially suggested using typological characteristics of the vessels.

Since glass chemical compositions determine the viscosity of glass at different temperatures (Doremus 1994: 99ff.), the deliberate use of specific raw materials can potentially have a marked effect on the working properties of the glass. These working properties could therefore determine the kinds of raw materials used. In this way the identity of characteristic raw materials is one way of defining specialisation, or lack of it, in glass production. The purity of the raw materials used, or the glass melted from them, is therefore reflected in the glass chemical compositions; in the long run the hope is to be able to provide a broad provenance for glasses by chemically analysing them.

3.13.3 The glass vessel forms

Scientific and archaeological characteristics of the goblets and beakers found in Lincoln will first be discussed in detail and the results of the chemical analysis of goblet fragments from London glasshouses will then be compared. Excavations in the city of Lincoln between 1972 and 1987 produced a wide range of Roman and early medieval glass and also some 500 fragments of medieval and post-medieval glass (Henderson *et al.* in preparation). The glass from Lincoln to be considered here derived from 16 different excavated sites, mostly within the area of

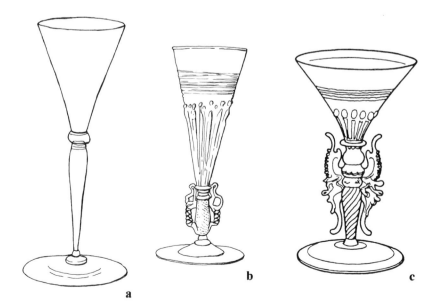

Figure 3.50 Examples of post-medieval goblets, (a) plain wine glass, 'Venice', late sixteenth–early seventeenth century; (b) ornate pincered decoration and applied ribs on a wine glass, 'Venice', first half of the seventeenth century; (c) ornately decorated *Façon de Venise* goblet, probably made in the Netherlands, first half of the seventeenth century.

a

b

c

the Lower city (Figure 3.49). The evidence was largely of domestic activity of relatively low social status, though some sites seem to have enjoyed a degree of wealth and social standing. Most of the glass was found in St Paul-in-the-Bail where an important post-medieval assemblage was associated not with the church itself, but with the seventeenth-century backfill of a disused well in the graveyard.

Much of the common post-medieval vessel forms found in Lincoln were probably manufactured in England, in areas such as Yorkshire, Lancashire, the west Midlands and London, with a smaller proportion being imported from the Low Countries. The balance of the glass, a small number of fragments, was probably imported directly from Venice or other centres in northern Italy.

Representative goblets and beakers of late sixteenth century and seventeenth century date are illustrated in Figures 3.50 and 3.51. A probable Italian import to

Lincoln is a fine finial from a goblet stem in transparent colourless glass outlined with turquoise blue glass, a typical Venetian technique from *c.* 1550 (Tait 1991: 166), though a Low Countries origin cannot be ruled out entirely. In general, such luxury items occur only rarely in Lincoln and the owners may well have been relatively wealthy burghers. Excavations have also produced a range of interesting thinly blown colourless vessel fragments, including six goblets with mould-blown knobs, other very thinly blown colourless goblet fragments, including bowl and base fragments and colourless vessel fragments decorated with opaque white (*vitro di trina*) cable decoration. In contrast to these fine vessels, excavations also produced the expected range of typical forms found on British urban sites, such as translucent pale greenish, brownish or greyish goblets with the usual range of decorative/strengthening devices (knobs and mereses) and mould-blown beakers in greenish and brown glass. Sixty-four individual fragments of goblets and beakers were found in Lincoln excavations.

3.13.4 Chemical investigations

Using electron probe microanalysis 39 samples of goblets and beakers from Lincoln were analysed (Henderson 1988a). Twenty-four goblet fragments from Lincoln were analysed chemically. They derived from post-medieval sites at St Paul-in-the-Bail, Steep Hill, St Mark's Church Dane's Terrace, Swan Street and Broadgate East; 16 of these 24 goblet fragments are from St Paul-in-the-Bail. Fifteen beaker fragments were analysed. Major components used to make the glass, (silica [SiO_2], calcium oxide [CaO], soda [Na_2O], potassium oxide [K_2O] and lead oxide [PbO]), may each be accompanied by impurities which can sometimes help to source the glass and/or the raw materials used. The glass used to make goblets and beakers found in Lincoln is of several different types which are listed in Table 3.1.

The four soda-lime-silica sub-types of Type a glasses are defined according to the impurities associated with the major components used and the soda levels. The existence of sub-types in soda-lime glasses reflects a variation in the raw materials used, and especially the impurity levels introduced. One of the soda-lime glass types (III) contains the highest soda level (with a mean value of 17.55%) and it is no

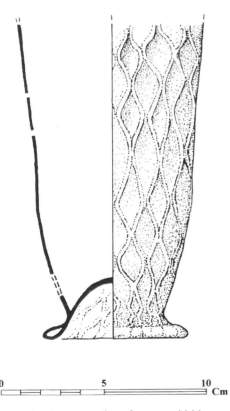

0   5   10
Cm

Figure 3.51 An example of a mould-blown late sixteenth-century–early seventeenth-century beaker.

Table 3.1 The major compositional types of glass currently found among the goblets and beakers analysed from Lincoln

a. soda-lime-silica; type III; type V, type VIII and type IX (high aluminia).

b. mixed-alkali with lowish calcium oxide and high potassium oxide; type IV

c. high calcium, variable but low total mixed-alkali; type VII.

These compositions for seventeenth-century goblets and beakers (excluding lead-rich glasses) are defined chemically elsewhere (Henderson 1998a).

coincidence that it was used to make glass of probable Venetian origin. It also contains relatively low impurity levels of magnesia (MgO) and phosphorus pentoxide (P_2O_5) and is characterised by relatively high chlorine levels: all three of these impurities would have been introduced with the alkali. Type III composition is typical of glasses analysed by Veritá (1985) which derived from seventeenth-century Venice.

Figure 3.52 is a bivariate plot of the nine compositional types for weight % magnesia oxide (MgO) *vs* weight % aluminium oxide (Al_2O_3). The plots clearly show how the soda-lime glasses of types III, V, VIII and IX can be distinguished by their impu-

rity levels. Elevated levels of magnesia are normally considered to characterise the soda-rich plant ashes used as an alkali (see Section 3.2.1), and aluminia (Al_2O_3) levels are often impurities in the silica (sand) sources used. A contribution to the aluminia level impurity may have resulted from corrosion of the crucible wall during glass-melting (Saleh *et al.* 1972; Merchant *et al.* 1997), but the predominant contribution would have derived from the sand source.

Instead of finding a compositional blurring brought about by glass recycling and trade, chemical analysis has produced some unexpected results. We can distinguish between different qualities of glass according to the impurity levels introduced with the soda and the sand. For high quality drinking glasses, in particular, it was considered important to produce a colourless glass if possible (see Section 3.13.6); Venetian 'cristallo' glasses of type III represent the highest quality of colourless glass from this point of view and the glass was often blown very thinly. The faintly-tinted glasses (type VIII), often not so thinly blown, can be distinguished, surprisingly, by their somewhat lower impurity level of magnesia from the more finely blown and/or more intricately decorated colourless glasses of type V. Another inference from these results is that the colourless and greenish brownish glasses have evidently not been mixed

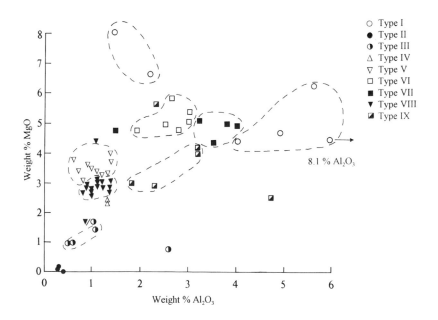

Figure 3.52 Weight % magnesia versus weight % aluminia in late sixteenth- and seventeenth-century Lincoln glass.

together as scrap: if this had occurred it would not have been possible to distinguish between them chemically. Although it may appear that there is no statistical distinction between types V and VIII based on the plotted points on Figure 3.52, the tabulated results (Henderson 1998a: Table 2) show that the standard deviations for compositional types V and VIII do not overlap.

3.13.5 Chemical composition and vessel form

It is now worth considering how these compositional types relate to vessel forms and colours. It is of interest to note that out of the 16 goblets from St Paul-in-the-Bail, 10 are of the types considered to have been manufactured in England. On the other hand the six goblets sampled which can be attributed the *Façon de Venise* (type V) chemical composition have a much wider range of site contexts: St Paul-in-the-Bail (2), St Mark's (1), Dane's Terrace (2) and Broadgate East (1). Given the relatively low level of use/preservation/retrieval of glass on sites other than St Paul-in-the-Bail, this may infer a relatively high social status for the *Façon de Venise* goblets from other sites. The fragments are mainly fine thinly-blown and all are colourless. One is a lion-mask stem from a goblet and many of these are regarded as having been made *à la Façon de Venise*; indeed there are examples of these thinly-blown lion-mask stems which are thought to have been made in Venice itself.

The four glass samples which fall into compositional type III are fine colourless or highly coloured (turquoise) glasses which are typical of the seventeenth-century Venetian composition (Veritá 1985) with the highest soda and silica levels. Two more samples of colourless glass but with distinctly lower soda levels (type IV in Figure 3.52) may have been manufactured in northern Europe to look like Venetian glass using Venetian techniques (*à la Façon de Venise)* and the six goblet fragments which form part of the grouping of type V in Figure 3.52, also all colourless, have lower soda and silica and higher magnesia and phosphorus pentoxide levels than found in type III. The different soda, magnesia and phosphorus pentoxide levels can be related to the use of a different soda source. It is therefore already apparent that the suggested different origins

of the glasses can be linked with their different chemical compositions.

It is worth trying to explain these compositional differences in terms of the potential origins of the alkali-rich plant ashes used. There is a historical reference to the import to northern Europe from Spain of *Barilla* ashes which are claimed to have provided the alkali for making cristallo glass *à la Façon de Venise* (Godfrey 1975: 159). An alternative plant-ash source would have been polverine or rochetta deriving from the Levant, Syria and Egypt (mentioned by Antonio Neri (1612) in his *Dell'Arte Vetraria*). If we assume, for the sake of argument, that the Venetian glasses of type III were made using *Barilla* and we compare the compositions of type V (glasses made *à la Façon de Venise*) with them, we might expect them to have the same compositions. As we have seen from this data set, they appear to differ. If the relative levels of soda and aluminia are considered it is apparent that the soda levels are, in fact, less diagnostic in grouping the glasses than the magnesia (an impurity in the soda ash used). So if *Barilla* was used for making both kinds of glass, different purification procedures would have been involved (Frank 1982: 76), producing higher levels of magnesia and phosphorus oxides in the *Façon de Venise* glass of type V than in the Venetian glass of type III. We can therefore, apparently, distinguish chemically between 'Venetian' products and those made in the 'Venetian fashion'. For earlier Venetian glasses, ashes of Levantine plants were also used, and the chemical compositions of the ashes of the soda-rich plant *Salsola kali* appear to fit the chemical compositions of eleventh–sixteenth-century Venetian glasses. The compositions of the ashes of this species are quite variable (Veritá 1985: 24–5, Tables III and IV) and since *Barilla* ash can *also* have a variable chemical composition, this is another possible explanation for the variations in seventeenth-century colourless glass compositions from Lincoln. In the fourteenth century the calcined residue of the plants was shipped to Venice in chunks (Jacoby 1993: 68, nn. 9, 12).

The two fine colourless goblet fragments, which, without chemical analysis might otherwise be labelled 'cristallo' (being completely colourless), and thus expected to fall into groups III or V (see Figure 3.52), contain high potassium oxide levels with a mean value of 14.65% and fall into compositional type IV. Normally post-medieval *cristallo* colourless glasses are considered to have a soda-lime composition such as type III (Charleston 1984: 106), so these two analyses illustrate that this can no longer be assumed to be the case.

In contrast to the colourless goblet fragments analysed, the balance were of a pale translucent brown, green or greyish hue; apart from two these fall into distinctive compositional types VIII and IX. The fourteen samples which belong to type VIII, of which eight are goblets are (with the exception of one) all plain forms with none of the decorative flourishes which are found on goblets of types III or V. The exception is a mould-blown goblet knob which forms an unexpected member of the group and may be an example of recycling.

If we compare faintly-tinted brown, green or grey goblet and beaker fragment compositions of types VIII and IX with the groups of colourless glasses already discussed, several differences are observable. Although the aluminia levels in the colourless glasses of types III, IV and V are within a similar range to the two colourless examples in type IX, the magnesia levels provide a distinction between the groupings (see Figure 3.52). The higher aluminia levels detected in type IX glasses vary considerably, with a mean and standard deviation of 2.92 ± 0.94; these also form a distinct group. It is likely that a sand source with high aluminia impurities was used leading to this compositional distinction (Henderson 1985: 270–1). This difference also infers that a different production zone or 'technological tradition' was involved. (Here the term *technological tradition* is used to suggest that the knowledge of glass-making may have moved with the artisans.)

Another interesting difference between colourless glass of type V and mainly translucent green, brown or greyish glass of type VIII is the impurity levels of lead oxide detected: only one sample of type V contains 0.1% lead oxide, with no lead oxide being detected in the remaining ones. In contrast ten of the fourteen type VIII glasses contain a mean of 0.3% lead oxide. This shows that purer raw materials (whether primary or recycled), in terms of the lead oxide impurity, were used to make most of the colourless glasses, and that the presence of a lead oxide impurity in most of type VIII glasses could indicate a level of mixing of different glass types. Nevertheless, type VIII data is relatively tightly clustered in Figure 3.52; it is possible that they were made in the Low Countries.

Other supporting evidence for the use of different sand sources can be found in the analytical data. Higher iron impurities are to be found in type IX; these glasses are also green and typical of Low Countries products. The fragments include a *berke-meier* or *roemer* base and a beaker decorated with a chequer-spiral design. Although soda-lime glasses, the samples of type IX contain relatively high aluminia and magnesia levels (see Figure 3.52); the elevated iron and aluminia levels in these glasses are characteristics of the use of specific sand sources.

The other mould-blown beaker fragments are distinctive and also fall into type IX with high aluminia and iron levels; they are probably of a Low Countries origin. A group of eleven distinctive seventeenth-century roemers (the 'spun-stem' variety) found in the excavations of various cities in north-western Europe are thought to have been made in the southern Netherlands. They conform to type IX composition, so this adds to the impression, if needed, that type IX glass was made using a Flemish recipe (Henkes and Henderson 1998).

Another source of information about the sources of seventeenth-century glass is to be found in the illustrations of vessels ordered by John Green of London in the 1660s (Thorpe 1949: 154; Fryer and Selley 1997: Plate 5). The goblet fragments (including mould-blown knops) from Lincoln of this form, including mould-blown ribbed knops, fall into type V. If the balance of this group were suspected of being Low Countries products it is likely that they were made from raw glass imported from Venice, or that the same (imported) primary raw materials were used and subjected to the same furnace conditions. A second possible inference is that this 'late' Venetian glass was made using the same recipe for several decades including (at the later end), the 1660s. Unfortunately the length of time during which vessels of particular shapes were made and were in use for in the seventeenth century is likely to be only datable to within a 25-year block (Bartels 1999). It is possible that future scientific excavations of well-dated post-medieval sites will provide dates which are precise enough to be able to state with confidence that type III glass was in use earlier than type V glass.

3.13.6 The importance of producing colourless glass

The fact that manganese oxide (potentially a glass decoloriser) occurs at higher levels in the faintly-tinted glasses of type VIII than in colourless glasses of types III and V, with iron impurity levels of c. 0.5%, indicates that the colour has been removed from the *colourless* glasses by controlling the furnace atmosphere carefully so that the manganese did in fact act as a decoloriser. In the faintly-tinted glasses the furnace atmosphere has clearly not been controlled so closely. The furnace atmosphere would have been determined by using a balance of fuel selection, air supply, crucible shape, the maximum temperature attained and the time that the melt was held at that temperature. Crossley (1990: 240) notes that in seventeenth-century England no attempts were made to use manganese as a decoloriser in the forest glass tradition; Sellner *et al.* (1979) have shown that the colours of seventeenth-century German forest glasses from two glass works were apparently produced as a result of controlling the melting conditions. This same inference can also now be drawn from this study of soda-lime glasses of types III, V and VIII from Lincoln. In order to produce colourless glass, it would also have been necessary to create a balance between the levels of iron and manganese in the glass so that the purple colour of manganese oxide compensated for the yellow colour from iron under fully reducing conditions. A significant difference from the forest glass technology was that manganese oxide was *not* present as an impurity in the alkali source used.

3.13.7 Glasshouse compositions?

From 1574 until 1606 Jacobo Verzelini, an Italian glass-worker, produced fine *cristallo* glass in London, though not much of this appears to have reached markets such as Lincoln. For the slightly later glasshouses of Aldgate (Charleston *et al.* in preparation) and Old Broad Street (Mortimer 1995) it is interesting to compare glass compositions with contemporary glass chemical compositions from Lincoln. A tight compositional grouping is observable for the distinctive colourless and highly coloured *Façon de Venise* products from Aldgate (Henderson 1998a) which includes the embedding of opaque white and other glass coloured canes into *cristallo* glass, especially in the decoration of goblets. When seen in the context of the Lincoln glass this is a third separable compositional group of *Façon de Venise* glass. The chemical analyses of glass from the Old Broad Street glasshouse, on the other hand, mainly of greenish or brownish glass, display a far wider compositional variation in impurity levels, with some (opaque white) glass apparently made at Aldgate found there. The Broad Street glasshouse was set up in the early years of the Mansell patent to produce 'crystal' glass (Crossley 1990: 241), but this is not evident from among the glass analyses, unless the same raw materials were used as at the Aldgate glass-house to make colourless 'crystal' glass. The high compositional variability probably means that glasses have been analysed from a range of sources or made using a range of raw materials (these are not *necessarily* mutually exclusive). It is, nevertheless of interest to note that much of the data for Old Broad Street greenish glass seems generally to contain lower alumina levels.

3.13.8 Summary of scientific investigations

The chemical analysis of seventeenth-century Lincoln and London glass has shown that, in spite of possible glass recycling, it is possible to define compositional groupings which are formed from distinct vessel types. Figure 3.53 provides a summary of this information for seventeenth-century goblets and beakers, showing how colourless glass from distinct groups (1 to 4), three of which are *Façon de Venise*, the fourth being from Venice. The groups have been arranged in this way so as to underline the contrasts in composition and in the geographical origins of the glasses as well as the grouping of the colourless and faintly-tinted glasses (compositional types are those refered to in Figure 3.53): group 1 = type VIII, group 2 = London glasses from the Aldgate glass-house, group 3 = type IV, group 4 = type III, group 5 = type VIII, group 6 = type IX and group 7 = type VII. It is

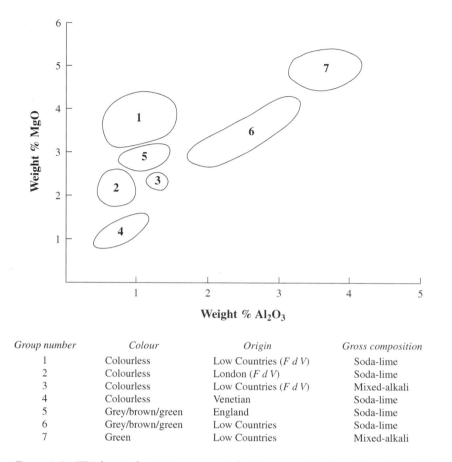

Group number	Colour	Origin	Gross composition
1	Colourless	Low Countries (*F d V*)	Soda-lime
2	Colourless	London (*F d V*)	Soda-lime
3	Colourless	Low Countries (*F d V*)	Mixed-alkali
4	Colourless	Venetian	Soda-lime
5	Grey/brown/green	England	Soda-lime
6	Grey/brown/green	Low Countries	Soda-lime
7	Green	Low Countries	Mixed-alkali

Figure 3.53 Weight % aluminia versus weight % magnesia in late sixteenth- and seventeenth-century Lincoln glass, showing the relationships between colour, likely origin and gross composition; note that the group numbers shown relate only to this diagram (*F d V* = *Façon de Venise*).

clear that one characteristic of colourless seventeenth-century glass is that it contains relatively low aluminia levels. Using these data alone, it is also clear that the glasses with a greyish, brownish or greenish tinge contain magnesia oxide levels of above 2.5%. Group 3 is mixed-alkali in composition whereas groups 1, 2 and 4 are soda-lime. Groups 5, 6 and 7 are composed of glass which has a green, brown or grey tinge. Group 5 is composed of typical English products, whereas groups 6 and 7 are typical products of the Low Countries. The relative levels of impurities of magnesia and aluminia can therefore be related to the colour of the glass as well as its origin.

3.13.9 Correlation of vessel form, economic value and chemical composition

In considering the inferred social value of the Lincoln glass provided by their archaeological contexts, the relative economic value of the glass is of critical importance. In order to examine the relative economic value a very useful list of the relative costs of imported glass at the port of Exeter is available. The data has therefore been used here, in the absence of similar comprehensive data from either Boston, which was Lincoln's main port in the earlier seventeenth century (Hinton 1956) or Hull for the later seventeenth century (Davis 1964). Allan (1984: 263)

Table 3.2 Relative glass values recorded in Books of Rates and Customs at the port of Exeter, 1610–1629

1.	Glasses 'of Venice making'	£1 per dozen	(1/8 each)
2.	Flemish glasses	6/8d per dozen	(6½d. each)
3.	Coarse Flemish glasses	£1 per gross	(1½d. each)
4.	Fine English drinking glasses	4/– per dozen	(4d. each)
5.	Coarse English drinking glasses	8d per dozen	(c. ½d. each)

From this list we can suggest possible correlations with the compositional types discovered in the glasses analysed from Lincoln (see Table 3.3).

Table 3.3 Relationships between port record descriptions, Lincoln glass compositions and vessel form/colour

Port record glass type	Suggested compositional type	Vessel type/colour
Glasses of 'Venice making'	III	Colourless/highly coloured Venetian
Flemish glasses	IV	Colourless; Low Countries (*Façon de Venise*)
	V	Goblets, colourless; Low Countries
	IX	Goblets of Low Countries types
Coarse Flemish glasses	VII	Green, brown Low Countries, mainly beakers
Fine English drinking glasses	VIII	Mid-seventeenth-century beakers possibly made in England
	V	Mid-seventeenth-century beakers
Coarse English drinking glasses	VIII	Includes green and brownish beakers

has reported on Books of Rates and Customs dating from between 1610 and 1629 respectively. The relative costs are listed in Table 3.2.

Some of the correlations between economic value and compositional type in Table 3.3 can be stated with confidence (types III and IX); other glass vessels, like those of compositional type VIII, may have been regarded as both 'fine' and 'coarse', depending on colour. Type VII can also be regarded as containing both 'high' and 'low' quality Flemish glasses, again an inference made on the basis of the vessel form and colour. In addition to Port records the Flemish *Façon de Venise* goblets, with important production centres in Liège and Brussels, were regarded as having five times the value of an 'ordinary' goblet (Tait 1991: 176), in this case a comparison of types 2 and 3 referred to in Table 3.2. For the higher value glass it is worth noting that in the late sixteenth century the inventories of the wealthy included mention of 'Verres' or 'Vennis' glasses. In Lincoln the economic value of the glass types listed in Table 3.2 may well have changed due to the

distances from ports such as Boston and later Hull, and the proximity to glass-houses such as those in Yorkshire and Tyneside. Nevertheless, in general it is considered that for glasses imported from Italy and the Low Countries their relative values would have remained about the same. During the post-medieval period Lincoln had lost much of the importance that it had had as an ecclesiastical centre in the Middle Ages, and its lines of communication were starting to become difficult to use. It can be suggested that any Italian glass products (for example) that reached Lincoln may have had an inflated value.

3.13.10 Summary

This research has generated some unexpected results. It has demonstrated that, in spite of potentially complex trade systems involving glass raw materials, glass ingots and chunks of raw glass, it is nevertheless possible to show that there are compositional relationships with vessel forms to be found. Since the finer glasses were colourless or highly coloured, this is reflected in the impurities which find their way into the glasses. During the late sixteenth and seventeenth centuries urban centres in Italy, the Low Countries and southern England had their own glass-making centres – and it is clear that they specialised in the manufacture of some fine goblets and beakers. Although it is not always clear precisely where the glass was fused from primary raw materials, there is evidence for the specialisation in the manufacture of specific forms and decoration – and these are shown to be linked to the raw materials used to make the original glass and therefore also their chemical compositions. It appears to be possible to distinguish compositionally between glass imported from Venice during the late sixteenth/early seventeenth centuries and that imported in the 1660s.

The relationships between vessel types and their chemical compositions suggest that the supply of raw materials used in glass-workshops to make the vessels was tightly controlled. In addition, the procedures used for purifying the glass raw materials (e.g. fritting) especially for (imported) alkalis varied according to the production centres involved. Of course if the fully-fused glass was imported as raw lumps, later to be blown into specific vessel forms, its composition would also reflect the use of a series of 'foreign' procedures. Colourless glasses are seen to have had a higher economic value than faintly-tinted glasses and the goblets made from colourless glasses can often be shown to have been made in particular production zones. Further research in the chemical analysis of well-dated vessel fragments of diagnostic form will contribute further and provide a means of tying up some of the loose ends generated by this research. Unless independently dated by the date of production scratched on the vessels, at this stage scientific research on glasses in museum collections which have been dated on art historical grounds may only serve to muddy the water.

References

Agricola, Georgius (1556) *De Re Metallica*, translated by H.C. Hoover and Hoover, L.H. (1950), New York: Dover Publications.

Al Khalaf, M. and Kohlmeyer, K. (1985) 'Untersuchungen zu ar-Raqqa-Nikephorion/Callinicum', *Damaszener Mitteilungen* 2: 133–62.

Allan, J.P. (1984) *Medieval and Post-medieval Finds from Exeter 1971–1980*, Exeter Archaeological Reports, 3.

Ankner, D. (1965) 'Chemische und physikalische untersuchungen an vori – und frühgeschichtlichen Glässera', *Technische Beiträge zur Archälogie*, II, Meinz.

Artis, E.T. (1828) *The Durobrivae of Antoninus identified and illustrated in a series of plates, exhibiting the excavated remains of that Roman station, in the vicinity of Castor, Northamptonshire*, London: privately printed.

Ashurst, D. (1992) *The History of South Yorkshire Glass*, Sheffield: J.R. Collis Publications.

Atkinson, D. (1929) 'Caistor excavations', *Norfolk Archaeology*, 108–12.

—— (1932) 'Caistor excavatons, 1929', *Norfolk Archaeology*, 24: 93–129.

Bamford, C.R. (1977) *Colour Generation and Control in Glass*, Amsterdam: Elsevier Scientific Publishing Co.

—— (1982) 'Optical properties of flat glass', *Journal of Non-crystalline Solids* 47, 1: 1–20.

Barag, D. (1985) *Catalogue of Western Asiatic Glass in the British Museum I*, London: British Museum Publications.

Barber, D. and Freestone, I.C. (1990) 'An investigation of the origin of the colour of the Lycurgus cup by analytical transmission electron microscopy', *Archaeometry* 32: 33–45.

Bartels, M. (1999) *Cities in Sherds*, Amersfoort: Rijksdienst voor het Oudheidkundig Bodemonderzoek.

Bass, G.F. (1986) 'A Bronze Age shipwreck at Ulu Burun (Kaş). 1984 campaign', *American Journal of Archaeology* 90: 269–96.

—— (1987) 'Oldest known shipwreck reveals Bronze Age splendours', *National Geographic* (December 1987): 693–734.

Bateson, D. and Hedges, R.E.M. (1975) 'The scientific analysis of a group of Roman-age enamelled brooches', *Archaeometry* 71: 177–90.

Baxter, M.J., Cool, H.E.M., Heyworth, M.P. and Jackson, C. (1995) 'Compositional variability in colourless Roman vessel glass', *Archaeometry* 37, 1: 129–42.

Bayley, J. (1990) 'Glass rings and the manufacture of high lead glass', in M. Biddle (ed.) *Object and Economy in Medieval Winchester*, Winchester Studies vol. 7, Oxford: Oxford University Press, pp. 268–9.

—— (in press) 'The Glastonbury Anglo-Saxon glass furnace', in J.A. Price (ed.), *Early Medieval Glass in the British Isles*, London: British Museum Press.

Beck, H.C. (1934) 'Glass before 1500', *Ancient Egypt and the East*, 7–21.

Bencard, M., Ambrosiani, K., Jørgensen, L.B., Madsen, H.B., Nielsen, I. and Näsman, U. (1979) 'Wikingerzeitliches Handwerk in Ribe. Ein Übersicht', *Acta Archaeologica* 49: 113–38.

Besborodov, M.A. (1975) *Chemie und Technologie der antiken und mittelälterlichen Gläser*, Mainz.

Biek, L. and Bayley, J. (1979) 'Glass and other vitreous materials', *World Archaeology* 11, 1: 1–25.

Bietti-Sestieri, A.M.B. (1977) 'Protovillanovan Italy and Frattesina', a paper delivered to the Prehistoric Society, London Conference: *Italian Prehistory: new perspectives* 1–3 April 1976.

—— (1980) 'Lo scavo del'abitato protostorico di Frattesina, Fratta Polesine (Rovigo)', *Bulletino di Paletnologia Italiana* 21: 221–56.

—— (1981) 'Economy and society in Italy between the late Bronze Age and Early Iron Age', in G. Barker and R. Hodges (eds) *Archaeology and Italian Society*, BAR S102, Oxford: British Archaeological Reports, pp. 133–55.

Bimson, M. (1983) 'Aspects of the technology of glass and copper alloys. A. Coloured glass and millefiori in the Sutton Hoo grave deposit' in R.L.S. Bruce-Mitford (ed. A. Care Evans), *The Sutton Hoo Ship Burial Volume 3*, London: British Museum Publications, pp. 924–44.

—— and Freestone I.C. (1983) 'An analytical study of the relationship between the Portland vase and other Roman cameo glasses', *Journal of Glass Studies* 25: 55–64.

Brill, R.H. (1963) 'Ancient glass', *Scientific American*: 120–30.

—— (1965a) 'Beth She'arim', *Israel Exploration Journal* 15,4: 261–2.

—— (1965b) 'The chemistry of the Lycurgus cup', *Proceedings of the 7th International Congress on Glass*, Brussels 1965, paper no. 223.

—— (1968) 'The scientific investigation of ancient glass', in *Proceedings of the Eighth International Congress on Glass*, Sheffield, pp. 47–68.

—— (1970) 'Lead and oxygen isotopes in ancient objects', in *The Impact of the Natural Sciences on Archaeology*, Philosophical Transactions of the Royal Society of London A 269, pp. 143–64.

—— (1970a) 'The chemical interpretation of the texts', in A.L. Oppenheim, R.H. Brill, D. Barag, D. and A. Von Saldern (eds), *Glass and Glassmaking in Ancient Mesopotamia*, Corning: The Corning Museum of Glass.

—— (1970b) 'Chemical studies of Islamic lustre glass', in R. Berger (ed.), *Scientific Methods in Medieval Archaeology*, Berkeley: University of California Press, Chapter XVI.

—— (1987) 'Chemical analyses of some early Indian glasses' in H.C. Bhardwaj (ed.), *Archaeometry of Glass*, Proceedings of the Archaeometry Session of the XI International Congress on Glass, 1986 New Delhi, India, Calcutta: The Indian Ceramic Society, pp. 1–25.

—— (1988) 'Scientific investigations of the Jalame Glass and related finds', in Weinberg, G.D. (ed.), *Excavations at Jalame Site of a Glass Factory in Late Roman Palestine*, Columbia: University of Missouri Press, pp. 257–94.

—— (1992) 'Chemical analyses of some glasses from Frattesina', *Journal of Glass Studies* 34: 11–22.

——, Shields, W.E. and Wampler, J.M. (1973) 'New directions in lead isotope research' in W.J. Young (ed.), *Applications of Science in Examination of Works of Art*, Proceedings of the Seminar 15–19 June 1970, Boston: Museum of Fine Arts, pp. 73–83.

—— and Shirahata, H. (1997) 'Laboratory analyses of some glasses and metals from Tell Brak', in D. and J. Oates (eds), *Excavations at Tell Brak vol 1*. Cambridge: The Macdonald Institute, University of Cambridge, pp. 89–94.

——, Shirahata, H., Lilyquist, C. and Vocke, R.D. Jr (1993) 'Part 3. Lead isotope analysis of some objects from Egypt and the Near East', in C. Lilyquist and R.H. Brill (eds), *Studies in Early Egyptian Glass*, New York: The Metropolitan Museum of Art, pp. 59–75.

Brown, D.H. (1997) 'The social significance of imported medieval pottery', in C.G. Cumberpatch and P.W. Blinkhorn (eds), *Not so Much a Pot, More a Way of Life*, Oxbow Monograph 83, Oxford: Oxbow Books, pp. 95–112.

Cable, M. (1998) 'The Operation of Wood-fired Glass-Melting furnaces', in P. McCray (ed.) The Prehistory and History of Glassmaking Technology, Ceramics and Civilisation, vol. VIII, Cincinatti: American Ceramic Society, pp. 315–30.

Caley, E.R. (1962) *Analysis of Ancient Glasses 1790–1957*, New York: The Corning Museum of Glass.

Callmer, J. (1977) *Trade Beads and Bead Trade in Scandinavia ca. 800–1000 A.D.*, Lund: University of Lund.

—— 1988) 'Pragmatic notes on the Early Medieval bead material in Scandinavia and the Baltic region', *Studia nad etnogeneza slowian* 1, Warszawa.

—— and Henderson, J. (1991) 'Glassworking at Åhus, S. Sweden (eighth century AD)', *Laborativ Arkeologi* 5, Stockholm: Stockholm University, Archaeological Research Laboratory, pp. 143–54.

Charleston, R.J. (1978) 'Glass furnaces through the ages', *Journal of Glass Studies* 20: 9–34.

—— (1984) *English Glass*, London: Allen and Unwin.

——, Grew, F. and Henderson, J. (in preparation) 'Archaeological and scientific investigations of the seventeenth-century glass-working site at Aldgate, London'.

Cool, H.E.M. (1996) 'Quantifying glass assemblages', in *Proceedings of the 13th Congress in the International Association for the History of Glass*, The Low Countries 28 August–1 September 1995, Lochem: International Association for the History of Glass, pp. 93–102.

—— and Price, J. (1995) *Roman Vessel Glass from Excavations in Colchester, 1971–1985*, Colchester: Colchester Archaeological Reports 8.

Cox, G.A. and Gillies, K.J.S. (1986) 'The X-ray fluorescence analysis of medieval durable blue soda glass from York Minster', *Archaeometry* 28, 1: 57–68.

——, Heavans, O.S., Newton, R.G. and Pollard, A.M. (1979) 'A study of the weathering behaviour of medieval glass from York Minster', *Journal of Glass Studies* 21: 54–75.

Crossley, D. (1987) 'Sir William Cavell's glasshouse at Kimmeridge, Dorset: the excavations 1980–81', *The Archaeological Journal* 144: 340–82.

—— (1990) *Post-Medieval Archaeology in Britain*, London: Leicester University Press.

—— and Aberg, A. (1972) 'Sixteenth-century glass-making in Yorkshire: excavations of furnaces at Hutton and Rosedale, North Riding, 1968–71', *Post-Medieval Archaeology* 6: 107–59.

Davis, R. (1964) *The Trade and Shipping of Hull 1500–1700*, East Yorkshire Local History Society Series, no. 17, Guisborough: J.T. Stokeld and Sons.

Davison, Weinberg G. (1940) 'A medieval glass factory at Corinth', *American Journal of Archaeology* 44: 297–324.

Dillon, E. (1907) *Glass*. London: Methuen.

Doppelfeld O. (1965) 'Die kölner Glasofen vom Eigelstein', *Proceedings of the Eighth International Congress on Glass*, Brussels, 1965, comptes rendu II, communication no. 236.

Doremus, R.H. (1994) *Glass Science*, New York: John Wiley.

Dussart, O. (1995) Les verres de Jordanie et de Syrie du Sud du IVe an VIIe siècle, nouvelles données chronologies in D. Foy (ed.) *Le Verre de l'Antiquité tardive et du haut Moyen Age*, Proceedings of the Association Française pour l'Archáeologie du Verre, huitième rencontre, Guiry-en-Vexin: Musee Archaeologique departmental du val d'Oise, pp. 343–59.

Engle, A. (1973) '3000 years of glassmaking on the Phoenician coast', *Readings in Glass History* 1, Jerusalem: Phoenix Publications, pp. 1–26.

Faraday, M. (1857) 'Experimental relations of gold and other metals to light', *Philosophical Magazine* 14: 401–17, 512–39.

Farnsworth, M. and Ritchie, P.D. (1938) 'Spectrographic studies on ancient glass. Egyptian glass mainly of the 18th Dynasty, with special reference to its cobalt content', *Technical Studies in the Field of the Fine Arts* 6, 3: 155–73.

Fischer, A. and McCray, W.P. (1999) 'Glass production activities as practised at Sepphoris, Israel (37 BC–AD 1516)', in J. Henderson, H. Neff and T. Rehren (eds), *Proceedings of the International Symposium on Archaeometry*, University of Illinois at Urbana Champaign (UIUC), Urbana, Illinois, 20–4 May 1996, *Journal of Archaeological Science* 26, 8: 893–906.

Folsach, K. von and Whitehouse, D. (1993) 'Three Islamic molds', *Journal of Glass Studies* 35: 149–53.

Forbes, R.J. (1957) 'Glass' in *Studies in Ancient Technology*, vol. 5, Leiden: Brill, pp. 110–231.

Foy, D. (1989) *Le verre mediéval et son artisanat en France mediterranéenne*, Paris: CNRS.

—— and Jézégou, M.-P. (1998) 'Commerce et technologie du verre antique le témoignage de l'épave "ouest embies 1"', in E. Rieth (ed.), *Méditerranée Antique. Pêche, navi-

gation, commerce*, Paris: Comité des travaux historiques et scientifiques, pp. 121–34.

Frandsen, L.B. and Jensen, S. (1987) 'Pre-Viking and Early Viking Age Ribe. Excavations at Nikolajgade 8, 1985–86', *Journal of Danish Archaeology* 6: 175–89.

Frank, S. (1982) *Glass and Archaeology*, London: The Academic Press.

Freestone, I.C. (1987) 'Composition and microstructure of early opaque red glass', in M. Bimson and I.C. Freestone (eds), *Early Vitreous Materials*, British Museum Occasional Paper no. 56, London: British Museum Press, pp. 173–91.

—— and Gorin-Rosen, Y. (1999) 'The great glass slab at Bet She'arim, Israel: an early Islamic glassmaking experiment', *Journal of Glass Studies* 41: 105–16.

——, Hughes, M. and Stapleton, C. (1999) 'Compositional studies of some Saxon glass', a lecture presented at a meeting of the Association of the History of Glass, *Current Research on the History of Glass through Scientific Analysis*, 29 March 1999.

Fremersdorf, F. (1965) 'Die Anfänge der Römischen Glashütten Kölns', *Kölner Jahrbuch für Vor- und Frühgeschichte* 8: 24–43.

Fryer, K. and Selley, A. (1997) 'Excavation of a pit at 16 Tunsgate, Guilford, Surrey, 1991', *Post-Medieval Archaeology*, Guildford, 31: 139–230.

Gam, T. (1990) 'Prehistoric glass technology', *Journal of Danish Archaeology* 9: 203–13.

—— (1993) 'Experiments in present and future' in *Proceedings of the 12th International Congress of the International Association for the History of Glass,* Vienna, August 1991, Amsterdam: AIHV, pp. 261–70.

Garner, H. (1956a) 'The use of imported and native cobalt in Chinese blue and white', *Oriental Art* 2, 3: 48–50.

—— (1956b) 'An early piece of glass from Eridu', *Iraq* 18: 147–9.

Gasparetto, A. (1965) 'Les fouilles de Torcello et leur rapport a l'histoire de la verrerie de la Venetie dans le haut Moyen Age', *Proceedings of the Eighth International Congress on Glass*, Brussels, comptes rendus II, communication no. 239.

Gauckler, P. (1915) *Necropoles puniques de Carthage*, Paris.

Godfrey, E.S. (1975) *The Development of English Glassworking 1560–1640*, Oxford: Clarendon Press.

Goerk, I.H. (1977) 'Glass raw materials and batch preparation', *Proceedings of the 9th International Congress on Glass*, Prague, vol. 2: 38–111.

Gorin-Rosen, Y. (1993) Hadera, Bet Eli'ezer, *Excavations and Surveys in Israel* 13: 42–4.

Gratuze, B. and Barrandon, J.-N. (1990) 'Islamic glass weights and stamps', *Archaeometry* 32: 155–62.

——, Soulier, I., Barrandon, J.N. and Foy, D. (1995) 'The origin of the cobalt blue pigment in French glass from the thirteenth to the eighteenth centuries', in D.R. Hook and D.R.M. Gaimster (eds), *Trade and Discovery. The Scientific Study of Artefacts from Post-Medieval Europe and*

Beyond. British Museum Occasional Paper 109, London: British Museum Press, pp. 123–34.

Grose, D.F. (1989) *The Toledo Museum of Art, Early Ancient Glass. Core-formed, Rod-formed, and Cast Vessels and Objects for the Late Bronze Age to the Early Roman Period*, New York: Hudson Hills Press.

Guido, C.M., Henderson, J., Cable, C., Bayley, J. and Biek, L. (1984) 'A Bronze Age glass bead from Wilsford, Wiltshire: Barrow G42 in the Lake Group', *Proceedings of the Prehistoric Society* 50: 245–54.

Hartmann, G., Kappel, I., Grote, K. and Arndt, B. (1997) 'Chemistry and technology of prehistoric glass from Lower Saxony and Hesse', *Journal of Archaeological Science* 24: 547–60.

Hatcher, H., Henderson, J., Kazmarzyck, A., Lakovara, P. and Vandiver, P. (forthcoming) 'Archaeological and technical studies of faience and faience making from Kerma, Sudan', Boston: Boston Museum of Fine Arts.

Heidemann, S. (1993) 'A report on the coins found on the glass tell 1993', unpublished manuscript.

Henderson, J. (1985) 'The raw materials of early glass production', *Oxford Journal of Archaeology* 4, 3: 267–91.

—— (1988) 'The nature of the Early Christian glass industry in Ireland: some evidence from Dunmisk Fort, Co. Tyrone', *Ulster Journal of Archaeology* 51: 115–26.

—— (1988a) 'Electron probe microanalysis of mixed-alkali glasses', *Archaeometry* 30, 1: 77–91.

—— (1988b) 'Glass production and Bronze Age Europe', *Antiquity* 62: 435–51.

—— (1989) 'The scientific analysis of ancient glass and its archaeological interpretation', in J. Henderson (ed.), *Scientific Analysis in Archaeology and its Interpretation*, Oxford University Committee on Archaeology Monograph no. 19, UCLA Institute of Archaeology Research Tools 5, Oxford: Oxbow Books, pp. 30–62.

—— (1990) 'Chemical and structural analysis of Roman enamels from Britain', *Archaeometry '90*, Proceedings of the International Symposium on Archaeometry, Heidelberg, April 1990, 285–94.

—— (1990a) 'The scientific investigation of the glass beads from Apple Down Anglo-Saxon cemetery and its archaeological interpretation', in A. Down and M. Welch (eds), *Apple Down and the Mardens, Chichester Excavations 7*, Chichester: Chichester District Council, pp. 156–68.

—— (1991a) 'Technological characteristics of Roman Enamels', *Jewellery Studies* 5: 65–76.

—— (1991b) 'The glass', in P. Armstrong, D. Tomlinson and D.H. Evans (eds), *Excavations at Lurk Lane, Beverley 1979–82*, fiche B6-C1, Sheffield: Sheffield Excavation Reports 1, pp. 124–30.

—— (1991c) 'Industrial specialisation in Late Iron Age Europe: organisation, location and distribution', *Archaeological Journal* 148: 104–48.

—— (1993) 'Aspects of early medieval glass production in Britain', *Proceedings of the twelfth Congress of the International Association for the History of Glass*, Vienna 26–31 August 1991, Amsterdam: International Association for the History of Glass, pp. 247–59.

—— (1995) 'Le verre de Dorestad: continuité technologique ou innovation', in D. Foy (ed.), *Le verre de l'antiquité et du Haut Moyen Age*, Eighth rencontre of the Association Française pour l'Archéologie du verre, Guiry-en-Vexin 1993, Musée Archéologique Départemental du Val d'Oise, pp. 51–6.

—— (1995a) 'An investigation of Early Islamic glass production at al-Raqqa, Syria', in P. Vandiver *et al.* (eds), *Issues in Art and Archaeology III*, Materials Research Society Proceedings, Cancun, Mexico 1994, vol. 352: 433–44.

—— (1995b) 'Investigations into marvered glass II', in J. Allan (ed.), *Islamic Art in the Ashmolean Museum*, Oxford Studies in Islamic Art, vol. 10, part 1, Oxford: Oxford University Press, pp. 31–50.

—— (1995c) 'Ancient vitreous materials', *American Journal of Archaeology* 99: 117–21.

—— (1996a) 'The analysis of ancient glasses Part II: luxury Roman and early medieval glasses', *Journal of Materials* 48, 2: 62–4.

—— (1996b) 'New light on early Islamic industry: excavations on al-Raqqa, Syria', in R.J.A. Wilson (ed.), *From River Trent to al-Raqqa*, Nottingham Studies in Archaeology 1, Department of Archaeology, University of Nottingham, pp. 59–71.

—— (1997) Scientific analysis of glass and glaze from Tell Brak and its archaeological significance, in D. and J. Oates (eds), *Excavations at Tell Brak vol. 1*, Cambridge: The Macdonald Institute, University of Cambridge.

—— (1998a) 'Post-medieval glass: production, characterisation and value', in D. Kingery and P. McCray (eds), *The Prehistory and History of Glass and Glass Technology*, Ceramic and Civilisation, Columbus, Ohio: The American Ceramic Society, pp. 33–60.

—— (1998b) 'Islamic glass production and the possible evidence for trade in a cobalt-rich colorant', in R. Ward (ed.), *Gilded and enamelled glass from the Middle East*, London: British Museum Press, pp. 116–21.

—— (1999a) Technological and scientific aspects of Anglo-Saxon glass beads', in M. Guido (ed.) *Anglo-Saxon Glass Beads in England*, Society of Antiquaries Research Report, London: Society of Antiquaries.

—— (1999b) 'Archaeological and scientific evidence for the production of early Islamic glass in al-Raqqa, Syria', *Levant* 31: 225–40.

—— (1999c) 'Una nueva caracterización? La investigación científica de las cuentas de fayenza encontradas en la Cova des Càrritx (Menorca, Sa Cometa des Morts I (Mallorca), Son Maimó (Mallorca) y Este (Véneto, Italia)', in V. Lull, R. Micó, C.R. Herrada and R. Risch (eds), *La Cova des Cárritx y la Cova des Mussol*, Ideología y sociedad en la prehistoria de Menorca, Barcelona: Universitat Autònoma de Barcelona, pp. 631–41.

—— (1999d) 'Scientific analysis of the glass and glass-bearing artefacts: technique, raw materials used and archaeological interpretation', in J.C. Besteman, J.M. Bos, D.A. Gerrets, H.A. Heidinga and J. de Koning (eds), *The Excavations at Wijnaldum, Reports on Frisia in Roman and Medieval Times, Volume 1*, Rotterdam: Balkema, pp. 287–97.

—— (2000) 'Chemical analysis of ancient Egyptian glass and its interpretation', in P.T. Nicholson and J. Shaw (eds), *Ancient Egyptian Materials and Technology*, Cambridge: Cambridge University Press, pp. 206–24.

—— (in press a) 'The production technology of Irish Early Christian glass, with specific reference to beads and enamels', in J.A. Price (ed.), *Early Medieval Glass in the British Isles*. London: The British Museum Press.

—— (in press b) 'Social context, technology and source: Post-medieval glass from Lincoln', *Antiquity*.

—— (in press c) 'Opaque red glasses in Iron Age Britain', in E.M. Jope, *Early Celtic Art in Britain*, Oxford: Oxford University Press.

—— (in press d) 'Localised production or trade? Advances in the study of cobalt blue and Islamic glasses from the Levant and Europe', in L. van Zelst, R. Bishop and J. Henderson (eds), *Pattern and Purpose, Essays in Honour of Edward V. Sayre*, Smithsonian Institution Press.

—— (in preparation) 'The scientific investigation of middle bronze age and later beads from Deir 'Ain 'Abata, Jordan', in D. Politis (ed.), *Deir 'Ain 'Abata, Jordan Excavations*, London: British Museum Press.

—— and Allan, J.A. (1990) 'Enamels on Ayyubid and Mamluk glass fragments', *Archaeomaterials* 4: 167–83.

—— and Holand, I. (1992) 'The glass from Borg, an early medieval chieftain's farm in Northern Norway', *Medieval Archaeology* 36: 29–58.

—— and Ivens, R. (1992) 'Dunmisk and glass-making in Early Christian Ireland', *Antiquity* 66, 250: 52–64.

—— , Janaway, R.C. and Richards, J. (1987) 'A curious clinker', *Journal of Archaeological Science* 14: 353–65.

—— and Ponting, M. (1999) 'Scientific studies of the glass from Frattesina', *Bead Study Trust Newsletter,* 32:3.

—— and Sablerolles, Y. (in preparation) 'A scientific investigation of fifth-century glass from Gennep, the Netherlands'.

—— , Tregear, M. and Wood, N. (1989) 'The technology of sixteenth- and seventeenth-century Chinese *cloisonné* enamels', *Archaeometry* 31: 133–46.

—— and Warren, S.E. (1981) 'X-ray fluorescence analysis of Iron Age glass: beads from Meare and Glastonbury Lake Villages', *Archaeometry* 23, 1: 83–94.

—— and —— (1983) 'Analysis of prehistoric lead glass', in A. Aspinall and S.E. Warren (eds), *Proceedings of the 22nd International Symposium on Archaeometry*, Bradford, pp. 168–80.

—— and —— (1986) 'Beads and rings; scientific analysis of the glass', in D. Tweddle (ed.), *Finds from Parliament Street and Other Sites on the City Centre*, Council for British Archaeology Research Report, The Archaeology of York, vol. 17/4, pp. 209–26.

Henkes, H.E. and Henderson, J. (1998) 'The spun-stem roemer, a hitherto overlooked roemer type', *Journal of Glass Studies*, 40: 89–104.

Heusch, J.-C. and Meinecke, M. (1989) *Die Residenz des Harun al-Rashid in al-Raqqa,* Damascus: Deutsches Archäologisches Institut.

Heyworth, M.P. (1991) 'An archaeological and compositional study of early medieval glass from North-West Europe', unpublished PhD thesis, University of Bradford.

—— , Hunter, J.R. and Warren, S.E. (1989) 'The role of inductively coupled plasma spectroscopy in glass provenance studies', in Y. Maniatis (ed.), *Archaeometry,* Proceedings of the 25th International Symposium, Amsterdam: Elsevier, pp. 661–70.

Highley, D.E. (1977) *Silica*, Mineral Dossier no. 18, London: HMSO.

Hinton, R.W.K. (1956) *The Port Books of Boston 1601–1640*, The Lincoln Record Society, vol. 50, Hereford: The Hereford Times Limited.

Hodges, H. (1970) *Technology in the Ancient World,* New York: Barnes and Noble.

Hodges, R. and Whitehouse, D. (1983) *Mohammed, Charlemaigne and the Origins of Europe,* London: Duckworth.

Holscher, H.H. (1968) *The Relationship of Viscosity to the Processing of Glass*, Owens-Illinois Technical Centre.

Hughes, M.J. (1972) 'A technical study of opaque red glass of the Iron Age in Britain', *Proceedings of the Prehistoric Society* 38: 98–107.

Hunter, J.R. and Heyworth, M.P. (1998) *The Hamwic Glass,* Council for British Archaeology Research Report 116, York: Council for British Archaeology.

Hutchins, J.R. III and Harrington, R.V. (1966) 'Glass', in *Encyclopaedia of Chemical Technology*, 2nd edn 10: 533–604.

Ilan, D., Vandiver, P. and Spaer, M. (1993) 'An early glass bead from Tell Dan', *Israel Exploration Journal* 43: 230–4.

Israeli, Y. (1991) 'The invention of blowing' in M. Newby and K. Painter (eds), *Roman Glass: Two Centuries of Art and Invention*, Society of Antiquaries Occasional Paper, vol. XIII, London: Society of Antiquaries, pp. 46–55.

Jackson, C.M. (1992) 'A compositional analysis of Roman and early Post-Roman glass and glassworking waste from selected British sites', unpublished PhD thesis, University of Bradford.

—— (1996) 'From Roman to early medieval glasses: Many happy returns or a new birth?', in *Proceedings of the 13th Congress in the International Association for the History of*

Glass, The Low Countries, 28 August–1 September 1995, Lochem: International Association for the History of Glass, pp. 289–302.

——, Nicholson, P. and Gneisinger, W. (1998) 'Glassmaking at Tell el-Amarna: an integrated approach', *Journal of Glass Studies* 40: 11–24.

Jacoby, D. (1993) 'Raw materials for the glass industries of Venice and the Terraferma, about 1370 – about 1460', *Journal of Glass Studies* 35: 65–90.

Jiazhi, L. and Xianqiu, C. (1987) 'A study on west Han PbO-BaO-SiO$_2$ glass and its corroded layer unearthed at Yang Zhou', in H.C. Bhardwaj (ed.), *Archaeometry of Glass*, Proceedings of the Archaeometry Session of the XI International Congress on Glass, 1986 New Delhi, India, (section II), Calcutta: The Indian Ceramic Society, pp. 21–6.

Jones, G.O. (1956) *Glass*, London: Methuen.

—— (1971) *Glass*, Gateshead: Penguin Books.

Kazmarzyck, A. (1987) 'The source of cobalt in ancient Egyptian pigments', in J.S. Olin and J. Blackman (eds), *Proceedings of the 24th International Symposium on Archaeometry*, Washington, DC: Smithsonian Institution Press, pp. 369–76.

—— and Hedges, R.E.M. (1983) *Ancient Egyptian Faience*, Warminster: Aris and Phillips.

Kock, J. and Sode, T. (1999) 'Glass bead making in India', a paper delivered to the Conference, *Traditional Glass Furnaces and Glass Production Technology Through the Ages*, Aarhus, Denmark, 11–14 August 1999.

Kunkel, von Loewenstern (1679) *Ars Vitrarii Experimentalis*, Leipzig.

Lappe, U. and Möbes, G. (1984) 'Glashütten im Eichsfeld', *Alt Thüringen* 20: 207–32.

Leciejewicz, I., Tabaczynska, E. and Tabaczynska, S. (1963–4) 'Ricerche archeologiche a Torcello nel 1962, relazione provisoria', *Boletino dell'Istituto di Storia della Societa e dello Stato veneziano*, V–VI.

——, —— and —— (1969–70) 'Commento archeologico ai reperti naturali', *Antichi e medievali scoperti a Torcello (1961–1962)*, Memorie di Biogeografia Adriatica, VIII.

——, —— and —— (1977) *Torcello, scavi 1961–2*, Rome.

Lilyquist, C. and Brill, R.H. (1993) *Studies in Early Egyptian Glass*, New York: The Metropolitan Museum of Art.

Lucas, A. (1934 [1921]) *Ancient Egyptian Materials and Industries*, London.

—— (1948) *Ancient Egyptian Materials and Industries*, London.

Matson, F.R. (1948) 'The manufacture of eighth-century Egyptian glass weights and stamps', in C. Miles (ed.), *Early Arabic Glass Weights and Stamps*, Numismatic Notes and Monographs, no. 111, The American Numismatic Society, New York, pp. 31–69.

—— (1951) 'The composition and working properties of ancient glass', *The Journal of Chemical Education* 28: 82–7.

May, T. (1904) *Warrington's Roman Remains*, Warrington: Mackie and Co.

McGovern, P.E. (1987) 'Silicate Industries of Late Bronze–Early Iron Age Palestine: Technical Interaction between New Kingdom Egypt and the Levant' in M. Binson and I.C. Freestone (eds), *Early Vitreous Materials*, British Museum Occasional Papers 56, London: British Museum Research Laboratory, pp. 97–114.

McGovern, P.E., Fleming, S.J. and Swann, C.P. (1991) 'The beads from Dinkha Tepe and the beginnings of glassmaking', *American Journal of Archaeology* 95: 395–402.

Meiguang, S., Ouli, H. and Fuzheng, Z. (1987) 'Investigation of some Chinese potash glasses excavated in Han Dynasty tombs', in H.C. Bhardwaj (ed.), *Archaeometry of Glass*, Proceedings of the Archaeometry Session of the XI International Congress on Glass, 1986 New Delhi, India, (section II) Calcutta: The Indian Ceramic Society, pp. 15–20.

Meinecke, M. (1991) 'Raqqa on the Euphrates: recent excavations at the residence of Harun er-Rashid', in S. Kerner (ed.), *The Near East in Antiquity*, vol. II, Amman, Chapter 2.

—— (1994) 'Al-Rakka', in C.E. Bosworth, E. van Donzel, W.P. Heinrichs and G. Lecomte (eds), *The Encyclopedia of Islam*, vol. VII, Leiden: E.J. Brill.

Mendera, M. (1991) 'Produrre vetro in Valselsa: l'officina vetraria di Germagnana (Gambassi-Fi) (sections XIII–XIV), in M. Mendera (ed.), *Archeologia e storia della produzione del vetro preindustriale*, Florence: Edizioni all'insegna del Giglio, pp. 15–50.

Merchant, I., Henderson, J., Crossley, D. and Cable, M. (1997) 'An examination of the chemical interaction of glass and ceramics in medieval glass technology', in A. Sinclair, E. Slater and J. Gowlett (eds), *Archaeological Sciences 1995*, Proceedings of a conference on the application of scientific techniques to the study of archaeology, Liverpool July 1995, Oxbow Monograph 64, Oxford: Oxbow Books, pp. 31–7.

Merrifield, M.P. (1849) *Original Treatises on the Arts of Painting*, London; reprint New York: Dover Publications.

Miglus, P.A. (1999) *Die Frühislamische keramik von tall Aswad*, Berlin: Phillip von Zabern.

Moorey, P.R.S. (1985) *Materials and Manufacture in Ancient Mesopotamia*, Oxford: The Clarendon Press.

—— (1994) *Ancient Mesopotamian Materials and Industries. The Archaeological Evidence*, Oxford: The Clarendon Press.

Morel, J., Amrein, H., Meylan, M.F. and Chavalley, C. (1992) 'Un atelier de verrier du milieu du 1er siècle après J.-C. à Avenches', *Archäologie der Schweiz* 15, 1: 2–17.

Moretti, C. (1983) 'Raw materials used by the Murano glass makers in the nineteenth century', *Glass Technology* 24, 4: 177–83.

Morey, G.W. (1964) 'Phase-equilibrium relations of the common glass-forming oxides except water', *US Geological Survey Professional Papers* No. 440-L, Washington, DC, Chapter L.

Mortimer, C. (1995) 'Analysis of post-medieval glass from Old Broad Street, London, with reference to other contemporary glasses from London and Italy', in D.R. Hook. and D.R.M. Gaimster. (eds), *Trade and Discovery: The Scientific Study of Artefacts from Post-medieval Europe and Beyond*, British Museum Occasional Papers, 109: pp. 135–44.

Morton, A.D. (1992) *Excavation at Hamwich*, vol. I. Southampton Archaeology Monographs 5, CBA Research Report no. 84. London: Council for British Archaeology.

Näsman, U. (1979) 'Die Herstellung von Glasperlen' in M. Bencard (ed.), 'Wikingerzeitliches Handwerk in Ribe', *Acta Archaeologica* (Københaven) 49: 124.

Neri, A. (1612) *Dell'Arte Vetraria*, Firenze. Translation and commentary by Christopher Merrett, *The Art of Glass*, New York: Dover Publications.

Newton, R.G. (1978) 'Colouring agents used by medieval glass-makers', *Glass Technology* 21, 4: 173–83.

—— (1980) 'Recent views on ancient glasses', *Glass Technology* 21: 173–83

—— and Davison, S. (1989) *Conservation of Glass*, London: Butterworths.

Nicholson, P.N. (1995) 'Glassmaking and glassworking at Amarna: some new work', *Journal of Glass Studies* 37: 11–20.

Oates, D., Oates, J. and McDonald, H. (1997) *Excavations at Tell Brak, Vol. I: The Mittanni and Old Babylonian Periods*, McDonald Institute or Archaeological Research and the British School of Archaeology in Iraq: Cambridge and London.

Oppenheim, A.L. (1973) 'Towards a history of glass in the ancient Near East', *Journal of the American Oriental Society* 93: 259–66.

——, Brill, R.H., Barag, D. and von Saldern, A. (1970) *Glass and Glassmaking in Ancient Mesopotamia*, Corning: The Corning Museum of Glass.

Painter, K. and Whitehouse, D. (1990a) 'IV Style, date, and place of manufacture [of the Portland vase]', *Journal of Glass Studies* 32: 122–5.

—— and —— (1990b) 'VI The Interpretation of the scenes [of the Portland vase]', *Journal of Glass Studies* 32: 130–6.

Peltenburg, E.J. (1971) 'Some early developments of vitreous materials' *World Archaeology* 3: 6–12.

—— (1987) 'Early faience: recent studies, origins and relations with glass', in M. Bimson and I.C. Freestone (eds), *Early Vitreous Materials*, British Museum Occasional Paper No. 56, London: British Museum Press, pp. 5–30.

Perrot, P.N. and Weinberg, G.D. (1968) 'A Late Hellenistic bead factory in Rhodes', *Studies in Glass History and Design*, International Commission on Glass, 1.

Petrie, W.F.M. (1894) *Tel el-Amarna*, London: Methuen.

Pliny (AD 77) *Natural History*, Book xxxvi, translated by Eichholtz (1962), Loeb Classical Library, p. 190.

Pollard, A.M. and Moorey, P.R.S. (1982) 'Some analyses of Middle Assyrian faience and related materials from Tell al-Rimah in Iraq', *Archaeometry* 24, 1: 45–50.

Price, J. (1998) 'The social context for glass production in Roman Britain', in P. McCray (ed.), The Prehistory and History of Glassmaking Technology, Ceramics and Civilisation, vol. III, Cincinatti: American Ceramic Society, pp. 331–48.

Price, J.A. (in press) 'The evidence for glass production in Roman Britain', in J.A. Price and J. Bayley (eds), *Glassworking Sites in Britain*, London: British Museum Press.

Rebourg, A. (1989) 'Un atelier de verrier Gallo-Romain à Autun', *Revue Archéologique de l'Est et du Centre* 156: 12–13.

Rednap, M. and Freestone, I.C. (1995) 'Eighteenth-century glass ingots from England and the post-medieval glass trade', in D.R. Hook and D.R.M. Gaimster (eds), *Trade and Discovery: The Scientific Study of Artefacts from Post-medieval Europe and Beyond*, British Museum Occasional Papers, 109, pp. 145–58.

Rehren, T. and Pusch, E.B. (1997) 'New Kingdom glass-melting crucibles from Qantir-Piramesses', *The Journal of Egyptian Archaeology* 83: 127–41.

Rogers, N.S.H. (ed.) (1993) *Anglian and Other Finds from Fishergate*, The Archaeology of York 17/9, York: Council for British Archaeology.

Rooksby, H.P. (1962) 'Opacifiers in opal glasses', *GEC Journal of Science and Technology* 29, 1: 20–6.

Ruprechtsberger, E.M. (ed.) (1993) *Syrien, von den Aposteln zu den Kalifen*, Mainz: zu Zabern.

Sablerolles, Y. (1992) *Het glas van Gennep. De glasvondsten van een nederzetting uit de volksverhuizingstijk te Gennep (Zuid-Limburg)*. Thesis for doctorate, University of Amsterdam.

—— (1993) 'A Dark Age glass complex from a Frankish settlement at Gennep (Dutch Limburg)', *Proceedings of the 12th Congress of the International Association for the History of Glass, Vienna 1991*, Amsterdam: AIHV, pp. 197–206.

——, Henderson, J. and Dijkman, W. (1997) 'Early medieval glass bead-making in Maastricht (Jodenstraat 30), the Netherlands', in U. von Freeden and A. Wieczorek (eds), *Proceedings of the International Bead Symposium, Mannheim*, November 1994, Kolloquien zur Vor- und Frühgeschichte Band 1, Römisch-Germanische Kommission, Bonn: Rudolf Habelt, pp. 293–313.

Saleh, S.A., George, A.W. and Helmi, F.M. (1972) 'Study of glass and glass-making at Wadi-el Natrun', *Studies in Conservation* 17: 143–72.

Salibi, N. (1954–5) 'Rapport préliminaire sur la deuxième campagne de fouilles à al-Raqqa', *Annales Archéologiques de Syrie* 4–5 (1954–5), pp. 69–76, 205–12.

Sanderson, D.C.W. and Hunter, J.R. (1981) 'Compositional variability in vegetable ash', *Science and Archaeology* 23: 27–30.

——, —— and Warren, S.E. (1984) 'Energy-dispersive XRF analysis of first-millennium AD glass from Britain', *Journal of Archaeological Science* 11: 53–69.

Sayre, E.V. (1964) *Some Ancient Glass Specimens with Compositions of Particular Archaeological Significance*, New York: Brookhaven National Laboratory.

—— (1965) 'Summary of the Brookhaven Program of analysis of ancient glass', in *Applications of Science in Examinations of Works of Art*, Proceedings of the Seminar held at the Boston Museum of Fine Arts, Boston, Mass., 7–16 September 1965, Museum of Fine Arts, Boston, pp. 145–54.

—— and Smith, R.W. (1961) 'Compositional categories of ancient glass', *Science*, 133, 9 June: 1824–6.

—— and —— (1963) 'The intentional use of antimony and manganese in ancient glasses', in F.R. Matson and G.E. Rindone (eds), *Advances in Glass Technology*, Part 2, New York: Plenum Press, 263–82.

—— and —— (1967) 'Some materials of glass manufacturing in antiquity', in M. Levey (ed.), *Archaeological Chemistry, a Symposium,* Third Symposium on Archaeological Chemistry, Atlantic City, New Jersey, Philadelphia: University of Pennsylvania Press, pp. 279–312.

Seibel, F. (1998) *Technologie und Fertigungstechniken römischer Glashütten am Beispiel der Ausgrabungen im Hambacher Forst: Aktualistische Vergleiche und Modelle*, Berlin: Galda + Wilch.

Sellner, C., Oel, H.J. and Camera, B. (1979) 'Untersuchung alter Gläser (Waldglas) auf Zusammenhang von Zusammensetzung, Farbe und Schmelzathmosphäre mit der Elektronenspektroskopie und der Elektronenspinresonanz (ESR)', *Glastechniche Berichte* 52: 255–64.

Shepherd, J. and Heyworth, M. (1991) 'Le Travail du Verre dans London Romain (Londinium): un état de la question', in D. Foy and G. Sennequier (eds), *Ateliers de Verriers de l'Antiquité à la période pré-industrielle*, Actes du 4ème Rencontres d'Association Française pour l'archéologie du Verre, Rouen 1989, Rouen: Association Française pour l'archéologie du Verre, pp. 13–22.

Shortland, A. and Tite, M.S. (1998) 'The interdependence of glass and vitreous faience production at Amarna', in P. McCray (ed.), The Prehistory and History of Glassmaking Technology, Ceramics and Civilisation, vol. III, Cincinatti: American Ceramic Society, pp. 331–48.

—— and —— (2000) 'Raw materials of glass from Amarna and implications for the origins of Egyptian glass', *Archaeometry* 42, 1: 141–52.

Stoch, Z., Pakulska, M. and Stoch, L. (1978) 'The influence of the structure and shape of grains of mineral raw materials upon the melting speed of soda-lime batches', *Szklo Ceramic* 29, 9: 238–41.

Stone, J. and Thomas, C. (1956) 'The use and distribution of faience in the Ancient East and Prehistoric Europe', *Proceedings of the Prehistoric Society* 22: 37–84.

Tabaczynska, E. (1965) 'Glashütte aus dem VII–VIII Jahrhundert auf Torcello bei Venedig Ausgrabungen 1961–1962', *Proceedings of the Seventh International Congress on Glass*, Brussels, 1965, communication 238.

Tait, H. (ed.) (1991) *Five Thousand Years of Glass*, London: British Museum Press.

Tatton-Brown, V. (1991) 'The Roman Empire', in H. Tait (ed.), *Five Thousand Years of Glass*, London: British Museum Press, Chapter 2.

Thorpe, W.A. (1949) *English Glass*, London: A. & C. Black.

Tite, M.S., Freestone, I.C. and Bimson, M. (1983) 'Egyptian faience: an investigation of the methods of production', *Archaeometry* 25: 17–27.

——, —— and —— (1987) 'The scientific examination of pre-Hellenistic faience from Rhodes', in M. Bimson and I.C. Freestone (eds), *Early Vitreous Materials*, British Museum Occasional Paper, No 56. London: The British Museum, pp. 39–46.

Tomasevic, T. (1977) 'Ein Glasschmelzofen in den Ausseren Reben, Kaiseraugst AG', in *Festschrift Elisabeth Schmid*, Basel, pp. 243–52.

Turner, W.E.S. (1954a) 'Studies of ancient glass and glassmaking processes. Part I: Crucibles and melting temperatures employed in Ancient Egypt at about 1370 B.C.', *Journal of the Society of Glass Technology* 38: 436T–44T.

—— (1954b) 'Studies of ancient glass and glass-making processes. Part II: the composition, weathering characteristics and historical significance of some Assyrian glasses of the eighth to sixth centuries B.C. from Nimrud', *Journal of the Society of Glass Technology* 38: 455–6.

—— (1956a) 'Studies of ancient glass and glass-making processes. Part V: Raw materials and melting processes', *Journal of the Society of Glass Technology* 40: 277–300.

—— (1956b) 'Studies of ancient glass and glass-making processes. Part III: The chronology of glass-making constituents', *Journal of the Society of Glass Technology* 40: 39–52.

—— (1956c) 'Studies of ancient glass and glassmaking processes. Part IV: The chemical compositions of ancient glasses', *Journal of the Society of Glass Technology* 40: 162–86.

—— and Rooksby, H.P. (1959) 'A study of opalising agents in ancient opal glasses throughout three thousand four hundred years', *Glastechnische Berichte*, 32K, VII: 17–28.

—— and —— (1961) 'Further historical studies based on X-ray diffraction methods of the reagents employed in making opal and opaque glasses', *Jahrbuch des Römisch-Germanischen Zentralmuseums* 8: 1–16.

—— and —— (1963) 'A study of the opalising agents in ancient glasses throughout 3400 years, part II', in F.R. Matson and G.E. Rindone (eds), *Proceedings of the 6th International Congress on Glass: Advances in Glass Technology*, New York: Plenum Press, pp. 306–7.

Van Es, W.A. and Verwers, W.J.H. (1980) *Excavations at Dorestad I. The Harbour: Hoogstraat I*, Nederlandse Oudheden 9, Amersfoort: ROB.

Vandiver, P.B. (1982) 'Mid-second-millennium B.C. soda-lime-silicate technology at Nuzi (Iraq)', in T.A. Wertime and S.F. Wertime (eds), *Early Pyrotechnology: The Evolution of the First Fire-using Industries*, Washington, D.C.: Smithsonian Institution Press, pp. 73–92.

—— (1983) 'Egyptian faience technology', in A. Kaczmarczyk and R.E.M. Hedges, *Ancient Egyptian Faience*, Warminster: Arris and Phillips.

Velde, B. (1990) 'Aluminia and calcium oxide contents of glass found in western and northern Europe, first to ninth centuries', *Oxford Journal of Archaeology* 9, 1: 105–17.

—— and Hochuli-Gysel, A. (1996) 'Correlations between antimony, manganese and iron content in Gallo-roman glass', in *Proceedings of the 13th Congress in the International Association for the History of Glass*, The Low Countries 28 August–1 September 1995, Lochem: International Association for the History of Glass, pp. 185–92.

Verità, M. (1985) 'L'Invenzione del cristallo muranese: una verifica analitica delle fonti storiche', *Rivista della Stazione Sperimentale del Vetro*, I: 17–36.

Watson, O. (1999) 'Report on the glazed ceramics', in P.A. Miglus, Die Frühislamische keramik von Tall Aswad, Berlin: Phillip von Zabern, pp. 81–7.

Wedepohl, K.H., Krueger, I. and Hartmann, G. (1995) 'Medieval lead glass from north western Europe', *Journal of Glass Studies* 37: 65–82.

Weinberg, G.D. (1969) 'Glass manufacture of Hellenistic Rhodes', *Archaiologikon Deltion* 24: 143–51.

—— (1983) 'A Hellenistic glass factory on Rhodes: progress report', *Journal of Glass Studies* 25: 37.

—— (ed.) (1988) *Excavations at Jalame site of a Glass Factory in Late Roman Palestine*, Columbia: University of Missouri Press.

Welch, M. (1992) *Anglo-Saxon England,* London: Batsford, English Heritage.

Werner, A.E. and Bimson, M. (1963) 'Some opacifying agents in Oriental glass', in F.R. Matson and G.E. Rindone (eds), *Proceedings of the 6th International Congress on Glass: Advances in Glass Technology,* New York: Plenum Press, pp. 303–5.

—— and —— (1967) 'Technical report on the glass gaming-pieces', in I.M. Stead (ed.), 'A La Tène III burial at Welwyn Garden City', *Archaeologia* 101: 16–17.

Weyl, W.A. (1937) 'The chemistry of coloured glass: II', *The Glass Industry* April 1937: 117–20.

—— (1951 [1992]), *Coloured Glasses,* Sheffield: Society of Glass Technology.

Whitehouse, D. (1991) 'Glass-making at Corinth: A reassessment', in D. Foy and G. Sennequier (eds), *Ateliers de verriers de l'antiquité à la période pré-industrielle*, Association Française pour Archéologie du Verre, Actes des 4ème Rencontres, 1989, Rouen: Association Française pour Archéologie du Verre, pp. 73–82.

Wood, E.S. (1965) 'A medieval glass-house at Blunden's Wood, Hambledon, Surrey', *Surrey Archaeological Collections* 62: 54–79.

Wright, A.C., Hulme R.A., Grimley, D.J., Sinclair, R.N., Martin, S.W., Prince, D.L. and Galeener, F.L. (1991) *Journal of Non-crystalline Solids* 129: 213.

Young, S. (1956) 'An analysis of Chinese Blue-and-White', *Oriental Art* 11: 43.

Zachariasen, W.H. (1932) 'The atomic arrangement of glass', *Journal of the American Chemical Society* 54: 3841–51.

4

CERAMICS

4.1 Introduction

As for metal and glass, the study of ceramics on its own can provide the substance for a book – and indeed it has. For example, a comprehensive publication by Prudence Rice (1987) has considered the full complexity of ceramic technology; a volume edited by Freestone and Gaimster (1997) provides a broad and informative consideration, based on short case studies, of the range of ancient ceramic technology. Even though this chapter focuses on the techniques of ceramic production, and the technology involved in forming and firing pottery, there are associated realms of study which should not be forgotten, and provide a more holistic approach. Certainly the 'evolution' of ceramic technology is undeniable, but there are many exceptions to what some people might call *progress*. There are certain assumptions in the study of pottery from an evolutionary perspective. Perhaps the most significant is the assumption that raw materials are chosen because they impart specific properties to the clays when they are being formed into a pot, when they are fired and when being used in one or more contexts. Of course in many cases this is true – simply because the behaviour of the pottery has been observed and the technology has developed on the strength of those observations. Related to the more deterministic area of pottery research is that of *ceramic ecology*, the study of ceramic production in relation to the exploitation of raw materials in the environment in which it occurs (Matson 1965; Kolb 1989).

However, as White (1972) and Wright (1986) have discussed, the interaction of style and techno-

logy is more complex than this: 'there is nothing inevitable about the acceptance of a new technology' (Wright 1986: 17); among other social groups, potters may have played an active role in creating stylistic changes. In addition to this, there is the study of pottery production in the context of the ways in which craft groups may determine the materials added to the pots that do *not* necessarily play a significant role in their performance but are determined by what was used or demanded by potters and consumers – so-called cultural factors (Wright 1986; Kilikoglou *et al.* 1998). Bishop (1992: 169) has stressed how important it is to keep 'central the archaeological problem under investigation ... thereby avoiding the centripetal tendency for methodological rather than archaeological statement, whether investigating changes in technology, production strategies, or ceramic exchange'. It is clear that the full range of potential sources of variation which produce the archaeological record should be considered. Tite (1999) has discussed a complex range of parameters which have led to the various modes of pottery production, distribution and consumption. Rather than discussing these parameters in isolation he has shown how the physical sciences can provide the means of investigating *some* of these questions; at the same time he accepts that 'sociopolitical and cultural–ideological factors are clearly of very considerable importance in explaining technological choice' (ibid.: 225). Something which often forms part of the archaeological investigation of ceramic composition is whether 'workshop compositions' of clays used can be identified. An analytical study of third- and second-millennia BC pottery from Iran

(Henrickson and Blackman 1992) has revealed links between typological characteristics such as vessel form, motif repertoire and decorative style, and the use of restricted ceramic compositions. It can be argued that indeed the products of workshop traditions have been identified – though there is still a further possible explanation: that for some (political) reason the raw material supply was controlled resulting in the same raw materials being used in a number of (nearby) workshops.

Part I of this chapter is a consideration of how clays originated, how clays were prepared for pottery production, how pottery was made and decorated, including the equipment needed and aspects associated with kiln use. Part II provides in-depth case studies: the changing mode of Iron Age pottery production in southern England; early medieval pottery production and the growth of towns; the manufacture of Chinese celadon; and Ottoman Iznik and the court patronage. All of these case studies are a reflection of the social and economic contexts in which the pottery was made, the level of archaeological research involved and the ways in which scientific investigations have been carried out.

4.2 The raw materials of pottery production

4.2.1 Clays and their origins

Although common clays are complex and need to be prepared before pots can be made from them, one of their more important properties, which people often take for granted, is their ability to absorb water. This allows clays to become plastic so that they can be shaped – the property of *plasticity*. Not all clays exhibit the same plasticity; this variation can be linked directly to their physical structure. Since plasticity is a critical property of clays, their physical structure and the ways in which they were formed are clearly worth considering in some detail since it is these which contributed to the property of plasticity.

Clays as materials can be defined in a range of ways. They are complex and are formed in many different contexts which, in turn, lead to their different physical (and chemical) properties. It is the existence of this wide range of clay types which

consequently leads to the manufacture of pottery of a correspondingly wide range of colours and properties. The potter's intervention in preparing and modifying the clays, including transformation by fire, also has an important impact on the finished product.

Clays can be defined in a variety of ways (see Section 4.2.3), but in order to define this most important component of pottery, it is necessary to start from basics: the composition of the earth's crust. It is the earth's crust which ultimately provides the raw materials from which clays are formed. The commonest elements in the earth's crust (expressed as oxides) are silicon dioxide – SiO_2 (60.1%) and aluminium oxide – Al_2O_3 (15.6%) with the balance of oxides, including the oxides of iron, magnesia, calcium, sodium, potassium, titanium and phosphorus being present at less than 5.1%.

4.2.2 The formation of clays from the earth's crust

Minerals are one of the principal components of clays. These are formed from a combination of oxides with a range of other compounds which occur in the earth's crust. A mineral is defined as any one of a number naturally occurring solid inorganic substances with a characteristic regularly ordered crystalline form. Different mineral types have different characteristics in addition to their crystalline form, which set them apart. These include colour, fracture, lustre (the way in which light is reflected from the surface of the mineral), hardness and specific gravity. The characteristic of fracture, for example, leads to crystal shapes which distinguish, in a very general way, between one family of minerals, quartz, feldspars and olivines and a second family, the pyroxenes and amphiboles. Following weathering and transportation (see Section 4.2.3) the first family are a blocky, squarish shape with equant forms, whereas the second family of minerals retain a stick-like, longer and thinner shape. Quartz tends to split (cleave) at its edges, pyroxenes split along their long axes (following cleavage planes) – a third family of mineral, the micas, cleave as sheets along the planes of their structures. In the chapter on metals the ore minerals are described (Section 5.2); those of relevance to the discussion here are rock-forming minerals because all clays are formed from rocks.

Thirty-nine per cent of the surface rock-forming minerals is composed of feldspars. Feldspars are a combination of silica (60.1% of the earth's crust) and other elements which form silicates. The mineral quartz forms 28% of the surface rock-forming minerals, clay minerals and micas 18% and ferro-magnesian silicates 2%; 9% are carbonates.

What bearing does the occurrence of these minerals have on the use of clay by a potter? The clays used by potters are essentially the result of sedimentation, but the sediments themselves have been formed by the weathering of rocks (igneous, metamorphic) which are composed of minerals. Since igneous rocks basically give rise to the formation of metamorphic and sedimentary rocks, it is worth considering them in some detail, because the properties of clays are fundamentally linked to them.

Igneous rocks are formed either by volcanic eruptions (produced by volcanos) or plutonic extrusions (formed deep in the earth and cooled slowly). Examples of fine grained volcanic rocks are obsidian (a natural glass; see Section 6.6), basalts and pumice; examples of coarse-grained plutonic rocks are granites and dolorites. Igneous rocks can also be classified according to a scale of acidity (high silica) and basicity (low silica). Thus acid rocks like granites have a pale colour, are coarsely textured (because they have cooled slowly) and have a low specific gravity; basic rocks like basalts have finer textures (because they have cooled faster) are darker in colour and have a high specific gravity. The greater weight and (darker) colour of basic rocks derive from the large quantities of mafic (magnesia and iron-rich) minerals.

As mentioned above, the most common rock-forming minerals are those which contain silica. The rock-forming minerals primarily with silicates can be graded according to their acidity or basicity, from the most acid minerals (micas), through quartz and feldspars to the ultra basic pyroxenes and olivines. Of course, rocks are made up of a variety of minerals.

Igneous rocks are the basis for metamorphic rocks (transformed by heat and/or pressure); sedimentary rocks are the result of the transport and deposition of igneous or metamorphic rocks. Some sedimentary rocks are formed by the compaction of millions of the shells (the 'carapace' of organisms that once inhabited them) and of the skeletons of diatoms – tiny single-celled algae which have skeletons impregnated with silica.

In describing the physical properties of igneous rocks and the minerals that compose them, their texture and acidity were mentioned. These properties will determine directly the susceptibility to weathering of igneous and metamorphic rocks (see Rice 1987: Table 2.3) and thus the kinds of clays that are formed from them, and their firing properties. However, having described the ways in which rocks and minerals can be classified, when we consider the most significant rocks for the formation of clays, it is the breakdown of those silicate rocks which contain significant aluminia, such as micas and some feldspars, that we are concerned with here. Feldspars contain a combination of silica and aluminia, and the balance of their compositions leads to a corresponding range of feldspar compositional types produced mainly by varying proportions of potassium, sodium and calcium. Thus feldspars can be classified into alkali (potassium) feldspars (orthoclase and microcline) and soda-lime (plagioclase) types: albite – is the sodic form and anorthite – the calcic form, depending on the proportion of these components. There are also plagioclase feldspars with intermediate compositions and different names (Velde and Druc 1999: 21–2).

The weathering and decomposition of rocks and minerals to produce clays involves mechanical, chemical and biochemical agents. Two processes are generally involved: fragmentation by wind, water and glacial ice and the chemical reaction of minerals with solutions of water (hydrolysis) to produce new minerals, sometimes involving weak acids. The processes of weathering (like any chemical reaction) are affected by temperature (extremes of temperature as well as the mean temperatures) and by rainfall, perhaps in the form of flooding. The biological agents that can play a part in breaking down rocks include bacteria, algae and rootlets. Extreme forms of chemical weathering remove elements from the rocks according to the solubility of the components – sodium first, followed by potassium, calcium and magnesia – which leaves relatively insoluble iron, aluminium and silicon. This kind of weathering occurs in humid tropical regions.

4.2.3 The definition of clays

Clays can be defined in several different ways, including the following features:

(I)   depositional situation;
(II)   particle sizes;
(III)   chemical composition and structure;
(IV)   mineralogy.

These definitions will be summarised here and the principles are described in each case, but it should be borne in mind that clays are extremely complex and a satisfactory agreement between researchers on how best to define them has not necessarily been reached in all instances.

These various ways of defining clays can be used to attempt to 'label' them. However people in the past who selected clays for pottery making would have done so with the experience of how the clays behaved when worked, especially their plasticity/the extent to which they absorbed water, how the clays were changed when fired (their shrinkage and thermal shock) and how different pottery colours were achieved when fired under a variety of conditions. In any case our labels obviously had no significance to past societies, but the behaviour of clays during the production process led to an enormously wide range of pottery types; clearly the development of firing technology and the mixing of clays both had their important roles to play. These (physical) definitions can be related to visual characteristics of pottery, including the ways in which the clays have been transformed in the fire and with the addition of other materials.

(I)   The depositional situation: close to the parent rock or transported and dumped

Primary (or residual) deposits of clay are those which have remained in more or less the same situation as the parent rock (such as granite, basalt, limestone and shale) from which they were derived as a result of various weathering processes described above. Sometimes when the parent rock is incompletely weathered these residual clays contain fragments of the parent rock such as feldspar, mica and quartz.

Secondary (sedimentary or transported) clay deposits are those which have been transported some distance from the parent rock by natural agencies such as wind, glaciation or streams. The largest sedimentary clays are those carried down to the coast and deposited as marine deposits. Because they are generally finer-grained, secondary clays they can be more homogeneous and can contain up to 10% organic components. Glacial clays generally contain a relatively high proportion of impurities and tend to be unsorted and are suitable to make earthenware from.

(II) The particle sizes of clays and the characteristics of a colloid

Different formation processes of clays lead to different particle sizes. These can be measured using a technique called granulometry (the measurement of grain size); it is generally agreed that clay contains particles of predominantly less than 2 micrometers (Rice 1987: 38, Figure 2.2). Because clays consist of such small particles they behave like colloids. A colloid is a mixture consisting of particles of one component suspended in a continuous phase of another which has the properties between those of a solution and a fine suspension. An example of an organic colloid is blood where haemaglobin (for example) is suspended in blood serum. This definition of clays, as colloids, provides a useful insight into how they behave when they are manipulated and worked, though not all particles in clays are a colloidal-size. According to several different (institutional) definitions of clays they contain the finest particle sizes, with silts, sands and gravels containing progressively larger particles. Soil maps frequently include silty clays and clayey loams, but fine-textured plastic clays are those deposited in lakes, streams and estuaries. For a soil to exhibit plasticity it should contain a minimum of 15% of fine particles.

(III) Chemical definitions: a variety of oxide combinations

Just as clays have distinctive properties which enable them to be made into pottery because they are colloids, their chemical compositions (and structures) are equally important. Clays are essentially composed of the two commonest oxides in the earth's crust, silica (SiO_2) and aluminia (Al_2O_3): it is no coincidence that these also happen to be the most resistant to weathering. When combined with water (H_2O) these oxides form what are generally described as hydrous aluminium silicates; most clays are composed of this substance, and obviously the existence of different clay types is connected to the different proportions of silica, aluminia and water they contain. The (atomic) structure of different clay types varies to the extent that the ratio of silica to aluminia can vary from 1:1 to 4:1, or higher, and the water component can vary between *c.* 13% and 35%. In addition, other oxides introduced by the presence of various minerals determine their chemical compositions. Iron and aluminium also combine with water, especially in tropical and subtropical zones, to produce iron and aluminium hydrous oxide clays, sometimes mixed with silicate clays.

These structural 'units', silica, aluminia and water, in fact are typically arranged in sheets, but not as discrete oxides. The 'water' component breaks down into oxygen and hydroxyl (OH–) components in clays and combines with silicon and aluminia in different ways, producing essentially two 'building blocks': (1) silicon combined with oxygen atoms and (2) aluminium combined with oxygen atoms or hydroxyl groups (see Figure 4.1). The relative number of these groups is determined by the kind of clays involved; as with any material the charged atoms or groups of atoms (ions) which constitute clays are held together with electrical charges. Silicon combines with oxygen atoms to produce tetrahedrons consisting of a central silicon atom combined with four oxygen atoms equally spaced around it; aluminium atoms combine with two oxygen and four hydroxyl ions forming octahedrons. The silicon-oxygen tetrahedra (the basic building blocks of silicate rocks) form sheets in clays which are typically composed of groups of tetrahedra with shared oxygens at their corners, producing hexagonal rings (Rice 1987, Figure 2.4b, c). In a similar way, sheets of octahedra are formed from aluminium, oxygen and hydroxyl groups. However, magnesia and iron ions (e.g. Mg^{2+}, Fe^{2+}, Fe^{3+}), among others, can replace ions of silicon and aluminium and this compositional range leads to a corresponding range of 50 clay mineral types. Trace components, such as titanium, calcium and sodium may also bond with clays.

Silicate clay minerals are often composed of sandwiches of alternating silica tetrahedra and aluminia-rich octahedra which are weakly-bound together. This clay structure produces *platelet* shaped particles and result in *easy cleavage* (see Section 4.2.3).

(IV) Mineralogical definitions

The use of optical petrology and X-Ray diffraction (see Section 2.2) has shown that clays basically consist of fine crystals with an internal structure such as silica and aluminia-rich sheets. Having said this, the existence of *'transitional'* clays illustrates the point that the definition and classification of clays is far from simple and there are still areas where no consensus of opinion has been reached. In addition, since in attempting to reconstruct past systems of pottery production we may want to relate the source of particular clays used to the fired result, it is worth bearing in mind that by firing the clays some of the mineralogical structure may be destroyed.

Most clay minerals or mineral groups can be classified as layered silicates (also known as phyllosilicates) (IV-1). Some clay minerals have a chain or lath structure (IV-2); a small number of clay minerals (allophane minerals) are amorphous to X-Ray diffraction.

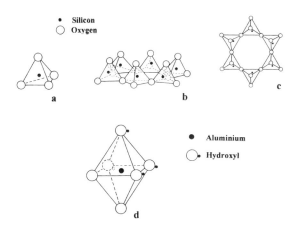

Figure 4.1 Some of the structural units found in clays: (a) silica and oxygen tetrahedron; (b) and (c) hexagonal arrangements of silica and oxygen tetrahedra; (d) aluminium, oxygen and hydroxyl octahedron.

IV-1 Layered silicate clays

Differences in the arrangement of the silicon- and aluminium-rich layers as well as the substitution of aluminium by various other groups, including those rich in potassium and magnesia, produces the variation which allows for a tripartite subdivision of layered silicate clays.

(A) KAOLINITE AND HALLYOSITE CLAYS These are two-layered structures, one each of silica tetrahedra and aluminia octahedra which are bonded relatively strongly. Kaolinite clays are mainly composed of the clay mineral kaolin. Kaolin results from the advanced weathering of rocks like acid granitic rocks (such as pegmatites and micaceous schists). Kaolin is normally high in aluminia – one of the characteristics of Chinese porcelain – and often occurs in the ratio of 2:1 with silica, combined with water. It normally occurs as flat hexagonal plates. Kaolins occur widely in temperate and tropical zones; the familiar conical hills of kaolin ('china clay') at St Austell in Cornwall are a memorable sight. These hills result from hydrothermal alteration of the granites which are characteristic of the area.

These clays are relatively low in plasticity, they are coarse and contain impurities including fragments of parent rock; the better sorted sedimentary kaolins tend to be relatively free of impurities, such as iron, which would colour the clay; the result is that they are white when fired. China clays have a high firing temperature (refractory), are low in impurities and, because of their relatively large particle size, are low in plasticity. They have a relatively low shrinkage when they are dry.

Hallyosite clays have developed from volcanic ash as recently as 4000 years ago (Hay 1960). They tend to be formed by hydrothermal action. Although they too have a two-layered structure, irregularities in the structure lead to more water in the mineral structure than kaolinite clays.

(B) SMECTITE CLAYS These clays have a three-layered structure consisting of two sheets of silica tetrahedra separated by a single layer of aluminia octahedra, again bonded loosely. Water molecules and a variety of atoms can easily penetrate the spaces between the unit layers which makes them expand, cleave apart and adsorb additional ions with ease; these water molecules are known as interlayer lattice water to distinguish them from chemically-bound water or the very weakly-bound water which contributes mainly to the plasticity of the clay (see Section 4.3.2 below). Smectites are formed mainly by the alteration of basic rocks and minerals which are high in calcium, magnesia and iron; examples are basalts or the decomposition of volcanic ash. Smectites are a relatively common component in arid regions and in recent sediments, but are not as highly weathered as kaolinites. If smectites are leached when high rainfall, high temperature and good drainage occurs, bases (such as magnesia, sodium and potassium) will be removed and this will lead to the formation of kaolinites. When compared to kaolinitic clays, smectites have a higher ratio of silica to aluminia (around 4:1), they contain more alkali metal ions such as sodium (Na^+) and potassium (K^+) and, because of the relatively lower level of aluminia, the clays are less refractory and melt/are fired at lower temperatures.

The most common member of the smectite group is montmorillonite. A number of ionic substitutions can occur within the clay: for example, if Al^{3+} is replaced by Mg^{2+} saponite is produced, or Al^{3+} by Fe^{3+} nontronite is produced. Smectite particles are thin and platey, but can be considerably smaller than kaolinite particles (0.05 μm–1 μm, rather than 0.6 μm–1 μm in diameter). The small particle size means that smectites are often plastic and sticky; their tendency to absorb water means that they display a high degree of shrinkage and have a tendency to crack when drying. Because they are able to adsorb other (colorant) ions they can be used as coloured slips.

(C) ILLITE CLAYS These also have a three-layered structure; they were named in 1937 after the state of Illinois in the USA, and are similar to smectites. About 15% of the silicon is replaced by aluminium in these clays, so they melt at even lower levels than smectite clays. At the same time, a charge deficiency, primarily in the outer silica layers of the unit structure, is balanced mainly by potassium ions (K^+), and in addition Ca^{2+}, Mg^{2+} and H^+ ions. Because the deficiency is close to the surface, rather than in the interior as with smectites, illite clays are non-expanding.

Illite minerals, like smectite minerals, are poorly-defined flakes with diameters ranging from 0.1 μm to 0.3 μm. These clays are also good for making coloured slips, such as used on Arretine/Samian ware and Greek black-figure ware.

Illite clays are produced in a variety of environments. They can form in offshore or deep alkaline marine environments by the alteration of kaolinites and smectites in the presence of calcium, potassium and magnesia and the absence of a leaching solution. These clay minerals can form by diagenesis. Over thousands of years illites may alter and become smectites.

IV-2 Chain or lath-like silicates

These are fibrous or lath-structured clay minerals which are found particularly in arid and desert regions; they can be weathered products of basalts. The clays consist of silica tetrahedra and the octahedra contain magnesia surrounded by oxygen atoms and hydroxyl groups. They are often found mixed with other clay minerals and with calcareous materials. They fall into two groups: the attapulgite-palygorskite group and the sepiolite group.

(A) ATTAPULGITE AND PALYGORSKITE CLAYS In attapulgite clays, the magnesia (magnesium ions in octahedral units) are mainly replaced by aluminia ions. The minerals are in the form of laths or bundles of laths, several microns in length, often in a bent and tangled pattern; they are highly absorbent. In palygorskite clays fewer magnesium ions are replaced by aluminia in the octahedra, than in attapulgite clays.

(B) SEPIOLITE CLAYS These clays contain octahedra with even fewer magnesia ions being replaced by aluminia than in palygorskite clays and the laths are thicker, shorter and denser than in attapulgite clays.

4.3 Pottery manufacture

4.3.1 The preparation of clays for potting

The preparation of clays can include mixing different kinds of clays and adding various kinds of inorganic or organic materials (known as temper). But before these processes occur preparation can also include forms of purification such as physically removing rootlets and stones, sometimes by drying the clay, crushing it and sieving it. Another technique that can be used is levigation, in which the clay is thrown into large tanks. The larger inclusions settle out and the finer particles are separated by remaining in suspension. Peacock (1982: 54, 122) describes a Roman levigation tank which had a 10,000 gallon capacity. Smaller installations were also used for decanting and evaporating clays from levigation tanks. During this process inclusions, like calcite, which could cause problems during the firing (see Section 4.3.10), can be removed.

This occurs prior to the physical techniques of wedging, kneading and foot-treading. These physical techniques of preparation eliminate air pockets and increase homogenisation of moisture and inclusions making the clay more workable. Wedging consists of repeatedly cutting the clay with a wire and pressing it together (see Figure 4.2a). Kneading, folding and pressing the clay are also used to eliminate air pockets (see Figure 4.2b). Foot-treading has the same effect as kneading but is carried out when large quantities of clay are involved (see Figure 4.3). These preparatory techniques ultimately aid in the successful firing of the pot and improve one of the most important physical properties of the clays, *plasticity*. Plasticity can be defined according to its yield point (the point at which compressive forces start to change the shape of the clay) and extensibility (the amount of deformation a clay can withstand beyond the yield point without cracking).

4.3.2 Plasticity and its effect on shaping the pot

With the adsorption of water, a clay can be shaped under pressure so that when it dries the vessel form is retained. When fired above certain temperatures the property of plasticity is eliminated. As mentioned above (Section 4.2.3 (II)) clay particles are very small, and a large proportion behave like colloids. The platelet shapes of the particles have large surface areas which lend themselves to the property of plasticity; the adsorbed water acts as a lubricant allowing the clay particles to slide over each other, while at the

Figure 4.2a
Wedging clay.

Figure 4.2b
Kneading clay.

Figure 4.3 Foot-treading clay at the Heracla brick works, northern Syria.

same time they are difficult to pull apart because the surface tension is sufficiently strong. Clay can be compared to two sheets of ice separated by water which slide past each other. Generally, the larger the surface area of colloid-sized platelets, correlated to the incidence of finer particles such as in smectites, the more plastic the clay; kaolinites have larger particles and tend to be less plastic. Excess water lowers the surface tension and makes the clay soft and weak.

Potters judge the workability of a clay (its plasticity) according to feel: its working range and plastic limits, both of which rely on the addition of water in order to create a workable clay from a dry clay. A clay which is to be wheel-thrown should have relatively wide plastic limits because it must be able to flow, while at the same time it should not dry out excessively. Hand-made pots can be made from stiffer clays with a higher yield point and lower extensibility. Some clays, such as montmorillonites are suitable for both wheel-throwing and hand-building and are described as 'fat'. There are various ways of

increasing the plasticity of a relatively stiff clay: the addition of organic material such as yoghurt, beer, bacteria or starch and acids (e.g. vinegar). Plasticity can be increased if a clay is aged so that bacteria and acids allow the water to reach all clay particles and cause flocculation (the agglomeration of particles in the clay, forming 'flocs') (Glick 1936). Another obvious way of increasing plasticity is to mix a relatively fine plastic clay with a stiff clay.

Layered silicates, especially smectite clays, can be easily worked and are therefore *plastic* because water can easily be adsorbed (and see Section 4.2.3 above). This water is so weakly-bound to the clay minerals that it turns to steam at low temperatures. This kind of water is distinct from the water (and hydroxyl groups) which is chemically-bound to the clay minerals and the water which forms between the lattice layers (Norton and Johnson 1944; Dal and Berden 1965).

Rice (1987: 55–7) describes the complex electrical properties of both the clay minerals and water molecules which result in the electrical 'attraction' of water to clays. The clay platelets have electrically charged surface sites, such as in kaolinites, for example, where ions of aluminium (Al^{3+}) and silicon (Si^{4+}) are located along the edges of the platelets and oxygen (O^{2-}) and hydroxyl (OH^-) ions on their surfaces; these ions are electronically 'unsatisfied'. These 'unsatisfied' sites bond with hydrogen and oxygen ions from the water, forming an adsorbed water layer around the mineral platelet. The adsorbed ions deriving from the water are organised ('immobilised') into a layer which in some senses is analogous to ice so that the layers 'slide' past each other (Pollard and Heron 1996: 122) and which clearly provide the important property of plasticity.

4.3.3 Shaping the pot

Thumb-pinched pottery is produced by inserting the thumbs into a lump of clay. The fingers are used to squeeze and pull the clay until it becomes thin enough to form the wall of the pot. It may be carried out on a flat surface so that the base in turn becomes flat, by pressing the clay down onto the surface. Taller and larger vessels are produced by drawing the clay upwards into the desired shape. If the shape of the pot base is to be conical or rounded, then a support/cradle is necessary; alternatively a mould can be used (see below).

Slab-building is carried out by flattening the clay on a flat surface to create an even thickness, perhaps with a roller, cutting it into slabs and then luting the slabs together with a thick suspension of clay (*slip*). Angular or cylindrical vessels are often built using this technique.

Coil-building is another commonly-used technique where the clay is formed into a series of rolls/fillets by rolling it on a flat surface. The coils are then built spirally on a pre-prepared base until the desired pot size is achieved. Rings and segments may be added to a pot which has been produced using another technique. As coils are added the clay needs to be squeezed to create a join; the addition of a slip to the surfaces may hide the features which are characteristic of the technique. Xeroradiography, however, will reveal clearly the coils used to build the pot (Rice 1987); any cracking which occurs will also

Figure 4.4 Part of an 'Abbasid mould for a pot, which itself is stamp-decorated, al-Raqqa, Syria.

Figure 4.5 Roman moulds for making *appliqué* bulls' heads and dancers (photo courtesy of R.J.A. Wilson).

be in characteristically horizontal lines following the arrangement of coils.

Moulded vessels are produced by pressing the wet clay into a pre-prepared fired ceramic or plaster mould. The mould fragment shown in Figure 4.4 was decorated using a stamp. The result of pressing the (leather-hard) pot into the *inside* of the mould is that the outside of the pot takes up the shape and/or the decoration (see Figure 4.6). Moulds can also be used for producing *appliqué* (see Figure 4.5). By noting slight imperfections in the mould it is easy to identify the existence of a series of pots made using the same mould. The moulds themselves may be single or in two parts. Buffering materials (between the clay and the mould) are sometimes used so that the decorated clay can be removed from the mould with ease. Examples are fine sand, powdered clay and ash. If the clay is applied to the *inside* of the mould, it should not be allowed to contract too quickly because this can cause cracking as it is compressed; if applied to the outside this is not a problem because it will separate itself by shrinking. If a two part

mould is used the seam line is visible on the pot; there is also a contrast in texture between the smooth moulded side and the rougher hand shaped side of the pot. Good examples of mass-produced decorated moulded wares are Roman Samian wares and early Islamic ʿAbbasid wares.

Wheel-thrown vessels

The first wheel-thrown pottery, as opposed to wheel-built, had come into common use by 2250 BC, the middle Bronze Age in Mesopotamia. The use of a wheel introduced a kind of control over pot-shaping which was difficult to achieve using other techniques. The distinction between a wheel-thrown as opposed to a wheel-built pot needs some explanation. Wheel-thrown pots are those which are shaped by using a wheel that can be turned mechanically, usually with the feet (at variable speeds, sometimes to rotate a cylinder below the wheel) leaving the potter's hands free to shape the pot. Alternatively it can be moved with a stick inserted in a hole in the rim of the wheel or with the hands as used by the Ibibio in Nigeria

Figure 4.6 Roman lamp mould and the lamp made from it (photo courtesy of R.J.A. Wilson).

(Nicklin 1981b). Wheel-built pots on the other hand are shaped on a simple turntable (*tournette*) and may, as a result, be quite symmetrical – because the pot will be *centred* on the wheel – but the wheel is used as a viewing surface.

To make a wheel-thrown pot the clay is thrown onto the centre of the face of a flat wheel where it sticks while it is rotated mechanically and, at the same time, the clay lump is formed into the desired shape with the potter's hands. The clay needs to be quite wet because the act of pressing and forming the clay tends to dry it. Initially the clay is opened as with a thumb-pinched pot (see Figure 4.7), the wheel is rotated rather slowly at this stage as increasing pressure is applied to the outside of the pot with a counter-pressure from the thumbs on the inside. The clay is normally pulled upwards (coning) and shaped with fingers and thumbs into a desired shape (see Figure 4.8) while at the same time the speed at which the wheel spins creates a centrifugal force which needs to be countered. More water may be added periodically in order to keep the clay plastic and shape the pot (Figure 4.9); if too much water is added the clay may become too soft and the wall of the pot may break away from its base, attached to the wheel. At some point the rim needs to be finished off (Figure 4.9). Once completed the pot can be sliced off the wheel with a wire. The clue for identifying a pot manufactured using the wheel-thrown technique is by the presence of fine concentric rings (*rills*) on the walls of the pot, if they have not been covered or obliterated by later finishing. A combination of moulding and wheel-throwing can be carried out. This is when wet clay is placed over a mould already located centrally on a wheel and the clay is pressed into the mould as the wheel rotates.

The kick-wheel consists of a small light upper wheel on which the clay is placed and shaped by the potter and a much heavier lower bearing or fly wheel. The weight of the fly wheel can provide so much momentum by being kicked judiciously that it can rotate continuously. The evidence for the earliest use of the potters wheel is meagre: its use has been inferred from the analysis of the layout of painted pottery designs dating to the end of the Halaf period in Mesopotamia (Nissen 1988: 46–7). From some-

Figure 4.7 Thumb-pinching the clay.

Figure 4.9 Finishing the rim of the pot.

Figure 4.8 Coning the clay.

what later contexts parts of a number of potters' wheels have been found: a basalt pivot which would have formed part of a bearing was found in a Canaanite (1200–1150 BC) potter's workshop (Magrill and Middleton 1997: Figure 6a). A fired clay potter's wheel weighing 44 kg (20 lb) was found in the potter's quarter at Ur. This had holes near its edge in which a stick would have been inserted in order to turn it (Woolley 1956: 28; Simpson 1997b: Figure 1). In medieval Haarlem, the Netherlands, van der Leeuw (1975) has suggested that a 'cart wheel' was used, with a turntable set in the middle.

Even though the potters wheel was introduced from a relatively early time in the development of pottery technology, hand-made pots were still, of course, being made. In spite of a lack of direct archaeological evidence for the kind of potters wheel used in medieval England, Singer *et al.* (1956: 288) published a thirteenth-century French illustration of a potter turning a potters wheel with a stick. Hand-made pottery was, however, still being produced at Ham Green, Bristol and Lyveden, Northamptonshire in the thirteenth century (Cherry 1991: 201).

Figure 4.10 Islamic (11th century) carved pot with *appliqué* from al-Raqqa, Syria.

4.3.4 Decorating the pot

Non-moulded surface finishing and decoration other than glazing

The *paddle and anvil technique* involves beating the outside of the vessel with a stick while a stone or clay 'anvil' is held at the opposite side. This can compact the clay, thin the walls, smooth or roughen the surfaces, remove the marks left by coil-building and improve bonding between separate segments used to make the pot; the technique has, for example, a long history in the manufacture of Chinese pottery (Wood 1999: 18–19). *Scraping* the leather-hard vessel surface will also remove imperfections and irregularities. A knife may be used to *trim* leather-hard pots of any excess, particularly from wheel-thrown and moulded vessels.

By using something like a damp cloth, the outside of a leather-hard clay vessel can be *smoothed*; alternatively the vessel may be wetted first. *Burnishing* leather-hard or dry clay may be achieved by rubbing the surface with something smooth, like a pebble or smooth piece of bone. Smooth pebbles were, for example, found in a Canaanite potter's workshop at Lachish (Tell ed-Duweir) in Palestine (Magrill and Middleton 1997: Figure 1). The process of burnishing actually realigns the fine clay particles as well as compacting the clay surface.

Various tools (often made from bone) can be dragged across the surface of a leather-hard clay vessel in order to decorate it. Combing, stamping, impressing, striating and rouletting are some possible techniques which can lead to an infinite combination of decorative designs. Cord has been impressed into the surfaces of beakers in order to produce the famous Beaker ware dating to about 4500 years ago. Stamping and impressing can be performed with the decorated end of a bone tool (akin to a die), a shell or a host of other possible objects that when repeatedly stamped into the surface repeat the same pattern in a controlled or random pattern. Rouletting is performed with a decorated cylindrical tool which is rolled across the pot surface (Balfet et al. 1983: 101).

The pot surface can also be carved, incised and perforated: all three of these techniques involve the removal of clay. These operations are generally carried out when the clay is leather-hard. Incised designs can, of course, be infinite. The kind of incisions produced, fine incisions, narrow grooves, or gouged lines, will depend on the kind of tool used. Incising leather-hard or wet clay can displace a small amount of clay along the margins which may remain when the pot is fired; incising which has been carried out once the pot has been fired causes chips to be removed from the margins of the lines. Examples of incising are *combing* and *scrafitto*; the former produces a series of 'combed' lines, the latter involves incising decoration through a slip layer which is then sealed with a layer of glaze and fired.

Carved decoration can either be carried out relatively deeply so as to remove areas of clay and to produce a decorative design or in a more shallow way (plano-relief, champlevé or excising) so that the remaining clay is seen to form the decoration in low relief. The clay may be cut away in chamfered sections so as to create panels which can be stepped.

Appliqué decoration involves the addition of small preformed elements to a pot surface such as fillets, pellets and spikes normally luted with a small amount of slip (see Figure 4.10). Handles, feet and bases may be similarly luted into place and can be both decorative and functional. *Barbotine* decoration is the application of a thick suspension of clay to the pot surface using a similar technique to that used for cake-decoration whereby the clay is carefully squirted into place on the pot surface creating raised designs.

Slip decoration is performed with a liquid suspension of fine clay particles which is often of a different colour from the pot being decorated. The slip may provide a smooth surface for subsequent decoration (including underglaze painting), but also a consistent, usually pale, colour providing a decorative contrast. An example of the use of slip to produce some highly decorated pottery in antiquity was that used for the manufacture of Roman red slip decorated *terra sigillata* (Roberts 1997: 189ff.), which includes Arretine and Gaulish Samian wares. Fine

textured illite clays were often used in the manufacture of *sigillata* and the particles, in that case, may be held in suspension because they are sheet-shaped. In compositional terms they often contain higher alkali (potassium or sodium) levels than the body of the pottery they decorate and as a result tend to fuse at (slightly) lower temperatures. The slip layer on *sigillata* is as thin as 30 microns. This family of pots is not only famous for the use of a brightly coloured red slip but is often decorated with moulded motifs or scenes.

Slips can be applied by dipping the pot into a slip, pouring the slip onto the surface or wiping it onto the pot surface. If a pot surface is irregular the application of slip will fill in those irregularities, and create a smooth surface. The slipped surface itself may be incised to reveal the underlying clay. As with glazing, the relative degree of contraction of the pot and slip need to be matched so that the slip adheres; some slips may be 'tempered' so as to come close to matching the contraction of the pot. If the coefficients of contraction and expansion are very different, the slip can easily flake off or 'craze' in the same way that glazes do. An example of the use of a white slip is in the production of Ottoman Iznik ware (see Figures 4.41 and 4.42; Section 4.7.8) in which a proportion of lead-rich 'frit' (actually glass fragments) is added to the slip so that its expansion and contraction matches both the pot body containing 'frit' and the translucent glaze which covers it.

If the pot is air-dried before the slip is applied it will extract water from the slip which produces a 'concentrated suspension' of clay particles on the pot surface (Velde and Druc 1999: 86). A slip can be distinguished from a 'wash' by the fact that the slip is fired on, whereas a wash is a pigment or lime-based solution which is applied to a fired pot (Rice 1987: 151).

4.3.5 Glazes: their technology, chemical compositions, colouring; the use of pigments

Glazes have the same material characteristics as many glasses. For a discussion of the chemical and 'structural' characteristics of glass see Section 3.1; needless to say glazes are amorphous, can be coloured by adding transition metal ions and can be opacified with various crystalline compounds. As with glasses, the chemical composition of glazes affects their melting temperatures, that is, the temperatures at which they become viscous. This is an important property if one is considering also the rate at which the pottery substrate contracts as it cools. Glaze chemical composition also affects its absorption of light. However, one obvious difference between glazes and glasses is that glazes are made specifically for their attachment to pottery surfaces. This difference in function can lead to glaze compositions which are not found among ancient glasses at all. Not only is the concept of the mechanical attachment of the glaze to the pottery surface important, but so are the ways in which wavelengths of light may be reflected from different glaze colorants and from pot surfaces. The raw materials that were used to make glasses and glazes will partly have been dependant on the *niche* that glazing and pottery technology occupied in the particular context being considered, bearing in mind the potential social, economic, ecological and ritual features of that production sphere. If both glazed pottery and glass production occurred in the same production zone, the glaze technology may have been viewed as a natural extension of glass technology or vice versa; alternatively conservative elements of production procedures, be they ritual, social or economic, may have prevented sufficient communication between artisans involved to have brought about cross-fertilisation between the uses of raw materials for making glass and glazes. On the other hand, fuel consumption and the raw materials used in the construction of kilns/furnaces are more likely to have borrowed from each other.

When a pot is glazed it typically undergoes two firings. The first, usually at *c.* 900–1100 °C is called the biscuit (or *bisque*) firing of the unglazed pot. It is designed to make the pot stronger, allows it to undergo most of its shrinkage and makes its surface more porous in order to promote interaction between glaze and pot surface. The second firing occurs after the pot has been allowed to cool down and the glaze is applied. This is carried out at a variety of temperatures, depending on the glaze and pottery types. A low melting point glaze may be applied to a high-fired pottery body, though it is clearly very difficult to apply a high melting point glaze to a pottery body with a low maturing temperature.

A critical temperature, which provides one way of classifying glazes, is their *maturing temperature*. This is the temperature at which the glaze is fused to the pot body and, as the pot cools, develops fully its characteristics of strength. It is, of course, dependent on the chemical composition of the glaze – the raw materials that have been mixed in order to create it and the 'impurities' that have been introduced. Another way of classifying glazes is by the kinds of pottery on which they are used.

Homogeneity of glaze recipes is equally important to the final colour achieved in glazing. Variations in firing temperature, firing atmosphere and firing cycles can all modify the glaze colour achieved as indeed does the basic glaze composition – whether colouring compounds have been deliberately introduced or not. To be able to coat a pottery body with glass in such a way as to make it stick is quite an achievement. The reason for this is that the expansion coefficient of the clay is normally much lower than that of the glaze. A crazed network of cracks (*crazing*) can be produced if the glaze contracts more than the body, *shivering* is when the glaze falls off the body because it contracts less or at a slower rate. The main aim is for the glaze to contract slightly more than the body of the pot so that it *fits* successfully and compresses the surface of the body slightly. Clearly the relationships between firing technology, and the structural and chemical characteristics of glazes and pottery bodies are both complex and intriguing. The other factors to be taken into account when producing a glaze are the maturing temperature of the glaze (determined by its chemical composition), its surface tension and, related to this, its wetting properties.

Various flaws in the glaze can be created if it is fired at the wrong temperature: if it is too high it may simply run off the pot surface or generate bubbles (though this may be a deliberately produced effect). Under-fired glazes may be dull and do not have a smooth glassy feel. Flaws in glazes can be produced if the *fit* of the glaze on the pot (i.e. the match of the expansion and contraction of the glaze and the pot as the two are heated up and cooled together) is not achieved.

4.3.5.1 The classification of ancient glaze chemical compositions

The classification of glaze chemical compositions (and their 'melting' behaviour) can be based on the relative levels of: (1) lead oxide (some of the lowest melting temperature glazes); (2) alkalis like potassium and sodium oxides; (3) alkaline earth metals especially calcium oxide; and (4) aluminium oxide – high levels create glazes with some of the highest melting temperatures.

The earliest pottery glazes date to *c.* the middle of the second millennium BC in the Middle East (Moorey 1994; Peltenburg 1971). Their basic composition was alkali-lime-silica. This is consistent with glass technology at the time – the principal alkali used was also soda. However, the result of using a soda-rich glaze was that it tended to produce cracks in the glaze as the glaze shrunk onto the pot (i.e. the glaze fit was poor). Indeed Hedges and Moorey (1982) were (at the time) surprised to find that all of the pre-Islamic glazed pottery dating from between 600 BC and AD 600 from Kish and Nineveh that they analysed had been made in the soda-lime tradition.

Freestone (1991) reports finding the same soda-lime technology in ninth-century BC glazes from the Neo-Assyrian sites of Nimrud, Ba'shiqa and Arban. During the eighth and seventh centuries BC there was a peak in the production of polychrome blue, white and yellow glazed pottery in Assyria and Babylonia. These findings were entirely consistent with the analysis of the glazes attached to Neo-Babylonian bricks from the Processional Way in Babylon (Matson 1986).

Although in the Middle East alkali-lime-silica glazes continued to be produced, some of the first lead-rich glazes were introduced by the Chinese in the Warring States period (475–221 BC) on earthenware jars; in this instance they are lead oxide-silica or lead oxide-baria-silica (Wood and Freestone 1995) and contained *c.* 20% lead oxide. Slightly later, in the Han Dynasty, glazes contained significantly higher lead oxide levels of typically *c.* 53–60% (Wood 1999: Table 78) which, with the balance of *c.* 29% to 33% silica and 3.5% to 6.7% alumina, is close to the eutectic. (A eutectic mixture is one which has the lowest freezing point of all possible combinations of its components.) The Romans, who also used lead glazes and perhaps introduced the technology independently, may have had a (late) influence on the development of Chinese lead glazes, but it seems likely that the Chinese were the first to introduce lead-silica glaze technology. The Roman glazes contained *c.* 45–60% lead oxide (Tite et al. 1998: 242). These lead-rich glazes continued to be manufactured in the Byzantine and Islamic worlds and sometime later, in the sixteenth century, high lead enamels used for *cloisonné* on metal vessels produced in China have been found to have a similar composition to the glazes used on *fahua* wares – the Chinese ceramic versions of *cloisonné* decoration on metal (Wood et al. 1989). This reminds us that there may have been a range of levels of technical interaction between those involved in vitreous technologies.

A lead-alkali glaze technology was first added to the alkali glaze technology, probably in Iraq, in the eighth century (Mason and Tite 1997). Although the Romans produced lead glazes in various shades of green due to the presence of iron, the use of lead by Islamic potters tended to be associated with the introduction of the earliest tin opacifiers in pottery – a gap of some 900 years since the introduction of tin as an opacifier in glasses (see Section 3.2.5.5); tin was also used intermittently by late Roman glassmakers. The lead oxide-soda-lime Islamic tradition continued in use and was employed for sixteenth- and seventeenth-century Iznik glazes (Henderson 1989b; Tite 1989). A 'western' equivalent was used in the manufacture of lead-rich glazes of the Italian Renaissance in which potassium oxide replaced soda (Tite 1991).

In the medieval west the familiar olive green colour of so many of the wares is due to the presence of iron in the pottery which interacted with the lead-silica glaze under reducing conditions. In addition to this, yellow and colourless glazes were produced under oxidising conditions (Newell 1995); the use of a colourless glaze would simply provide the pot with a glassy appearance with the orange or reddish clay being visible behind it. The darker green hues found in this medieval pottery were produced by using copper and brass filings. The addition of iron oxide produced a darker brown colour in the glaze under reducing conditions. Because these glazes sometimes contained high (< 60%) lead oxide levels, the potter had to be careful not to reduce the glaze to the extent that the lead was reduced to metal; this would have produced a matt metallic finish.

The glaze would have been applied in the form of a paste by brushing it onto the pot (as powdered litharge or lead sulphide – galena PbS), dipping the pot in the glaze or sprinkling a powder on it. In the eleventh and twelfth centuries glaze appears to have been splashed on (Cherry 1991: 202). Analytical investigations of medieval pottery found at a kiln site of Hanley Swan, Worcestershire, UK has revealed that lead oxide was added in its 'raw' state to the body of the pot and a white layer formed as a result of the lead reacting with the body (Hurst and Freestone 1996). However, one result of brushing a powdered lead compound onto the pot is the toxic lead fumes which are produced when the pottery is fired. A way of preventing this is to fuse the lead with glass and then powder the glass, which is then applied to the pottery surface. This material is labelled 'frit' by some potters and art historians, but strictly speaking frit is defined as the partly fused raw materials of glass production, so the label is incorrect in this context. Fusing the lead in the glass prevents further lead fumes from being generated, but they may still be produced when the glass is made in the first place. There is however another advantage to applying powdered glass to a pot surface to produce a glaze: the resulting glaze will be homogeneous with fewer flaws.

Another type is salt (NaCl) glaze. This was produced by introducing salt into the kiln at high temperatures. A proportion of the salt decomposes with the alkali (Na) combining with the aluminium and silica in the pottery to produce a soda-rich high-temperature glaze; the chlorine in the salt combines with hydrogen in the water (H_2O) molecules in the pot to produce an acidic hydrogen chloride gas (Starkey 1977: 2).

In the Far East the glazes used on stoneware and porcelain tended to mature at high temperatures (up to as high as 1350 °C) having different chemical compositions from the soda-lime and lead-rich glazes used in the west (Wood 1999: 38; see Section 3.6). The principal compositional difference is the inclusion of a high alumina content with relatively low (resulting) levels of calcium oxide, soda and potassium oxide. In some Chinese pottery between c. 1500 BC and AD 900 the alkalis, a mixture of soda (Na_2O) and potassium oxide (K_2O), although at a maximum level of 5%, was provided by wood ash applied to the surface, which interacted with silica in the pot and produced a mottled colour. Some glazes contain elevated magnesia which increases their durability; this was certainly necessary given the low calcium oxide levels. After about AD 900 in China 'lime' glazes are supposed to have supplanted 'wood ash' glazes (Wood 1999: 32). However, in compositional terms the two 'compositional families' are virtually indistinguishable (Wood 1999: Tables 6 and 7), with calcium oxide levels of c. 16–20% and total alkali levels of between c. 2 and 3% in both. Further scientific research into the recipes used and the production procedures employed is clearly necessary.

4.3.5.2 Glaze colorants and the use of pigments

Many of the colorants used in glazes were also used in glasses (see Section 3.2.5). Moreover many of the factors which determine the colour of glazes are the same as those which affect glass coloration, the only differences being (a) that some glaze chemical compositions are not found among glasses and (b) the presence of a pottery body. The actual physical explanation for coloration in glasses and glazes, in terms of the chemical environment in which the colorants act is given in Section 3.2.5. The application of painted designs for which pigments are ground up and painted on generally relies on the pigment particles *not* dissolving in the glazes.

Painted designs can be applied either before or after firing. The pigments used can either be inorganic (made from ground up coloured minerals), or organic. Pigments are often made into a suspension with water, fine clay and a binder, and then painted onto the pot surface. Of the mineral-rich pigments, iron-, manganese- and carbon- (ground charcoal) based colorants can survive the firing process. The iron-rich minerals produce brown, red and black colours; an example of a black colorant is iron-titanite (ilmenite). Manganese-rich minerals can be used to produce black or brown colours. The colours of these mineral-rich colorants essentially remain the same throughout firing (Goffer 1980). Such minerals were used to produce paint colours for decorating prehistoric pots in the Middle East and present day Pakistan (Wright 1986). Other mineral-rich colorants are used in glazes (see Section 4.3.5). Organic paints are often applied with a brush after the pot has been fired. These break down and lose their colour in the kiln. An example of such a paint is Maya blue which consists of a suspension of clay mixed with metallic oxides; the organic dye is absorbed onto the clay substrate (José-Yacaman et al. 1996). On the other hand resist painting involves the use of a protective coating of something like wax over the parts of the pots which are not to be painted – and which is removed by heat (Shepard 1976: 206ff.). Slips can also be 'painted' on.

There are, however, studies of pottery glazes which underline some of the differences (and similarities) between glass and glaze coloration. Discrete changes in the use of cobalt-rich colorants have been identified in the glazes produced between *c.* 1430 and 1650 found in Turkey, including Iznik (Henderson 1989b: 67). Both manganese-rich and arsenic-rich cobalt ores were used at different times. The use of colorants not used in glasses can be noted: in Neo-Assyrian ninth-century BC pottery Freestone (1991) found that a black colour was caused by a Mn (Fe) pigment. However other colorants he found are also found in contemporary and earlier glasses: the white (opacifying) colorant used was calcium antimonate, the yellow (opacifying) colorant was lead antimonate and an opaque green glaze was produced by a combination of iron and opacifying crystals of calcium antimonate. In Partho-Sassanian glazes Hedges (1982) found that a blue colour was due to reduced iron, green was due to iron (with or without copper), darker browns due to iron and manganese and a black colour due to iron sulphide which had been produced under reducing conditions.

Kingery (1986) has underlined the importance of painted underglaze pigment technology in the Italian Renaissance, making the point that before the fifteenth century (in the west) most glaze colorants dissolved in the glaze and had blurred boundaries. Although, as mentioned above, the use of crystalline opaque colorants in glazes was not new, the defini-

tion of the areas to be decorated was. In around 1557 Cipriano Piccolpasso (1980) published *The Three Books of the Potter's Art*, an invaluable source of information about the kinds of raw materials used to make the glazes and glaze colorants for Renaissance pottery. In it there is a description of the preparation of two pigments used: lead antimonate (yellow) and tin oxide (white). Neither of these opacifiers were new to vitreous technology, the former being used first in the mid second millennium BC and the latter used first in the second century BC (Henderson 1985). However in this context the opaque crystals could be applied as a paint in areas defined by sharp lines. Other opaque colours were produced by mixing copper with lead antimonate (green) and iron with lead antimonate (orange), again both effects which had already been achieved in ancient glass coloration. A new pigment, called bole red, a ferruginous material, was used both in the coloration of Iznik underglaze decoration (see Section 4.7.9) and in pottery made in Renaissance Italy, appearing for the first time in Iznik pottery in 'Rhodian' style pots of about 1580. It was found to consist of finely ground particles of an iron-rich pigment mixed with fine silica particles, producing a red colour under the correct furnace conditions (Henderson 1989b: 68, Table 2). The opaque yellow/orange colour sometimes observed in 'bole red' suggests that furnace conditions played an important part in determining the final colour achieved.

Another pigment used by the potters of Iznik for creating (and defining) an outline was a mixture of iron, nickel, copper and cobalt (Henderson 1989b), quite possibly ground-up smalt, a pigment used for colouring medieval glass and also used by artists. A very dark green coloured pigment also used for outlining applied decoration was chromite (Tite 1989). This continued to be used for colouring Iznik glazes into the mid seventeenth century, though at this time the glaze technology had declined (Henderson 1989b: 68). It is not until the nineteenth century that chromium was introduced into the repertoire of true glaze colorants.

4.3.6 Clay drying

Various factors affect the ways in which clay dries: the amount of water in the clay, humidity in the immediate environment, other characteristics of clay particles (their size, flocculated or deflocculated and their orientation), the temperature at which the drying occurs, any variations in temperature, and the air currents. The ways in which pottery dries will now be described, especially what happens to the water in relation to the physical structure, and the manner in which this affects the strength of the pot.

When pottery dries in air the *adsorbed water* which surrounds the clay platelets and which provided lubrication when the pot was being shaped, starts to evaporate. In so doing the clay platelets draw together until they are no longer separated, increasing the density of the clay and small cracks may develop (Kingery and Francl 1954). The clay is now 'leather-hard' and is no longer plastic, so it can be easily handled. Some of the water which was added to make the clay plastic is held in *pores* in the clay and this takes longer to evaporate; the finer the particle size in the clay the finer the pores and the longer it takes for this water to evaporate. Pore water is replaced by air and when this water evaporates no further contraction occurs (i.e. the bulk volume remains the same). Evaporation through pores starts at the surface with water being continuously drawn out and evaporating as a moisture gradient comes into being. One potential result of fine clays drying too fast is that water evaporates from the surface of the pot faster than it can be supplied from the interior; the result is that the surface contracts faster than the interior sometimes producing compression of the surface which can lead to cracking. This process can be controlled if the clay is allowed to dry slowly. As the clay dries the moisture gradient may also draw out salts and organic particles which will be deposited on the surface as a scum which can affect the colour, density or hardness of the pot (Brownell 1949). The occurrence of *non-clay inclusions* such as sand or shell particles produces a more open structure, even if there are fewer pores (Mehren et al. 1981). These particles have no water films around them, so less water is held per unit volume than found in fine clays, but because shrinkage of the clay is relatively low and movement of water through to the surface is easier, drying is easier. What is of particular significance is that when inclusions which have no water films around them are added to clays,

shrinkage of the clay is minimised and so therefore is the potential of the pot warping and cracking.

Water is also held in a layer one molecule thick on the clay surface (*surface adsorbed water)* even when the clay may appear to be 'dry' (Rice 1987: 65). The water held in the mineral lattice of the clay (see Section 4.3.2) is lost when the pottery is fired.

The distribution of water in the body of the pot, and the orientation of the clay particles within it, are both factors which affect the way in which the pot shrinks as it dries. When a pot is produced by wheel-throwing the continuous addition of water to the outside leads to differential water content; when the pot dries the outside will shrink more than the interior which can lead to cracking. When clay particles are in a random arrangement the clay is more likely to crack or warp. However, when a pot is shaped by coil-building or wheel-throwing the clay particles can line up into patterns known as *preferred orientation*. This is when the particles are dragged into particular orientations by stroking the clay repeatedly while shaping the pot; even when a pot is moulded the absorption of water by the mould can realign the clay mineral particles into particular orientations. This helps to reduce shrinkage and cracking. *Anisotropic shrinkage* is another cause of cracking. As the pottery dries and contracts the pot may contract at different rates because during the formation of the pot different proportions of water and/or different alignments of clay particles are concentrated in different parts of the pot.

The term *green strength* when applied to pottery refers to its resistance to cracking and warping as it dries in the unfired state (Ryan 1965). The parameters which may add to this strength are particle size (the finer the particles the greater the strength), the presence of sodium ions (Na^+) and organic materials (like gums and milk solids) and a deflocculated state (where the particles do not form agglomerations [flocs]). Green strength is at its greatest when clay is completely dry. However, a balance needs to be struck between shrinkage and the attainment of green strength: deflocculated clays have lower shrinkage than flocculated clays as well as greater green strength. Fine clays, which have greatest green strength, also shrink more than clays containing coarser particles. A compromise is to add coarser particles so as to promote evaporation of water and the movement of water from the interior to the exterior; the result is to reduce the risk of cracking. Obviously in practice different potters get to know how different clays behave and modify the preparation procedures accordingly.

4.3.7 The texture of clay and clay inclusions

The texture of clay can be assessed simply by rolling a small quantity between the fingers; if it feels smooth or 'slimy' then it is usually a fine clay, whereas a stiff clay may feel coarse and gritty. The clay can also be nibbled in order to test it. Particle-size fractions of clays can be measured using the suspension or sieving method. The texture is mainly determined by the proportion of coarse grains – the clastics – as well as their size and shape. Clastics are not to be confused with the material that potters add to clays deliberately known as *temper* or *grog* (see Section 4.3.8). Clays can contain a wide range of inclusions ranging from pebbles and gravels to the more frequent sand and silt. Sand often contains more than just quartz: micas, feldspars and ferric minerals commonly occur and contribute to the impurities which end up in man-made glass (see Section 3.2.2). Sedimentary geologists distinguish between two sedimentary size ranges: 'mud' (containing particle sizes of less than 0.06 mm) and 'muck' (sediments associated with peat deposits and other wet environments containing 50% or more fine organic matter).

In the past, potters may have deliberately exploited clays which contained angular inclusions in a range of sizes, since these would bond and dry well, and confer strength on the final fired pot. Modern potters add materials to commercially produced refined clays, producing strength and plasticity in triaxial bodies (Norton 1970: Figures 12.2, 12.3 and 12.4). The three components are: clay(s), a filler (the same as a temper providing limited shrinkage, reduced cracking and reduced drying time) and a flux – normally an alkaline mineral which is a 'cementing' component.

The smallest size range of clay inclusions includes *colloids* which are particles of 0.001 mm (1 μm) or less in diameter suspended in another medium (for example, clay minerals in water) which repel each other because of their electrical charges (see Section 4.2.3(II)). Colloids have the property of being able to adsorb ions (Rice 1987: 76); the finer the clay the greater the potential for this. Ions fill the electronically 'unsatisfied' sites on particle surfaces and in so doing affect the arrangement of clay particles which may cause either clustering of particles (flocculation) or the opposite (deflocculation) (Johnson and Norton 1941). This therefore has an effect on the working properties of the clays. In deflocculated clays, where the particles repel each other, the particles are stable suspensions that resist settling, but when the clay dries or the clay particles settle the clay has a low shrinkage and a high green strength; deflocculated clays are therefore ideal to make *slips* from (see Section 4.3.4). The presence of organic colloids changes the acidity of clays and this (the pH balance) can affect its plasticity and flocculation/deflocculation. In general their presence increases the clay's plasticity. Most clays contain a small amount of organic matter in any case, with sedimentary clays containing as much as 10%.

4.3.8 Additions to clays (temper) and cultural choice

Clay is composed of a range of constituents which determine its properties as it is worked, dried and as the kiln or furnace temperature rises. Materials can also be added to clays in order to improve these properties, for example the all-important property of thermal shock resistance. While residues of parent rocks in primary clays and the introduction of particulate material during re-bedding of clays can provide inclusions, there are also some materials which are relatively easily identified as having been added intentionally as temper. However, because of the range of possible origins of the inclusions found in pottery – and in spite of *sometimes* being able to identify with certainty the inclusions that have been added intentionally – identifying temper has its own problems (Rice 1987: 408). The identity, size, shape and relative amount of the inclusions help to characterise the clays.

Over and above the straight 'deterministic' approach to the study of the choice of temper – that is the assumption that raw materials (temper) were selected because they determined the appropriate physical property of the pot when fired and when used (O'Brian et al. 1994: 261) – there are the important considerations of ceramic ecology and cultural considerations. Professor Fred Matson, one of the 'founding fathers' of ceramic investigations, has pointed to the *availability* of ceramic raw materials for pottery production as clearly being an important parameter in determining what raw materials were used (Matson 1965) – a branch of ceramic investigations that has become known as 'ceramic ecology' (Kolb 1989). Just as important, and in some cases, even more important, are the *cultural* choices that a potter may make as to what kind of raw materials are used. Craft practice in this case may be tied to the manufacture of specific technological *styles*, which themselves can drive production as part of the identity of the craft group involved (Wright 1986). These cultural choices in using particular styles may just as much be tied to traditions of place and time of production as other factors, as has been demonstrated by a study of changing fabric types of prehistoric pottery in the East Midlands in England (Allen 1991). As Sterner (1989: 458) has pointed out, the re-use of pre-fired pot ('grog') may have been a way of transmitting the life of an older pot and associated traditions from one generation to another, as found among the Sirak Bulahay of North Cameroon. Akin to this practice is the discovery of a recycled Bronze Age pottery fragment in a Deverel-Rimbury vessel at the cremation cemetery of Pasture Lodge, Long Bennington, Lincolnshire, England (Allen 1991) and in Bronze Age accessory cups (Allen, forthcoming).

Temper can either be inorganic or organic in nature: organic temper includes dung, straw and chaff, but perhaps the commonest kind is inorganic. Among inorganic temper (also described as aplastic inclusions) there are many possibilities: shell, sponge spicules, (quartz) sand, sandstone, limestone, basalt and volcanic ash. Small fragments of pot are also added – known as *grog*. The material which can be identified with some confidence as having been added deliberately is *grog*. On the other hand, some volcanic ash and vegetable matter burns away completely during firing, leaving only their casts (spaces) in the pottery. The materials which can be both added as temper and which occur naturally include quartz, calcite, sponge spicules, shell and mica. The distinction between the use of temper and the natural occurrence of the same material in the clays used can however often be made by determining the size, shape (angularity) and amount found – there is generally far more shell, for example, if added as temper (up to 30%). Magetti (1982) has gone further using size as a criterion alone in an attempt to distinguish between deliberately added and naturally occurring inclusions.

Shell or calcite has been used quite extensively as temper (Rye 1976; Arnold 1985). In low-fired clays while calcite expands at about the same rate as the clay, quartz expands at a greater rate. With the close match in expansion one might therefore expect calcite to have been used in preference to quartz as a temper (Rice 1987: 410), but Woods (1986), for example, has found that in the production of cooking pots, this has not always been the case. Quartz is often considered to have been added as a temper to clay if it is angular (because it has been prepared by crushing it) rather than having a rounded profile due to natural wear during transport and deposition in the environment. However, angular quartz also occurs naturally in primary or in sedimentary clays.

4.3.9 The conditions of firing

Three important factors will affect the changes which take place in a pot as the temperature rises: (1) the length of firing; (2) the temperature of firing; (3) the atmosphere in which the firing and cooling take place. All three of these factors must be considered together; to consider them separately is a somewhat artificial distinction since they can be interrelated and changing one factor can have an effect on the others. For example, mineralogical and chemical changes in the pottery may occur at lower temperatures if the atmosphere is reducing (oxygen-deficient) rather than oxidising.

(1) *The length of the firing* is very important and it can be broken into three stages: the period when the temperature is being raised, the period during which it is held at the maximum temperature and the period during which the temperature falls. Obviously fuel is used during the first and second periods but it is not likely to be used during the third. A critical

expression of the conditions in which various physical and chemical changes can occur in the clay is known as the 'work heat'. It is the 'effect' (however that is measured) of a given amount of heat on the ceramic in a given amount of time. It is in fact difficult to divorce time and temperature of firing.

(2) *The temperature of firing* as already described can change during different parts of the firing cycle; defining the length of time that the maximum temperature was held at is certainly important. In the past, potters could be described as being at the mercy of the burning characteristics of the fuels used: some will burn faster and give greater heat than others. Having said this, inevitably the burning characteristics of fuels used would ultimately have been experimented with and used to best effect. The determination of the maximum temperature of firing can be achieved using a number of analytical techniques such as differential thermal analysis (Grim 1968). Of course different clays can withstand different firing temperatures before they vitrify and lose their structural integrity. Indeed different wares can be distinguished according to the temperatures at which they have been fired, such as earthenware, stoneware and porcelain. In firing stoneware and porcelain the combination of the high temperatures and raw materials used brought about a degree of vitrification in the body of the pot.

A further point to bear in mind is that the relative position of the pot in the kiln will determine the temperature that it is subjected to: it may vary by as much as 150 °C (Simpson 1997b: 52). Terracottas which are 'normally' fired in open firings are heated to below 1000 °C; earthenwares between 900 °C and 1200 °C and stonewares, at between 1200 °C and 1350 °C. Porcelains, being most refractory, with the highest aluminia content, will fire as high as 1400 °C. Bonfire firings are generally quicker than kilns and a deal less controlled, with their maximum temperatures being held briefly. Although lower temperatures were achieved in bonfires, this doesn't necessarily mean that all low temperature firing was carried out in them (see Section 4.3.11).

Today potters use clay pyrometric cones of known compositions which bend at specific temperatures. By watching them during the firing cycle it is possible to hold the kiln at the appropriate temperature.

(3) *The atmosphere of firing* is important because it can affect the colour and hardness of the pot, and, in addition, its shrinkage and porosity. In discussing, or attempting to reconstruct, kiln technology it is important to know what the firing atmospheres were during the period when the kiln was held at its maximum temperature, but also during the cooling phase. The atmosphere may be affected by the differential air flows at different times, the use of different kinds of fuel at different times (such as different species of wood – see Section 5.6.2) and a covering of ash over the pots. The kind of firing set-up used is obviously important in determining the firing atmosphere achieved. The firing atmosphere is defined as the balance of gases (such as oxygen, carbon monoxide and carbon dioxide) during the firing procedure. An *oxidising* atmosphere is one in which oxygen predominates, whereas a *reducing* atmosphere is oxygen-deficient (i.e. carbon dioxide and carbon monoxide predominate) and is often smoky. A kiln in which air is able to circulate freely will normally be an oxidising atmosphere (though will obviously contain the other gaseous components of air, such as nitrogen). Sulphur-rich fuel combustion may produce sulphur dioxide gas and water vapour; the pottery itself may produce water vapour and the sulphur-rich and carbon-rich components of the clay minerals in the pots being fired when oxidised during firing may also produce their respective gases – SO_2, CO_2 and CO. When open firing was used, such as in bonfire firings (see Section 4.3.11.1), the control over air supply and the rate of fuel consumption would have been more difficult than in a pottery kiln. The net result (e.g. pottery colour) would have been less predictable. In open firings the atmosphere is often a compromise between oxidising and reducing, being neither completely oxidising nor reducing; to produce a completely reduced black colour caused by the oxidised (ferric) iron being reduced to its reduced form (ferrous), prolonged firing in a reducing atmosphere above 825 °C is necessary (Sheppard 1976: 219). On the other hand, in a kiln, control over the atmosphere was easier: a completely oxidising atmosphere was possible if a free flow of air was attained; to achieve a completely reducing atmosphere was more difficult – the fuel needed to be 'smothered'.

4.3.10 What happens when clay is fired?

Irrespective of the firing technology used, when a dry pot is heated, the remaining water held in the clay is gradually lost and at the same time the clay mineral structure and its chemical characteristics will be altered. During these processes the clay becomes harder.

Most weight loss on firing is due to the loss of surface adsorbed water and pore water from the clay (see Section 4.3.2 above). Cracking may occur if this process occurs too fast. The chemically combined water is driven off at higher temperatures, the process being dependent on the kinds of clays involved and therefore the ways in which water is held within the lattice structures (as hydroxyl groups). The effect of mixing clays appears to make the loss of hydroxyl groups more gradual and reduces the temperature at which it occurs. The volatilisation of organic components as gases (carbon monoxide and carbon dioxide) also contributes to weight loss; a high proportion of organics in the clay will lead to a correspondingly relatively high degree of shrinkage. Incomplete oxidation of organic-rich clay components may lead to ceramics with a dark core when seen in a broken section.

Other causes of contraction include the breakdown of *inorganic inclusions*: for example, sulphates, sulphides and carbonates, such as calcite ($CaCO_3$), dolomite ($CaMg(CO_3)_2$) pyrite (FeS) or gypsum ($CaSO_4.2H_2O$), which, when heated, give rise to gases such as sulphur dioxide and carbon dioxide. Chlorides can react with iron in the clay producing iron chloride. As these changes occur above temperatures of 500 °C, the increasing density of the clay is accompanied by decreasing porosity (the pores contract and close).

At still higher temperatures *new minerals form* and *vitrification* within the clay starts to occur, eventually producing a glassy phase. New minerals mainly form at temperatures above 900 °C, so are not normally observed in pottery fired in bonfires. Above 900 °C clay minerals lose all water, they break down and form new silicates. For example in kaolins the metakaolin formed at *c.* 500 °C breaks down into spinel, an aluminium-rich alteration product, and silica, both of which cause increased shrinkage (Grim

1968). It is normally claimed that spinel forms needles of mullite ($3Al_2O_3.2SiO_2$) between 1050 °C and 1275 °C and at even higher temperatures between around 1275 °C and 1460 °C, yet more shrinkage occurs as more high-temperature minerals are formed such as cristobalite. However, clay impurities, such as potassium oxide and calcium oxide reduce the temperature at which these minerals form (Johnson et al. 1982). A.C. Dunham (1992) has pointed out that the *soaking time* is an important factor in the development of high-temperature crystallites in the ceramic: mullite spinel assemblages form at 950 °C after only two hours soaking at that temperature; at higher temperatures the amounts of mullite spinel assemblages increase. So the combination of factors which affects the formation of minerals in a ceramic as the temperature is raised is not straightforward.

These changes in ancient ceramics can be investigated using two principal techniques: differential thermal analysis and X-ray diffraction.

The mineralogical transitions, which have mainly been noted as a result of work with kaolinites, obviously also apply in general to other clay types, such as smectites. The transitions occur at different temperatures in smectites because the clays have a different mineralogical/chemical composition (see Section 4.2.3); their different compositions have the overall effect of lowering the temperatures at which 'high-temperature' minerals form – smectites are also less refractory. Montmorillonites retain their lattice structures until *c.* 800–900 °C. In excess of these temperatures the pathways of mineral development differ according to their compositions: in those with Al^{3+} ionic substitutions, spinel forms; in those which are generally low in iron, quartz develops instead. As with kaolinites the presence of alkalis (lithium, sodium and potassium) reduces the temperature at which minerals develop and the maximum temperature up to which they survive.

Another group of changes that can occur in pottery as the temperature is raised is what happens to inclusions that may have been added by the potter (as a *temper* – see Section 4.3.8) or which occur in the clay naturally. The main effect that these inclusions have on the pot, as a result of modifying the microstructure of the clay, is on its expansion and contraction during firing. Finely divided particles of reduced iron, mica and lead minerals can all act as low temperature fluxes. When three types of commonly occurring inclusions – quartz, feldspar and calcium – are heated to sufficiently high temperatures they have specific roles in initiating and developing the partial fusion or fusion of grains. Since this process can have an important effect on the strength, thermal shock resistance, porosity, colour and hardness of pottery, a summary will be provided here.

This fusion process can be defined both as *sintering* and *vitrification*. Sintering is defined as a process when particle surfaces (in this case clay particles) *begin* to fuse or stick to others – either as a solid state or liquid phase reaction (i.e. although the material does not melt completely it forms a coherent mass). In the former a 'neck' is formed from the surface diffusion of atoms between the particles – but no liquid phase or melting is involved (Kingery et al. 1976: 469–79). The rate at which solid state sintering occurs is approximately inversely proportional to the particle size involved. Sintering usually leads to a reduction in mass with pores becoming more spherical or being eliminated. In liquid phase sintering, as the name suggests, a liquid phase *is* involved because components with lower melting temperatures (such as fluxes like alkaline feldspars) melt. More of the solids melt (are 'fluxed') as sintering proceeds, and the particles are drawn together as the pores get smaller. This shrinkage increases the density of the pot. Vitrification is an extension of this process as heating continues leading to a glassy phase (Kingery et al. 1976: 490), the elimination of pores occurs and the mass increases even more.

The classic *wasters* from kiln sites are those where the pots have been heated to such high temperatures that they have become glassy (vitrified), have slumped and in so doing have lost their original shape. With fine-textured ceramics sintering and vitrification occur at the lowest temperatures – an important property when it comes to using slips.

Quartz/silica

Quartz is a mineral which contains the highest proportion of silica – the quartz sand of glass-makers. Silica is also found in flint, chert, jasper, agate and chalcedony (see Chapter 6). Sandstone, a sedimentary rock and quartzite, a metamorphic rock, both contain a high proportion of quartz. Occasionally the silica-rich skeletal remains of single-celled marine organisms, diatoms, and of sponges occur in pottery. Another form of silica which is found in pottery is organic: phytoliths are present in trees and grasses and remain in pottery once they are burnt. Quartz has been studied in particular in relation to the effect its presence has on the strength, porosity and shrinkage of pottery. A recent study of the mechanical performance of quartz-tempered ceramics (Kilikoglou et al. 1998), mainly with reference to Aegean examples, focused on energy dissipation during fracture and, refreshingly, the discussion covered some of the *contextual* and cultural considerations for the choice of raw materials. Vekinis and Kilikoglou (1998) have shown that a combination of the Hertzian point loading test and the abrasion wear resistance test on relatively small samples can provide a means of characterising earthenware ceramics which contain quartz and other inclusions. Toughness, an important characteristic of ceramics if determined by the Young's test, and hardness measurements, can both be related to the results of the Hertzian point loading test.

The presence of quartz in pottery *can* reduce firing shrinkage, but it can also reduce the strength of the pot when fired. In order to be of benefit it needs to be present as small particles, or in small amounts.

Although quartz is a mineral, and has a high melting point of 1710 °C, when heated it undergoes three kinds of changes in its atomic structure (inversions) which can effect the ceramic structure and its properties. The first occurs at 573 °C when there is a change from α- to β-quartz accompanied by a volume increase of 2%. Around this temperature the removal of a large amount of water from the clay occurs so it counterbalances any volume increase. The second change occurs at 867 °C, from β-quartz to tridymite and the third, at 1250 °C, from tridymite to cristobalite. The formation of tridymite and cristobalite occur very slowly, because major rearrangements of silica-oxygen tetrahedra occur; their formation is accelerated by the presence of fluxes. The occurrence of tridymite and cristobalite in pottery is therefore dependent on the temperature being held for long enough during the kiln firing cycle for them to form. Open firing may produce the change from α- to β-quartz, but may not even promote the formation of tridymite. Crystals which are incompletely dissolved in the glass which forms at high temperatures have a large expansion coefficient which, on cooling and contracting, may cause stresses resulting in cracks in large crystals and microcracks in the pottery. Between 200 °C and 270 °C any β cristobalite which formed at 1250 °C reverts to α cristobalite resulting in a volume contraction of 2%.

Feldspars

Feldspars occur in rocks such as granites and lavas. As mentioned above (Section 4.2.2) they are the most common minerals in the earth's crust forming 39% of rock-forming minerals. They contain a combination of silica and aluminia and the balance of their compositions leads to a corresponding range of feldspar compositional types. They are the primary parent material for clay minerals and can be present at low levels in clays due to incomplete weathering, imparting some of the properties to the clay described below. In commercial ceramic production clay, (alkaline) feldspars and quartz are mixed.

The three main categories of feldspars which form a continuum of aluminosilicate minerals are characterised by substitutions of potassium (K^+), sodium (Na^+) and calcium (Ca^{2+}) ions. The proportion of these ions in the different feldspar minerals varies, the result being that potassium oxide feldspars contain an *average* of 64.7% silica and the calcium oxide feldspars 42.8% silica (Cardew 1969: 44).

Examples of potassium feldspars are orthoclase, microcline and sanidine which have very similar chemical compositions; these are often found in intrusive rocks like granites. Plagioclase feldspars (see Section 4.2.2) can either be sodic or calcic, that is the end member of the sodic feldspar is sodium (Na) and that of the calcic feldspar is calcium (Ca). An example of a sodic feldspar is albite and of a calcic feldspar, anorthite. The continuum of aluminosilicates that these form a part of reminds us that there are plagioclase feldspars with intermediate compositions. Potassium feldspars and sodic feldspars are found in granites and other metamorphic rocks; calcic feldspars, on the other hand, are found in lavas.

The alkaline ions (Na^+ and K^+) which characterise some feldspars act as fluxes during pot firing, reducing the temperature at which sintering and melting will occur, and they form a thick viscous liquid; this is also helped by their small particle size. Potassium oxide feldspars melt at c. 1150 °C and soda feldspars at c. 1118 °C. The alkaline earth ion (Ca^+) in calcium oxide feldspars melts at the much higher temperature of c. 1550 °C (due to the relatively high aluminia levels) – though this is reduced if other feldspars are present.

Calcium

When calcium oxide or calcium occur in clays naturally, the clay is known as *calcareous* or *marly*. The calcium is present in the form of calcium carbonate ($CaCO_3$) as limestone, shell (perhaps as aragonite) and calcite. Calcium is sometimes added deliberately to clays in the form of animal bone ash. The use of bone ash was probably patented by Thomas Frye, a proprietor of the Bow, London Porcelain Factory, leading eventually to the production of bone china (Freestone 1999: 15).

When calcium carbonate is heated it decomposes into calcium oxide and carbon dioxide. The temperature at which this occurs in pottery varies according to the oxidising-reducing atmosphere, the grain size of the crystals and the heating regime, but normally it occurs between c. 700 °C and 900 °C (Velde and Druc 1999: 103). If this occurs above c. 1000 °C, as is the case in many kilns, the calcium forms part of the liquid glassy phase and it can form calcium silicate minerals like wollastonite ($CaSiO_3$) or calcium ferrosilicates. Tite and Maniatis (1975) found that the melting of calcium compounds is accelerated in a reducing atmosphere. Below 1000 °C a potential problem occurs. Calcium oxide absorbs atmospheric water (it is hygroscopic) and eventually reacts with the water to form quicklime ($Ca[OH]_2$). In so doing heat is released, the volume of the pottery increases and this causes the pot to crack and to spall; the strength of the pot is therefore reduced. This effect is particularly marked in clays which contain large lime particles – if they are fine it is less of a problem, and also if the pot is fired in a reducing atmosphere. If the calcium is present in the form of aragonite it will be transformed into calcite at temperatures between 400 and 500 °C (Deer, Howie and Zussman 1962).

4.3.11 Types of firing and the use of kilns

4.3.11.1 'Open' firing

'Open' pottery firing is also known as bonfire firing and 'clamp' firing (see Figure 4.11, 1). Although some authors regard 'open' firing to have also occurred in a pit (see Figure 4.11, 2) presumably because there was no superstructure, the definition of 'open firing' here only includes bonfire and 'clamp' firings. It has recently been pointed out (Gibson and Wood 1997: 58) that there are no ethnographic examples or reliable archaeological evidence for 'clamp' kilns. 'Firing installations' in which partially-fired vessels are buried in a pit under a mound of soil or turves and which would therefore have reached temperatures of *c.* 900 °C will not be considered further.

Open firings tend to be short lived and achieve only relatively low temperatures of *c.* 800–900 °C, with a minimum temperature of *c.* 600 °C. Cardew (1969: 11) claims that the chemical and physical structures of clays demand a minimum temperature of 550 °C in order to make serviceable pottery, but obviously this varies according to the clays used. By using a pyrometer to measure temperatures in kilns, there is still a somewhat open question as to whether the temperatures measured are those achieved by the pots or the atmosphere surrounding them (Nicklin 1981a). Open firing probably produced some of the earliest pottery – the thirteenth-millennium BC Japanese Jomon pottery (Harris 1997: 20), the tenth-millennium BC Middle Nile pottery of Egypt (Welsby 1997: 27) and the Proto-Hassuna wares of the late seventh millennium BC found in small villages in Mesopotamia (Simpson 1997a: 38).

The pottery to be fired is placed on a bed of fuel and more fuel is placed on top of it. The whole is ignited, and once the firing is over the pots are removed (see Figure 4.11, 1). Ethnographic examples show that individual firing events can include hundreds of pots, such as those assembled by potters in Gogunda, Rajasthan (Rice 1987: Figure 5.17).

However, open firing is least easy to control and must have been one reason why pottery kilns were introduced. Evidently if the level of control over the firing is deemed to be sufficient and the products are acceptable in an open firing then there are none of the problems of servicing a kiln. However, open firing is subject to the widest range of problems because it is not contained. As the fuel burns it tends to shift which, in turn, may cause the pottery to shift, raising the possibility of damage. The pottery can be marked by direct contact with the fire as well as by rapid temperature changes which can cause it to crack or to become dented. The extent to which pottery may be overfired or underfired can be related to the way in which it is stacked, and this, in turn, can be linked to an uneven supply of heat, sometimes caused by draughts. As part of the lack of control over the firing process, a lot of heat can be lost to the atmosphere through radiation and convection. In general, non-kiln firings tend to be short, the rate of heating usually not controlled and rather fast, and the time during which the maximum temperature is sustained (the soaking period) tends to be brief before cooling begins (Shepard 1976: 87, 89). One of the most striking characteristics of open firings is the very rapid initial rise in temperature to *c.* 900 °C – which is attained after about twenty minutes, usually just after the fuel which covers the firing has been consumed. After this the temperature declines rapidly to begin with to about 500–600 °C, and then more slowly. Given the variations of the conditions within an 'open' firing, different parts heat up and cool down at different rates, so these figures are generalisations. For these reasons, quite apart from the variations in gaseous atmosphere which could change the glaze colour (see Section 4.3.5), and because of possible physical damage to the outside of the pot, glazed wares are not generally fired in the 'open'.

Having said this, the technique of 'open' firing has been used successfully for millennia to fire cooking and storage pots. The thermal shock referred to above can be avoided by pre-heating the pottery. In the context of a bonfire if the fuel is heated from above then heat is transmitted downwards, although initially a lot is lost to the atmosphere. In any high-temperature process the density of the wood (if used) and therefore

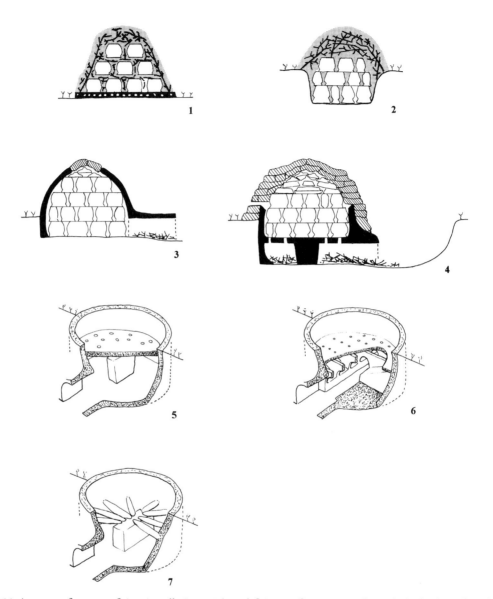

Figure 4.11 A range of pottery firing installations: 1 'open' firing; 2 firing pit; 3 through draft; 4 up-draught; 5, 6 and 7 examples of three Roman up-draught kilns (1–4 reconstructed sections); 5–7 cut-away sections showing support structures).

its calorific value has a direct effect on the amount of heat produced and the rate at which it burns; experience and experiment would eventually have led to a reduction in the number of unsuccessful firings (see Section 4.3.11.2). Shepard (1976: Figure 4) has shown that a temperature of *c.* 900 °C can be achieved using dung, coal and juniper wood as fuel.

4.3.11.2 Pottery kilns

In order to reach higher temperatures than those achieved in a pit the fuel supply was carefully controlled in the context of a carefully constructed kiln. The idea was to enclose the pottery to be fired in a chamber. As for the furnaces used in glass production (Section 3.4), pottery kilns were constructed out of bricks which could withstand the temperatures and the consequent expansion and contraction when being heated up and cooled. Kilns could also be built out of stone, as in Pereuela, Spain (Peacock 1982: 21).

There are three basic kiln types to be considered: pit kilns, updraft kilns and downdraft kilns (see Figures 4.11, 4.12 and 4.14).

Pit kilns

Pit kilns are, as the name suggests, elaborations of pit-fired installations, but they do not have the super-structure which distinguishes them from the more familiar updraft kilns (see Figure 4.11, 2). In a pit kiln the fuel is placed below and above the pottery and not clearly separated as in updraft kilns. The most prominent difference between pit kilns and firing pits is that in pit kilns (not illustrated) the firing is carried out within a pit which is enclosed by mud or brick walls on three or four sides. The effect of the enclosure walls is to allow the kiln to reach higher temperatures and for longer, than in a firing pit (Shepard 1976: Figure 4). If dug into a slope the draught can be channelled into the pit kiln. Postgate and Moon (1982: 127) report an early Dynastic (early third millennium BC) example from Abu Salabikh, Iraq, lined with bricks which was probably fired with dung cakes or straw. Postgate and Moon (1982: 109) also describe (unlined) pit kilns, each with individual flues from Abu Salabikh dating to the Uruk (fourth millennium BC) period. Because of the proximity of the fuel to the pottery, there would be a risk of disturbing the glaze so unglazed pottery is generally fired in them.

Updraft kilns

The most familiar kind of kiln is the two-chambered updraft kiln (see Figures 4.11 and 4.12). This is generally a cylindrical construction, sometimes with a domed roof, which is divided into two chambers. The lower chamber contains the fuel; the chambers are divided by a floor in which flues are constructed and through which the heat rises to fire the pottery. The pottery is carefully stacked on the floor of the kiln. The reason why they are called updraft kilns is fairly clear: the draught rises from the fuel into the upper chamber of the kiln. Fresh fuel is either fed directly into the firing chamber or through openings in the side of the kiln. Some of the earliest updraft

kilns, with circular plans, were developed in Mesopotamia *c.* 6000 BC (Simpson 1997a: Figure 2). Those found in agricultural villages such as Yarim Tepe I (Oates and Oates 1976: 42) were used to fire decorated globular jars and open bowls.

Earlier versions of the updraft kilns were not necessarily roofed over but open-topped with broken sherds providing the cover, but which, nevertheless, acted as a 'chimney'. Apart from the heat which was needed to fire the pots, the other important feature of these kilns was the gases produced by the burning fuel. Because the kilns essentially have open tops a lot of the heat is wasted because it escapes through the top. Another disadvantage is that hot spots can be created, depending on how the pots are stacked in the kiln, although this is almost inevitable in any kiln form. The vessels lying at the bottom of the load receive the greatest heat and there is a gradient of heat, falling off towards the top. When carbon-rich materials in the fuel are oxidised they can produce carbon monoxide and carbon dioxide gases; it is the balance between these gases and oxygen in the kiln which is critical in determining the colour of the (glazed or unglazed) pottery produced (see Section 4.3.5). An advantage of the 'open' topped kiln was that the pottery could be loaded from the top. The top of the kiln could have been constructed from pot

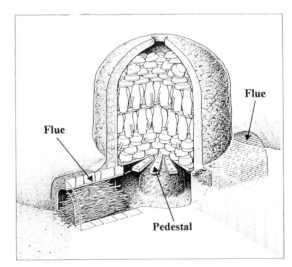

Figure 4.12 A medieval updraft kiln with two flues © The British Museum.

sherds piled on top (see above) or closed off with a temporary brick-built dome.

In loading the kiln, pottery is sometimes deliberately separated during firing by using ceramic objects called *saggers* (or *setters*). Saggers also allowed pottery to be stacked; the saggers containing the pottery sometimes fitted into each other so that a larger number could be stacked. The pots also sometimes stood on kiln plates within the saggers. For obvious reasons the saggers would have been made from a high-firing ceramic materials (see for example the scientific investigations of saggers used in the production of Chinese celadon wares in Section 4.6.5.4). It was especially important that glazed pots were separated during firing, and there are many examples (up until very recently) where one can observe the telltale use of tripods (*stilts*) which leave three small indentations on the underside of the pot; these were used to separate glazed pots (Figure 4.13).

A wide range of updraft kiln structures may well have been used (see V.E. Swan's comprehensive publication, *Pottery Kilns of Roman Britain* (Swan 1984: 34–8, Figures II and III)). Swan describes four different kinds of kilns that were used in the Britain during the Roman period (in addition to 'open'

firing): (i) a single-chambered sunken kiln with a permanent domed superstructure; (ii) a kiln built on the ground surface with open-topped temporary superstructure; (iii) a sunken kiln with a permanent open-topped superstructure; (iv) a sunken kiln with an open-topped superstructure made from a combination of temporary and permanent materials. In addition to this Swan distinguishes between nine different systems of support for the kiln floors which were either perforated floors or an arrangement of radiating bars from a central support (see Figure 4.11, 5–7). Forms of support for the floors included a free-standing pedestal, cross-walls, corbels, pilasters and an inverted pottery vessel. Another shape of updraft kiln is square in plan.

Downdraft kilns

Downdraft kilns are often elongated in plan and the fire is located at one end with the chimney at the other (see Figure 4.14). The fire may or may not be set in a separate chamber. Downdraft kilns differ in one obvious way from updraft kilns: instead of the draught being drawn immediately through the pottery stacked in the upper chamber the draught initially passes around (not through) the pottery, up the inside of the kiln wall and then downwards off the roof of the kiln onto the pots. It then passes through the kiln chamber holding the pottery and is vented through an exterior chimney. It is the chimney which draws the draught through the kiln. The effect of a downward draught is that the development of hot spots in the kiln is minimised. Perhaps the greatest development of downdraft kilns was in the Far East where downdraft kilns were built 'in series' as multi-chambered climbing kilns ('dragon' kilns), such as at Longquan, China (see Figure 4.15). Here the kiln is built on a slope with the firing chamber at the bottom and a series of kilns built next to each other, linked by openings at the bases of the walls on the uphill side. The draught heat therefore emanates from the fire box and is drawn towards a chimney at the top end passing over the pots, being deflected from the kiln rooves, and then through into the next kiln via the hole in the base of the uphill kiln. Clearly the wind direction was important, whether feeding an updraft or a downdraft kiln, so the kilns would have been constructed

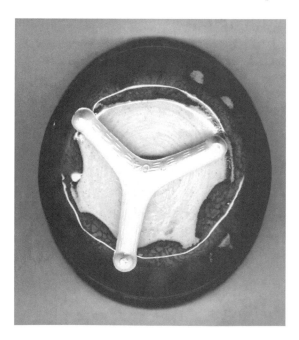

Figure 4.13 Tripod attached to the base of a glazed pot.

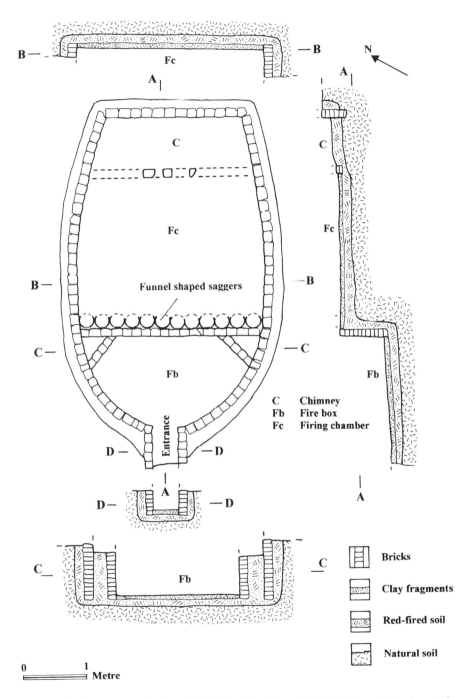

Figure 4.14 A plan of the remains of a downdraft kiln, Five Dynasties (907–60 AD), Yaozhou, China.

Figure 4.15 A Chinese dragon kiln constructed on the side of a hill, Longquan, China (photograph courtesy of Nigel Wood).

with the prevailing wind direction in mind. Pots could be inserted through external openings in the kilns and these openings could also be used to examine the pots being fired. Very large kilns of this kind can take as long as two weeks to fire (Leach 1976: 186).

The construction of pottery kilns, like glass-melting and metal-smelting furnaces, involves the manufacture of large numbers of bricks which can withstand the temperatures involved; it was therefore just as critical to select clays to make the kiln bricks and kiln saggers with the appropriate properties as it was to select clays to make the pottery. Inevitably the bricks became vitrified by the development of hot spots on the inside of the kiln, with a breakdown of the brick structure. In addition, as with other pyrotechnologies, each time the kilns are heated up the bricks expanded and each time they cooled they contracted. The kilns therefore had a finite lifespan, sometimes needing to be patched up with clay when the walls cracked and sometimes buttressed when the cracking was severe. After all, if a kiln collapsed

during a firing the time and energy which had been invested in making the pottery load would be completely lost.

Rye and Evans (1976: 167) found that during a kiln firing the atmosphere of the kiln changed from oxidising just before the addition of new fuel to reducing just after the fuel was added (see Sections 4.3.9 and 4.3.11.3). So this was something taken into account when quite specific pottery glaze colours were required (which might rely on the furnace atmosphere for full colour development), given that the kiln would need to be stoked at regular intervals during the firing. Another very important consideration was the way in which the pottery was stacked inside the kiln (see p. 138). Indeed when dealing with mass-produced wares the arrangement of pottery and saggers inside the kiln was carried out by specialists.

If pottery firings go wrong for some reason the pots may break or may be indented (Figure 4.16), or alternatively it may be impossible to identify their original form. If pottery over-heats badly the clay will begin to bloat and the pot will collapse.

Figure 4.16 Wasters from an 'Abbasid kiln, al-Raqqa, northern Syria; note the cracks and indentations.

4.3.11.3 The fuels used

The kind of fuel used is clearly important – whether it is slow- or fast-burning – and the density of one kind of fuel (hard or soft) wood, determines the amount of heat produced. Soft woods burn faster and therefore release their heat at a faster rate – an important consideration in bringing about a quick rise in temperature at the start of a firing (Rhodes 1969: 61). The fuel that can be used includes wood (branches, bark, brush, sawdust), charcoal, peat, palm fronds, reeds, bamboo, coconut husks, agricultural by-products such as straw, chaff, corncobs, cattle or sheep dung and the bones of animals and fish (Cockle 1981: 94, Moorey 1994: 144; Rice 1987: 154). The size of the fuel is also clearly important; logs burn more slowly than twigs so they are often placed below the pottery. Peat, dung, reeds and straw are most appropriate for 'open' firings and dung in particular because it burns rapidly and evenly, holding its shape as a glowing ember. Smaller fuel and dung placed on top quickly produces a layer of ash which can insulate the pottery and reduces the heat loss by convection. In Italy in the sixteenth century Cipriano Piccolpasso described the use of straw in kilns in order to produce an initial intense heat (Piccolpasso 1980).

The management of fuel resources is clearly something that is relevant to efficient pottery production, especially if it occurs on a large scale (as discussed in the context of metal production in Section 5.6.2). Writing about the Romano-British pottery industries, Swan (1984: 7) has suggested that 'areas of woodland, properly managed to grow small and medium-sized trees, would have been essential both for the fuel needs of any larger industrial establishment and for the construction of its associated buildings, such as workshops and stores'. She arrived at the same conclusion, by inference, as Figueral (1992) did when she examined scientifically the evidence of fuel consumption involved in Romano-British iron-smelting: that permanent coppicing must have been involved. In the case of pottery production this must have been true especially for large-scale production which operated over long periods, such as in the Oxfordshire region and at Colchester, for example (Swan 1984: 7). Another perceptive point made by

Swan is the possible relationship between kiln design and the type of fuel used. Some of the Romano-British kilns excavated at the Alice Holt/Farnham, New Forest, which were twin-flued kilns had letter-box shaped apertures at the junction of the flue and furnace chambers. These apertures have been interpreted as an indication of the use of fuel with a small diameter (Swan, 1984: 7), although, if this was the case, clearly only a small quantity could have been added relatively slowly at some stage of the firing cycle. There is, however, no question that kiln design and fuel availability must have been linked to both scale of production and demand.

Arguably, fuel was the most 'expensive' raw material. Wood selection and charcoal burning are both labour intensive. Depending on the scale of production, it was therefore critical to construct a kiln in which the heat was used effectively and efficiently. Although the pottery was enclosed in a kiln, the initial heating up of the kiln itself (as for any furnace structure) required a lot of heat energy – and this is one reason why it can be more efficient to use a large kiln rather than a small one, in that each time a kiln is loaded with pottery to be fired, the kiln must be cooled down – so the larger the kiln, the larger the volume of pottery loaded into it. Cardew (1969: 182) calculated that even in a large kiln 30% to 40% of heat is lost through radiation, convection and conduction. For open firings the figures get far worse – only 10% of the energy potential of the wood is used (National Academy of Sciences 1980: 28). Indeed the availability of fuel may have had a direct effect on pottery technology: Matson (1971: 74) has even suggested that a shortage of fuel in the early first millennium AD may have been responsible for the lowering of pottery firing temperatures at Seleucia.

4.4 The changing modes of Iron Age pottery production in Britain

4.4.1 The socio-economic context

The late Iron Age in western and central Europe was a time of great social and economic change. Economic centralisation and an increase in the population are reflected in changes in the strategies of production, trade, exchange and, to some extent, set-tlement, albeit with a level of continuity from the earlier Iron Age. Although it cannot be claimed that the features which characterise the system of large defended areas called *oppida* in parts of Europe are also found in Britain – with centralised populations, clearly identifiable production areas in some and occasionally a 'hierarchy' of structures – there are, nevertheless, signs that Britain increasingly came within the ambit of what was happening on the continent of Europe. Very large sites, often on valley sides, although of a wide variety of types (Bradley 1984; Cunliffe 1991: 366; Millett 1990: 23), surrounded by banks and ditches and which mainly date from after 50 BC, did exist in Britain. Within some of these, coin mints have been found (Rodwell 1976; Crummy 1980). High status burials tend *not* to be associated with these *oppida* and this gives us a clue as to the status of (some of) the sites (Millett 1990: 23). With one or possibly two exceptions, there is not the same evidence for the intensification and centralisation of a *range* of industries, as found in some European *oppida* (Collis 1984). The first exception is the site of Hengistbury Head in Dorset. Here excavations have revealed evidence for the working of iron, copper alloy, silver and shale, for salt extraction and for possible glass-working (Cunliffe 1991; 1987). By apparently being at the edge of the *oppida* system Hengistbury benefited from exchange and trade in a range of materials and products. Those which formed part of the processes of production included raw glass, shale, lead (which was cupelled to produce silver) and copper (Cunliffe 1987). Hengistbury can, however, be regarded as anomalous in a British context; no other late Iron Age site, including those labelled as *oppida*, have revealed such a *range* of industries. Indeed in Britain only the earlier Iron Age site of Meare Lake Village, Somerset, can be claimed as producing evidence for such a wide range of industries (Bulleid and Gray 1948; 1953; Gray 1966 and Coles 1987). The other possible exception is the site of Silchester, where excavations of an *oppidum* have produced evidence of coin moulds (Fulford 1987: 275) and revealed the evidence for the manufacture of copper alloy horse-riding furniture and for iron-working in contexts dating to the first half of the first century BC (Fulford, personal communication). Silchester/Calleva, enclosing 35 ha, may also turn out to provide evidence for industrial production on a scale comparable to that found in continental *oppida* (Fulford 1987). The *oppidum* of Stanwick and the associated site of the Tofts in Yorkshire have produced evidence for copper alloy working, including the production of horse-riding furniture, and other copper alloy working, but no evidence for industrial installations (Spratling 1981; Haselgrove, personal communication).

This picture of relatively dispersed (non-centralised) industrial production in late Iron Age Britain and the lack of correlation between large sites and centralised focal places in society (Haselgrove 1986) is further underlined by the evidence for the largest scale of coin production in Iron Age Europe. This has been found in Lincolnshire, at Old Sleaford (Elsdon 1997), where 3,000 coin moulds have been found, and at Dragonby (May 1996). Neither of these sites can, strictly speaking, be classified as *oppida*. In Europe it is possible to identify incipient urbanism reflected in the features of production industries in what can be described as industrial villages (Collis 1979; 1982; 1984; Pieta 1982). *Some* heavily-defended European *oppida* have produced evidence for specialised industries, sometimes on a large scale, such as at the 3 sq km site of Gradistea Muncelului, Rumania (Daicoviciu and Daicoviciu 1963) and at Manching, Bavaria (Piggott 1965: 216; Krämer and Schubert 1970; Jacobi 1974; Collis 1984; Ralston 1988). Although this pattern of industrial centralisation, with the inferred control over raw material supply that this involved, may have been true for areas like Bavaria, it was by no means the case for all of late Iron Age Europe. In central Bohemia, for example, excavations of the late Iron Age settlement of Mšec revealed nineteen iron-smelting furnaces (Pleiner 1977; 1980). These furnaces must have been producing far more iron than was needed for local consumption. Moving westwards, to Burgundy, the range of settlement sizes, including small *oppida*, that have been observed (Ralston 1988), though not proven to be contemporary, also suggests a lack of centralisation.

In Britain it has been claimed that industrial centralisation occurred in another large settlement type somewhat earlier: fortified hillforts. However, if the evidence for middle and late Iron Age industry in Britain is examined closely, it becomes apparent that a large part of it is to be found outside hillforts in much smaller settlements (Henderson 1984; Henderson 1991: 112; Morris 1994a: 384) which often specialised in single materials (Henderson 1991). A definite exception to this is the distribution of middle Iron Age pottery from hillforts in western England (Morris 1994a: 378). Where it can be shown that hillforts are contemporary with smaller industrial settlements in the same region, the supply of raw materials *may* have been controlled from these larger sites. However, at the moment this cannot be demonstrated. Hillforts were important settlements in other ways and probably acted as meeting places and grain stores, as has been suggested for the most extensively excavated hillfort at Danebury in Hampshire (Cunliffe 1995). It is, nevertheless, irrefutable at present that evidence for iron-working from hillforts, for example, is scant when compared to the massive amount of evidence which has been discovered at smaller sites which specialised in iron production such as at Gussage-all-Saints, Hampshire, Weelsby Avenue, Lincolnshire, and Bryn-y-Castell, Snowdonia. Compared to pottery, iron is less easy to characterise and it is less easy to build up distribution patterns, but the large scale of production evidence speaks for itself (see, for example, Section 5.12.2.1). It is unlikely that iron produced at relatively small settlements was solely for local use. This is in accordance with the production of exotic Iron Age materials, like glass, where the products, even in the middle Iron Age, spread well beyond production zones (Henderson 1991: 125, Figure 4) so it is likely that an excess of iron was produced for local consumption. On the other hand in the late Iron Age, especially after *c.* 50 BC, a range of pottery fabrics and forms was being produced in Britain and imported from abroad.

Given that the remains of shaft furnaces used for iron-smelting have been found in Iron Age Europe, the technology of their construction and of achieving sufficiently high temperatures, with the necessary fuel/draught supply, was clearly understood. We might therefore expect to find extensive evidence for Iron Age pottery kilns in Britain and in Europe, but up to now no such evidence has been found. This might be because the high temperatures involved in iron-smelting of *c.* 1300 °C would have led to more durable vitrified ceramics at the end of the smelt than would have resulted from firing pottery. But just because the temperatures necessary for iron-smelting were achieved, this does not by itself indicate a priori that similar developments would have occurred in pottery manufacture. A range of social/political and ritual factors may determine tight norms in the development of industries in which technological aspects of particular specialisations may *not* have been shared.

4.4.2 Ceramic production in southern Britain during the late Iron Age

One of the fascinating aspects of Iron Age society towards the end of the first millennium BC was the links which existed with the Classical Roman world. Although the 'Celts' (referred to as the Gauls by Livy)

had invaded Italy and sacked Rome in 387 BC, they also imported very fine ceramic and metal products from the Classical world. While these have been found on high status sites (especially burials) in Europe dating to the fifth and fourth centuries BC, the adoption and use of a higher proportion of Roman products *on a regular basis* did not really occur until the second century BC. It is no coincidence that this occurred at the same time as the emergence of settlements displaying a range of (different) proto-urban features in Britain and Europe and that increasingly firm trading contacts with the Roman world developed. In no way did Roman technology dominate. Iron Age industries in Europe manufactured some outstanding products, reflecting great skill and understanding of the properties of the raw materials – witness the highly complex modelling in metal of early Celtic art involving the use of the lost-wax technique (Stead 1985; Hodson 1995) the evidence for

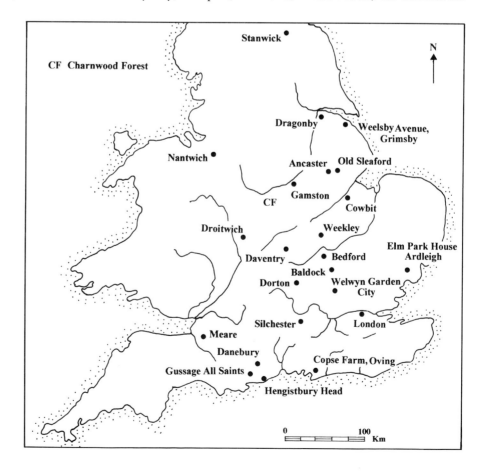

Figure 4.17 The locations of the principal Iron Age sites mentioned in the text.

which has been found at sites like Gussage-all-Saints, Dorset (Foster 1980) and Weelsby Avenue (Foster 1995) (see Figure 4.17).

However, there are clear signs that late Iron Age pottery technology experienced some significant changes from about the first century BC; though on a generally smaller scale, there is evidence that a level of non-local production can be traced back as far as the early and middle Iron Age (fifth–second centuries BC). Peacock (1968; 1969) showed relatively early on in the technological investigation of Iron Age pottery that it was possible to characterise the products of pottery made in south-western Britain because it contained exotic mineral suites which characterised the rocks found there (Peacock 1969: 52–3). The assumption has been that the petrological characterisation of pottery in eastern Britain, where there are not the same deposits of igneous rocks which could provide a characterisation, would prove to be a lot more difficult. The reason for this is that the clays and tempers which are available in eastern Britain are unlikely to be as easily characterised as those in the west because, typically, the shell-tempered wares, which are particularly common in the region, are difficult to characterise due to the occurrence of fossil shells at numerous sites along the Jurassic escarpment (Elsdon 1997: 124). In very few instances, where the nearest source of fossil shell is at some distance from a site a non-local source can be suggested. At Cowbit, Lincolnshire, for example, where the distance is 14 km, regional distribution of the pottery or the shell temper can be suggested in connection with seasonal exploitation of salt at the site (Knight 1999). Petrological analysis of a range of pottery from Lincolnshire sites was carried out (Middleton 1996) in order to examine the relationship between fabric and pottery decorated with specific techniques, which has led to the suggestion that they were specialised products (May 1996: 436; Elsdon 1997: 108). In the event, no clear link was detected. However, the use of neutron activation analysis to investigate pottery from Ancaster and Dragonby did show a distinction in the clays used; it is clear that further investigations using a technique which is capable of detecting elements at low levels may provide a means of characterising the pottery, but not necessarily help to identify analytically a clay source.

In Lincolnshire, therefore, a tacit assumption that it is impossible to characterise late Iron Age pottery using petrological and chemical analysis has been found to be only partially correct: there are promising avenues of research which confound this assumption. Work in the counties of Nottinghamshire, Derbyshire, Leicestershire and Northamptonshire has shown that initially during the middle Iron Age (fifth/fourth–second century BC) pottery was produced which was tempered with igneous inclusions which possibly derived from diorite sources in Charnwood Forest (Leicestershire), or at its fringes – as suggested by Dr John Carney of the British Geological Survey (Allen et al. 1999: 129). This is the same area that is thought to be the source for group XX stone axes (see Chapter 6), some early medieval pottery (Williams and Vince 1997; and see Section 4.5.2.2) and its study may provide evidence for 'trade' in stone querns (Knight 1992). The coarse angular inclusions are derived from medium-grained rock of granitic texture, further characterised by pink to grey feldspar, abundant grey quartz and flakes of biotite. It was first recognised at Gamston, Nottinghamshire, in quartz-gritted and grog-tempered sherds (Williams 1992; Knight 1992). This granodiorite temper was found to be similar to the outcrop close to Mountsorrel on the eastern part of Charnwood Forest. Knight (1992: 42) has suggested that the pottery or temper was transported over a distance of 35 km from Charnwood to Gamston. Other pottery tempered with granodiorite derived from Charnwood has been found in Derbyshire, Leicestershire and Northamptonshire (Knight 1999). In addition, pottery made from gabbroic clays, typical of the Lizard peninsula in Cornwall, has been found as far afield as Weekley, Northamptonshire, about 380 km distant from the source of gabbroic clays (Knight 1999) and at Crick, Daventry (A. Woodward, personal communication). The same clear distribution has not been achieved for pottery moving in the opposite direction.

4.4.2.1 Introduction of the potters wheel and its effect on local production

There is one clear sign of Roman influence on ceramic technology in the Iron Age and that is the introduction of the potters wheel (Thompson 1982;

Morris 1994a: 383; Rigby and Freestone 1997: 57). Whereas the native pottery of Iron Age Britain had been hand-made and had a variable composition including temper of vegetal matter and grog, the results of using a potters wheel are clearly visible among the more sinuous forms, such as pedestalled urns, with the characteristic series of spiral rills on their interiors (see Section 4.3.3). In parts of southern Britain during the first century BC these wheel-made pots formed a high proportion of the assemblages found at Skeleton Green (Partridge 1981), Elm Park House, Ardleigh (Thompson and Barfield 1986), Ursula Taylor Lower School, Bedford (Dawson 1988) and Baldock (Stead and Rigby 1989). The pottery had more sinuous forms compared to the local hand-made wares, clearly as a result of being produced using a wheel (Figure 4.18). Although made using a new technique, the raw materials (grog and vegetal temper) are often indistinguishable from those used to make hand-built traditional wares (ibid.). Production was still very much of a regional character, and occasionally it is possible to characterise the raw materials used to the extent that it is clear that not only 'local' raw materials (i.e. those which derived from an area

within the vicinity of the site) were used, but a proportion derived from some distance from the site.

An example of this is Hamilton's (1985) study of seven Iron Age fabrics identified from the excavations at the second–first-century BC late Iron Age farmstead of Copse Farm, Oving, West Sussex, England (Bedwin and Holgate 1985). The pottery encompassed both 'saucepan' pottery with a date span of *c.* late second–early first century BC (Hamilton 1985: 225) and the succeeding Aylesford-Swarling types, traditionally dated to between 50 BC and 43 AD (Cunliffe 1991: 132ff.) with the Copse Farm material likely to date to the late first century BC. The 'saucepan' pots were largely barrel-shaped and some had tooled horizontal lines just below the rim and above the base angle; some had more elaborate decoration. The forms of the wheel-thrown Aylesford-Swarling pots consisted of jars and bowls, often with out-turned rims and many had cordoned decoration. An example of a corrugated urn made in the Aylesford-Swarling tradition of Birchall's type II (Birchall 1965: Figure 4, no. 34) is shown in Figure 4.19. The site produced what have been identified as hand-made copies of Aylesford-Swarling types. In this context it should therefore have been possible to investigate the extent to which fabric-use related to the technique of forming – and whether raw materials used for 'the more specialised' wheel-thrown pots derived from further afield than the hand-made pottery. This presupposes (potentially falsely) that a high proportion of wheel-thrown pottery was made locally for 'local' consumption. Hamilton found that two fabrics, a wheel-thrown quartz sand-tempered fabric (fabric 3) and a hand-made flint-tempered fabric (fabric 1) represented 55% and 28% respectively of the sherds examined. The quartz sand used for wheel-thrown pottery (fabric 3) was regarded by Hamilton as so fine as to be a 'glass sand' and to have derived from up to 7 km away from the site. On the other hand the raw materials used to make hand-made 'saucepan' pots may have included clays derived from local Woolwich or Reading beds. However, it is suggested that the flint temper used in these pots may have been coastal pebbles – and these would have derived from about 10 km away. There is no question that fine sand rather than razor-sharp flint temper is more suited to wheel-throwing – the

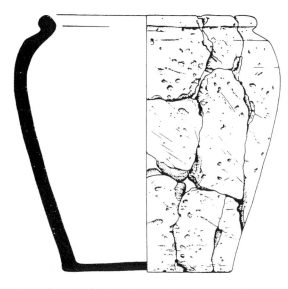

Figure 4.18 A wheel-made later Iron Age ovoid jar with a bead rim from Gamston, Nottinghamshire (after Knight 1992).

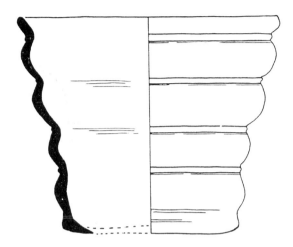

Figure 4.19 An imported corrugated urn of first century BC date made in the Aylesford-Swarling tradition from Old Sleaford, Lincolnshire of Burchall's (1965: 245) type II (after Elsdon 1998).

presence of flint would cut into the potter's hands – and in that sense the change in raw materials does, in this case, reflect a change in technology. Even though there is an absence of evidence for local pottery production, it is still possible to infer that the hand-made pot was made locally due to the petrological identification of the clays used to make pots and mineralogical links to locally-occurring clays. On the other hand the more standardised fabrics used to make the wheel-thrown pottery are more likely to have been imported to Copse Farm. This concurs with the model for a more centralised mode of production, whereby a smaller number of centres produced wheel-thrown pottery, sometimes in finer fabrics, in the late first century BC and early first century AD, anticipating the arrival of Roman production practices.

This could be described as contributing to a greater degree of production specialisation, especially if the raw materials were seen to 'improve' the appearance (as may be suggested for wheel-thrown pottery) or of its firing behaviour. Both the wheel-thrown and hand-made pottery were also clearly fired in open firings rather than in kilns. The temperatures did not reach those which were necessary to burn out the vegetal inclusions, suggesting that the firings were short and relatively reducing; no kilns

have been found during excavations of British late Iron Age sites. Had kilns been used one might suggest that the workshop mode of production was involved, rather than that of 'the household' (Peacock 1982: 8–9).

From about 25 BC a range of wares which reflects the adoption of Romanised dining customs, are found on some British Iron Age sites. In contrast to the locally-made wheel-thrown pottery, these imports include some made with fabrics which can be characterised by the presence of exotic volcanic and metamorphic rocks, suggesting a source for the pottery in central Gaul (Rigby and Freestone 1985). These imports are found in high status burials such as at Welwyn Garden City, Hertfordshire (Stead 1967) and a mirror burial at Dorton, Buckinghamshire (Farley 1983). These wares contrasted with the locally-made British wares in being of an even pink colour, sometimes having mica-dusted coatings and occasionally white slips. They were clearly mass-produced in permanent kilns using a finer fabric and were a far more standardised product. Although these finer wares were available, it is interesting that locally-made wares were still produced throughout the Roman period in Britain.

Rigby and Freestone (1985) note that the pottery forms made in the latest (pre-Roman) Iron Age are typologically and technically identical to those found in the Belgic assemblages of northern France. It is only by using scientific analysis that they can be distinguished. This very close similarity seems to suggest something that is rare to be able to pinpoint in an archaeological context: that the British products were first made by immigrants or itinerant Gallic potters who used locally-occurring raw materials.

4.4.3 Salt briquetage production and distribution

In total contrast to the manufacture of pottery made on the wheel, rather coarse hand-made ceramic containers were produced specifically for drying and transporting salt. One of the better-known sources for salt, which continued to be exploited from prehistory into the medieval and later periods, is in Cheshire at sites like Droitwich (Hurst 1997) and Nantwich. Another recent publication of the site excavations in Droitwich (Woodiwiss 1992) reports the discovery of coarse ceramic containers, simple hearths with bars and pedestals, water channels and plank-lined pits used for storage. The evidence published here is both Iron Age and Roman in date and relates to the extraction of salt from saline springs in Droitwich. Some of the evidence that has been found for salt production, at sites like Brean Down, can now be dated to the late Bronze Age, and the known number of Iron Age sites that were involved in salt production is growing all the time. During a survey of the south-western fen edge in an area of approximately 20 sq km, 192 saltings were found, mainly in south-western Lincolnshire (Lane 1992: 218). The dates of these saltings ranged from late Bronze Age (with a carbon-14 date of 810–415 cal. BC at the 95% confidence limit) at Billingborough, to (middle) Iron Age, Roman and medieval. The sites are normally identified by the presence of fired clay fragments and dated by associated pottery, where present. Salt extraction from saline water was normally carried out at low energy inland parts of tidal creeks (saltwater marsh) close to the freshwater fen which could provide peat or wood for fuel. During this extensive survey various roughly-made baked clay artefacts associated with salt extraction were found. Bars, supports and vessels (mainly 'non-circular') constituted the principal types (Lane 1992: 221–6). It is suggested that the crudity of the clay indicates that the equipment was produced on site. Some of the clays used to make this briquetage had undergone preparation with the addition of chopped vegetation, including cereal waste from threshing in some cases; such additions have been found also in Hampshire briquetage (Bradley 1975: 23). Further south, on the coast of Essex, by 1990, 315 individual 'red hill' (saltings) sites had been discovered, mainly of late Iron Age and Roman date (Fawn et al. 1990). Excavations in the Red Hills produced evidence of settling tanks (to allow the water to clear), and hearths (some of which had become vitrified).

The actual reconstruction of the processes of evaporation and crystallisation of saline water, while simple processes physically, is relatively difficult using the available archaeological evidence of hearths and briquetage. Clearly the saltwater was heated in pans in order to drive off the water. However, it is likely that evaporation would have occurred as a continuous process, with the tank being topped up with saline water before the salt crystals were completely dry. The reason for this is the presence of what medieval producers called 'bittern', the dissolved matter which produced a bitter taste in the salt: if all the water was driven from the saline solution the bittern would be mixed in with the salt crystals. It is likely therefore that the salt crystals were scooped out as they formed. The crystals would have been transferred for drying and moulding into cakes. However at the Essex Red Hills sites no suitable candidates for drying hearths have been found, though fragments of suitably low-fired vessels have been.

Studies of salt production in Wessex (Bradley 1975; 1992; Morris 1994b) have provided a model for changes in the intensity and scale of the industry over time. The production of salt on the south coast of Wessex in the earliest known phase during the early–middle Iron Age was seasonal and on a small scale. During the late Iron Age several salt-producing sites appeared on previously uninhabited shores, a reflection of a more intense, larger scale of production for a wider network of consumers. Production was probably part-time, even in the late Iron Age, and it only really 'came of age' in the Roman period. The ceramic moulds and other equipment used in the Iron Age salt-producing industry were coarse and presumably produced when the need arose. In the Roman period however permanent inland brine springs, which were already concentrated salt solutions, were exploited and metal cauldrons were used for heating the salt solution (Bradley 1992).

Salt production was a relatively widespread activity but we are still not quite certain about why salt was being produced; nonetheless, one suggestion, that salt was used for drying meat which could then be stored (Cunliffe 1991: 466) must be correct. Because the fabric of the containers which salt was transported in is coarse, it becomes possible to characterise the fabric using thin-section petrology. Morris (1985) in the examination of briquetage from Droitwich and the central Cheshire plain, has found that the inclusions it contains are often sufficiently characteristic to be able to relate it to a production site, or area of production, and that as a result it is possible to build up distribution zones for the material. The briquetage produced in Droitwich, in the vicinity of the saline springs there, was made in two fabrics: one characterised by sandy marl and the other by sandy marl with organic inclusions (ibid.: 346). The briquetage (known as very coarse pottery, VCP) produced on the Cheshire plain was characteristically also of two (different) fabrics. One has a sandy clay matrix containing angular crushed hard rock fragments (the most common being igneous devitrified porphyritic rhyolite and rhyolitic tuff). The other most common type was a fabric characterised by the presence of a microgranite/granophyre rich in alkaline feldspar and poor in plagioclase. Although Nantwich and Middlewich, Cheshire are possible production centres for this ware because the volcanics and granites occur there, there is, at present, no absolute proof for its production at these places.

Bradley (1975) has shown that salt containers made on the coast of the Hampshire-Sussex borderland were distributed up to 60 km from the source, and there is evidence for the distribution of briquetage from inland sites over greater distances. The salt containers which originated at Droitwich, Hereford and Worcestershire, for example, have been found up to 85 km away from a source (Figure 4.20). The pattern produced is referred to as a 'restricted' spatial distribution, though it is far from being highly localised. Briquetage made in the Cheshire plain, in the Nantwich area, has been found up to 140 km away (see Figure 4.21). There is also now evidence for the distribution of briquetage from Cheshire further away still, as far as Nottingham in the East Midlands (Knight 1999). Although these distribution patterns provide powerful evidence for a sphere of interaction, the *period* over which these interactions occurred is very important to the archaeologist because society changed during the middle/late Iron Age, and interactions as reflected by briquetage distribution during different phases of the Iron Age would clearly be articulating with potentially different social structures. Thus, the distribution of VCP during the early Iron Age extends up to 47 km from mid-Cheshire, whereas during the late Iron Age it is distributed as far as Nottingham (Knight 1999a). This is clearly a reflection of the ways in which exchange and trade in such materials operated in a more open system over longer distances in the late Iron Age than in the earlier Iron Age. Morris's work on salt containers from this source in mid-Cheshire (see Figure 4.22 for material of later Iron Age date) shows that the distribution pattern for the later Iron Age is similar to that found in a down-the-line exchange system (Renfrew 1975). By plotting raw numbers of characterised briquetage fragments against distance from source, one is extracting that particular ceramic from a wider technological context. In order to, in effect, normalise the occurrence of salt briquetage to the occurrence of pottery Morris (1994a: 385–6) uses what she refers to as the 'Salt index'. This is a calculation of the ratio of salt container fragments to pottery fragments by weight from a site by phase; this accounts for a variety of archaeological factors such as the amount of deposition activity on the site (see Figures 4.23, a–c).

Whereas clearly the study of the distribution of Iron Age salt briquetage and its occurrence in relation to the deposition of pottery on archaeological sites is instructive on one level, a further consideration is the extent to which briquetage distributions coincide with other dated Iron Age materials and what this tells us about social groupings. Different materials, such as pottery, coins and glass, will have had different social meaning and socio-economic values. In western Britain Morris's (1981: 70) petrological study of very coarse pottery shows a distribution which coincides with chemically characterised glass made at Meare Lake Village in Somerset (Henderson 1991: 125, Figure 4), falling as it does within a 'tribal' zone attributed to the Dobunni, based on the distributions of Dobunnian coins (Sellwood 1984: Figures 13.1, 13.2). The fact that these three distribution patterns for three very different materials, very coarse pottery, glass and coins, coincide ought to tell us a range of things.

The first point to make is that the range of factors which determines distribution patterns may be wide indeed. Plog (1977: 129), for example, suggests that the range of movement of commodities, the amount exchanged, the time span involved, the direction and intensity of flow, the degree of centralisation of the distribution and the overall complexity of the system are important variables. Although these variables certainly will have played important roles in

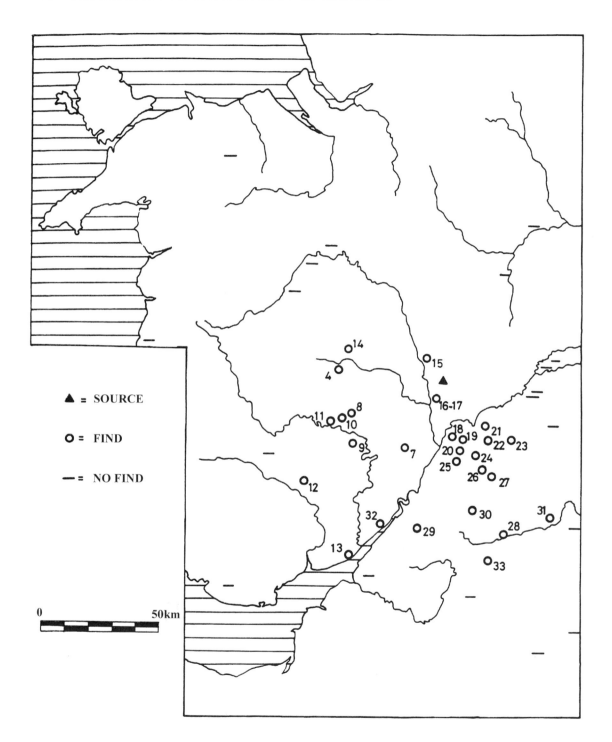

Figure 4.20 Distribution map of later Iron Age Droitwich salt containers and the location of the source (after Morris 1985).

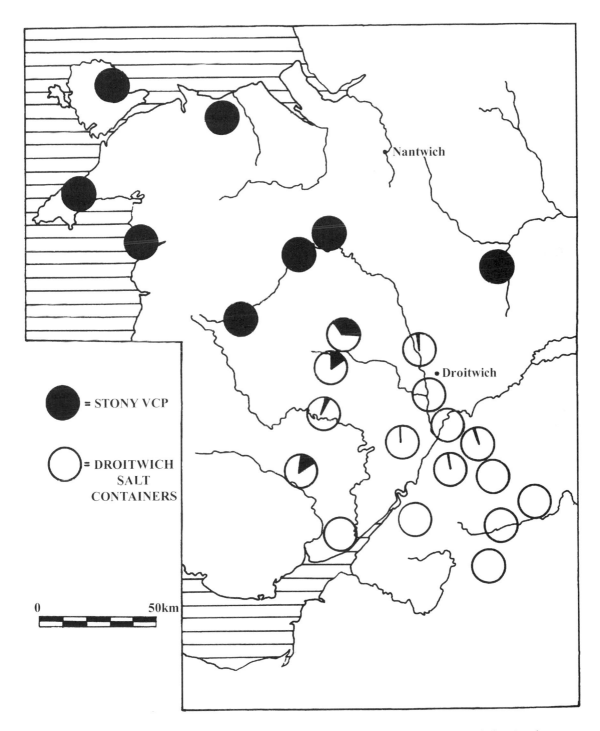

Figure 4.21 The distribution of Droitwich salt containers and stony VCP (very coarse pottery) showing, by means of pie diagrams the relative proportions and the location of the source of the salt containers at Droitwich (after Morris 1985).

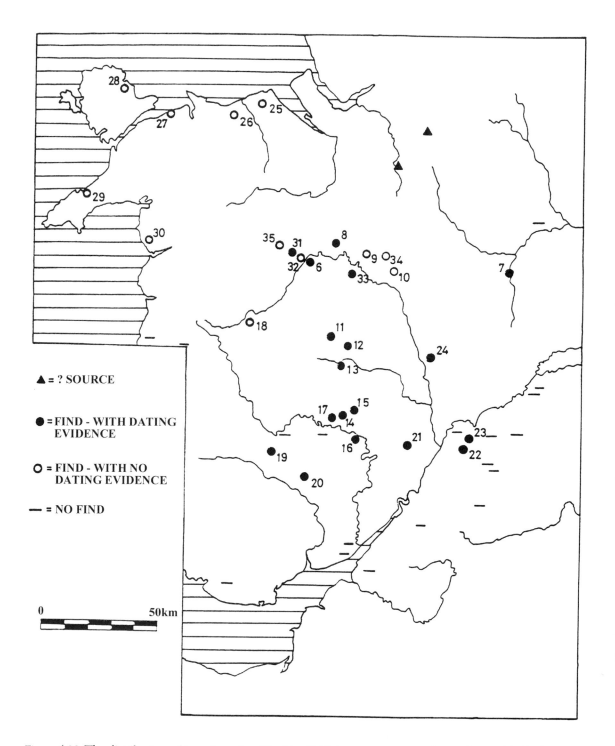

Figure 4.22 The distribution of later Iron Age Cheshire VCP (very coarse pottery) containers with the location of possible sources (after Morris 1985).

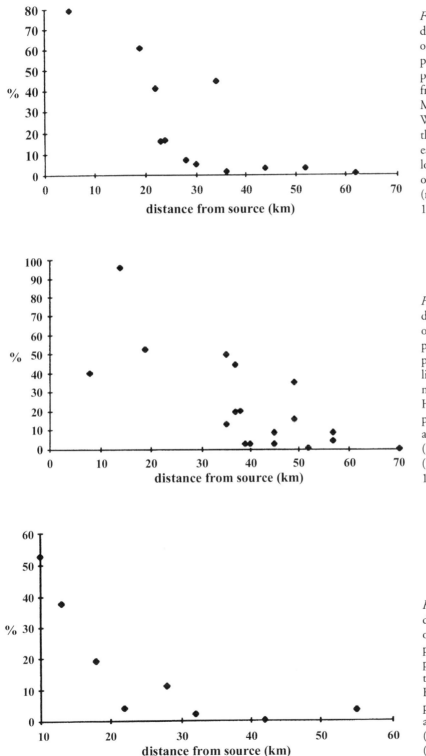

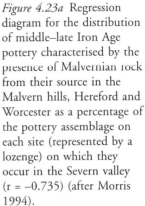

Figure 4.23a Regression diagram for the distribution of middle–late Iron Age pottery characterised by the presence of Malvernian rock from their source in the Malvern hills, Hereford and Worcester as a percentage of the pottery assemblage on each site (represented by a lozenge) on which they occur in the Severn valley (r = −0.735) (after Morris 1994).

Figure 4.23b Regression diagram for the distribution of middle–late Iron Age pottery characterised by the presence of Paleozoic limestone from their source near the Woolhope Hills in Hereford and Worcester as a percentage of the pottery assemblage on each site (represented by a lozenge) (r = −0.723) (after Morris 1994).

Figure 4.23c Regression diagram for the distribution of middle–late Iron Age pottery characterised by the presence of dolerite from their source at the Clee Hills, Shropshire as a percentage of the pottery assemblage on each site (represented by a lozenge) (after Morris 1994).

determining the distribution patterns which we plot for materials, several of these factors, such as 'the amount exchanged' and the 'intensity of the flow' may sometimes be impossible or very difficult to determine archaeologically (given that we can never be sure that we are dealing with a representative proportion of the amount in circulation or associated with the event which led to the formation of the archaeological deposit yielding the pottery). It is nevertheless well worth examining the data available to see whether these factors can be determined, even if only partially. One of these factors – the intensity of flow – may lead, if it varies over time, to distribution patterns with fluctuating fringes through time according to the intensity of contact, exchange and distribution; the precision of dating techniques available to archaeologists may prevent the detection of these fluctuations, so that what we normally observe is the summed (partial) results of human interaction.

The second point to make is that Iron Age coin distributions are of late Iron Age date because they were first produced in the late Iron Age; the distributions of pottery and glass are of middle Iron Age dates. This provides us with evidence that in this region a putative Dobunnian tribal territory existed some 200 to 150 years before the coins were minted (Henderson 1991: 125). Thirdly, *if* we regard very coarse Iron Age pottery as having a relatively low value (although its social value may have been potentially high if the salt they contained was used for meat storage), it is perhaps surprising to find an exotic material such as glass falls within the same zone, the materials being distributed from different sources. This would appear to underline how tightly bounded the territory was and, on this occasion, the distribution of very coarse pottery hints at the likelihood that intensity of distribution/contact was quite high. Finally it is worth pointing out that whereas the study of the distribution of petrologically characterised Iron Age pottery contributes in an important way, it is only by comparing its distribution with that of other materials that a more integrated impression of production and distribution can be gained.

4.4.4 Conclusions

In late Iron Age Britain there are a number of factors which contributed to the change in pottery produc-

tion and which affected the level of specialisation: the availability of raw materials; the use of open firing rather than a permanent kiln; the effect on parts of Britain of the important social and economic changes on the continent of Europe both before and after various areas had been conquered by the Romans in the first century BC; the adoption of Roman drinking vessels – and presumably their dining customs; and local conservatism among both potters and those who used the pots.

The study of other pottery production in the British middle and late Iron Ages has shown that the production of distinctive pottery types became more centralised than during the early Iron Age with pottery being distributed some distance from the production sites. Also there are distinctive regional developments, for example in the west Midlands (Elsdon 1992), with petrological studies successfully revealing complex production and exchange systems in the west country (Peacock 1968; 1969) and the Severn Valley basin (Morris 1981; 1982; 1983; 1991). The result of the comprehensive study of middle–late Iron Age pottery production and distribution by Morris and other workers has provided the evidence for down-the-line exchange systems for traded wares. Figures 4.23a–c show regression analyses for the percentage of traded wares for each site considered characterised by petrology against the distance from the geological source area to sites in different areas. This provides clear evidence for down-the-line exchange, which is apparently independent of the size or form of the site on which it was used. The chemical investigation of the pottery which constitutes the important Iron Age style zones of southern England (Cunliffe 1991) would provide an additional layer of interpretation relating to Arnold's (1985) resource exploitation territories.

4.5 The production and distribution of early medieval pottery in Britain

4.5.1 Introduction

Between *c.* 410 and 650 the Anglo-Saxons occupied England. They were skilled metalworkers, but they did not continue to make the rather high quality pottery produced by their Roman predecessors. Their hand-made pottery can therefore be described as less technically sophisticated. Most pottery of this date has been found in large cemeteries, with a lesser contribution from settlements. The overwhelming majority of complete vessels come from cremation cemeteries, such as Spong Hill in eastern England, with a smaller number surviving where inhumation burial was practised. When ceramics from burials are examined, rather than those associated with settlements, it is very much a case of studying the 'way of death' rather than the way of life and this should be taken into account in any interpretation.

The hand-made early Anglo-Saxon pottery technology involved fabrics which were probably fired at relatively low temperatures, *c.* 500 °C, or slightly higher, in bonfires (Brisbane 1981: 234). The estimate of this firing temperature was based on the fact that their structurally-bound water had not been lost – for this particular kind of clay (Rice 1987: 103). Most have a black 'reduced core' – although this may also be due to the presence of organic materials which were increasingly used in the sixth and seventh centuries (Hamerow 1993: Chapter 3). Pottery was either decorated manually or was stamped (Myres 1969; Briscoe 1981). Aside from the pottery itself, the evidence for the manufacture of early Anglo-Saxon pottery is sparse. Two examples serve to reflect the level of evidence. One piece of evidence is a probable firing area found near Pakenham in Suffolk,

where two circular hearths lined with gravel were found. They contained partly baked sherds which had a similar character to clay deposits found within 100 m of the site (Haith 1997: 150). Pot dies, a pottery trial piece and a 'clay reserve' were found at West Stow in Suffolk (West 1985). However no remains of kilns have been found there. The implication from this evidence, at least, seems to be that the scale was that of a household industry (Peacock 1982), though there is evidence that this is not necessarily strictly true. There is inferential evidence for more than just a 'household' level of industry: the distribution of pots which have a characteristic stamped decoration on them, produced with deer antler, has led to the suggestion that they are the products of the 'Illington-Lackford workshop' (Campbell 1982: 36). The distribution of these pots, which occur on ten sites, is in East Anglia and Cambridgeshire. However there is no direct industrial evidence for their manufacture and a study of their fabrics indicates that a variety of clays were used in their manufacture (Welch 1992: 110). This has led to the suggestion that production was indeed on a household scale, perhaps with daughters taking the stamp with them when they moved to a new settlement when they married. Vince's (1989: 165) view that 'the low technological level of early Saxon pottery manufacture and its minor role in society has led to a minimal view of its mode of production'

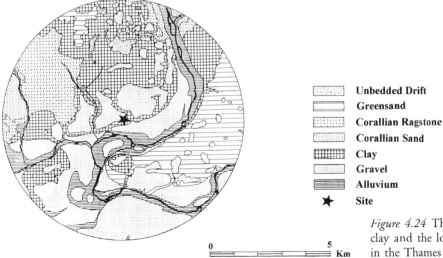

	Unbedded Drift
	Greensand
	Corallian Ragstone
	Corallian Sand
	Clay
	Gravel
	Alluvium
★	Site

0   5
                        Km

Figure 4.24 The distribution of Gault clay and the location of Barrow Hills in the Thames valley, Oxfordshire.

bears investigation in relation to his large-scale petrological research into pottery production in the Thames valley and especially in view of the common use of cremation urns in cremation cemeteries. By the role of pottery in 'society' one is referring to pottery used in both functional and ritual contexts.

4.5.2 The study of Anglo-Saxon and later pottery production in the Thames valley

The geological characteristics of the Thames valley *might* suggest that a petrological study would not be a promising approach: sedimentary rocks and clays which outcrop in some areas are covered elsewhere mainly by river-lain sand and gravel with mixed rock inclusions from well beyond the Thames valley (Figure 4.24). However, the combination of careful excavation with petrological analysis of large numbers of samples has produced some intriguing results, especially since the study contributes to the interpretation of the growth of proto-urban and urban centres.

The raw materials for pottery production in the Thames valley included Jurassic Oxford and Kimmeridge clays and Tertiary London clays. These clays contain a very low quartz content and therefore needed to be tempered in order to fire them effectively; this was even more critical when a clay with a high organic component was used which led to an 'open' fired texture. 'Self-tempered' Cretaceous Gault clays also occur. These contain quartz, muscovite and iron-rich compounds such as hematite and glauconite (Vince 1989: 164). The Gault clays are located at the base and top of the London clay and the Reading beds at the base of the Tertiary deposits. The clay from the Reading beds were used in the high medieval period, but they have a high maturing temperature (the maturing temperature is the maximum hardness and minimum porosity of a particular ware or composition). Thus the potters used either 'self-tempered' clays or added temper to clays themselves; the distinction between added temper and natural inclusions can sometimes be difficult to identify using petrology. One kind of temper that can be identified with certainty, however, is chaff, and its presence has been used as evidence for the manufacture of pottery in agricultural communities using locally available raw materials. Research into Anglo-Saxon pottery found in the excavation of settlements has tended to focus on questions relating to domestic pottery production. The small number of decorated pots which have characteristic forms and stamps may be considered to be specialist products, though some plain pots have very regular shapes and some decorated pots have very irregular shapes and are poorly made. In addition fabric differences indicate that some variations in raw materials were involved even for 'similar' pots; this could suggest that they were *not* made in one specialised workshop.

4.5.2.1 Early Saxon pottery (fifth–seventh centuries)

Barrow Hills

Vince (1989) has carried out an intensive petrological study of early Anglo-Saxon pottery from the site of Barrow Hills, Radley to the north-west of Abingdon, Oxfordshire (see Figure 4.24). More than forty Anglo-Saxon buildings have been found dating to between the fifth and seventh centuries. During the excavations more than 10,000 sherds of pottery were found. Vince studied 3,000 of these sherds petrologically using a binocular microscope and each fabric type was studied more intensively using a petrological microscope. The potential raw materials used, including the gravel terrace on which the settlement was built, and local Kimmeridge clay, were also examined petrologically.

The terrace gravel was found to be typical of that found in the Oxford region, containing abundant rounded fragments of oolitic, fossiliferous and fine-grained limestones, a moderate number of fossil shell fragments, sparse red iron compounds and rounded quartz. Lenses of finer forms of silica (sand) are present. It might therefore be anticipated, given that gravel may be heterogeneous, that it would be inappropriate for use as pot temper, though separation of the finer gravel would have been possible and the sands could have been used. There are, however, minor variations in the composition of the terrace gravels depending on its location: those at the foot of the chalk south of Radley contain a noticeable proportion of flint and those in north Wiltshire apparently contain no shell or iron compounds (Vince 1989: 167). These features therefore offered an interesting potential for characterising some of the Barrow Hills pottery. Vince found that the most common fabrics were those tempered with inclusions typical of the Cretaceous Greensands containing quartz grains and some with a glauconitic, micaceous, silty clay matrix typical of Gault clay (see Figure 4.25). These outcrop especially to the east of the site. Other fabrics are typical of gravel deposits in Warwickshire or north Oxfordshire: crushed calcite characterised one fabric, abundant phosphate fragments another.

Vince found that the Barrow Hills pottery fabrics did contain gravel terrace temper and that the types of inclusion varied, some with elevated levels of quartz and some with sparse to moderate levels of flint. Although impossible to state where the gravel temper derived from precisely, the important inference is that the gravel temper (and therefore the pottery) was *non-local*, the assumption being that the temper did not travel and that the pottery was made where the temper occurred. The pottery industry at Barrow Hills was not purely a domestic craft using locally-occurring raw materials; the pottery was clearly made in a supra-local zone, some distance beyond the current parish boundaries of Radley. The question of *where* precisely this range of pottery fabrics used at Barrow Hills was made is still an open one because the outcrops that were used are widespread, although it would appear that several places were involved.

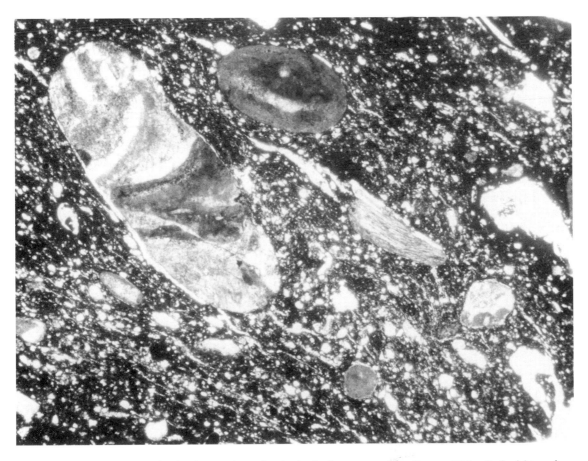

Figure 4.25 Photomicrograph of a thin-section of early Anglo-Saxon ware from Barrow Hills, Oxfordshire, characterised by limestone, iron ore and quartz inclusions (photographed at × 40).

The vessels are likely to have travelled over both short and long distances to reach the site. The majority travelled over distances of more than 10 km and some for up to 40–50 km to reach Barrow Hills. Trade, market exchange and other mechanisms can be suggested as possible explanations for the distribution patterns of early Anglo-Saxon pottery around Barrow Hills. Carrying this further Vince (1989: 168) has argued that since the settlement was reliant on non-local supplies of pottery it is likely that it relied on non-local sources for other materials; a surplus would have been produced for trade. The research, which has benefited (by a process of elimination) from the use of identifiably non-local temper to make pottery, has therefore provided a model for pottery production in other areas of the early Anglo-Saxon world.

Midlands pottery

A comprehensive consideration of granitic-tempered pottery by Williams and Vince (1997) using a combination of thin-section petrology and ICPS has also now shown that early to middle Saxon wares with a particular distinctive granitic inclusion are widely distributed. The most likely source of the inclusions in much of the pottery is an area focused on the Mountsorrel granodiorite outcrop in Leicestershire (Allen et al. 1999: 129) with a possible limit at the sand deposits in the Coventry and Warwick areas. This basically coincides with the pre-Cambrian rocks of the Charnwood Forest area; Mountsorrel is located east of Charnwood Forest. (There is also the possibility that the parent rock may have been moved by glacial action.) It is of interest to note that such inclusions were also used in Iron Age pottery from Nottinghamshire and Derbyshire (Williams 1992) showing how long the source of a pottery raw material can be used for (see Section 4.4.2 above). A petrological thin-section of the pottery revealed 'a clay matrix which is dominated by large discrete grains of plagioclase feldspar, quartz, potash feldspar, biotite, mica and with occasional small pieces of granitic rock composed of quartz, feldspar (predominantly plagioclase but with some orthoclase) and brown biotite'. Occasional grains of other minerals were also present (Williams and Vince 1997: 218).

Williams and Vince found that the 'Charnwood Forest' wares were distributed widely in the Midlands with granitic inclusions coming from a 'single' source. This therefore provides another example to add to the results of the Barrow Hills study which shows that (some) early Saxon pottery was definitely not produced within a 'domestic' local mode of production since it is widely distributed and not simply made for local consumption. Indeed 'Charnwood ware' was used both in domestic and religious contexts; Williams and Vince suggest that the pottery may have been exchanged and distributed on the occasion of religious festivals.

4.5.2.2 Other studies of early–middle Saxon 'plain' wares

Russel (1985: 130) had difficulty classifying Anglo-Saxon plain pottery from West Stow using petrological analysis, finding that identified 'groupings' of fabric types tended to be somewhat subjective and that statistical analysis (Clustan) did not help. At Mucking the thin-section programme also experienced difficulties in that in some cases sherds which had been assigned separate petrological types were found to join, again suggesting that the process of assigning petrological groupings was somewhat subjective (Hamerow 1993: 27). Blinkhorn (1997: 118), however, has noted that a broad distinction can be made between chaff-tempered ware and fabrics characterised by containing mineral temper (mica and haematite) as well as 'chalk/limestone' and sandstone. By plotting their occurrence at Mucking he found that the greatest amounts of chaff-tempered wares occurred in the northern area of the site. His interpretation of the distributions of decorated wares is that they are partly a reflection of a retention of cultural identity of the Germanic settlers in England; many of the styles of pottery decoration are similar to those found in their continental homelands (Myres 1977). Blinkhorn (1997) notes that 'although the decoration developed along a divergent path over the next hundred years or so, the pottery remains within the Germanic tradition, presumably indicating a strong retention of cultural identity'.

In his study of 7,000 sherds of early/middle Saxon wares from Raunds, Northamptonshire, Blinkhorn identified three broad fabric classes (bringing together ten fabric types) based on the treatment of sand, grit or organic temper, added. The distribution of these fabric classes revealed that the sand-tempered wares were more common on the part of the North Raunds site where there was a focus of middle Saxon activity; the inference being that although both quartz- and sand-tempered wares were used in the early Saxon period when the site was founded, by the middle Saxon period the less time-consuming use of sand, which did not need crushing, was adopted. This appeared to be a sensible functional interpretation.

Thirty kilometres away the Saxon site of Penny-land, Milton Keynes (Blinkhorn 1993) produced pottery fabrics which were very similar due to the use of similar geological raw materials. However, in spite of the use of both sand- and grit-tempered wares in the early Saxon period, the opposite situation to that found at Raunds was discovered to have occurred with the use of the grit-tempered wares rising from 51% of the plain pottery assemblage in the early occupation phase, to 72% by the latest occupation phase. This evidence therefore clearly contradicts the functional interpretation of pottery-use at Raunds. Blinkhorn's interpretation of this pattern of production and use is a combination of a continuing use of continental traditional practices and that the differing tempering techniques were used by people of differing cultural origins who continued to used the accepted procedures established in their homelands. He even feels that the distributions of pottery produced using a variety of temper is a reflection of 'the rise and fall of the populations of the various cultural groups within the settlement'.

Blinkhorn's discussion of the petrological analysis of Anglo-Saxon pottery therefore provides us with an intriguing level of interpretation, indicating that a close scrutiny of the distribution of petrologically characterised 'plain' wares can generate more than purely a functional interpretation, and indeed, taking residuality in the archaeological record into account, the functional interpretation in this case appears not to make sense. At the very least this approach reminds us that there are cases where functionality *must* have played an important part in the selection of ceramic raw materials, but that in some cases what

was perceived as the cultural norm may have played a more important role in determining the raw materials and other procedures used. It would be very interesting to investigate the use of temper in Anglo-Saxon pottery in the region which includes Pennyland and Milton Keynes, and how any patterns that would be discerned, could link with those established. Clearly there must also have been situations where the cultural norm and functional considerations were one and the same thing.

4.5.3 Mid-Saxon pottery (seventh–ninth centuries) in the Thames valley

London

Most Thames valley settlements including Barrow Hills and Mucking were abandoned in the seventh century. Since mid-Saxon rural settlements in the Thames valley are scarce, Vince turned to an important gravel terrace urban site, London, to investigate pottery production (see Figure 4.26). Unlike the area around Barrow Hills the gravel terraces of the Thames in the London area are capped in places with brick earth, and under the gravel is fine-textured London clay. This sequence would have been visible to potters looking for raw materials in the sides of river and stream valleys. Blue clays were also forming under anaerobic conditions at the time.

As in the early Saxon period, chaff-tempered wares were manufactured and commonly used during the mid-Saxon period along with Ipswich-type ware found throughout East Anglia and other wares such as northern and southern Maxey-type wares in Lincolnshire, Northamptonshire and Cambridge-shire. Imported wares came from the Rhineland, northern France and Belgium. Using petrological analysis Vince (1989: 169) found that the chaff-tempered wares contained quartz, muscovite and iron compounds, but these minerals, individually or in combination, are not sufficiently distinctive to be able to characterise the wares to a source. On the other hand the wares containing temper of rounded quartz with polished surfaces are similar to the temper used in Barrow Hills wares; the London quartz temper differs from the Barrow Hills quartz temper because it is covered with a layer of red iron ochre which extends into the cracks of the quartz grains and

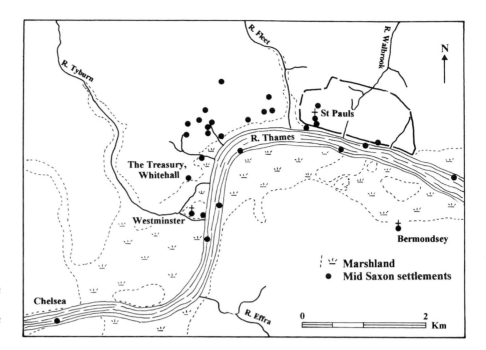

Figure 4.26
Location of middle
Saxon sites in the
London area of the
Thames valley.

remains visible even if the grain is polished. Cretaceous Greensand is likely to be one possible source for this quartz temper in the London wares because the Greensand is cemented with iron to form an ironstone. Another is where the Woburn sand outcrops in Buckinghamshire and south Bedfordshire.

The hinges of shells which survive in pottery can provide an interesting means of identifying the species of the shell (Cooper 1982) if thin-sectioned. A small group of London mid-Saxon wares contain bivalve mollusc shell fragments which would be characteristic of the littoral zone (see Figure 4.27). These can be further characterised by the presence of opaque streaks running parallel to the surface of the shell caused by iron pyrite crystals secreted by the mollusc. It might be suggested that this characteristic when found in pottery could be used to link the production of the pottery to a quite specific source of clay containing such shells. However, pottery containing fragments of such shells not only occurs in London, but also in Beverley (east Yorkshire), York and Waltham Abbey (Essex), as well as at Dorestad (Holland) and Flanders. Such a wide distribution suggests otherwise. Research by Hamerow, Hollevoet and Vince (1994) has shown that a typical seventh-

century fabric (chaff-tempered ware), with a highest occurrence in England south of the Thames is also found in substantial quantities in Flanders. It is considered most likely that this pottery was copied in Flanders as a parallel technological development (ibid.: 16); on this occasion it has been found that thin-section petrology has not proved to be sufficiently sensitive to establish whether indeed the pottery from Flanders was made there or in southern England.

A single pottery sherd which is characterised by the presence of biotite and igneous rock fragments (together with limestone) suggests a source in the east Midlands where the Charnwood Forest granite and Croft syenite outcrop – the gravels surrounding the area – have these characteristic inclusions.

Unlike the study of Barrow Hills pottery the use of petrology in the investigation of the production and distribution of mid-Saxon pottery is therefore rather mixed; at least for Barrow Hills wares it was possible to contribute in a substantive way to new models of pottery production and distribution. One reason is that the London gravels and brickearths are less easy to characterise than those on which Barrow Hills was located. In spite of this, it has been possible

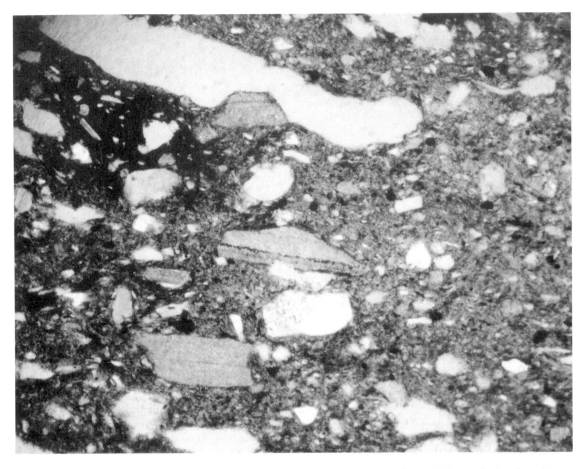

Figure 4.27 Photomicrograph of a thin-section of middle Saxon Shelly ware from Jubilee Hall, London characterised by abundant shell fragments (photographed at × 40).

to state that some 'fineware' pottery was probably obtained from the continent and that coarsewares were obtained from as far afield as the east Midlands – though at this stage the relative numbers of samples are rather limited. Vince notes (1989: 171) that the distances over which pottery travelled are comparable to those found in the late Roman and high medieval periods and that because the appearance of mid-Saxon pottery is somewhat unsophisticated, there has been a preconception that its supply occurred over relatively short distances. The suggestion is (ibid.) that the pottery distribution is symptomatic of an integrated economy in which rural goods were traded for imported goods (of which the continental pottery is an indication). This evidence concurs with the

mid-eighth-century coin distribution from the London mint and with surviving documentary evidence. Although clearly in such circumstances there may be strong indications that there is evidence for an integrated economy using coins, if an entirely different level of evidence, such as the production and distribution of pottery agrees with it, the level of interpretation becomes an increasingly more powerful one.

Looking again beyond the shores of England, the Saxon 'Charnwood Forest' pottery described by Williams and Vince (1997) has been found to have a very similar fabric and surface treatment to that used in Scandinavia and the Baltic coastlands between the fifth and the ninth centuries. Thin-section petrology was unable to distinguish between the wares found in the two areas, so ICPS was used as an investigative tool instead. Analyses of seventh- to tenth-century pottery samples of this granitic-tempered ware showed that sherds found in Poland could be distinguished from some found in the Malaren valley in Sweden and from Catholme, Derbyshire; results from the Birka, Sweden, material, however, are less easy to interpret. In the main it seems that the Baltic and English granitic wares could be distinguished. However, no information is provided about what elements cause the clustering of ICPS data, and how it might, or might not, be relatable to characteristics observable in thin-section.

4.5.4 Late Saxon and early medieval pottery (ninth to eleventh centuries) and early towns

London

The discovery of coin hoards and Scandinavian artefacts in the ninth century are a testament to the fact that London was raided a number of times by the Vikings. The Saxons built timber fortresses at a number of locations along the Thames valley to protect themselves: at Oxford, Wallingford, on an island near Cookham called Sashes, Southwark and London. These places were towns which controlled trade and from the mid-tenth century they had their own mints, which later provided *danegeld*. By the time the Domesday Book was written, about 10% of the population lived in towns and was engaged in trade or providing services to other members of the urban population. The economy of the mid-eleventh century provided the foundations for the high medieval period.

To what extent is this clear development towards a fully integrated medieval economy reflected in the production and distribution of late Saxon and early medieval pottery in the Thames valley? The pottery which characterised the mid-Saxon period was replaced by another (different) kind of *shelly* ware: a fabric which contains fossil shell fragments. The ware is widely distributed along the Thames valley and northwards as far as the west Midlands; in spite of having the same appearance and petrology in a range of areas it is known variously as Stafford-type ware,

Cheddar E ware, Lincoln ware, Oxford B ware and late Saxon Shelly (LSS) ware. Vince examined forty-five thin-sections of pottery which derived from London and five samples from Oxford. All were characterised by the occurrence of fragments of an oyster-like shell of the species *gryphaea* which is characteristic of the Oxford clay (Vince 1989: 173). The presence of a single species of shell may be due to its robustness following partial weathering, or because marginal habitats are prone to have a more restricted species range, but as yet the exact clay source(s) has not been located, so neither hypothesis can be proven. The occurrence in LSS of shell fragments of a 'recent' freshwater species and sparse rounded quartz pebbles several millimetres across suggests that deposition in a recent alluvium has occurred.

Although widely distributed, there are problems dating LSS. For example, Oxford B came into use in the late eighth century to early ninth century, though neither carbon-14 dating and especially not thermoluminescence are able to provide sufficiently accurate dates to better other kinds of (archaeological-stratigraphic) dating. The pottery probably ceased being used in the eleventh century when Oxford was sacked: dendrochronological dates for the London waterfront, a far more precise dating technique, when available, has shown that LSS formed more than half the assemblage in use *c.* 1040 but had gone out of use *c.* 1055. With a wider range of pottery fabrics, and in spite of some problems of generating the necessary decade-by-decade dating framework, it would have been possible to suggest how the production of pottery and the mechanisms for its distribution changed through this important period for the Thames valley. However, at present this is not the case. As the dating framework becomes tighter it will become possible to at least sample LSS from well-dated contexts, which may lead to the recognition of subtle variations in its production technology and use over time. Since LSS is found on all site types – the centres of Domesday *vills*, towns and minor settlements – the identification of closely-dated technological variations and the changing distribution patterns that can be assembled using these identifications, are potentially very important archaeologically in providing evidence for spheres of interaction using pottery distributions.

In contrast to the late Saxon 'monopoly' of wares, during the course of the eleventh century a range of other wares replaced LSS in the Thames valley. At this time the ware types begin to show greater concentrations around towns like Oxford and London rather than the same ware being distributed along the Thames valley; continental imports start to reappear. Vince has also studied petrologically these early medieval coarsewares. He was able to show that in two wares the potters used the same temper as in the early Saxon period: Oxford AC contains limestone gravel 'which matches precisely the limestone gravels of Barrow Hills and elsewhere around Oxford' (Vince 1989: 174). The pottery used in London known at the time as early Surrey coarseware was characterised by Vince (ibid.) as containing iron-coated quartz and

iron-rich cement fragments of Greensand origin. The balance of mid- to late-eleventh-century coarsewares used in London have variable temper containing mainly well-sorted quartz sand, some with mainly fossil shells from the Woolwich beds, and some a mixture of the two. The same forms and fabrics are also found in north-east Kent; it is no coincidence that the distribution of a fabric with these characteristics coincides with a suitable parent rock.

Another coarseware is characterised by calcareous blue-green algae, originally mistakenly identified as chalk and mistakenly labelled 'early medieval chalky ware'. The fossiliferous algae were accompanied by polished rounded quartz grains, angular chert and flint sitting in a micaceous, silty clay matrix (see Figure 4.28). The presence of algae suggests strongly

Figure 4.28 Photomicrograph of a thin-section of London early medieval 'chalky' ware characterised by inclusions of blue-green algae (× 40).

that the clay was recently deposited; the presence of freshwater pea mussels supports this. The distribution of these fabrics is mainly to the north-west of London in St Alban's, Aylesbury and Cublington, so the suggestion is that the source of clay lies in that area – the most likely parent clay being Gault (Vince 1989: 175).

4.5.5 Conclusions

The use of ceramic petrology alone to examine early medieval pottery in the Thames valley has provided results which contribute to the discussion of how local and regional economies developed during the second half of the first millennium AD. Although examination of the fabrics which derived from the area of Barrow Hills in the Thames valley did not provide a suite of exotic minerals which might unambiguously provide a clay source, by examining very large numbers of sherds it has become possible to show that they were probably non-local in origin. Although a survey of the distribution of gravel deposits revealed where they might have been 'dropped' by glacial action, a consideration of possible re-deposition by river action has not apparently been considered. Nevertheless, taking into account that a proportion of the gravels would *not* have been affected by river action, this is an important result. A further qualification is that although grain size and angularity of inclusions have been taken into account, the relative proportions of different materials used in the pots were not described. This is far from being a severe criticism, since the overall results are perfectly valid, but it would be interesting to examine thin-sections of the pottery with this in mind.

This research demonstrates that the tacit assumption of the 'household' production mode for pottery, made within the settlement for consumption there, is now no longer tenable for all of the pottery of the early Saxon period. This conclusion has been supported further by analytical research of early medieval pottery in the west Midlands based on a different means of characterising the pottery, the occurrence of 'exotic' inclusions. Indeed, by examining other wares in the Thames valley from mid-Saxon, late Saxon and early medieval periods it is clear that not only the sources of clays changed through time, but that a proportion of the wares were imported from a zone outside 10 km in all the periods considered. It is also interesting to note that the same temper was used in early Saxon coarsewares found at Barrow Hills, Oxfordshire, as in early medieval coarsewares (Oxford AC) found in Oxford, and in this case this observation could be a result of the gravel having been moved by river action. Clearly, as the population increased, and the fully-fledged market economy of the high medieval period came into existence, pottery tended to be exchanged or traded over longer distances; wares made in England *may* have been exported to Flanders in the seventh century, though this is difficult to prove (Hamerow et al. 1994). Vince's study has shown several things: first, how important it can be to examine large numbers of samples, when they are available; second, how important it is to frame the research questions so that it has the greatest potential for contributing to mainstream archaeology; and third, the value of using several different (technical and archaeological) approaches in the investigation of the same problem.

4.6 The manufacture of celadons

4.6.1 Oriental ceramic bodies: proto-porcelains, porcelains and stonewares, including celadons

The production of Yaozhou celadons will be described here in detail because comprehensive archaeological research has revealed one of the most complete series of ninth- to eleventh-century workshops and kilns ever found in the ancient world. To be able to relate the excavated workshops to the kilns they almost certainly supplied with unfired pots is unique. In addition, few researchers have compared the technologies of the ceramic materials used to make kiln materials, such as saggers, with the pottery itself. The scientific research which has been carried out has gone some way in helping to define the degree of industrial specialisation and refinement. In this instance, both had clearly attained a high level. However, before these fascinating archaeological and scientific investigations are presented, the technological context onto which celadons fit will be described.

Celadons are known in the west by that name because of their green glaze; their bodies are made of stoneware. Before discussing in detail the excavated evidence for celadon production and its scientific investigation, it is useful to consider where celadon 'sits' in the developments which occurred in Oriental high-fired ceramics. Amongst oriental ceramic products one can include low-fired pottery, glazed and vitrified pottery (stonepaste wares) produced at higher temperatures, and translucent porcelain produced at still higher temperatures of *c.* 1280–1400 °C. What is known as Chinese protoporcelain was first manufactured during the Shang Dynasty – seventeenth–eleventh centuries BC (Chen Tiemei et al. 1999: 1003) using 'porcelain stone' (petuntze, china stone), a sericitised or kaolinised feldspathic rock containing kaolinite, muscovite, illite and quartz which can apparently be fired directly into porcelain (Guo Yangi 1987), although work by Yap and Younan Hua (1995) suggests otherwise; one such production centre may have been Wucheng in south-east China (Chen Tiemei et al. 1999). However, it is still not clear if Shang porcelain was ancestral to eastern Han Dynasty porcelain (221–25 BC) (Medley 1986). According to Li Jianzhi (1986: 129–33) the first true white porcelains were being manufactured *c.* 575 AD at the Gongxian site in Henan province at temperatures of around 1350 °C.

True porcelain is made from high-firing refractory kaolin clays ('china clays') mixed with a (partially decomposed) feldspathic rock and quartz. The alkali feldspar melts and fuses to the quartz and also vitrifies the aluminium-rich clay (acting as a flux), so these ceramics, in the same way as Islamic 'fritware' and Iznik (see Section 4.7.8) rely for their strength, in part, on having vitrified bodies. The northern Chinese kaolin deposits which were used to make Ding ware porcelain bodies are sedimentary and lack the alkali fluxes which promote vitrification (Guo Yangi 1987) and there is not the same translucency which is associated with the formation of glass in the bodies. The southern Jingdezhen products used kaolin which occurred in association with rocks composed of quartz, mica (sericite) and feldspar (albite – a soda-lime type). The presence of feldspar-rich rocks provided the flux which led to the glassy

phase which produced the translucency seen in the famous Jingdezhen porcelains dating from as early as the Five Dynasties period (907–60 AD). The characteristic white colour of true Chinese porcelain can partly be attributed to the purification of the clay used: in the eighteenth century the potters of the famous production centre of Jingdezhen in Jiangzi province used kaolin from sixty miles away which was washed, crushed and re-washed several times. It was then strained through a horse hair sieve and through a bag made out of a double thickness of silk (Staehelin 1965: 22–6).

Stonewares generally fire above 1150 °C and are characterised by having an opaque glassy body. As a result of the vitrification that occurs in the body at these temperatures their bodies have a high density and a low porosity. They are noted for their strength and are generally made from clays which are low in fluxes (like alkalis, iron and calcium) and high in aluminia. Because low levels of flux are present in the clays used, the wares fire at high temperatures, and mullite crystals (an aluminium silicate) form which provide the strength. Celadons are examples of stonewares.

The composition of southern Chinese celadon bodies are characterised by containing relatively high quartz and relatively low aluminia levels when compared to Ding and other northern Chinese white-wares (Pollard and Hatcher 1994). The Yue bodies contain iron oxide which causes them to turn a grey colour when fired and the maturing temperature of southern Chinese celadons is relatively low in comparison with northern wares. There appears to have been a relatively simple recipe for making the bodies using a pulverised altered igneous rock called porcelain stone. This stone consists of clay and fine-grained mica (sericite) – a hydrous silicate of potassium and aluminium (see above). The potassium, although at relatively low levels in Yue ware bodies, for example, acts as a flux and, in addition to the clay, provides the necessary plasticity to form the pot. It is suggested that the lower levels of flux in northern Ding (porcelain) whitewares is due to the use of kaolins. The presence of the flux promotes vitrification of the bodies which gives them a translucent quality.

Scientific and archaeological investigations of the earliest celadons in Korea of the Koryo dynasty

(918–1392 AD) have provided evidence that, while the appearance of the pottery itself was clearly inspired by Chinese Yue technology in the late tenth century (Vandiver et al. 1989: 375; Koh Choo et al. 1999: 54), the technology was locally developed (Vandiver et al. 1989: 348, 365; Koh Choo et al. 1999). The kilns were made of mud and rocks: this unusual combination of raw materials was revealed by chemical and mineralogical analysis. There is primary archaeological evidence for the development from the use of bricks as found in Chinese kilns to the use of kilns made from mud and rocks at Sŏri in Korea. Here a 40 m long brick kiln has been found stratified beneath several mud and rock kilns. Microstructural and chemical analysis of Korean celadons suggest that they were probably fired at relatively low temperatures (1050–1150 °C) and cooled rapidly. There is, however, evidence for a two-step firing method producing a biscuit-fired body for Koreo celadons and this technique clearly distinguishes Koreo from Chinese production methods (Koh Choo et al. 1999: 64). The Korean (Koreo) ceramics were fired in hill-climbing dragon-type kilns (see Figure 4.15) of about 1 m wide and 7–17 m long (Soontaek Choi-Bae 1984) and were smaller than the southern Chinese type. The earlier types consisted of a fire box which was located at the base with stoke holes at one side; exhaust gases and smoke escaped from the top. The hot exhaust and flue air rises to fire the pottery. Later Korean dragon kilns were constructed with separate firing chambers.

4.6.2 Green glazed wares and the development of glaze colour in celadons

The Chinese were involved in making green glazed ware for a span of some 3,500 years from the middle of the Shang Dynasty (c. 1500–1050 BC). Given the generic term 'green glaze' there are subtle differences in the colours which need to be explained. Apart from the iron present which clearly contributes in a significant way to the greenware glaze colour (a range of 0.65–1.36% in Guan wares) another potential colorant is manganese oxide, but this generally occurs at low levels, of less that 0.1%. As mentioned in Section 4.3.5.2 an iron-green colour in glass and glazes can usually be attributed to ionic forms of iron,

and normally to the presence of the reduced form, ferrous iron (Fe^{2+}) (Portal 1997: 103). However, not only is it likely that, in fact, the iron is normally present as a mixture of two valances, ferrous and ferric (Fe^{3+}), with a higher proportion of ferrous ions in some celadons, but the chemical environment in which it sits needs to be considered (see Section 4.3.5.2). For instance the total level of alkali in the glaze has an important effect because the higher the proportion of potassium oxide as opposed to soda, the greater the amount of light absorption occuring and hence the darker the hue.

In fact consideration of the atomic structure in silicate glazes reveals just how complex the coloration of transition metal ions, like those of iron, can be. When a transition metal assumes an ionic state, the ligand (the ions surrounding the colorant) depends on both the field strength and negative charge (i.e. provided by the oxygen). In transition metals, one of the energy shells (in this case the 3d sub-shell) is only partly filled with electrons and it is this which produces some of the colouring characteristics. When co-ordinated with other ions, such as Si^{4+} and Al^{3+} in celadons, the energy levels of the d electrons in transition metals are split (distorted) by the electric field produced by the co-ordinating ions. This splitting is sensitive to the arrangement of surrounding ions (the chemical environment); the result determines the glass colour. The theory of these effects is called the 'ligand field' theory. When higher energy level orbits in the iron ions are unoccupied, the electrons in lower energy level orbits absorb different wavelengths of light quanta in order to move up to the higher energy level quanta. It is this last energy transition that causes the glaze to appear green: the negative charge is bigger on the Fe^{3+} ligand than on Fe^{2+} and Fe^{3+} and this changes the quantum light resulting in a big absorption in the ultraviolet area.

Naturally other potential colorants make an important contribution. Glazes made at Longquan and Yaozhou have a yellowish brown colour, probably due to the formation of an iron-sulphur chromophore in the glaze (Scheurs and Brill 1984), which would occur under reducing conditions. In celadons made at Yue, translucency is augmented by the precipitation of white anorthite crystals at the glaze–body interface which screens the underlying grey body; sometimes anorthite crystals are precipitated in the glaze itself in areas which are rich in aluminium and potassium oxides (Vandiver et al. 1989: 358; Li Wenchao et al. 1992). The sub-micron sized particles add to the glaze brilliance by bending and scattering the light. In addition, because of intentional poor mixing of coarsely ground raw materials used in Guan and Longquan green glazes, residual raw materials which formed the original batch are frozen in place due to the incomplete fusion. Adding further to the scattering of light from beneath the glaze surface, wollastonite crystals were precipitated in calcium oxide-rich areas of the glazes during cooling in Longqaun celadon glazes of the Song Dynasty (Vandiver and Kingery 1984: 615).

Any crazing which may have resulted from a poor glaze fit in Yue and Guan ceramic glazes may also produce an internal reflection of light which results in a 'shimmering' effect. As described in Section 4.3.5, crazing of glaze, in which a series of cracks appear, results from a mismatch in the contraction of body and glaze as they cool together after being fired. Although glaze is characterised by a certain tensile strength, when crazing occurs it is exceeded. The relatively high lime composition of Chinese celadon glazes means that they contract faster than the bodies of the pots. Below 960 °C the glaze behaves like a brittle solid because it ceases to flow or relax. As with any glassy material if, during the period when the glaze is becoming increasingly viscous, the cooling rate is reduced, the amount of crackling may be reduced.

The relatively low-firing Yue glazes tend to be well mixed, finely ground and homogeneous; Guan and Longquan glazes tend to be heterogeneous. The more highly fired northern Yaozhou glazes tend to be homogeneous.

Although Chinese celadon glazes clearly have visual features in common, there are differences in the glaze technologies used in the southern and northern traditions. Among the southern wares (Guan, Yue and Longquan), for instance, Guan glazes have major components of relatively low silica with high aluminia and calcium oxide (with respective mean values of 61.54%, 16.56% and 13.96%). Their alkali (soda and potassium oxide) component is low, with respective mean values of 0.19% and 3.35% (Vandiver et

Table 4.1 The principal Chinese dynasties referred to in the text

Southern dynasties of China	
Tang	618–907 (north and south)
Five Dynasties	907–960
Song Dynasty	
Northern Song	960–1126 (north and south)
Southern Song	1127–1279 (south China)
Jin	1115–1234 (northern China)
Yuan	1279–1368 (north and south)

al. 1989: Table III, including samples from Tang, Five Dynasties and Song; see Table 4.1). Of the three southern celadon glazes the Yue wares, in general, contain the highest calcium oxide levels irrespective of date, with the levels of Guan approaching those of Yue; some Longquan celadon glazes on the other hand approach the low levels of calcium oxide found in northern celadons, which tend to contain more magnesia and titania. Yap and Younan Hua (1995) performed a Principle Components analysis on nine greenware glazes – Yue, Longquan, southern Song, Guan, Ru, Linru, Jun, Yaozhou and Ge. In this statistical analysis they included the relative oxide levels of silicon, aluminium, iron, calcium, magnesia, potassium and sodium in the glazes. They discovered that the northern (Ru, Yaozhou, Jun and Linru) clustered separately but close together and that most of the southern glazes could be distinguished from the northern glazes inferring, not entirely unexpectedly, that different raw materials were used in the two regions to make glazes. They were unable to separate some of the southern products using this form of statistical analysis.

Chinese celadon glazes tend to be relatively resistant to weathering, although Yue and Guan glazes contain relatively low silica and high levels of calcium oxide (c. 60% silica and 18–24% calcium oxide) and tend to weather to an iron-stained brown colour; any craze lines allowing the water to penetrate.

Re-firing of millimetre-sized pieces of celadon glazes makes it possible to estimate the temperatures at which they were fired, mainly from their behaviour and appearance. Some of these determinations are for kiln wasters, which, in general, tend to be over-fired. Re-firing of southern Chinese Guan and Yue ware glazes between 1000 °C and 1100 °C shows that they rounded at this temperature, with a probable firing temperature of around 1100 °C; this produces the desired translucent effect in the glaze. Above *c.* 1200 °C the translucency of the glaze is lost because the bubbles in the glaze become larger. These relatively low firing temperatures, a slightly lower total flux and inclusions of unmelted raw materials all limit the degree to which the Guan celadon glazes flow. However, Longquan ware celadon glaze appears to have had slightly higher optimal firing temperatures of between 1100 °C and 1200 °C. Still higher temperatures were used to fire northern Chinese Yaozhou, Ding and Jun celadon wares – optimal temperatures of between 1150 °C and 1250 °C were used; Guo and Li (1986: 157) state that 1300 °C was used. On the other hand, Yue wares tended to be fired at 1100 °C, have pinholes and few large bubbles, indicating that they had a low viscosity.

4.6.3 The archaeological evidence for celadon production at Yaozhou

At the kiln complex of Yaozhou in Hungbao township at Tongchuan ('Bronze valley') in Shaanxi Province northern China (see Figure 4.29), some quite exceptional evidence for the production of celadon has been found. During the early and middle Tang Dynasty this complex supplied the nearby capital of China, Changan, at a time when its population exceeded one million. Not only has a series of kilns been unearthed at Yaozhou, but the excavators have discovered the workshops which were associated with the kilns, together with evidence for the processing of clay, emplacements for the wheel and evidence of producing moulded decoration. This high level of evidence is very rare indeed in a world context.

Although the evidence for pottery production at Yaozhou stretches back to Neolithic times, the most comprehensive evidence starts in the late Tang Dynasty (618–907 AD), continued in the Five Dynasties (907–960) and flourished in the years of Xining (1068–1077) in the Northern Song Dynasty and continued in the Jin (1115–1234) and Yuan (1279–1368) dynasties. The celadon made there was hard and eggshell-thin with elegant decoration under the characteristic olive green glaze colour.

Tang Dynasty (618–907 AD)

Since the evidence for pottery production is unusually comprehensive, it is worth considering here the chronological development of the evidence, which starts with the production of Tang Dynasty glazed wares. It is suggested that these *mantou* kilns were used for firing lead-glazed porcelain, but there is no apparent evidence that this is definitely the case. Wood (1999: 110–11) notes that in north China 'proto-celadons' were produced and that these were not of a particularly notable quality; the developmental focus was more on developing the technology of whitewares, blackwares and lead-glazed *sancai* wares (lead-glazed earthenwares). The kiln and workshop evidence is discussed here because it is clearly antecedent to a discussion of the evidence for celadon production.

Four areas were excavated at Yaozhou, two most extensively: area I measuring approximately 81 × 28 m and area II approximately 42 × 22 m. A series of pottery workshops and kilns were discovered in both areas. In one workshop – cave dwelling 3 in area II – a remarkable range of evidence was discovered: the shaft hole for a potters wheel towards the southern end of a workshop and at the northern end a deposit of lion figurines and bowls near a deposit of 'clay paste'; about 2 m east of the clay deposit was a pottery jar with a groove running away from it, both presumably were used in the preparation of clay (Institute of Archaeology 1992: 16). The workshop in cave dwelling 5 in area II contained lumps of clay, another potters wheel shaft hole, more clay paste, a sagger and a deposit of unfired lamps. In cave dwelling 6, area II, evidence for the manufacture of specific pot forms was found: a deposit of spouts for handled ewers, as well as a deposit of ewers themselves. In a further workshop (Z12, area I), an area of trampled clay was discovered adjacent to pits full of clay and pottery vats, which presumably contained water. In yet another workshop (Z20, area I) a tub about 2 m long set into the floor has been interpreted as a levigation vessel, although it might be regarded as rather small for this purpose (Institute of Archaeology 1992: 32).

The kilns that were discovered are claimed to have been used for the production of lead-glazed wares, because of their proximity to the workshops in which

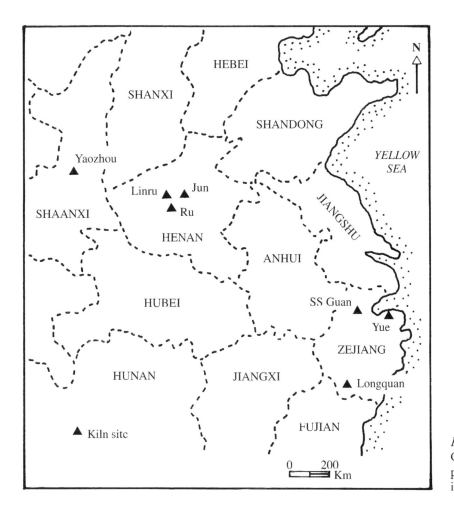

Figure 4.29 Map of Chinese provinces, and principal sites mentioned in the text.

such pottery was (probably) produced. One kiln (Y10 in area II) measured *c.* 3 m × 1.5 m. It consisted of a fire box at the south-west end next to a firing chamber about 50 cm higher, and, at the north-eastern end, a chimney. Two other kilns were of the same type. Kiln Y12 (in area II), though not well preserved, is smaller, about 2 m long, consisting of a double chamber with a chimney at one end, the fire box presumably missing (Institute of Archaeology 1992: 40). Although there is no direct evidence for it, perhaps this smaller furnace was used for fritting the glaze components. One of the best preserved kilns (Y28, area IV) was of a similar form to Y10 and a square shape measuring about 4.5 m × 5.5 m. A series of pillars, found to be still *in situ* in the firing chamber, would have supported pots; the back wall

of the kiln was especially well preserved providing evidence for the way in which gases and smoke was drawn out of the kiln. A pair of vents on both sides of the wall fed into the bases of the chimneys (Institute of Archaeology 1992: 41); the internal length of the largest chimney was 1.5 m so the draw on the gases must have been significant. The kiln must have been an updraft type in which the hot air and gases emanating from the fire reverberated off the roof of the kiln down onto the pottery (which was presumably located on pillars), the entire structure being of a square shape and possibly encased in a layer of clay to retain the heat within. Depending on how the pots were stacked within the kiln, the roof may have been relatively low. Having passed over the pots being fired, the gases would have been drawn down to the bottom of the back wall, through the vents and up the chimneys.

It is clear that evidence for almost all the different processes of pottery production have been found, possible levigation, trampled clay, the balls of clay which have presumably been physically prepared, the potters wheel, unfired pots, saggers for firing the pots in and the kilns with pedestals. No evidence for kiln bars was mentioned and the primary evidence for the manufacture of lead glazes appears to be lacking. The kiln form, with the fire box at one end of the firing chamber at a lower level, rather than underneath it, may be linked to a kiln tradition which included climbing (dragon) kilns with the fire box at one end.

The Five Dynasties (907–60 AD)

Seven areas belonging to the Five Dynasties were excavated at Yaozhou, two of which produced most evidence: area IV measuring about 343×383 m and area VI measuring about 466×57 m (Institute of Archaeology 1997: 6).

As for the Tang kilns, the workshops belonging to this period also display an interesting range of evidence for the production of pottery, in this case celadons. In workshop Z20 in area IV the position for potters wheels, a vat in which water would have been stored, and deposits of (unspecified) clay paste were found. It is claimed that in workshop Z66, area IV an area was discovered where the clay was kneaded and a 'washing' tub was found – perhaps for the potters themselves. In Z17 a 'precipitation' (i.e. levigation) tub was found.

Five Dynasties kilns have much in common with the Tang examples described above, with a fire box lower than the firing chamber at one end and two square chimneys at the opposite end. As with the Tang kilns, different features are preserved to different extents. Kiln Y15 in area IV measures about 5 m $\times 4.5$ m, is an enclosed horseshoe shape and is therefore of a similar size to (some) Tang kilns. This kiln, together with kiln Y29 in area VI, had a blocked entrance to the fire box. This might either indicate that the kiln was sealed during its last firing, to starve it of air, or that this was the (normal) way of producing a reducing atmosphere. Excavation of a boat-shaped kiln (Y31, area VI) revealed a line

of twelve funnel-shaped saggers still *in situ* at the front of the firing chamber just behind the wall at the back of the fire box (Figure 4.14). This kiln also had remains of what *might* be the base of vents which would have transmitted the gases upwards towards the roof of the kiln. The area just behind the fire box was evidently sufficiently hot to fire pots in the saggers. A corridor-shaped entrance to the fire box (a stoke hole), would have contained the heat effectively. The arrangement of vents into the what was probably a single chimney in kiln Y43, area VI, was apparently far more complex than the other kilns: five vents along the base of the wall with other smaller square vents higher up, including seven in a second register, and although poorly preserved, more in a third register about 1.2 m above the kiln floor (see Figure 4.30). One affect of this arrangement of flues would be to draw the gases over the pots at a variety of levels, the highest being at 1.2 m. One possible inference is that the pots may have been stacked somewhat higher than in kilns with vents into the chimneys at lower levels.

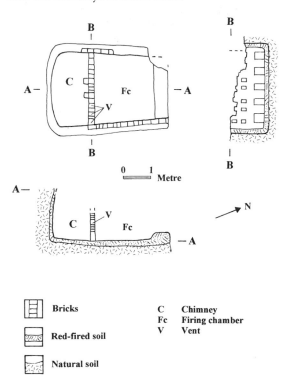

Figure 4.30 Kiln Y43 a Five Dynasties kiln at Yaozhou.

Clearly it cannot be assumed that the Tang Dynasty production technology for lead-glazed wares was the same as for northern Song celadon, although, if lead-glazed wares were being produced, the kiln designs are basically the same. Considering the very much lower maturation temperatures needed for Tang Dynasty lead glazes this might be considered surprising. There is, however, a likely explanation: that the pottery bodies themselves were fired at high temperatures, the glaze applied by dipping the pot, and the glazed pot fired at lower temperatures in saggers in the same kilns – perhaps using fuel which burnt at lower temperatures.

The northern Song Dynasty
(960–1127 AD)

Six areas were excavated: area II of 82 × 20 m, area III approximately 90 × 14 m, area IV, approximately 70 × 66 m, and area VI, a series of four slip trenches with a minimum width of 2.5 m wide × 60 m long (Institute of Archaeology 1998). The evidence for the production of northern Song celadon is on a massive scale, including workshops where glaze was probably applied to the pottery, and kilns with more complex designs and/or better preservation than those which date to the Shang Dynasty or Five Dynasties. There is so much excavated evidence that only a proportion will be discussed here, where it serves to illustrate differences and builds on the evidence described above.

At various points around the inside of the workshop walls were post holes, presumably for supporting a wooden roof. Workshops Z1–1 and Z1–2 in area I were constructed next to kiln Y1. Although the kiln is basically of the same type as ascribed to Tang pottery production the two workshops have new and fascinating pieces of evidence for celadon production. Workshop Z1–1 contained three large 'glaze vats', the largest measuring 85 cm across which was set into the floor (see Figure 4.31). Adjacent to the vats was a 'heatable brick bed' with a stoke hole beneath it. Without being sure about the identity (chemical composition) of the glaze, it is difficult to suggest what function precisely the 'glaze vats' had. If there was no way of heating the glaze, it must have been removed in raw chunks for subsequent re-use. It is difficult to know what the

'heatable brick bed' was used for. The long-section of the 'heatable brick bed' is not drawn to scale (Institute of Archaeology 1998: 18). In Workshop Z1–2 the balance of equipment that was necessary to produce celadon was discovered (Figure 4.32): a tub which was considered to have been used for kneading the clay, a potters wheel pit, with a deep narrow hole into the ground which would have been used for holding the 'spindle' of the wheel in place, a stone mortar for grinding raw materials, with a water vat next to it. The turntable itself was found at the north-western end of the workshop, on a stone platform next to a deposit of saggers (Institute of Archaeology 1998: 20). A similar heatable brick bed to that in Z1–1 was found in workshop Z11 and a large one measuring 1.4 × 1.9 m in workshop Z22. Another long narrow workshop measuring 7.5 × 1.5 m (workshop Z37) contained the evidence for a similarly wide range of production activities: a deposit of 'body paste', a tub for kneading the clay, two pits for potters wheels, and a pottery vat, presumably to contain the water needed by the potters in building pots on the wheels. At the north-eastern end of the workshop was a brick and stone platform. A pit containing fine sand was found in workshop Z42 (Institute of Archaeology 1998: 42).

Yet another workshop (Z45) contained the elusive evidence for the production of saggers, the vessels which protect (especially) glazed pottery from variations and excesses of kiln conditions. Unfired saggers were found near both a kneading tub and a potters wheel. The scientific investigation of some saggers was carried out (see Section 4.6.5.4), but not of these unfired examples. In workshop Z71 two stone seats were found near two wheels which were interpreted as potters' seats. More evidence for levigation of clay was found in workshop Z78 in the form of two large 'tubs' measuring 4.4 × 3.6 m and 4.7 × 4.1 m (maximum) respectively.

Eighteen northern Song kilns were found. Most are of the same design and lay-out as Tang and Five Dynasties kilns, basically divided into three functional areas: an entrance leading into a firing pit at the lowest level, a stepped firing chamber in front of this and, at the far end, two chimneys connected to the firing chamber by vents. Where they survive, in some cases there appear to be more than one register

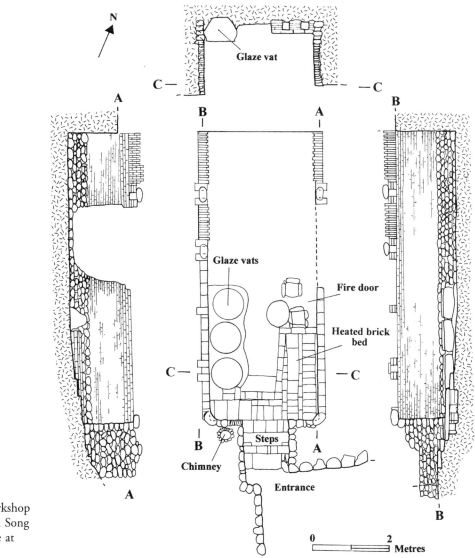

Figure 4.31 Workshop Z1–1 a northern Song Dynasty kiln site at Yaozhou.

of vents connecting the firing chamber to the chimneys as found in Tang kilns.

The survival of especially complex 'air-inlet' (i.e. forced draught) systems among the northern Song kilns illustrates added sophistication when compared with this aspect of Five Dynasties kiln technology. The surviving length of the ventilation duct for kiln Y56 is 3.26 m, which serves a kiln of 3.6 m in length. The (complete) and most complex ventilation duct for kiln Y63 is 3.3 m long (i.e. nearly the same length as for Y56) serving a kiln of 4.4 m in length. It is

about 35 cm deep and 35 cm wide at its narrowest point, and was presumably capped with flat stones, as seen in other ventilation duct constructions. It has a bifurcating mouth widening to about 70 cm presumably into which bellows and tuyères were inserted and perhaps driven with water power. The opposite end of the duct widens to 1.07 m and has a series of three dividing walls forcing the draught through three flues over a 1.5 m deep ash pit. A similar arrangement was also found in kiln Y21, but with a duct that split into five flues, with the draught

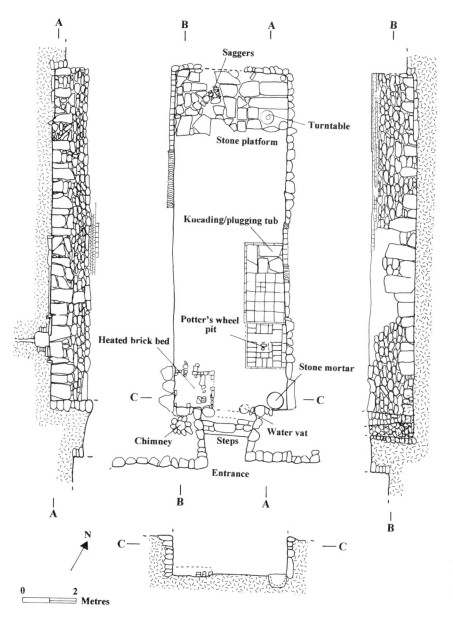

Saggers

Turntable

Stone platform

Kneading/plugging tub

Potter's wheel pit

Stone mortar

Heated brick bed

Chimney   Steps   Water vat

Entrance

N

0   2
Metres

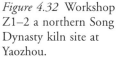

Figure 4.32 Workshop Z1–2 a northern Song Dynasty kiln site at Yaozhou.

being swept over an ash pit into the kiln. Yet another (incomplete) arrangement for the air inlet system was found in kiln Y36. The evidence from the illustrations suggests that the air was forced into two separate ducts at either side of the kiln over the leading edge of the ash pit – presumably helping the fuel lying on the grate to burn. In this case the kiln was of a stepped construction. At the 'end' of the air inlet system in kiln Y47 is a wall across the duct which

has a series of six holes near the top in order to channel the air (at higher pressure) into the fire box; each hole is only 10 cm square.

A structure, measuring about 2.3×2 m, was found attached to the end of the ventilation duct for kiln Y2. Although no details are given of what was found inside the box which was, according to the drawn section, only about 40 cm deep, this appears to have been the location of the bellows system. This

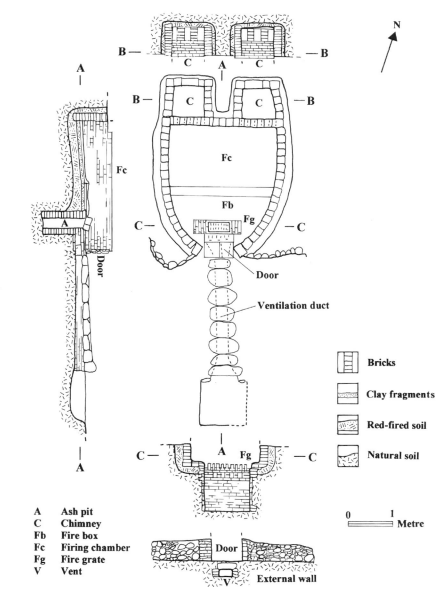

Figure 4.33 Kiln Y5 a northern Song Dynasty kiln site at Yaozhou.

A	Ash pit
C	Chimney
Fb	Fire box
Fc	Firing chamber
Fg	Fire grate
V	Vent

ventilation duct was capped with flat slabs. The constructional details of the brick-built ash pit for kiln Y2 are also helpful in reconstructing what others probably looked like: the 1 m deep pit was brick built with an opening at the base for raking out the ash. Another well-preserved grate over an ash pit was found in kiln Y4. Perhaps the most complete kiln is Y5: here the full arrangement of the grate lying over an ash pit and the way that the ventilation duct fed

the air into the firing chamber can be seen. The duct fed air so that when it hit the far wall of the ash pit it would have been forced upwards through the burning fuel and also downwards, presumably compacting ash in the ash pit which was lined with a vitreous 'sintered' layer of slag. A door in the external wall of the kiln allowed fuel to be inserted; the door lay over the below-ground air duct (see Figure 4.33). Evidence for the use of saggers, which

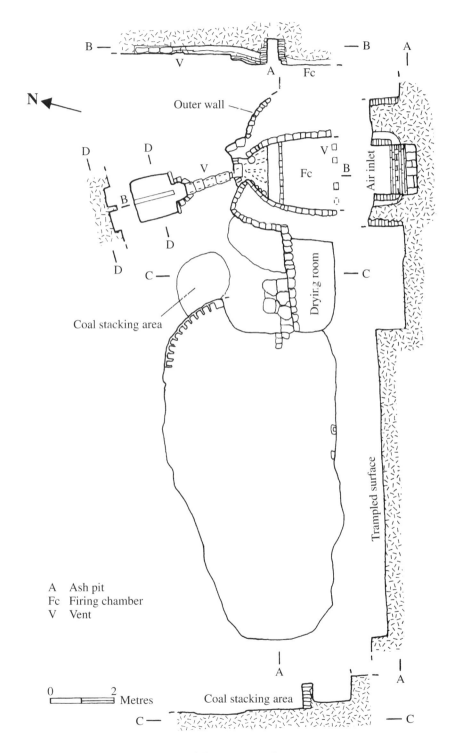

B — B
V A Fc
N
Outer wall
D D
V Fc V
Air inlet
B B
D
D
C — C
Drying room
Coal stacking area
Trampled surface

A Ash pit
Fc Firing chamber
V Vent

0 2 Metres
Coal stacking area
A
A
C — C

Figure 4.34 Kiln Y44 a northern Song Dynasty kiln site at Yaozhou.

were normally removed after use, were found as imprints in the floor of kiln Y19, towards the back of the kiln and funnel-shaped saggers were found at the front of kiln Y31 (Figure 4.14).

The evidence for the fuel used is slim, except in northern Song kiln Y3, where a deposit of coal cinders was found at the bottom of the ash pit and adjacent to kiln 44 where an area in which coal was heaped was identified – and nearby a dump of 'furnace slag' deposited against the outer wall of the kiln (Figure 4.34). Li Guozhen et al. (1992) claim that wood was used as a source of fuel in the Tang Dynasty and Five Dynasties. The use of coal as a fuel source may have had an affect on the kiln atmosphere with the introduction of sulphurous fumes which could have led to the development of yellowish iron-sulphur chromophore in some of the glazes and the use of saggers.

Kiln furniture

As mentioned above, saggers have been found *in situ* in the kilns and also imprints of the saggers were found in the floor of kilns. Two types of saggers have been found: cylindrical and 'ware'-shaped (You Enpu 1986: 282, Figures 1, 2). The cylindrical saggers have perforated holes in the side walls in order to allow water vapour and other gases to escape. Either single pots or stacked pots could be placed inside the saggers. The 'ware'-shaped northern Song saggers have their rims turned downwards with a groove underneath – also used by Ding potters and very similar to those used today. When pots were placed in saggers, the potters always used a spacer of some sort, called setters. During Tang production a tripod was used to separate pots inside cylindrical saggers, as is clear from the three pin marks found on the pot bases. In the Song dynasty either one or two vessels were placed in a sagger. One kiln (Y28) had the remains of supporting posts presumably so that the gases could interact with pot and sagger comprehensively. The posts had various diameters and were either hollow or solid.

Decoration – and the use of moulds

During the Tang, Five Dynasties, Song, Jin and Yuan dynasties moulds were used to produce intricate decoration on wares produced at Yaozhou. Some 200 complete moulds or mould fragments were found during the excavations at Yaozhou, of which the majority were used for the production of bowls and plates. More than eighty Tang dynasty moulds were found which were for producing, among other forms, human figures, animals, bottles, handleless cups and bell pillows; more than 90% of these were for determining the complex object shapes. They were mainly two-part moulds and some had the potter's surname or full name carved on them. Sixteen-and-a-half Five Dynasties moulds were found at Yaozhou. Some of the moulds formed a set, having been produced from the same original. The highest quality moulds are those which date to the Song Dynasty, particularly the middle Song Dynasty: more than 90% were used for stamping decoration and many of the others were copied from the original mould (son moulds) for the mass-production of bowls, plates, cups and pillows. The impressed technique is claimed as a technical advance which was introduced in the middle Song dynasty when robust forms were decorated with fluid and elegant incised decoration (Guo Yanyi et al. 1995: 320). Compared with Song moulds, Jin moulds were heavy and the patterns less complicated. The patterns on the Jin moulds included fish, lotus and peony flowers and peacocks. Fewer Yuan moulds were found and the main pattern was peony flowers.

Guo Yanyi et al. (1995) have studied the characteristics of these moulds and identified three basic types: (1) the original mould; from which (2) the remoulding mould is copied – also known as a son mould; and (3) a body mould which is taken from an existing decorated pot body. The function of the moulds was also designated: (1) the 'moulding' mould, for forming complicated body shapes; (2) moulds for stamping a pattern on the pot – often the same mould as (1); (3) the 'dressing' mould to correct/perfect the shape of a damp pottery body.

4.6.4 Evidence of celadon production organisation from mould inscriptions

By studying closely inscriptions on Yaozhou pottery moulds Wang Lanfang (1995) has found that it is possible to show how parts of the production were organised there. The inscribed character 'guan' indicates that the pots were objects of tribute and since both 'guan' and 'xin guan' wares have been excavated from graves belonging to high-ranking people this makes sense. Celadon sherds with the 'guan' character inscribed on them have been found in Five Dynasties contexts at Yaozhou, showing that the kilns were involved in producing ware for the imperial tribute system. Although made of white porcelain, two 'guan' ware bowls and two dishes were excavated from the tomb of the King of Wei state, who was the son-in-law of Emperor Muzong of Liao and buried in the ninth year of Yingli reign (959) in Chifengdayingzicuin. It is not stated whether any of these 'guan' or 'xin guan' wares have been found in lower status contexts. Nevertheless it is clear that they were definitely used in high status contexts and were produced as part of an imperial tribute system.

Other Five Dynasties wares are inscribed with the 'Ding jia' character on the back. Either a surname or a full name are also inscribed, which could either be that of the master potter or of the craftsman himself (Wang Lanfang 1995). During the Tang Dynasty at Yaozhou surnames are inscribed on tools; during the Song Dynasty many of the moulds, especially those decorated with children at play, have a full name inscribed in negative in cursive handwriting on the base. It is suggested that because individual's names occur on the tools and moulds, that the workshops were run by individuals as opposed to institutions, like local authorities, though clearly they were 'driven' by the demand for high status wares. The Five Dynasties moulds inscribed with 'Ding jia' probably received an assignment to produce tribute for porcelain and when finished continued to produce 'popular' wares. During the Song Dynasty, especially between 1078 and 1106, covering the reigns of Yuanfeng and Chongning, Yaozhou specialised in the production of tribute wares for the imperial house.

During the late Song Dynasty small bowls which all have trumpet mouths, straight inclined walls and a small foot ring with a diameter of c. 9.5 cm were one of the specialised products. These were inscribed with 'Daguan' (1107–10), 'Zhenghe' (1111–17) and Xining (1068–77). The same is true of other (southern) Song kilns, and is surely not unexpected given that predetermined shapes and decorations were produced with moulds in both the Five Dynasties and the Song Dynasty.

4.6.5 Scientific investigation of Yaozhou technology

4.6.5.1 The glazes

Although the glaze is mainly a transparent olive green colour, some is also yellowish brown. The colours are achieved by a combination of the chemical composition of the glazes, the firing temperatures, the cooling cycle and (changes in) kiln atmosphere. Guo Yenyi and Li Guozhen (1986: Table 2) showed by re-firing experiments that the Yaozhou glazes were fired at temperatures as high as 1300 °C; Yang Zhongtang et al. (1995) have determined the firing temperature to be between 1223 and 1309 °C as reflected in the physical characteristics of relict quartz crystals. Using a laser Raman microprobe Yang Zhongtang et al. (1995: 75) investigated the silicate 'structural units' (e.g. monomer and dimer units) present in celadon glazes and used the degree of broken bonds and number of non-bridging oxygens per tetrahedral cation (which tend to increase with temperature) as an aid in the interpretation of firing temperatures, though, given the complex chemical environment involved, the interpretation remained tentative.

Yaozhou celadon glazes are characterised by high silica, aluminia and calcium oxide levels and a low level of total alkali (the oxides of potassium and sodium) with a maximum content of around 5%: c. 65–72% SiO_2; 13.6–15.3% Al_2O_3; 5.6–12.6% CaO; 1.6–2.2% MgO; 1.9–3.1% K_2O; 0.31–0.6% Na_2O; 1.5–1.9% Fe_2O_3; 0.1–0.37 TiO_2; 0.47–0.77% P_2O_5 (Guo Yenyi and Li Guozhen 1986).

Using ICPAES Li Wenchao et al. (1992) considered the ratio of silica to aluminia molecules in celadon glazes. Figure 4.35 shows a clear correlation between aluminia and silica in the glazes (with a correlation coefficient of 0.88). Some distinction is seen between the compositions of the glazes, indicating that slightly different recipes were used. Most Tang (618–906) glazes are above the straight line; the Five Dynasties and Song below it. The molecular ratio of silica/aluminia progressively increased from Tang to Jin (1115–1234) dynasties, and then decreased in the Yuan Dynasty (1279–1368). The implication here is that the relative amount of aluminia increased; the biggest improvement occurring especially between the Tang and Five Dynasties wares, with a change in

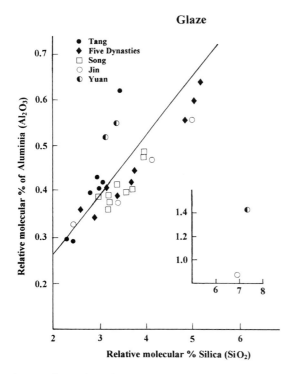

Figure 4.35 The relative molecular % of aluminium oxide versus silica in celadon glazes of Tang, Five Dynasties, Song, Jin and Yuan periods (after Zhang Zhigang *et al.* 1995).

the (average) ratio from 7.2 to 8.16 (Zang Zhigang et al. 1995: Table 3). Although all celadons contained calcium oxide the average level appears to fall moving from Tang to Song Dynasty from 15.19% to 10.14% (Zang Zhigang et al.1995: 63, Table 4). One of the compositional differences between southern and northern Song celadons is the higher phosphorus pentoxide levels in southern celadon glazes; the southern glazes are also sometimes bluish green. A larger proportion of crystallites in some south Guan-Ru and Ru-Jun northern Song which are contemporary with Yaozhou glazes can be explained by a longer and slower cooling rate than for Yaozhou glazes. There are, however, many bubbles, some unreacted quartz as well as the 0.02 mm thick layer of anorthic crystals (see Section 4.6.2 above) (Go Yen and Lie Gouge 1986: 157) in Yaozhou celadons.

The reflectivity of Tang Dynasty, Five Dynasties and Song Dynasty celadon glazes from Yaozhou was

determined (Zhang Zhiang et al. 1995: 64), each in the range of 400–800 mμ. For example, Tang had a bias towards bluish green (Figure 4.36), Five Dynasties ginger yellow (Figure 4.37) and Song olive green. A bluish-green colour has a stronger reducing atmosphere than the ginger yellow colour (i.e. there is a higher proportion of ferrous than ferric ions present). Infrared absorption spectra reveal that ferrous (Fe^{2+}) ions have a strong absorption, but for visible light wavelengths the absorption is weaker making the glaze appear blue. Ferric (Fe^{3+}) ions have a strong absorption spectrum in the ultraviolet area, but in visible light the glaze appears yellowish. Both are dependent on the relative proportions of reducing, as opposed to oxidising, gases in the kiln atmosphere during firing. The typical olive green celadon colour was achieved by a balance of reducing gases somewhere between Tang and Five Dynasties; these findings are supported by an analysis of gas bubbles in the glazes.

Investigation of the *gas bubbles* in the glazes in Yaozhou celadon samples from Tang Dynasty, Five Dynasties and Song Dynasty can help to determine the firing atmosphere *at the temperature when the glaze became too viscous for the bubbles to escape.* By the time the high-temperature glaze had been heated to the maximum temperature to be used in the firing operation, gases released by breakdown of raw materials in the pottery and glaze would have ceased; the main contribution would have been from the kiln atmosphere itself. The determinations showed that the size of the gas bubbles increased by the time of the Song Dynasty and their density decreased (Yang Zhongtang 1992: Table 1). Chemical analysis of the gas bubbles in the glazes using laser Raman microprobe analysis was also performed. The results are mixed, mainly because the author was aware that there was a degree of variation in the glaze colours both within a dynastic production period as well as between the periods. The main result is that in all the samples there was a greater proportion of reducing gases (e.g. CO, CH_4, H_2, H_2O) than oxidising gases (e.g. O_2, CO_2 and SO_2). However, overall the lowest proportion of reducing gases was in Tang wares, the Five Dynasties contained the highest and the Song Dynasty material contained an intermediate proportion (i.e. it was weakly reducing).

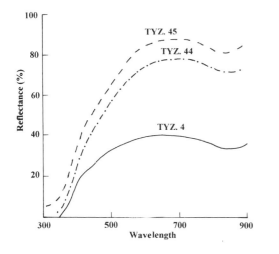

Figure 4.36 The percentage reflectance of Tang Yaozhou celadon glazes (after Zhang Zhigang *et al.* 1995).

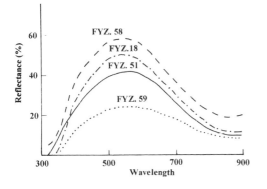

Figure 4.37 The percentage reflectance of Five Dynasties Yaozhou celadon glazes (after Zhang Zhigang *et al.* 1995).

The variation in glaze colours showed that in Tang glazes, the most oxidising atmosphere was responsible for producing greyish (bluish) green and ginger yellow colours; in Five Dynasties the most reducing atmosphere produced olive green and jade green colours; in the northern Song the intermediate atmosphere between Tang and Five Dynasties produced olive green and yellowish green colours.

4.6.5.2 The pottery bodies

Yaozhou bodies are characterised by relatively high aluminia and relatively low silica contents; the reverse

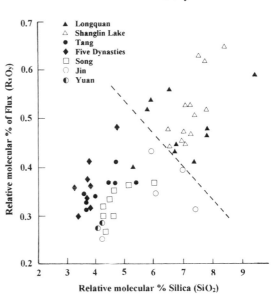

Figure 4.38 Relative molecular % of fluxes versus silica in Yaozhou ware of a range of Dynasties (after Zhang Zhigang *et al.* 1995).

being true of (southern) Longquan wares. The sedimentary rocks which would have been used to make the Yaozhou wares contained iron and titanium impurities. By examining the different proportions of silica, aluminia and the 'flux' component using 'traditional' chemical analysis and inductively coupled plasma emission spectroscopy, Zhang Zhigang et al. (1995) found that some differences in compositions were observable for Yaozhou wares of different dynasties. Figure 4.38 shows relative levels of 'fluxing' components and silica for body compositions of Yaozhou wares dating to the Tang, Five Dynasties, northern Song, Jin and Yuan dynasties; it also includes results of body analyses for southern (Longquan and Shanghlin lake) bodies. The first thing to note is the compositional distinction between northern and southern wares (indicated by a broken line). The second is that, although northern celadons fall in the same area there is a clear chronological shift in the compositions, and therefore the raw materials used. From among the Yaozhou wares there was a (generally) lower relative level of flux used in some (but not all) northern Song wares, with many of the Five

Dynasties wares containing the highest proportion. The Tang products occupy an intermediate position between Five Dynasties and Song wares. There are several exceptions to these generalisations, but a major inference that slightly different combinations of raw materials were used still stands.

4.6.5.3 The moulds

The material used for moulds is characterised by high levels of silica and aluminia at levels which are indistinguishable from the bodies of Yaozhou celadons (compare Guo Yenyi: Table 1; Guo Yanyi et al. 1995: Table 2). The silica levels in the Song Yaozhou moulds range between 62.5% and 71.62%, and aluminia levels between 20.7% and 32.71%. They also contained very low calcium oxide levels of mainly less than 1% and, as with the pottery, a low total alkali of up to a maximum of 3.6% (Guo Yanyi et al. 1995: Table 2). Yaozhou bodies contain between 65.7% and 72.2% silica and between 20.3–29.8% aluminia. Indeed these compositional similarities carry through for most of the other components, especially levels of magnesia and phosphorus pentoxide. Some variation in levels of calcium oxide in the moulds when compared with the pot bodies (a range of 0.37–1.13 in the moulds compared to 0.2–0.53 in the pot bodies) is unlikely to have affected the properties of the raw materials used; even the levels of iron and titanium are comparable. It is clear that very similar materials were used for making the moulds and the pot bodies which is a somewhat unexpected result. Wang Fang and Wang Lanfang (1995: 311) have noted the use of a buffering material which appears as a thin yellow layer on the moulding surface; no more specific identification has yet been carried out. However, Anderson and Guo Yanyi (1995: 100) have noted, during experiments designed to reproduce the process of using celadon moulds, that a good releasing agent could either consist of a layer of dusted ash or a mixture of ash and dry clay. The firing temperature of the moulds is claimed to have been between 1100 °C and 1200 °C (Wang Fang and Wang Lefang 1995: 311), yet this is a similar composition to the pots, so a higher firing temperature is likely.

For moulds with fine decoration the porosity of the moulds is a significant factor. The apparent porosity (the proportion of voids in a material) and water absorption of the moulds have been worked out for celadon material. Guo Yanyi et al. (1986: 322, Table 3) found that the decorated plate and bowl moulds (n = 11) had apparent porosities of 27–35%, whereas the undecorated simple animal moulds (n = 2) had apparent porosities of 14–17%. Greater porosity might enable a better quality mould to result, though 'excessive' porosity has been found to prevent a precise impression being made (Zhang Zhigang et al. 1995: 100). In any case, a similar level of porosity for Yaozhou saggers suggests that while fine clays were undoubtedly used to make moulds, they were not necessarily selected/prepared from clearly distinguished special clays.

4.6.5.4 The saggers

The opportunity to compare the chemical and mineralogical composition of saggers with the mould and pottery bodies has not, as yet, apparently been fully realised. Li Wenchao et al. (1992) report the average silica and aluminia contents of Yaozhou saggers as 58.25% and 37.24% respectively. As might be expected for a ceramic material which is used for the protection of the pots which it contains, the aluminia level is apparently higher than the maximum level of 32.71% for northern Song Yaozhou wares; the silica level is correspondingly lower. You Enpu (1986) has not published the full chemical analyses of the saggers, nor stated the numbers of analyses involved. The 'average' porosity of Yaozhou saggers is similar to that for moulds – 14.59%. When compared to results for Ding saggers, Yaozhou saggers apparently contain on average about 10% higher aluminia levels and can therefore be described as more refractory.

4.6.5.5 Analysis of Yaozhou raw materials

As mentioned in the description of the workshop excavations, deposits of clay were found which, quite reasonably, were labelled as raw materials used for the production of celadons in those kilns; these do not appear to have been scientifically tested. However, Guo Yenyi and Li Guozhen (1986: 159) have carried out chemical analyses of 'typical' raw materials from places 'near Yaozhou kiln sites'. Some clays tested contained a mixture of quartz, mica, feldspar and kaolinite; there are some similarities with the composition of the bodies analysed, but this is not absolute proof that they were used. Work by Guo Yanyi (1987) has suggested that Nichi refractory clay, Chenlu refractory clay, Chenlu limestone and Fuping glaze stone, consisting of silty sand, kaolin, calcite, quartz and feldspar (Li Guozhen and Guan Peiying 1979: 196) could all have been used as Yaozhou glaze raw materials. As with many instances of pottery production, raw materials are often mixed. In 'The stele of Marquis De Ying' of the Xining reign (1068–1078) 'at the beginning the body was made with combined clays', so, in spite of a range of experiments with clay mixing by Li Guozhen and Guan Peiying (1979) only a best estimate can be determined using clay found in the northern Chinese Central Plain near Yaozhou; as Li Guozhen and Guan Peiying (1979) mention, the range of clays and 'glaze stones' in the vicinity of the Yaozhou kilns is very wide indeed.

4.7 Iznik: Ottoman court ceramics and the development of 'fritware'

4.7.1 Introduction

Turkish Iznik pottery which has been decorated with one of the most exuberant ranges of designs with one of the widest range of glaze colours. Its study raises a number of research questions such as what features of the ceramic technology can be seen as being specifically Iznik in origin and what social, economic or political features of the society may have contributed to its production.

Iznik ware was used in Ottoman Turkey between c. 1480 and 1650; copies were made in the nineteenth century and are still being made today. Both prior to the introduction of Iznik decoration on pottery, and after it, the interiors of the mosques and minarets of Ottoman Turkey were sometimes highly decorated using glazed tiles. One hypothesis is that artisans from Tabriz in Iran, who manufactured tiles before 1480, contributed in some way to the emergence of Iznik pottery. However, before describing Iznik ceramic technology in detail, and discussing some of the other features of fifteenth-century ceramic technology, it is necessary to consider what kinds of ceramic technology may have influenced the emergence of Iznik before the fifteenth century, in order to place the technology of Iznik ceramic bodies into a broad context.

4.7.2 The possible origins and the characteristics of stonepaste/fritware and maiolica/'faience' technology

The bodies of 'Iznik' ware are a kind of stonepaste, also known as 'fritware'. Stonepaste is a ware which consists of crushed silica combined with a small amount of clay and crushed glass (Henderson 1989b; Tite 1989). It is debatable whether *frit*, the partially fused primary raw materials of glass-making (see Section 3.3), was in fact added to the silica and clay instead of ground up glass. Whichever was used, it led to the formation of a glass network in the pottery body as it was fired. When the pottery body was fired in the kiln the glass (or frit which was transformed into glass), and the small amount of clay fused together producing the glassy network which extended between some of the quartz crystals. Hence the name of the fabric: *stonepaste*.

A recent consideration of the origins of stonepaste technology has suggested that some of the earliest wares resulted, not in tandem with the ninth-century development of high lead tin-glazed wares (see Section 4.3.5.1), but that, slightly later, Iraqi potters working in the tenth- and eleventh-century court of Fatimid, Egypt, introduced proto-stonepaste wares (Mason and Tite 1994: 88). It is thought that in these contexts the practice of adding quartz and ground up glass to clay-rich bodies eventually led to the development of true stonepaste bodies.

The term *faience* is sometimes mistakenly used to describe Iznik stonepaste wares. The production of true faience goes back to 4000 BC in the Near East and Egypt, and several different techniques of faience production were used to make beads and vessels in these areas and elsewhere (see Section 3.9.2; Tite and Bimson 1986; Kingery and Vandiver 1986). Italian *maiolica* is also sometimes described as 'Faenza', the latter word having a French derivation which probably comes from the popularity in sixteenth-century France of wares made at Faenza, Italy. Maiolica was made by coating a calcareous earthenware pot with a white tin-opacified glaze, a technique now thought to have its origins in eighth-century Basra, Iraq (Mason and Tite 1997). However, one of the compositional differences between the glazes used in Islamic tin-glazed wares and of maiolica was caused by the probable use of wine lees as a source of the alkali in

Faenza, introducing potassium rather than sodium (Tite 1991); Kingery and Smith (1985) refer to European (faience) products as 'soft porcelains'. Medici porcelain is also quite different from Iznik pottery (Kingery 1986). Maiolica was produced in Spain and later in other Mediterranean and northern European countries, and as far afield as Mexico and South America. Maggetti et al. (1982) found that by combining an (semi-quantitative) X-Ray diffraction analysis with petrological investigation of the temper used they were able to distinguish clearly between European, Mexican and other products.

Compositional investigations, using neutron activation analysis, of maiolica bodies produced in the early sixteenth century in Castel Durante, Deruta, Faenza, Gubbio, Venice and Urbino in Italy shows a high degree of compositional similarity in the products (Myers 1992: 149–54). There is, however, a 'tendency for objects painted in the same workshops to be compositionally similar to one another rather than to other objects in the group' (ibid. 149). Given this intriguing tendency, a compositional investigation of the brilliant glazes used for decorating the wares from these same workshops in order to establish whether they, too, reflect the use of *slightly* different raw materials would be very interesting. Wilson (1987) has pointed out that those who signed, inscribed and dated their work regarded themselves not as artisans, but as *artists*. Some of the finest maiolica products acted as a means of marking the reconciliation between two elite families (Watson 1986: 56). It is clear from the highly fortified landscape of walled towns and cities in some of the areas of Italy in which maiolica was made and used, that competition and even war was not unusual.

The development of maiolica glaze technology included the precise application of pigments and the development of pigment technology. As Kingery (1993) has pointed out, prior to the fifteenth century manganese purple and copper green colorants were dissolved in the glazes. The development in the use of the painted pigment technology particularly in fifteenth-century maiolica, but also in the context of Iznik glazes, especially in the sixteenth century, characterised the impressive achievements of elite maiolica used as tableware. Although many of the

crystalline pigments that were used, such as lead antimonate, were not new in the context of glass and glaze technology (see glass colours and glaze colours in Sections 3.2.5.5 and 4.3.5.2), painted designs using a wide range of colours (and including new pigments) was (Thornton 1997: 17).

In contrast to the earthenware body of maiolica, the bodies of Iznik pottery and other Islamic stonepaste wares contain a much higher silica content and are much harder. Because of their high silica content these pottery bodies are characteristically an opaque white colour. The kind of silica chosen was often naturally-occurring quartz, especially if low in iron, resulting in the desired white colour. A small proportion of clay was also added, which provided plasticity. Although hard, the pottery can contain quite a number of pores (i.e. it is porous) which means that, unlike Chinese porcelain, it may be weak. Although, as mentioned above, tin was introduced into some other Islamic glazes and maiolica as an opacified layer which provided a white background, in Iznik pottery and tiles the tin oxide is usually completely dissolved in the glaze so that the glaze remains translucent (see Section 4.7.9). A white *background* for glaze decoration in Iznik pottery is provided instead by a clean white slip. It is therefore clear that the technology of Iznik pottery is very different from the much earlier material faience, and from maiolica (Faenza).

The manufacture of Iznik can be regarded as an attempt to manufacture a hard white body, perhaps in response to the demand for Chinese porcelain. However, even though the visual results were impressive, as will become clear, neither the hardness nor the translucency of true porcelain was achieved.

4.7.3 Iznik

Iznik is a city in western Asia Minor with a Nicaea in the fourth century BC (see Figure 4.39 for its location). It subsequently became a Roman and then a Byzantine city before coming under Ottoman rule in 1331, at which point it became known as Iznik. Iznik was the first major Ottoman capital to be relegated to second capital when the Ottomans conquered Constantinople. Documented estimates of the number of kilns in Iznik vary between an unbelievable 300

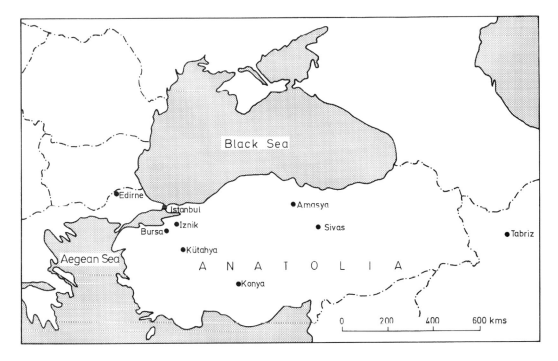

Figure 4.39 Location map of Iznik and other sites in Ottoman Turkey and beyond.

kilns during the reign of Sultan Ahmed (1607–17) to 9 kilns by the mid-seventeenth century when the industry had certainly declined. The highly decorated glazed products made in the distinctive Iznik style (which could also have been made at Kütahya) are likely to have been manufactured for relatively high status consumption, against a background of rusticated wares.

As mentioned above the term *fritware* is sometimes used to describe Iznik (and other Islamic pottery). It is worth considering whether the term is appropriate in rather more detail. Frit refers to a semi-fused mass of primary raw materials which are brought together in an initial stage of the manufacture of glass (see Section 3.3). Frit is formed from silica (either sand or quartz), an alkali (either mineral or plant ash) and often calcium oxide, aluminium oxide and sometimes lead oxide. In the case of Iznik ceramics, the addition of frit or of glass to the pottery raw materials leads to the formation of a glassy network once the material is fully melted into the body of the pottery (see Section 4.7.2 above).

4.7.4 The research questions

A number of connected questions about the technology of Iznik form a focus for a broad investigation as to why Iznik appeared when it did, and under what conditions. Starting with the slim evidence of production, including kiln sites, historical references to Iznik production will be briefly reviewed in order to shed light on the context in which the pottery was made. The scientific examination of Iznik wares will then be linked to the archaeological and historical sources. Clearly, however, in adopting this methodology, it is necessary to have a series of specific research questions to focus on.

One question which relates to the development of the technology is to establish how the range of colours used in the superbly decorated range of Iznik wares was achieved and how these pigments developed over time, from the initial blue-and-white pottery, through to the exotic polychrome pots incorporating the striking bole red and finally ending in the seventeenth-century decline of the industry, producing second-rate products. Another aspect of the study is to examine the pot bodies in order to try and establish the raw materials used. The use of body and glaze raw materials can reflect different aspects of the same industrial organisation. The sources of exotic colorants used in the glazes may have changed over time, being sensitive to changing political allegiances or the exhaustion of colorant mineral deposit. The principal substances used for making the ceramic bodies on the other hand are likely to have been easier to obtain and to have involved contacts which were more localised than those involved in obtaining colorant minerals. The processes involved in the manufacture of glazes and ceramic bodies can therefore be the end result of a complex network of contacts between the person mining the colorant-rich minerals, the middlemen who supplied them to potential tradesmen who may then have sold them to, or exchanged them with, the potters. Scientific analysis can help to contribute in the investigation of these questions, provided that well-dated artefacts and those representative of the range of decorative styles are examined.

Another important source of information comes from the historical evidence. If texts are available, it may be possible to augment the scientific findings. As in all of the case studies reported in this book, one of the aims is to define the niche, or role, that the industry and its products played in society; the social and economic systems of Anglo-Saxon and early medieval Europe were worlds apart from those of Ottoman Turkey, so there would have been both similarities but also significant differences in the ways in which the organisation and function of the industries articulated with society.

Given the sudden appearance of high quality Iznik products, it is appropriate to examine a variety of possible contributory reasons, not just historical/socio-economic but also the *origins* of the industry from a technological viewpoint. This last involves a consideration of pottery and tiles that were used in Turkey before 1480, and a comparison of their technologies with the products of Iznik from its inception *c.* 1480, until its decline in *c.* 1650. The wares to be compared include, first, Chinese porcelain, second, rusticated 'Miletus' ware, a glazed earthenware, and third, the products of a group of potters known as the 'Masters of Tabriz'. There is an obvious

stylistic connection between the blue-and-white Chinese porcelain products and the early (and later) Iznik blue-and-white products, but the technology behind these different products needs to be compared. Little work has been carried out on the local 'Miletus' earthenware, so it is worthwhile investigating the technology involved in order to examine any possible influence on the origin of Iznik.

With respect to this third possible influence, there is historical evidence that a group of potters from Iran called the 'Masters of Tabriz' were invited by the Ottomans to oversee the massive production of tiles to decorate mosques and minarets prior to the appearance of Iznik, so in these investigations it was hoped to identify any technological characteristics which they may have introduced. They were involved in a highly ambitious project, the production of glazed tiles for the mosque complex of Sultan Mehmed I in Bursa, one of the first capitals of the Ottoman state, built between 1419 and 1424, which showed clear Iranian aesthetic (Atasoy and Raby 1989: 83). After this, in 1425, they focused their attention on the tile-work for the mosque of Murad II also in Bursa. Subsequently they had commissions to tile the mosques in Edirne, also an early capital of the Ottoman state: they tiled the Şah Malek Paşa Camii completed in 1429, the mosque of Murad II near Edirne completed in 1436 and Murad II's mosque, Üç Şerefeli datable to between 1437–8 and 1447–8. Their last work was the so-called tomb of Cem Sultan in Bursa which was originally built in 1479. A completely different group of tilers were responsible for producing tiles for the famous 'Tiled Pavilion', the Çinili Köşkü, in Istanbul, dated 1473 (Atasoy and Raby 1989: 89).

Finally, a non-technological reason needs to be offered as to why it was that Iznik pottery appeared when it did. What was it that brought about its introduction?

4.7.5 Evidence for the production of Iznik and other 'fritware'

Excavations of kilns at Iznik have revealed two kinds of structures. The first was the lower parts of what were probably two-chambered circular kilns (see Figure 4.40): the firing chambers (Aslanapa 1969:

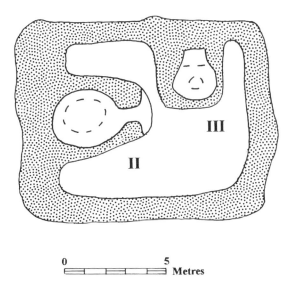

Figure 4.40 Plan of the kilns found at Iznik (after Aslanapa 1969).

146, Figure 5). The second kind was described as rectangular measuring 1.5 × 1.8 m in plan, surviving to a height of 2.5 m and described as 'small'. Recesses were visible inside this second kiln type which, it is claimed, were for shelves; one illustration shows that this kind of kiln had a rounded end (Aslanapa 1969: Figure 3). It is suggested that this rectangular kiln type had 'transverse arches' and is reminiscent of such kilns found in other Islamic contexts, such as Merv, Turkmenistan (Dr St J. Simpson, personal communication) and eighth–ninth-century Islamic contexts in al-Raqqa, Syria (Henderson et al. forthcoming). It is notable however that no Iznik wasters were found in these excavations at Iznik, only those of Miletus ware (Aslanapa 1969: 142) together with many Iznik sherds. However, although the Iznik kilns are primary evidence for pottery production, there is no *direct* evidence that these kilns were used for the manufacture of stonepaste wares and it is likely, though not proven, that they would have been used for the manufacture of earthenware. Although a higher temperature would have been necessary for the production of Iznik stonepaste wares, the question of what precise structural differences there may have been in the kilns used to fire fritware rather than earthenware (if any) must remain speculative until a kiln for firing stonepaste wares is excavated.

Abū'l Qāsim's treatise, consisting of two manuscripts dated 1301 and 1583 respectively, describes Iranian fritware technology (Allan 1973) which would probably have been that used for the production of Iznik ware. The treatise includes reference to both kiln bars and saggers (ibid.: 114): the complete pots each inside its own lidded sagger would have been placed on a kiln bar which would have been inserted into the kiln wall. The saggers would have protected the pots from variations in kiln atmosphere, from vitreous fuel-ash and from the dripping glaze derived from other pots. The kilns were fired for twelve hours using wood such as hyssop, walnut and willow. The willow was stripped of its bark so that it did not smoke – had it been allowed to it could have created a more reducing atmosphere and may have reduced the lead oxide found in (Iznik) glazes to lead metal and in so-doing blacken the pots. The pots were allowed to cool down for a week.

No evidence for the use of these techniques has so far been found at Iznik, though fritware pots definitely made at Iznik (according to their dated inscriptions) do not bear the telltale cockspur marks that would have been left as a result of using tripods for separating and stacking the pots, so saggers are very likely to have been used. Whitehouse mentions the use of kiln bars at Siraf (Whitehouse, 1971: 15) and saggers were used at Takht-i Sulimān. Recent excavations of a pottery dump from an eleventh-century workshop at al-Raqqa, Syria, has provided more evidence for the use of kiln bars and saggers in an Islamic context (Tonghini and Henderson 1998). Abū'l Qāsim's treatise describes the procedure for making the 'frit' component of the pottery (the partially fused primary raw materials of glass which is mixed with ground up silica), as opposed to fritware pottery, in a kiln called a *biraz*. The process takes eight hours during which the mixture is well mixed. The structures described and illustrated by Whitehouse (1971: 15, Plate VIa), which he excavated at Siraf, were quite possibly fritting kilns: 'Each comprised a fire box and a chamber containing an oval earthenware tray.' He suggests that they would have been used for making glaze, but the discovery of earthenware trays suggests that there may be an alternative explanation: that they were used for fritting. Normally the mixture to be fritted would be raked from time to time in such trays (see Section 3.3). Glazes/glasses are normally melted in crucibles or in tanks (see Section 3.4). Abū'l Qāsim mentions the mixing of the frit with the clay (Allan 1973: 114).

With one exception, all the kiln debris and wasters from Iznik so far published derive from the manufacture of Miletus earthenware: the exception is the discovery of small ceramic fragments which had been used as testers, including for the testing of distinctive bole red glaze. These fragments have holes drilled through them and it is thought that the potters were able to hook them out of the kiln without disturbing the rest of the pots (Atasoy and Raby 1989: Figure 44). At Kütahya, another probable production centre for Iznik fritware, Şahin (1981) has published excavations of (earthenware) painted pottery and tile kilns where the minimum internal diameter is 1.2 m, but again no kilns unquestionably associated with fritware production have been found.

4.7.6 Historical evidence for the production of Iznik

It is clear from the registers relating to the Topkapi Palace treasury and kitchens in Istanbul that Iznik pottery was regarded as a prestigious ware. A reference is made to the purchase of 541 Iznik plates, dishes and bowls from the bazaar in Istanbul in 1582 for the sumptuous banquets which were held to celebrate the circumcision of Prince Mehmed, the son of Sultan Murad III, which lasted 52 days and nights (Atasoy and Raby 1989: 14). Although regarded as prestigious, Iznik was never regarded by the Sultan as being in the same class as Chinese porcelains: 10,600 pieces of porcelain are held in the Topkapi Palace today. The historical research into Iznik pottery by Nurhan Atasoy was largely based on three types of documents: schedules of fixed prices, inventories of the effects of deceased persons and palace registers. The last category includes records of gifts presented to the sultan, items deposited and issued by the palace treasury and the payrolls of craftsmen employed by the palace. Specific wares are referred to as 'porcelain', 'celadons' and 'pottery' and whether they are Ottoman products. For some of the later

Iznik wares, the production centre is recorded. Apart from Istanbul and Kütahya, Iznik is mentioned exclusively in documents dating to between the end of the fifteenth century and the early eighteenth century. In 1570 four master potters were even brought from Iznik to Istanbul, along with the tools of their trade (Atasoy and Raby 1989: 23). However, the position of Kütahya as a production centre in relation to Iznik and to Istanbul still needs to be examined scientifically, and if possible archaeologically, in detail; given that the 'Iznik' wares made at Kütahya are indistinguishable technologically from those made at Iznik itself, it must have formed a significant part of the production and distribution network.

By the mid-seventeenth century the quality of Iznik ware had declined, and it is only from about this time that in the schedules of fixed prices Iznik is referred to explicitly as the place of origin (Atasoy and Raby 1989: 25). An explanation for this is that Iznik would have been competing with other centres of provincial production, such as Kütahya. Among the probate inventories studied, one in which Iznik wares are mentioned specifically is worth describing in detail in order to provide a flavour of its status and relative 'social' and economic value. A probate inventory dated 1548 for Hâce İshak bin Abdürrezzak, a draper and clothier who had stocks in the Cloth Merchants' Hall in Edirne and the Caravanserai of Halil Paşa, and who owned houses in Edirne and farms in the country, mentions Iznik pottery. He can certainly be regarded as rich and owned eleven Iznik dishes and four pieces of Chinese porcelain (Atasoy and Raby 1989: 26). Among the other inventories are those for members of the military class, who also owned Iznik ware; members of this class could practise farming and stock-raising and often owned slaves.

The payrolls of craftsmen employed by the palace might be expected to provide some fascinating insights into the organisation of Iznik pottery and tile production. However, as Attasoy and Raby (1989: 32) note, although documents are available in which, for example, the name of the master tiler, the names of his apprentices, their daily wages, the name of the sultan who took them into the palace, and even their ethnic origin, is stated, information about whether they made the tiles themselves or whether they were only responsible for setting the tiles in places on walls is lacking. Nevertheless, such information is of great interest in that it provides a clear description of the hierarchy of the production organisation within the Palace.

As for documents relating to the technology of production of Islamic fritware, one of the most important is the treatise by Abū'l Qāsim (Allan 1973) written in 1301 (mentioned above) which includes a section on pottery in the chapter on precious stones. The recipe for the production of fritware cited by him is ten parts of silica, one part of glass frit and one part of fine white clay; it is presumed that the 'parts' are by volume, rather than by weight. Abū'l Qāsim's recipe describes a special fritting furnace in which the primary raw materials of glass production were 'melted' together. However as noted in Section 3.3 the intention when fritting is to arrest the fusion of raw materials before a glass is produced, though the treatise suggests that glass was produced:

> This [*shakhār* from Baghdad or Tabriz] is cooked over a slow fire [for six hours], and is stirred from morning till night with an iron ladle made as large as the diameter of the kiln until it is well mixed [and becomes white] and it becomes one, like molten glaze, and this is the material for glass vessels. After eight hours they take out the brew by the ladleful. Below, in front of the oven, is a pit full of water, into which they put the glass frit. When water and fire meet there is a great noise and roaring like thunder, which for all the world could be real thunder and lightning [such that everyone who has not seen it and hears the noise falls on his knees shuddering and trembling]. The craftsmen call this mixture *jawhar* and store it, until the time comes to compound it, in a broken up, powdered and sifted form.

> (Allan 1973: 113)

It is apparent that once the raw materials were fully fused they were thrown into a pit with water where it would have shattered (devitrified) into silicate crystals. The material produced (glass or silicate crystals) is therefore not the same thing as a true frit, which would be partially fused glass raw materials with a granular consistency. It is interesting though that during the fritting process the frit is also thrown into cold water, several times. In this case it only occurs once – presumably the shattered glass produced is easier to store and to mix with the other ingredients in the manufacture of Iznik. Finished Iznik pots contain a network of glass which could either have derived from the addition of (re-)melted silicate crystals or frit which would have melted fully into glass during the firing process. If the material described above was used then clearly real frit was *not* used. Although this procedure would probably have been followed in principle by Iznik potters, another stage would have been the addition of lead (and tin) at some point in the production process: this is also described by Abū'l Qāsim (Allan 1973: 113).

Fuel consumption for firing the Iznik kilns is discussed by Anhegger (1941: 176–77). He refers to a document dated 1719 which describes the demand for fuel for the kilns. Demand for pine wood was such that the *naib* (judge) of Iznik and the governor of the province of Kocaeli were asked to provide 50,000 kilos for the kilns at Tekfur Sarayi. It was clear that only a certain quality of wood would be accepted because of its combustion characteristics: without resin or knots. The presence of knots would tend to cause the wood to burn at differential rates causing hot spots in the kiln and potentially resulting in some failed pots. The amount of smoke produced would have a direct effect on the atmosphere of the kiln and therefore the resulting colour of the pottery and its glazes; in Abū'l Qāsim's recipe it is noted that bark can sometimes cause too much smoke (Allan 1973: 114).

4.7.7 The date and range of decorative types

Iznik pottery follows a relatively well-dated developmental sequence of glaze decoration. The date ranges applied to this development are based on the building dates of Ottoman mosques decorated with tiles which display the same designs (see Table 4.2). Because the dates are relatively secure, it is possible to trace the 'emergence', development and decline of

Table 4.2 List of Ottoman pottery samples taken for microprobe and SEM analyses

Date	Description
1430	'Masters of Tabriz' blue-and-white
c. 1460	Miletus ware blue-and-green
1480	Blue-and-white from Iznik
1510	Blue-and-white from Iznik
1520	Blue-and-white from Iznik
1530	Tugrakes spiral blue-and-white from Iznik
1540	Potters' style Grape dish fragment blue-and-white with turquoise from Iznik
1550s	Damascus ware dark, blue, olive green, turquoise, 'black' outlines from Iznik
1560–70	Slip-painted. Red slip, blue-and-white from Iznik
1580	Rhodian ware. Bole red, blue and emerald green from Iznik
1580	Rhodian ware. Bole red, blue, turquoise, emerald green and 'black' from Iznik.
1580	Late blue-and-white from Iznik.
c. 1650	Emerald green, blue, 'black' and red.

Figure 4.41 Typical example of potters' style ware (after Atasoy and Raby 1989).

Figure 4.42 Typical example of 'Damascus' ware (after Atasoy and Raby 1989).

Iznik pottery. From *c*. 1480 to 1520 a tight introverted form of (mainly) spiral blue-and-white decoration is used, known as *early blue-and-white* which, like all the other Iznik types of decoration, has a colourless overglaze. From *c*. 1520 to 1540 an extra colour – turquoise blue – was added and this decoration in a more open form is known as *the two blues*. An example of this ware dating to *c*. 1530 is shown in Figure 4.41, a typical example of potters' style ware. The third variety of glaze decoration in the sequence is known as *Damascus ware*. This type of decoration which was used during the 1550s involves the use of a much wider range of colours among which are an aubergine purple, deep cobalt blue and a sage green (see Figure 4.42). The fourth kind, *slip-painted* ware, as the name suggests, incorporates a second colour of slip as well as blue, 'black' and other colours of glaze. Rhodian glaze decoration used between 1570 and 1580 incorporates the widest range of decorative colours and includes a colour which is applied in relief and can vary between a tomato-coloured red and a yellow orange colour; this is known as bole red. The next decorative variety, *late blue-and-white*, consists of a far more open and exuberant pattern than used in early blue-and-white. It was in use between *c*. 1580 and *c*. 1600. Iznik pottery was still being produced in the seventeenth century, but by 1650 the products were second-rate with the glaze no longer adhering to the pot properly and the slip no longer having the brilliant white colour of sixteenth-century Iznik (see below).

4.7.8 The technology of typical Iznik ceramic bodies examined

It was with these archaeological and historical considerations in mind that small samples of the tiles and pottery were mounted in epoxy resin discs so that that could be examined analytically using an electron microprobe and visually under magnification using a scanning electron microscope (SEM). Using the SEM individual inclusions could be photographed and analysed in ceramic bodies, slips and glazes. As well as this, by using an SEM, variations in the chemical composition of the glazes, such as the presence of a cobalt-rich painted design (as reflected in the grey level/average atomic number – see Section 2.3) could be photographed. A glaze rich in a heavy compound, like lead oxide, will appear a paler grey colour than a lighter compound, like silica. High quality quantitative analyses could be obtained for the glazes using an electron microprobe.

First, the technological characteristics of Iznik products from 1480 to 1650 will be described. The possible technological influences of Chinese blue-and-white, 'Miletus' earthenware and the 'Masters of Tabriz' products will then each be considered in turn.

In the scientific analysis of Iznik ceramics thirteen pottery samples were examined, all of which derived from Iznik, or were derived from dated Turkish monuments. They ranged in date from 1430 to 1650 and included examples which represent the full stylistic range of Iznik pottery. In addition to the pottery, a series of fifteenth- and sixteenth-century Turkish tiles were examined for comparison and in order to investigate links between pottery and tile technologies (Henderson and Raby 1989). The samples examined are listed in Table 4.2 with their likely production dates.

From an analytical point of view it was seen to be important to determine how the pottery body was made, how the white background to the glaze was achieved and what was used for colouring the glazes. A discussion of the colorants will follow a consideration of the major compositional characteristics of the bodies.

Figure 4.43 is a photomicrograph of a thick section through a typical Iznik pot, revealing a (lower) zone of pale body, a clearly delineated thinner slip layer lying on top of this and, virtually invisible under the conditions of illumination, a thin translucent glaze layer. If a specimen of Iznik pottery is examined under a scanning electron microscope using a back-scattered detector to display contrasts in average atomic number (i.e. chemical composition; see Section 2.3) its different structural characteristics come into sharp focus (see Figure 4.44).

1 the lowest layer shown (above the micron scale bar) is the silica-rich body, with a network of lead-rich glassy 'frit' showing as a pale grey colour (see Figure 4.45). Within the body fabric are larger dark areas which are voids in the fabric;
2 above the body layer is a generally darker grey silica-rich layer – the slip. It contains noticeably smaller silica crystals than the body and a smaller proportion of lead-rich frit;
3 above the slip layer is the interface (or interaction) layer showing as silica crystals bathed in a white lead-rich glaze;
4 the surface layer showing as white is a high lead translucent glaze.

The first two and the fourth of these structural characteristics are detectable in all Iznik pottery types. The depth of the interaction zone can vary (Henderson 1989b; Tite 1989).

Analysis of the body of Iznik blue-and-white pot sherds dating to c. 1520–40 showed that in addition to the high proportion of silica (ground quartz or sand) and the frit, there was also a small proportion of clay which when combined with the frit produced variations in composition (depending on the type and composition of the clay used). The occurrence of magnesia, aluminium and calcium in the body frits can be attributed to the use of the clay component. This feature was also found in other Iznik pottery bodies. Occasionally tin was detected in the *body* of Iznik ceramics, specifically in the glassy 'frit' phase of a blue-and-white pot tested. If one takes a closer look at the glassy frit phase in the ceramic body (Figure 4.45) it can be seen that the pale grey angular silica crystals are mainly surrounded by a

Figure 4.43 A photomicrograph of a mounted section of typical Iznik pottery body and glaze. The distinction between the white slip layer (which incorporates a large black void) and the body can be seen clearly.

white glassy layer and interspersed between (black) voids in the potsherd.

Close examination of the glaze showed that a few relict silica crystals were often suspended in the glaze and occasionally a few small (white) tin crystals. In fact it was found that normally between about 3% and 6% tin oxide was completely dissolved in Iznik glazes. In general the principal components of Iznik glazes are the oxides of sodium, silicon, lead and tin, with traces of magnesia and aluminium. Indeed this type of lead oxide-soda-silica plus tin glaze is typical of all the Iznik sixteenth-century glazes analysed and found in samples of all the stylistic variations analysed.

The second stylistic type of Iznik pottery considered was multicoloured Damascus ware (see Figure 4.42). Although the 'style' of glaze decoration is obviously quite different, not only is the technique of making the body the same as for blue-and-white, but so is the basic composition of the glaze.

The sample of slip-painted ware analysed has a complex series of layers. The ceramic consists of a central silica-rich body (a pale buff colour), with white slip layers on both inner and outer surfaces. On top of the white slip is a further (red) slip layer. Covering this is a glaze consisting of a bluish underglaze, the whole thing being sealed by a colourless glaze. The red slip decoration is only used on part of the pot surface, so the white slip is revealed in places. X-Ray fluorescence spectroscopy has revealed that all the layers are rich in lead, including the glaze, both slip layers and the frit in the body; a lead map showed the highest 'relative' lead level in the glaze, slightly less in the interaction layer, a variable and lower level in the slip layers, with slightly more in the outer red slip layer than in the inner white slip layer and apparently least of all in the silica-rich body. In general, most Iznik pottery analysed contained a higher proportion of lead frit in the body than in the slip layer. There can be no question that the presence of lead in all

Figure 4.44 A back-scattered scanning electron micrograph of a typical Iznik body showing the surface ('white') glaze, the interaction layer containing ('black') silica crystals, the slip layer with fine silica crystals and the body containing larger silica crystals, voids and a higher proportion of 'white' glassy phase than in the slip.

components of Iznik ware helps the fit of the glaze. This slip-painted ceramic presents a challenge to the potter because of the complex structural considerations associated with two slip layers which could potentially reduce the possibility of achieving the appropriate relative contraction of each component as it cooled – a proper glaze fit.

Rhodian samples incorporate the use of bole red used in relief, and display a wide range of glaze colours. The bole red is evidently produced as an application of a kind of red iron-rich slip, probably modified by the development of a translucent reddish glass. Variation in the colour of 'bole red' and the orangey reds found in other Iznik pottery (described

as 'bole') are probably attributed to the different firing characteristics of the colorants (particularly copper) in the red glassy phase. Further research is needed in order to sort this problem out properly. Chemical analysis using proton-induced X-Ray emission shows a high iron content and some copper associated with the slip. Examination of the bole red layer using a scanning electron microscope (see Figure 4.46) shows that it consists of silica and iron-rich crystals bathed in a lead glaze, with a higher proportion of larger silica crystals (appearing grey) lying at a lower level in the glaze, as would be expected. An interesting feature of bole in Figure 4.46 (an interpretative illustration is provided in Figure 4.47) is

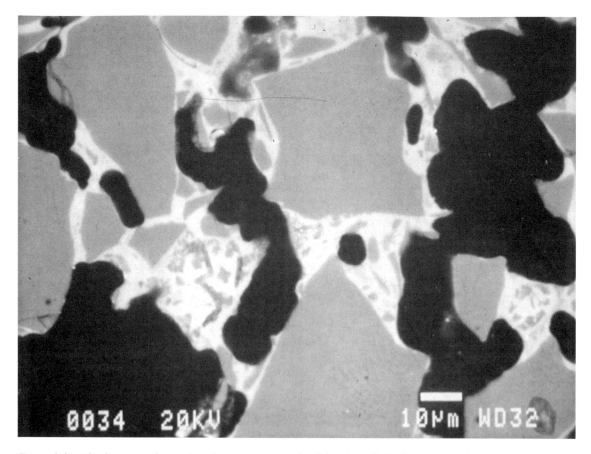

Figure 4.45 A back-scattered scanning electron micrograph of the glassy ('white') phase that has developed between silica crystals in an Iznik body.

the basal layer of minute spinel crystals, which would have formed a dark paint applied to the surface of the white slip and used to mark out the area within which the bole was to be applied. The spinel crystals appear in the electron micrograph as a layer of small white crystals lying on and partly in the underlying silica slip layer in Figures 4.46 and 4.47. The white layer lying over the bole is the base of a lead-rich glaze. Without mounting a section of this kind, and examining it under the SEM, it would not have been possible to identify dark paint used for laying out the decoration, since it was completely covered by the bole red decoration.

The sample of late blue-and-white Iznik pottery analysed which dates to about 1580 and an Iznik tile dating to around 1600 both have the familiar three-component structure: a lead-frit body, lead-rich slip and lead oxide-soda-silica glaze. The latest pot examined from Iznik dates to *c.* 1650. In spite of some similarities in the attempted decoration from that achieved in preceding Iznik pottery styles, by this time it is evident that the technology of ceramic production was in decline. In the production of this mid-seventeenth-century pot the silica used was coarser, with maximum crystal size increasing to *c.* 400 microns, compared to *c.* 100 microns in mid-sixteenth-century Iznik ceramics. Another technological feature which distinguishes this pottery from the finer earlier material is the occurrence of bone ash in the body, where the calcium in the bone ash probably acted as a flux, and the phosphorus possibly as a glass-former, producing a random distribution

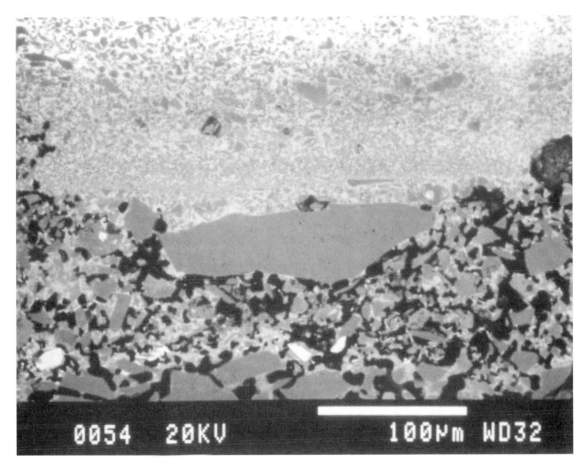

Figure 4.46 A back-scattered scanning electron micrograph of a section through bole red pigment decorating the surface of an Iznik pot.

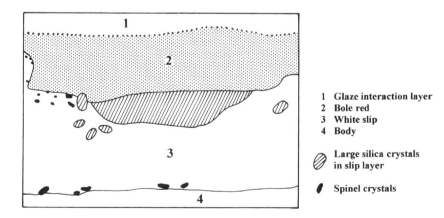

1	Glaze interaction layer
2	Bole red
3	White slip
4	Body

Large silica crystals in slip layer

Spinel crystals

Figure 4.47 An explanatory diagram of Figure 4.46.

of glassy areas. This is an early example of its use in a European context. Although lead- and tin-rich glassy inclusions are present in the seventeenth-century sample, they do not form part of the full interconnected glassy network seen in the earlier Iznik pottery, as if the knowledge of production techniques had only been partly remembered. A poorly formed glaze, which 'rolls' off the surface of the pot is a further technical characteristic which illustrates the decline of this ceramic technology. This pottery clearly marks the decline in quality of Iznik production.

4.7.9 Fifteenth- and sixteenth-century glaze technology and the development of colours

Various features of ceramic technology are important in the effective development of glazes and glaze colours. Although discussed in Section 4.3.5, some of these bear repeating in the context of Iznik glaze technology. The gross composition of the glaze will directly affect the colour which is achieved in the glaze; for example when copper is used as a colorant, the colour will vary between turquoise in lead oxide-soda-silica glazes (as in Iznik glaze), green in lead-silica glaze and blue-green in alkali-silica glazes. The depth of the observed colour will also be affected by the average atomic number of the major constituents; a high proportion of lead oxide will lead to a greater absorption of light wavelengths so that the colour will appear to be of a darker hue. Apart from the gross composition of the glaze, the maximum temperature reached by the kiln, the oxidising-reducing conditions, and the cooling cycle will all affect the successful adherence of the glaze to the ceramic body (its fit). The chemical composition of the body of the pot, and by inference, the crystalline composition and water content of the original clay used, will all affect the fit of the glaze, as will the fineness of the slip, if used. In the case of Iznik pottery the presence of lead in the body, slip and glaze allows the glaze to fit efficiently by reducing the potential differences of contraction on cooling and minimising random cracking or shivering of the glaze. The presence of lead in Iznik glaze provides elasticity which helps the glaze fit. The fit may also be improved by the presence of dissolved tin.

In spite of the wide range of decorative styles employed by Iznik potters the composition of the glazes employed varied little until the decline occurred in the seventeenth century. The glaze composition used in all cases was found to be a lead oxide-soda-silica type (Henderson 1989b: Table 2). Another feature which is characteristic to Iznik is that tin oxide is dissolved in the glaze at a level of c. 5% Henderson 1989b; Tite 1989). The lead oxide dissolved in Iznik glazes imparts a brilliant translucence which shows off the decoration, mainly underglaze, to its best advantage.

Electron microprobe analysis can determine what colorant-rich minerals have been used in order to develop coloured underglazes. As we have seen, the Iznik potters used a white slip as background with cobalt blue or pale green underglaze, which often also coated the internal face of the pot. They used a whole range of glaze colours: turquoise, sage green, emerald green, bole red and purple (apparently black), which produced some intricate and beautiful results. Cobalt blue is a colour that was used throughout the Iznik tradition. Cobalt occurs in nature as a cobalt-rich mineral (i.e. cobalt when used as a colorant has a suite of chemical impurities associated with it: see Section 3.2.5.1). The levels of these impurities changed over time in Iznik ceramics and since they can sometimes be related to mineralogical deposits exploited we can infer that the source for the cobalt mineral used also changed. In the late fifteenth and early sixteenth centuries the impurities detected with the cobalt were iron, nickel and copper. This suggests that a manganiferous cobalt source was used. From c. 1530–60 an arsenic-rich cobalt source was apparently used in Iznik blue glazes. The blue-black pigment used for the linear decoration of a mid-sixteenth-century tile contained cobalt, manganese and arsenic which infers that arsenical cobalt was used, and that the manganese may have been introduced as an additional impurity from an alternative source. One arsenic-rich source for cobalt is the Black Forest in Germany, and there are others in Europe, associated with ancient Massifs; cobalt is also found in Persia and this source was probably used for decorating Kashan wares. Manganiferous sources are found in China but without more analyses, we cannot at this stage establish with confidence which precise sources were used in Iznik blues.

Manganese by itself was found to be the cause of the colour of the translucent purple Iznik glazes. Green colours were produced by iron oxide combined with copper oxide, with occasional detection of chromium; the emerald green glazes were found to contain more iron oxide and less copper oxide. The dark, apparently black, outlines used from about the mid-sixteenth century are due to a high density of pigment particles: the dark green outline in Rhodian pots was found to be coloured by iron and copper, and have been identified by Professor Michael Tite as chromite particles (Tite 1989). Chromite particles were also found to have been used as an applied pigment which was used for defining areas of decoration, as in the case of the application of bole red, described above.

4.7.10 Did local Miletus ware, imported Chinese porcelain, Masters of Tabriz tiles and pottery, and Abraham of Kütahya ware influence the development of Iznik?

In order to examine how other ceramic technologies may have influenced the emergence of an apparently fully-fledged Iznik pottery technology in 1480, the technology of other locally produced 'rusticated' wares or 'peasant wares' (Carswell, in Petsoploulos 1982) needs to be examined. Examples of this are the so-called Abraham of Kütahya wares (Carswell and Dowsett 1972) and Miletus earthenware (Figure 4.48). In addition, other possible influences on the emergence of Iznik pottery need to be examined, especially Chinese porcelain and the bodies of Masters of Tabriz tiles and pottery.

Figure 4.49 shows a back-scattered electron micrograph of a fragment of Miletus earthenware dating to about 1460. If this micrograph is compared with Figure 4.44, a section of Iznik, several differences can be seen. In the Miletus pottery there is no frit component at all, and a series of cracks through the body shows the presence of structural weakness not generally found in Iznik pottery. We can therefore say with confidence that the origins of the bodies of Iznik pottery are unrelated to that of Miletus ware, even if some similar colorant minerals were used.

In view of the use of blue-and-white glaze decoration from the earliest phase of Iznik production,

Figure 4.48 Typical example of Miletus ware (after Atasoy and Raby 1989).

one might suspect that Chinese porcelain technology contributed to the development of Iznik. However, as can be seen in Figure 4.50 the microstructure of high aluminia Chinese porcelain is also entirely different from Iznik pottery with a lack of slip layer and more finely ground silica crystals. Perhaps a more likely source of technological influence might be that attributed to the 'Masters of Tabriz'. Some of the 'Masters of Tabriz' tile glazes analysed were all found to be of a lead oxide-soda-silica composition. Like Iznik glazes the 'Masters of Tabriz' glazes contained tin, but it was not only generally found at slightly higher levels, but mostly present as crystals in suspension (Figure 4.51). Since tin-opacified glazes were introduced much earlier in the Islamic world (Mason and Tite 1997) these glazes are therefore to be regarded as forming a continuation of an earlier tradition. Iznik potters used a far wider range of glaze colours than the 'Masters of Tabriz' who used only monochrome dark blue, turquoise and blue-and-white for tile decoration. While the mineral colorants used were basically the same as used by Iznik potters to make these colours (cobalt, copper and tin oxide respectively), the use of the colorants is often excessive, for example by using excessive cobalt to produce an apparently 'black' glaze instead of cobalt blue. It is also clear that the firing conditions sometimes went

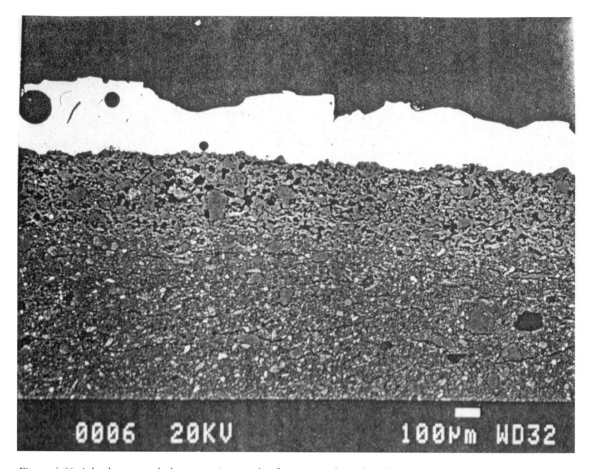

Figure 4.49 A back-scattered electron micrograph of a section through Miletus ware.

wrong. An example of this is where metallic lead was found to be in a suspension of a pale blue glaze decorating a tile from Mahmud Pasa Turbesi dated 1474 (see Figure 4.51). This indicates that the glaze was fired under reducing conditions changing the lead oxide (in a translucent glaze) to droplets of lead metal producing a partially opaque glaze. Although there are similarities in the glaze technologies of Iznik and 'Masters of Tabriz' tiles there are clearly also significant differences.

The results for the analyses of a series of fifteenth-century Turkish tile bodies dating to between 1426 (the mosque of Murad II in Bursa) and 1474 (the so-called tomb of Cem Sultan in Bursa) are published elsewhere (Henderson and Raby 1989), so a summary will be given here. Figure 4.52 shows a polished sec-

tion of a tile from the Muradiye in Edirne dated to 1436, a typical example of 'Masters of Tabriz' work. A very limited development of an alkali-lime frit is visible (appearing white) covering some of the (grey) silica crystals. The development of this glassy phase is very limited when compared to its full development in Iznik pottery. The randomly distributed bright (higher atomic number) inclusions have lead oxide, tin oxide, lead oxide-silica-calcium oxide and lead oxide-silica-tin oxide compositions. The microstructure and composition of this tile body attributed to the 'Masters of Tabriz' is therefore quite different from that of the 'Iznik' potters (compare with the body of Figure 4.43). From the series of tile analyses carried out, the technology used for making the body of *cuerda-seca* tiles and underglaze blue-and-white tiles in

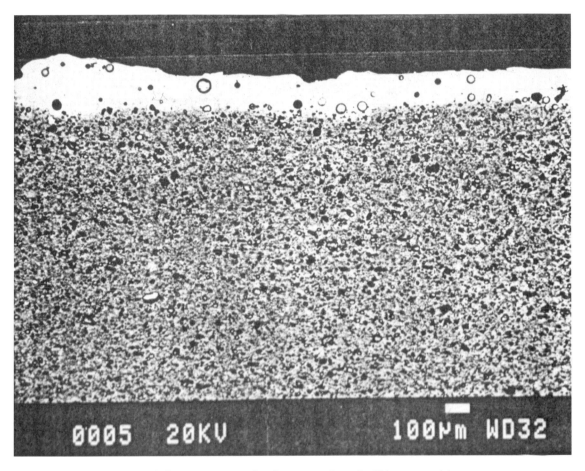

Figure 4.50 A back-scattered electron micrograph of a section through Chinese porcelain.

the Muradiye mosque in Edirne was the same, differing little from the technique used for making tiles in the so-called Cem Sultan Tomb in Bursa – these last tiles are attributable to the tradition of the 'Masters of Tabriz' and so they might be expected to be closest in technology to Iznik products.

It could be argued that the occurrence of a random distribution of lead-rich glassy 'frit' of similar composition to the lead oxide-soda-silica glazes found in *some* of the tiles tested (but not all) suggests that the technology was undergoing an experimental or transitional phase. The evidence for this is very weak, especially since most 'frit' that occurs in the tile bodies is of the alkali-silica composition and is not lead-rich as found in Iznik. The alkali-silica frit is more likely to represent a form of

continuity from an existing Islamic ceramic tradition. Some tiles examined contained no detectable frit at all, so it is not possible to detect a clear developmental phase in tile body technology through the period up to *c.* 1480.

The analysis of a single sherd of blue-and-white pottery dating to *c.* 1430, which can be attributed to one of the painters who decorated the blue-and-white tiles in the Muradiye Mosque in Edirne, shows that in the occasional production of such pottery by the 'Masters of Tabriz' the same alkali-silica frit with a smaller number of randomly distributed lead-rich glassy areas was used as can be found in their tilework.

When compared to Iznik compositions the 'Masters of Tabriz' glazes are mainly similar in being

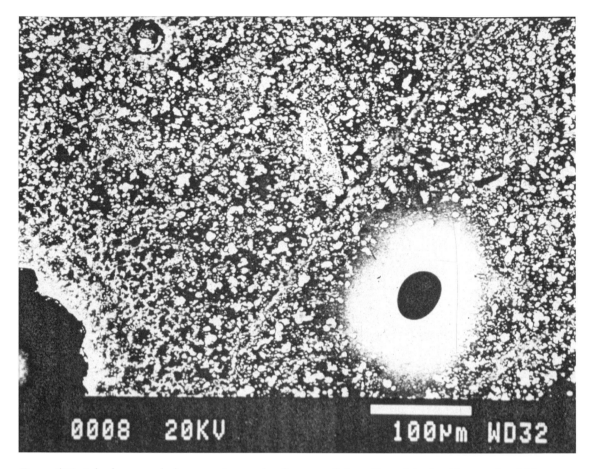

Figure 4.51 A back-scattered electron micrograph of masses of tin oxide and lead oxide crystals which appear white. The glaze is pale blue in colour and is from Istanbul, Mahmud Pasa Turbesi dated to 1474. The fact that the lead has crystallised out of solution indicates that the glaze is 'unsuccessful' because the firing conditions have been too reducing.

a lead oxide-soda-silica (+ tin oxide) type, but in addition there is some marked variation in the composition of the glazes found in the tiles used for decorating Mahmud Pasa Turbesi, Istanbul, dated to 1474 where lead oxide-potassium oxide-silica (+ tin) and a lead oxide-silica (+ tin) were found. In the glaze of the pottery fragment attributed to the 'Masters of Tabriz', the major components were lead oxide, soda and silica, but the lead oxide was present at a significantly lower level, at 4%, than found in Iznik glazes (at 20–30%).

So we can suggest with some confidence that the locally-produced Miletus ware and the Masters of Tabriz tile and pottery technology did not lead directly to the development of Iznik pottery, and also that Chinese blue-and-white porcelain technology is entirely different. Around 1480–90, we might expect the earliest Abraham of Kütahya ware to provide a clue. A blue-and-white potsherd of this type from Iznik was found to be made with a fully developed lead-rich frit. However, the frit was found to contain a lower lead content and can be regarded as transitional in technological terms from the fully-developed Iznik frit technology, which appears around 1510. The body of a tile from Bursa dating from 1512–13 shows characteristics of a non-standardised technology, or possibly one in transition, with multiple layers of ceramic raw

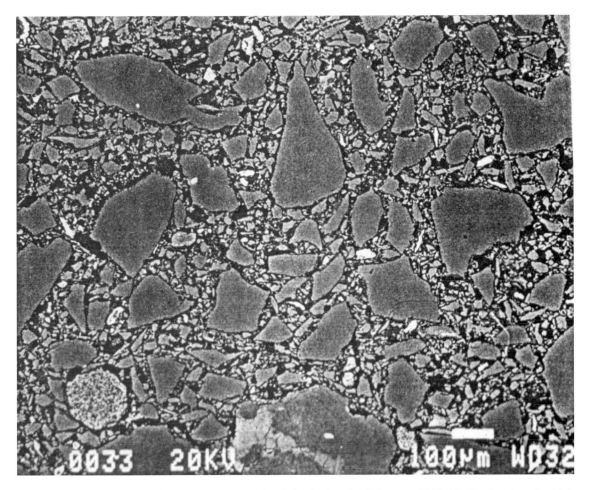

Figure 4.52 A back-scattered electron micrograph of the body of a 'Masters of Tabriz' tile showing the high proportion of large silica crystals and a very limited development of a glassy phase.

materials, including a layer of 'slip-like' material sealed beneath a layer containing larger crystals (see Henderson and Raby 1989 for further discussion). So although pottery technology was standardised by *c.* 1510, tile technology was perhaps still in a state of flux at this time. It is however worth considering the possibility that there was not the same need to produce a perfect tile body with the right weight and thickness as in the manufacture of Iznik pottery; it was, after all, only the glazed tile surfaces which were seen – and some at a distance.

Thus here we have apparent evidence for the origins of the manufacture of Iznik pottery; though it clearly resulted from a very complex situation in which location and chronology should be seen as two very important parameters. The technological development appears to have resulted from new local, rather than external, factors. Court patronage would certainly present the most likely motivation for new developments and near perfection in Iznik technology.

4.7.11 Production and the 'art of the state'

Although the technology of Iznik, and of some of the wares which preceded it and were contemporary with it, are relatively well known the evidence for production sites and a discussion of its internal dynamics are relatively thin on the ground. In the absence of the discovery of kilns that were definitely used for firing Iznik, other sources of evidence must be considered. For this period one important source of evidence is historical.

Atasoy and Raby (1989: 74) note that Iznik was certainly not the only pottery production centre in the sixteenth century. Diyarbakir in eastern Turkey produced provincial imitations of Iznik; in the early eighteenth century Iznik potters working at the Tekfur Sarayi kilns in Instanbul produced Iznik-style tiles; the potteries of the Golden Horn in Istanbul, at least in the seventeenth century, produced earthenware. John Carswell (Carswell and Dowsett 1972) has made the point that there is documentary evidence for Kütahya being an important production centre in the sixteenth and seventeenth centuries. Two vessels bear inscriptions in Armenian which date the vessels to 1510 and 1529 and both refer to Kütahya as the centre of production. The critical point to make here is that these pots might easily be classified as products of Iznik since the same technology is involved (Tite 1989). Given that only a small number of these products are inscribed with primary evidence of where they were manufactured, there is every reason for suspecting that a large number of other wares were made at Kütahya.

The Palace of Sultans at Topkapi in Istanbul was the centre of a vast well-administered Ottoman empire; thousands of people lived and worked in the palace. It was from the palace that the highly centralised government of the empire was run and one part of this organisation was the manufacture of Iznik, by dictat.

Designs for Iznik pottery and the patronage of the court in Istanbul are irrefutable facts. However, demand for Iznik was such that during some periods, such as in the late sixteenth century, the Sultan had to issue an imperial decree which reprimanded the potters of Iznik for delaying the delivery of tiles caused by the demands for Iznik ware used in domestic consumption and for export.

4.7.12 Conclusions

The structural and microstructure features of Iznik pottery bodies can now be defined as consisting of a high silica body (mistakenly referred to as 'faience') containing a lead frit and a small amount of clay, a white slip layer normally containing lower lead levels than the frit, and a lead oxide-soda-silica surface glaze in which tin was dissolved. This technology was used for the manufacture of the Abraham of Kütahya wares, Golden horn wares, Damascus wares, Slip-painted wares, Rhodian wares and Iznik tiles of the sixteenth century. The range of colorant raw materials increased over this period, with the fullest range being used in Rhodian wares which included bole red applied in relief. The origins and initial development of this technology lie somewhere in the late fifteenth century, and apparently locally; this is the time when the principal structural characteristics of Iznik ceramics were first developed, followed in the mid-sixteenth century by the full development of a very wide range of colorants in the glazes. Earlier technologies of the 'Masters of Tabriz' tile-work and the local Miletus pottery bear little relation to the technology of Iznik, even though some characteristics of the glaze technologies are common to both. Technologically there is little to relate Chinese blue-and-white porcelain to Iznik even though it is likely to have provided the stimulus for the production of Iznik blue-and-white. Court patronage is likely to be the explanation/motivation behind the new technological developments, and since these developments occurred over an apparently relatively short time, any possibility that the features associated with the 'Masters of Tabriz' technological tradition contributed to the emergence of Iznik technology is small. By the mid-seventeenth century the technology of Iznik pottery is clearly in decline; the quality of the glaze, its fit and the technology of the pottery body were in stark contrast to the near perfection and brilliance of Iznik at its peak.

References

Allan, J.W. (1973) 'Abū'l Qāsim's treatise on ceramics', *Iran* 11: 111–20.

Allen, C.S.M. (1991) 'Thin sections of Bronze Age pottery from the East Midlands of England', in A. Middleton and I.C. Freestone (eds), *Recent Developments in Ceramic Petrology*, British Museum Occasional Paper 81, London: British Museum Publications, pp. 1–15.

—— (forthcoming) 'Accessory cups of the Bronze Age in Lincolnshire', submitted to *Proceedings of the Prehistoric Society*.

——, Knight, D. and Williams, D.F. (1999) 'Vessel fabrics', in L. Elliott and D. Knight (eds), 'An early Mesolithic site and first-millennium BC settlement and pit alignments at Swarkestone Lowes, Derbyshire', *Derbyshire Archaeological Journal* 119: 79–153.

Anderson, R.P. and Guo Yanyi (1995) 'Imitating Song Dynasty Yaozhou ware: a potter's perspective', in *Science and Technology of Ancient Ceramics*, Proceedings of the 1995 International Symposium, Beijing: Science Press, pp. 99–101.

Anhegger, R. (1941) 'Quellen zur osmanischen keramik', in Otto-Dorn, K. *Das Islamische Isnik*, Berlin, pp. 165 95.

Arnold, D.E. (1985) *Ceramic Theory and Cultural Process*, Cambridge: Cambridge University Press.

Aslanapa, O. (1969) 'Pottery and kilns from the Iznik excavations', in *Forsuchungen zur Kunst Asiens. In Memoriam Kurt Erdmann*, Istanbul: Istanbul University.

Atasoy, N. and Raby, J. (1989) *Iznik the pottery of Ottoman Turkey*, London: Alexandria Press.

Balfet, H., Fauvet-Berthelot, M.-F. and Monzon, S. (1983) *Pour la normalisation de la description des poteries*, Paris: CNRS.

Bedwin, O. and Holgate, R. (1985) 'Excavations at Copse Farm, Oving, West Sussex', *Proceedings of the Prehistoric Society* 51: 220–8.

Birchall, A. (1965) 'The Aylesford-Swarling culture: the problems of the Belgae reconsidered', *Proceedings of the Prehistoric Society* 31: 241–367.

Bishop, R.L. (1992) 'Comments on Section II: variation', in H. Neff (ed.), *Chemical Characterization of Ceramic Pastes in Archaeology*, Monographs in World Archaeology no. 7, Madison: Prehistory Press, pp. 167–70.

Blinkhorn, P.W. (1993) 'Early and Middle Saxon Pottery from Pennyland and Hartigans', in R.J. Williams (ed.), *Pennyland and Hartigans. Two Iron Age and Saxon Sites in Milton Keynes*, Buckinghamshire Archaeology Monograph Series 4.

—— (1997) 'Habitus, social identity and Anglo-Saxon pottery', in C.C. Cumberpatch and P.W. Blinkhorn (eds), *Not So Much a Pot, More a Way of Life*, Oxbow Monograph 83, Oxford: Oxbow Books, pp. 113–24.

Bradley, R. (1975) 'Salt and settlements in the Hampshire Sussex Borderland', in K.W. de Brisay, and K.A. Evans, (eds), *Salt – The Study of an Ancient Industry*, Colchester: The Colchester Archaeological Group, pp. 20–5.

—— (1984) *The Social Foundations of Prehistoric Europe*, London: Longman.

—— (1992) 'Roman salt production in Chichester Harbour: rescue excavations at Chidham, West Sussex', *Britannia* 23: 27–44.

Brisbane, M. (1981) 'Incipient markets for early Anglo-Saxon ceramics: variations in levels and modes of production', in H. Howard and E.L. Morris (eds), *Production and Distribution: A Ceramic Viewpoint*, British Archaeological Reports, International Series 120, Oxford: British Archaeological Reports, pp. 229–42.

Briscoe, T. (1981) 'Anglo-Saxon pot stamps', in D. Brown, J. Campbell and S. Chadwick-Hawkes (eds), *Anglo-Saxon Studies* 2, Oxford: British Archaeological Reports, pp. 1–36.

Brownell, W.E. (1949) 'Fundamental factors influencing efforescence of clay products', *Journal of the American Ceramic Society* 32, 12: 375–89.

Bulleid, A, and Gray, H. St G. (1948) *The Meare Lake Village*, vol. 1, Taunton: privately printed.

Campbell, J. (1982) 'The lost centuries: 400–600', in J. Campbell (ed.), *The Anglo-Saxons*, London: Phaidon, pp. 20–44.

Cardew, M. (1969) *Pioneer Pottery*, New York: St Martin's Press.

Carswell, J. (1982) 'Ceramics' in Y. Petsopoulos (ed.) *Tulips, arabesques and turbans. Decorative Arts from the Ottoman Empire*, London: 73–96.

—— and Dowsett, C.J.F. (1972) *Kütahya Tiles and Pottery from the Armenian Cathedral of St. James, Jerusalem*, 2 vols, Oxford: Oxford University Press.

Chen Tiemei, George (Rip) Rapp, Jr and Zhichun Jing (1999) 'Provenance studies of the earliest Chinese proto-porcelain using instrumental neutron activation analysis', in J. Henderson, H. Neff and Th. Rehren (eds), *Proceedings of the International Symposium on Archaeometry*, University of Illinois at Urbana Champaign (UIUC), Urbana, Illinois, 20–24 May 1996, *Journal of Archaeological Science* 26, 8: 1003–16.

Cherry, J. (1991) 'Pottery and tile', in J. Blair and N. Ramsey (eds), *English Medieval Industries*, London: The Hambledon Press, pp. 189–209.

Cockle, H. (1981) 'Pottery manufacture in Roman Egypt. A new papyrus', *Journal of Roman Studies* LXXI: 87–97.

Coles, J.M. (1987) *Meare Village East*, Somerset Levels Papers 13, Somerset Levels Project.

Collis, J.R. (1979) 'City and state in pre-Roman Britain', in B.C. Burnham and H.B. Johnson (eds), *Invasion and Response, The Case of Roman Britain*, British Archaeological Reports 73, Oxford: British Archaeological Reports, pp. 231–43.

—— (1982) 'Gradual growth and sudden change – urbanisation in Temperate Europe', in C. Renfrew and S. Shennan (eds), *Ranking, Resource and Exchange, Aspects of the Archaeology of Early European Society*, Cambridge: Cambridge University Press, pp. 73–8.

—— (1984) *Oppida, Earliest Towns North of the Alps*, Sheffield: Department of Archaeology and Prehistory.

Cooper, J. (1982) 'The research potential of molluscan shell in shell-tempered pottery', in A. Middleton, I.

Freestone, C. Johns and T. Potter (eds), *Current Research in Ceramics: Thin-section Studies*, British Museum Occasional Paper 32, London: British Museum Publications, pp. 161–2.

Crummy, P. (1980) 'Camulodunum', *Current Archaeology* 7: 6–10.

Cunliffe, B. (1987) *Hengistbury Head Dorset. Volume 1: The Prehistoric and Roman Settlement, 3500 BC–AD 500*, Oxford University Committee for Archaeology, Monograph no. 13.

—— (1991) *Iron Age Communities in Britain*, London: Routledge and Kegan Paul, 3rd edn.

—— (1995) *Danebury Volume 6: A Hillfort Community in Perspective*, Council for British Archaeology Research Report 102, York: Council for British Archaeology.

Dal, P.H. and Berden, W.J. (1965) 'Bound water on clay', *Science of Ceramics* 2: 59.

Daicoviciu, I. and Daicoviciu, H. (1963) *Sarmizegethusa*, Bucharest.

Dawson, M. (1988) 'Excavations at Ursula Taylor Lower School', *Bedfordshire Archaeology* 18: 6–24.

Deer, W.A., Howie, R.A. and Zussman, J. (1962) *Rock-forming Minerals V: Non-silicates*, London: Longman.

Dunham, A.C. (1992) 'Developments in industrial mineralogy: I. The mineralogy of brick-making', *Proceedings of the Yorkshire Geological Society* 49, 2: 95–104.

Elsdon, S.M. (1992) 'The Iron Age pottery' in P. Clay (ed.), 'An Iron Age farmstead at Grove Farm, Enderby, Leicestershire', *Transactions of the Leicestershire Archaeological and Historical Society* 66: 83–91.

—— (1997) *Old Sleaford Revealed*, Oxbow Monograph 78, Oxford: Oxbow Books.

Farley, M. (1983) 'A mirror burial at Dorton, Bucks.', *Proceedings of the Prehistoric Society* 49: 269–302.

Fawn, A.J., Evans, K.A., McMaster, I. and Davies, G.M.R. (1990) *The Red Hills of Essex. Salt-making in Antiquity*, Colchester: Colchester Archaeology Group.

Figueral, I. (1992) 'The charcoals', in M.G. Fulford and J.R.L. Allen (eds), 'Iron-making at the Chesters villa, Woolaston, Gloucestershire: Survey and Excavation 1987–91', *Britannia* 23, 1: 59–215.

Foster, J. (1980) *The Iron Age Moulds of Gussage All Saints*, British Museum Occasional Paper no. 12, London: British Museum Publications.

—— (1995) 'Metalworking in the British Iron Age: the evidence from Wesley Avenue, Grimsby', in J. Raftery (ed.), *Sites and Sights of the Iron Age, Essays on Field work and Museum Research presented to Ian Mathieson Stead*, Oxbow Monographs 56, Oxford, Oxbow Books; London: Council for British Archaeology Research, pp. 49–61.

Freestone, I.C. (1991) 'Technical examination of Neo-Assyrian glazed wall plaques', *Iraq* 53: 55–8.

—— (1999) 'The science of early English porcelain', *Proceedings of the Sixth Conference and Exhibition of the European Ceramic Society*, 20–24 June 1999, Brighton, British Ceramic Proceedings no. 60, Abstracts vol. 1: 11–17.

—— and Gaimster, D. (eds) (1997) *Pottery in the Making*, London: British Museum Press.

Fulford, M. (1987) '*Calleva atributum*: an interim report on the excavations of the oppidum', *Proceedings of the Prehistoric Society* 53: 271–8.

Gibson, A. and Wood, A. (1997) *Prehistoric Pottery for the Archaeologists*, Leicester: Leicester University Press.

Glick, D.P. (1936) 'The microbiology of ageing clays', *Journal of the American Ceramic Society* 19: 169–75.

Goffer, Z. (1980) *Archaeological Chemistry*, New York: Wiley.

Gray, H. St G. (1966) *The Meare Lake Village*, vol. III, M.A. Cotton (ed.), Taunton: privately printed.

—— and Bulleid, A. (1953) *The Meare Lake Village*, vol. II, Taunton: privately printed.

Grim, R.E. (1968) *Clay Mineralogy*, 2nd edn, New York: McGraw-Hill.

Guo Yangi (1987) 'Raw materials for making porcelain and the characteristics of porcelain wares in north and south China', *Archaeometry* 29: 3–20.

—— and Li Guozhen (1986) 'Song Dynasty Ru and Yaozhou green glazed wares', in *Scientific and Technological Insights on Ancient Chinese Pottery and Porcelain*, Proceedings of the International Conference on Ancient Chinese Pottery and Porcelain, Shanghai Institute of Ceramics, Beijing: Science Press, pp. 153–60.

——, Zhang Zhigang, Chen Shiping and Zuo Zhexxi (1995) 'Ancient ceramic moulds of Yaozhou kiln', in *Science and Technology of Ancient Ceramics*, Proceedings of the 1995 International Symposium, Beijing: Science Press, pp. 320–4.

Haith, C. (1997) 'Pottery in Early Anglo-Saxon England', in I.C. Freestone and D. Gaimster (eds), *Pottery in the Making*, London: British Museum Press, pp. 146–51.

Hamerow, H. (1993) *Excavations at Mucking, volume 2: The Anglo-Saxon Settlement*, English Heritage Archaeological Report 21.

——, Hollevoet, Y. and Vince, A. (1994) 'Migration period settlements and Anglo-Saxon pottery from Flanders', *Medieval Archaeology* 38: 1–18.

Hamilton, S. (1985) 'Iron Age pottery', in O. Bedwin and R. Holgate 'Excavations at Copse Farm, Oving, West Sussex', *Proceedings of the Prehistoric Society* 51: 220–8.

Harris, V. (1997) 'Jomon Pottery in Ancient Japan', in I.C. Freestone and D. Gaimster (eds), *Pottery in the Making*, London: British Museum Press, pp. 20–5.

Haselgrove, C.C. (1986) 'Central places in British Iron Age: a review and some problems', in E. Grant (ed.) *Central Places, archaeology and history*, Sheffield: J.R. Collis Publications, pp. 3–12.

Hay, R.L. (1960) 'Rate of clay formation and mineral alteration in a 4000-year-old volcanic ash soil on St. Vincent, B.W.I', *American Journal of Science* 258: 354–68.

Hedges, R.E.M. (1982) 'Early glazed pottery and faience in Mesopotamia', in T.A. Wertime and S.F. Wertime (eds), *Early Pyrotechnology*, Washington, DC: Smithsonian Institution Press, pp. 93–104.

—— and Moorey, P.R.S. (1982) 'Pre-Islamic ceramic glazes at Kish and Nineveh in Iraq', *Archaeometry* 17, 1: 25–43.

Henderson, J. (1984) 'Beads of glass', in B.W. Cunliffe *Danebury, an Iron Age Hillfort in Hampshire, volume 2: The Excavations 1969–1978: The Finds*, Council for British Archaeology Research Report no. 52, London: Council for British Archaeology, pp. 396–8.

—— (1985) 'The raw materials of early glass production', *Oxford Journal of Archaeology* 4 (3): 267–91.

—— (ed.) (1989a) *Scientific Analysis in Archaeology and its interpretation*, Oxford University Committee for Archaeology Monograph no. 19; UCLA Institute of Archaeology, Archaeological Research Tools 5, Oxford: Oxford University Committee on Archaeology; Los Angeles: UCLA Institute of Archaeology.

—— (1989b) 'Iznik ceramics: a technical examination' and 'A technical examination of Ottoman ceramics', in N. Atasoy and J. Raby, *Iznik. The Pottery of Ottoman Turkey*, London: Alexandria Press, Chapter 6.

—— (1991) 'Industrial Specialization in late Iron Age Britain and Europe', *The Archaeological Journal* 148: 104–148.

—— and Raby, J. (1989) 'The technology of fifteenth-century Turkish tiles: an interim statement on the origins of the Iznik industry', *World Archaeology* 21 (1), 115–32

——, Challis, K., Cumberpatch, C., Larson, S. and Towle, A. (forthcoming) 'Excavations at al-Raqqa, 1998'.

Henrickson, R.C. and Blackman, M.J. (1992) 'Scale and paste: investigating the production of Godin III painted buff ware', in H. Neff (ed.), *Chemical Characterization of Ceramic Pastes in Archaeology*, Monographs in World Archaeology no. 7, Madison: Prehistory Press, pp. 125–44.

Hodson, F.R. (1995) 'A Münsingen Fibula', in Raftery (ed.), *Sites and Sights of the Iron Age, Essays on Field work and Museum Research presented to Ian Mathieson Stead*, Oxbow Monographs 56, Oxford, Oxbow Books; London: Council for British Archaeology Research, pp. 62–6.

Hurst, D. and Freestone, I.C. (1996) 'Lead glazing technique from a medieval kiln site at Hanley Swan, Worcestershire', *Medieval Ceramics* 20: 13–18.

Hurst, J.D. (ed.) (1997) *A Multi-period Salt Production Site at Droitwich: Excavations at Upwich*, Council for British Archaeology Research Report 107, York: Council for British Archaeology.

Institute of Archaeology – Shaanxi province (1992) *Tang Dynasty Huangbao Kiln Site*, vol. 1, Beijing: Cultural Relics Publishing House.

—— (1997) *Five Dynasties Huangbao Kiln Site*, Beijing: Cultural Relics Publishing House.

—— and Yaozhou Kiln Museum (1998) *Song Dynasty Yaozhou Kiln Site*, Beijing: Cultural Relics Publishing House.

Jacobi, G. (1974) *Werkzeug und Gerät aus dem oppidum von Manching*, Die Ausgrabungen in Manching, vol. 5, Wiesbaden: Steiner.

Johnson, A.L. and Norton, F.H. (1941) 'Fundamental study of clay. 2. Mechanism of deflocculation in the clay-water system', *Journal of the American Ceramic Society* 24, 6: 189–203.

Johnson, S.M., Pask, J.A. and Moya, J.S. (1982) 'Influence of impurities in high-temperature reactions of kaolinite', *Journal of the American Ceramic Society* 65, 1: 31–5.

José-Yacaman, M., Rendon, L., Arenas, J. and Serra Puche, M.C. (1996) 'Maya blue paint: an ancient nanostructural material', *Science* 273: 223–5.

Kilikoglou, V., Vekinis, G., Maniatis, Y. and Day, P.M. (1998) 'Mechanical performance of quartz-tempered ceramics: Part I, Strength and toughness', *Archaeometry* 40,1: 261–80.

Kingery, W.D. (1986) 'The development of European porcelain', in W.D. Kingery (ed.), *High Technology Ceramics Past, Present and Future*, Ceramics and Civilisation vol. III, Westerville, Ohio: The American Ceramic Society, pp. 153–80.

—— (1993) 'Painterly maiolica of the Italian Renaissance', *Technology and Culture*: 28–48.

——, Bowan, H.K. and Uhlmann, D.R. (1976) *Introduction to Ceramics*, 2nd edn, New York: John Wiley.

—— and Francl, J. (1954) 'Fundamental study of clay. 13. Drying behaviour and plastic properties', *Journal of the American Ceramic Society* 37, 12: 596–602.

—— and Smith, D. (1985) 'The development of European soft-paste (frit) porcelain', in W.D. Kingery (ed.), *Ancient Technology to Modern Science*, Ceramics and Civilisation vol. 1, Columbus, Ohio: American Ceramic Society, pp. 273–93.

—— and Vandiver, P.B. (1986) *Ceramic Masterpieces*, New York: The Free Press.

Knight, D. (1992) 'Excavations of an Iron Age settlement at Gamston, Nottinghamshire', *Transactions of the Thornton Society of Nottinghamshire* 96: 16–90.

—— (1999) 'A regional ceramic sequence: pottery of the first millennium BC between the Humber and the Nene', in J.D. Hill and A. Woodward (eds), *Prehistoric Britain: The Ceramic Basis*, Oxford: Oxbow Books.

—— (1999a) 'Iron Age Briquetage and Miscellaneous Fired Clay', p. 137 in L. Elliott and D. Knight 'An early Mesolithic site and first millenium BC settlement and pit alignments at Swarkestone Lowes, Derbyshire', *Derbyshire Archaeological Journal* 119: 79–153.

Ko Choo, C.K., Kim, S., Kang, H.T., Do, J.Y., Lee, Y.E. and Kim, G.H. (1999) 'A comparative scientific study of the earliest kiln sites of Koryŏ celadon', *Archaeometry* 41, 1: 51–70.

Kolb, C.C. (1989) 'Ceramic ecology in retrospect: a critical review of methodology and results', in C.C. Kolb (ed.), *Ceramic Ecology in Retrospect, 1988: Current Research in Ceramic Materials*, British Archaeological Reports International Series 513, Oxford: British Archaeological Reports, pp. 261–375.

Krämer, W. and Schubert, F. (1970) *Die Ausgrabungen in Manching 1955–1961. Einfuhrumg und Fundstellungübersicht*, Wiesbaden: Steiner.

Lane, T. (1992) 'Iron Age and Roman Salterns in the South-Western Fens', in P.P. Hayes and T.W. Lane (eds), *The Fenland Project Number 5: Lincolnshire Survey, The South-West Fens*, East Anglian Archaeology Report no. 55, pp. 218–29.

Leach, B. (1976) *A Potter's Book*, London: Faber and Faber.

Li Gouzhen and Guan Peiying (1979) 'Research on Yaozhou blue-green ware', *Silicate Study Journal* 7, 4: 192–7.

——, Wang Jian, Li Wenchao, Qin Jianwu, Zhuang Youqing and Meng Shufeng (1992) 'Discussion of the technology on Yaozhou ware glaze of successive Dynasties', in Li Jiazhi and Chen Xianqiu (eds), *Science and Technology of Ancient Ceramics*, Proceedings of the 1989 International Symposium, Shanghai: Shanghai Science and Technology Press, pp. 285–93.

Li Jianzhi (1985) 'The evolution of Chinese pottery and porcelain technology', in W.D. Kingery (ed.) *Ancient Technology to Modern Science*, Ceramics and Civilisation vol. 1, Columbus, Ohio: American Ceramic Society, pp. 135–62.

Li Wenchao, Wang Jian and Li Guozhen (1992) 'Mechanism on formation of transition layer in ancient ceramics of Jun, Ru and Yaozhou wares in the Song Dynasty', in *Science and Technology of Ancient Ceramics*, Proceedings of the 1992 International Symposium, pp. 280–5.

Magetti, M. (1982) 'Phase analysis and its significance for technology and origin', in J.S. Olin and A.D. Franklin (eds), *Archaeological Ceramics*, Washington, DC: Smithsonian Institution Press, pp. 121–33.

Magrill, P. and Middleton, A. (1997) 'A Canaanite potter's Workshop in Palestine', in I.C. Freestone and D. Gaimster (eds), *Pottery in the Making*, London: British Museum Press, pp. 68–73.

Mason, R.B. and Tite, M.S. (1994) 'The beginnings of Islamic stonepaste technology', *Archaeometry* 36: 77–92.

—— and —— (1997) 'The beginnings of tin-opacification of pottery glazes', *Archaeometry* 39, 1: 41–58.

Matson, F.R. (1965) *Ceramics and Man*, London: Methuen.

—— (1971) 'A study of temperatures used in firing ancient Mesopotamian pottery', in R.H. Brill (ed.), *Science and Archaeology*, Cambridge: MIT Press, pp. 65–80.

—— (1986) 'Glazed brick from Babylon – historical setting and microprobe analyses', in W.D. Kingery (ed.), *Technology and Style, Ceramics and Civilisation II*, Columbus, Ohio: American Ceramic Society, pp. 133–56.

May, J. (1996) *Dragonby. Report on Excavations at an Iron Age and Romano-British Settlement in North Lincolnshire*, Oxbow Monograph 61, Oxford: Oxbow Books.

Medley, M. (1986) *The Chinese Potter – A Practical History of Chinese Ceramics*, Ithaca, New York: Cornell University Press.

Mehren, F., Muller, K.A. and Fitzpatrick, W.J. (1981) 'Characterization of particle orientations in ceramics by electron paramagnetic resonance', *Journal of the American Ceramic Society* 64, 10: C129–30.

Middleton, A. (1996) 'Petrology', in J. May (ed.), *Dragonby. Report on Excavations at an Iron Age and Romano-British Settlement in North Lincolnshire*, Oxbow Monograph 61, Oxford: Oxbow Books, pp. 419–21.

Millett, M. (1990) *The Romanization of Britain*, Cambridge: Cambridge University Press.

Moorey, P.R.S. (1994) *Ancient Mesopotamian Materials and Industries. The Archaeological Evidence*, Oxford: The Clarendon Press.

Morris, E.L. (1981) 'Ceramic exchange in western Britain: a preliminary view', in H. Howard and E. Morris (eds), *Production and Distribution: A Ceramic Viewpoint*, Oxford: British Archaeological Reports 120, pp. 67–81.

—— (1982) 'Iron Age pottery from western Britain: another petrological study', in I.C. Freestone, C. Johns and T. Potter (eds), *Current Research in Ceramics: Thin-Section Studies*, London: British Museum Occasional Paper 32, pp. 15–27.

—— (1983) 'Petrological report, Droitwich briquetage containers, seriation analysis by fabric type of the Iron Age pottery', in A. Saville and A. Ellison (eds), *Excavations at Uley Bury Hillfort Gloucestershire 976*, Bristol: Western Archaeological Trust Excavations Monograph 5.

—— (1985) 'Prehistoric salt distributions: two case studies from western Britain', *Bulletin of the Board of Celtic Studies* 32, 336–79.

—— (1991) 'The pottery', in P. Barker, R. Haldon and E. Jenks, Excavations on Sharpstones Hill near Shrewsbury 1965–71, in M.O.H. Carver (ed.), Prehistory in Lowland Shropshire, *Transactions of the Shropshire Archaeological Society* 67, 15–57.

—— (1994a) 'Production and distribution of pottery and salt in Iron Age Britain: a review', *Proceedings of the Prehistoric Society* 60, 371–93.

—— (1994b) 'The organisation of salt production and distribution in Iron Age Wessex', in A.P. Fitzpatrick and E.L. Morris (eds), *The Iron Age in Wessex: Recent Work*, Salisbury: The Trust for Wessex Archaeology, pp. 14–16.

Myers, E.J. (1992) 'Compositional standardization in sixteenth-century Italian maiolica', in H. Neff (ed.), *Chemical Characterization of Ceramic Pastes in Archaeo-*

logy, Monographs in World Archaeology no. 7, Madison: Prehistory Press, pp. 145–57.

Myres, J.N.L. (1969) *Anglo-Saxon Pottery and the Settlement of England,* Cambridge: Cambridge University Press.

—— (1977) *A Corpus of Anglo-Saxon Pottery of the Pagan Period,* 2 vols, Cambridge: Cambridge University Press.

National Academy of Sciences (1980) *Firewood Crops: Shrub and Tree Species for Energy Production,* Washington, DC: National Academy of Sciences.

Newell, R.W. (1995) 'Some notes on "splashed glazes"', *Medieval Ceramics* 19: 77–88.

Nicklin, K. (1981a) 'Ceramic pyrometry: two Ibibio examples', in H. Howard and E. Morris (eds), *Production and Distribution: A Ceramic Viewpoint,* British Archaeological Reports, International Series 120, Oxford: British Archaeological Reports, pp. 347–59.

—— (1981b) 'Pottery production and distribution in southeast Nigeria', in H. Howard and E. Morris (eds), *Production and Distribution: A Ceramic Viewpoint,* British Archaeological Reports, International Series 120, Oxford: British Archaeological Reports, pp. 169–96.

Nissen, H.J. (1988) *The Early History of the Ancient Near East,* Chicago: University of Chicago Press.

Norton, F.H. (1970) *Fine Ceramics, Technology and Applications,* New York: McGraw-Hill.

—— and Johnson, A.L. (1944) 'Fundamental study of clay. 5. Nature of the water film in a plastic clay', *Journal of the American Ceramic Society* 27, 3: 77–80.

Oates, D. and Oates, J. (1976) *The Rise of Civilization,* Oxford: Oxford University Press.

O'Brien, J., Holland, T.D., Hoard, R.J. and Fox, G.L. (1994) 'Fracture toughness determinations of alumina using four-point-bend specimens with straight-through and chevron-notches', *Journal of the American Ceramic Society* 63: 300–5.

Partridge, C. (1981) *Skeleton Green: A Late Iron Age and Romano-British Site,* London: Britannia Monographs 2.

Peacock, D.P.S. (1968) 'A petrological study of certain Iron Age pottery from western England', *Proceedings of the Prehistoric Society* 34: 414–27.

—— (1969) 'A contribution to the study of Glastonbury Ware from south-western Britain', *The Antiquaries Journal* 49: 41–61.

—— (1982) *Pottery in the Roman World,* London: Longman.

Peltenburg, E. (1971) 'Some early developments of vitreous materials', *World Archaeology* 3, 1: 6–12.

Piccolpasso, C. (1980) *The Three Books of the Potter's Art: A Facsimile of the Manuscript in the Victoria and Albert Museum,* (R. Lightbown and A. Caiger-Smith, eds), 2 vols., London: Scolar Press.

Pieta, K. (1982) *Die Puchov-Kultur,* Studia Archaeologica Slovaca, Instituti Archaeologici Academiae Scientiarum Slovacae, 1, Nitra: Academiae.

Piggott, S. (1965) *Ancient Europe,* Edinburgh: Edinburgh University Press.

Pleiner, R. (1977) 'Neue Grabungen frühgeschichtlicher Eisenhüttenplatte in der Tschechoslowakei und die Bedeutung des Schachtofens fur die Entwicklung des Schmelzvorganges', in A. Ohrenberger and K. Kaus (eds), *Archäologische Eisenforschung in Europa,* Graz: Burgenalandisches Landesmuseum, pp. 107–17.

—— (1980) 'Early iron metallurgy in Europe', in T.A. Wertime and J.D. Muhly (eds), *The Coming of the Age of Iron,* Yale: Yale University Press, pp. 375–415.

Plog, F. (1977) 'Modelling economic change', in T.K. Earle and J.E. Ericson (eds), *Exchange Systems in Prehistory,* New York: Academic Press, pp. 127–40.

Pollard, A.M. and Hatcher, H. (1994) 'The chemical analysis of oriental ceramic body compositions, part 1: wares from north China', *Archaeometry* 36: 41–62.

—— and Heron, C. (1996) *Archaeological Chemistry,* Cambridge: The Royal Society of Chemistry.

Portal, J. (1997) 'Korean Celadons of the Koryo Dynasty', in I.C. Freestone and D. Gaimster (eds), *Pottery in the Making,* London: British Museum Press, pp. 98–103.

Postgate, J.N. and Moon, J.A. (1982) 'Excavations at Abu Salabikh 1981', *Iraq* 44: 103–36.

Ralston, I. (1988) 'Central Gaul at the Roman Conquest: conceptions and misconceptions', *Antiquity* 62: 786–94.

Renfrew, C. (1975) 'Trade and action at a distance: questions of integration and communication', in J. Sabloff and C.C. Lamberg-Karlovsky (eds), *Ancient Civilization and Trade,* Albuquerque: University of New Mexico Press, pp. 3–59.

Rhodes, D. (1969) *Kilns: Design, Construction and Operation,* Philadelphia: Chilton Books.

Rice, P.M. (1987) *Pottery Analysis: A Sourcebook,* Chicago: The University of Chicago Press.

Rigby, V. and Freestone, I.C. (1985) 'The petrology and typology of the earliest identified central Gaulish imports', *Journal of Roman Pottery Studies* 1: 6–21.

—— and —— (1997) 'Ceramic changes in late Iron Age Britain', in I.C. Freestone and D. Gaimster (eds), *Pottery in the Making,* London: British Museum Press, pp. 56–61.

Roberts, P. (1997) 'Mass production of Roman finewares', in I.C. Freestone and D. Gaimster (eds), *Pottery in the Making,* London: British Museum Press, pp. 188–93.

Rodwell, W.J. (1976) 'Coinage, oppida and the rise of Belgic power in south-eastern Britain', in B. Cunliffe and T. Rowley (eds), *Oppida: The Beginnings of Urbanism in Barbarian Europe,* British Archaeological Reports, Supplementary Series 11, Oxford: British Archaeological Reports, pp. 181–7.

Russel, A.D. (1985) 'Petrological report on the West Stow Saxon Pottery', in S.E. West (ed.), *West Stow: The Anglo-Saxon Village,* 2 vols, East Anglian Archaeology, vol. 24.

Ryan, W. (1965) 'Factors influencing the dry strength of clays and bodies', *Transactions of the British Ceramic Society* 64: 275–85.

Rye, O.S. (1976) 'Keeping your temper under control', *Archaeology and Physical Anthropology in Oceania* 11, 2: 106–37.

—— and Evans, C. (1976) *Traditional Pottery Techniques of Pakistan: Field and Laboratory Studies*, Smithsonian Contributions to Anthropology no. 21, Washington, DC: Smithsonian Institution Press.

Şahin, F. (1981) 'Kütayha seramik teknolojisi ve çini firinlari hakkinda görüşler', *Sanat Tarihi Yilli ği* 11, 133–51.

Scheurs, J.W.H. and Brill, R.H. (1984) 'Iron and sulfur-related colours in ancient glasses', *Archaeometry* 26, 2: 199–209.

Sellwood, L. (1984) 'Tribal boundaries viewed from the perspective of numismatic evidence', in B. Cunliffe and D. Miles (eds), *Aspects of the Iron Age in Central Southern Britain*, University of Oxford Committee for Archaeology Monograph 2, Oxford: University Committee for Archaeology, pp. 191–204.

Shepard, A.O. (1976) *Ceramics for the Archaeologist*, Washington, DC: Carnegie Institution of Washington.

Simpson, St J. (1997a) 'Prehistoric ceramics in Mesopotamia', in I.C. Freestone and D. Gaimster (eds), *Pottery in the Making*, London: British Museum Press, pp. 38–43.

—— (1997b) 'Early urban ceramic industries in Mesopotamia', in I.C. Freestone and D. Gaimster (eds), *Pottery in the Making*, London: British Museum Press, pp. 50–5.

Singer, C., Holmyard, E.J., Hall, A.R. and Williams, T.J. (1956) *A History of Technology*, vol. II, Oxford: Clarendon.

Soontaek Choi-Bae (1984) *Seladon-Keramik der Koryo-Dynastie*, Köln: Museum für Ostasiatische Kunst, pp. 918–1392.

Staehelin, W. (1965) *The Book of Porcelain: The manufacture, transport, and sale of export porcelain in China during the eighteenth century, illustrated by a series of contemporary Chinese watercolours*, London: Lund Humphries.

Starkey, P. (1977) *Saltglaze*, London: Pitman.

Stead, I.M. (1967) 'A La Tène III burial at Welwyn Garden City', *Archaeologia* 101: 1–62.

—— (1985) *Celtic Art in Britain before the Roman Conquest*, London: British Museum Publications.

—— and Rigby, V. (1989) *Verulamium: The King Harry Lane Site*, London: English Heritage Archaeological Monographs 12.

Sterner, J. (1989) 'Who is signalling whom? Ceramic style, ethnicity and taphonomy among Sirak Bulahay', *Antiquity* 63: 451–9.

Swan, V.G. (1984) *The Pottery Kilns of Roman Britain*, Royal Commission on Historical Monuments, Supplementary Series 5, London: Her Majesty's Stationery Office.

Thompson, I. (1982) *Grog-Tempered 'Belgic' Pottery of South-Eastern England*, Oxford: British Archaeological Reports 108.

—— and Barfield, P. (1986) 'Late Iron Age pottery and briquetage from Elm Park House, Ardleigh, 1981', *Essex Archaeological and Historical Society* 17: 166–70.

Thornton, D. (1997) 'Maiolica production in Renaissance Italy', in I.C. Freestone and D. Gaimster (eds), *Pottery in the Making*, London: British Museum Press, pp. 116–21.

Tite, M.S. (1989) 'Iznik pottery: an investigation of the methods of production', *Archaeometry* 31, 2: 115–32.

—— (1991) 'Technological investigations of Italian Renaissance ceramics', in T. Wilson, (ed.), *Italian Renaissance Pottery: Papers written in association with a Colloquium at the British Museum*, London: British Museum Publications, pp. 280–5.

—— (1999) 'Pottery production, distribution, and consumption – the contribution of the physical sciences', *Journal of Archaeological Method and Theory* 6: 181–233.

—— and Bimson, M. (1986) 'Faience: an investigation of the microstructures associated with the different methods of glazing', *Archaeometry* 28, 1: 69–78.

——, Freestone, I.C., Mason, R., Molera, J., Vendrell-saz, M. and Wood, N. (1998) 'Lead glazes in antiquity – methods of production and reasons for use', *Archaeometry* 40, 2: 241–60.

—— and Maniatis, Y. (1975) 'Scanning electron microscopy of fired calcareous clays', *Transactions of the British Ceramic Society* 74: 19–22.

Tonghini, C. and Henderson, J. (1998) 'An eleventh-century pottery production workshop at al-Raqqa, Preliminary report', *Levant* 30: 113–27.

Van der Leeuw, S.E. (1975) 'Medieval pottery from Haarlem: a model', in J.G.N. Renaud (ed.), *Rotterdam Papers* II, Rotterdam: Coördinatie Commissie van Advies inzake Archeologisch Onderzoek binnen het Ressort, pp. 67–87.

Vandiver, P.B, Cort, L.A. and Handwerker, C.A. (1989) 'Variations in the practice of ceramic technology in different cultures: a comparison of Korean and Chinese celadon glazes', in P.E. McGovern and M.D. Notis (eds), *Cross-craft and Cross-cultural Interactions in Ceramics*, Ceramics and Civilisation vol. IV, Westerville, Ohio: The American Ceramic Society, pp. 347–88.

—— and Kingery, W.D. (1984) 'Composition and structures of Chinese Song Dynasty celadon glazes from Longquan', *Bulletin of the American Ceramic Society* 63, 4: 612–16.

Vekinis, G. and Kilikoglou, V. (1998) 'Mechanical performance of quartz-tempered ceramics: Part II, Hertzian strength, wear resistance and applications to ancient ceramics', *Archaeometry* 40, 2: 281–92.

Velde, B. and Druc, I.C. (1999) *Archaeological Ceramic Materials*, Berlin: Springer.

Vince, A. (1989) 'The petrography of Saxon and early medieval pottery in the Thames valley', in J. Henderson (ed.), *Scientific Analysis in Archaeology and its interpretation*, Oxford University Committee for Archaeology Monograph no. 19; UCLA Institute of Archaeology, Archaeological Research Tools 5, Oxford: Oxford University Committee on Archaeology; Los Angeles: UCLA Institute of Archaeology, pp. 163–77.

Wang Fang and Wang Lefang (1995) 'The manufacture technology of Yaozhou porcelain mould and its characteristics', in *Science and Technology of Ancient Ceramics*, Proceedings of the 1995 International Symposium, Beijing: Science Press, pp. 313–19.

Wang Lefang (1995) 'Five Dynasties ceramic moulds recently discovered at Yaozhou kiln site', *Kaogu yu Wenwu* (Archaeology of relics) 3: 50–5 (in Chinese).

Watson, W.M. (1986) *Italian Renaissance Majolica from the William A. Clark Collection*, London: Scala Books.

Welch, M. (1992) *Anglo-Saxon England*, London: Batsford.

Welsby, D. (1997) 'Early pottery in the Middle Nile Valley', in I.C. Freestone and D. Gaimster (eds), *Pottery in the Making*, London: British Museum Press, pp. 26–31.

West, S. (1985) *West Stow: The Anglo Saxon Village*, East Anglian Archaeology 24.

White, L. (1972) 'The act of invention', in M. Kranzberg and W.H. Davenport (eds), *Technology and Culture. An Anthology*, New York: New American Library, pp. 274–91.

Whitehouse, D. (1971) 'Excavations at Sīrāf. Fourth interim report', *Iran* 9: 1–18.

Williams, D. (1992) *A Note on the Petrology of some Late Iron Age Sherds from Gamston, Nottinghamshire*, Ancient Monuments Laboratory Report 14/92, London: English Heritage.

—— and Vince, A. (1997) 'The characterization and interpretation of early to middle Saxon granitic tempered pottery in England', *Medieval Archaeology* XLI, 214–20.

Wilson, T. (1987) *Ceramic Art of the Renaissance*, London: British Museum Publications.

Wood, N. (1999) *Chinese Glazes*, London: Black.

—— and Freestone, I.C. (1995) 'A preliminary examination of a Warring States pottery jar with so-called "glass paste" decoration', in Guo Jinkum (ed.), *Science and Technology of Ancient Ceramics 3; Proceedings of the International Symposium on Ancient Ceramics (ISAC '95)*, Shanghai, pp. 12–17.

——, Henderson, J. and Tregear, M. (1989) 'An examination of Chinese *fahua* glazes', *Proceedings of the International Symposium on Ancient Ceramics* (ISAC '89), Shanghai, pp. 172–82.

Woodiwiss, S. (ed.) (1992) *Iron Age and Roman Salt Production and the Medieval Town of Droitwich*, London: Council for British Archaeology Research Report 81.

Woods, A.J. (1986) 'Form, fabric and function: some observations on the cooking pot in antiquity', in W.D. Kingery (ed.), *Technology and Style,* vol. II, Columbus, Ohio: American Ceramic Society, pp. 157–72.

Woolley, C.L. (1956) *Ur Excavations IV: The Early Periods*, London and Philadelphia: The British Museum and University Museum.

Wright, R.P. (1986) 'The boundaries of technology and stylistic change', in W.D. Kingery (ed.), *Technology and Style,* Ceramics and Civilisation, vol. II, Columbus, Ohio: The American Ceramic Society, pp. 1–20.

Yang Zhongtang (1992) 'Study on gas composition of ancient Yaozhou celadon glaze and its archaeological significance', in *Science and Technology of Ancient Ceramics*, Proceedings of the 1992 International Symposium, pp. 201–10.

——, Li Yueqin, Wang Zhihai and Xu Peicang (1995) 'Research on the molecular network structure in glass phases of glaze from ancient Yaozhou celadon and blackware', in *Science and Technology of Ancient Ceramics*, Proceedings of the 1995 International Symposium, Beijing: Science Press, pp. 72–7.

Yap, C.T. and Younan Hua (1995) 'Chinese Greenware glazes of eight famous wares: Yue, Longquan, Southern Song Guan, Ru, Linru, Jun, Yaozhou and Ge', in *Science and Technology of Ancient Ceramics*, Proceedings of the 1995 International Symposium, Beijing: Science Press, pp. 155–62.

You Enpu (1986) 'Kiln furniture and methods of ware-setting used in Yaozhou kiln and Ding kiln', in *Scientific and Technological Insights on Ancient Chinese Pottery and Porcelain*, Proceedings of the International Conference, Shanghai Institute of Ceramics, Beijing: Science Press, pp. 282–6.

Zang Zhiang, Li Jiazhi and Zuo Zhenxi (1995) 'Study on celadon technology of Yaozhou kiln in successive dynasties', in *Science and Technology of Ancient Ceramics*, Proceedings of the 1995 International Symposium, Beijing: Science Press, pp. 60–5.

5

METALS

5.1 Metals as materials

Apart from mercury, which is a liquid, metals are solid at room temperature. The atoms from which metals are constructed are held together by *metallic bonds*. It is these metallic bonds which give metals some of their distinctive properties. The usual metallic state consists of a number of regularly-spaced crystals formed into a lattice. Metals are therefore quite different from materials like glasses which are amorphous because the atoms which make up metals are ordered so that the distance between them is the shortest possible – for maximum compactness (Guinier 1989: 88). Whereas metals exhibit long-range order, glasses, on the other hand, only exhibit short range order (that is they are only ordered over short distances) and their 'structure' is not predictable.

The unit that makes up metals is a positively charged ion. Detached electrons move freely in the metal and form a negatively-charged 'sea'. This is responsible for the cohesion of the metallic structure as a whole, and guarantees the neutrality of the whole assemblage. Each unit within the lattice has a specific number of atoms per unit cell, which differs accordingly to the element concerned. An example is the so-called *face-centred cubic (fcc)* structured unit (see Figure 5.1).

One of the reasons why metals can be used by man is that they can be deformed. Because the metal need not break when it is deformed, this kind of deformation is known as *plastic deformation* and occurs when the metal is stretched or hammered. Obviously being able to stretch a metal is a very important property when making metal objects.

Another important property of metals (and other materials) is known as *elastic deformation*. Both glass and metal can undergo this form of deformation, even if they have no ability to deform at room temperature. Glass can only be stretched by elastic deformation up to a point before it breaks. Metals can also be elastically deformed, but do not break because they can undergo *plastic deformation*. This is a critical property because it is the kind of deformation which occurs when metal objects are manufactured. Copper, for example can be drawn through dies into thin wires and thin sheets of copper can be created in rolling mills. During these processes

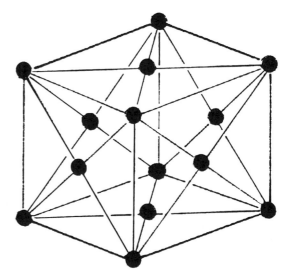

Figure 5.1 A face-centred cube, one of the possible structural units of metals.

the volume of copper remains unchanged. Metals deform because planes of atoms in the lattice can slip past each other to produce a movement in the metal without losing contact. This kind of movement cannot take place in glasses because they crack. When metals such as pure copper or iron are stretched, they will in fact eventually break or fracture, but only after a certain amount of deformation has occurred.

It is rare that metal crystal lattices have a perfect structure; there are usually imperfections present, such as edge dislocations. Because these irregularities are present in the structure, it enables the metal to be deformed at a lower applied stress (because the irregularities allow the metal to slip) than would be possible if the lattice was a perfect structure. In order to understand how the structure of metal (as it is formed) affects its working properties, it is necessary to describe what happens to a metal as it cools during the casting process – a principal way of manipulating the metal.

All ancient metals are impure and can be made from a deliberate *alloy* of two or more metals, such as bronze or brass. The fact that they are impure affects the way that crystals grow as the molten metal cools. Many ancient cast metals show what is known as *dendritic* structures. Dendrites look like tiny fern-like growths scattered at random throughout the metal (Figure 5.2); the faster the rate of cooling the smaller the crystals produced. The dendritic structures are described as forming a separate *phase* from the matrix in which they sit; their growth is what is referred to as a form of *segregation*. That is, the chemical composition of the dendrites is slightly different from the matrix metal. Thus an alloy is very often a mixture of different phases, that is, of different types of crystals with sizes that vary greatly from a micrometre to several centimetres, each being characterised by a definite composition and structure.

These different parts of the metal (phases), exist at different states of equilibrium when the metal has cooled down. We can use a phase diagram to predict

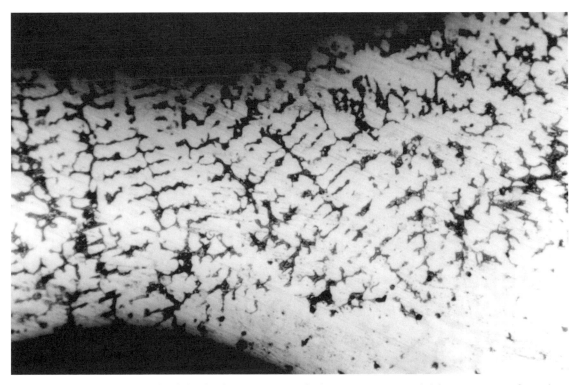

Figure 5.2 A photomicrograph of the dendritic structure which can occur in metal (photo courtesy of Matthew Ponting).

what phases are present in an alloy at equilibrium and at any particular temperature. Put simply, a phase diagram provides information about the phase compositions of a metal at any given temperature.

5.2 The range of metals used and their ores

Copper

Ancient man initially used metals as found (native metals). The first objects made were small trinkets such as pins and rings – from copper or arsenical copper in the Chalcolitic period; copper was the earliest metal to have been used, certainly as early as the eighth millennium BC (see Section 5.8.1). The ores may have been identifiable by mining communities from the plant species which grew in the soils enriched by the copper-bearing minerals. Malachite has a bright green colour and azurite a brilliant blue colour, so it is clear that their colours would have been noted by early prospectors. The

salts of copper are often a turquoise green colour, so this must also have attracted the attention of those prospecting for metal.

Primary native copper forms from the reduction of sulphidic copper minerals in hydrothermal solutions in the presence of iron. One environment in which this process can occur is in reducing (relatively oxygen-free) environments like swamps. Primary copper occurs as huge masses, but also as small particles and plates lining cavities. Secondary native copper forms from weathering of oxidised copper minerals near the primary sulphidic deposits (Figure 5.3). The primary copper which would have been available to early man occurred near the surface, having already been spread and re-deposited by glacial action. Coughlan (1962) lists Talmessi in Iran, Ergani Madan in south-east Turkey and the Mitterberg in the Austrian Alps as deposits of native copper that were probably exploited at the inception of metallurgy. Tylecote (1992: 1) notes that native copper is extremely heterogeneous and often contains deposits such as calcite which would prove to be

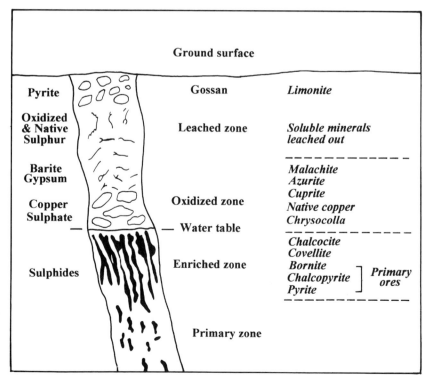

Figure 5.3 Section through a copper ore, showing the distribution of primary ores, the oxidised zone and leached zone.

problematical if included in the worked metal – it can also contain elements such as iron, nickel and arsenic. Minerals may dissolve and then run down into ore bodies or percolate off and, together with clay, fill up voids and fissures. They may run into the base of the weathered ore horizon where they will precipitate forming clayey ores, generally known by the German term *Fahlerz* – faded or discoloured ores (Craddock 1995: 28). These fahlerz ores include copper-rich sulphur tetrahedrite (which also contains antimony and lead) and tettanite (which also contains iron and arsenic).

It is claimed that a small pendant found in the Shanidar cave in the Zagros mountains, Iraq, in ninth-millennium BC contexts (Solecki 1969) is made from mineralised copper and would therefore be the earliest metal artefact known. However, it is now missing and the identity of the material used to make this exceptional artefact may never be ascertained (Craddock 1995: 98). There is, however, no doubt that malachite and native copper were used in the eighth millennium BC at the early Neolithic settlement of Cayönü Tepesi in south-east Turkey (Maddin *et al.* 1991). This early use of copper would have involved hammering the metal into sheets and rolling it into tight tubes; beads were also made from malachite.

Iron

The native iron used by ancient man occurs as meteoritic iron. Knox (1987) categorises these as siderites, pallasites and mesosiderites. Only siderites are completely composed of iron, the other two contain about 50% iron. The pallasites could have been used as a source of iron by ancient man; the mesosiderites are unusable. Some very large American meteorites show signs of early use; the Descubridora meteorite from Mexico has a broken copper chisel point embedded in a crack (Friend 1926: 11). The iron-rich meteorites found in Greenland by the Inuits have been given names: the woman (3 tons), the Tent (30 tons) and the Dog (0.4 tons). There are no clear examples of meteorite use in the Old World; Craddock (1995: 104–109) discusses the problems associated with (mis-)identification in detail. Tylecote (1987: 103–4) has noted that the structure of meteoritic iron is surprisingly resistant to heat.

Iron ores such as hematite (Fe_2O_3), geothite ($HFeO_2$) and limonite ($FeO(OH)_n.H_2O$) are found in enormous lodes. Magnetite (Fe_3O_4) and siderite ($FeCO_3$) are less common. Iron pans and bog iron ores would also have been available and exploitable by ancient man. Some slags produced by early solid state processes would have contained about 50% of iron and could have been re-smelted by a more efficient process. But in most cases such material, including low grade ores would not have been used until the industrial revolution. Tylecote and Clough (1983) have suggested that weathered marcasite nodules found in chalk could have been used as a source of iron in the European Iron Age.

Iron appears to have been first used in the later centuries of the third millennium BC, though it was not exploited in any quantity until *c.* 1200 BC, when it was used for the manufacture of tools and weapons (see Section 5.11.2). Iron has a melting point of 1540 °C which would have been too high for ancient smelting furnaces. The actual smelting temperature was around 1200 °C when a liquid slag was formed from the impurities with the iron; the iron would have been reduced to metal by the presence of charcoal. The same kind of furnaces would have been used for both copper and bronze smelting, but in the initial stages copper would have been smelted in crucibles, something which was not possible for iron (see Section 5.6). The ores of iron, such as hematite, are more widespread than those of copper but the spread of the knowledge of iron-use took a considerable time, with bronze still continuing to be used in the areas where iron was introduced. The slow introduction of iron may be partly explained by the fact that because it could not be worked cold in the same way that copper could; however, a more likely explanation is that iron could not be smelted in crucibles.

Tin

The principal mineral ore of tin is cassiterite (SnO_2). In 1540 Vannuccio Biringuccio in his *Pirotechnica* (Smith and Gnudi 1942) describes available sources of tin in the following way: 'I have heard from people who know that the largest quantities and best tin found in Europe is what is mined in England; I have heard that it is also found in parts of Flanders and

Bavaria, but the bizarre place-names are too diffi-cult for me' (Wilson 1987: 24). It is assumed that the English tin sources referred to are those in Devon and Cornwall, those in 'Bavaria' are the deposits in Saxony-Bohemia (the Erzgebirge). Tin deposits occur with certain kinds of granite in other parts of the word: Afghanistan, Malaya, China, Bolivia and Nigeria (Tylecote 1992: 18; Stech and Pigott 1986).

The discovery of tin deposits at Kestel, Anatolia, and crucible fragments with a tin-rich silicate layer adhering to them of up to 20 μm thickness at early Bronze Age (3000–2000 BC) Göltepe (2 km away from Kestel) (Adriaens et al. 1999) has led to detailed and sometimes fractious discussions in the literature (Muhly et al. 1991; Hall and Steadman 1991; Muhly 1993). However, Yener and Vandiver (1993: note 32) provide early Bronze Age carbon-14 dates for the Kestel mine; a late fifth to early third-millennium ther-moluminescence date for a crucible from Göltepe (Vandiver et al. 1993) further substantiates the im-portance of tin exploitation and processing in the area. A description by Willies (1993) of early Bronze Age tin mines cannot leave any doubt about the importance of the deposit. However, although tin was definitely being processed, presumably as part of a process to make a copper alloy, the question of whether the Göltepe site was used for tin-smelting has not been proven absolutely (Adriaens et al. 1999: 1073).

Zinc

Smithsonite or calamine ($ZnCO_3$) was the principal zinc ore in the west, whereas sphalerite, a zinc sulphide (ZnS), occurs as far east as Asia Minor. Metallic zinc was not produced before the seven-teenth century in the west, though it was somewhat earlier in the east where it was used to make coins in the sixteenth century in the Ming Dynasty (1368–1644). It was imported by the East India Company from the east from about 1605 onwards (Tylecote 1992: 119). Some of the most compre-hensive evidence for ancient zinc production from sphalerite has been found at Zawar in India (Craddock et al. 1990) – see Section 5.7.3.

Lead

Lead is still a widespread mineral and was exploited from an early stage in man's use of metal. It is char-acterised by having a relatively low melting point which means lead metal can be separated from its ores in simple hearths. The commonest of the lead minerals is galena (lead sulphide, PbS) with others being cerussite ($PbCO_3$) and anglesite ($PbSO_4$).

Lead was used in the Chalcolithic period of the eastern Mediterranean and Middle East; the earliest lead artefacts are a bracelet from Yarim Tepe I in the Sinjar plain of northern Mesopotamia in present Iraq (Merpert et al. 1977), a bead from Jarmo in the Zagros Mountains, Iraq (Braidwood et al. 1983), and other beads from Çatal Hüyük, Turkey (Muhly 1983) – all date to the sixth millen-nium BC.

Gold

Unlike copper, gold does not harden when ham-mered, and it is possible to beat the metal out into very thin sheets without the need to reheat it so as to prevent cracking. Early gold objects were, neverthe-less, very small. This is a reflection of the rarity of the metal; the technique of hammering two pieces of gold together was discovered relatively early and is known as fusion bonding. The earliest evidence for the use of gold comes from fifth-millennium BC Neolithic cemeteries in Varna, Bulgaria; here the gold has been hammered and cast.

Gold is found in veins, usually in quartz rock and also within pyrites and arseno-pyrites. When gold-bearing rock weathers, the metal is carried away by streams; the larger pea-sized fragments are seldom carried far by water and become deposited in allu-vial gravels in the upper reaches of rivers, known as placer deposits. Vein gold – the metal embedded in quartz rocks – was certainly worked, as is clear from workings at Dolaucothi in central Wales (Lewis and Jones 1969: 90). The gold associated with pyrites was also exploited by the Romans.

The occurrence of the platinum group elements (PGE) in gold (platinum, iridium, osmium, palla-dium, ruthenium and rhodium) is a clear indication when gold is derived from a placer deposit. The rea-son for this is that these elements weather out of asso-ciated formations and tend to collect in the same bed as the gold, forming part of the gold nuggets. Platinum inclusions are sometimes found in ancient gold-work, partly because the PGE metals are extremely unreactive. PGE inclusions were usually not removed from ancient gold-work and caused problems for gold-workers. The chemical analysis (Meeks and Tite 1980) of PGE inclusions (Ogden 1977) has produced some interesting results, but it is unlikely that the chemical characterisation is specific enough to be a provenancing tool.

Silver

Silver occurs far less frequently than gold, though the two metals are sometimes found together as a natural alloy, electrum. There is evidence for the separation of silver and gold as early as the seventh century BC from Sardis, capital of Lydia in western Asia Minor (Ramage 1970), which seems to be intimately linked to the development of coinage. Various argentiferous (silver-rich) lead ores could have been used as sources of silver: galena and cerussite and the non-plumbate ore jarosite (mixed hydrated sulphates of a variable composition and variable colour ranging from red to ash-coloured). One of the better-known sources of jarosite is the Rio Tinto mine in Spain. At Laurion, Greece (dating to between the fifth and third centuries BC), silver was removed from argentiferous lead by smelting and cupellation (Jones 1988) (see Section 5.7.6). Silver could also have been obtained from gold as a by-product of parting (removing silver and copper from the gold). Patterson (1971) provides a comprehensive assessment of potential silver sources in a New World context. In addition to the sources already mentioned these include 'dry ores' such as cerargyrite (AgCl), aregentite (Ag_2S), stephanite (Ag_5SbS_4), argentiferous fahl ores, and silver-rich pyrite ores (combined with FeS).

Bronze

Gradually metalsmiths became aware that by making *alloys* such as bronze, a mixture of copper and tin, the properties and workability of the metals could be improved. Bronze is a harder metal than copper. It is also more easily worked. The effect of alloying a small quantity of tin with copper is also to reduce the melting point of the copper. At the same time, tin acts as a de-gassing agent leading to a higher proportion of successful castings. In practice this meant that bronzesmiths found that bronze was a metal which was easier to cast than copper. With the introduction of bronze at different times in different parts of the world, the quality of casting improved dramatically. Lead was added to copper and tin as early as the middle Bronze Age (from *c.* 2000 BC) in the Syro-Palestinian area. Lead would have improved the fluidity of the metal and aided the casting of metal (Craddock 1977), although its erratic levels during the earlier phases of its use suggest that it is unlikely that lead was employed systematically (Craddock 1986a).

Brass

Brass, a mixture of copper and zinc, was first introduced in any quantity in the first century BC (Craddock 1978). A technological reason for adding zinc to copper would be to make it stronger; bronze also has greater mechanical strength and is a harder metal than pure copper. Also, brass has a yellower appearance and is closer in appearance to gold, something which may have been of special concern in antiquity.

By the end of the first millennium BC brass was being produced in some quantity (Craddock 1978), with the first brass coinage containing about 20% zinc occuring in the first century BC (Craddock *et al.* 1980). Craddock (1995: 297) suggests that the areas where these first brass coins were minted, Bithynia and Phrygia, in north-west and central Asia Minor, were also the areas where the first zinc was deliberately produced, between the fourth and first centuries BC, using predominantly zinc sulphide, ZnS (sphalerite). Earlier zinc-rich copper alloys of late second millennium BC date have been found in the Middle East such as two Assyrian bowls from Nimrud (Hughes *et al.* 1988) both of which contained about 6% zinc together with tin. The metal was a more golden colour than found in the normal tin bronze. A brass twisted bracelet of eighth century BC date from Cavustepe, eastern Turkey (Geçkinli *et al.* 1988) with 11% zinc (and no tin) may have been made from 'natural' brass – the Assyrian 'copper of the mountain' (Halleux 1973). Farnsworth *et al.* (1949) reported the rather surprising occurrence of a thin sheet of metallic zinc of fourth century date from the Athenian agora. In 23 BC in Rome the Emperor Augustus initiated the minting of brass coins which had small but significant compositional differences (such as higher iron levels) from the earlier series in Asia Minor, suggesting a different zinc ore was used (Burnett *et al.* 1982). The earliest recorded Roman zinc mines in the west are at Stolberg near Aachen (Gechter 1993) where calamine (zinc carbonate, $ZnCO_3$, also known as callamine) was mined.

5.3 Locating and mining ores

The winning of metal ore and its subsequent preparation involved a range of not especially complex skills. The recognition and identification of suitable mineral-bearing rocks was perhaps initially one of the more demanding aspects of metal production. As Phillips (1980) has pointed out, plant colonies consisting of quite specific species which thrive on metal-rich soils would have provided an important clue as to the location and extent of surface mineral-bearing deposits. Ores either occur as veins in rocks or as deposits which have been weathered out of veins and reconcentrated elsewhere, often as a result of hydrothermal processes. These processes involve the filling of fractures within the main strata of with saline mineral-bearing aqueous solutions; the result is that the minerals are deposited in between the strata. The processes occur under great temperature and pressure. As the temperature and pressure fall silica (quartz) and carbonates (such as calcium carbonate – calcite) crystallise out of the solution, being deposited together with compounds of metals. Iron minerals are often present and deposited with non-ferrous minerals – the latter are often either carbonates or sulphides. The early copper mine at Rudna Glava in the Balkans was re-worked by the Romans in order to mine the iron which had been deposited with the copper (Jovanović 1982: 109). It is an interesting thought that early copper miners would have observed a brown (iron-rich) mineral in the same location as the copper mine but did not actually exploit it for metallurgical processes.

Nevertheless, the colour of metal-bearing ores must have been an important means of locating them – perhaps in combination with the specific plant colonies which might be associated with them. The typical bright green colour of weathered copper carbonates, like malachite, bright blue azurite or the bluish chrysocolla (a copper silicate), for example, can wash out of the rocks and stain the surrounding area with brilliant colours.

Once the ore was located, it needed to be extracted from the ground in some way. The open cast technique of mining needs little explanation other than the fact that the mineral-bearing rocks still needed to be broken up. The technique of heating up the mineral-bearing rock by fire-setting next to the outcrop and then throwing cold water on it in order to shatter it would have provided a ready source of broken mineral-bearing rocks. The second-millennium BP mine at Copa Hill in central Wales, where Comet Lode provided the copper-bearing mineral chalcopyrite, was associated also with lead and silver ores. The tips associated with the working of Copa Hill contained charcoal which probably derived from fire setting operations (Timberlake and Mighall 1992). The wood used for the charcoal was mainly oak, with some ash and hazel; the charcoal made from the woods was dated to the early and mid-second millennium BC.

One of the earliest mines in Europe, at Rudna Glava, consists of a nest of closely-spaced surface pits which follow the deposits of malachite copper ore. Forty shafts, of 15–20 m depth and 0.7–2.0 m across, lead from the pits. A step was often cleared above the vein itself to provide easy access to quartz-rich copper ore lodes and the iron and copper secondary minerals (associated with the limestone and marble country rock). The shapes of the shafts were apparently determined mainly by the extent of the lodes (Jovanović 1979). A possible ritual dimension is provided by the discovery of a large quantity of relatively fine early and middle Vinča period potsherds and the presence of an altar with one group of sherds. The pottery suggests a date of the first part of the fourth millennium BC for the mine which, with Ai Bunar in Bulgaria (Černych 1978), makes it one of the earliest in Europe.

The earliest dated evidence for copper production in the west is currently that from Ross Island, Killarney, Co. Kerry, Ireland (O'Brian 1990; 1994; O'Brian *et al.* 1990). This evidence dates to between

2400 and 2200 BC and into the early centuries of the second millennium (O'Brian 1994: 229–30). Here the copper ore which must have been sulphidic occurred in thrust fractures associated with quartz micro-veining in the lower carboniferous limestone at its junction with old red sandstone of the Hercynian Orogeny. The excavations were associated with Bell Beaker and All Over Corded (AOC) pottery tradition. Grooved hammers of old red sandstone and shovels or rakes of ox scapulae were found. The non-slagging technique of copper-smelting was apparently carried out nearby in a shallow hearth. The other principal group of mine shafts in the same area of south-west Ireland is at Mount Gabriel, but these date to the second millennium BP and the pits follow a series of faulted deposits as discrete pits. The

ore mined was probably malachite together with adventitious sulphides; it was probably crushed near the mines and then picked out by hand (Jackson 1980; O'Brian 1994).

Metal ores were formed in ancient rocks and mining often occurred in mountainous areas, sometimes with poor communications. Even during the Bronze Age in the west, mines became increasingly more complex than the small shafts connected with surface pits mentioned above, although the Neolithic flint mines such as those at Grime's Graves in Norfolk, were far from simple (see Section 6.2.1). The complexity of a copper mine revealed by a three-dimensional reconstruction of part of the Great Orme's Head, Anglesey (Figure 5.4) shows clearly not just the contrast between the nineteenth-century

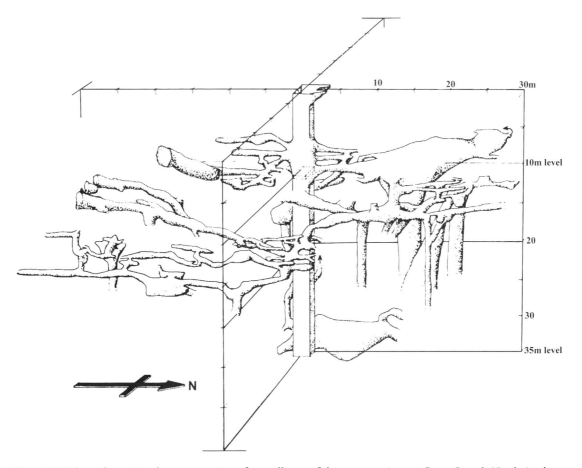

Figure 5.4 Three-dimensional reconstruction of a small part of the copper mines at Great Orme's Head, Anglesey; the square nineteenth-century shaft is clearly visible.

shafts with square sections and the Bronze Age ones with circular sections, but also the potential danger of the operation. Usually, the early mines consisted of localised, restricted 'workings' which radiated from the main shaft. The mining of ores in these restricted spaces would have been awkward and potentially cumbersome. In addition, the available oxygen would have been used up quickly, especially when lamps were used as the source of light. The lack of oxygen would explain the reason why a number of relatively short tunnels are found in mines without a supply of 'forced' air.

The famous well-preserved Timna mines in the Arabah valley (in modern day Israel) have been extensively studied. The Arabah valley cuts through limestone to expose metalliferous Nubian sandstone which has been penetrated by epigenic deposits of copper mineralisation, typically as malachite nodules with residual chalcocite, brochantite and bornite. The Nubian sandstone which has been permeated by copper mineralisation lies beneath the Arabah limestone cliffs (which are several hundred metres high). Ancient mining galleries where the ores have been followed back into the sandstone are visible today (Rothenberg 1972; 1988; 1990). Many galleries were re-worked in the late Bronze and early Iron Ages. However, from the fourteenth until the twelfth century BC the Egyptians mined and smelted the copper on an enormous scale with over 9,000 mining shafts spread over several square kilometres. The Egyptians not only re-worked existing shafts, but created new ones where erosion may have exposed fresh deposits, and also exploited the horizontally bedded ores by sinking vertical shafts. Typically the shafts were 60–80 cm in diameter and up to 10 m deep. The triangular wedge-shaped marks from the use of picks and running scratches produced by chisels are so well-preserved that some of the techniques of mining can be reconstructed. The shafts were excavated by chiselling out an annulus of rock to about 10 cm in depth , breaking up the stump of rock produced and then repeating the operation (Conrad and Rothenberg 1980: 74). The horizontal galleries were apparently excavated by undercutting the rock face at floor level for about 1 m beyond the working place; this is why chisel marks remain on the walls of the galleries. Given that there is only

restricted evidence for ventilation shafts – with only one being discovered (Conrad and Rothenberg 1980: 165) – it is unlikely that there was ever any intention of creating a system that was more extensive than the thousands of small mines which have survived so well. As such, Craddock (1995: 69) has pointed out that the technology of mining at Timna was at a similar level to the workings investigated in temperate Europe.

Relatively recent research into Anatolian tin mines at Kestel has uncovered a backfilled shaft with a fill of pottery dated to c. 3000 BC, crucibles and a mining chamber re-used as an early Bronze Age mortuary chamber. The mining had been achieved with fire setting and stone tools. The cassiterite was low grade and Willies (1993: 263) makes the point that iron could also have been mined there, though this suggestion needs to be confirmed. Ten kilometres to the east in the Aladağ range, silver, gold, iron, lead and copper mines occur. There is associated evidence of tin-smelting at Göltepe 2 km from Kestel (Yener and Vandiver 1993), which includes nodules of tin, large crucible fragments with tin-rich accretions, ore-processing ground stones and a multi-faceted stone mould possibly used for casting tin ingots (ibid.).

As Shepard (1993) makes clear, in the first millennium BC the technology associated with mining improved radically across a broad swathe of the ancient world from the Mediterranean, Middle East and India to China. The mines were worked below the water table and were extended outwards for hundreds of metres from the vertical shafts, necessitating drainage and ventilation. The use of timber supports or pillars of ore was introduced in order to extract what would have previously been regarded as inaccessible metalliferous material. Of course the first millennium BC saw the widespread introduction of iron, so one should pose the question as to whether demand for the metal which could be used for a wider range of tools than copper alloys actually drove the advancement of mining technology. One answer would seem to be that the demand for metal is likely to have been partly responsible for creating the impetus for improved mining technology, with the need to mine in increasingly inaccessible places.

The principle behind draught control in mining was to light a fire at the base of one shaft, the rising

Figure 5.5 A form of ventilation system using a linen cloth in a mine.

hot air would then draw air from other connected parts of the mine to be replaced by fresh air. Galleries could be blocked off by using waste or shutters. An illustration in Agricola's *De re Metallica* (1556) shows that fans made out of linen cloths were also used to help the induction of fresh air through the workings (see Figure 5.5).

The evidence for using drainage control in mining operations that has survived in mines shows a high degree of sophistication. One of the best preserved series of water-raising wheels was found at the Roman lead-silver (jarosite) mine of Rio Tinto, Spain (Palmer 1926/7; Weisgerber 1979). The manually operated wooden wheels were held together with wooden pegs and had leaded bronze axles. The wheel rims were compartmentalised with scoops, each of which deposited the water at a higher level on a launder from where it flowed to the sump under the next wheel, and so on, until the water was eventually raised to the surface of the mine. The vertical

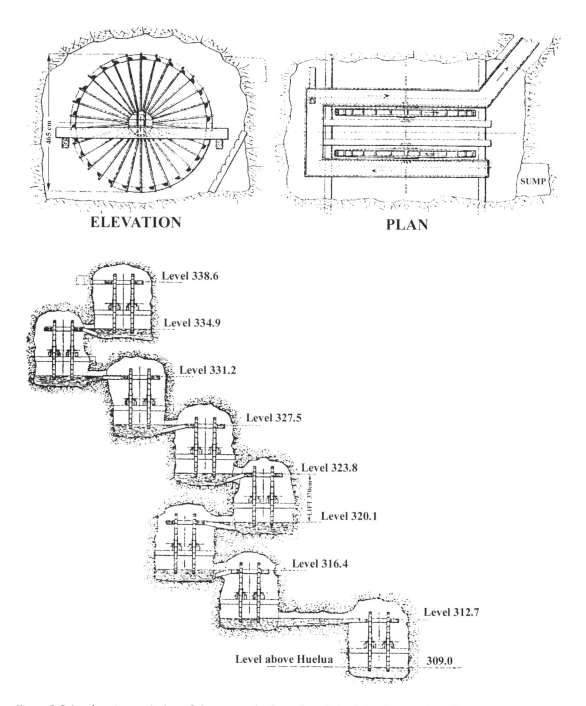

ELEVATION   **PLAN**

Figure 5.6 An elevation and plan of the water wheels used to drain (raise the water) in the Roman mines at Rio Tinto, Spain, together with a cross-section of the full vertical arrangement of water wheels.

distance by which the water was raised by a single wheel was typically 3 to 4 m (see Figure 5.6).

Water was also deliberately used for mining as part of a process called *hushing*. This was a system where water stored, uphill from metalliferous deposits, was released and directed with maximum force at the ore-bearing deposits using straight-sided channels. The technique was used especially where loose material like glacial scree or alluvium needed to be removed in order to provide access to a metalliferous deposit. Further removal of loose material would be carried out if necessary in order to expose more deposits of interest. The technique was certainly used in the Roman period, such as at the gold mines in north-west Spain (Lewis and Jones 1970) and at Dolaucothi in central Wales (Lewis and Jones 1969; Annels and Burnham 1986). The technique was still in use in eighteenth- and nineteenth-century Pennine lead mines (Foster 1883). Ground

sluicing also provided a means of separating minerals such as gold or tin from the matrix, though the archaeological evidence for this technique in antiquity is limited.

The use of stone hammers is attested at a number of prehistoric copper mines such as Rudna Glava and Rudnik in the former Yugoslavia (Jovanović 1988), the Mitterberg in Austria (Pittioni 1948 and 1951) and Ross Island, Co. Kerry, Ireland (Jackson 1980). The hammers often have grooves mid-way along them which were used for hafting. The most complete example of a mining hammer was found with the famous mummified Chilean 'copper man' thought to date to *c.* AD 600 (see Figure 5.7). The hammers frequently have fractured ends so it is likely that they were used for delivering a blow to the ore-containing rock which can be matched with the distinctive pecked walls of mine shafts (Craddock 1979: Plate 8.4).

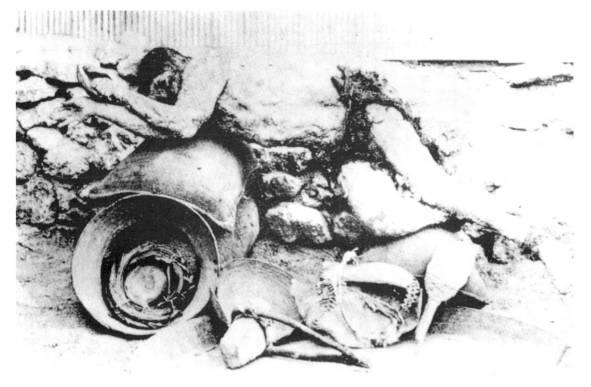

Figure 5.7 The 'copper man' found in 1900 in the copper mine of Chuquicamata, Chile. The man is associated with various mining implements, some of which have been found on prehistoric sites such as a wooden shovel, mining hammers (including one with an 'open' wooden handle in the foreground) and ore baskets.

5.4 Ore sorting

Once mined, the ore would then be sorted. The separation of the ore-rich rocks from the matrix rock would have been based on the experience that mineral crystals have distinctive colours (see Section 5.3 and 5.10.4.2). Quality control at this stage would be largely based on a combination of experience and trial-and-error, but where debitage from this separation process has been found it is clear that separation was often highly successful. For most ores the aim was to produce pea-sized particles of ore. The processes of crushing and sorting are known as *beneficiation*. Sometimes the ore would have been ground down to a finer grade by a rubbing action – 'as fine as flour' as Diodorus put it (Oldfather 1933) – especially when the mineral was finely-dispersed, such as in all gold and in some tin ores. Crushing of the flat surfaces of (sometimes imported) hard rocks may have been carried out. Fire setting when mining the ores could have partly roasted the ores; roasting was a necessary preliminary stage before effective smelting could occur, especially in the early phase of copper-smelting. The process drives off the oxides of sulphur and carbon in converting the metal sulphides and carbonates into their respective gaseous oxides (sulphur dioxide and carbon dioxide); it also drives off the chlorine and the water of crystallisation, both of which would form part of the minerals (see Section 4.2.3). The experimental beneficiation of Timna ores by Merkel increased the copper content from *c.* 12% to between 30% and 40% which is ideal as a charge for the furnace (Merkel 1985).

Washing, especially of gold and tin ores, in wooden washeries or *buddles* also occurred: they are simple sluice boxes or wooden tubs. Investigation of the third- to fifth-century BC Greek silver mines at Laurion has produced some of the best-preserved evidence for washing installations (Jones 1984; 1988). Ethnographic evidence indicates that this was often done by women and children. At or near the quarry site the ore may have been further broken up or refined by being reheated (roasted) in a hearth – the ore-rich rocks were then picked out. For example, at Great Orme's Head, Anglesey (Smith 1989), where there was an epigenic sulphidic mineralisation principally consisting of chalcopyrite (a copper pyrites mineral), stone mortars were found at the mining site suggesting that the ore was crushed there. Craddock (1995) has suggested that most ore was separated manually once crushed. Heaps of crushed rock and vein stuff with flecks of charcoal, fragments of bone and stone tools have been found near springs a few hundred metres from the mine at Great Orme, which suggests that some ore washing was carried out – though a radiocarbon date of 1200 BP suggests that this deposit was associated with a late phase of use. The initial mine-working at Great Orme appears to date to the later part of the second millennium BC (ibid.: Table 2.1). The dates of these two phases illustrate how long such sites can continue to be used. It is only with painstaking excavations of representative deposits and a full understanding of the stratigraphy together with scientific analysis of the materials found that the history of mining at such sites can start to be understood.

5.5 The heat-treatment of metals: the process of smelting

One copper ore, chalcopyrite (copper iron sulphide $CuFeS_2$), melts at 880 °C and it has recently been discovered (Rostoker *et al.* 1989) that after suitable beneficiation and pre-treatment it was possible to produce copper metal in crucibles without strongly reducing conditions (under charcoal) and without a formal furnace, but at temperatures of *c.* 1250 °C. Reduction of copper ore can occur at 1100 °C, but once liquid it needs a superheat of at least 20 °C above 1100 °C (Tylecote 1992: 22).

The process of smelting involves heating the metal-bearing raw materials to a sufficiently high temperature to allow 'impurities' (gangue minerals) associated with the metal to form and to reduce the ore to metal. Some 'impurities' are added in order to assist the smelting process. The atmosphere also needs to be sufficiently reducing (oxygen-free) to allow the metallic element to be separated from its associated 'impurities'. This usually occurs in furnaces; the principal aim being to recover a high proportion of metal when low grade ores are being melted so as to require less beneficiation: however,

Figure 5.8 Photomicrograph of annealed copper. Note the characteristic eqiaxed crystals called annealing twins.

the Matte smelting process described in Section 5.7.1 produces a rather impure metal. In the case of iron a bloom of metal is produced as a result of the smelting process; for metals like mercury and zinc the metal is collected by condensing a gas with the gangue minerals forming a liquid slag. As the discussion below indicates, there is also evidence for smelting being carried out in crucibles. Firstly, however, we need to consider the tentative identification of the earliest evidence for smelting.

Metal artefacts can be examined microscopically to investigate their crystal structures. This can provide information about how the metal was heat-treated in order to make the metal object suitable for its function. For example, native copper artefacts were sometimes hammered and annealed at high temperatures: both processes would produce characteristic crystal forms in the metal (see Figures 5.8 and 5.9). The processes of hammering and annealing could be carried out at a temperature of 1100 °C, a temperature that could be produced in a charcoal hearth (with bellows); the melting point of copper is 1083 °C. Craddock (1995: 122) is clear that where only these processes are found, smelting has not necessarily occurred, while at the same time hammering and annealing would certainly have led to the development of metal melting and smelting technologies.

The evidence for early smelting is unlikely to have left significant archaeological remains; even the associated debris is similar to the processes of melting (Tylecote 1982). Muhly (1988) considered that the *scale* of production would, in the end, turn out to be the best indicator of whether copper-smelting had occurred. The sixth-millennium lead artefacts referred to above (Section 5.2) are made of the lead minerals galena and cerussite (Sperl 1990) and therefore not smelted.

High-temperature industries often produce vitreous (glassy) debris because (fuel) ashes in the environment combine with silica, which is found in ceramic materials such as bricks and crucibles

Figure 5.9 Photomicrograph of a repeatedly hammered and annealed metal.

and sometimes in metal-bearing materials being processed. The vitreous (fuel-ash) slags which were produced often became absorbed into the slag metal during smelting.

Thus, a vitrified fragment from Çatal Hüyük of the right date may be related to some of the earliest copper-smelting technology (Neuninger *et al.* 1964). Similar (later) material has been found at Feinan in Jordan (see Sections 5.5.1 and 5.8), and in fifth-millennium BC contexts at Tepe Ghabristan, north-west Iran and Tal-i-Iblis, southern Iran (Caldwell 1968). It is also possible that early (sixth-millennium) smelting occurred at Yarim Tepe, northern Mesopotamia (Craddock 1995: 126).

5.5.1 The non-slagging process

The earliest firm evidence for smelting technology comes from Feinan, southern Jordan. Rothenberg and Merkel (1995) discuss very early copper-smelting in a late Neolithic (Qatifian) phase of site 39 in the Timna valley, now dated to 4460 BC. The earliest

evidence from the site is for a non-slagging process, possibly only involving crucibles in a hearth rather than a furnace. This would have occurred under reducing conditions in order to produce the metal rather than one of its oxides. Experiments using a source of 'forced' air directed at the hearth through blowpipes have been successful (Scheel 1989). The rough bowl-shaped vessels that have survived prob-ably formed primitive hearths and were heated from above. They *may* have formed the bases of primitive furnaces, but there is no clear evidence of super-structures; blowpipes were probably used in the early stages. By the early third millennium BC true slag-forming processing had developed in the Middle East. It is clear that a crucial difference in the devel-opment of the technology was made by the intro-duction of bellows which would have allowed sufficiently high temperatures to have been reached. It is, however, worth making the point that if suffi-ciently high grade copper ore is smelted (such as high grade malachite) little or no slag is produced

(Craddock and Gale 1988). The incentive for smelting ores, and for the high quality ores to be smelted, would have been driven by the demand for metal. This could have formed part of a complex of social, political and economic developments, such as occurred in the Middle East in the third millennium BC (Moorey 1994: 13–17).

A factor which limited how long this non-slagging process could be used was that the crucible (or simple furnace) eventually became choked with gangue. By studying the by-products of high-temperature industries, the level of efficiency of that industry can sometimes be judged; the more primitive process produced semi-vitrified gangue and half-smelted ore which were rich in copper prills and copper minerals. The slags produced were also rich in copper prills; the prills were picked out by hand after crushing. This is a reflection of the relatively low level of efficiency in terms of maximising copper production from a given amount of copper-bearing ore. It is clear that the use of primitive hearths could neither reach the high temperatures necessary nor were they sufficiently reducing to produce liquid free-flowing slag. They nevertheless formed the basis for the first copper production.

5.5.2 *The slagging process*

The fully-fledged smelting technology converted the solid gangue into a liquid (slag) so that it could be tapped off, while at the same time it allowed the metal to form and separate, something which would have been impossible by simply using beneficiation alone. Because the slag produced had a low viscosity (being silica-rich) it accumulated at the base of the furnace – this was very important for metalsmiths. Since a high temperature was needed during the smelting process, it was more efficient to keep the process going once the temperature was achieved – in order to feed the high demand for metal. In Merkel's (1990) experimental smelts typically 20 kg of charcoal was necessary in order to bring the furnace up to temperature, about 25% of the fuel consumed during the full period of use. This principle, where a large proportion of fuel was used in order to reach the 'working' temperature of a furnace, applies to all other high-temperature industries which involve the use of furnaces. Clearly, the kind

of fuel used and its calorific value are important considerations here.

The direct archaeological evidence for smelting copper is rather 'thin on the ground'. Nevertheless, examination of the metal itself that was produced by smelting can provide evidence for the conditions used. The metal's chemical composition reflects the extent to which 'impurities' associated with the metal have been effectively removed, although others are added which formed part of the fluxes. Volatile metals such as arsenic associated with copper can still be associated in the finished object (Budd *et al.* 1992). The element which is especially helpful, in that its level can provide an indication of the efficiency of the smelting process, is iron. The iron minerals which may have been associated with the copper ores subjected to the earlier process will not necessarily have been sufficiently reduced to have become incorporated in the forming copper. Under the higher temperatures and more highly reducing conditions of the later smelting process, the iron minerals may have combined with the silica present to form iron silicates and run off as a liquid slag at relatively low temperatures; the mineral texture of the slag will be dependent on its rate of cooling. Under sufficiently reducing conditions some of the iron minerals would combine with the copper to produce copper-iron alloys. Iron is soluble in copper and even low levels of sulphides promote the process (Rosenqvist 1983: 326).

The result is that the copper which collects below the slag in a smelting process, such as found at sites like Timna, contains several percentages of iron which would have acted as a flux (Craddock 1988). The iron levels can be reduced from between 1 and 2% to a workable 0.5% by re-melting in an open crucible (Tylecote and Boydell 1978): the iron-rich phase floats to the surface where it can be easily removed. Merkel (1990: 107) achieved this by blowing air across the surface to produce iron oxide. It is clear that, in general, products from the earlier production process contain much lower (though highly variable) iron levels than the later, more advanced, one. Craddock (1995: 139) stresses that this is a broad trend and that there are therefore exceptions to this rule in individual cases. It is interesting to note that the low iron levels found in western European Bronze

Age copper objects are typical of the 'earlier' poorly reducing process; no evidence of smelting has been found at any of the western European copper mines. The only early western European (non-mining) copper-smelting site that has been excavated is the Beaker copper mine at Ross Island, Co. Kerry, Ireland, where no slag was found, so this agrees with the overall picture of the more primitive (non-slagging) smelting process occurring in western Europe at the time. The same picture has been found in Iberia at Millarian copper-smelting settlements (Hook *et al.* 1991). In the Middle East, at Feinan, a relatively small proportion of ore was smelted close to the mines themselves.

5.6 The evidence of furnaces, their construction and use

A range of fragmentary furnace remains have been excavated, providing evidence for the existence of both bowl and shaft furnaces. The evidence from Timna suggests that the later shaft furnaces were constricted quite sharply just above the reaction zone. The minimal evidence for ancient furnaces clearly needs an explanation. Furnaces are unlikely to survive the smelts; all that often remains on metal production sites is just furnace bases and broken fragments of furnaces (see, for example, Figure 5.21 in Section 5.12.2.1). Killick (1992) has pointed out that the wide range of furnace shapes that have been identified from African ethnographic examples makes it very difficult to suggest (the full range of) reconstructed ancient furnace shapes given the paucity of evidence (and see Craddock 1995: 170). Cultural rather than technological considerations may have played an important rôle in determining the furnace shape such as the use of African iron furnaces in the shape of women. The reconstruction of two Viking age iron-smelting shaft furnaces is shown in Figure 5.10. Careful excavations of an iron-smelting site at Stanley Grange, Derbyshire, part of a medieval grange, has

Figure 5.10 A model of two Viking-age iron-smelting shaft furnaces.

Figure 5.11a The excavated remains (in plan) of one of the medieval iron-smelting furnaces found at Stanley Grange, Derbyshire, England.

provided some interesting suggestions for the reconstruction of the remains of shaft furnaces found there. Figure 5.11a is a photograph of one of the excavated plans of a slag-tapping shaft furnace from the site; the bands of coloration around the furnace are due to the clay from which it was built being oxidised and reduced (see Figure 5.11b). Figure 5.12, b–d shows a series of reconstructions of the types of shaft furnaces found at Stanley Grange, based on the excavated evidence; also included is a computerised reconstruction of the feature in Figure 5.11a (Figure 5.12a). One especially interesting possibility which is included (Figure 5.12d) is a furnace which involves a spiralling effect on the draught (Keith Challis, personal communication). This information on the Stanley Grange iron-smelting operation is provided here in order to

underline the potential complexities of the possible archaeological and technological interpretations of such industrial evidence. More detailed consideration of specific archaeological examples of ancient metal mining and smelting sites are given below in the form of case studies.

Furnaces in which smelting occurred were being used as early as the late third millennium by the Harrapan and post-Harrapan civilisations of north-west India (Bhardwaj 1979). The form of these smelting furnaces for iron, copper, tin and lead would have been roughly cylindrical (a shaft) and built with clay, stones or bricks. If built of brick or stone the structure would have been mortared; the clay would have been plastered on the outside to help to retain the heat as well as on the inside to protect the bricks/stones (a 'sacrificial' layer). The clay used for covering the outsides and insides of furnaces would often have been of a refractory nature, tempered with larger fragments of quartz, crushed mine waste or slag, so as to withstand the temperatures that the furnaces attained without melting themselves. It is likely that in antiquity metal-smelting furnaces were re-lined or repaired after each firing; hot spots would still sometimes cause the lining to vitrify and to 'corrode'. Merkel (1990) found that erosion of his experimental furnace caused problems and that it even modified the chemistry of the process. The ideal material for protecting the furnace would have been graphite, but there is no evidence for its use in that context, in spite of its occurrence in central European Iron Age crucibles and domestic pottery (Kappel 1969). In the African early Iron Age, clay from ant and termite nests was used for luting iron-smelting furnaces (Childs 1989). In the sixteenth century Agricola mentions that carbon was used deliberately as an admixture to the clays used for lining furnaces (Hoover and Hoover 1950: 376). These furnaces would have been built to hold several hundred kilograms of charge (ore mixed with fuel) and to withstand thermal shock and mechanical stress, but they were not expected to have had particularly long lives. One of the best preserved remains of an Iron Age shaft furnace was found at Scharmbeck near Harburg, Germany (Craddock 1995: Figure 7.5).

The furnace, when first constructed from clay, would generally need to be baked, or at least allowed to dry out, as exemplified by the Pokot in Kenya in

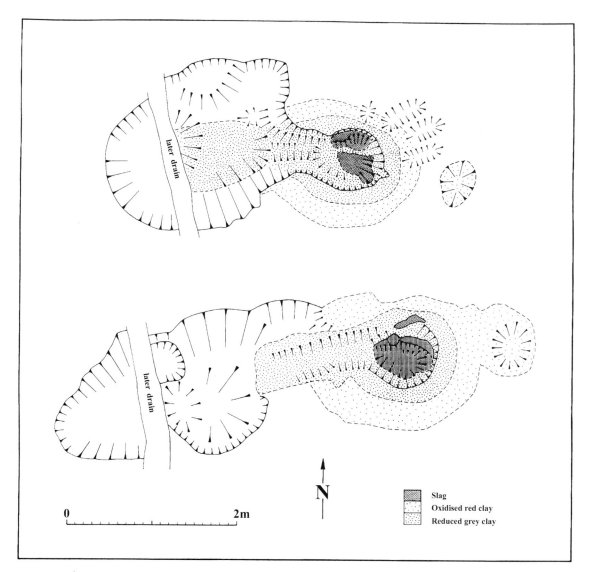

Figure 5.11b Interpretative plans of excavated remains of two medieval iron-smelting furnaces at Stanley Grange, Derbyshire, England.

building their iron-smelting furnace (Brown 1995: 61). The ore, fluxes and fuel would then have been added in the correct proportions to promote smelting (reduction of the ore to metal), depending on the kind of ore and on furnace construction. Some iron and copper ores would already contain sufficient silica to be self-fluxing; occasionally the iron ore used would need to be mixed with a silica flux. In the case of copper ores, Merkel used one part beneficiated ore to four parts iron oxide flux in his experimental melt.

The reason so much iron oxide flux was added was due to its high silica content, but also because iron is required in the smelting system regardless of the metal smelted so as to produce a tappable fayalite slag.

Various *reaction zones* can be defined in a 'typical' shaft furnace. In the top zone the charge was dried and heated. The combustion zone was just on the inner end of the tuyère where the primary reactions occurred. The reducing gas, carbon monoxide,

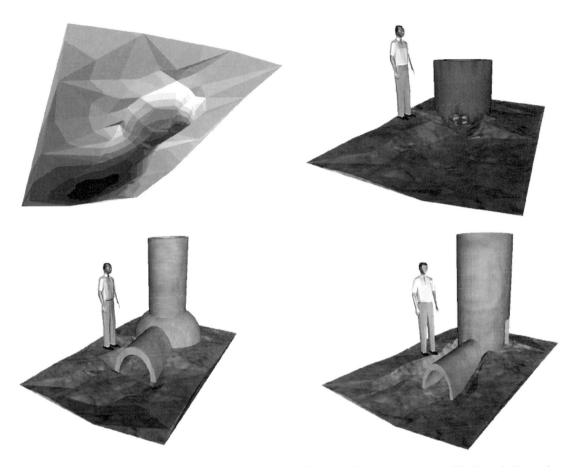

Figure 5.12 (a) The computer simulated three-dimensional feature in Figure 5.11b (top); (b), (c) and (d) are three possible computer simulated reconstructions of the excavated remains of the features shown in Figures 5.11a and 5.11b (top) at Stanley Grange, Derbyshire.

produced by oxidisation of the fuel, reduces the ore to metal which sinks down through the furnace. While this is happening, silica and/or iron in the flux reacts with gangue mineral oxides to form a liquid slag. It is important to make sure that the slag is of the right composition in order for it to be sufficiently liquid for the reduced metal to sink through it; the attack by slags on the furnace lining, which would increase the silica level in the slag and thereby increase its viscosity, can also be an important consideration. Fulford and Allan (1992) discovered the anticipated glassy fuel-ash slags which resulted from the vitrification of the furnace lining during iron-smelting at Chesters Roman villa; they estimated

that in order to re-use the furnaces they needed to be re-lined with a layer of clay of between 10 and 30 cms thick. The iron-smelting slag would have been tapped periodically. Excavations of iron-smelting sites of the early Iron Age period (c. 350 BC–500 AD) at Fjergen in Nord-Trøndelag, north of Trondheim, Norway, revealed a series of pits surrounding the remains of the furnace with a groove leading from the furnace into the pits. The pits had been re-lined with clay several times indicating that the site was a relatively permanent installation (Prestvold 1996: 46). It would have been clear when it was necessary to remove slag from the furnace by the bubbling sound that the slag made when it had accumulated to the level of the tuyère mouth. During smelting accumulations of slag would need to be removed from the end of the tuyère near the primary reaction zone, something which has been found during experimental smelts (Joosten *et al.* 1997: 83).

During copper- and tin-smelting, in the area just below the reaction zone, the metal which sinks too close to the bottom of the furnace coalesces into droplets which in turn sink through the accumulated slag to form an ingot in the base. For iron, the metal bloom tends to attach itself to the furnace wall just below the tuyère. The upper surface of the metal is protected from being re-oxidised by a layer of slag sitting in it. The time needed for a smelting opera-tion can be estimated by examining the penetration of vitrification into the furnace walls (Tite *et al.* 1990). Examination of ancient furnace walls in this way suggests that 5–10 hours is a typical length for a smelting operation. When smelting was complete using a non-slag-tapping iron furnace the bloom was pulled out through the top, or the front was dismantled; it is apparent that as one moves from Iron Age to Roman iron-smelting, slag tapping was increasingly used. When a slag-tapping furnace was used, the bloom was pulled out through the slag-tapping arch.

Over most of the Occidental ancient world the smelting of iron produced a bloom from a shaft furnace. Iron melts at a temperature of 1550 °C, a temperature which can be reduced in the presence of phosphorus and carbon; the result is that iron was smelted (and worked) in the solid state. The bloom is an accumulation of impure iron metal which contained some slag. Some iron was also present in the slag which resulted. The proportion of slag in the bloom depended on the efficiency of the slag-ging process. The bloom needed to be repeatedly hammered and annealed (smithed) in order to squeeze out the slag and other extraneous material to produce what is called *wrought iron*. From a prac-tical point of view, however, it can be difficult to distinguish between smithing and smelting slags unless their chemical and mineralogical composition and their morphology are determined (McDonnell 1984: 52). Small amounts of slag inevitably remained in the iron, becoming 'stringers' as the metal was smithed, and indeed made the metal easier to weld.

In essence, the furnace was therefore used for an initial smelt of the iron-bearing minerals, but a second series of smithing processes actually produced the workable iron.

During the smelting operation it was important to keep the supply of air at the appropriate level (see Section 5.6.1) as well as the balance and supply of fuel (see Section 5.6.2), ore and flux. The more fuel that was added, the hotter and more reducing it became. If too reducing, iron used in the flux might become liquid metal which could contaminate the metal being smelted, although this was sometimes a desired phenomenon. One of the ways of judging furnace conditions was by observing the colour of the furnace flame. The ideal flame should be colourless with some blue near the base, showing that carbon monoxide was being burnt in the top part of the furnace. By peering through the tuyère it was possi-ble to observe conditions in the base of the furnace and in large African furnaces spy holes were used for the purpose (van der Merwe and Avery 1988).

5.6.1 Air supply

There are no obvious advantages to using a natural draught furnace (Craddock 1995: 174), except when relatively low temperatures would have been needed as in lead-smelting furnaces. Ninth- to eleventh-century iron-smelting furnaces in the central southern highlands of Sri Lanka were sited facing the July and August mon-soon winds so there was at least some guarantee of the draught during these times of year; bellows were also used. It is interesting to note that an intermittent blast was more useful than a continuous one for smelting metals in a shaft furnace, because it penetrated further into the furnace (Merkel 1990: 103).

Draught would have been forced through bellows into the lower part of the furnace in order to heat the fuel. Given that a necessary minimum volume of air needed to be injected using manually-operated bellows (with a known blast pressure) and the temperatures needed to be maintained at between 1100 and 1200 °C for smelting, Bamberger and Wincierz (1990) have shown that the internal diam-eter of bellows would need to be between 15 cms and 40 cms. Updraft furnaces operated because of their height – up to 3.5 m in parts of sub-Saharan Africa (Miller and van der Merwe 1994) – using the same principle as a chimney, but even here tuyères were also used.

Evidence for the use of blowpipes has been reported in much of Chalcolithic and Bronze Age Europe (Roden 1988), though it is likely that bellows would have eventually replaced them. Blowpipes were certainly used in sixteenth-century South America to melt copper and gold (Raleigh 1848). Various kinds of bellows using animal skins would have been used but the archaeological evidence for their use is the survival of tuyères. Bag bellows were replaced by pot bellows in some areas; the latter have been found in late Bronze Age metalworking sites in the eastern Mediterranean and the Middle East. Tuyères (tapering ceramic pipes) acted as conduits for the air, with the nozzle from the bellows inserted in one end and the tuyère directing the air into the reaction zone (the hottest part of the furnace) at the other. The tuyère was often set at an angle of about 30 or 60 degrees to the vertical through the furnace wall so as to direct the blast into the bed of the furnace. A single tuyère used opposite the slag-tapping area was an ideal solution. However, if it became blocked (on the inside), the whole smelting process could be jeopardised. During his experimental smelts Merkel (1990) used three tuyères at 120 degrees to each other and it was still possible to tap the slag. Unlike the clay with filler used to line the furnaces, the thermal properties of tuyères must have been tried and tested well in advance; a single tuyère which was used during iron-smelting operations in the northern Cameroon and Nigeria still corroded, but at the correct rate for the pace at which the smelting progressed (Killick 1992). During experimental smithing Sim (1998: 30) found that the volume of air is more important than the pressure applied; when charcoal is the fuel, high pressure can even be disadvantageous because the fuel is easily blown away in the air blast.

5.6.2 Fuel supply and its effect on the environment

The fuel used to charge the furnace was obviously important in that the calorific value (a measure of the heat produced) when it was burnt needed to be sufficient to drive the smelting process. The fewer times a furnace needed to be fuelled, the more effi-

cient the process was in terms of man hours. Charcoal was the principal fuel in antiquity: it has a high calorific value (this depends on the density of the wood that it is derived from – hard woods being the preferred kind), it has a great affinity for oxygen and for absorbing vapours. Charcoal is the material produced as a result of the incomplete combustion of wood. In the process of production wood is converted into almost pure carbon. Typically the volume of the wood is reduced by c. 30% and its weight will have been reduced by about 25% of the original. It burns at about 900 °C and with an air blast much higher temperatures can be reached – though this also depends on the type and size of wood. Charcoal was produced by covering a stack of wood with turves leaving a central flue, or by controlling the amount of air in another way, for instance by burning wood in a pit. Charcoal burning leaves few signs, and no archaeological evidence for the activity has been recognised.

The size of the charcoal was important to a successful firing because of the effect it had on the circulation of gases through the furnace charge. Charcoal can reduce metal oxides easily, while at the same time it contains few impurities. Tite et al. (1990: 174–5) noted that a relatively high zinc level on the surfaces of refractories used at Timna was probably derived from the zinc originally present in the charcoal used. Tylecote et al. (1977) noted that some charcoals contain magnesia and calcium, but these had little effect on the final metal composition produced.

At the Romano–British iron-smelting site at Chesters villa on the Severn estuary the kind of wood needed was poles of 10–15 years growth (Figueral 1992); it is suggested that coppices in Roman Britain could have produced one tonne of charcoal per hectare per year in a 15-year cycle. Large deposits of charcoal which belonged to a charcoal store acted as fuel for the iron-smelting furnaces which were excavated at Chesters. For example, the contexts associated with furnace F24 produced 324 charcoal samples which were identified as alder, hazel, maple, ash, elm, sallow or willow, oak, holly, *Rosaceae*, birch, hawthorn, poplar and chestnut. Oak charcoal was the most frequently occurring among the charcoal examined from the contexts (Figueral 1992: 190) with hazel charcoal coming second. Further to this, because some complete cross-sections of small branches had survived, it was possible to establish that the wood had been cut outside its growing season. By using dendrochronology the ages of the majority of carbonised branches were established as 7 or 8 years old; fragments of larger, older trees were very rare. The inference was that the iron furnaces at Chesters were mainly active during the winter and early summer outside the sowing and harvesting season. Anatomical features of wood were well preserved showing that it was well dried before being converted into charcoal. Because the outer rings were very close together, it was also possible to suggest that growth had slowed down. This could either be explained because of the onset of adverse environmental conditions during the last year of growth or because tree-cutting would interrupt its growth each time. At Chesters the 'interruption in growth' may well have been due to organised growth management such as pollarding and/or coppicing specifically linked to the iron-smelting operation. It would be interesting to investigate the impact that Roman bloom smithing furnaces in the Holy Cross Mountains, in south-eastern Poland (south of Warsaw), had on the environment. Here the industry was on a massive scale (Bielenin 1984), with the remains of 131 smithing furnaces being found at one site (Jeleniow site 1) alone.

Figures relating to consumption of charcoal during metal-smelting have been derived from experimental work carried out by Merkel (1990: 86–7) based on Timna furnaces. He found that between 20 and 50 kg of charcoal was needed in order to produce 1 kg of copper; the more reliable fuel:slag ratio was 1 kg of slag required to c. 2 kg of fuel. An experimental slag-tapping furnace used for smelting bog ore consumed a similar ratio of 1.5:1 charcoal to ore (Joosten et al. 1997: 89).

The identification of plant charcoals found in the slags during different periods of copper production at Feinan on the opposite side of the Wadi Arabah from Timna in Jordan by Engel and Frey (1996) has shown juniper (*Juniperus phoenicea*), oak (*Quercus calliprinos*), olive (*Olea europaea*) and pistachio (*Pistacia* cf. *atlantica*) were used as fuel in the early Bronze Age. The plants were probably growing in a heavily vegetated area at the time. By the end of the Bronze Age, however, more shrubby species such as tamarix were used which provided a lower calorific yield than the more mature woods used during the early Bronze Age. The two possible interpretations of this pattern are that the climate had changed and/or that the environment had been over-exploited for fuel due to metallurgical activities in the area (Engel 1993).

If metal production (or indeed any other high-temperature industry) was carried out on a sufficiently large scale, the supply of wood for the preparation of charcoal may have been controlled by coppicing, which might be detectable using pollen samples taken from the environs of the smelting sites or by the impact coppicing had on the density of tree rings (Figueral 1992). Horne (1982) has suggested that the denudation of north-eastern Iran was due to the demand for fuel used in ancient metalworking. However, other recent work focusing on the impact of metallurgy on the environment in temperate climes, where it might be expected that the environment would be able to recover more quickly, has shown that until the industrial revolution the impact was not as severe as might be assumed. Marshall et al. (1998) have investigated the environmental impact of the mining and smelting sites in the Ramsau valley, Eisenerz, Austria (Doonan et al. 1996). They took cores at Neuburgsattel, Austria, 3 km away from the smelting and mining operations. In spite of the relatively large scale of industrial activity the sequence dating back to 2000 BC revealed a decline in beech (*Fagus*) in the later medieval period which can be linked to documentary evidence for the preferential exploitation of beech as a source of charcoal for the nearby Radmer copper works. They also detected an increased incidence of lead in the Roman period which they interpret as a possible increase in lead production at the time. While lead content increased, there is no significant impact of copper and zinc in the cores tested (the other two chemicals sought by atomic absorption spectroscopy). Apart from the impact on the growth of beech and the occurrence of lead in the cores, the results published by Marshall et al. (1998) do not reveal any evidence for widespread woodland clearance. They concluded that in this case, at least, damage to the environment was not as great as might have been expected. Coring closer to the Bronze Age copper production site may have produced evidence for a Bronze Age impact on the environment.

Mighall (1990) has shown that the effects of Bronze Age mining at Copa Hill, Cwmystwyth in Wales, was reflected in a local depletion in trees, but no long-term effects; this would seem to reflect periodic small-scale activities which allowed vegetational communities to recover. In contrast, Mighall and Chambers (1989; 1997) have carried out palynological research in the vicinity of Bryn y Castell hillfort in Merioneth, Wales (see Section 5.12.2.1) and inferred that the iron production operations there in the late Iron Age and Romano–British periods had an effect on the (local) vegetation which at first was thought to have been marked (Mighall and Chambers 1989). Later it was realised that the apparent effect was more localised – dating to the late Bronze Age (Mighall et al. 1990). The woodland decline could, it seems, be correlated with the occupation of Bryn y Castell. It had a marked effect on the vegetation of a nearby wetland basin where alder carr woodland became an open valley mire. So, in contrast to the findings (above) this study clearly revealed a marked result of a metal industry on the vegetational communities in the landscape. At Crawcwellt West (see Section 5.12.2.2) Chambers and Lageard (1993) found definite evidence in the late Iron Age (and the late Bronze Age) for high concentrations of charcoal implying the use of fire; this is especially clear in the late Iron Age corresponding with iron-working at Crawcwellt. The charcoal is *prima facie* evidence for the use of fire which is quite possibly linked to smelting and smithing activities at Crawcwellt.

Such research is far from simple: the problems of inferring human activity from changes in pollen spectra are complex. Edwards (1982) suggests that pollen cores should be taken within 30 m of a disturbed woodland in order to detect the disturbance. The other consideration is that it can be difficult to be confident of selecting the appropriate magnitude of 'indicator' pollen taxa count in order to suggest or infer that observed changes in their proportions are linked to disturbances caused by

humans (Edwards 1982; 1983); even the type of site may influence the pollen rain.

Another fuel, coal, was apparently used for forging iron in the Roman world (Schubert 1957: 44), but there is very limited evidence for its use elsewhere in the ancient world.

5.6.3 Pollution

Both the mining and smelting of metals can produce significant levels of pollution in the environment. Recently published research into environmental pollution of metal exploitation in Jordan serves to illustrate the potential impact that such industrial activities had. Hauptmann et al. (1992) and Adams (1999) note that there is early evidence for the exploitation of the sedimentary copper ore deposits at Feinan starting in the fourth millennium BC and continuing into the Iron Age and Roman periods (see Section 5.8). Tips of industrial debris which result from the exploitation of metal can lead to heavy metal pollution in either particulate form or in solution. Such pollution can be transported and deposited in the landscape by processes such as sheet and gulley erosion (Pyatt and Birch 1994). Pyatt et al. (1999) have examined the environmental pollution associated with the spoil and slag tips on the southern side of Wadi Dana adjacent to Khirbet Feinan in Jordan. The technique used to measure the copper content of soils was the use of Merck Merckoquant strips. Sampling occurred along a transect from the spoil heap into an area where no apparent metallurgical activity had occurred. Copper was found even in the modern environment in sheep urine (5 ppm) and sheep faeces (10 ppm) as well as in goat's milk (3 ppm). As one might expect, the measured level of copper on the surface of the spoil heap was 200 ppm; no copper was detected on the control site (Pyatt et al. 1999: Table 3). At a sampling site to the north of Wadi Feynan, associated with a twelfth- to ninth-century BC stratified slag tip, sheep faeces were found to contain c. 25 ppm copper. Pyatt et al. (1999) note that copper pollution clearly has an effect on the production of barley grains today. Moreover they suggest that it is likely that the measured effect of pollution on plant growth would have had a similar effect in the past and would have entered the food eaten by slaves mining the copper (for example) causing physical weakness.

5.7 The heat-treatment of metals: refining and purification

Freshly smelted metal is liable to have contained a range of impurities, such as iron in copper derived from both the flux and ore, and other metallic impurities in the ore, such as nickel and arsenic. These impurities needed to be removed from iron, especially, in order to avoid the metal being brittle. In addition, by re-melting the metal, droplets coagulate. The copper mines at Timna had crucible furnaces in which this last process occurred (Rothenburg 1972: 80, plates 38–41; Craddock 1995: Figure 5.33). Smelted copper ('black' copper) containing arsenic, antimony, bismuth and iron, could be oxidised so as to form a removable layer by melting the metal in an open crucible. Iron oxides would have reacted with the crucible wall to form a glassy slag which would be helped by the addition of sand. These slags typically contain delafossite, $CuFeO_2$, and are found on sites where the metal was purified in the first stage of alloying (Tylecote 1982). Lead and tin, which melt at relatively low temperatures, may have been pure enough to use directly after smelting.

5.7.1 The matte smelting process (for copper)

In this process low grade primary sulphidic ores are transformed by successive concentration operations to produce a rather impure metal, which itself needs refining. Crushed and sorted (beneficiated) copper ores are first partially roasted so as to remove sulphur and sulphur dioxides and to convert iron sulphides into oxides which can then be slagged with crushed quartz. The partially roasted ore was smelted in a furnace with a limited air supply (the matting stage) which converted remnant chalcopyrite ore to molten copper sulphide with a proportion of iron sulphides and iron oxides, which could then be slagged off. The copper and iron sulphides produced by this process are called the 'matte'. This is smelted to convert it into the respective oxides by slagging with crushed quartz in order to remove the iron oxide and produce *black* copper, which can then be refined. The origins of this process are hazy, but it is fully described in Renaissance texts by Agricola (Hoover

and Hoover 1950) and Biringuccio (Smith and Gnudi 1942). There is a limited amount of evidence for a multi-stage process from ancient sites, such as at the Bronze Age copper-smelting site at Acqua Fredda, Trentino, Italy (Piel *et al.* 1992).

5.7.2 Iron alloys (and steel 'working')

Cast iron contains 2–5% of carbon, often accompanied by 1–3% silicon; the carbon content can reduce the melting temperature of the iron from 1550 °C to between 1150 °C and 1200 °C. Wrought iron is what is 'wrought' from the iron bloom after repeated hammering and annealing to force out extraneous material like slag.

Pure iron is a relatively soft metal which can be hammered into shape and can also be welded together. The iron bloom needed to be smithed repeatedly, that is, it was heated until it became an orange yellow colour, and hammered in order to squeeze out the slag. By reheating the bloom between episodes of hammering it was annealed and the slag kept molten. One of the results of repeatedly smithing the bloom was a loss of iron; about 75% of the original due to the oxidised surface flaking off as hammer scale (Crew 1991; see below, Section 5.12.2.4). Crewe's experimental work suggests that 45 reheatings were involved in converting a bloom into usable iron via a billet. Once smithed and annealed, the iron could then be modified in a range of ways including welding. In this process, pieces of iron were joined by hammering while they were white hot at *c.* 1100 °C. The slag spread over the hot surfaces during this process and prevented oxidisation.

Because iron was soft, and because of the 'purity' of some of the iron produced in antiquity, some of it needed to be alloyed before it could be cast. When iron is alloyed with levels of less than 2% carbon, *steel* is produced. Three distinct forms of steel are found: the most common is called *ferrite* in which the carbon is dissolved in the solid solution, but only up to 0.02%. The second, *austentite*, contains up to 2% carbon, but is unstable below 723 °C. Below this temperature, if the steel is *quenched* (plunged into water), the austentite is transformed into *acicular* (needle-like) crystals known as martensite, and if allowed to cool slowly in air a ferrite-pearlite (see below) structure forms. A third kind is a steel in which an inter-metallic compound is present called *cementite* (iron carbide – Fe_3C), which exists as discrete particles or plates. When the cementite plates alternate with ferrite plates as a lamellar structure the result is called *pearlite*. Some steels were apparently produced adventitiously, as for example in some parts of Africa (Gordon and Killick 1993), where some iron blooms can be described as 'natural steel'; they contain carbon in the form of ferrite and pearlite.

Examination of the metallurgical structure of steel (i.e. the way in which the crystals have formed) can provide evidence of how the metal was heat-treated and an indication of its composition. For example, a steel which contains 0.8% of carbon and which has been slowly cooled is reflected by the presence of a (typical) microstructure of ferrite and pearlite. The important thing is that, as a result, the working properties of the metal are changed. One property which changes is the reduction in its melting temperature, from an unalloyed iron at 1550 °C to between a more manageable 1150 °C to 1200 °C. In order to produce a steel successfully, appropriate heat-treatment and working at the correct temperatures are critical. If the metal is heated to red heat between 750 °C and 900 °C the austentite formed is stable and should be cooled slowly. However, as mentioned above, it becomes unstable below 723 °C: the crystals are transformed according to the cooling rate used (a fundamental property which is what determines the working properties of metals). If the steel cools *too slowly* (in air) the ferrite-pearlite microstructure forms; if cooled *too quickly*, which can be achieved by plunging the hot metal into water, then a hard needle-like (acicular) series of crystals or a plate-like series of crystals are formed. The rate of quenching can be changed by using solutions other than water, such as salt, oil or urine. The plate-like crystals are called martensite; if they are found in a steel, then they offer clear evidence that quenching has occurred. The formation of martensite can sometimes only affect the outer layer of the metal (depending on its thickness), so that the interior cools more slowly. The object produced with a martensitic structure would be too brittle a steel for most uses and would need to be reheated at below red heat so that the martensite forms iron carbides.

While the strength of the metal decreases, its toughness increases during re-heating, though the brittleness is also affected by the use of higher temperatures and the period during which the quenching is carried out. Early metalsmiths may have been able to judge the degree of tempering by observing the change in colour of the oxidised surface: straw yellow for lightly tempered steel or a blue colour for more heavily tempered steel. The earliest martensitic steel dates to the late second millennium BC.

The physical process by which carbon steel is normally produced is called *carburisation*; it is also known as case hardening and forge hardening. It is a diffusion process which is a kind of *cementation*. This slow solid state reaction (whereby the two materials are heated together until one is absorbed by the other) would have involved heating the iron at red heat in a clay container packed with charcoal dust (Tylecote and Gilmore 1986). Theophilus (Hawthorne and Smith 1963: 93–4) and Biringuccio (Smith and Gnudi 1942: 372) both mention how carburisation should occur under reducing conditions by wrapping the iron in a variety of organic materials such as charred plant remains, hoofs, horn and leather and then in clay or powdered glass. In China, steel was produced by mixing wrought and cast iron so that the cast iron partially melted and some carbon diffused in. The fused metal was then forged and heated again to further homogenise the whole.

In the context of discussing the production of crucible steel (*wootz*) in India, Bronson (1986) distinguishes between *in situ* carburisation and co-fusion. At the time he noted that there was little reliable evidence for crucible steel before the mid-first millennium AD, though Craddock (1998) reports evidence for the production of crucible steel in Asia several centuries earlier than this. The use of both co-fusion and *in situ* carburisation are first mentioned in the early Islamic period; it was the segregated cementite structure which had been allowed to form which produced the Damascus pattern. There is also recently discovered evidence for the production of crucible steel in early Islamic (ninth century) contexts of Merv, Turkmenistan (Herrmann *et al.* 1996; 1997). Lang *et al.* (1998) report the discovery of a Sasanian sword made from crucible steel of sixth–seventh century date in the collections of the British Museum. The assumption that crucible steel was only used for the production of prestigious Damascus-patterned blades is now seen to be false; Lang *et al.* (1998: 13) found that none of the crucible steel used to make early pieces they examined had the distinctive Damascene structure. Damascus-pattern blades were labelled in this way because it was thought that medieval Damascus steel 'entered the west' through this town (zaffre, a cobalt-rich pigment used in the medieval period is also known as 'Damascus pigment', perhaps for the same reason).

Another alloy of iron, with phosphorus, would have lowered the melting point of iron (in the same way as carbon steel). Ehrenreich's (1985) research into the use of phosphorus-rich iron ores showed that, although the inclusion of phosphorus could potentially cause embrittlement, the metal tools made from this metal were of good quality (see Section 5.12.1 below); Tylecote and Gilmore (1986: 7–9) established that low levels of phosphorus enhanced the working properties of wrought iron. Much later phosphoric iron was used to make music wire (Goodway 1987).

Cast iron is also an alloy of iron and carbon; it also contains sulphur and phosphorus. The last two elements can cause brittleness, while at the same time the melting point, already depressed by the content of 2–5% carbon in cast iron, is reduced still further. A form of cast iron called white cast iron also contains less than 1% silicon and if cooled quickly will promote the formation of cementite, the iron carbide crystals mentioned above. This produces a very hard steel which is basically unworkable. The brittle quality can be reduced by heating for long periods at just below the melting temperature, a process called malleablisation. It lowers the carbon content by oxidation, and the cementite is converted into graphite which is much less likely to cause cracking than the structure of white cast iron. Another form of cast iron, grey cast iron, contains above 2% silicon; if cooled slowly the carbon is precipitated as graphite. Most of these forms of cast iron have been found in early China (Wagner 1989; 1993: 361–2) but they are rare in the west.

5.7.3 *Zinc*

As mentioned in Section 5.2 smithsonite ($ZnCO_3$) was the principal zinc ore in the west, whereas sphalerite, a zinc sulphide (ZnS) was the main ore further east. Like mercury, zinc is produced using distillation. Some of the earliest (historical) references to the process are to be found in India dating to the last few centuries of the first millennium BC (Craddock 1990; 1995: 309) in which a metal known as *rasa* was burned to produce an eye salve. One of the more complete references to the process of producing zinc was the *Rasaratnākara* ascribed to Nāgārjuna, a fourth-century Indian scientist; the text was probably written in the eighth century AD. In this text the zinc ore (*Rasaka*) was digested repeatedly with fermented 'paddy water', natron (a mineral evaporite source of soda), ghee (clarified butter), wool, lac (*terminalia chebula*) and borax (a boron-sodium oxide compound). This mixture is roasted in a covered crucible (a retort) so as to retain reducing conditions and produce zinc metal rather than zinc oxide. In the third century AD Galen described how zinc was prepared by throwing a (sulphidic) zinc ore into the fire (Walsh 1929) and collecting the zinc vapour from above. In the eleventh century AD Al-Birūni, an Iranian writer described how zinc oxide was prepared. Zinc ore was placed on a fire in a furnace and the 'condensed' oxide was collected from bars made of clay which were suspended above; the same process was still in use two centuries later (Allan 1979: 39–40). Other Iranian authors describe the use of clay bars coated with zinc ores or made from zinc ore. Tylecote (1970: 287) observed that there were so many furnace bars at Deh-Qualeh 200 km south-west of Meshed, northeastern Iran, that a village was built on them. Barnes (1973) carried out an analytical investigation, using an electron microprobe and XRF, of Iranian furnace bars deriving from a furnace site about 3 km from the lead-zinc mine of Kushk. He found indisputable evidence for a zone of zinc enrichment extending to 40 μm below the surface. The survival of muscovite in some of the bars suggested that the temperature achieved during the process did not exceed 800 °C (Barnes 1973: 9). Even though described only as 'ancient', the research does provide evidence for the function of these bars for zinc condensation.

Archaeological evidence for producing zinc shows that the mixture was placed in a clay retort (tubular crucible) perhaps by rubbing it against the side and a condenser tube with a long neck was fitted over the open end of the crucible. When heated from below, carbon monoxide was formed from the oxidation of the organic components in the mixture, which in turn reduced the zinc compound in the ore to metallic zinc; while this was happening the gas burnt off with a blue flame. An indication that the reaction was complete was the appearance of white smoke: metallic zinc was being oxidised. At this point the mouth of the retort was held with a pair of tongs and inverted in order to pour out zinc metal.

One of the best preserved archaeological examples of a more sophisticated mass-production of zinc metal is the remains of furnaces and retorts used for zinc distillation found at the ancient Indian mines at Zawar, Rajastan, of fourteenth and fifteenth century AD date (Craddock *et al.* 1990). The ore from Zawar is a mixed sphalerite (ZnS) – galena (PbS) deposit, the two compounds being visually distinct so they can be separated by eye. The sphalerite would have been roasted first to oxidise the sulphide. All the retorts were made in the shapes of aubergines and had volumes varying between 750 cc and 1200 cc. A conical condenser was luted onto the end of the retort. Excavations showed that a stick was inserted into the charge to hold it in place.

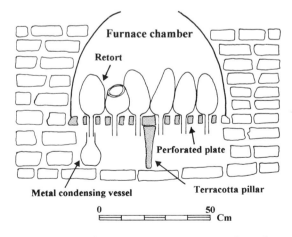

Figure 5.13 A diagrammatic cross-section through a furnace for smelting zinc, based on evidence found at Zawar, India.

The stick eventually burnt away leaving a channel for the zinc vapour to pass through to the condenser. A loaded furnace would therefore consist of banks of inverted retorts in the upper chamber with their necks attached to a conical condenser passing through perforations in the floor to a lower cool chamber in which the zinc vapour cooled and condensed as metal, probably in small collecting vessels. At Zawar each furnace held thirty-six retorts (Figure 5.13).

The remains of the material within the retorts found at Zawar seemed to consist of the remains of organic pellets (perhaps cow dung) which had been heated until they had started to fuse at the edges (sinter). Salt was found inside the 'spent' retorts. A fourteenth-century description of the kinds of materials used in the zinc-smelting mixture included lac, treacle, white mustard, the myrobalans, natron and borax, boiled with milk and clarified with butter (Ray 1956: 191) – this is similar to the eighth-century list of ingredients mentioned above. The salt found at Zawar may represent a relict unreacted component of natron.

In China, for some reason, the early technical books make no mention of zinc, even though, strangely, the distillation of mercury is described in detail. Sixteenth-century Chinese accounts refer to the use of 'new tin' for the manufacture of coins, at a time when the first brass coinage was introduced (Bowman *et al.* 1989; Cowell *et al.* 1993). By the end of the sixteenth century Chinese zinc was being exported to Europe. The process by which it was produced consisted of aqueous distillation with an internal condenser, the Mongolian still (Needham 1980: 81). Each jar is filled with zinc ore (smithsonite) and sealed with mud which is allowed to dry. The jars are then piled with alternate layers of coal and charcoal brickettes. A fire is burnt below the jars and when the retorts become red hot, the ore will melt. When cooled the jars are broken open to produce zinc; the metal is easily burnt off. Craddock (1995: 317) has noted that this 'same' process is still used in remote areas of Yunnan and Guizhou provinces, with an internal condenser. The zinc ore is mixed with powdered coal, mud and ashes. The 'jars' are arranged in a trough-like furnace, the heating process continuing for several hours; once

Figure 5.14 Scraping calamine from the walls of a furnace at Rammelsberg, Germany.

complete a collecting saucer is inserted in each jar and a loose lid fitted. The fire is them extended to the top of the jars so that the re-suction and distillation can be completed. A flame colour is observed; when it no longer burns blue (the carbon monoxide is no longer burning off) the process is considered to be complete.

Similarly in the west it was not until rather late that zinc was recognised as a separate metal (Craddock 1995: 317–18). In the thirteenth century Albertus Magnus (Wyckoff 1967: 250) referred to a white smoke collected from furnace flues and a special dark sort which sank to the bottom known as *Indian Tutt*. Small amounts of calamine were collected from the flues of the silver/lead smelters at Rammelsberg in Germany (Figure 5.14).

5.7.4 Lead

The density and compactness of galena, the commonest lead ore, make it easy to separate from gangue minerals such as iron and copper. It contains 80% lead and was normally smelted directly in a moderately oxidising atmosphere to produce lead oxide and gaseous sulphur dioxide. The lead oxide then reacted with more galena, while being reduced to lead and more sulphur dioxide. The actual reduction of the lead oxide is liable to have been promoted by the presence of carbon monoxide (Craddock 1995: 206). Sulphur dioxide was not the only gas to be produced: lead itself is both volatile and also noxious, as is the arsenic which is sometimes associated with lead.

One of the best preserved lead-smelting hearths from the west is a small stone-lined rectangular structure from Scarcliffe Park, near Duffield on the Derbyshire–Nottinghamshire border in England of only 20 cm in depth. This is of a Roman date and was found near a Roman villa (Lane 1973; 1986: 85–90). It had an open front. A small fire, probably fuelled by charcoal, was built within it and the lead ore sprinkled on it. The ore would have been reduced to metallic lead in the way described above and would have run out of the front. Silica-rich slags formed if the temperature was high enough and if the lead ores contained gangue minerals. Roman slags tend to contain relatively high lead levels, reminding us that there was little need to 'recycle'

the ore because it occurred widely. In medieval England, lead was smelted in very large hearths, typically of 1–2 sq m. These were known as *bailes* or *boles* (Barker and White 1992) and consisted of stone-built hearths on which logs, ore and brushwood were laid in layers. They were built in positions where they could receive natural draughts such as on the crests of hills in the Pennines, with a tap hole on the opposite side to drain the smelted lead. Agricola's description (Hoover and Hoover 1950: 391–2) of sixteenth-century lead-smelting in Westphalia describes the use of charcoal and straw as fuel and the recovery of lead from slags. In the Middle East, Allan (1979) has recorded the use of small shaft furnaces in the Nahlak and Tars regions of central Iran. These were about 2 m in height and varying between 20 cm and 100 cm in width, with bellows. The litharge (lead monoxide) produced by silver cupellation (see Section 5.7.6), but which had also absorbed other metals such as arsenic, bismuth, antimony and copper could be resmelted, but was much harder (Craddock 1995: 211). Indeed argentiferous lead ores had to be smelted at higher temperatures and under better reducing conditions to reduce the silver, the result being the use of somewhat more complex smelting furnaces found at Laurion, Greece (Craddock 1995: Figure 6.8).

5.7.5 Gold

The purification of gold involved its separation from copper and silver. Some of the earliest (seventh century BC) evidence has already been discussed in Section 5.2, under silver. The removal of silver from gold, was achieved by a process called *cementation*. Cementation is a process in which a solid is mixed with a powder so that they chemically combine. In addition to removing silver from gold, it is also used in brass production and is one of the techniques used to make faience (see Section 3.9.2). For gold it involves the use of chlorides and sulphides. Lechtmann (1971; 1973) showed that both copper and silver could be removed from gold by using aqueous solutions of ferrous sulphate and sodium chloride (common salt). American excavations at sixth-century BC Sardis in Turkey revealed a refinery for purifying electrum – a natural gold-silver alloy (Ramage 1970). The processes involved were very

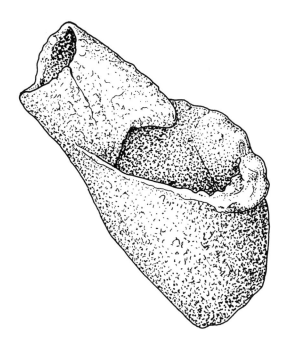

Figure 5.15 Illustration of a cupel with the tubular tuyère attached. The vessel was probably used for assaying ores; from the silver production site of Agucha, Rajasthan.

similar to those described by Agricola who published *De re Metallica* in 1556 (Hoover and Hoover 1912: 453–7). Together the processes are referred to as *parting*; the vessel in which the finely-divided grains and foils are placed is known as a *parting vessel* (see Figure 5.15). Electrum was placed in the parting vessel packed with salt and a silica-rich material, such as brick dust which formed the 'cement'. This was heated up in a small square furnace where a slow *solid state* reaction occurred; it was critical that the metal was not heated to a temperature where it melted. The process allowed the silver to react with the chlorine in the salt to produce silver chloride, the silver moving from the electrum into the cement. The gold could be removed and the silver recovered by cupellation. Touchstones could be used to test the purity of the metal (Oddy 1986 and 1993). Bayley (1991) has recognised the presence of parting vessels from Roman, Anglo-Saxon and medieval metalworking sites, but none of the small furnaces have survived. A sixteenth-century illustration by Agricola of a simple gold-refining furnace is shown in Figure 5.16.

5.7.6 Cupellation of lead-silver ores

Cupellation is a process whereby a silver-rich lead ore is separated into its constituents thereby purifying one of the metals (Forbes 1964: 193). The silver is extracted from a silver-containing lead ore such as jarosite, found at Rio Tinto, which consists of mixed hydrated sulphates of a very variable composition – including arsenic, antimony and bismuth. These sulphates form at the junction between the oxidised and primary deposits of the ore and vary widely in colour, but are usually of an earthy hue. In order to extract the silver, lead had to be imported. A lead ingot has been found at Rio Tinto marked NOVA CARTHAGO (Carthagena); lead isotope determinations of lead found in the Rio Tinto slags showed that the lead was not derived locally (Craddock *et al.* 1985), so both sources of evidence agree. More typically, however, galena or cerussite (lead ores) would have been cupelled.

The first stage was to smelt – then cupellation was carried out. During the smelting stage all the silver is reduced into the lead, some of the lead being evaporated off. Examination of the slags from this process reveal a very low silver level and that strongly reducing conditions have been used. The silver and lead produced also contained other heavy metals if present in the ore, such as gold, copper, zinc, arsenic, antimony and bismuth. The vessels in which the process was carried out are known as cupels, and can have a very small volume; at the third-century BC Mauryean silver mine of Agucha, Rajashtan, they held a maximum of 8–9 cc (Craddock *et al.* 1989; Craddock 1995: 223). The cupels have an extended lip which accommodates the tuyère supplying the air blast (Craddock 1995: Figure 6.10). The iron minerals in the bricks/clay which make up the furnace react with the arsenic and antimony to produce arsenides and antimonides (known as *Speiss*). The argentiferous lead with its impurities of other heavy metals would then be placed in the cupellation vessel and air blasted over it. The lead oxide produced would absorb the copper, arsenic, antimony and some bismuth; the balance (gold and most bismuth) would combine with the silver. Repeated cuppellation could remove the bismuth, but it is clear that this did not always occur. Cowell and Lowick (1988) found that Islamic silver coins from the Panjhir mines in the Hindu Kush

Figure 5.16 An illustration of a gold-refining furnace from Georgius Agricola's *De re Metallica* (1556).

region of Afghanistan contained traces of bismuth which sometimes rose to several per cent. Pernicka and Bachmann (1983) have investigated the partitioning of trace elements during cupellation at the famous Greek mines of Laurion (Conophagos 1980).

5.7.7 Brass

Brass is a golden coloured alloy of zinc and copper. Zinc has a boiling point of 917 °C (Pollard and

Heron 1996) and copper of 1083 °C. The earliest (deliberately made) zinc would have been produced using the cementation (calamine) process by heating finely-divided copper with zinc ore (zinc carbonate = smithsonite) under charcoal in a closed crucible. The zinc vapour will be absorbed into the copper; an example of a solid-gaseous cementation process (calamine). During this process clouds of dense white zinc oxide fumes would be produced. It is clear that the process must be carried out above 917 °C, so that zinc vapour could form; on the other hand, if the temperature was too high, the brass forming on the surface of the crucible could melt completely and then sink to the bottom. This would leave only a small surface area of the brass exposed to further adsorption and would slow the process down. In post-medieval Europe a temperature of *c*. 1000 °C was used (Sisco and Smith 1951: 257).

No furnaces in which brass was made using the cementation process have been found. The main archaeological evidence is that reported by Bayley (1984; 1990) and Rehren *et al.* (1993). This evidence consists of crucibles with lids in which the cementation process for making brass may have been carried out. The Roman crucibles discussed by Bayley were found to be heavily impregnated with zinc salts. They are small and are found on a number of sites in Britain and Germany. The medieval examples from Dortmund discussed by Rehren *et al.* are larger. Theophilus describes the cementation process used in making 'coarse brass' for the production of cauldrons, kettles and basins (Hawthorne and Smith 1963: 139–45).

Pollard and Heron (1996: 216–26) discuss the technological changes which occurred in brass production, as reflected in the chemical compositions of *jetons* and European scientific instruments between the late fourteenth century and the early twentieth century AD. By monitoring the levels of zinc over time they have compared the levels they detected with the levels supposedly associated with the maximum uptake of zinc using the 'classical' and 'granulated' calamine process: 28% and 33% (Pollard and Heron 1996: Figures 6.5 and 6.9). They found that 28% was reached by 1450 and exceeded by 1560, 160 years *before* the patent for the granulation process was introduced. After 1675, when 33% is exceeded quite commonly, it is suggested that brass was made by direct mixing.

5.7.8 Other alloys of copper – with arsenic, antimony and nickel

Northover (1998) has reviewed the technology of what he refers to as 'exotic alloys' in antiquity. In addition to bronze (copper-tin) and copper-zinc (brass) he also discusses copper-arsenic, copper-arsenic-antimony and copper-nickel.

Copper-arsenic metals were the first copper alloys to be made. They are discussed further below (Section 5.9). Some copper ores contain arsenic which is retained in the copper metal. Northover (1989) has noted that even if a copper contains levels of up to 25% it may not have an effect on the properties of the metal, because it will all be concentrated in the metallic inclusions. Indeed Budd and Ottaway (1991: 135) noted a substantial level of micro-segregation of arsenic in European copper-arsenic alloys. Shalev and Northover (1987) have stated that the lowest arsenic concentration which can produce a two-phase alloy in 'normal cooling' is 2.5%. It was found that copper-arsenic alloys, which contain between 2–6%, are most suitable for cold-working metal in its as-cast condition, being ductile, so that it does not crack, and having elevated hardness values. There is little to be gained in terms of work hardenability if a level of 2% arsenic or less is present in a copper-arsenic metal.

5.7.9 Mercury

Mercury is produced by distillation and has a very low boiling point of 357 °C. The metal occurs naturally as cinnabar (mercury sulphide, HgS). When roasted in air, cinnabar decomposes at between 600 °C and 700 °C and this produces poisonous mercury vapour. The Roman author Dioscorides described the process in *Materia Medica* in the first century AD. This involved the insertion of cinnabar in an iron spoon (crucible), heating it up, and collecting the condensed vapour from the underside of the vessel which covered it. This 'soot' consisted of mercury globules, mercury chlorides, sulphides and soot. An iron crucible would have been used instead of a ceramic one because mercury penetrates easily into clays. Various archaeological sites have produced evidence, or probable evidence, for this process. In Anatolia at Ladik Koy, near Konya, Barnes and Bailey (1972) claim to have found Roman condensers; mercury was mined at Izmir in western Anatolia (Granger 1934: 115) and in Spain (Rackham 1952). Craddock (1995: 303–5) outlines the late first-millennium BC evidence from India and China and the texts which describe the sublimation and condensation of mercury. Agricola (Hoover and Hoover 1912: 429) describes the distillation of mercury vapour in an external receiving vessel and he also described a second process whereby the large surface areas of leaves were used to allow mercury vapour to condense on them. In the latter process the mercury was heated in a small chamber in which there were branches or small trees. The mercury ran down and could be collected below the chamber, or by shaking the branches.

5.8 Early copper production at Wadi Feinan, Jordan

5.8.1 Introduction

The first use of copper to make beads in the Palestinian area dates to the eighth–seventh millennia (Garfinkel 1987). Powdered copper used for cosmetic purposes at Jericho and Nahal Hemar, for example, appeared in Neolithic times, another reflection of the exploitation of native copper in oxidised zones of native ores. The use of a copper-rich pigment (diopsite, a copper silicate) was even found to have been used on some of the earliest statuary in the world from the pre-pottery Neolithic B phase of Ain Ghazal (Rollefson *et al.* 1985). On the basis of a comparison of copper: nickel and antimony: arsenic ratios in Feinan copper ores, Hauptmann (1989: Figure 14.3) claims that the copper ores used to make beads at Jericho in the pre-pottery Neolithic B and middle Bronze Age periods derived from Feinan.

Although earlier claims (Hauptmann 1989) that the earliest copper and copper alloys appeared for the first time in the Chalcolithic period at Tell Abu Matar and Bir Safadi in Palestine (Hauptmann 1989: 119), there is now clear evidence for earlier copper exploitation with a carbon-14 date of 4460 BC for an ash sample from site 39 in the Wadi Nehushtan along the western fringe of the Arabah valley, at the entrance to the modern Timna Mines Company (Rothenberg and Merkel 1995; 1998). The dating of Wadi Fidan 4 has been discussed by a range of scholars. Hauptmann's surface survey and the probable misidentification of the pottery found on the surface as 'Qatifian' pottery (Gilead 1990: 60; Goren 1990) thought to date to the Neolithic/Chalcolithic transition led to a suggested date of the fifth–fourth millennia for the copper-smelting there. Excavations at Wadi Fidan 4, however, have now provided four calibrated carbon-14 dates which fall in the second half of the fourth millennium BC, and therefore belong to the earliest phase of the early Bronze Age (Adams 1999: 112–13). This suggests that the Chalcolithic dates for metallurgical activities at Wadi Fidan 4 dates are too old. Evidence for metalliferous activities also occurred in the area in early Bronze Age II and III, and to a more limited extent in the middle Bronze Age II; most evidence from Feinan dates to the Iron Age II and from the Roman period, with limited evidence from the early Islamic period (Hauptmann *et al.* 1992: Table 5).

5.8.2 The ore deposits

Detailed descriptions of the Chalcolithic and early Bronze Age copper metallurgy by Hauptmann (1989) and Hauptmann *et al.* (1992) stand as comprehensive discussions of important phases of early metal production in the Middle East, concentrating on metallurgical activities, especially in the area of Wadi Feinan, Jordan (Figure 5.17). The copper ores exploited were found to have derived from Cambrian and more recent sedimentary environments; those at Feinan 'genetically' linked to the geological formations along the western side of the Wadi Arabah at Timna. Although Wadi Arabah is part of a fault extending from the Red Sea to the Zagros-Taurus mountains, the metal-bearing geological formations at Timna and Feinan or between individual sites where copper was worked or smelted (Hauptmann 1989: 120) were not expected to be distinguished using compositional and isotopic studies. In the event some differences in the crystalline textures were observed for contemporary formations, and differing levels of silver, gold and selenium appear to distinguish between copper ores in the dolomite-limestone-shale formations at Feinan and Timna (Hauptmann *et al.* 1992: 16). Fieldwork established that the Feinan industrial deposits extended over an area of 20×25 km with an estimated 150,000 to 200,000 tons of slag. The area was clearly very important as a copper supply in the southern Levant. A further Cambrian (copper-manganese) deposit was Maadi, at Bir Nasib on the western side of the Sinai peninsula. These three deposits appear to have been the only possible sources for copper in the Chalcolithic or later periods in this

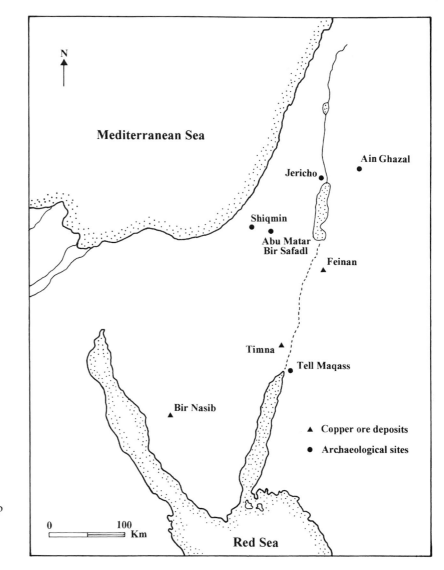

Figure 5.17 Location map of metallurgical sites and other sites mentioned in the text.

area. The formation date of other copper ores, in the Eastern Desert of Egypt for example, occur in pre-Cambrian rocks and are therefore not related to those used at Feinan.

There is evidence at Feinan for prehistoric mining of copper ores concentrated along joints and faults in Cambrian sandstones and in underlying dolomitic limestone-shale deposits which were also rich in manganese ores (Hauptmann *et al.* 1992). The evidence for early mining at Feinan consists of pottery and grooved hammerstones (Hauptmann

et al. 1985). At Feinan, copper ores are found in two geological environments (see Figure 5.18). The principal copper source apparently used in the Chalcolithic and Roman periods was the geologically younger of the two in the Cambrian ('Massive Brown') sandstone in the Wadis Khalid, at Abiad and Ratiye, and at Khirbet el-Jariye. These ores consisted of malachite (copper hydroxycarbonate), 'tile' ore (malachite and iron hydroxides), chalcocite (copper sulphide), (par)-atacamite (copper chloride) and a minor proportion of copper-silicates. Some of the

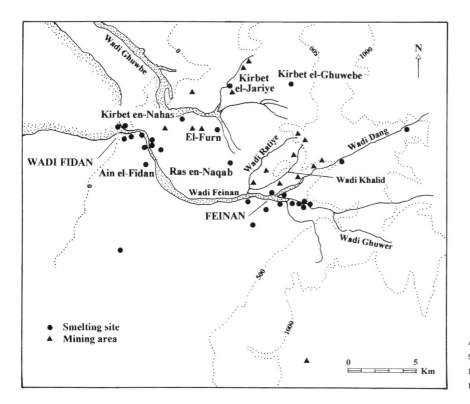

Figure 5.18 Map showing smelting and mining locations in the Feinan area.

copper ore samples analysed contained up to 51.8% copper. The older dolomitic-limestone-shale environment was exploited later in the Bronze Age and in the Iron Age, outcrops in the Wadis Khalid and Dana, and at Khirbet en-Nahas and Khirbet el-Jariye. These outcrops contained secondary copper ores, chrysocolla (amorphous and cryptocrystalline copper-silicates) and malachite. Corresponding modifications of chrysocolla are observable in the Timna formation to the west.

Due to their differing formation histories, the two deposits of ores are visually distinct. The ore deposits which were mined in the early Bronze Age and Iron Age were those in the dolomite-limestone-shale deposits. At Timna, mining appears to have concentrated on mineralised Cambrian sandstone.

5.8.3 Evidence for early ore exploitation and metallurgical activity in Palestine

Although industrial deposits extend over an area of 20 × 25 km at Feinan, the evidence of the metallur-gical activities, which apparently date to the early Bronze Age, is on a rather small scale. Before describing it in detail, it is worth noting briefly the occurrence of evidence from other sites where, in some cases, it is clear that ore from the Arabah was imported – and this may be the explanation for limited evidence of early smelting at Feinan. Hauptmann (1989) has listed the sites where evidence of the occurrence for 'Chalcolithic' metallurgical activities have been found in Palestine (Tell Abu Matar, Bir Safadi, Wadi Ghazzek and Shiqmin), the Jordan valley (Jericho) and in lower Egypt (Maadi) (see Figure 5.17).

The ores found at Tell Abu Matar and Bir Safadi match closely the texture of the mineralisations in the Cambrian limestone in Feinan. The 'tile ores' with chalcocite from Bir Safadi apparently derived from either Timna or Feinan. It is suggested that the ores found at Shiqmin, and smelted there between 4400 and 3300 BC, were probably derived from Feinan (Shalev and Northover 1987; Shalev 1991). Figure 5.19 shows the distribution of the evidence

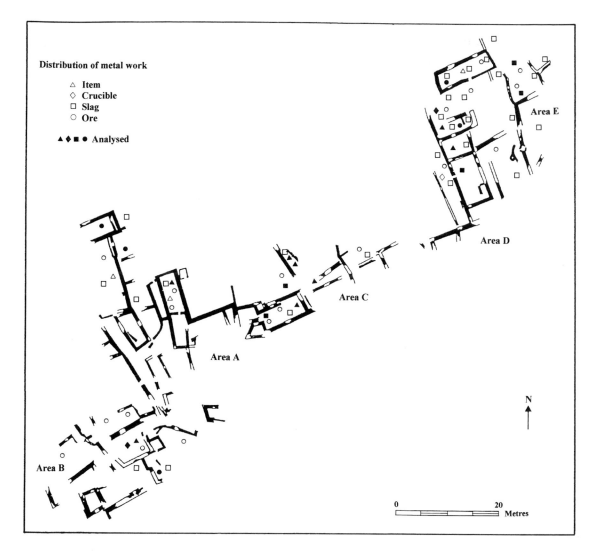

Figure 5.19 The distribution of industrial debris at Shiqmin, Palestine (after Shalev and Northover 1987).

for metalworking activities at Shiqmin and illustrates the type of evidence found on such a site. Those ores found at Wadi Ghazzeh, however, were interpreted as deriving from both Feinan and Timna. The characteristic of microcrystalline chrysocolla partly replacing malachite and atacamite ores, was observed in ores found at pre-pottery Neolithic B Jericho. This is an identical characteristic found in the dolomitic limestone-shale environment in which ores formed at Feinan. The same, mineralogical, links can be made between the ores found at the Maadi and Feinan copper deposits. As well as Feinan, it is suggested that Bir Nasib on the western side of the Sinai peninsula provided the copper-manganese pyrolucite deposit found at Maadi. It is clear that copper-rich minerals which derived from Feinan and Timna were traded quite widely, early in the history of metal production, including in the Neolithic and Chalcolithic periods in a zone of some 200 km through Palestine, the Jordan valley and lower Egypt.

5.8.4 The characteristics of metallurgical activity at Wadi Feinan

The archaeological evidence for early copper metallurgy at Feinan consists of lumps of copper ore, discarded 'host' rock, metalliferous slags, copper prills, crucible fragments (see Figure 5.20), copper beads and incomplete copper beads (Adams 1999: 127–8). Amongst the crucible fragments found during the excavations at Wadi Fidan 4 were some 'brick-shaped' ones with a depression at one end which could possibly have acted as a handle (Adams 1999: 140, Figures 5.35–5.37). Grooved hammer stones have also been found in the settlements. These pieces of evidence were found in settlements in the

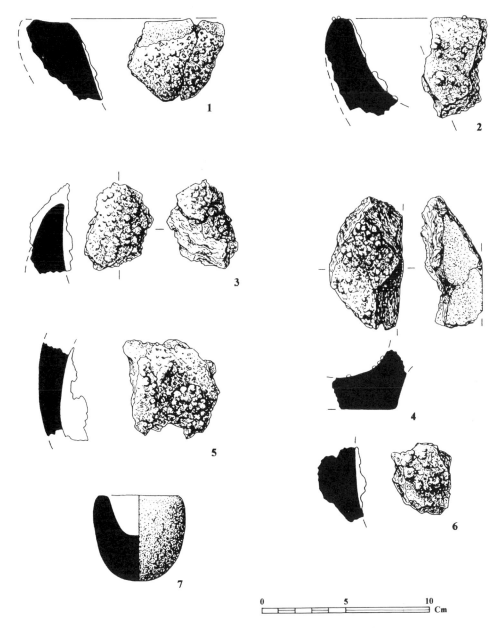

Figure 5.20 Crucible fragments from early Bronze Age Wadi Fidan, Jordan (Adams 1999).

Wadi Fidan (see Figure 5.18) – labelled Wadi Fidan 4 and A – about 10 km north-west of Feinan and in the Wadi Feinan itself, labelled Feinan 17 and Tell Wadi Feinan. Hauptmann *et al.* (1996) have described the metallurgical activity at Wadi Fidan 4 as 'household metallurgy'.

The ores found were mainly considered to be carefully selected malachite, (par)-atacamite with cuprite, chalcocite and copper silicates from both geological formations at Feinan. Study of the slags has provided a clear idea of the smelting procedures employed. Prills of copper were separated from gangue by crushing and so was cuprite. Prills and cuprite were apparently combined in a second operation during which cuprite was reduced to metallic copper (Hauptmann *et al.* 1996). There is no evidence for tuyère use, but the contents of crucibles were heated by superheating charcoal in the vessels using blow-pipes (Rehder 1994). Rehren (1997: 115) has noted that it was not until the late Bronze Age that the outsides of crucibles were heated.

One compositional characteristic of the slag found at Feinan was the almost total absence of manganese. It was commonly found in early Bronze Age copper slags at Feinan (but not at Timna) where it was used as a fluxing agent in the formation of slags. A range of phases was identified in the slags by using scanning electron microscopy: metallic copper, cuprite (Cu_2O), delafossite ($Cu^+Fe^{3+}O_2$), magnetite (Fe_3O_4), and chalcocite (Cu_2S). Based on the presence of these phases the slags can, overall, be classed as oxidic. This means that the slagging process occurred in an environment in which some oxygen was available. However, had it been fully oxidising, clearly no metallic copper would have been produced.

Because the mining environment has been researched, including the chemical/mineralogical/ textural characteristics of the ores found at Timna and Feinan, it has been possible to relate the ores found there to the remnant and modified minerals in the slags from Wadi Fidan 4. One of the principal reasons why this has been possible is due to the nature of the metallurgy practiced: it is clear that the different phases found in the slag were only partially crystallised from the melt. One such was delafossite in a glassy matrix (Hauptmann 1989:

Figure 14.10). The cuprite which was present would have resulted from the decomposition of malachite or from melting 'primary' cuprite. Iron-rich magnetite in the slag resulted from using areas of copper ore rich in limonite which were not added deliberately to form the flux. Hauptmann *et al.* (1992: 12) mention that the ores from the sandstone environment 'are remarkably low in manganese (< 0.02 per cent) although the iron content occasionally reaches 15 percent'. Rothenberg and Merkel (1995: 2) claim that the iron oxide present in Timna slag 'proved that fluxing with iron oxide was already known at Site 39'; a possible limonite source is mentioned. Like Hauptmann, Shalev (1991: 416) – in discussing the chemical compositions of slag from the Chalcolithic village at Shiqmin – is less confident that iron found in copper prills was added as a flux.

Hauptmann (1989: 124) suggests that slight desulphurisation of chalcocite (Cu_2S) in the Feinan copper sources produced cuprite and sulphur dioxide:

$$Cu_2S + 3/2 \ O_2 \rightarrow Cu_2O + SO_2$$

The formation of 'high' temperature species which form under reducing conditions such as iron silicates, fayalite (Fe_2SiO_4) and pyroxenes, was only rarely observed.

Overall, it is clear that there was only a partial formation of the slag and that ores were not completely decomposed by heat. The lack of the reducing conditions necessary for the formation of copper metal, and the apparent relatively low temperatures can be suggested as the main reasons for the partial decomposition of the ore and the reasons why it would not have been fully molten. Similar partially decomposed ore and partial vitrification was found during the examination of some partly vitrified material from nearby Wadi Madsus (Craddock 1995: 128, Figure 4.2), though the conditions appear to have been even less reducing than those detected at Wadi Fidan 4, with no formation of fayalite.

As mentioned in Section 5.5.1 there has been some discussion of the 'non-slagging' process of copper production (Craddock and Meeks 1987). Tylecote (1974) and Craddock (1986b) discussed the relative ease with which liquid copper could be produced, especially with high grade ores. By identifying of the different phases in slags, it is possible to establish the temperatures achieved using a crucible in a smelting hearth: in this case temperatures of around 1130 °C were apparently achieved, presumably with the aid of tuyères (a forced draught). This can be stated because, for example, in order for cuprite to melt, 1080 °C needs to be exceeded; copper-iron oxides with 80% Cu_2O have a melting point of 1130 °C. However, the overriding factor would be whether the temperature was sufficiently high for reduction of the metal to have occurred.

Because the ore samples analysed were relatively pure, containing up to 51.8% copper, usable metal was still produced with low impurity levels. It is clear, therefore, that high purity copper did not necessarily derive from the use of native copper, but, as in this case, from smelting simple copper ores containing high copper contents (Tylecote *et al.* 1977). Nevertheless, this is, perhaps, precisely what we might expect to find during the early stages of copper production. Coughlan (1962) has shown that malachite could be smelted at 800 °C.

While predominantly bowl-shaped hearths were used for the production of copper metal in the Chalcolithic in Timna (Rothenberg and Merkel 1995: Figure 3), during early Bronze Age II and III periods (2900–2300 BC) smelting furnaces had been introduced producing slag. Two Iron Age IIB and IIC (*c*. 900–500 BC) smelting sites at Feinan and Khirbet en-Nahas (the 'ruins of copper') have produced more than 100,000 tons of slag constituting evidence for massive smelting activity (Hauptmann *et al.* 1985).

In early Bronze Age II and III contexts at Feinan Hauptmann (1989: 129) describes the discovery of a battery of twenty-seven fragmentary furnaces in which more-or-less self-fluxing copper-manganese ores were smelted at temperatures between *c*. 1200 °C and 1250 °C (Hauptmann and Roden 1988: 511, Abb. 1). These were re-used as many as twenty-seven times (see Figure 5.21). It is apparent that higher temperatures were achieved within the suggested 'open fronted' furnaces but not in the production of copper in Chalcolithic hearths. The furnaces were about 60 cm in diameter and possibly 40 cm tall (an estimate). They were located also as to benefit from the prevailing wind direction just below the crests of ridges. A number of fragmentary clay bars have been found at Timna (Rothenberg and Shaw 1990), some bearing a vitrified layer. Since it is clear that they would have been vertical when used, it is suggested that these originally formed a grill on the front of the furnaces to hold the smelting charge and the fuel (charcoal) in position – and possibly to hold a front wall in position (Craddock 1995: 130).

Another contrast with early Bronze Age I production is that the copper produced contained higher levels of lead, zinc and iron, with traces of cobalt and nickel also being detected. The lower sulphur content in early Bronze Age II and III metal supports the suggestion that the ores smelted contained a lower sulphur content. Hauptmann has suggested that the development of the true furnace technology was a response to attempts to smelt silicate ores which were exploited for the first time in the early Bronze Age of the region. The silica could not have been removed by beneficiation; a flux (manganese) was added to remove the silica from the copper ore in the context of smelting at Feinan; at Timna iron was added.

By investigating ancient production on such a large scale, further questions are generated as research proceeds. Although the link between the use of ores containing high copper content and Chalcolithic 'non-furnace' metallurgy has been made, later results from lead isotope determinations of Chalcolithic slags appear to suggest that during the Chalcolithic period copper minerals were exploited from both the dolomite-sandstone-shale and the sandstone units, and therefore include ores with lower copper contents (Hauptmann *et al.* 1992: 27). The issue of whether the development of furnace technology was driven by the exploitation of ores with lower copper content, or whether the furnace development led to the realisation that ores with a lower copper content could be exploited is therefore not quite resolved. Beneficiation obviously had an important role to play.

The emergence of smelting technology in this part of southern Palestine and Transjordan may have acted as a catalyst for the emergence of urbanism in the early Bronze Age (Ilan and Sebanne 1989). The knowledge of industrial processes appears to have

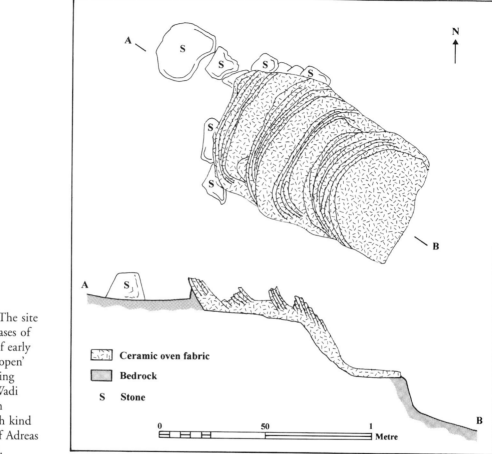

Figure 5.21 The site of several phases of re-building of early Bronze Age 'open' copper-smelting furnaces at Wadi Fidan, Jordan (redrawn with kind permission of Adreas Hauptmann).

been restricted at the time (Levy 1995) and as the scale of manufacture increased, the nature of production also changed during the early Bronze Age. The mode of production changed from the manufacture of 'elite' objects to more utilitarian forms (Adams 1999: 153). Results from excavations at Wadi Fidan 4 seem to support the idea that in the early Bronze Age a development and expansion of features of the earlier Chalcolithic copper metallurgy occurred. As Craddock (1995: 147–8) has noted, one of the more important aspects of the evidence for metallurgical processes at Feinan and Timna is that it is possible to follow the development of a very small-scale and intermittent crucible process through small slag-tapping shaft furnaces via the use of an open-sided low furnace or hearth producing manganese or iron

slags. Here the earliest phase has been described because of its importance as one of the earliest places that copper metallurgy developed.

5.9 Scientific studies of copper and bronze in Europe – the potential for characterisation

5.9.1 Introduction

The analysis of unalloyed copper could provide an ideal opportunity for characterising and studying the exploitation of metal sources. Ottaway, for example, made an important start in the analysis of Chalcolithic artefacts from the Alpine zone (1978). Doran and Hodson (1975: 250) have noted the existence of geographically localised groups of arsenical copper compositions. There are, however, certain significant difficulties to be considered. One of these is the identification of the copper ore itself. Figure 5.3 is an idealised section through a sulphide copper ore deposit illustrating the chemical and mineralogical variation moving from the weathered upper portion of the deposit, through the leached and oxidised zones, into the primary sulphide ore zones. This figure illustrates some of the complexities in the mining conditions. Various investigators have noted the problems of attempting to distinguish between the use of the two main types of copper ore, the sulphide and oxide ores, in the production of copper and copper-based artefacts (Ericson *et al.* 1982).

As Craddock (1995: 285) has pointed out, there is also a continuing debate among archaeologists and scientists as to whether there was any attempt to produce copper with a predetermined level of arsenic which could affect the properties of the metal (Charles 1967: see Section 5.9). Under reducing conditions in a furnace, small quantities of naturally-occurring arsenic could be retained in the metal (McKerrell and Tylecote 1972). Analytical work on arsenical copper artefacts has shown that the distribution of arsenic in the metal can often be heterogeneous and that it becomes impossible to predict the properties of the metal using bulk compositions alone. This is because segregation of arsenic may occur at the surface or within the non-metallic inclusions (Northover 1989; Budd and Ottaway 1991: 135). The disequilibrium of arsenic within the solid solution with copper is yet another basic problem when it comes to interpreting/predicting the properties of arsenical coppers (Budd 1991). As mentioned above, even in copper-arsenic alloys which contain arsenic levels of up to 25%, where the arsenic is concentrated in the inter-metallic inclusions its presence may not have an effect on the working properties of the metal. A level of 2–6% arsenic was found to be most suitable for cold-working the copper-arsenic alloy in its as-cast condition: it is ductile with elevated hardness values (Shalev and Northover 1987). Britton and Richards (1969) conducted an analytical survey using optical emission spectrometry which included southern British Wessex early Bronze Age copper alloys and showed (appar-ently) that the highest levels of arsenic were to be found in daggers which would therefore benefit from increased hardness.

The debate about whether arsenic was deliberately alloyed with copper has been approached by: (1) comparing the composition of the copper metal with that of the ore; (2) relating the arsenic levels to other minor and trace elements in the copper; and (3) examining any relationship between arsenic content and artefact type.

Hook *et al.* (1987) have examined the late third-millennium BC Chalcolithic smelting and casting debris at the Millarian site of El Malagón in south-east Spain. The evidence includes copper ores, droplets of metallic copper, crucibles, hearths, moulds and metalwork. The process of metal-smelting did not seem to include the use of tuyères and no metal slag was identified. It has been suggested that simple bowl furnaces with updraft chimneys were used; since no such chimneys have ever been found this part of the interpretation is inferential. An analytical investigation by Hook *et al.* (1987) of the malachite ores found on the site showed that they were basically free of arsenic, whereas the metalwork contained several per cent of arsenic. Furthermore, and the analysis of a complete used clay mould showed the contact surfaces to be rich in arsenic. At the time the conclusion of this investigation was that the arsenic had been added deliberately to the copper metal. However, a later consideration of the evidence (Hook *et al.* 1991) showed that the local ores do in fact contain arsenic in sufficient quantities to be carried through the smelting process into the metalwork found.

The association of arsenic with other elements such as antimony, bismuth, nickel or silver in both ores and metalwork is a second approach to attempting to answer the question of whether arsenic was deliberately alloyed with copper. Craddock (1979) has pointed out that the arsenic in Bronze Age copper from the British Isles and western Europe is generally related to the presence of other trace elements; this strongly suggests that any arsenic was introduced with the copper ore. Craddock (1995: 288) argues that the presence of other trace elements suggests that arsenic was *not added separately* and even if unaccompanied by trace elements still does not prove that it was added separately. Budd *et al.* (1992) also points out some of the problems in attempting to relate the composition of the metal ore to the objects made from it.

As already mentioned, there does nevertheless seem to be some (limited) relationship between the occurrence of elevated arsenic levels and certain artefact types – especially those with blades (Craddock 1995: 288). However, the sample for which a comparison has been made for Agaric culture metalwork in Spain, is small (only four blades were analysed, and three of these contained high arsenic levels: Craddock; 1995: Figure 8.1), so further work is needed to examine this closely. Moreover, in metallographic examinations reported by Budd *et al.* (1992) they found that there was no simple correlation between high arsenic levels and artefacts type. A potential silvery surface colour could be caused by sweating which would create arsenic-rich surface phases. This possibly indicates that the smiths were more concerned with the decorative effects produced than the working properties of the metal. Elevated arsenic contents increase the hardness of the alloy which would create a sharp cutting edge, though this would have been balanced against the embrittlement of the metal if not annealed correctly.

The best evidence for the use of sulphide and oxide copper ores in metal production is the primary archaeological evidence of copper mining as at, for example, the early Eneolithic mines of Rudna Glava in north-eastern Yugoslavia (Jovanović 1971; 1988). These mines date to the second half of the fourth millennium BC. Their exploitation followed the copper oxide ore veins which resulted from the decomposition of chalcopyrite (a sulphide ore) oxide and carbonate minerals. It was possible to date the use of the shafts from the discovery of high quality black burnished amphorae and a clay altar crushed *in situ* on an access platform in one of the mines. About forty shafts have so far been found ranging from 15 to 20 m in depth and 0.7 to 2 m across. More than 200 mining hammers made from hard rock river cobbles have been found, many of which have a continuous groove around the middle so that they could be attached to a handle (Jovanović 1982: 135–40); such artefacts have been found associated with other mines (Craddock 1995: Figure 2.14).

At a copper-working site, the ideal situation can be illustrated by Lechtmann's (1976: 26) find of a deserted furnace of alternating layers of wood and malachite (a copper carbonate ore) near Chiclayo in Peru (Lechtmann 1976: 26). Archaeological evidence for the use of sulphide copper ores would be sulphur-rich slags or unmelted sulphide mineral fragments. There are other factors which can affect the impurity patterns of the copper used. These are:

1 the degree of metal/ore segregation;
2 contamination from the furnace wall;
3 the use of fluxes that contribute manganese, iron or arsenic;
4 the fact that molten copper can absorb sulphur from the fuel (dry wood may contain 0.1–0.2% weight % sulphur);
5 the mixing of ores and the variation of impurity patterns in ore bodies.

In spite of these factors, Junghans *et al.* (1960; 1968; 1974) have claimed some definite relationships between copper ores and the artefacts made from them through the determination of levels of nickel, bismuth, arsenic, antimony and silver impurities using optical emission spectrometry. Groupings such as EO1 and EO1A for Copper Age Iberian metals, C2 in early Bronze Age Austria and EIIA in early Bronze Age Scotland and Ireland have emerged. However, there has not been any attempt to interpret comprehensively their European distributions. Since the *Studien zu den Anfangen der Metallurgie* (SAM) involved some 12,000 chemical analyses of copper-containing artefacts, it is important to ask if the overall methodology and interpretation are acceptable. The aim of the research was in fact to identify 'workshops'. One result was that it was possible to distinguish between nearly 'pure' copper, used to make Copper Age artefacts when native copper/secondary ores were worked, and the early Bronze Age use of Bohemian and central German *fahlerz* ores (see Section 5.2). Thus the aim of identifying workshops, with accompanying potential inferences about the location and organisation of industries within them, was not really achieved, and, in any case, the definition of a workshop should surely include the production of specialised artefact types and this was not taken into account either. Some kind of contribution has however been made in distinguishing broadly between 'industries' through chemical analysis. Though such a distinction could also be made on typological grounds, chemical analysis has distinguished between the use of different ore types. However by using bulk wet chemical analysis there is no possibility of identifying any segregation or enrichment of elements. Segregation of bismuth, lead and nickel during heat-treatment of the metal would lead to compositional heterogeneity and a single chemical analysis might be unrepresentative of the rest of the artefact (Charles 1973); if supported by metallography and the use of a scanning electron microscope this problem, and the potential complication of corrosion, may be overcome.

By using electron probe microanalysis it is possible to locate zones of enrichment. Northover (1982a) has identified a primary and several secondary production areas for the copper-using period in the British Isles through analysis of copper artefacts, though not ores, leading to the implication that local ores were in use. A careful study by Needham *et al.* (1989) focused on early Bronze Age metallurgy in southern Britain, when copper and arsenical copper were replaced by tin bronze. The technique of analysis used was atomic absorption spectroscopy, so that metallurgical structures were not considered. They suggested that the trace element pattern detected was unlikely to reflect closely the composition of the ore sources but was more likely to be a record of typical smelting and melting practices and the procedures adopted of alloying, mixing and recycling metal. By examining the structure of the data with multivariate statistics (principal components analysis) it was found that the majority of the analytical results belonged to a rather diffuse mixture of distributions, the components of which could be shown to change over time. Overall, they interpreted the variation in trace elements as reflecting irregular features of the supply, exchange and mixing of what might originally have been compositionally distinct metals. There was a shift from the primary Irish-like pattern of fairly high arsenic, antimony and silver contents in the copper

(Coughlan and Case 1957) – though determined with optical emission spectrometry – through various stages to a higher nickel and slightly increased lead composition; the latter possibly indicating greater continental influence. This can be regarded as a careful study which took the full range of archaeological complexities into account when interpreting the data. The case study described in Section 5.9.4, in which the results of lead isotope analysis and chemical compositions of copper are considered, goes well beyond this study by Needham *et al.* (1989).

In earlier work Doran and Hodson (1975: 251) claimed that by applying multivariate statistical analysis to the results of analysing copper-bronze alloys, it should eventually be possible to distinguish clusters that represent common, natural and widely-distributed combinations of elements from those that have at least some regional significance. Needham *et al.* (1989) started the process whereby the chemical characterisation of regional early Bronze Age copper-bronzes became apparent. Doran and Hodson (ibid.) also suggested that distinctive workshop clusters may be distinguished from general ore-clusters, the latter reflecting the use of a major ore type. Again, the work by Needham *et al.* (ibid.) suggest that it is difficult to distinguish such workshop clusters, since the data is obscured by a number of irregular components in the supply, exchange and mixing of metal, at least in their study area of southern England.

5.9.2 *The role of lead isotope analysis*

When almost any technique is used for measuring the physical properties of archaeological materials, the interpretation can often be complicated. The use of lead isotope analysis is no exception. Some complex discussions about the applicability and use of lead isotope analyses have recently been published (Reedy and Reedy 1992; Sayre *et al.* 1992; Gale and Stos-Gale 1992; Pernicka 1993). It is difficult to identify a consensus of opinion between the research groups involved as to the 'correct' interpretation of the use and limitations of lead isotopes in the investigation of ancient metal production. Nevertheless, there are a number of features of the methodology which must be investigated in order to tackle geological, metallurgical and archaeological features of the systems involved. Such features will be discussed in more detail below but they include the need to perform isotope determinations for a sufficient number of samples from individual lead-bearing metal sources in order to attempt to link them with the isotope signatures determined for the artefacts. A second consideration is the possibility that scrap metal mixing has occurred, leading to a potential blurring of isotope signatures. Rather than present all the complex arguments that have been addressed, brief summaries of some work with Mediterranean metal will be presented to provide an idea of some of the problems and possibilities (Section 5.9.3), followed by a much more detailed discussion of recent work (Section 5.9.4). The intention is to present a range of positive results .

5.9.3 Some studies of Mediterranean metalwork

In discussing well-stratified earliest Bronze Age metal artefacts from Poliochni on Lemnos, Pernicka *et al.* (1990: 278) stressed the serious potential problems produced by the possibility that two different ore deposits may have indistinguishable lead isotope signatures, and that it would never be possible to gather sufficient data for ores (presumably because of their potentially massive horizontal and vertical extents). It is, nevertheless, obviously important to attempt to identify specific deposits of metal which were exploited by ancient metalworkers (in the context of a thorough survey), though there is always a possibility that much of the evidence has already been destroyed by more modern mining activities (Craddock 1989).

Pernicka *et al.* (1990: 283) suggested that assignment by isotopic composition to a *geographical region* in the Aegean and Anatolia is possible, however. They even found variations in lead isotope abundance ratios in copper-based artefacts from different periods. The changes in lead isotope values were related to changes in the geographical origin of the ore used, and *in this sense it provides provenance information* for the lead used. They suggested that sources of copper in the Troad were used in the second and third sub-periods of the early Bronze Age at Poliochni, which changed to lead isotope signatures of copper ores characteristic of central Anatolia and

the eastern Pontids later in the early Bronze Age.

A potentially more powerful approach to provenancing metals is to combine chemical analyses of the metal with lead isotope determinations. Discussion of the metallurgy of late Neolithic and early Bronze Age Greece (McGeehan-Liritzis and Gale 1988) broached the important question of whether or not metallurgy developed independently in mainland Greece. Determination of lead isotope ratios of lead in copper sources, which might support the suggestion of a 'local' use, was used to help to answer this question. In the discussion it was stated that an earring from Dimini had isotope data consistent with the Laurion (Greece) source, though it was also pointed out that the copper-based earring had typological parallels with a gold earring from late Neolithic Sesklo and a copper earring from Emborio, Chios. A local Thessalian source for the copper was suggested as a possibility instead of the Laurion source (ibid.: 214). However, the lead isotope determinations stand by themselves as objectively-measured scientific data and, while archaeological characteristics are important, until such an alternative copper source in Thessaly is located with the appropriate lead isotope signature, on one level the Laurion source provides the necessary scientific proof for the origin of the lead in the copper. McGeehan-Liritzis and Gale (ibid.) noted that artefacts plotted with the Cypriot or Laurion fields using the lead-207 to lead-206 ratio versus lead-208 to lead-206 ratio. However, they moved outside the field or moved from the Cypriot to the Laurion field using lead-207/lead-206 ratio versus lead-206/lead-204 ratio. This makes it difficult to interpret the use of specific ores for the manufacture of specific artefacts, and, as noted below, a regional approach may be more appropriate in some cases, coupled with comprehensive determinations for lead isotope signatures for ore bodies. In this case the chemical analysis of the metal artefacts did not help either.

Where trace compositions of metals are close, but lead isotope ratios vary widely between metals, the (past) existence of chemically similar deposits with different isotopic compositions can be suggested. The two techniques, chemical analysis and lead isotope determinations, therefore provide two separate (useful) levels of information; there is no a priori reason why the two techniques should yield results which 'agree' (the same is true for a material such as glass). The studies by McGeehan-Liritzis and Gale (1988) and Pernicka *et al.* (1990) were chosen for discussion here because they show a contrast in interpretation: Pernicka *et al.* emphasise the problems of relating the lead isotope ratios determined in artefacts to those for individual metal sources, pointing out that regional characterisation of the ores is as good as we can hope for. McGeehan-Liritzis and Gale, on the other hand, prefer to attempt to link specific ore bodies to metal artefacts. The technique of lead isotope determination is by no means as straightforward as early investigations of archaeological materials led us to believe and its impact on the development of archaeology can, in no way, be compared with the enormously important impact that carbon 14 dating has made, as attempted by Dayton. Distribution, exchange and interaction patterns based on the chemical analysis of metal artefacts are of value, but do not realise their greatest potential until they are closely related to such patterns of interaction provided by other Bronze Age materials, such as stone and pottery. After all, it is not very likely that metal circulation and exchange formed an isolated system. By building up such relationships, several interrelated spheres may become apparent (Pèrles 1992). Ideally such work should be done on a regional basis.

5.9.4 The chemical analysis and lead isotope analysis of Bronze Age metalwork found in Britain

5.9.4.1 Introduction

Rohl and Needham (1998) have investigated a range of lead-rich ores in England, Wales and beyond using lead isotope analysis. They discuss lead isotope signatures for 382 lead ore (galena) samples and 95 copper mineral samples from deposits in the British Isles. For a range of reasons it was not always possible to collect representative samples or enough samples from each deposit. The overall result of their lead isotope determinations of samples from England and Wales led them to suggest that it would be impossible, using lead isotope determinations alone, to determine the provenance of the metal that was used

to make an artefact unequivocally. One of the reasons, already mentioned in Section 2.2, is not only whether the samples from the lead-bearing ores sampled might be representative, but also the extent to which the metal may have been derived from other ore sources outside England and Wales (with which there is archaeological evidence for interaction – such as Scotland, Ireland, Brittany, northern France, the Low Countries and the Rhineland) (Rohl and Needham 1998: 36) and which could be used as scrap. In the investigation of the lead isotope signatures from these areas it was found that there were substantial overlaps in the isotope signatures. It was noted, however, that in spite of similarities in the lead isotope signatures between different ore regions, a distinction was achieved between Lower Palaeozoic and Carboniferous limestone lead-bearing deposits. One critical way of refining such an investigation is to sample ore sources for which there are secure dates and to exclude those from the analysis for which there is no evidence of any ancient exploitation; inclusion of the latter making the interpretation overly complex.

Having said this, as with the Aegean research, if archaeological parameters and chemical compositions of the metals are taken into account as well, a far more informative result can be generated. In any case, the likelihood that only a single source of metal was used in a controlled and conservative way by a production centre (workshop) is very unlikely in most archaeological contexts; there is, nevertheless, a possibility that metal could be recycled within the same production sphere and that even if a range of metals were included, this would nevertheless give the *appearance of homogeneity.*

Rohl and Needham (1998: 175) make the important point that by the time a degree of homogeneity has been achieved by recycling of metals the net result in terms of the lead isotope signature produced is not (necessarily) to be able to source the metal to the ores used, but it becomes more a means of characterising the metal stock used to make a particular artefact type. This raises the question of whether the metalworkers themselves were able to identify the metal type (and by inference its working properties). Nevertheless, in such an analytical survey, if the artefact type selected is then compared to other types a measure of difference in terms of the isotope signature may be obtained.

By comparing the lead isotope signatures of copper mines which are clearly of a Bronze Age date with the isotope signatures of Bronze Age metalwork, some of the sources can either be confirmed or discounted. Rohl and Needham, for example, compared the isotope signatures of copper derived from the Great Orme mine in Gwynedd, that at Mount Gabriel, Co. Cork, Ireland, as well as several copper mines in the English south-western peninsula (another suggested source of copper used in the Bronze Age), with those of Bronze Age metalwork. Many of the isotope signatures of the bronze artefacts do not match those of the putative copper sources. There are certain factors which can explain these apparent mismatches. At Great Orme it was found that the copper ore was not radiogenic in a consistent way in the lode: pockets of uranite were distributed throughout the mineralised zone. This therefore would make it very difficult to relate the ore source to the metal used, even though there is no doubt that the mine was used.

A further interesting consideration is the impact/contribution that a particular source of metal had on the metal supply used to make the artefacts for which lead isotopes have been measured. Gale *et al.* (1991) found in the Eneolithic Balkans, somewhat unexpectedly, few of the copper artefacts were apparently composed of the famous source of copper at Rudna Glava (Pernicka *et al.* 1993) and Ai Bunar for which there is plenty of evidence for mining. The suggestion is that once a metal source, such as at Mount Gabriel, came to be exploited it did not contribute to the metal supply used to make British Bronze Age metal in a significant way and therefore the isotopic signatures of the Mount Gabriel metal and British artefacts did not match.

5.9.4.2 Chemical compositions of British Bronze Age metalwork

The British Bronze Age has benefited from an extensive programme of metal analyses performed primarily by Peter Northover (Northover 1980a; 1982a; 1982b; 1988a) and supplemented by, among others, Rohl and Needham (1998). It is worth considering some of the principal analytical/archaeo-

logical results so as to be able to highlight the significance of a comparison with lead isotope determinations. One thing is clear: that there is no doubt that there were changes in the kind of metal used to make artefacts during the Copper and Bronze Ages in Britain. In spite of the variations in concentration associated with the smelting procedures affecting the presence of arsenic (Pollard *et al.* 1991; Budd *et al.* 1992), antimony, zinc and lead (Tylecote *et al.* 1977), as well as the segregation of lead and bismuth in copper (Hughes *et al.* 1982; Slater and Charles 1970), the tendency of cobalt, iron (and zinc) to segregate in the slag, and impurities which may be introduced with alloying components such as tin and lead, Northover's (1980) classification of Bronze Age metals using variations in the concentrations of arsenic, silver, nickel, cobalt, zinc, bismuth and lead appears to stand up in archaeological terms. By carefully selecting samples for dating using accelerator mass spectrometry from reliable archaeological contexts Needham *et al.* (1998) have shown that the chronological sequence of development of Bronze Age metalwork that has been assembled is essentially correct, with some slight refinement. Clearly to establish a solid chronological framework is very important before embarking on a study of how the metal supply changed over a period of 1,800 years. Without a solid dating framework inferences would be, at best, weak. The changes are seen in the *dominant* metal used, often with new kinds of metal or a 'new balance of inputs' (Rohl and Needham 1998: 177, Figure 41).

Bronze Age metalwork can be classified mainly according to *specific assemblages* which contain characteristic types. The *copper* artefacts dating to between *c.* 2500 and 2100 BC include axes, halberds and knives/daggers. Various specialists have presented different classifications of these artefact types (Needham 1996; Burgess 1980; Harbison 1969a; 1969b). Figure 5.22 illustrates the range of copper and copper alloy axe forms which were manufactured and used through the chronological phases to be discussed. What follows is an overview of some of the artefact types, including axes, found in the assemblages and their chemical characteristics; this is by no means an exhaustive survey of artefact types and compositional variation.

The chemical characteristics of the type of copper used is mainly of Northover's type 'A' unalloyed copper (with characteristic impurity pattern of arsenic, antimony and silver) which continued to be used in some areas until *c.* 1900–1800 BC. This kind of copper is considered to have had an Irish origin (Case 1966; Northover 1982a). The dated evidence for south-western Irish copper being processed in the Copper Age at Ross Island, Co. Kerry (O'Brian 1994) supports this. Another type of copper is characterised by high arsenic and low/medium levels of nickel impurities, but its source is difficult to define.

During the early Bronze Age the *Brithdir Assemblage* dating to *c.* 2150–2000 BC contains similar metalwork forms to those made of copper, but with the addition of armlets. This earliest tin-bronze assemblage is, however, morphologically distinct from the copper equivalents. Rohl and Needham (1998: 89) found that the impurity pattern of arsenic, antimony and silver detected was very similar to that of type A, suggesting the continued use of the same metal source. Other early Bronze Age metal has impurities of Northover type B with elevated arsenic and nickel impurities.

From *c.* 2000–1900 BC the *Mile Cross Assemblage* contains two axe types which are rarely found in Ireland or Scotland. The axes analysed have shown a range of metal compositions. Northover's group F/F* appears during this period: the metal is characterised by principal impurities of arsenic and silver.

The *Willerby Assemblage* dates to *c.* 1900–1700 BC; its hoards tend to contain only axes, many of which have punched designs. Most of the objects analysed by Rohl and Needham (1998: 91) contain low impurity levels of arsenic, nickel, antimony and silver. They suggest that the low silver levels are due to mixing with low impurity metal, possibly deriving from central Wales as well as another indigenous source.

The *Arreton Assemblage* dates to *c.* 1700–1500 BC and is characterised by an increase in the number of hoards, especially in southern England. The assemblage has some distinct differences from the morphology of artefacts found in the Willerby Assemblage, with the introduction of new types,

such as the spearhead. One type of metal used contained low impurity levels like in the Willerby Assemblage metal. It was during this time that the Great Orme and Mount Gabriel sources of copper were exploited; one gallery at Great Orme used at this time is liable to have produced low impurity malachite and azurite oxide ores (Ixer and Budd 1998). Some of the rest of the metal used for Arreton metalwork contained quite broad ranges of impurity levels of arsenic, antimony, silver and nickel.

The *Acton Assemblage* dates to the earliest part of the middle Bronze Age and is characterised by the appearance of palstaves, dirks and socketed spearheads. Metal of this phase contains characteristic levels, especially of arsenic and nickel (Northover 1980: 230), and also iron and cobalt. Most of the chemical analyses are for objects which have derived from Wales and the Marches. Northover considers that the metal probably derived from (north) Wales, especially in the first two phases of the middle Bronze Age from *c.* sixteenth century BC. Rohl and Needham (1998: 94–5) note that the principal impurity levels of arsenic and nickel in Acton metalwork fall into two groups, one containing much lower levels than the other.

Taunton Assemblage metalwork commonly occurs as hoards across southern England (Rowlands 1976). A range of small tools such as razors, awls, sickles, hammers, punches and chisels appear at this time as well as rings, pins, torcs and armlets. Taunton metal contains medium levels of arsenic and nickel (in line with one of the Acton impurity patterns), accompanied by low levels of silver and antimony – the suggestion here is the continued use of Acton metal. Another impurity pattern consists of similar levels of arsenic and nickel, though nickel is higher than arsenic. The metal may be derived from across the Channel.

There was a severe decline in the volume of newly smelted metal in circulation during the middle–late Bronze Age transition, from *c.* 1250–1000 BC (Needham 1996) with a greater dependence on imported continental metal and on recycling (Northover 1982a).

The *Penard Assemblage* dating to *c.* 1275–1140 (Needham *et al.* 1998) includes early imported swords and other flange-hilted types which may have been local products (Colquhoun and Burgess 1988); slightly later regional sword types definitely developed. In the Penard Assemblage, a much higher proportion of weaponry occurs, with far fewer of the ornaments seen in the Taunton Assemblage. The main impurities are still arsenic and nickel; metal-work found at some distance from south-eastern England sometimes contains higher tin and arsenic levels (Northover 1982a). Rohl and Needham (1998) note two compositional types based on impurity patterns: one contains medium levels of arsenic and nickel, relatively low antimony and silver levels, with low to medium lead levels; the suggested source for this metal is north-west England. The second type contains generally higher levels of arsenic, antimony, silver and nickel with lead levels increasing to around

1% (Northover 1988a). This latter type of metal is close in composition to that used in the succeeding Wilburton Assemblage.

The *Wilburton Assemblage* dates to *c.* 1140–1020 (Needham *et al.* 1998). This assemblage saw the appearance of the sword chape (a device attached to the end of the scabbard) as well as horse harness and cart fittings. However, the volume of newly smelted metal still continues to be rather low compared with the Taunton Assemblage and the succeeding Ewart Assemblage. Some Wilburton hoards can contain an enormous number of pieces, such as the 6,500 pieces in the Isleham hoard (Britton 1960b). One compositional characteristic of Wilburton metalwork is the presence of lead at levels which normally exceed 3%, sometimes being as high as 30% (Hughes *et al.* 1982;

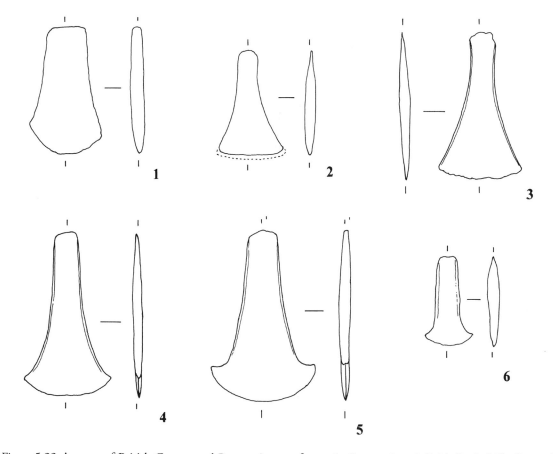

Figure 5.22 A range of British Copper and Bronze Age axe forms: 1, Copper Age; 2, Brithdir; 3, Mile Cross; 4, 5 and 6, Willerby; 7, Arreton; 8, Acton; 9, Taunton; 10, Penard; 11, Wilburton; and 12, Ewart.

Northover 1982b). Whereas some of the metal used in the Penard Assemblage contained lead levels of up to 1%, which is unlikely to have been added deliberately, the lead in Wilburton metal is all liable to have been added deliberately as part of a new lead-copper-tin alloy with good casting properties.

Northover's (1982b) S-metal was found to be dominant in the Wilburton Assemblage, with quite characteristically tight impurity levels of arsenic, antimony, silver and nickel. There is evidence for a continuity in the use of this kind of metal in the Penard metalwork. Another metal contains arsenic as the principal impurity (Northover's H metal) with lead

levels generally being over 5%. There is also some evidence for the mixing of S and H metals. Northover's S metal is rich in the four impurities derived from the western Alpine zone, in the area of Switzerland and specifically in Austria (Pittioni 1957); Rychner (1981) has found these elements in Swiss metal objects of c. 900–750 BC. Rychner and Kläntschi (1995: 78) note that metal with these impurities occurs over quite wide areas in Europe; they explain its widespread appearance as being the result of a new exploitation of fahlerz-type coppers. If this interpretation is accepted, Rohl and Needham (1998: 105–6) suggest that (it) 'would allow the Armorican/north French/southern British metal

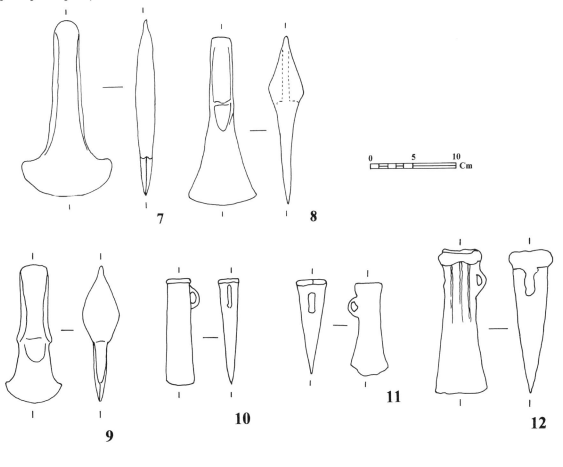

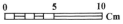

Figure 5.22 (continued)

pool of this period to be of more local origin'. This kind of interpretation clearly underlines the need to build up a mosaic of regional studies.

The *Ewart Assemblage*, having once been dated to between *c.* 1000–750 BC, can now be dated more precisely to *c.* 1020 – 800 BC (Needham *et al.* 1998). The metalwork is widespread and includes a wide range of types. The sword types show some morphological development with a recognition of a northern and southern series (Colquhoun and Burgess 1988) and the carp's tongue sword of possible French origin (O'Connor 1980), with axes displaying regionalised distributions leading to the suggestion of regional industries (Burgess 1968). It was towards the end of the period that iron was introduced, and which probably explains the reason why large quantities of metal of this date have been recovered; the appearance of iron led to a progressive redundancy of bronze. The first appearance of copper ingots during this phase provided another source of metal, for which lead isotope determinations could potentially provide important information.

The chemical composition of Ewart metalwork is mainly leaded bronze. This kind of metal has been classified by Northover (1982b) as T metal. The principal impurities are arsenic, antimony, silver and nickel, with arsenic and antimony not being detected in a number of examples. It is compositionally similar to the preceding Wilburton metalwork and probably includes an admixture of that metal stock. Rohl and Needham (1998: 108) make the important point that since the volatile impurities of arsenic and antimony correlate with stable ones, nickel and silver, it is unlikely that the low levels of volatile impurities can be attributable to recycling. They suggest, in fact, that two sources of impurities are involved: one with higher levels for all four elements, the other with impurities at the lower end (with some arsenic variation). Craddock *et al.* (1990) produced supporting results for this interpretation. The occurrence of hoards which often contain low impurity metal in south-eastern England and northern France may be linked to the occurrence of copper ingots (which contain low impurities) in the region. The chemical compositions of the copper ingots generally include low impurity levels (Northover and Craddock 1990: 102); any lead present is thought

to have been introduced in the ore. One Bronze Age copper source, which contains these low impurity levels, is Alderley Edge (Ixer and Budd 1998). Davey *et al.* (1999: 59) claim that Irish late Bronze Age copper alloys tend to contain greater arsenic and antimony levels than those found in north Wales, in particular the Llyn Fawr Assemblage.

The *Llyn Fawr Assemblage* is thought to have been introduced *c.* 800 BC, but it is difficult to define for how long it was in circulation (Rohl and Needham 1998). The lower number of Llyn Fawr finds which have been made is almost certainly due to the displacement of bronze by iron, especially for tools and weapons. Among the wide range of types, razors and sickles are diagnostic, as is the specialisation of swords and socketed axes. The classic Hallstatt C bronze Gundlingen sword is frequently found in Britain, especially in wet contexts. There are compositional results from a single hoard (Tilshead) of metalwork and a small number of other Llyn Fawr objects. The impurity levels of arsenic, antimony, silver and nickel are generally low with high lead levels. Non-leaded bronzes have also been detected. Northover (1980a; 1988b) has suggested that there are possible regional and chronological variations in the use of lead types. It is suggested that it is unlikely that recycled Ewart metalwork could have contributed to the metal available, or that northern France (Armorica) was a source, with its relatively high impurity levels (Northover 1988b).

5.9.4.3 The relationships of chemical compositions to lead isotope determinations

The relationships of the chemical compositions of British Bronze Age metalwork to their lead isotope signatures have provided some very important insights into the relationships of these independent characteristics of metal. Lead isotope signatures are a reflection of the age at which the metal was formed, the environment (temperature, pressure) and the source material – as well as any recycling of the metal that may have occurred. The chemical composition of the metal is also dependent on the environment in which the original mineralisation occurred, but in addition the degree of or kind of alloying and recycling of the metal that has occurred. The two kinds of characteristics are not quite the same and measure rather different attributes. They can therefore be treated as partially independent measures of the 'history' of the metal and the ways in which it has been modified or treated.

Rohl and Needham (1998) provide one of the few considerations of how matches and mismatches between lead isotope signatures and chemical analyses of copper and copper alloys can generate useful, sometimes quite specific, archaeological information about the metal supply and metal circulation during the British Bronze Age. Since the two sets of results measure separate characteristics of the metal, the results do not always support each other. Although an earlier investigation by Needham *et al.* (1989) into early Bronze Age copper and bronze suggested that it was difficult to distinguish between workshop clusters using chemical analyses because of a number of irregular components in the supply, exchange and mixing of metal, this consideration of

Bronze Age metalwork on a larger scale has provided a number of more specific inferences.

Bearing in mind the outline description of some of the compositional characteristics of Bronze Age bronzes given above, a number of examples have been selected here in order to highlight the range of information that can be obtained from a comparison of lead isotope signatures and chemical compositions and how this can affect the interpretation. Not all of the results from metalwork assemblages are considered.

It can be claimed that some lead in copper objects is derived from the copper ore used. The early copper used in British copper objects is traditionally claimed as deriving from Ireland, such as the Ross Island, Co. Kerry, source (O'Brian 1994), and indeed the comparatively restricted lead isotope ratios in the metalwork supports this (Rohl and Needham 1998: 87). Although this lead isotope clustering is not

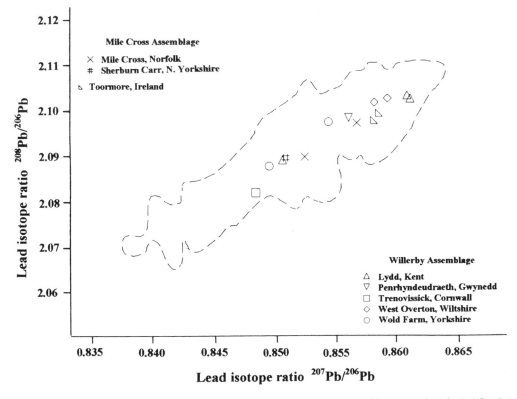

Figure 5.23 The isotopic spread of Willerby assemblage and Mile Cross assemblage metalwork © The British Museum.

a priori evidence for the use of a restricted ore source, the well-defined compositional type of copper used to make the metalwork found all over Britain and Ireland supports the interpretation. However, a compositionally distinct copper with characteristic arsenic and nickel levels that was used to make copper metalwork may, according to lead isotope determinations, derive from south-west England. Some of the characteristic Brithdir metalwork is of the characteristic composition found in earlier copper which strongly suggests a continued use of the same ore, whether recycled or not. Some of the Willerby metalwork forms a coherent compositional type, but there is a linear spread of isotopic determinations (see Figure 5.23) which has been interpreted as the mixing of metals from two or more principal sources. Lead may have been added both inadvertently and deliberately. For one group of six Arreton objects their low impurity levels are basically

comparable to the principal Willerby metal. This might suggest a similar metal source. However, the lead isotope characteristics of Arreton bronzes are quite different from those of Willerby bronzes – this is a clear example of a mismatch between the results of the two techniques.

Rohl and Needham's (1998: 96–7) careful consideration of the possible sources of metal used for the production of the Taunton Assemblage further underlines the subtle approach that needs to be adopted to this kind of investigation. The isotopic plot occupies a continuous linear spread which could suggest the mixing of two 'dominant' metals with very different isotopic ratios (see for example Figure 5.24). Most objects from metal-bearing regions in Britain are located at one end of the spread but some lie outside the 'England and Wales Lead Isotope Outline' suggesting another (external) source was used. When these 'clear' isotopic distinctions are

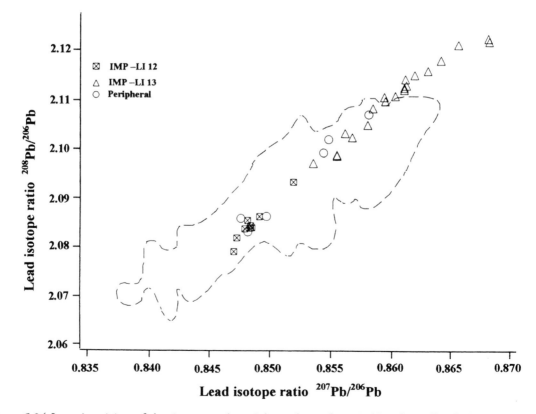

Figure 5.24 Isotopic mixing of dominant metals mainly made up from Rohl and Needham's (1998) impurity groups L1 12 and L1 13 © The British Museum.

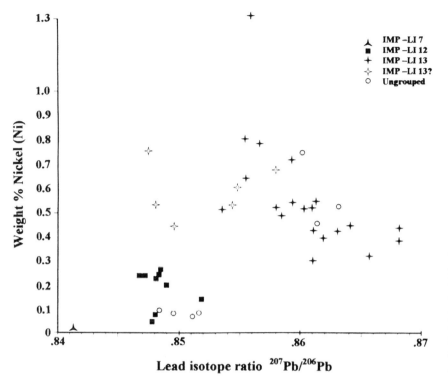

Figure 5.25 Weight % nickel content versus lead isotope ratio for Rohl and Needham's impurity groups L1 7, L1 12, L1 13, L1 13? and ungrouped samples © The British Museum.

compared with the chemical compositions of the metalwork it might be suggested they should be broadly correlated. When nickel was chosen as a means of monitoring this, they did indeed find levels of 0.3–0.4% at one end which steadily increased to 0.5–0.8% at the other, though those metals at the 'low' end contained nickel levels of below 0.3% (see Figure 5.25). This is something which is difficult to explain, even though other impurities do tend to reflect that two dominant sources were mixed.

When considering the Penard Assemblage a similar spread of lead isotope plots is seen as that found in the Taunton metalwork. This might therefore suggest, as for the Taunton metalwork, that a mixture of two principal metal sources has produced the pattern. However, this does not sit easily with the results of chemical analyses: the main grouping of lead isotope determinations includes the two main impurity patterns. Another interesting feature of Penard metalwork is that some objects show a (negative) correlation between percentage lead content and the position on isotopic plots. Impurities of anti-

mony and silver support this interpretation. There seems to be a link with the succeeding Wilburton metalwork in that the Penard material with higher lead contents has lead isotope plots which are shifted towards the signature for the Wilburton metalwork. This suggests that there was a source of lead which was common to both assemblages. The analytical results for Ewart Assemblage copper ingots show that most have low impurities with slight variations which could be attributed to that found in a single copper ore source or region.

Yet again, results of lead isotope determinations provide a rather different strand of evidence: the results are very widely spread, to the extent that it is very unlikely that a single source region was involved. The most likely interpretation, provided by Rychner and Kläntschi (1995), is that different sources of similar fahlerz ores (see Section 5.2) were exploited at the same time, providing apparently similar impurity patterns in the metal, but which derived from a range of locations.

5.10 Early copper and copper alloy production in Thailand

5.10.1 Introduction

One of the key questions to ask about the emergence of metallurgy in south-east Asia is: when did copper alloy metallurgy first appear in the famous cultural horizon of Ban Chiang? White (1986) believes that this first happened *c.* 1700 BC and she reminds us (1988: 175) that the appearance of metallurgy in south-East Asia was relatively recent in the history of its discovery. It is, nevertheless, of great interest to investigate some of the contexts in which it first appeared, because the evidence is comprehensive and

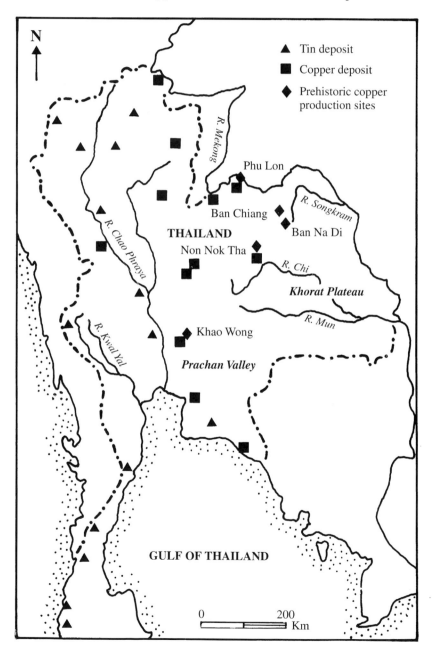

Figure 5.26 The distribution of metal resources in the region of Thailand together with the principal sites mentioned in the text.

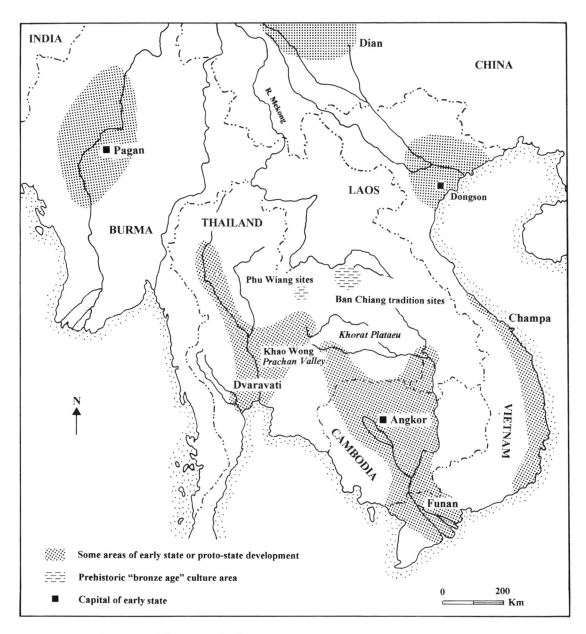

Figure 5.27 The locations of the zones of cultural traditions.

it also provides a contrast with metallurgical investigations in the west. Figure 5.26 is a map of metal resources in Thailand. The early period of metal usage in south-eastern Asia is *c.* 1700–1000 BC. Currently, however, the earliest published evidence for the use of bronze objects is from the site Non Nok Tha, at some time during the third millen-

nium (Bayard 1984: 165). Figure 5.26 is a map of the main sites mentioned in this section, together with areas of early state or proto-state development shown in Figure 5.27.

White and Pigott (1996) contend that craft specialisation since the prehistoric period in southeast Asia developed largely within a community-based mode of production. They use the definition for this offered by Costin (1991: 8) as 'autonomous individual or household-based production units, aggregated within a single community producing for unrestricted regional consumption'.

Excavations of prehistoric village sites in north-east Thailand at Non Nok Tha, Ban Chiang, Non Chai and Ban Na Di, have revealed important evidence for the emergence of prehistoric metal use in the area. Research has shown the sophistication of copper-based metallurgy from possibly as early as 2000 BC.

5.10.2 North-east Thailand: Ban Na Di and Ban Chiang

Higham (1988) has described some important findings from the excavations at Ban Na Di, a lowland settlement in north-east Thailand in the Sakon Nakon basin of the northern Khorat Plateau between Phu Lon and the Khao Wong Prachan valley (see Figure 5.27) forming part of the innovative Ban Chiang cultural tradition. White and Pigott (1996: 155) state that part of this cultural horizon dates to at least the third and probably the fourth millennium BC. There is an absence of copper and tin ore deposits from the Sakon Nakon basin (Pigott 1985; see Figure 5.27), so the minerals must have come from at least 100 km away. Mining, and probably smelting, must have taken place several days' journey from the villages where the objects were used; a major copper-smelting site is yet to be discovered in this area.

In the later period (B) at Ban Na Di (Bayard 1984), which dates to between 1200 and 100 BC, the excavations revealed almost the entire sequence of bronze-working activities involved in the conversion of bronze ingots into artefacts. Level 7 (c. 900–500 BC) revealed the presence of a furnace. The remains consisted of a series of clay blocks arranged around a central hollow which was full of large pieces of charcoal, and there was a channel through the furnace wall which would have been the location of a tuyère. The furnace was 0.6–0.75 m in diameter and was surrounded by two lenses of dense charcoal, the probable rake-out from the furnace which contained fragments of crucibles and bronze. In level 5 (c. 100 BC–200 AD), eight further furnaces were found built of loosely packed blocks of clay set in shallow pits and typically of 0.4×0.3 m in diameter.

Moulds were made of clay and of stone and found in levels 5, 6 and 7 (c. 900 BC–200 AD); some were fragments of bivalve moulds. It is apparent that artefacts such as decorated bracelets and bells were cast. In level 5 (c. 100 BC–200 AD) a tin-lead alloy fragment of metal was found attached to the pouring cone of a mould (Rajpitak and Seeley 1984) with an estimated very low melting point of between 180 °C and 270 °C. It is suggested that this might have been used to create a template which was later covered in clay prior to bronze casting. The lost-wax technique was certainly used; some wax survived and was identified by using thin layer chromatography and gas liquid chromatography as a relatively unrefined insect wax. This may have been used for polishing the bracelet it was found attached to, but it is nevertheless a remarkable find. Two complete crucibles were found in level 6 (c. 500–100 BC) with capacities of 80 ml and 75 ml. Other crucible fragments in levels 8 to 6 were made of clay, liberally tempered with rice chaff; by level 5 sand temper was used instead.

5.10.2.1 Scientific analysis of the metal

It is evident that from 1200 BC at Ban Na Di bronze was imported and melted down in crucibles to be cast into objects. Bangles (with lost-wax decoration), beads, fishhooks and projectile points were made there. There were four alloys employed (Rajpitak and Seeley 1984). Most objects, especially the arrowheads and bracelets, were made from low-tin bronze (with tin levels of 2–14%). The second alloy, a leaded copper, was used to make a comma-shaped bead and bracelets; the third alloy was a leaded-tin bronze, which was used for the manufacture of rings and bracelets. The last alloy, was a high-tin bronze with arsenic, which contained tin levels of up to 24%. The tin levels produced a gold-like finish and the metal was extremely brittle; it was used to make wire (Maddin and Weng 1984). By using factor analysis Higham (1988: 135–6) highlighted that the metallurgy in levels 8–6 (1200–100 BC) displayed far less compositional variability than in levels 5 and 4 (c. 100 BC–post 200 AD). Almost all of the metal from earlier contexts was made of low-tin bronze and only two specimens apparently have a significant lead content. In the later period, the low-tin bronze is retained, lead alloys were introduced and four specimens contained very high tin levels. There was evidently a significant change in metal technology in level 5 which may be related to the first appearance of iron-smelting.

5.10.2.2 The social significance of bronze metallurgy at Ban Na Di

Higham (1988: 142) has commented on the context in which metal is first used at Ban Na Di. There were two groups of burials at the site; exotic or unusual artefacts were concentrated in one of these (Higham 1983). These objects included imported stone bracelets which were sometimes repaired with bronze wire. There were also marine shell bracelets and beads, cattle figurines, and, in two late graves, eight objects of iron. Several graves contained the remains of silken garments. Dalton has suggested that the economy, alliance networks and social organisation were mutually embedded and that the circulation of exotic goods probably cemented the maintenance of alliances between ('autonomous') communities. The production of copper and tin would have added another dimension to the existing exchange networks; bronze goods were rare in mortuary contexts to begin with, so it is likely that they were used for display. The community and its leader that lived at Ban Na Di evidently controlled the supply of metal, and the control of this supply would have been important in maintaining wealth and status (even if not especially high) in the area.

5.10.2.3 Ban Chiang

The metallurgy at Ban Na Di was not developed there; it was fully developed from the earliest level (c. 1200 BC). The evidence for metallurgy at Ban Chiang c. 24 km to the north of Ban Na Di (see Figure 5.26) is in most respects identical to that recovered in levels 6–8 in Ban Na Di (Wheeler and Maddin 1976), but they also found a socketed spearhead, a type not found at Ban Na Di. The initial presence of bronze at Ban Chiang was perhaps as early as 1700 BC, and is therefore very important in the emergence of copper alloy metallurgy in south-

eastern Asia (White 1982). Two of the graves found at Ban Chiang produced a socketed spearhead (Figure 5.28, 1) and a socketed axe (Figure 5.28, 2); no socketed implements were found at Ban Na Di. Again the presence of crucibles at Ban Chiang, though associated with very small amounts of slag, suggests that whilst casting of artefacts may have occurred, if smelting occurred only a small volume of metal was involved. Eighty crucible fragments were found at Ban Chiang (Figure 5.28, 3), including some which suggest that they were slightly larger than those found at Phu Lon (White et al. 1991: 201). Scientific analyses of six early period (1700–1000 BC) artefacts have been reported by Stech and Maddin (1988) with elemental analysis having been performed on five of these. All those analysed were of a tin-bronze, their casting was competently handled, and they had been worked and annealed. Their overall conclusion is that the basic techniques of copper-working appeared to be in full use at Ban Chiang; no specific dates were given for the artefacts analysed within the 700-year early period. Taking all the Sakon Nakon basin settlements together, it is likely that the casting which took place was mainly for small implements and for jewellery. The nature of the production (and consumption) was apparently mainly for a social subset in an average village; there were no apparent restrictions on the distribution and no obvious elite association of the artefacts has been identified (White and Pigott 1996: 157), though the artefacts did form part of a display ritual.

5.10.3 The Phu Wiang region

In the north-east corner of the Khorat basin, in the Phi Wiang region, excavations have produced possible evidence for a sub-regional specialisation of the production of axes during the second millennium BC. This is in contrast to Ban Chiang and Ban Na Di. The sites of Non Nok Tha (see Figure 5.26) and Non Pa Kluay have produced axes, complete sandstone bivalve axe moulds sets for casting socketed implements, axe mould blanks and crucibles of a larger size than found at Phu Lon and in the Sakon Nakon basin (White et al. 1991: 201). It is of interest that many of the artefacts produced were recovered from graves at Non Nok Tha, which in this case may have had a bearing on the status of the individuals

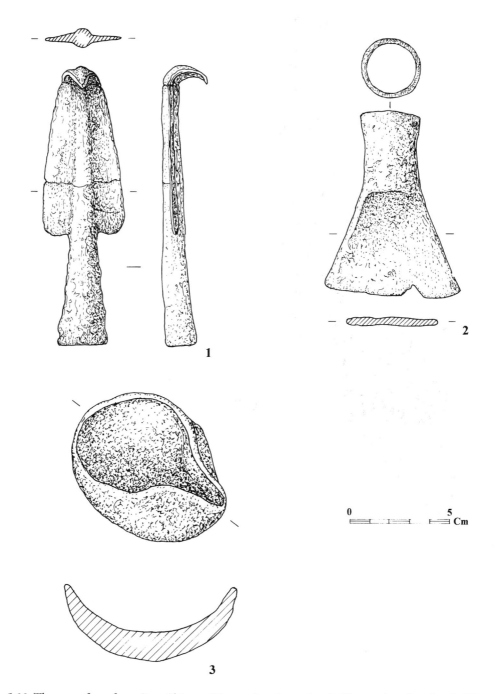

Figure 5.28 Three artefacts from Ban Chiang: (1) a socketed spearhead; (2) a socketed axehead; (3) a crucible (re-drawn, with permission, from White and Pigott 1996).

buried. One significant factor which might determine where socketed implements were cast is the availability of sandstone to make the moulds. The Phu Wiang sites are a few kilometres away from the outcrops of sandstone used to make the moulds (Bayard 1980: 193). It is suggested by White (1988) that the bangles of the Ban Chiang tradition were produced using the lost-wax method. However, this does not explain the location of specialised industries completely. The sandstone moulds, or even the sandstone would not have weighed much, so could have been re-used, and could easily have been transported to areas of the Ban Chiang tradition. Rather than suggest that the distribution of moulds or moulding materials was a passive one, perhaps there was a degree of control over the production processes, even if it did not lead to the accumulation of wealth.

5.10.4 North-east Thailand in the first millennium BC: evidence from Phu Lon

Pigott and Natapintu (1988a) have reported on a survey of the ore sources and associated metal-working sites in a mountainous area in north-east Thailand in Loei and western Nong Khai provinces. It is an area rich in mineral resources. Dates from the early second millennium BC and the first millennium BC make the early activities contemporary with metal-consuming sites of the Ban Chiang cultural tradition on the adjacent Khorat plateau. The most significant pre-industrial site surveyed was Phu Lon, a prehistoric copper mining complex on the southern bank of the Mekong river (see Figure 5.26). The ore being mined was a copper sulphide with an indigenous oxide (gossan) zone exposed at the surface. Prehistoric mining apparently exploited the upper reaches of the ore body where malachite ore was deposited in quartz veins disseminated in the iron-rich skarm rock. The site of Phu Lon has evidence for a complex of metallurgical activities; investigations concentrated on primary mining areas of Lower and Peakock flats and on a secondary mining area, Bunker Hill. Adjacent to Bunker Hill, the Pottery flat revealed evidence for ore crushing and copper processing. The stratigraphy at Phu Lon suggests that intermittent exploitation by several groups occurred (Pigott et al. 1992).

5.10.4.1 The mining evidence

The undisturbed evidence for mining occurred only at certain locations as shallow pits which had been mined with stone mauls. Hundreds of broken or worn stone mauls were found in the mining area; they were of hard intrusive rock and therefore ideal for mining and ore crushing. It is thought that metal tools were also used for mining. The areas around the remnant mining shafts revealed extensive pulverised deposits of host rock, some crushed to a relatively uniform size (Pigott and Natapintu 1988b: 5), anvil stones associated with small crushers and some bits of malachite. The enormous scale of activities was reflected in the accumulation of mining rubble in the area. At Lower flat and other locations a 10 m depth of mining rubble was found. There appears to have been periodicity in mining activities in some areas, where layers of clean sand alternate with mining rubble. Dating of the Phu Lon mining activity, as at most other mines was problematic. A small pocket of charcoal from otherwise sterile layers of clean sand and mining rubble yielded a carbon-14 date of the first half of the first millennium BC which is in general agreement with other dates obtained for the mining activity.

5.10.4.2 The Pottery flat ore-dressing and metal casting area

Prior to excavation this area produced cord-marked pottery and evidence for ore-crushing activity. Excavations revealed comprehensive evidence of ore dressing in a stratum of 15–50 cm thick and covering an area of 100 m in length and 30 m wide. Charcoal from the basal deposit provided a range of dates in the first millennium BC. The deposit consisted of crushed host rock, ore-crushing hammers, anvils of intrusive rock and a few pieces of malachite. The malachite would have been hand sorted.

Fragments of two different bivalve moulds were found, one ceramic and the other stone. In addition, seventy rice chaff-tempered crucible fragments were found. A small quantity of what was presumed to be smelting slag was recovered. Tylecote (1974) and Craddock (1995: 135) have made the point that the reduction of malachite could have been achieved in the crucibles themselves or in a bowl furnace; for well-dressed malachite freed of most of its gangue and with low impurities, little slag would be expected to be generated. Petrological examination of the cord-marked pottery found at Phu Lon revealed that three basic fabrics in local clay had been used.

Other ore-dressing locations were found at the site called Bunker Hill and at Ban Noi. At the latter site the ore-crushing evidence was contained in a deposit which was over 1 m deep and finely stratified, suggesting, in contrast to Pottery flat, that the activities occurred for short periods, but over a considerable period of time. A single carbon-14 date fell into the first half of the first millennium BC. Crucible fragments and slag were found at Ban Noi, as well as small circular depressions in which the crucibles might have rested.

5.10.4.3 Social distinctions and the degree of industrial specialisation in north-east Thailand

A review of the archaeological evidence for social hierarchy in north-east Thailand (White and Pigott 1996) has revealed a lack of an elite class, with some archaeological sites having somewhat more well-to-do areas than others, but no exceptionally rich graves which might be expected from the presence of a 'chiefdom'. In other words the evidence is for a society with weak ranking, but with evidence of some social differentiation (Higham and Kijngam 1984: 441; Bayard 1984). The grave assemblages reveal that age, sex and social and economic roles played an important part in providing social distinctions (White 1995). The production equipment found in the Non Nok Tha graves indicates that metal artisans were buried there and that they were regarded as socially distinct in the second millennium BC, something already identified for potters in central Thailand (Higham 1988). There is even little evidence that there was a hierarchy among sites of different sizes in north-east Thailand in the first millennium BC. Metal artefacts found in burials at Ban Na Di and Non Nok Tha tend to be associated with more well-to-do individuals, but this is not exclusive and their incidence is not especially prominent. White and Pigott (1996: 157) are of the opinion that the metal objects were used by social sub-sets within villages who had a somewhat higher social status than average. Access to the metal objects

may have been through social convention. The question is: to what extent did consumers of the objects 'control' the supply in some way?

The archaeological evidence suggests that independent communities of specialists provided a regionalised 'service' for consumers. The small and somewhat modest items of jewellery produced, which could be linked potentially to the display of wealth, indicate that little 'power' would have been generated by controlling the processes of production. The utilitarian objects did not apparently have a secondary function which might have indicated that the owner had an elevated rank in society. None of the more 'prestigious' objects, which might indicate a display of wealth are present (White and Pigott 1996: 158). The evidence for the function of artisans in society is suggestive of independent economically-motivated specialists, but there is no evidence for a patron-driven system. Most villages apparently had *casters*, but the absence of permanent settlements which were related to tin and copper mining operations, together with variation in the ceramics from the mining sites, suggests that more than one group visited the sites (White and Pigott, ibid.). Indeed the fact that some aspects of moulding operations were found in some areas and not in others, such as the use of sandstone moulds to produce socketed artefacts, suggests the existence of a 'differentiated web of metal makers undertaking different stages and aspects of the production' (ibid.). It is suggested that between 2000 and 300 BC increasing specialisation and exchange occurred at the same time and that they formed part of economic growth and greater industrial complexity.

5.10.5 Central Thailand: evidence from Non Pa Wai and Nil Kham Haeng of the Ban Chiang cultural tradition

A group of sites in the Khao Wong Prachan valley in central Thailand (see Figures 5.26 and 5.27) has provided comprehensive evidence for prehistoric copper ore processing, as well as large-scale smelting. Non Pa Wai or 'Rattan Hill' was the most important of the three sites excavated by Pigott and Natapintu (1988a: 159; White and Pigott 1996). The site covered c. 50,000 sq m (5 ha) with deposits of up to 3 m deep clearly presenting a sampling problem to the aspiring investigator. The site dates to between the mid-second millennium BC and 700 BC. The deposits consisted predominantly of copper production debris with an admixture of habitation material. Thousands of thick-walled rice-tempered crucible fragments were found, of a larger size than found in the north-east, which it is presumed were used for smelting; furnace chimney fragments and ceramic moulds were also found. Some fragments of thick arc-shaped ceramic rims from Non Pa Wai have been interpreted as the rims of bowl 'furnaces', though this is still to be confirmed. Crushed ore and smelting slag were also found. The ores from Non Pa Wai were the copper-silicate (chrysocolla) and weathered copper sulphide ores. Bennett's

(1990) research indicates that numerous plano-convex slag cakes resulted from pouring off the contents of large crucibles. Hundreds of fragments of sandstone bivalve moulds were found in large quantities, including for the production of socketed axes and arrow points which, in general were smaller and thinner than those found in the contemporary north-east Thailand (see Figure 5.29, 1). Tens of thousands of ceramic moulds described as cup/conical moulds were found (see Figure 5.29, 2, 3) which are considered to have been used for casting ingots (White and Pigott 1996: 161).

Because no furnaces were found, Pigott has interpreted this technology as crucible-smelting in which oxidic and sulphidic ores were smelted in a crucible

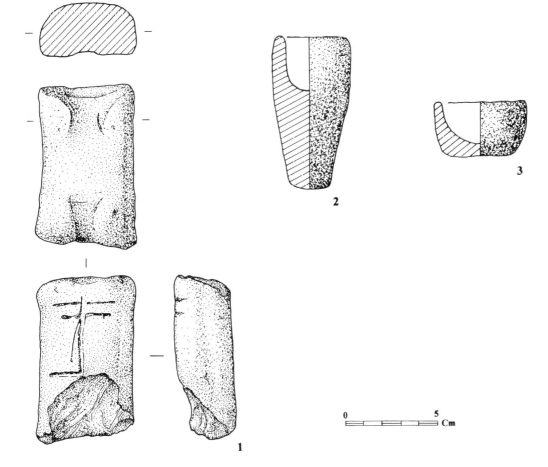

Figure 5.29 Three moulds from Non Pa Wai: (1) bivalve mould for the manufacture of socketed axes; (2) ingot mould; (3) ingot mould (re-drawn, with permission, from Pigott and Natapintu 1988 and the MIT Press).

and embedded in a bonfire of fuel. The crucible would then have been placed below a portable chimney within which the fuel was placed, the draught being supplied by bellows. Only copper ingots and artefacts were produced; no tin was apparently imported for bronze production. Overall the industrial deposits were found to be homogeneous and thought to reflect numerous spatially flexible small operations which operated contemporaneously.

5.10.6 Nil Kham Haeng

The industrial deposits at Nil Kham Haeng are dated between 1100 BC and 300 BC and overlap chronologically with the Non Pa Wai deposits. The deposits contained crushed ore waste, rock and slag, but crucibles and cup/conical moulds were relatively rare. The presence of small (20 cm diameter) clay-lined pits, however, suggest that small bowl furnaces were probably used. At some point in the first millennium BC a lower grade sulphur-rich ore was used which involved increased man-hours for its smelting. However, because the technology did not, apparently, involve the production of crucibles and cup/conical moulds the man hours involved overall would have been reduced. The use of small furnaces would have simplified production procedures. There was no evidence for the occurrence of spatially defined areas in which specialists were located.

5.10.7 The degree of specialisation in central Thailand

The apparent lack of a workshop organisation for copper production in the Khao Wong Prachan valley does not exclude the possibility that there was some kind of interaction between specialised artisans, even if there was no apparent control by political elites. It is suggested that these activities were kin-based 'with no obvious association with a political centre' (White and Pigott 1996: 165) and that they occurred seasonally. The scale of production was enormous and much larger than would have been necessary purely for local consumption. However, the distribution of copper ingots and artefacts made from the production centre provides little helpful information about demand (ibid.). One characteristic of the Nil Kham Haeng production is the mass-production, in standardised mode, of cordiform implements which

Pigott has pointed out are probably too thin to have been used mechanically. This has led him to suggest that perhaps they were a special sort of ingot readily recognisable as to their source by their shape (as in with Iron Age currency bars in Europe – see Section 5.12.2.5 below). Although iron was introduced in the period 700–300 BC it had no obvious impact on copper production in this region. The associated artefacts in graves at Nil Kham Haeng indicate that some importance was apparently placed on the social status of those buried. One way of interpreting the evidence is that the producers controlled their industry (White and Pigott 1996: 167) and were therefore somewhat autonomous, remaining unaffected by any external control.

5.11 Technological innovation and the case of iron

5.11.1 Technological innovation

The concept of technological innovation is a complex one and one which is often difficult to explain using available archaeological and technological evidence. If high-temperature industries such as metal, glass and ceramic production are considered, there are a number of features which all three technologies sometimes have in common. These include the transformation of raw materials by heat into something different, the use of fuel in a measured way and the use of an enclosed structure (furnace or kiln) in which the technological transformation occurred. It might therefore be suggested that a 'later' industry (such as glass production) might have been heavily influenced by an existing one (such as copper alloy production). Although, unquestionably, some elements of glass production would have been 'borrowed' from the production of copper alloys, such as the use of fuels and the manufacture and use of sufficiently refractive bricks to build the furnaces involved, in many ways the production technologies are very different. Simple assumptions about the 'evolution' of high-temperature industries can potentially be misleading. Various new technological processes would need to be introduced in order to deal with new materials and this is where different levels of innovation would be involved. Another important feature of ancient technology is not standardised production procedures but the fact that the characteristics of a range of materials can be unpredictably variable and can lead to the existence of imperfections in the technology. Smith (1981) argued that the existence of an imperfection at one level in a technological hierarchy allows the next higher level of structure to exist (i.e. it leads to its development and serves as a nucleus for change). The nucleus for change is present in those points in the original structure which are undergoing some form of strain; they are 'least contented' (Smith 1981: 382).

The use of raw materials, the ways the materials are (heat-)treated, because they would behave very differently when hot, and subsequent forms of decoration would all have been distinctly new. Over and above these purely technological factors, the social, economic, ritual and political *milieu* in which new industries were invented and developed would clearly have had a powerful influence (Renfrew 1978: 93).

Looking at it from another viewpoint, that of a development economist, an increase in the population generally correlates with an increase in the scale of industrial output (particularly mass-production of utilitarian objects), which in turn would result in the intensification of production and technological innovation (Fisk and Shand 1969). Considering the nearly infinite range of conditions in which ancient production occurred – and the social/economic/religious and political factors which affected it – this model is probably only applicable to a small proportion of the cases and ignores the potentially strong influences that *tradition* may have had on decision-making processes in the development of technologies. Indeed, Adams (1981) pointed out that technology can be an unpredictable variable, and that human behaviour can be modified in the process of applying a new technology and therefore adaptive when it comes to basic skills, knowledge and method. It is considerations such as these which make it necessary to be wary of applying generalised models for the processes involved in technological innovation.

Barnett (1953: 7) defined an innovation as 'any thought, behaviour or thing that is new because it is qualitatively different from existing forms . . . every innovation is an idea or constellation of ideas some of which may be given overt and tangible expression'. The introduction of the earliest metal production *could* be seen to have developed out of the older pyrotechnology of pottery making (with the provisos mentioned above). Although, obviously, for pottery production there is no need to gather minerals in quite the same way, or to smelt them, the same concept of heating raw materials in an enclosed space (kiln or furnace) using (a range of) fuels which had specific properties and calorific values were involved. When iron-smelting was introduced for the first time a new development of an existing pyrotechnological continuum involving lead and copper probably took place. The important thing is that, in all likelihood, though not in all contexts, certain modifications of existing production processes were made, especially for iron, which resulted in a new technological configuration (Bee 1974: 174).

5.11.2 Innovation and iron

Pigott's (1982: 21) important point about the development of iron metallurgy in these terms is that iron existed as an impurity in copper ores and that copper and iron ores co-occur in the same geological deposits. Iron oxide was also a primary fluxing agent in the processes of copper-smelting and bronze-making. As Pigott also pointed out (ibid.) it is a foregone conclusion that metalsmiths became familiar with the basic properties of by-products rich in iron (furnace slags) long before iron was intentionally smelted. Indeed one might be tempted to infer a similar technological link between early faience and glass, since early faience production involved at least some familiarity with a vitreous (glassy) material. However, that is where the comparison ceases; in no way can it be claimed that glass was an 'impurity' of faience. Wallace (1972: 477), Smith (1981: 381) and Pigott (1982: 22) suggest that technological innovation can sometimes occur by manipulation of raw materials in an environment which is 'aesthetically sensitive'; this suggests that skilled artisans may have had the freedom (from control) and sufficient time to innovate. Another source of motivation (in the appropriate socio-political context) may have derived from the realms of ceremonial or religious practice. In the ancient Near East Pigott (ibid.) notes that 'early iron artefacts from Bronze Age contexts, as well as many from the bimetallic phase just prior to the widespread adoption of iron, are often, though not exclusively, artefacts designed for decorative/ceremonial purposes'.

Iron was being intentionally produced by the later centuries of the third millennium BC in the eastern Mediterranean (Waldbaum 1980). Maxwell-Hyslop (1974) considers that a text dating to *c.* 1900 BC from an Assyrian trading colony of Karum Kanesh at Kültepe refers to a material known as *amutum* which is now thought to be iron. Although iron evidently was being produced intentionally at this time, it was not until *c.* 1200 BC that iron artefacts began to occur in quantity. This occurred at about the same time in the Middle East as it did in Europe (Champion 1980). The time lag between when iron was first introduced and when it was first used on a large scale can partly be explained by the fact that although iron minerals are more common than copper minerals, far more energy is necessary to work iron (Smith 1971: 51); smelting and forging iron requires far more time and energy than the mass-production of cast copper and bronze artefacts. The technological difficulty with iron was not with obtaining high temperatures, but in developing the new techniques necessary to hot-forge the bloom. Snodgrass (1980: 368) emphasises that he considers economic factors led to the mass-production of iron. It is interesting to note that in the fourth millennium BC in Mesopotamia changes in metal technology are revealed by the presence of objects in temples and graves, with a sharp increase in the quantity of precious and base metals. In this context Moorey (1988: 31) suggests that the reasons for innovation and experimentation were threefold: (1) the first appearance of population concentrations in a small number of large fortified settlements with monumental mud-brick buildings; (2) clear evidence of social stratification and craft specialisation; (3) the use of written administrative records, especially in the south (Sumer). These factors had obviously changed radically by the time the first mass-production of iron occurred.

The Chinese distinguished between the 'lovely metal' (bronze) and the 'ugly metal' (iron) (Keightley 1976). Iron first appeared in China in the seventh to fifth centuries BC (Huang Zhanyue 1976; Blunden

and Elvin 1983). Taylor and Shell (1988) point out that a usable iron bloom can be produced at temperatures close to or even below that needed to melt copper or gold if it contains a large amount of carbon, so whether the appropriate temperatures could be reached for these carbon-rich blooms at least, is not at issue. From a technical point of view, a significant new development was hot-forging the iron bloom. Taylor and Shell (ibid.) suggest that there are two factors which distinguish the introduction of iron in China from other areas. First, once introduced, iron was used quite soon for the manufacture of tools, implements and weapons on a large scale. This contrasts with Egypt, for example, where iron was used for a long time just after it was introduced to make small, rare luxury items (Coughlan 1956: 66). Second, in northern China, where it is suggested that bronze was hardly used for tools and implements, the initial use of iron is very likely to have involved comparisons by artisans between the working properties/hardness and fracture characteristics of iron, stone, bone and wood (Cheng 1963).

Different types of iron are generally held to be more-or-less well suited to different uses: wrought iron or steel for most weapons and cast iron for ornaments, pots and, less ideally, tools and implements. Raw cast iron is virtually useless for making objects (Trousedale 1975: 65). Chinese finds do fit this pattern: weapons are virtually all made from wrought iron; tools and implements from cast iron. (Hua *et al.* 1960: 73). The range of products expanded from white cast iron, early malleable cast iron, possibly steel, and forged wrought iron around the fifth century BC, to a sophisticated matching of different types of iron with the uses to which they are put. This was well established by the Han Dynasty (206 BC–220 AD) (Wang 1982: 128). A survey of the uses to which iron was put in its early stages shows that the major impact of the introduction of iron in China was on agricultural production, water management and other public works.

It is interesting to surmise as to whether the introduction of iron had a broader impact on Chinese society. Ch'ao (1936: 63) and Thorpe (1980–1) are of the opinion that the introduction of iron in China was a major factor, if not the most important factor, in bringing about changes in land ownership, trade and social structure, as well as the increase in population which occurred in the Warring States period (475–221 BC) and early Han Dynasty. Put the opposite way round, Hsu (1978: 260) suggests that it is an increase in population that caused the technological innovation and that the production of iron became widespread because the socio-economic environment generated a demand for it. To suggest that the introduction of a single material had such an impact on society and to ignore other environmental or political parameters would seem to be an oversimplification. Iron production and use were intimately related to other aspects of the society and economy and, as in any such context, it is difficult to tease these interrelated aspects apart. In any case, there were variations in the production and use of iron in different parts of China (Taylor and Shell 1988), something which was also true of bronze production (Rawson 1988), so this alone makes it difficult to generalise.

5.12 The production of iron in Iron Age Britain

5.12.1 Iron Age iron

The scientific analysis of iron of British Iron Age date, where it only began to be used in a limited way in the seventh century BC, has produced some meaningful implications by studying slag inclusions. Hedges and Salter (1979) analysed slag inclusions in iron bars of the kind known as 'currency bars' and they were able to link the differences they found to differences in ore types used. The Danebury group was especially tight in composition and was therefore quite probably made from a single source or a number of very similar sources. As with copper ores, the problem comes when one attempts to relate the metal used in specific artefacts to the parent ores. Ehrenreich (1985) has also noted that the sword-shaped bars from Danebury and Gretton (Figure 5.33, A and C) were high in phosphorus, whereas the spit-shaped bars from Beckford had a low phosphorus content (Figure 5.33, B). He suggests that this distinction in shape, which could have been correlated with the phosphorus content in the bars, could have been a way of distin-

guishing the kind of iron ore used, and the bars would therefore have been instantly recognisable to the Iron Age blacksmith. (A more detailed discussion of currency bars is included below in the description of the experimental production of such a bar.)

This brings us to the broader question of whether phosphorus-rich ores were mined especially for the properties of hardness that phosphorus may give to the cutting-edge of tools. From Ehrenreich's analytical survey of iron artefacts of Iron Age date from southern England, it is possible to suggest that by 100 BC adzes, ploughshares and sickles were certainly produced using high-phosphorus iron, and production of these tools at regionalised centres is suggested as a possibility. The use of phosphorus-rich iron for the manufacture of ploughshares could however be seen as inappropriate, since implements made from phosphorus-rich iron are liable to be brittle, and such a ploughshare might shatter on hitting a stone. In the case of ploughshare production then, a softer iron would seem to be more appropriate, and the use of a phosphorus-rich iron for their production seems to indicate a lack of understanding of its properties. For other objects which could shatter when used, such as swords, daggers and chariot tires, the use of appropriate low-phosphorus iron for the objects sampled indicates an awareness of the correct use of iron ore type, but that perhaps this awareness was somewhat limited. It may only have existed among the more skilful or higher status artisans (a status inferred from the fact that the objects they made were designed for the higher echelons of society). By the first half of the first century AD, as Ehrenreich notes, iron ores were definitely selected for their working properties, and by this time a limited amount of steel (i.e. iron containing a significant amount of carbon) was produced as well.

Up to the first century BC in England there appears to have been a system of discrete iron-working centres, perhaps with their own technical secrets and specialisations. After this, one could suggest that the systematic selection of iron ores for their properties, and the appearance of mild carbon steel on a small scale, implies greater communication and interaction between artisans. This pattern is also seen in other industries such as bronze, glass and enamel production. To illustrate how such chemical data can properly be assessed archaeologically, the relationship between settlement type and iron ore use was investigated (Ehrenreich 1985: 80). It seems that low-phosphorus ores (which were used for prestigious items such as swords, daggers and chariot tires) were selectively imported and used predominantly in hillforts in southern England. Even where hillforts were near phosphatic iron sources, low phosphorus iron was imported. Although there are exceptions to the rule, Ehrenreich suggests that high phosphorus iron was available to all members of society, whereas low-phosphorus iron was only available to the higher echelons. We should however consider the idea that hillforts were not the only places associated with the higher levels of society, and if one uses the evidence of artefacts as reflecting the presence of different levels of society one cannot ascertain such a thing.

Indeed, if this was the case we should have to consider the possibility that a hierarchy of artisans existed, with higher-status iron-workers operating from hillforts; this cannot currently be proven in an English context. This brings in the relationship between artisan status and the value put on the artefact and/or the material it is made from; this complicated issue has been discussed elsewhere (Henderson 1991).

5.12.2 Prehistoric iron production in north-west Wales

5.12.2.1 Bryn y Castell
Peter Crew's exemplary work in the excavation of iron-smelting sites in Wales has linked experimental

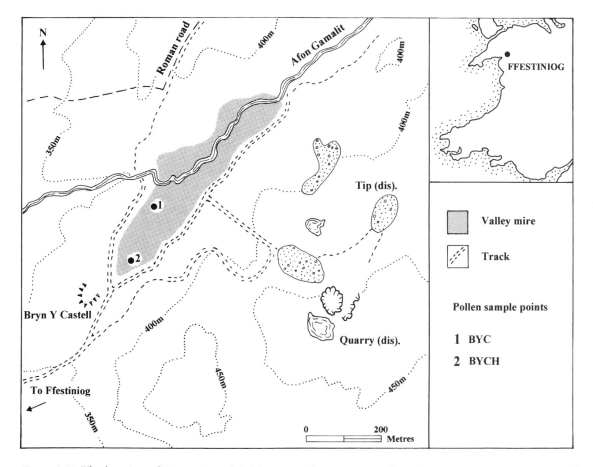

Figure 5.30 The location of Bryn y Castell hillfort near Ffestiniog in north Wales, in relation to environmental sampling locations.

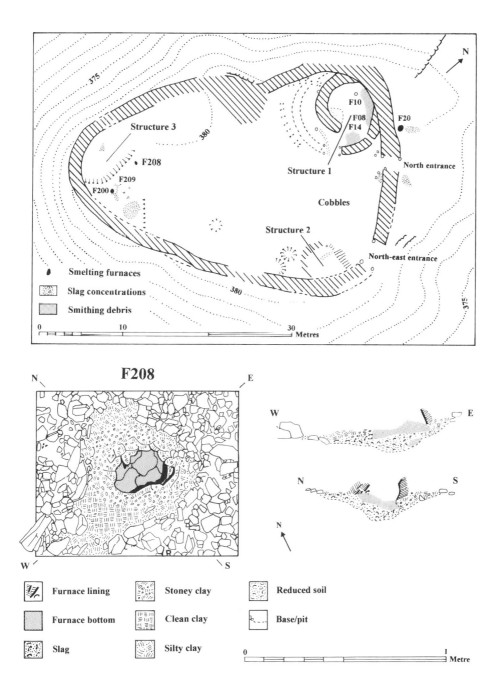

Figure 5.31 The Bryn y Castell hillfort and archaeological context F208, the remains of an Iron Age iron-smelting furnace.

iron production to scientific research. It has focused the minds of those interested in ancient iron technology. The study of the hillfort site of Bryn y Castell in north-west Wales is set in an environmental context (see Figure 5.30). The hillfort was bounded by a dry stone wall rampart of 40 m × 25 m and had two entrances (Crew 1988: 91). Prior to excavation two structures were visible, an apparently circular hut and a platform of stone adjacent to the rampart. Using archaeomagnetic and carbon-14 dating two main phases of production could be identified: an early phase in the first century BC and a late phase in the second/third century AD.

The excavation of this small hillfort revealed that there was ample evidence for iron production including the remains of several smelting furnaces (see Figure 5.31). The best preserved of the two furnaces shown in Figure 5.31 was F208. The base of the furnace was a shallow pit excavated into the bedrock; this was full of fragments of furnace bottom. Unusually, part of the superstructure survived as a furnace lining which was *in situ* and could be dated. The internal shape of the furnace probably approximated to an eccentric cone which would have narrowed to a throat of *c.* 15 cm in diameter. Crew (1988: 96) suggests that there may have been a chimney which would have extended the height of the furnace. These furnaces had internal diameters of *c.* 25–30 cm with a possible total height of *c.* 80 cm. From the remains of furnace linings it was evident that the furnaces had been re-lined several times.

A snail-shaped structure in the north corner of the hillfort (Figure 5.31) contained dense spreads of charcoal and 35 kg of slag and furnace lining. Two carbon-14 dates of 40±70 BC and 170±70 BC indicate a late Iron Age date for the structure, there being two phases of use. The structure produced a large quantity of small iron-working residues consisting of smelting slag which had fresh breaks; Crew (1988: 93) suggests that the slag was being broken up to recover small quantities of iron. Apart from this, the occurrence of hammer-scale and small pieces of spherical slag indicate that bloom smithing occurred there. Despite the evidence of bloom smithing at Bryn y Castell, no blooms have been found there. However, sub-rectangular billets of iron,

each weighing approximately 2 kg, were found at nearby settlement sites; one was of a third century date so it was not *necessarily* related to the activities at Bryn y Castell, despite the evidence of a continued iron industry into the third century AD. The occurrence of iron billets *may* therefore indicate the kind of product being manufactured at Bryn y Castell.

The excavations of a small structure outside the hillfort (Crew 1988: 96–8) produced evidence for a complex of features associated with iron-working. The structure itself had at least two structural phases, both of which related to processes of iron-working which are reflected in the dumps of material outside it. Archaeomagnetic dates for an interior deposit of silty soil packed with charcoal and iron-working debris range from 150±10 AD to 240±25 AD, so this site may indeed have produced the iron billets mentioned above. Only the latest furnace had any superstructure intact, consisting of a low bank of clay packed with numerous flakes of slate which were set on edge; its heavily vitrified lining produced an archaeomagnetic date of 240±25 AD.

Excavation of the central area produced evidence for a probable smithing hearth. An earlier feature was a shallow oval pit of *c.* 1 m in length surrounded by a thick bank of clay. It had become slightly vitrified under oxidising conditions and was associated with vesicular 'crispy' slags.

A dump of *c.* 1200 kg of iron-working debris outside the structure consisted of smelting slags and a large number of smithing hearths. This constitutes a considerably greater quantity than found on any previously excavated Iron Age site. The evidence provided an opportunity to carry out a quantitative study of the different proportions of slag which derived from the activities at the site. It is rarely possible to do this using the evidence of an ancient industrial site, so the results from the study are especially significant.

The research that has been carried out on the determination of the environmental impact of iron-smelting at Bryn y Castell is considered in section 5.6.2.

5.12.2.2 Crawcwellt West

The upland settlement of Crawcwellt West is located on the eastern flank of the Rhinog mountains (Crew

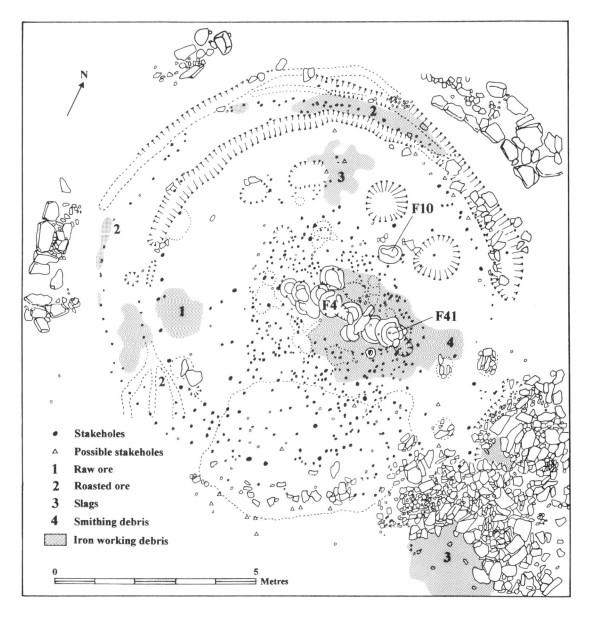

N

F10

F4

F41

- • **Stakeholes**
- △ **Possible stakeholes**
- **1** **Raw ore**
- **2** **Roasted ore**
- **3** **Slags**
- **4** **Smithing debris**
- ▓ **Iron working debris**

0   5
⊢───────┼───────┼───────┤ **Metres**

Figure 5.32 Platform A at Crawcellt, north Wales, showing zones where deposits related to the iron-smelting industry there were located.

1989; 1998). It consists of a series of large enclosures covering about 4 ha. A large platform 12 m in diameter (site A) was the site of a timber structure (Figure 5.32). A continuous slot dug in short segments and which may have originally held vertical timbers was superseded by a sequence of three stake-wall houses, approximately 10.5, 9.5 and 8 m in diameter, each built on a slightly different alignment with their entrances in slightly different positions. The three houses were represented by some 200 stake holes. Gulleys were located to the west and north of the houses. Because the site, in its upland location, had not been ploughed and there had not been modern stone clearance, the surviving evidence was good. Nevertheless, the archaeological features excavated on the inside of the building were often difficult to assign to any particular structure because the stratification was thin and many of the deposits fragile. Excavations were supplemented by magnetic susceptibility surveys of slag dumps in order to map them and also as a means of estimating the total weight of slag in them (Crew 1998).

Excavations of the platform revealed a long and complex sequence of iron-working activity. The structural evidence consisted of a sequence of ten smelting furnaces, several of which had been reconstructed on several occasions. The latest two were best preserved (F4 and F41 in 5.32) and consisted of heavily vitrified clay-lined 'bowls' with internal diameters of 25–30 cm, surviving wall thicknesses of 15–20 cm and with a 15 cm break in the clay lining indicating that there had been an arch in the superstructure. Both furnaces had clear evidence for a 3.5 cm diameter blowing hole at ground level lying at 90 degrees to the suggested arches. All the other furnace remains had the same orientation with 'arches' facing the building entrances (Crew 1989: 14). F41, the latest of the furnaces, had been substantially reconstructed on at least two occasions. It is likely that F4 and F41 were used together. Further excavations (on site H) revealed the remains of a well-preserved furnace built in the centre of a building. The furnace was set above ground, unlike most others found at Crawcwellt. The reason for this position became clear with the discovery of tap slag found in the slag dump. The furnace was well preserved because it had been protected by large stones which had been carefully set around it once it had fallen out of use (Crew 1998: 26). It had been re-lined, reducing its internal diameter from 35 cm to 25 cm.

The furnaces were evidently used for iron-smelting; reheating iron for smithing is thought to have occurred in the bases of redundant furnaces. The raw material used was bog iron ore and two dumps of roasted ore were recovered from the platform. In total, 200 kg of iron-working residues were found in the interior and 400 kg outside. Apart from bog ore, large quantities of clay and vitrified furnace lining were recovered as well as smelting and smithing slags. An estimate of the total slag from a magnetic susceptibility survey and an excavated dump (including some not yet excavated) was c. 1400 kg. More than 100 plano-convex smithing hearth bottoms were recovered; these form just below the blowing hole in the smithing hearth. They form from fuel slags, clay fluxing from the hearth lining, iron oxides burning off and falling from the bloom and smelting slag trapped in the bloom liquating in the hearth.

The dating of Crawcwellt West relied on archaeomagnetic dates: the results indicate that the furnaces were fired between 200–100 BC if one standard deviation is used, or 250–50 BC if two standard deviations are used (Crew 1989: 15). This is therefore entirely within the Iron Age.

5.12.2.3 The experimental reconstruction of iron-smelting

Peter Crew and his team have carried out experimental reconstructions of smelting and smithing processes using phosphorus-rich bog iron. The work has provided a solid basis for the interpretation and quantification of the excavated debris from iron-making sites. The experiments were based closely on the excavated evidence for iron-working: the use of bog iron ore, a low shaft furnace, smithing hearths and a range of slag types produced. The principal aim was to reproduce the conditions in which the slags found were formed.

The slags from both sites were of two basic types: prills and runs of black, non-magnetic iron-rich slag with well-defined cooling surfaces which accumulated as loose agglomerations in the charcoal bed of the furnace. The second type is dense and homogeneous with a characteristic blocky fracture, resulting from interaction with the furnace lining (Crew 1991: 21).

The furnace reconstructions used locally-occurring clays of similar refractory character to those found in the excavated furnaces: there was no sign of thermal deformation at temperatures up to 1200 °C. The evidence for the use of various charcoals, including oak and alder was reflected in pollen profiles – at Bryn y Castell and Crawcwellt West. Commercially-produced charcoal was used in the experiment. The bog ore was collected in 20 kg batches from northern

Shropshire. It has a combined iron-manganese oxide content of over 84% and low silica of 7%; the potential yield is 45%. The phosphorus content is *c.* 1% which is similar to Bryn y Castell ore, though more than the content of Crawcwellt ore. This was roasted and then crushed.

The furnaces were built above ground on a stone and clay plinth to reduce the drying time between campaigns. It had been found that furnaces whose bases lay beneath the ground level absorbed water and had to be reconstructed between smelts; not a problem in the Iron Age because the furnaces would have been constructed inside buildings. The only surviving full wall thickness was below ground (15 cm), but this was found to be too thin for the furnace superstructure leading to heat loss and cracking. It was found that a bed depth of 35 cm was the minimum for the production of an iron bloom with a layered charge. Piston bellows were used to provide a forced draught, mainly so as to control precisely the air input, a very important parameter in such an experiment. The bloom was removed from the top of the furnace; a low furnace was especially appropriate for this operation (Crew 1991: 23).

5.12.2.4 An iron-smelting experiment based on excavated evidence

The operation of the furnace provided some extremely interesting information about the production of iron under conditions based on archaeological evidence It was found to be necessary for the furnace to be at a full operating temperature before any ore was added. The furnace (in experiment XP27) was pre-heated with wood for 30 minutes using a natural draught, until the fire bed was high enough to use piston bellows. Charcoal was then progressively added until the furnace was full. Pre-heating continued for a further 2.5 hours and in total the process consumed 14 kg of charcoal. By this time the exhaust gases burnt as a blue flame. Handfuls of ore were added after 3.5 hours mixed with charcoal in a ratio of 1:1 by weight; a total of 7.6 kg of ore and 8 kg charcoal were added over a period of 4.5 hours. The total charcoal consumed should have been about 28 kg. After 5.25 hours slag blocked up the blowing hole and was cleared using a rod; a sign that a bloom was forming with slag on top of it. The same clearance operation needed to be carried out after 6 hours and in the process a tube was created through cool slag, allowing the smelt to continue with slags accumulating down the rear of the bloom. If the blowing hole became blocked, the smelt had to be abandoned.

In the base of the furnace some 1600 g of loose prills and flows of black iron-rich furnace slags had accumulated. These were similar to the archaeological slags. No furnace bottoms were produced using these experimental conditions; Crew (1991: 28) suggests that many slags labelled as 'furnace bottoms' were in fact cakes of smithing slag. The raw bloom (including slag) weighed 4680 g. The resulting cleaned bloom weighed 1700 g, an equivalent yield of 40% taking into account other loose prills of metal.

The success of this experiment was confirmed by the production of a currency bar weighing 500 g, a yield of 12% from the ore. The global quantification of this experiment (Crew and Salter 1991), subsequently confirmed by others, indicated that each new smelt requires some 100 m of charcoal and about 25 man-days work.

The calculations of the amount of archaeological slag produced indicates that each furnace, if repaired, could last for at least 20 smelts and result in the production of at least 20 blooms of *c.* 20 kg each. The surviving structural evidence suggests that a minimum of 300 blooms were produced and that a calculated minimum quantity of 1600 kg of slag residues would have been produced (not including the possibility that slags were recycled).

5.12.2.5 Scientific study of iron-working: the production of a currency bar

Scientific study of residues from iron-smelting can provide a range of information. The extent of vitrification and the formation of high-temperature crystallites can indicate the temperatures involved in specific industrial processes. The relict minerals in the slags may provide a means of linking the slag to the original iron ore and the form of other crystallites in the slags may provide information about the temperature conditions in which they were formed. This kind of research is discussed in the context of copper production (Section 5.8.2), so will not be repeated here. Instead the experimental production of an Iron Age currency bar will be described.

Iron currency bars have distributions in Iron Age Britain according to their distinctive shapes. Sword-shaped currency bars account for over 40% of the known examples and spit-shaped bars for some 50% of the total. These main types can be divided into sub-types which have their own metallurgical characteristics and are seen to be regionally distributed (Crew 1993). For example, the currency bars which have been found at Danebury, Beckford and Gretton (types A, B and C: see Figure 5.33) have superficially similar sockets, but determination of the chemical compositions of the slags which they contained showed that they were distinctive (Hedges and Salter 1979). Metallurgical analysis of a relatively large number of bars (Ehrenreich 1985) shows that there is a strong correlation between bar shape and the metal type used. One qualification of some of this earlier analytical work is that phosphorus levels,

for example, can vary considerably across a bar which would not have been revealed by the small samples taken (Crew and Salter 1993). However, in spite of this qualification, using only phosphorus contents as an indicator seems to suggest that the iron used contained high, low or moderate phosphorus contents.

Crew and Salter (1993) have produced experimental currency bars by smithing blooms. A bloom weighing 1700 g was smithed to a short bar (labelled XP27) weighing 630 g using an experimental hearth and charcoal as a fuel source. The final drawing of the bar was done under a power hammer. Because the XP27 was produced under known conditions, analytical work provided a means of explaining the patterns and the 'circularity of argument which is inevitable to some degree in the study of ancient iron' could be avoided (Crew and Salter 1993: 14). The composition of the ore, the furnace clay and the charcoal used were all known as well. Any heterogeneity of the resulting composition could be confidently linked to heterogeneity of the bloom, but as a result of piling metals having different compositions. The ores used had consistent phosphorus and arsenic contents, with some variation in manganese levels. The roasted ore contained 80% ferric oxide, about 4% manganese oxide, 7% silica, about 2.3% phosphorus pentoxide and about 0.04% arsenious oxide.

As anticipated, phosphorus was found at levels varying between 0.1% and 0.9%. The highest levels of phosphorus coincide with a localised area of large grain size the presence of which has been interpreted as an extreme variation in the smelting conditions. Segregation of phosphorus may also be brought about by forging and, in any case, the reducing conditions can vary in different positions in the furnace and during the smelt. Crew and Salter also found that the width of enrichment zones depended on the way in which the metal was smithed. A difference noted between smithing by hand and using a power hammer was a less enriched metal was produced with the power hammer. The explanation offered was that the power hammer may not have been stronger but it was quicker, so the enrichment zone may not have had time to develop. Variation of the smelting conditions would also be reflected in the charcoal consumption rate and the blowing rate.

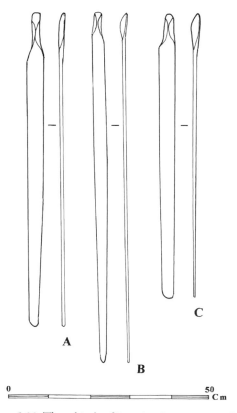

Figure 5.33 Three kinds of Iron Age iron currency bars.

The levels of arsenic in the bar varied between 0.05% and 0.25%, indicating that although the ore contains about 0.04% there is a six-fold enhancement in the metal. Clearly not much arsenic can have been lost in the smelting operation. The carbon content of the bars was also examined. The carbon was present mainly as pearlite (see Section 5.7.3) varying from 0.2% to 0.7% in concentration through the bar. The enriched zones of carbon coincided with the higher levels of phosphorus. The bloom would probably have been carburised to some extent and the carbon would have been burnt out from the surface during the forging process. Bands of phosphorus would however inhibit carbon loss. It was noted that carbon-rich zones were bounded by strings of slag especially in longitudinal section. These carbon-rich zones have been noted in archaeological currency bars (Tylecote 1986: 147–8).

The slag produced from smelting the metal used for the currency bar was examined. The slag contained 2.94% phosphorus pentoxide. Piaskowski's work on the relationship between phosphorus levels in ore, metal and slag suggests that the level should be between 0.3 and 1% in the metal: the mean level in the bar was found to be about 0.4%.

The experimental production of a currency bar has been especially valuable, since by carrying out scientific analysis on the bar, the observed results could be linked to the composition and structure of both the metal and slag, as well as to the smithing and smelting conditions. In some instances physical characteristics of the currency bar produced can be related directly to archaeological examples.

5.12.2.6 Technological implications

As a result of collecting all the available evidence for the iron industry at Bryn y Castell and Crawcwellt West, Crew (1995: 222–3) has been able to estimate the resources necessary for iron production, based on the recovered slags. Over eighty experimental smelts have also been carried out which have provided direct evidence for the resources required, being based firmly on the excavated evidence of the smelting of bog ores in low shaft furnaces. By carrying out experimental iron production it has been possible to reproduce most of the slag types – of course under well-defined conditions. As a result

of this, information can be gained directly about the amount of ore and fuel required.

By comparing the total weight of slag recovered from each excavated site with that recovered from the experiments for a known amount of iron ore, it is possible to estimate what quantity of iron would be produced in billet form. Thus 1200 kg of slag from Bryn y Castell could have been produced from 220 cycles of iron production, requiring about 2 tons of raw bog ore and about 120 tons of wood for making charcoal. The net result would be to produce about 340 kg of billets or 150 kg of finished objects. The resources of iron ore would therefore only have been about 10 sq m of a bog ore deposit of 10 cms in depth. Using the same calculations the scale of production at Crawcwellt West would have been up to three times this amount. If the estimated 300 blooms from the site of Crawcwellt West had been smithed to artefacts it would have resulted in the production of between 600 and 900 plano-convex hearth bottoms (PCBs), depending on the number of smithing cycles. Indeed because quantification of the residues found on platform A at the site has been carried out, it has been possible to suggest strongly that only smelting and primary bloom smithing occurred there; this is supported by scientific work on the PCBs which, despite a wide variation in size, seem to be of a very similar chemical composition and microstructure.

Crew (1989: 16) has suggested that preparation of the raw materials (charcoal, iron ore), furnace construction, drying, emptying and repairing was carried out on a seasonal basis. Associated with the smelting would have been smithing activities. Each campaign would have needed 0.25 ton of raw iron ore and 1 ton of charcoal, producing 30 kg of billets and 20 kg of finished objects per smelting episode. Not more than fifteen campaigns of iron-working would have been necessary to produce the debris found, which is much less than the potential life span of the structures themselves.

Crew's work has also shown that smelting iron *within* a building is a positive advantage because smelting and smithing are operations which are monitored by the colour of the flame or of the iron, so the reduced light levels of a building would have been ideal. The charcoal and ore would also have been stored dry.

Because Bryn y Castell and Crawcwellt West were partly contemporary they must have formed part of an interrelated production system. Crew originally suggested that Bryn y Castell within its hillfort was a high status settlement, but it would seem that the organisation of the industry, while being connected to the supply of bog iron, was less centralised than first envisaged.

Few sites in prehistoric Britain have produced this comprehensive evidence for iron-working. Crew (1998: 30) has estimated that in excess of 6.5 tonnes of slag was produced at Crawcwellt, more than five times the amount recovered from Bryn y Castell and far more than found on any other prehistoric British site. A range of other sites have provided evidence for iron production, but on a much smaller scale; very few have produced more than 100 kg (Salter and Ehrenreich 1984: 151–2). It is clear that, in order to provide Iron Age Britain with sufficient iron, Bryn y Castell and Crawcwellt, both relatively small sites even though producing iron very effectively, must represent only a very small part of a complex situation. Salter has estimated that about 1 tonne of iron per year would have been sufficient to supply central southern Britain, assuming a loss of only 200 g of iron per settlement per year. One obvious explanation for the shortfall of evidence for the primary production of iron is that, in the past, there has been a lack of interest and a lack of motivation in researching the iron industry.

5.13 The chemical characterisation of precious metals?

5.13.1 Introduction

Gold might be conceived of as being relatively uncomplicated in terms of the analysis of its native sources and the artefacts derived from them. However, this is not always the case. Up to 38% silver can be present in naturally occurring gold (Tylecote 1976: 3–4) and various percentages of silver can be added as a form of 'adulteration' and to produce electrum alloys. Copper may be added to counteract the whitening effect of silver, to produce a hardening effect, or as adulteration. The study of

Irish gold, which will be considered briefly here, illustrates how controversies can develop around the analysis of metal raw materials. Hartmann (1970) carried out 1,425 analyses of European prehistoric gold objects including 507 from Ireland. From several compositional groupings there is one ore labelled 'PC' by him which he partly 'characterised' by its content of platinum. Scott (1976) has noted, however, that 25% of these objects actually contain no platinum at all. There has been much discussion of the suggestion that the source of the gold in gold objects from Ireland was the Upper Rhine rather than Ireland (Harbison 1971). Hartmann (1970) sees the German placer deposits as the most likely source for PC gold, with the import of ingots or scrap for the manufacture of typically Irish objects. Only five analyses of Irish native gold were carried out by Hartmann and many more need to be made of German, Irish and particularly Scottish native gold, where little work appears to have been done, before anything approaching a firm statement can be made. It is worth noting that early Bronze Age gold lunulae (Taylor 1970; 1979) have been found in regions with stream deposits of gold but not, for example, in Wessex (which has no indigenous sources of gold), and we might be tempted to draw some conclusions about the sources of the gold from this. Hartmann (1979) suggests that only the early Bronze Age Irish objects (including lunulae and sun discs) were made from Irish gold deposits and that the similarity in composition between many of his Iberian and Irish gold samples suggested to him that strong trade relations existed between the two areas. As noted above, comprehensive chemical analyses of the European ores themselves would need to be carried out before a convincing interpretation could be accepted. This brief reference to one important area of research, which needs further intensive study, shows how important the comprehensive analysis of the raw materials is and the need for constructing comprehensive sampling strategies. What follows, however is an account of a research project which is an investigation of gold deposits where the presence of unambiguous trace elements has allowed the gold to be sourced and its uses in the production of coins monitored over time.

5.13.2 Compositional links between the New World and Europe through the use of gold and silver

It is rarely possible to relate the composition of a coin, whether its trace components or one of its major constituents, to its date of manufacture. In one of the earliest successful studies, Hall and Metcalf (1972) showed that the fineness (% gold) of Carolingian coins decreased in a very specific way from 702 until 756, inferring that there was evidently a deliberate control over the amount of gold added to the coins over this period. From an earlier period, however, Butcher and Ponting (1998) show how chemical analysis of Roman silver coinage provides information about debasement over time and relationships between contemporary but different coinages. In sixteenth-century Europe another study (Barrandon et al. 1995) has shown that it is not only possible to chemically characterise the sources of South American silver and gold, but also to be able to trace the use of these metals over time in European coinage.

Trade in precious metals played an important part in the links between the Americas and Europe from the sixteenth to the late eighteenth centuries. Enormous amounts of silver and gold were brought to Europe by the Spanish and Portuguese (Hamilton 1934). The profits which accrued from these imports contributed substantially to the development of agriculture, mining and manufacturing industries; the bullion was an incentive for the industrial revolution (Braudel and Spooner 1967). While there has not been any question that precious metals were imported from the New World, and indeed this was one of the principal reasons for colonising these new lands, it is difficult to reconstruct the precise role that precious metals played in the monetary history of Europe using incomplete contemporary commercial or monetary statistics (Barrandon et al. 1995: 171). Cipolla (1989: 69) states that while the origin of the treasure is known, once it reached Spain the uses to which it was put and where it was eventually used are unknown.

The introduction of precious metals into European coinage brought with them trace elements which characterised the use of the precious metal ores. Because the amount of the tracer (impurity) in the precious metal is carried through to its final use in the coin it becomes possible to assess the amount of silver or gold used and at the same time establish where the ore derived from.

As mentioned above, to be able to characterise metal in this way is exceptional and to be able to trace its use in the final objects made from it is also very unusual indeed. Even if metal was mixed or recycled, as long as the characteristic element remained in the metal, and the element was only found in the ore, as claimed, it is possible to trace the use of the ore comprehensively. Barrandon et al. (1995) did this by using two techniques: thermal neutron activation analysis produced by a mini-reactor associated with a cyclotron for the analysis of silver coins and proton activation for the gold coins.

Barrandon et al. (1995) studied two sources of ore which were known to have been exploited: 'Peruvian' silver from Potosí (Le Roy Ladurie et al. 1990) and gold from Brazil. Geochemical data for these sources was available and the research team was able to show that indium (In) or the indium:silver ratio was characteristic of Andean silver, and palladium (Pd) or the palladium:silver ratio is characteristic of Brazilian gold.

These trace elements were found to occur at much higher levels in the 300 European coins analysed of sixteenth to eighteenth century date than in the European coinages before the arrival of the American gold and silver. Fortunately for Barrandon et al. (1995) the levels of these trace elements were not only sufficiently high in the original ore but remained at levels that could be detected using the techniques of analysis that they used.

5.13.3 The silver coins

About 120 American, Spanish and French coins and 62 coins from Genoa and Milan were chemically analysed using thermal neutron activation analysis. The feature of the Potosí coins that has made this study significant is that the silver coins contain indium at c. 7 ppm; when silver coins struck in Mexico and in Spain at the end of the fifteenth and the beginning of the sixteenth centuries were chemically analysed no indium was detected. By plotting the log scale of indium measured in parts per million

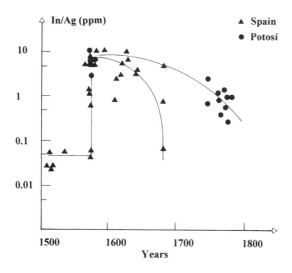

Figure 5.34 The relative levels in parts per million of indium and silver (log scale) found in coins struck in Potosí or Lima, Peru (1556–1784) and Spain (1512–1686) (after Barrandon *et al.* 1995) © The British Museum.

relative to the silver content (i.e. the ratio) of coins struck in Potosí or Lima between 1556 and 1784 and Spain between 1512 and 1686 (Figure 5.34) it becomes clear that the appearance of indium in Spanish coins of Philip II of Spain (1556–98) marks the fact that Potosí silver as an ore had crossed the Atlantic to Spain from *c.* 1570. Nine out of eleven Philip II silver coins contained Potosí silver. From a technological point of view, the date of 1570 roughly coincides with the date of introduction into Peru of a more productive metal extraction technique of mercury amalgam (see Section 5.7.9) in 1573 after the mercury mines at Huancavelica had been opened.

Although there was a flow of Andean silver across the Atlantic, it was relatively short-lived; from the reign of Charles II (1665–1700) onwards, coins struck with silver considered to have had a European origin appeared in the population. By the middle of the seventeenth century output of Potosí silver had fallen by roughly 30% and the Mexican mines were starting to contribute in a more substantial way (Cross 1983: 409). The French situation in the sixteenth century lends itself to this kind of study because there was a decree of 1549 stipulating that all coins should be marked with their date of issue. Barrandon *et al.*

(1995: 172) found that by focusing on the products of the so-called 'Atlantic group' of mints (Spooner 1972) at Bayonne, Bordeaux, La Rochelle and Nantes, they were able to show that Potosí silver was frequently present in coins dated to 1575 onwards with a peak at the end of the sixteenth/early seventeenth century and a final decrease starting in the 1640s. This study of the French coinage is unusual in that it is possible to relate clearly the dates of the coins to their compositions. The influence of Andean silver appears in the Italian mints of Genoa and Milan (Barrandon *et al.* 1992) from 1575 onwards, ending in the 1640s. There is a slight recovery after this which may represent a re-minting cycle.

5.13.4 The gold coins

While Barrandon *et al.* (1995) found that seven ppm of indium characterised silver from Andean sources, the levels of palladium present in gold coins struck in Brazil and which characterises them unambiguously is much higher with a mean and standard deviation value of 866±530 ppm. This palladium value is approximately 100 times higher than found in gold coins struck in Portugal before 1700 (Figure 5.35). The study focused on *c.* 100 gold coins from Brazil, Portugal, Britain and France. From 1750 onwards the peak visible in Figure 5.35 suggests a re-minting cycle among existing European metal rather than among new American arrivals.

From 1703, the date of the Methuen Treaty, Britain was the European nation which was most involved in trade with Brazil. It has been estimated that between 1700 and 1760 Britain absorbed some 30% of Brazil's output of gold (Fisher 1971: 20, 21, 128). Although only twenty coins were included in the study, the pattern of increased palladium levels from the early eighteenth century is clear (Figure 5.35), increasing from a mean of 23 ppm before 1703 to 718 ppm for coins minted between 1703 and 1752. It was possible to estimate what is presumably an average palladium concentration in Brazilian gold of 1,115 ppm with an associated error of about 25%. By comparing this value to that found in British gold coins Barrandon *et al.* (1995) were able to estimate that the true contribution of Brazilian gold to British coinage of *c.* 1700–50 was around 61%. Gold from Portugal, which originally derived from Brazil, played

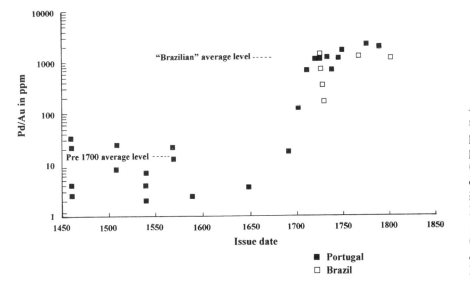

Figure 5.35 The relative levels in parts per million of palladium and gold (log scale) by issue date for coins struck in Portugal and Brazil between 1460 and 1802 (after Barrandon *et al.* 1995) © The British Museum.

a very important role in the British economy. Coins were minted from ingots or re-minted from coins.

The study of the use of Brazilian gold in French eighteenth-century coins provides a more detailed picture. The availability of gold was responsible for a slowly increasing number of total issues between 1702 and 1725 from 7.2% to 37.5%. An *arrêt* on 26 May 1726 produced a decrease in 1726 and 1727 to 25.6% and 18.1% respectively. During this time all coins were withdrawn from circulation and re-minted. The percentage of total issues increased in the 1730s again, reaching a peak of 62% in 1770–4. The peak may have been caused by an increasingly smaller proportion of 'pre-Brazilian' gold entering the melting pot combined with re-melting of the original French Brazilian issues which had been withdrawn from circulation.

References

Adams, R.B. (1999) 'The development of copper metallurgy during the early Bronze Age of the southern Levant: evidence from the Feinan region, southern Jordan', unpublished PhD thesis, University of Sheffield.

Adams, R. McC. (1968) 'The natural history of urbanism', *Smithsonian Annual* 2: 41–59.

—— (1981) *Heartland of Cities*, Chicago: Aldine.

Adriaens, A., Yener, K.A. and Adams, F. (1999) 'An analytical study using electron and ion microscopy of thin-walled crucibles from Göltepe, Turkey', in J. Henderson, H. Neff and T. Rehren (eds), Proceedings of the International Symposium on Archaeometry, University of Illinois at Urbana-Champaign (UIUC), Urbana, Illinois, 20–4 May 1996, *Journal of Archaeological Science*, 8: 1069–74.

Allan, J.W. (1979) *Persian Metal Technology*, London: Ithaca Press.

Annels, A.E. and Burnham, B.C. (1986) *The Dolaucothi Gold Mines*, Cardiff: University of Wales.

Bachmann, H.-G. and Rothenburg, B. (1980) 'Die Verhüttungsverfahren von Site 30', in H.-E. Conrad and R. Rothenburg (eds), *Antikes Kupfer im Timna-Tal*, Der Anschnitt Beiheft 1, Bochum: Deutsches Bergbau Museum, 215–36.

Bamburger, M. and Wincierz, P. (1990) 'Ancient smelting of oxide copper ore', in R. Rothenburg (ed.), *The Ancient Metallurgy of Copper*, London: IAMS, pp. 123–57.

Barker, L. and White, R. (1992) 'Early smelting in Swaledale' in L. Willies and D. Cranstone (eds), *Boles and Smeltmills*, London: Historical Metallurgy Society, pp. 15–18.

Barnes, J.W. (1973) 'Ancient clay furnace bars from Iran', *Bulletin of the Historical Metallurgy Group* 7, 2: 8–17.

—— and Bailey, E.H. (1972) 'Geologists discover ancient retort – evidence points to world's oldest mine', *World Mining (US Edition)*, April, 49–55.

Barnett, H.G. (1953) *Innovation: The Basis of Cultural Change*. New York: McGraw-Hill.

Barrandon, J.-N., Guerra, M.F., Le Roy Ladurie, E., Morrison, C. and Collin, B. (1992) 'La diffusion de l'argent du Potosí dans les monnayages européens à partir du XVIe siècle: le circuit méditerranéen', *Gaceta Numismatica* 107: 15–22.

—— , Le Roy Ladurie, E., Morrison, C. and Morrison, Ch. (1995) 'The true role of American precious metals transfers to Europe in the sixteenth to eighteenth centuries: new evidence from coin analyses', in D.R. Hook and D.R.M. Gaimster (eds), *Trade and Discovery. The Scientific Study of Artefacts from Post-Medieval Europe and Beyond*, British Museum Occasional Paper 109, London: The British Museum Press.

Bayard, D.T. (1980) *The Pa Mong Archaeological Survey Programme, 1973–75*, University of Otago Studies in Prehistoric Anthropology 4, Dunedin.

—— (1984) 'A tentative regional phase chronology for north-east Thailand', in *Southeast Asian Archaeology at the XV Pacific Science Congress*, University of Otago Studies in Prehistoric Anthropology, vol. 16, Dunedin: University of Otago, pp. 161–8.

Bayley, J. (1984) 'Roman brass-making in Britain', *Journal of the Historical Metallurgy Society* 18, 1: 42–3.

—— (1990) 'The production of brass in Antiquity with particular reference to Roman Britain', in P.J. Craddock (ed.), *Two Thousand Years of Zinc and Brass*, British Museum Occasional Paper 50, London: British Museum Press, pp. 7–28.

—— (1991) 'Archaeological evidence for parting', in E. Pernicka and G.A. Wagner (eds), *Archaeometry '90*, Basle: Birkhauser Verlag, pp. 19–28.

Bee, R.L. (1974 *Patterns and Processes,* New York: The Free Press.

Bennett, A. (1990) 'Prehistoric copper smelting in Central Thailand', in I. Glover and E. Glover (eds), *Southeast Asian Archaeology 1986*, Oxford: British Archaeological Reports, pp. 109–20.

Bhardwaj, H.C. (1979) *Aspects of Ancient Indian Technology*, Delhi: Motilal Banarsidass.

Bielenin, K. (1984) 'Bloom smithies on early historic smelting sites in the Holy Cross Mountains', in B.G. Scott and H. Cleere (eds), *The Crafts of the Blacksmith*, Essays presented to R.F. Tylecote, in Proceedings of the 1984 Symposium of the UISPP Comité pour la Sidérurgie Ancienne, Belfast: UISPP Comité pour la Sidérurgie Ancienne and the Ulster Museum, pp. 35–46.

Blunden, C. and Elvin, M. (1983) *Cultural Atlas of China,* Oxford: Phaidon.

Bowman, S.G.E., Cowell, M.R. and Cribb, J. (1989) '2,000 years of coinage in China: an analytical study', *Journal of Historical Metallurgy Society* 23, 1: 25–30.

Braidwood, L.S. *et al.* (1983) *Prehistoric Archaeology along the Zagros Flanks*, Oriental Institute Publications 105, Chicago: University of Chicago.

Braudel, F. and Spooner (1967) 'Prices in Europe from 1450 to 1750', *The Cambridge Economic History of Europe 4,* Cambridge: Cambridge University Press.

Brill, R.H. and Wampler, J.M. (1967) 'Isotope studies of ancient lead', *American Journal of Archaeology* 71: 63–77.

Britton, D. (1960) 'The Isleham hoard, Cambridgeshire', *Antiquity* 34: 279–82.

—— and Richards, E.E. (1969) 'Optical emission spectrometry and the study of metallurgy in the European Bronze Age' in D. Brothwell and E. Higgs (eds), *Science in Archaeology*, London: Thames and Hudson, pp. 603–13.

Bronson, B. (1986) 'The making and selling of wootz, a crucible steel of India', *Archaeomaterials* 1, 1: 13–51.

Brown, J. (1995) *Traditional Metalworking in Kenya*, Oxbow Monograph 44 and Cambridge Monographs in African Archaeology 38, Oxford: Oxbow books.

Budd, P.D. (1991) 'A metallographic investigation of Eneolithic arsenical copper', PhD thesis, University of Bradford.

—— , Gale, D., Pollard, A.M., Thomas, R.G. and Williams, P.A. (1992) 'The early development of metallurgy in the British Isles', *Antiquity* 66, 252: 677–96.

—— and Ottaway, B.S. (1991) 'The properties of arsenical copper alloys: implications for the development of Eneolithic metallurgy', in P. Budd, B. Chapman, C. Jackson, R. Janaway and B. Ottaway (eds), *Archaeological Sciences 1989*, Proceedings of a conference on the application of scientific techniques to archaeology, Bradford, September 1989, Oxbow Monograph 9, Oxford: Oxbow Books pp. 132–42.

Burgess, C.B. (1968) 'The later Bronze Age in the British Isles and north-western France', *Archaeological Journal* 125: 1–45.

—— (1980) *The Age of Stonehenge*, London: Thames & Hudson.

Burnett, A.M., Craddock, P.T. and Preston, K. (1982) 'New light on the origins of *orichalcum*', in T. Hackens and R. Weiller (eds), *Proceedings of the 9th International Congress of Numismatics*, Berne 1979, Association Internationale des Numismates Professionels, Publication 6: 263–8.

Butcher, K. and Ponting, M. (1998) 'Atomic Absorption Spectrometry and Roman Silver Coins' in A. Oddy and M. Cowell (eds) *Metalurgy and Numismatics*, vol. 4, Royal Numismatic Society Special Publication No. 30, London: Royal Numismatic Society, pp. 308–334.

Caldwell, J.R. (1968) 'Pottery and cultural history on the Iranian plateau', *Journal of Near Eastern Studies* 27: 178–83.

Case, H. (1966) 'Were Beaker people the first metallurgists in Ireland?' *Palaeohistoria* 12: 141–77.

Černych, E.N. (1978) 'Ai Bunar – a Balkan copper mine of the fourth millennium BC', *Proceedings of the Prehistoric Society* 44: 203–18.

Chambers, F.M. and Lageard, J.G.A. (1993) 'Vegetational history and environmental setting of Crawcwellt, Gwynedd', *Archaeology in Wales* 33: 23–5.

Champion, T.C. (1980) 'The early development of iron-working', *Nature* 284: 513–14.

Ch'ao, Ting-chi (1936) *Key Economic Areas in Chinese History*, London: Allen and Unwin.

Charles, J.A. (1967) 'Early arsenical bronzes – a metallurgical view', *American Journal of Archaeology* 71: 21–6.

—— (1973) 'Heterogeneity in metals', *Archaeometry* 15, 1: 105–14.

Cheng, Te-K'un (1963) *Archaeology in China. Volume 3, Chou China*, Cambridge and Toronto: Heffer and University of Toronto Press.

Childs, S.T. (1989) 'Clays to artefacts: resource selection in African early Iron Age iron-making technologies', in G. Bronitsky (ed.), *Pottery Technology: Ideas and Approaches*, Boulder, Colorado: University of Colorado, pp. 139–64.

Cipolla, C.M. (1989) 'American treasure and the Florentine coinage in the sixteenth century' in E.H.G. Van Cauwenberghe (ed.), *Precious Metals, Coinage and the Monetary Structures in Latin-America, Europe and Asia*, Leuven: University of Leuven.

Cleere, H. (1970) *Iron Smelting Experiments in a Reconstructed Roman Furnace*, London: The Iron and Steel Institute.

Colquhoun, I. and Burgess, C.B. (1988) *The Swords of Britain*, Munich, Prähistorische Bronzefunde, IV, 5.

Conophagos, C.E. (1980) *Le Laurium Antique*, Athens: Ekdotike Hellados.

Conrad, H.-G. and Rothenberg, B. (eds) (1980) *Antikes Kupfer im Timna-Tal*, Der Anschnitt Beiheft 1, Bochum: Deutsches Bergbau Museum.

Costin, C. (1991) 'Craft specialisation: issues in defining, documenting and explaining the organisation of production', in M.B. Schiffer (ed.), *Archaeological Methods and Theory 3*, Tucson: University of Arizona Press, pp. 1–56.

Coughlan, H.H. (1956) *Notes on Prehistoric and Early Iron in the Old World*, Oxford: Oxford University Press.

—— (1962) 'A note upon native copper: its occurrence and properties', *Proceedings of the Prehistoric Society*, 28–57.

—— and Case, H.J. (1957) 'Early metallurgy of copper in Ireland and Britain', *Proceedings of the Prehistoric Society* 23: 91–123.

Cowell, M.R., Cribb, J., Bowman, S.G.E. and Shashoua, Y. (1993) 'The Chinese cash: composition and production', in M.M. Archibald and M.R. Cowell (eds), *Metallurgy in Numismatics* 3, Royal Numismatics Society Special Publication 24, London: Royal Numismatics Society, 185–98.

—— and Lowick, N.M. (1988) 'Silver from the Panjhīr mines', in W.A. Oddy (ed.), *Metallurgy in Numismatics* 2, London: Royal Numismatics Society, pp. 65–74.

Craddock, P.T. (1977) 'The composition of the copper alloys used by the Greek, Etruscan and Roman civilisations 2. The Archaic, Classical and Hellenistic Greeks', *Journal of Archaeological Science* 4: 103–24.

—— (1978) 'The composition of copper alloys used by the Greek, Etruscan and Roman civilisations', *Journal of Archaeological Science* 5: 1–16.

—— (1979) 'Deliberate alloying in the Atlantic Bronze Age', in M. Ryan (ed.), *Proceedings of the 5th Atlantic Colloquium*, Dublin: Stationery Office, pp. 369–85.

—— (1980) (ed.) *Scientific Studies in Early Mining and Extractive Metallurgy*, British Museum Occasional Paper 20, London: British Museum Press.

—— (1986a) 'The metallurgy and composition of Etruscan bronze', *Studi Etruschi* 52: 211–71.

—— (1986b) 'Evidence for Bronze Age metallurgy in Britain', *Current Archaeology* 9, 4: 106–9.

—— (1988) 'The composition of the metal finds', in B. Rothenberg (ed.), *The Egyptian Mining Temple at Timna*, London: IAMS, pp. 169–81.

—— (1989) 'The scientific investigation of early mining and smelting', in J. Henderson (ed.), *Scientific Analysis in Archaeology and its Archaeological Interpretation*, Oxford University Committee on Archaeology, Monograph 19 and UCLA Institute of Archaeology, Archaeological Research Tools 5, pp. 178–210.

—— (1990) 'Zinc in Classical Antiquity', in P.T. Craddock (ed.), *Two Thousand Years of Zinc and Brass*, British Museum Occasional Paper 50, London: British Museum Press, pp. 1–6.

—— (1995) *Early Metal Mining and Production*, Edinburgh: Edinburgh University Press.

—— (1998) 'New light on the production of crucible steel in Asia', *Bulletin of the Metals Museum of the Japan Institute of Metals* 29: 41–65.

——, Burnett, A.M., Preston, K. (1980) 'Hellenistic copper-base coinage and the origins of brass' in W.A. Oddy (ed.), *Scientific Studies of Numismatics*, British Museum Occasional Paper 18, London: British Museum Press, pp. 153–64.

——, Freestone, I.C., Gale, N.H., Meeks, N.D., Rothenburg, B. and Tite, M.S. (1985) 'The investigation of a small heap of silver smelting debris from Rio Tinto, Huelva, Spain', in P.T. Craddock and M.J. Hughes (eds), *Furnaces and Smelting Technology in Antiquity*, British Museum Occasional Paper No. 48, London: The British Museum, pp. 199–218.

——, ——, Gurjar, L.K., Middleton, A. and Willies, L. (1989) 'The production of lead, silver and zinc in Ancient India', in A. Hauptmann *et al.* (eds), Proceedings of the International Symposium, *Old World Archaeometallurgy*, Heidelberg 1987, Der Anschnitt, beiheft 7, Bochum: Deutsches Bergbau-Museum, pp. 51–70.

—— and Gale, D. (1988) 'Evidence for early mining and extractive metallurgy in the British Isles', in E.A. Slater and J.O. Tate (eds), *Science and Archaeology, Glasgow 1987*, Oxford: BAR British Series 196.

—— and Hughes, M.J. (eds) (1985) *Furnaces and Smelting Technology in Antiquity*, British Museum Occasional Paper No. 48, London: The British Museum.

——, Leese, M., Matthews, K. and Needham, S.P. (1990) 'The composition of the metalwork', in S. Needham, *The Petters Lane Bronze Age Metalwork: An Analytical Study of Thames Valley Metalworking in its Settlement Context*, British Museum Occasional Paper 70, London: British Museum Publications, p. 77–89.

—— and Meeks, N.D. (1987) 'Iron in Ancient Copper', *Archaeometry* 29: 187–204.

Crew, P. (1988) 'Bryn y Castell hillfort – a late prehistoric iron working settlement in north-west Wales', in B.G. Scott and H. Cleere (eds), *The Crafts of the Blacksmith*, Essays presented to R.F. Tylecote, in Proceedings of the 1984 Symposium of the UISPP Comité pour la Sidérurgie Ancienne, Belfast: UISPP Comité pour la Sidérurgie Ancienne and the Ulster Museum, pp. 91–100.

—— (1989) 'Excavations at Crawcwellt West, Merioneth, 1986–1989, a prehistoric upland iron-working settlement', *Archaeology in Wales* 29, 11–16.

—— (1991) 'The experimental production of prehistoric bar iron', *Historical Metallurgy* 25, 1: 21–36.

—— (1993) 'Currency bars in Great Britain', in M. Mangin (ed.), *La sidérugie ancienne de l'Est de la France dans son contexte européen*, Colloque de Besançon 10–13 Novembre 1993, Annales littéraires de l'Université de Besançon 536, Série Archéologie 40, pp. 345–50.

—— (1995) 'Decline or prohibition? The end of prehistoric iron working in north-west Wales', in P. Benoit and P. Fluzin (eds), *Paléométallurgie du fer & Cultures*, Actes du Symposium International du Comité pour la sidérurgie ancienne de l'Union Internationale des Sciences Préhistoriques et Proto-historique, Institut Polytechnique de Sévans 1–3 November 1990, Belfort-Sévenans, Belfort Cedex: Vulcain, pp. 217–27.

—— (1998) 'Excavations at Crawcwellt West, Merioneth, 1990–1998: a late prehistoric upland iron-working settlement', *Archaeology in Wales* 38: 22–35.

—— and Crew, S. (eds) (1990) *Early Mining in the British Isles*, Maentwrog: Plas tan y Bwlch Snowdonia Study Centre.

—— and Salter, C.J. (1991) 'Comparative data from iron smelting and smithing experiments', in E. Nosek (ed.), *From Knife to Bloom, Materialy Archeologiczne* XXVI: 15–22.

—— and —— (1993) 'Currency bars with welded tips', in A. Espelund (ed.), *Bloomery Ironmaking during 2000 years*, vol. 3, *In Honorem Ole Evenstad*, Comité pour la sidérugie ancienne de l'UISPP, Trondheim: Budal-seminaret, pp. 11–30.

Cross, H.E. (1983) 'South American bullion production and export 1550–1750', in J.F. Richards (ed.), *Precious Metals in Later Medieval and Early Modern World*, Durham, North Carolina: Carolina Academic Press.

Davey, P.J., Northover, P., O'Connor, B. and Woodcock, J.J. (1999) 'Bronze Age metallurgy on the Isle of Man: a symposium', in P.J. Davey (ed.), *Recent Archaeological Research on the Isle of Man*, British Archaeological Reports, British Series 278, Oxford: British Archaeological Reports, pp. 39–62.

Doonan, R.P.C., Klemm, S., Ottaway, B.S., Sperl, G. and Weinek, H. (1996) 'The east Alpine Bronze Age copper smelting process: evidence from the Ramsau valley, Eisenerz, Austria', in S. Demirçi, A.M. Özer and G.D. Summers (eds), *Archaeometry '94*, Ankara, pp. 17–22.

Doran, J.E. and Hodson, F.R. (1975) *Mathematics and Computers in Archaeology*, Edinburgh: Edinburgh University Press.

Edwards, K.J. (1982) 'Man, space and the woodland edge – speculations on the detection and interpretation of human impact in pollen profiles', in S. Limbrey and M. Bell (eds), *Archaeological Aspects of Woodland Ecology*, British Archaeological Reports International Series S146, Oxford: British Archaeological Reports.

—— (1983) 'Quaternary palynology: multiple profile studies and pollen variability', *Progress in Physical Geography* 7: 687–709.

Ehrenreich, R.M. (1985) *Trade, Technology and the Ironworking Community in the Iron Age of Southern Britain*, British Archaeological Reports, British Series 144, Oxford: British Archaeological Reports.

Éluère, C. and Mohen, J.-P. (eds) (1991), *Découverte du Métal*, Paris: Picard.

Engel, T. (1993) 'Charcoal remains from an Iron Age copper smelting slag heap at Feinan, Wadi Arabah (Jordan)', *Vegetation History and Archaeobotany* 2: 205–11.

—— and Frey, W. (1996) 'Fuel resources for copper smelting in Antiquity in selected woodlands in the Edom Highlands to the Wadi Arabah, Jordan', *Flora* 191: 29–39.

Ericson, J.E., Pandolfi, L. and Patterson, C. (1982) 'Pyrotechnology of copper extraction: methods of detection and implications', in T.E. Wertime and S.F. Wertime (eds), *Early Pyrotechnology, The Evolution of The First Fire-using Industries*, Washington, DC: The Smithsonian Institution Press, pp. 193–204.

Farnsworth, M., Smith, C.S. and Rodda, J.L. (1949) 'Metallographic examination of a sample of metallic zinc from ancient Athens', *Hesperia* (supplement) 8: 126–9.

Figueral, I. (1992) 'The charcoals', in M.G. Fulford and J.R.L. Allen (eds), 'Iron-making at the Chesters villa, Woolaston, Gloucestershire: Survey and Excavation 1987–91', *Britannia* 23, 1: 59–215.

Fisher, H.E.S. (1971) *The Portugal Trade. A Study of Anglo-Portugese Commerce 1700–1771*, London: Methuen.

Fisk, E. and Shand, R. (1969) 'The early stages of development in a primitive economy: the evolution of subsistence to trade and specialisation', in C. Wharton (ed.), *Subsistence Agriculture and Economic Developments*, Chicago: Chicago University Press, pp. 257–74.

Forbes, R.J. (1964) *Studies in Ancient Technology*, vol. VIII, Leiden: Brill.

Foster, W. (1883) *A Treatise on a Section of the Strata from Newcastle-on-Tyne to the Mountain of Cross Fell, in Cumberland,* 3rd edn, revised W. Nall, Newcastle.

Friend, J.N. (1926) *Iron in Antiquity*, London: Griffin.

Fulford, M.G. and Allan, J.R.L. (1992) 'Iron-making at the Chesters villa, Woolaston, Gloucestershire: survey and excavation 1987–91', *Britannia* 23, 1: 59–215.

Gale, N.H. and Stos-Gale, Z.A. (1992) 'Lead isotope studies in the Aegean (The British Academy Project)', in A.M. Pollard (ed.), *New Developments in Archaeological Science*, Proceedings of the British Academy 77, Oxford: Oxford University Press, pp. 63–108.

—— and ——, Lilov, P., Dimitrov, M. and Todorov, T. (1991) 'Recent studies of eneolithic copper ores and artefacts in Bulgaria', in C. Eluere and J.-P. Mohen (eds), *Découverte du Métal*, Paris: Picard, pp. 49–75.

Garfinkel, Y. (1987) 'Bead manufacture on the pre-pottery Neolithic B site of Yiftahel', *Journal of the Israel Prehistoric Society* 20: 79–90.

Gechter, M. (1993) 'Römischer Bergbau in der Germania Inferior, Eine Bestandsaufnahme', in H. Steuer and U. Zimmermann (eds), *Montanarchäologie in Europa*, Sigmaringen: Jan Thorbecke Verlag, pp. 161–66.

Geçkinli, A.E., Bozkurt, N. and Basaran, S. (1988) 'Metallographic studies of archaeological metal artefacts from Çavus tepe', *Aksay Ünitesi-Bilimsel Toplanti Bildinileri* 1 (23–25 November), Ankara: Middle East University, pp. 229–46.

Gilead, I. (1990) 'The Neolithic-Chalcolithic transition and the Qatifian of Northern Negev and Sinai', *Levant* 22: 47–63.

Goodway, M. (1987) 'Phosphorus in antique music wire', *Science* 236: 927–32.

Gordon, R.B. and Killick, D.J. (1992) 'The metallurgy of the American bloomery process', *Archaeomaterials* 6, 141–67.

—— and —— (1993) 'Adaption and technology to culture and environment: bloomery smelting in America and Africa', *Technology and Culture* 34, 2: 243–70.

Goren, Y. (1990) 'The 'Qatifian Culture' in Southern Israel and Transjordan: additional aspects for its definition', *Journal of the Israel Prehistoric Society* 23: 100–12.

Granger, F. (trans.) (1934) *Vitruvius: On Architecture*, Loeb Edition, London: Heinemann.

Guinier, A. (1989) *The Structure of Matter from Blue Sky to Liquid Crystals*, London: Edward Arnold.

Hall, E.T. and Metcalf, D.M. (1972) *Methods of Chemical and Metallurgical Investigation of Ancient Coinage*, Royal Numismatical Society Special Publication 8, London: Royal Numismatical Society.

Hall, M.E. and Steadman, S.R. (1991) 'Tin and Anatolia: another look', *Journal of Mediterranean Archaeology* 4: 217–34.

Halleaux, R. (1973) 'L'orichalque et la laiton', *Antiquité Classique* 42: 64–81.

Hamilton, E.A. (1934) *American Treasure and the Price Revolution in Spain 1501–1650*, Cambridge, Massachusetts.

Harbison, P. (1969a) *The Axes of the Early Bronze Age in Ireland*, Munich: Prähistorische Bronzefunde IX, 1.

—— (1969b) *The Daggers and the Halberds of the Early Bronze Age in Ireland,* Prähistorische Bronzefunde VI, 1.

—— (1971) 'Hartmann's gold analyses: a comment', *Journal of the Royal Society of Antiquaries of Ireland* 101: 159–60.

Hartmann, A. (1970, 1982) *Prähistorische Goldfunde aus Europa: spektralanalytische Untersuchungen und deren Auswertung*, 2 vols, Römisches-Germanisches Zentralmuseums, Studie zu den Anfangen der Metallurgie, 3.5, Berlin: Mann.

—— (1979) 'Irish and British gold types and their West European counterparts', in M. Ryan (ed.), *The Origins of Metallurgy in Atlantic Europe*, 5th Atlantic Colloquium, Dublin 1978, pp. 215–28.

Hauptmann A. (1989) 'The earliest periods of copper metallurgy in Feinan, Jordan', in A. Hauptmann, E. Pernicka and G.A. Wagner (eds), Proceedings of the International Symposium, *Old World Archaeometallurgy*, Heidelberg 1987, Der Anschnitt, Beiheft 7, Bochum: Deutsches Bergbau-Museum, pp. 119–35.

——, Bachmann, H.G. and Maddin, R. (1996) 'Chalcolithic copper smelting: new evidence from excavations at Feinan', in Ş. Demirci, A.M. Özer and G.D. Summers (eds), *Archaeometry '94: The Proceedings of the 29th International Symposium on Archaeometry*, Ankara: Tübitak.

——, Begemann, F., Heitkemper, E., Pernicka, E. and Schmitt-Strecker, S. (1992) 'Early copper produced at Feinan, Wadi Araba, Jordan: the composition of ores and copper', *Archaeomaterials* 6: 1–33.

——, Pernicka, E. and Wagner, G.A. (eds) (1989) Proceedings of the International Symposium, *Old World Archaeometallurgy*, Heidelberg 1987, Der Anschnitt, Beiheft 7, Bochum: Deutsches Bergbau-Museum.

—— and Roden, C. (1988) 'Archäometallurgische Untersuchungen zur Kupferverhüttung der frühen Bronzezeit in Feinan, Wadi Arabah, Jordanien', *Jahrbuch den Römisches-Germanisches Zentralmuseums* 35: 510–16.

——, Weisgerber, G. and Knauf, E.A. (1985) 'Archäometallurgische und bergbauarchäologische Untersuchungen im Gebiet von Fenan, Wadi Arabah (Jordanien)' *Der Anschnitt* 37: 163–95.

Hawthorne, J.G. and Smith, C.S. (eds) (1963) *On Divers Arts: The Treatise of Theophilus*, Chicago: University of Chicago Press.

Hedges, R.E.M. and Salter, C.J. (1979) 'Source determination of iron currency bars through the analysis of slag inclusions', *Archaeometry* 21: 161–75.

Henderson, J. (1991) 'Industrial specialisation in late Iron Age Europe: organisation, location and distribution', *The Archaeological Journal* 148: 104–48.

Herrmann, G., Kurbansakhatov, K. and Simpson, St J. (1996) 'The International Merv Project; preliminary report on the fourth season (1995)', *Iran* 34: 1–22.

——, —— and —— (1997) 'The International Merv Project; preliminary report on the fifth season (1996)', *Iran* 35: 1–33.

Higham, C.F.W. (1983) 'The Ban Chiang culture in wider perspective', *Proceedings of the British Academy* 69: 229–61.

—— (1988) 'Prehistoric metallurgy in Southeast Asia: some new information from the excavation of Ban Na Di', in R. Maddin (ed.), *The Beginning of the Use of Metals and Alloys*, Papers from the Second International Conference on the Beginning of the Use of Metals and Alloys, Zhengzhou, China 21–6 October 1986, Cambridge: The MIT Press, pp. 130–55.

—— and Kijngam, A. (eds) (1984) *Prehistoric Investigations in Northeast Thailand*, British Archaeological Reports, International Series 231, Oxford: British Archaeological Reports.

Hook, D.R., Arribas, Paulau, A., Craddock, P.T., Molina, A. and Rothenburg, B. (1987) 'Copper and silver in Bronze Age Spain', in W.H. Waldren and R.C. Kennard (eds), *Bell Beakers of the Western Mediterranean*, British Archaeological Reports, International Series 331 (ii), Oxford: British Archaeological Reports, pp. 147–72.

——, Freestone, I.C., Meeks, N.D., Craddock, P.T. and Morento Onorato, A. (1991) 'The early production of copper alloys in South-East Spain', in E. Pernicka and G.A. Wagner (eds), *Archaeometry '90*, Basel: Birkhauser Verlag, pp. 65–76.

Hoover, H.C. and Hoover, L.H. (trans.) (1912, 1950) *Agricola: De re Metallica*, New York: Dover Publications.

Horne, L. (1982) 'Fuel for the metalworker', *Expedition* 25, 1: 6–13.

Hsu Cho-yun (1978) 'Agricultural intensification and marketing agrarianism in the Han Dynasty', in D.T. Roy and T.H. Hsien (eds), *Ancient China: Studies in Early Civilization*, Hong Kong: Chinese University Press.

Hua Jue-ming, Liu, S.Z. and Yang, G. (1960) 'Preliminary report of a metallographic examination of some Warring States and Han iron objects', *Kaogu* 1: 73–87.

Huang Zhanye (1976) 'Some questions concerning the beginnings of iron smelting and the use of iron implements in China', *Wenwu* 8: 62–9 (in Chinese).

Hughes, M.J., Lang, J.R.S., Leese, M.N. and Curtis, J.E. (1988) 'The evidence of scientific analysis: a case study of the Nimrud Bowls', in J.E. Curtis (ed.), *Bronze-working Centres of Western Asia*, London: Kegan Paul, pp. 311–15.

——, Northover, J.P. and Staniaszek, B.E.P. (1982) 'Problems in the analysis of leaded bronze alloys in ancient artefacts', *Oxford Journal of Archaeology* 1, 3: 359–64.

Ilan, O. and Sebanne, M. (1989) 'Copper metallurgy, trade and the urbanization of southern Canaan in the Chalcolithic and Early Bronze Age', in P. de Miroschedji (ed.), *L'urbanisation de la Palestine à l'âge du Bronze ancien*, vol. 1, British Archaeological Reports International Series 527, Oxford: British Archaeological Reports, pp. 139–62.

Ixer, R.A. and Budd, P. (1998) 'The mineralogy of Bronze Age copper ores from the British Isles: implications for the compositions of early metalwork', *Oxford Journal of Archaeology* 17: 15–41.

Jackson, J.S. (1980) 'Bronze Age copper mining in counties Cork and Kerry, Ireland', in P.T. Craddock (ed.), *Scientific Studies in Early Mining and Extractive Metallurgy*, British Museum Occasional Paper 20, London: British Museum, pp. 9–30.

Jones, J.E. (1984) 'Ancient Athenian silver mines, dressing floors and smelting sites', *Journal of the Historical Metallurgy Society* 18: 65–81.

—— (1988) 'The Athenian silver mines of Laurion and BSA excavations at Agrileza', in J.E. Jones (ed.), *Aspects of Ancient Mining and Metallurgy*, Bangor: Department of Classics, University College of North Wales, pp. 11–22.

Joosten, I., Nie, M. van and Rijk, P. de (1997) 'Experiment with a slag-tapping furnace at the historical-archaeological experimental centre, Lejre', in L. Chr. Nørbach (ed.), *Early Iron Production – Archaeology, Technology and Experiments*, Proceedings of the Nordic Iron Seminar, Lejre, 22–28 July 1996, Technical Report no. 3, Leyre: Historical-Archaeological Experimental Centre, pp. 81–91.

Jovanović, B. (1971) 'Early copper metallurgy of the central Balkans', *Actes du VIIe Congrès Internationale des Sciences Prehistorique et Proto-historique*, 1971: 131–40.

—— (1979) 'The technology of primitive copper mining in south-east Europe', *Proceedings of the Prehistoric Society* 45: 103–10.

—— (1982) *Rudna Glava*, Muzej Rudarstva I Metalurgie, Bor/Beograd: Arheološki Institut.

—— (1988) 'Early metallurgy in Yugoslvia', in R. Maddin (ed.), *The Beginning of the Use of Metals and Alloys*, Papers from the Second International Conference on the Beginning of the Use of Metals and Alloys, Zhengzhou, China, 21–6 October 1986, Cambridge, Mass.: The MIT Press, pp. 69–79.

Junghans, S., Sangmeister, E. and Schröder, M. (1960) 'Metallanalysen Kupferzeitlicher und frühbronzezeitlicher Bodenfunde aus Europa', *Studien zu den Anfängen der Metallurgie*, vol. 1, Berlin: Mann.

——, —— and —— (1968) 'Kupfer und Bronze in der frühen Metallzeit Europas', *Studien zu den Anfängen der Metallurgie* vols 2.1–2.3, Berlin: Mann.

——, —— and —— (1974) 'Kupfer und Bronze in der frühen Metallzeit Europas', *Studien zu den Anfängen der Metallurgie*, vol. 2.4, Berlin: Mann.

Kappel, I. (1969) *Die Graphittonkeramik von Manching, Die Ausgrabungen in Manching 1955–1961*, Band 2, Römisch-germanische Kommision des Deutschen Archäologischen Instituts Zu Frankfurt, Wiesbaden: Steiner.

Keightley, D. (1976) 'Where have all the swords gone? Reflections on the unification of China', *Early China* 2: 31.

Killick, D. (1992) 'The relevance of recent African iron-smelting practice to reconstructions of prehistoric smelting technology', *MASCA Research Papers in Science and Technology* 8, 1: 8–20.

Knox, R. (1987) 'On distinguishing man-made from nickel-iron in ancient artefacts', *MASCA Journal* 4, 4: 178–84.

Lane, H.C. (1973) *Field Surveys and Excavations of a Romano-British Settlement at Scarcliffe Park, East Derbyshire*, Research Report no. 1, Derwent Archaeological Society.

—— (1986) *The Romans in Derbyshire*, 2, Bolsover, Derbyshire: Veritas.

Lang, J., Craddock, P.T. and Simpson, St J. (1998) 'New evidence for early crucible steel', *The Journal of the Historical Metallurgy Society* 32, 1: 7–14.

Lechtmann, H. (1971) 'Ancient methods of gilding silver: examples from the Old and New Worlds', in R.H. Brill (ed.), *Science and Archaeology*, Cambridge, Mass.: MIT Press, pp. 2–31.

—— (1973) 'The gilding of metals in pre-Columbian Peru', in W.J. Young (ed.), *Application of Science in the Examination of Works of Art*, Boston: Boston Museum of Fine Art, pp. 38–52.

—— (1976) 'A metallurgical site survey in the Peruvian Andes', *Journal of Field Archaeology* 3: 1–42.

Le Roy Ladurie, E., Barrandon, J.N., Collin, B., Guerra, M. and Morrison, C. (1990) 'Sur les traces de l'argent di Potosí', *Annales ESC*: 483–505.

Levy, T. (1995) 'Cult, metallurgy and ranked societies – Chalcolithic period (ca. 4500–3500 BC)', in T.E. Levy (ed.), *The Archaeology of Society in the Holy Land*, Leicester, Leicester University Press, pp. 226–44.

Lewis, P.R. and Jones, G.D.B. (1969) 'The Dolaucothi gold mines I', *The Antiquaries Journal* 49, 2: 244–72.

—— and —— (1970) 'Roman gold-mining in North-West Spain', *The Journal of Roman Studies* 60: 169–85.

Maddin, R. (ed.) (1988) *The Beginning of the Use of Metals and Alloys*, Papers from the Second International Conference on the Beginning of the Use of Metals and Alloys, Zhengzhou, China, 21–6 October 1986, Cambridge, Mass.: The MIT Press.

—— , Stech, T. and Muhly, J.D. (1991) 'Cayönü Tepesi', in C. Éluère and J.P. Mohen (eds), *Découverte du Métal*, Paris: Picard, pp. 375–86.

—— and Weng, Y.Q. (1984) 'The analysis of bronze "wire"', in C.F.W. Higham and A. Kijngam (eds), *Prehistoric Investigations in Northeast Thailand*, British Archaeological Reports, International Series 231, Oxford: British Archaeological Reports, pp. 112–16.

Marshall, P.D., O'Hara, S.L. and Ottaway, B.S. (1998) 'Early copper metallurgy in Austria and methods of assessing its impact on the environment', *Der Anschnitt*, Beiheft 9: Bochum: Deutsches Bergbau-Museum, pp. 239–49.

Maxwell-Hyslop, K.R. (1972) 'The metals *Amutu* and *Asi'u* in the Kültepe texts', *Anatolian Studies* 22: 159–62.

McDonnell, J.G. (1984) 'The study of early iron smithing residues', in B.G. Scott and H. Cleere (eds), *The Crafts of the Blacksmith*, Essays presented to R.F. Tylecote, in Proceedings of the 1984 Symposium of the UISPP Comité pour la Sidérurgie Ancienne, Belfast: UISPP Comité pour la Sidérurgie Ancienne and the Ulster Museum, pp. 47–52.

McGeehan-Liritzis, V. and Gale, N.H. (1988) 'Chemical and lead isotope analysis of Greek Late Neolithic and Early Bronze Age metals', *Archaeometry* 30, 2: 199–226.

McKerrell, H. and Tylecote, R.F. (1972) 'The working of copper-arsenic alloys in the Early Bronze Age and the effect on the determination of provenance', *Proceedings of the Prehistoric Society* 38: 209–18.

Meeks, N. and Tite, M.S. (1980) 'The analysis of platinum-group element inclusions in gold antiquities', *Journal of Archaeological Science* 7: 267–75.

Merkel, J.F. (1985) 'Ore beneficiation during the Late Bronze Age/Early Iron Age at Timna, Israel', *MASCA Journal* 3.5: 164–9.

—— (1990) 'Experimental reconstruction of Bronze Age copper smelting based on archaeological evidence from Timna', in B. Rothenberg (ed.), *The Ancient Metallurgy of Copper*, London: IAMS.

Merpert, N., Munchaev, R.M. and Bader, N.O. (1977) 'The earliest metallurgy of Mesopotamia', *Sovtskaya Arkheologiya* 3, 154–65.

Mighall, T. (1990) 'Copa Hill, Cwmystwyth: preliminary palaeoecological observations', in P. Crewe and S. Crewe (eds), *Early Mining in the British Isles*, Maentwrog: Plas tan y Bwlch Snowdonia Study Centre, pp. 65–8.

—— , Blackford, J.J. and Chambers, F.M. (1990) 'Bryn y Castell – Late Bronze Age clearances or climatic change', *Archaeology in Wales* 30: 14–16.

—— and Chambers, F. (1989) 'The environmental impact of iron-working at Bryn y Castell hillfort, Merioneth', *Archaeology in Wales* 29: 17–21.

—— and —— (1997) 'Early iron-working and its impact on the environment: palaeoecological evidence from Bryn y Castell hillfort, Snowdonia, North Wales', *Proceedings of the Prehistoric Society* 63: 199–220.

Miller, D.E. and van der Merwe, N.J. (1994) 'Early metal-working in sub-Saharan Africa', *Journal of African History* 35: 1–36.

Moorey, P.R.S. (1988) 'Early metallurgy in Mesopotamia', in R. Maddin (ed.), *The Beginning of the Use of Metals and Alloys*, Papers of the Second International

Conference on the Beginning of the Use of Metals and Alloys, Zhengzhou, China, 21–6 October 1986, Cambridge, Mass.: The MIT Press, pp. 28–33.

—— (1994) *Ancient Mesopotamian Materials and Industries. The Archaeological Evidence*, Oxford: Clarendon Press.

Muhly, J.D. (1983) 'Kupfer B. Archaölogisch', *Reallexikon der Assyriologie und Vorderasiatischen Archäologie* 6, Berlin: de Gruyter, 348–64.

—— (1988) 'The beginnings of metallurgy in the Old World', in R. Maddin (ed.), *The Beginning of the Use of Metals and Alloys*, Papers from the Second International Conference on the Beginning of the Use of Metals and Alloys, Zhengzhou, China, 21–6 October 1986, Cambridge, Mass.: The MIT Press, pp. 2–20.

—— (1993) 'Early Bronze Age tin and the Taurus', *American Journal of Archaeology* 97: 239–53.

——, Begemann, F., Öztunali, Ö., Pernicka, E., Schmitt-Strecker, S. and Wagner, G.A. (1991) 'The bronze metallurgy of Anatolia and the question of local tin sources', in E. Pernicka and G. Wagner (eds), *Archaeometry '90*, Basel: Springer Verlag.

Needham, J. (1980) 'The evolution of iron and steel technology in East and Southeast Asia', in Wertime and Muhly (eds), *The Coming of the Iron Age*, New Haven: Yale University Press.

Needham, S. (1990) *The Petters Lane Bronze Age Metalwork: An Analytical Study of Thames Valley Metalworking in its Settlement Context*, British Museum Occasional Paper 70, London: British Museum Publications.

—— (1996) 'Chronology and periodisation in the British Bronze Age' in K. Randsborg (ed.), 'Absolute chronology: archaeological Europe', *Acta Archaeologica* 67: 121–40.

——, Bronk Ramsey, C., Combs, D., Cartwright, C. and Pettitt, P. (1989) 'An independent chronology for British Bronze Age metalwork: the results of the Oxford Radiocarbon Accelerator programme', *Archaeological Journal* 154: 55–107.

Needham, S., Leese, M.N., Hook, D.R. and Hughes, M.J. (1989) 'Developments of the Early Bronze Age metallurgy of southern Britain', *World Archaeology* 20, 3: 383–402.

Neuninger, H., Pittinoni, R. and Siegl, W. (1964) 'Frühkeramikzeitliche Kupfergewinnung in Anatolien', *Archaeologia Austriaca* 35: 98–110.

Northover, J.P. (1980) 'The analysis of Welsh Bronze Age metalwork' in H.N. Savory (ed.), *Guide Catalogue to the Bronze Age Collections*, Cardiff: National Museum of Wales, pp. 229–43.

—— (1982a) 'The exploration of long-distance movement of bronze in Bronze and Early Iron Age Europe', *Bulletin of the Institute of Archaeology* 19: 45–72.

—— (1982b) ' The metallurgy of the Wilburton hoards', *Oxford Journal of Archaeology* 1, 1: 69–109.

—— (1988a) 'The analysis and metallurgy of British Bronze Age Swords', in I.A. Coloquoun and C.B. Burgess (eds), *The Swords of Britain*, Munich, Prähistorische Bronzefunde, IV, 5, pp. 130–46.

—— (1988b) 'The Late Bronze Age metalwork: general discussion', in B. Cunliffe (ed.), *Mount Batten, Plymouth: A Prehistoric and Roman Port*, Oxford University Committee on Archaeology Monograph no. 26, Oxford: Oxbow Books, pp. 75–85.

—— (1989) 'Properties and use of copper-arsenic alloys', in A. Hauptmann, E. Pernicka and G.A. Wagner (eds), *Proceedings of the International Symposium on Old World Archaeometallurgy* 1987, Bochum: Deutsches Bergbau-Museum.

—— (1998) 'Exotic alloys in antiquity', in T. Rehren, A. Hauptmann and J.D. Muhly (eds), *Metallurgica Antiqua In Honour of Hans-Gert Bachmann and Robert Maddin, Der Anschnitt,* Beiheft 8, Bochum: Deutsches Bergbau-Museum, pp. 113–21.

—— and Craddock, P.T. (1990) 'Smelting practices', in S. Needham (ed.), *The Petters Lane Bronze Age Metalwork: An Analytical Study of Thames Valley Metalworking in its Settlement Context*, British Museum Occasional Paper 70, London: British Museum Publications, pp. 99–103.

O'Brian, W.F. (1990) 'Prehistoric copper mining in southwest Ireland', *Proceedings of the Prehistoric Society* 56: 269–90.

—— (1994) *Mount Gabriel: A Bronze Age Copper Mine in South West Ireland*, Galway: University of Galway Press.

——, Ixer, R. and O'Sullivan, M. (1990) 'Copper resources in prehistory: an Irish perspective', in P. Crew and S. Crew (eds), *Early Mining in the British Isles*, Maentwrog: Plas tan y Bwlch Snowdonia Study Centre, pp. 30–6.

O'Connor, B. (1980) *Cross-channel Relations in the Later Bronze Age*, British Archaeological Reports, International Series 91, Oxford: British Archaeological Reports.

Oddy, A. (1986) 'The touchstone: the oldest colorimetric method of analysis' *Endeavour* 10, 4: 164–6.

—— (1993) 'The assaying of gold by touchstone in antiquity and the medieval world', in C. Éluère (ed.) *Outils et Ateliers d'orfèvres des Temps Anciens*, Soc. des Amis du Musée des Antiquities Nationales, Paris.

Ogden, J.M. (1977) 'Platinum group metal inclusions in ancient gold artefacts', *Journal of the Historical Metallurgy Society* 11, 2: 53–72.

Oldfather, C.H. (trans.) (1933) *Diodorus Siculus: Works,* Loeb Classical Library, London: Heinemann.

Olin, J.S. and Franklin, AD (eds) (1982) *Archaeological Ceramics*, Washington, DC: Smithsonian Institution.

Ottaway, B.S. (1978) 'Aspects of the earliest copper metallurgy in the northern sub-alpine area in its cultural setting', unpublished PhD thesis, University of Edinburgh.

Palmer, R.E. (1926/7) 'Notes on some ancient mine equipment and systems', *Transactions of the Institution of Mining and Metallurgy* 36: 299–336.

Patterson, C.C. (1971) 'Native copper, silver and gold accessible to early metallurgists', *American Antiquity* 36: 286–321.

Perlès, C. (1992) 'Systems of exchange and organisation of production in Neolithic Greece', *Journal of Mediterranean Archaeology* 5: 115–64.

Pernicka, E. (1993) 'Evaluating lead isotope data: further observations – comments III', *Archaeometry* 35, 2: 259–62.

—— and Bachmann, H.-G. (1983) 'Archäometallurgische Untersuchungen zur antiken Silbergewinnung', in *Laurion III, Erzmetall* 36, 12: 592–7.

——, Begemann, S., Schmitt-Strecker, S. and Grimanis, A.P. (1990) 'On the composition and provenance of metal artefacts from Poliochni on Lemnos', *Oxford Journal of Archaeology* 9, 3: 263–98.

——, ——, —— and Wagner, G.A. (1993) Eneolithic and Early Bronze Age copper artefacts from the Balkans and their relation to Serbian copper ores', *Prähistorische Zeitschrift* 63, 1: 1–54.

Phillips, P. (1980) *The Prehistory of Europe*, London: Allen Lane.

Piaskowski, J. (1982) 'A study of the origin of the ancient high-nickel iron generally regarded as meteoric' in T.A. Wertime and S.F. Wertime (eds), *Early Pyrotechnology*, Washington, DC: Smithsonian Institution Press, pp. 237–44.

Piel, M., Hauptmann, A. and Shröder, B. (1992) 'Naturwissenschaftliche Untersuchungen an bronzezeitlichen Kupferverhüttingschlacken von Acqua Fredda/Trentino', *Universitätsforschungen zur Prähistorischen Archäologie* (Universität Innsbruck) 8: 463–72.

Pigott, V.C. (1982) 'The innovation of iron. Cultural dynamics in technological change', *Expedition* 25 (1): 20–5.

—— (1985) 'Pre-industrial mineral exploitation and metal production in Thailand', *MASCA Journal* 3, 5: 170–4.

—— and Natapintu, S. (1988a) 'Archaeological investigations into prehistoric copper production: the Thailand archaeometallurgy project, 1984–86', *The Beginning of the Use of Metals and Alloys*, Papers from the Second International Conference on the Beginning of the Use of Metals and Alloys, Zhengzhou, China, 21–6 October 1986, Cambridge, Mass.: The MIT Press, pp. 156–62.

—— and —— (1988b) 'Investigating the origins of metal use in Prehistoric Thailand', in N. Barnard (ed.), *Proceedings on Ancient Chinese and Southeast Asian Bronze Age Cultures*, Canberra: Australian National University.

——, —— and Theeiparivatra, U. (1992) 'Research in the development of prehistoric metal use in Northeast Thailand' in I. Glover,P. Suchitta and J. Villiers (ds) *Early Metallurgy, Trade and Urban Centres in Thailand*

and Southeast Asia, Bangkok: White Lotus, pp. 47–62.

Pittioni, R. (1948) 'Recent researches on ancient copper mining in Austria', *Man* 48: 120.

—— (1951) 'Prehistoric copper mining in Austria: problems and facts', *Institute of Archaeology*, Seventh Annual Report: 16–43.

—— (1957) 'Urzeitlicher Bergbau auf Kupfererz und Spuranalyse', *Archaeologica Austriaca* 24: 67–95.

Pollard, A.M. and Heron, C. (1996) *Archaeological Chemistry*, London: Royal Society of Chemistry.

——, Thomas, R.G. and Williams, P.A. (1991) 'Some experiments concerning the smelting of arsenical copper', in P. Budd, B. Chapman, C. Jackson, R. Janaway and B. Ottaway (eds), *Archaeological Sciences 1989, Proceedings of a conference on the application of scientific techniques to archaeology, Bradford, September 1989*, Oxford: Oxbow Books, pp. 169–74.

Prestvold, K. (1996) 'Iron production and society. Power, ideology and social structure in Inntrøndelag during the Early Iron Age: stability and change', *Norwegian Archaeological Review* 29, 1: 41–6.

Pyatt, B.F., Barker, G.W., Birch, P., Gilbertson D.D., Grattan, J.P. and Mattingley, D.J. (1999) 'King Solomon's miners – starvation and bioaccumulation? An environmental archaeological investigation in Southern Jordan', *Ecotoxicology and Environmental Safety* 43: 305–8.

—— and Birch, P. (1994) 'Atmospheric erosion of metalliferous spoil tips: Some localised effects', *Polish Journal of Environmental Studies* 4, 3: 51–3.

Rackham, H. (1952) (trans.) *Pliny: The Natural History* IX, Loeb Classical Library, London: Heinemann.

Rajpitak, W. and Seeley, N.J. (1984) 'The bronze metallurgy', in C.F.W. Higham and A. Kijngam (eds), *Prehistoric Investigations in Northeast Thailand*, British Archaeological Reports, International Series 231, Oxford: British Archaeological Reports, pp. 102–12.

Raleigh, Sir W. (ed. R.H. Schomburgh) (1848) *The Discoveries of the Large, Rich and Beautiful Empire of Guiana*, Hakluyt Society (London) Series I, 3.

Ramage, A. (1970) 'Pactolus North', *Bulletin of the American Schools of Oriental Research* 199: 16–28.

Rawson, J. (1988) 'A bronze-casting revolution in the western Zhou and its impact on provincial industries', in R. Maddin (ed.), *The Beginning of the Use of Metals and Alloys*, Papers from the Second International Conference on the Beginning of the Use of Metals and Alloys, Zhengzhou, China, 21–6 October 1986, Cambridge, Mass.: The MIT Press, pp. 228–38.

Ray, P. (1956) *History of Chemistry in Ancient and Medieval India*, Culcutta: Indian Chemical Society.

Reedy, T.J. and Reedy, C.L. (1992) 'Evaluating lead isotope data: comments on E.V. Sayre, K.A. Yener, E.C. Joel and I.L. Barnes "Statistical evaluation of the presently accumulated lead isotope data from Anatolia and surrounding regions"', *Archaeometry* 34, 1: 73–105.

Rehder, J.E. (1994) 'Blowpipes versus bellows in ancient

metallurgy', *Journal of Field Metallurgy* 21: 345–50.

Rehren, T. (1997) 'Tiegelmetallurgie – Tiegelprozesse und ihre Stellung in der Archäeometallurgie', unpublished abilitation manuscript, Facultät der Werkstoffwissenschaft und Werkstofftechnologie der TU Bergakademie Freiburg.

——, Lietz, E., Hauptmann, A. and Deutmann, K.H. (1993) 'Schlacken und Tiegel aus dem Alderturm in Dortmund', in H. Steuer and U. Zimmermann (eds), *Montanarchäologie in Europa*, Sigmaringen: Jan Thorbecke Verlag, pp. 303–20.

Renfrew, C. (1978) 'The anatomy of innovation', in D. Green, C. Haselgrove and M. Spriggs (eds), *Social Organisation and Settlement: Contributions from Anthropology, Archaeology and Geography*, British Archaeological Reports, International Series 47, Part I, Oxford: British Archaeological Reports, pp. 89–117.

Roden, C. (1988) 'Blasrohrdüsen', *Der Anschnitt* 40, 3: 62–82.

Rohl, B. and Needham, S. (1998) *The Circulation of Metal in the British Bronze Age: the application of lead isotope analysis*, British Museum Occasional Paper, no. 102, London: The British Museum.

Rollefson, G., Simmons, A., Donaldson, M., Gillespie, W., Kafafi, Z., Köhler-Rollefson, I., Mcadam, E. and Rolstau, E. (1985) 'Excavation at the pre-pottery Neolithic B village at Ain Ghazal, Jordan', *Mitteilungen der Deutschen Orient-Gesellschaft* 117: 69–116.

Rosenqvist, T. (1983) *Principles of Extractive Metallurgy*, 2nd edn, New York: McGraw-Hill

Rostoker, W., Pigott, V.C. and Dvorak, J.R. (1989) 'Direct reduction to copper metal by oxide-sulfide mineral interaction', *Archaeomaterials* 3, 1: 69–87.

Rothenberg, B. (1972) *Timna*, London: Thames and Hudson.

—— (1988) *The Egyptian Mining Temple at Timna*, London: IAMS.

—— (ed.) (1990) *The Ancient Metallurgy of Copper*, London: IAMS.

—— (1990a) 'Copper smelting furnaces, tuyères, slags, ingot-moulds and ingots in the Arabah: the archaeological data', in R. Rothenburg (ed.), *The Ancient Metallurgy of Copper*, London: IAMS, pp. 1–74.

—— and Merkel, J. (1995), 'Late Neolithic copper smelting in the Arabah', *Institute of Archaeo-Metallurgical Studies Newsletter* 19: 1–7.

—— and —— (1998) 'Chalcolithic, 5th millennium BC, copper smelting at Timna', *Institute of Archaeo-Metallurgical Studies Newsletter* 20: 1–3.

—— and Shaw, C.T. (1990) 'The discovery of a copper mine and smelter from the end of the Early Bronze Age (EB IV) in the Timna valley', *Institute of Archaeo-Metallurgical Studies Newsletter* 15/16: 1–8.

Rowlands, M.J. (1976) *The Production and Distribution of Metalwork in the Middle Bronze Age in Southern Britain*, British Archaeological Reports no. 31, Oxford: British Archaeological Reports.

Rychner, V. (1981) 'Le cuivre et les alliages du Bronze Final en Suisse Occidentale', *Musée Neuchatelois* 3: 97–124.

—— and J. Kläntschi (1995) *Arsenic, Nickel et Antimoine: une approchée de la métallurgie du Bronze Moyen et Final en Suisse par l'analyse spectrométrique*, Lausanne: Cahiers d'Archéologie Romande, 63.

Salter, C. and Ehrenreich, R.M. (1984) 'Iron Age iron metallurgy in central southern Britain', in B. Cunliffe and D. Miles (eds), *Wessex and the Thames Valley in the Iron Age*, Oxford University Committee for Archaeology Monograph 2, Oxford.

Sayre, E.V., Yener, K.A., Joel, E.C. and Barnes, I.L. (1992) 'Statistical evaluation of the presently accumulated lead isotope data from Anatolia and surrounding regions', *Archaeometry* 34: 73–105.

Scheel, B. (1989) *Egyptian Metalworking and Tools*, Aylesbury: Shire Egyptology.

Schubert, H.R. (1957) *History of the British Iron and Steel Industry from c. 450 BC to AD 1775*, London: Routledge and Kegan Paul.

Scott, B.G. (1976) 'The occurrence of platinum as a trace element in Irish gold: comments on Hartmann's gold analyses', *Irish Archaeological Research Forum* III, 2: 21–4.

Shalev, S. (1991) Two different copper industries in the Chalcolithic cultures of Israel', in C. Éluère and J.P. Mohen (eds), *Découverte du Métal*, Paris: Picard, pp. 413–25.

—— and Northover, J.P. (1987) 'Chalcolithic metal and metalworking from Shiqmin', in T. Levy (ed.), *Shiqmin I: Studies concerning Chalcolithic Societies in the Northern Negev Desert, Israel (1982–4)*, British Archaeological Reports, International Series 356, Oxford: British Archaeological Reports, pp. 357–71.

Shepard, R. (1993) *Ancient Mining*, London: Institute of Mining and Metallurgy.

Sieveking, G. de G. (1979) 'Grimes Graves and prehistoric European flint mining', in H. Crawford (ed.), *Subterranean Britain*, London: John Baker, pp. 1–43.

Sim, D. (1998) *Beyond the Bloom. Bloom refining and iron artifact production in the Roman world*, British Archaeological Reports, International Series 725, Oxford: Archaeopress.

Sisco, A.G. and Smith, C.S. (1951) (trans.) *Lazarus Ercker: Treatise on Ores and Assaying*, Chicago: University of Chicago Press.

Slater, E.A. and Charles, J.A. (1970) 'Archaeological classification of metal analysis', *Antiquity* 44: 207–13.

Smith, C.S. (1971) *A Search for Structure. Selected Essays on Science, Art and History*, Cambridge, Mass.: The MIT Press.

—— and Gnudi, M.T. (eds) (1942) *The Pirotechnica of Vannoccio Biringuccio*, Chicago: Basic Books.

Smith, W.D.F. (1989) *The Great Orme Copper Mines*, Llandudno: Creuddyn Publications.

Snodgrass, A.M. (1980) 'Iron and early metallurgy in the Mediterranean', in T.A. Wertime and J.D. Muhly (eds), *The Coming of the Age of Iron*, New Haven, Connecticut: Yale University Press, pp. 335–74.

Solecki, R.S. (1969) 'A copper mineral pendant from northern Iraq', *Antiquity* 43: 311–14.

Sperl, G. (1990) 'Zur Urgeschichte des Bleies', *Zeitschrift fur Metallkunde* 81, 11: 799–801.

Spooner, F.C. (1972) *The International Economy and Monetary Movements in France, 1493–1725*, Cambridge, Mass.: MIT Press.

Stech, T. and Maddin, R. (1988) 'Reflections on early metallurgy in Southeast Asia', in R. Maddin (ed.), pp. 163–74.

—— and Pigott, V. (1986) 'The metals trade in Southwest Asia in the third millennium B.C.', *Iraq* 48: 39–64.

Steuer, H. and Zimmermann, U. (eds) (1993) *Montanarchäologie in Europa*, Sigmaringen: Jan Thorbecke Verlag.

Stos-Gale, Z. (1989) 'Lead isotope studies of metals and the metal trade in the Bronze Age Mediterranean', in J. Henderson (ed.), *Scientific Analysis in Archaeology and its interpretation*, Oxford University Committee for Archaeology, Monograph no. 19 and UCLA Institute of Archaeology, Archaeological Research Tools 5, Oxford: Oxbow Books, pp. 274–301.

Taylor, J.J. (1970) 'Lunulae reconsidered', *Proceedings of the Prehistoric Society* 36: 38–81.

—— (1979) *Bronze Age Goldwork of the British Isles*, Cambridge: Cambridge University Press.

Taylor, S.J. and Shell, C.A. (1988) 'Social and historical implications of early Chinese iron technology', in R. Maddin (ed.), *The Beginning of the Use of Metals and Alloys*, Papers from the Second International Conference on the Beginning of the Use of Metals and Alloys, Zhengzhou, China, 21–6 October 1986, Cambridge, Mass.: The MIT Press, pp. 205–21.

Thorpe, R. (1980–1981) 'The Chinese Bronze Age from a Marxist perspective', *Early China* 6: 97–102.

Timberlake, S. and Mighall, T. (1992) 'Historic and prehistoric mining on Copa Hill, Cwmystwyth', *Archaeology in Wales* 32: 38–44.

Tite, M.S., Hughes, M.J., Freestone I.C., Meeks, N.D. and Bimson, M. (1990) 'Technological characterisation of refractory ceramics from Timna', in B. Rothenburg (ed.), *The Ancient Metallurgy of Copper*, London: IAMS, pp. 158–75.

Trousedale, W. (1975) *The Long Sword and Scabbard Slide in Asia,* Smithsonian Contributions to Anthropology 17, Washington, DC: Smithsonian Institution.

Tylecote, R.F. (1970) 'Early metallurgy in the Near East', *Metals and Materials* 4: 285–93.

—— (1974) 'Can copper be smelted in a crucible?', *Journal of the Historical Metallurgy Society* 8: 54–83.

—— (1976) *A History of Metallurgy*, London: The Metals Society.

—— (1982) 'Metallurgical crucibles and crucible slags', in J.S. Olin and A.D. Franklin (eds), *Archaeological Ceramics*, Washington, DC: Smithsonian Institution, pp. 231–42.

—— (1986) *The Prehistory of Metallurgy in the British Isles*, London: Institute of Metals.

—— (1987) *The Early History of Metallurgy in Europe*, London: Longman.

—— (1992) *A History of Metallurgy*, 2nd edn, London: The Institute of Materials.

—— and Boydell, P.J. (1978) 'Experiments on copper smelting', in B. Rothenburg (ed.), *Chalcolithic Copper Smelting*, London: IAMS, pp. 27–49.

—— and Clough, R.E. (1983) 'Recent bog iron ore analyses and the smelting of pyrite nodules', *Offa* 40: 115–18.

——, Ghaznavi, H.A. and Boydell, P.J. (1977) 'Partitioning of trace elements between ores, fluxes, slags and metal during the smelting of copper', *Journal of Archaeological Science* 4, 4: 305–33.

—— and Gilmour, B.J.J. (1986) *The Metallography of Early Ferrous Edge Tools and Edged Weapons*, BAR British Series 155, Oxford: BAR.

van der Merwe, N.J. and Avery, D.H. (1988) 'Science and magic in African technology', in R. Maddin (ed.), *The Beginning of the Use of Metals and Alloys*, Papers from the Second International Conference on the Beginning of the Use of Metals and Alloys, Zhengzhou, China, 21–6 October 1986, Cambridge, Mass.: The MIT Press, pp. 245–60.

Vandiver, P.B., Kaylor, R., Feathers, J., Gottfried, M., Yener, K.A., Hornyak, W.F. and Franklin, A. (1993) 'Thermoluminescence dating of a crucible fragment from an early tin processing site in Turkey', *Archaeometry* 35, 2: 295–8.

Wagner, D.B. (1989) *Toward the Reconstruction of Ancient Chinese Techniques for the Production of Malleable Cast Iron*, East Asian Occasional Papers 4, Copenhagen: University of Copenhagen.

—— (1993) *Iron and Steel in Ancient China*, Leiden: Brill.

Waldbaum, J.C. (1980) 'The first archaeological appearance of iron and the transition to the Iron Age', in T.A. Wertime and J.D. Muhly (eds), *The Coming of the Age of Iron*, New Haven, Connecticut: Yale University Press, pp. 69–98.

Wallace, A.F.C. (1972) 'Paradigmatic Processes in Culture Change', *American Anthropologist* 74, 3: 467–78.

Walsh, R. (1929) 'Galen visits the Dead Sea and the copper mines of Cyprus (166 AD)' *Bulletin of the Geographical Society of Philadelphia* 25: 92–110.

Wang, Z.S (1982) *Han Civilisation* (trans. K.C. Chang and collaborators), New Haven, Connecticut: Yale University Press.

Weisgerber, G. (1979) ' Das römische Wasserheberad aus Rio Tinto in Spanien im British Museum, London', *Der Anschnitt* 31, 2–3: 62–80.

—— (1992) 'Der Kupfermann', in *Amerika 1492–1992 Neue Welten – Neue Wirklichkeiten*, Braunschweig, pp. 159–67.

Wheeler, T.S. and Maddin, R. (1976) 'The techniques of the early Thai metalsmiths', *Expedition* 18: 38–47.

White, J.C. (1982) *Ban Chiang: Discovery of a Lost Bronze Age*, Philadelphia: University of Pennsylvania Press.

—— (1986) 'A Revision of the Chronology of Ban Chiang and its implications for the Prehistory of Northeast Thailand', PhD dissertation, University of Pennsylvania.

—— (1988) 'Early East Asian metallurgy: the southern tradition', in R. Maddin (ed.), *Prehistoric Investigations in Northeast Thailand*, British Archaeological Reports, International Series 231, Oxford: British Archaeological Reports, pp. 175–81.

—— (1995) 'Incorporating heterarchy into theory on sociopolitical development: the case from Southeast Asia', in R.M. Ehrenreich, C.M. Crumley and J.E. Levy (eds), *Heterarchy and the Analysis of Complex Societies*, Arlington, Virginia: The American Anthropological Association.

White, J.C. and Pigott, V.C. (1996) 'From community craft to regional specialization: intensification of copper production in pre-state Thailand', in B. Wailes (ed.), *Craft Specialization and Social Evolution: in memory of V. Gordon Childe*, Philadelphia: University of Penn-sylvania, pp. 152–75.

——, Vernon, W., Fleming, S., Glanzman, W., Hancock, R. and Pelcin, A. (1991) 'Preliminary cultural implications from initial studies of the ceramic technology at Ban Chiang', in Indo-Pacific Prehistory 1990, Proceedings of the 14th Congress of the Indo-Pacific Prehistory Association, Yogyakarta, Indonesia, vol. 2, *Bulletin of the Indo-Pacific Prehistory Association* 11: 188–203.

Willies, L. (1993) 'Appendix: Early Bronze Age tin working at Kestel', in K.A. Yenere and P.B. Vandiver, 'Reply to J.D. Muhly, "Early Bronze Age Tin and the Taurus"', *American Journal of Archaeology* 97: 255–64.

—— and Cranstone, D. (eds) (1992) *Boles and Smeltmills*, London: Historical Metallurgy Society.

Wilson, T. (1987) *Ceramic Art of the Renaissance*, London: British Museum Publications.

Wyckoff D. (trans.) (1967) *Albertus Magnus: Book of Minerals*, Oxford: Clarendon Press

Yener, K.A. and Vandiver, P.B. (1993) 'Tin processing at Göltepe, an Early Bronze Age site in Anatolia', *American Journal of Archaeology* 97: 207–38.

Zwicker, U. (1989) 'Untersuchungen zur Herstellung von Kupfer und Kupferlegierungen im Bereich des östlichen Mittelmeeres', in A. Hauptmann, E. Pernicka and G.A Wagner (eds), Proceedings of the International Symposium, *Old World Archaeometallurgy*, Heidelberg 1987, Der Anschnitt, Beiheft 7, Bochum: Deutsches Bergbau-Museum, pp. 191–202.

6

STONE

6.1 Introduction

The scientific study of archaeological 'stone' includes obsidian, chert, flint, marble, turquoise, jade and so on. Each rock type can be identified and classified according to its mineralogy, structure, texture and, when present, its fossil content. This may allow the pressures, temperatures and other environmental conditions in which it was formed to be deduced. The nature of minerals and their development is discussed in the section on ceramic raw materials (see Sections 4.2 and 4.2.3), so will not be repeated here.

6.2 Flint and chert

Flint is basically a silica-rich (siliceous) material. Silica is often also the chief component of glass, but instead of being entirely *amorphous* like glass, flint and chert are composed of masses of minute interlocking quartz crystals and fibres with water-filled micropores between them (i.e. it is cryptocrystalline like chalcedony and chert). Flint can also contain amorphous silica called *opal*. Chert is characterised by a splintery fracture and flint by a marked conchoidal fracture, the latter giving millions of man-made flint artefacts their characteristic appearance. Sometimes the quartz crystals can be replaced by other substances; flint also contains microfossils. It is probably formed as part of a post-depositional process in carbonate sediments in which silica is redistributed. Chalk is composed of fossilised skele-

tons of millions of minute marine organisms. Some non-carbonate minerals are also preserved in the flint. The chemical composition of the flint is therefore partly a reflection of its formational mechanism, partly the chemical composition of its host sediment and also partly the extent to which the formational mechanism has 'gone to completion'. Flint and chert occur in a variety of forms. In Britain chert occurs most often in tabular masses and flint in nodules, though at Grimes Graves in Norfolk tabular masses of flint were worked as well as some nodular wallstone. Flint and chert cannot be distinguished by their crystallinity.

6.2.1 *Flint and chert mining*

One of the better known sources of flint in Europe is the Neolithic site of Grimes Graves in Norfolk which is thought to have been used for a short period around 2000 BC. This mine is in a well-drained heathland environment in eastern England which is rich in chalk and in the Cretaceous was a flat sea bed. The only visible clue on the disturbed ground surface for the existence of subterranean flint mines is a series of shallow depressions. These depressions are where the vertical shafts have been backfilled with material and a certain amount of subsidence has occurred. There were between 350 and 500 shafts so the activities were on a massive scale. However, this scale of activity was not, by any means, especially unusual with at least 250 mine shafts at Easton Down and Martin's Clump in Hampshire. The mining of flint would have been like mining many other materials that occur in horizontal seams, either rock or mineral. At Grimes Graves a series of vertical conical shafts of 10–15 m have been dug through the surface frost-shattered flint down into better quality unaltered flint.

In following the beds of flint, miners dug horizontal galleries from the vertical shaft of between 3–7 m in length. In some environments the flint could be broken away from the walls by heating it up by lighting fires next to the walls of the galleries. Once the flint was hot, cold water would have been thrown onto it, causing it to crack. Some evidence of fire has been found at the foot of the shafts at Grimes Graves which may have been used to break up large masses of

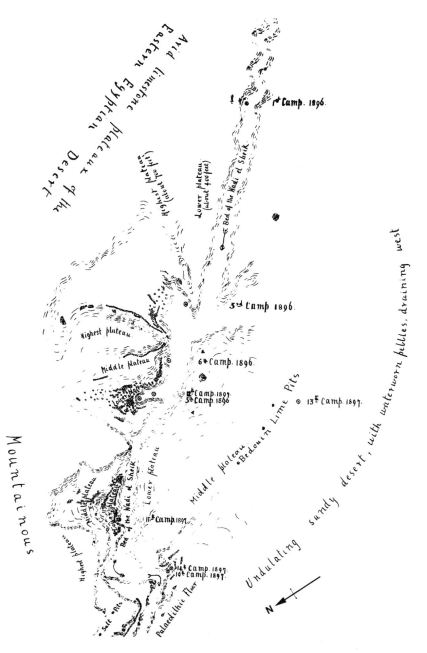

Figure 6.1 The nineteenth-century map of chert mines at Wadi el Sheikh, Egypt.

extracted flint. However, the softness of the chalk and the brittleness of the flint at Grimes Graves suggests that fire would not necessarily have been used as a means of breaking up the flint in the galleries. Once broken into suitably sized chunks the flint would have been loaded into baskets and hauled up ladders resting on the sides of the shafts to the surface. The large chunks would later have been broken down into suitably sized *nodules* for working into implements. It is clear from archaeological investigations in flint mines that Neolithic man was only interested in a small proportion of the many layers of flint through which the shafts were sunk.

Although Grimes Graves has been researched in some detail, the level of production based on the number of filled-in mine shafts detected is dwarfed by the site of Rijkholt-St Geertruid in the Netherlands which dates to *c.* 3000 BC. Here some 5,000 mining shafts have been found. On the assumption that *all* the mines were used for 500 years and *continuously* (both rather big assumptions) the excavator, P.W. Bosch calculated that some 150 million Neolithic flint axes would have been produced.

In the case of the chert mine at Wadi el-Sheikh some 160 km south of Cairo in Egypt, the complexity of how the working deposits accumulated over time was considered (see Figure 6.1; Weisgerber 1987). Here both open and underground quarrying techniques were used with a primary phase in the New Kingdom, and with some evidence of older workings. Some of the tool marks found in the mines have different characteristics from those found in European mines: they appear to have been made with metal tools. It is suggested that this strengthens the interpretation that there were both stone- and metal-using phases of mining. The mining activity produced large dumps of debris of up to 3 m in height – which is likely to have been the original appearance of other ancient quarries such as Grimes Graves in England, Rijkholt-St Geertruid in the Netherlands or Spiennes in Belgium. The preservation at Wadi el-Sheikh is so good in the desert environment that 'it is as if they have only recently been abandoned' (Weisgerber 1987: 168). Interestingly, stone grooved hammers similar to those found in European prehistoric copper mines were found in the mining debris, but the groove was close to the end rather than in the middle, as in European examples. Chert picks were also found.

6.3 Sourcing stone

Some archaeologists rely on a visual identification of stone but the results which include their perception of colour can not only be arcane but also difficult to communicate. A chert type, for example, is obviously formed as a result of a natural process and although a degree of visual homogeneity may result, this is not guaranteed. Chert is a siliceous material deposited or formed by secondary solution and re-deposition over a restricted period of time in a restricted geographical area. One way through the minefield of subjective perception of colour is to use colour charts. But colour is only one attribute of stone and often an unreliable source indicator. A more comprehensive characterisation of stone is usually required. For example, Luedtke (1978) has found that if chert types were formed close in time and space they tended to have similar proportions of trace elements, as determined by neutron activation analysis; by using discriminant analysis she was able to distinguish between cherts with different sources in the North American mid-west.

As with other work which attempts to source rocks in order to build up exploitation and distribution patterns during different periods of prehistory and history, it is important to properly sample geological sources so as to include the full range of physical variation for the chert type. By doing this the aim is to determine the full range of compositional variation of the source before archaeological samples are investigated scientifically. Although of course it is still possible to chemically analyse archaeological artefacts made out of rock in an attempt to identify different compositional groupings, for rocks like cherts only the degree of compositional variation within and around a source may provide the evidence necessary to begin to identify the source's chemical signature. Chemical variations can exist within formations and this is why it is so important to sample sources such as quarries adequately. Once adequately characterised, it becomes possible to show, through the analysis of artefacts, how quarries were used over time.

A recent example of this is where scientific analysis has accompanied one of the most comprehensive investigations of a stone quarry, on a large scale. This has been the Roman quarry at Mons Claudianus in the Eastern Desert of Egypt (Peacock and Maxfield 1997). Here survey and excavation of the quarries as well as adjacent buildings, settlements and fort has placed the quarrying activities in a solid regional and environmental context. Chemical and petrological analysis of the grey plutonic rocks has been very successful and has produced a means of sourcing the rock and therefore distinguishing it from similar rocks in other regions.

However, a comprehensive study of chert and chalcedony use and distribution in Belize has made a contribution which illustrates both the potential and the limitations of using an appropriate trace analytical technique to study geological reference groups and associated artefacts made from it (Cackler et al. 1999). As with flint, the colour of the chert did not have a particularly significant role to play in its characterisation (Cackler et al. 1999: 394). In this case, variations in chert colour were found to be due to weathering. By investigating statistically the geological samples, the only distinction that could be identified analytically was a distinction between northern Belize chert, Crooked Tree chalcedony (which was lower in most trace elements than chert) and an unidentified material from Kichpanha. Hudler et al. (1996) were however able to distinguish between chert quarries at Colha in Belize due to micro-variation in its composition, but this would have a restricted applicabilty to the sourcing of archaeological artefacts.

By using neutron activation analysis and examining the structure of the data produced using factor analysis, Hoard et al. (1992; 1993) have shown that it is possible to distinguish between groups of siliceous materials from the White river valley in the USA. These cryptocrystalline siliceous materials (chalcedony and chert) of the central Great Plains were used to make chipped stone tools. Since specimens from the three known sources at Flattop Butte in north-east Colorado, Table Mountain in east central Wyoming and the White river badlands of South Dakota are visually indistinguishable, this was a distinct step forwards (Hoard et al. (1993) Figure 2) showing the value of such work.

6.4 Steatite

Steatite (or soapstone) is a rock mainly composed of talc and minor amounts of other minerals such as chlorite. It was used for the manufacture of objects such as beads in Mesopotamia (Moorey 1994: 75–6). It was probably used for the manufacture of vessels on sites of the Halaf period through to the fifth millennium BC (ibid: 39–40). Kohl et al. (1979) used X-ray diffraction analysis and other means to investigate 375 samples of 'soft stone', predominantly from carved artefacts (but including specimens from potential sources) of the late fourth millennium to early second millennium BC from south-west Asia, including Mesopotamia.

In the eastern United States steatite was extensively mined in prehistory. It was used in the late Archaic period and possibly in the early Woodland period for the manufacture of lugged bowls. Sedentary farmers later used it for the manufacture of smoking pipes and decorative items. The use of neutron activation analysis to attempt to source steatite in the area has met with success. Allan et al. (1975) used the relative concentrations of rare earth elements (the lanthanide group of chemical elements with atomic numbers of between 57 and 71) to chemically characterise steatite according to the quarry that it came from. Even the analysis of steatite from the same zone but from quarries several miles apart could be distinguished. They used a technique familiar to geochemists: first the rare earth concentrations are normalised to average chondritic values, then the ratio of the steatite values to chondrites is plotted again the atomic number of rare earth elements such as lanthanum (La), samarium (Sm) and europium (Eu). The reason why normalised values are used is that elements with even atomic numbers tend to occur at higher concentrations than those with odd atomic numbers. This is due to relative nuclear stability and relates to the origin of the element. The average concentration of each element in chondritic meteorites is used for normalising the results, because the abundance of elements in these meteorites is usually taken as the average abundance in the solar system. Geological processes cause fractionation of rare earth elements and it is this fractionation of one relative to the others that can provide a means of linking their chemical characteristics to a source for the steatite. Test analyses on steatite artefacts from the Shenandoah valley has provided useful evidence for two groups exploiting widely separated sources (Allan *et al.* 1975: 80).

6.5 Answering archaeological questions through the scientific analysis of flint

Flint was used to manufacture some of the earliest tools used by man that have survived. Because it can be worked to produce sharp blades with characteristic conchoidal fractures, it was used to make, among other artefacts, including hand axes, blades, scrapers and arrowheads. Some of the questions which archaeologists are keen to answer in relation to flint use and characterisation are:

- How was flint used in ancient societies?
- Why were particular flint sources used rather than others?
- Over what distances did the flint travel from its source?

Programmes of archaeological science research can be constructed to answer these questions. To answer how flint was used in ancient society, a wide range of archaeological features must be taken into account, including where the flint was found on the site, the kind of site the flint was found on, how the flint artefacts were made, what 'significance' they held in the archaeological assemblage, what the flint artefacts were used for and what other lithics were used (e.g. stone axes) on the site? Abrasion studies, cut marks on bones and forensic archaeology can all contribute to the overall interpretation in different ways.

One of the questions that can be investigated with chemical analysis is an attempt to establish what distance the flint travelled from its source. This relies on the premise that it is possible to source the flint

chemically to a particular location or zone, and to build up a distribution zone from it to the archaeological sites on which it was used or worked. To some extent this also assumes that no flint mines have been destroyed by natural processes, such as by coastal erosion. It would be hoped that the geological conditions in which the flint formed would be such that the trace elemental composition would be characteristic of the geological stratum or age. As mentioned above, slight differences in the characteristics of formation, such as the chemical structure of the host sediment and the degree to which its formational process has gone to completion, *should* lead to specific compositional signatures for flint found at different (vertical and horizontal) locations. Indeed Cowell *et al.* (1980) found a consistent compositional variation between layers of flint at Grimes Graves.

Some of the earliest chemical work on flint was carried out using emission spectrometry (Sieveking *et al.* 1970) and neutron activation analysis (NAA), which is capable of measuring some elemental concentrations to below 1 ppm. Both techniques have been used to investigate the possibility of chemically characterising flint sources in Britain (Aspinall and Feather 1972; Aspinall *et al.* 1975; De Bruin 1972). This showed that it was sometimes possible to distinguish in general between broad geological areas in which flint occurs, such as the relatively high levels of thorium detected in flint from Grand Pressigny (France) which distinguished it from the flint from Dutch sites of St Gertrude and Rijkholt, from all the English flint tested and from Spiennes in Belgium. Also, the thorium concentrations found in Grimes Graves flint has a mean and standard deviation which was diagnostic. However, subsequent research using atomic absorption spectroscopy (AAS) (Craddock *et al.* 1983) has found that it is possible to chemically characterise flint more precisely, linking chemical compositions to specific areas within England: East Anglia, the South Downs and Wessex. One of the reasons why this work was more fruitful is that AAS can be used to detect a somewhat different suite of elements. In this case the elements detected were aluminium, iron, magnesia, potassium, sodium, calcium and lithium, at levels above 50 ppm. Apart from the obvious high silica levels the elements which provided the characterisation were thought to be present in the non-carbonate minerals (alumino-silicates, phosphates etc.), unreplaced low magnesia calcite and trapped interstitial water (Cowell 1979; Craddock *et al.* 1983: 138).

They chemically analysed flint derived from 11 mining areas (including 2 nearby mines in their 'South Downs A' group and 4 in their 'South Downs B' group). Craddock *et al.* (1983) compared these to the chemical compositions of 400 polished flint axes, of which 300 derived from the presumed 3 main areas in which the flint mines are located: the South Downs, Wessex, and East Anglia. Through the chemical analysis of 100 axes derived from excavated Neolithic sites within these areas Craddock *et al.* showed an apparent discrimination between the flint derived from these mines based on their relative concentrations of iron and aluminium. They were able to indicate, on the basis of the proportion of flint axes found in each region, which mine the flint was derived from. This produced some intriguing and some unexpected results. Although it *might* be

assumed (somewhat simplistically) that the area in which the axeheads were found would have supplied the flint to make them, in two of the three cases this was not so (see Figure 6.2). In the South Downs region more than 50% of the flint axes analysed derived from the South Downs area. However, more than 50% of the axes found in the Wessex region were also made from South Downs flint and rather more than a third of the axes found in the East Anglia region were made from South Downs flint.

Grimes Graves (an East Anglian mine) apparently supplied less than 10% of the flint used for axes in the East Anglian area which is about the same proportion as the Wessex flint used. In all, 67% of the axes were assigned to a South Downs source. One explanation for these unexpected findings is one of dating. Grimes Graves was used for a short period in the latest Neolithic. Other flint mines were exploited much earlier: for example, some of the South Downs flint mines in the fourth millennium BC. Since considerably fewer axes were apparently used in the late Neolithic, it is perhaps not surprising that few axes made from

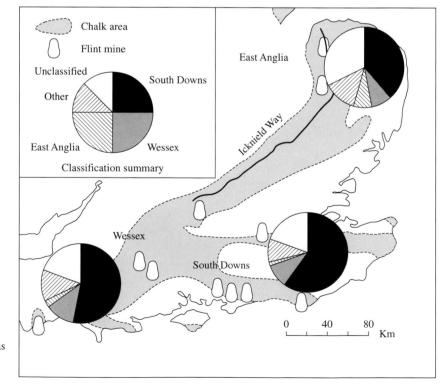

Figure 6.2 The relative proportion of different kinds of flint (from the South Downs, Wessex, East Anglia, other areas and unclassified sources) used for making flint axes which have been found in these same areas of flint sources © The British Museum.

flint mined in the late Neolithic have been found. About one quarter of the flint axes which were analysed in this study remained unsourced, indicating that further work is necessary to locate the sources, though they may now be destroyed. However, the results clearly provide an excellent step forward showing that flint which was used to make axes travelled some distance from its source. Nonetheless, as Craddock *et al.* point out (1983: 160) chemical analysis of flint artefacts other than hand axes *might* have produced the allusive analytical proof for the use and distribution of Grimes Graves flint. When compared to the results of stone axe provenance studies (see Section 6.8 below), reasons other than the working properties of the flint may need to be put forward for the use of 'alien' flint, such as cultural, in areas where flint is already available. Another result of this research is that it shows how important it is to use an analytical technique which can measure the appropriate range of elements at the appropriate level of sensitivity for the characterisation of the material. (This may only become clear when research has already shown that the results

from using a particular technique are inappropriate or unpromising.) Clearly a comparison of the chemical compositions of flint artefacts from dated archaeological contexts with those from (where possible) seams of contemporary dated flint which have definitely been exploited by man is a priority.

Subsequently, inductively coupled plasma atomic emission spectroscopy has been used for the chemical analysis of flint with another successful outcome. Thompson *et al.* (1986: 247) showed that some elements, such as barium and beryllium, for example, provided a distinction between flint deriving from Cissbury and flint deriving from Black Patch, Church Hill and Harrow Hill.

Consigny and Walter (1997) provide a promising set of results for the chemical analysis of flint and chert from the Paris basin. Although not fully published, they indicate that by using particle-induced X-ray emission (PIXE) they are able to chemically distinguish siliceous materials from the same geological layer but different geographical regions (see Figure 6.3). Most work had focused on the central part of the Paris basin in the Ile-de-France using techniques such

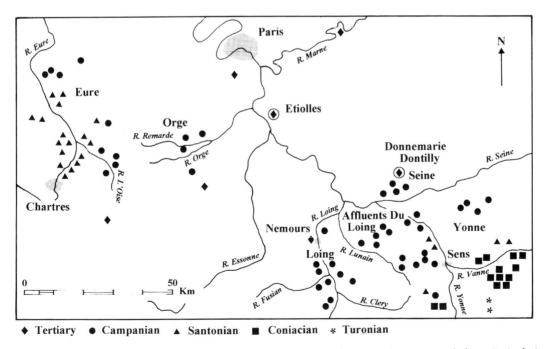

Figure 6.3 The distribution of chert and flint in the Paris basin and surrounding area and the principal sites mentioned in the text.

as micropalaeontology. The results showed that Upper Cretaceous (Senonian and Turonian) cherts associated with chalk and Tertiary cherts associated with lake limestone had been used. It is easy to distinguish between the two kinds, but it was found to be much more difficult to distinguish between cherts of the same type from different locations. In order to address this problem the research involved sampling geological deposits from a range of geographical locations, including from the valleys of the rivers Eure, Orge, Loing, Lunain, Yonne and Vanne. Both Upper Cretaceous and Tertiary formations were sampled. The research involved taking samples of raw chert and flint, where possible, from the same and different geological formations (i.e. both horizontal and vertical sampling). It was found that the further apart the deposits of the same geological stratum were, the greater the difference in trace elements detected in each (Consigny 1992). This was found to be true of chert and flint deposits of the same geological age: the trace element characteristics were found to gradually change as the sampling point moved away from a location along a single geological stratum.

Three groups of chert which probably derived from Champigny limestone were examined. They derived from the archaeological sites of Etiolles and Donnemarie-Dontilly, La Fouillotte and from another site, Villejuif. Etiolles is a late Magdalenian site in the centre of the Paris basin, on the right bank of the Seine to the south-east of Paris. There is evidence here for the manufacture of flint blades from large cores (Pigeot 1987). Donnemarie is situated 80 km to the south-east of Paris. It is an Upper Palaeo-lithic open air settlement which used long blades. Chemical analysis of the cherts found at the sites, probably associated with Champigny limestone, showed that they could be distinguished chemically. The chert from Donnemarie is characterised by the presence of germanium and uranium, that from Etiolles by the presence of germanium, uranium and zirconium, and that from another location, Villejuif (for which no locational information is given), by unusually high levels of uranium. These elements have been used in the principal components plot in Figure 6.4.

Flint from two phases of use at Etiolles was also analysed which led to a more complex and

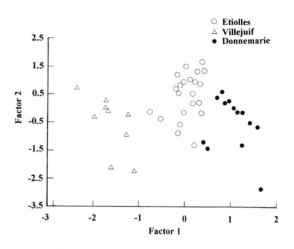

Figure 6.4 A principal components analysis of chert from Etiolles, Villejuif and Donnemarie.

only partially-resolved set of results. They used the same criteria to chemically characterise the flint as for the chert: presence or absence of elements and/or the levels of trace elements. Consigny and Walter discovered three compositional types. One group characterised by uranium, arsenic and germanium could only be broadly sourced to the Tertiary limestone (Consigny and Walter 1997: 341). Analysis of the second type, a golden brown flint, revealed three compositional types of which only one could be sourced to the valley of the river Loing which had been suggested before the analysis had been carried out on the basis of macroscopic characteristics. A source for the second compositional type of golden coloured flint could not be suggested. The third type, which is characterised by niobium, could not be matched with any geological samples examined, but it was found that flint from a Magdalan-ian site of Abri du Lagopède at Arcy-sur-Cure about 150 km to the south-east was also characterised by this element. The authors suggest that the sites are unlikely to be linked, but more sensibly they suggest that flint found at the two sites was derived from the same source of flint. However, in spite of the fact that niobium is a rare trace element in flint, until the source of flint containing niobium is located, it is difficult to be sure how close together the sources were which provided flint for the two sites.

This research by Consigny and Walter provides a glimpse of what might be possible: it provides a possible framework for research in other flint-rich environments, such as across the English Channel in England. Given that a level of flint characterisation has been achieved using neutron activation analysis, ICPAES and especially AAS there appears to be a great potential to build on this work. Clearly a thorough geological survey of flint and chert sources is an important component in the investigation of the sources that may have been used in antiquity.

To the north of these French geological formations, but of associated age, Holmes and Harbottle (1994) have used neutron activation analysis to examine Lutetian limestone from the area around Paris. They found that while petrography was able to localise it to a stratum belonging to several quarries, NAA was able to produce finer distinctions between quarries belonging to the same geological stratum. They also mention that their findings can have significant art-historical implications in sourcing the limestone used to build and embellish Nôtre-Dame Cathedral, for example.

6.6 Obsidian research: a microcosm of the development of archaeological science

Research into the sourcing of obsidian, a stone which it might be claimed is one of the better candidates for chemical characterisation, has produced some exceptional results. Obsidian studies can be viewed as representing a microcosm of the way in which archaeological materials research has developed and progressed, starting with the use of relatively small data sets due to the limiting and time-consuming nature of the scientific techniques used, through to the use of more highly automated techniques which are able to generate archaeologically coherent data sets (Jope 1989). Importantly if the research project is set in an appropriately broad framework, results from the chemical analysis of obsidian have not only enabled it to be sourced, but have also provided evidence for the ways in which obsidian from different sources was used during different periods of prehistory.

Obsidian was one of a range of lithics used to make tools. By taking the use of other lithics into account the study of chemically characterised obsidian use brings a range of archaeological factors into play. These include the proportion of tools from a dated site assemblage made from obsidian; the changes in obsidian source exploitation over time; the size and function of the sites on which the obsidian was found; the kind of trade/exchange networks involved in the distribution of obsidian; the reasons why a specific type of obsidian was preferentially used. Combined with an archaeological survey and excavation of obsidian-using sites, as well as a comprehensive survey of the obsidian sources, the complex archaeological information which can be derived from such studies contributes in an important way to mainstream prehistoric archaeology. Some of the early work with obsidian had already provided important inferences about trade/exchange systems (Renfrew *et al.* 1965; 1966; 1968).

Obsidian is a naturally-occurring glass which is formed during volcanic eruptions. It is almost entirely a glass which formed as a result of rapid chilling at the earth's surface; some obsidians contain up to 15% crystals. The lavas which produce obsidians generally contain greater than 66% silica (they are rhyolitic in composition), and are therefore classified as acid rocks. Some have a more basic composition and are called dacite or trachyte. Chemically, obsidians can be defined according to the balance of alkalis (soda and potassium oxide), silica, aluminia and calcium oxide; the ratio of alkalis to aluminia distinguish between 'peralkaline' and 'subalkaline' obsidians, for example (Macdonald *et al.* 1992). One of the main compositional differences between obsidian and a typical man-made soda-lime glass is the much higher level of aluminia in obsidian, which normally occurs at levels above 10% (as opposed to about 2–5% in most man-made glass) and the much lower levels of calcium oxide (generally less than 2%, as opposed to 6–8%). One result of these compositional differences (especially the differences in alkali and aluminia levels) is that obsidian melts at *much* higher temperatures than man-made glass. It is therefore a material which man has not, until recently, attempted to modify by heat-treatment. Obsidians weather at their surfaces as a result of interaction with water in the environment (hydration) and under some (restricted) circumstances this can be used as a form of dating (Ericson 1988), although any success has mainly been restricted to its application in the US.

Obsidian has been used for the manufacture of blades and arrowheads, and also for the manufacture of bowls. The quality of obsidian is clearly important in determining what it was used for and Renfrew et al. (1965) noted that in Classical contexts it was used for the manufacture of seals, tesserae, mirrors and statues.

In some instances obsidians are apparently sufficiently homogeneous and chemically distinct for them to be characterised chemically in terms of each eruption and lava flow (Gordus et al. 1968; Michels 1982). The reason for this homogeneity is its rapid solidification from a liquid state, preventing any mixing. Bowman et al. (1973) have however discovered variability in some elements due to magmatic mixing prior to eruption, although for the characterisation of archaeological obsidians and their sources this has apparently not yet proved to be a problem. Having said that, those who collected obsidian in prehistory may have only returned to a limited number of loci on an obsidian flow (or perhaps a single locus), which would lead to limited variation in the chemical composition of the obsidian used to make artefacts. Jack (1976) used less than five analyses as a means of 'characterising' most of the major obsidian sources in California because it was assumed that its compositional homogeneity made a more detailed geochemical survey unnecessary. Hughes (1994) has however investigated closely the variation in the chemical composition of obsidian in the Casa Diablo region of California. Although this obsidian source had been assumed to be geochemically homogeneous, analysis of 200 samples from twenty different locations revealed the existence of two or possibly three potentially different sources (Lookout Mountain, Sawmill Ridge and Prospect Ridge). Hughes (ibid.: 268) points out that this more specific characterisation provides archaeologists with the opportunity to resolve temporal, spatial and production histories involving each obsidian type. It could also allow archaeologists to investigate whether more than one source of obsidian was used by a

prehistoric community at any one time; currently the obsidian artefacts which can be traced to the Casa Diablo source were derived from sites which appear only to have used a single source at a given time. These kinds of studies alert us to the possibilities of geochemical variations, perhaps even within 'single' flows (Pollard and Heron 1996: 87). Hughes (1994) working in California, Tykot (1997a) working with Sardinian obsidian, and Yellin (1995) working with Anatolian obsidian, all emphasise the importance of chemically analysing a sufficient number of obsidian samples to monitor any geochemical variations at different volcanic sources; these three authors also underline the importance of recording precisely the locations from which samples of obsidian are removed for analysis during field surveys.

Because some geological sources of obsidian are identifiable in the field today, it can be possible to relate the composition of a specific obsidian source to the composition of obsidian artefacts made using material from that source. Obsidian was used at least as early as Mesolithic times in the Mediterranean (Hallam et al. 1976; Blackman 1984), and earlier still in other parts of the world (Michels et al. 1983; Merrick and Brown 1984; Gowlett and Henderson, forthcoming; Perlès 1987).

The first techniques used for obsidian analysis were optical emission spectroscopy and petrology, and these were later followed by techniques such as neutron activation analysis, electron probe microanalysis, X-ray fluorescence spectroscopy and, most recently, inductively coupled plasma emission spectrometry (Heyworth et al. 1988). The results of these analytical techniques have indicated that trace and minor element compositions have most discriminative value for obsidians in the Mediterranean area. In the western Mediterranean, traces of lanthanum, scandium and caesium in particular have provided a means of fingerprinting obsidian sources. In the analysis of middle Stone Age East African obsidians minor levels of calcium and iron have distinguished between sources. It follows therefore that it should be possible from the chemical analysis of obsidian to work out distribution zones in a particular period, the use of obsidian relative to other chipped stone resources, and to suggest mechanisms of distribution. Much of the work by Renfrew and co-workers and by Ammerman has attained these objectives. One result of these studies is clear: the contacts which can be inferred between the source of the obsidian and the points at which the obsidian (artefacts) have been found, based on their chemical constituents are in most cases completely new.

6.6.1 Obsidian use in the Middle East

It was not until *c.* 7500 BC that obsidian artefacts were moved in any quantity, or with any regularity, beyond the immediate environs of the source areas in the Near East. Cann and Renfrew (1964) and Renfrew *et al.* (1966; 1968) discerned two principal source areas for obsidian in the Near East and the sites which they supplied during the seventh and sixth millennia BC. Chemical characterisation was based on trace levels of caesium, thorium and scandium. Renfrew and co-workers referred to these sources and the sites in their immediate vicinity as 'supply zones'. The supply zone in central Anatolia was labelled the Cappadocian source, based on the volcanoes near Agicol and Çiftlik. The second supply zone, in eastern Anatolia (Armenia), is based on the volcanic sources of Nemrut Dag and Bingol. *Supply zones* were defined as the area within which sites have chipped stone industries consisting of greater than 80% obsidian (expressed in terms of the number of artefacts). It is worth emphasising the importance of this idea of *proportion* for the chipped stone industry, because it is a way of standardising data so that different site assemblages can be directly compared, irrespective of the numbers of artefacts involved.

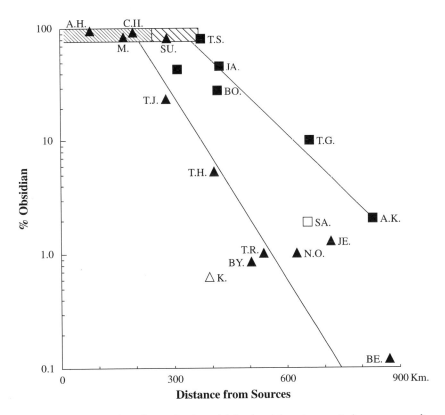

Figure 6.5 The percentage of obsidian (logarithmic scale) in the chipped stone industry versus distance from source for early Neolithic sites in the Near East. The shaded area is the supply zone; the straight lines indicate approximately exponential fall-off of obsidian from the contact zones. Triangles represent sites in central Anatolia and the Levant supplied by the Cappadocian source; squares represent sites in the Zagros mountains area supplied by Armenian sources. T.S. = Tell Shemsharah; JA = Jarmo; BO = Bouqras; TG = Tepe Guran.

Wright (1969: 48) has suggested that, in some instances, the total weight of obsidian would provide an alternative means of defining the proportion of material involved, although even this suggestion has potential problems; both sets of information provide different levels of meaning and one way forward is to present both % weight and % number of artefacts with distance from source. However, chemical characterisation is the basis of this work. From the work of Renfrew *et al.* (Figure 6.5), it is apparent that the central Anatolian supply zone extends up to 250 km from the source, whereas the Armenian supply zone extends over 300 km from the source. Beyond the supply zone is the 'contact zone', where the fall-off in the amount of characterised obsidian is exponential and is therefore plotted on a logarithmic scale in Figure 6.5. (This means that the scale on the left [% obsidian] increases by a factor of 10 with each major subdivision).

It is evident that with the sharp fall-off in % obsidian beyond 250 km or 300 km, at the edge of the supply zone, the mechanisms involved in its distribution in the contact zone must be somewhat different. Where there is a higher percentage of obsidian around the source within the supply zone it can be suggested that any trade that occurred was intensive, and possibly that the obsidian consumers travelled to the source themselves. At least it can be suggested that the people who procured the obsidian probably formed an integrated and dependent part of the supply system (Figure 6.5). In the contact zone band the trade falls off, and indeed it is possible that the amount of obsidian traded was deliberately withheld to inflate its value. The term Renfrew (1975; 1977) has applied to this form of trade or exchange is 'down-the-line'. This form of trade involves the transmission of 'goods' from one settlement to another in a linear fashion and is normally applied to land trade. It is unfortunate that other components of the chipped stone industry in the same regions of the Near East have not apparently been studied in the same way, since this could partially provide us with a fascinating series of competing zones for different types and qualities of materials. It would then be possible to broach the tricky concept of relative value.

Wright (1969: 51) has suggested that this model of supply and contact zone would not work for Armenian material if obsidian from separate phases of sites are considered. Wright (ibid.: 51) also suggested that a consideration of different *functions* of sites in the study area might make a difference; sites which specialised in obsidian artefact production could have a significantly larger number and weight of obsidian artefacts, including debitage associated with production, and in making comparisons with non-production sites the artefact types should be included. Torrence (1986: 97–8) has also emphasised this approach combined with a consideration of relative proportions of stone type found in specific site phases. Thus, a comparison of % obsidian (however this is expressed) between contemporary sites which specialise in obsidian artefact production and between those which have other functions in the zones(s) around the source of obsidian would appear to offer a means of comparing like with like, where the % weight of artefact assemblages (including debitage) can be directly compared. Nevertheless, the distribution patterns published by Renfrew *et al.* reflect *regular* but not necessarily *regulated* behaviour during the seventh and sixth millennia BC and there need not *necessarily* have been any formal exchange or trade organisation involved. Their research blazed the trail for subsequent research in obsidian analysis and is especially significant for its contribution to modelling distribution mechanisms.

In an analytical study of Anatolian obsidian by Gratuze (1999) using a very sensitive analytical technique, ICP-MS with the sample being introduced by laser ablation, he claims to have detected nine separate Cappadocian sources. By comparing his results with those produced by other workers who have used neutron activation analysis and X-ray fluorescence spectrometry he has also been able to confirm some attributions they made to specific sources where there had been an element of doubt. Gratuze (ibid.) also claims that laser ablation ICP-MS will replace NAA and XRF as a virtually non-destructive technique (see section 2.2). However, the level of destruction that is involved in using NAA/XRF and ICP-MS in liquid mode, as used by Tykot (1997a), is evidently acceptable.

6.6.2 *Obsidian use in southern Europe*

In Italian contexts (Ammerman 1979) has followed an inclusive approach to the sourcing and distribution of stone, one which takes into account the types of site which produced the stone (and whether they specialised in working it), the different artefact types and the relative sizes that have been found, the proportion of different stone types found on each site as well as the distance from stone sources. Early work on obsidian sources in the western Mediterranean has shown that four principal obsidian sources could be chemically defined, mainly by using neutron activation analysis and based on the lanthanum to scandium and caesium to scandium ratios. Figure 6.6 shows a plot of ppm of barium

versus ppm of zirconium in obsidians from a range of sources in the Mediterranean and Africa. The figure underlines how obsidian from Sardinia, Lipari and Pentellaria can be distinguished, but also the extent that they differ compositionally from Anatolian sources. Hallam *et al.* (1976) later showed that it was possible to distinguish compositionally between the four basic sources which are all on islands near Italy: Sardinia, Lipari, Pantelleria and Palmarola, the latter in the Pontine islands. Let us now look at these four main geochemical groupings in terms of their geographical distribution (Figure 6.7). The four zones given are what Hallam *et al.* (1976) have referred to as *obsidian interaction zones*. These are defined as 'the area within which sites

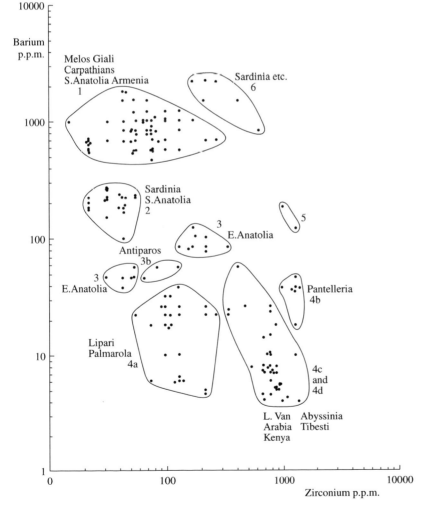

Figure 6.6 Parts per million barium versus parts per million zirconium detected in obsidian samples from a range of sources in the Middle East, in the Mediterranean and in Africa.

Figure 6.7 The distribution of chemically characterised obsidian in and near Italy and southern France; SA = Sardinian A obsidian; SB = Sardinian B obsidian; SC = Sardinian C obsidian; P.l = Palmarolan obsidian; Pa = Pantellarian obsidian. The different zones are obsidian interaction zones (Cann *et al.* 1968; reproduced with kind permission of the authors and the Prehistoric Society).

derive 30% or more of their obsidian from the same specific sources'. Of course by increasing the percentage for the definition of an interaction zone from 30% to 50%, we could produce a rather different, more contracted pattern leading to a different archaeological interpretation. Since Hallam

et al. (1976) published their paper, Thorpe *et al.* (1984) have shown that Pantellerian obsidian reached southern France, where it was excavated from Copper Age contexts.

Francaviglia (1988) noted that Neolithic and late Bronze Age peralkaline obsidian found in Sicily could also be sourced at Pantelleria. Francaviglia (ibid.) analysed 143 obsidian samples from Pantelleria, a considerable sample size, and found that there were at least five different obsidian sources on the island, though the exact location of some were uncertain. Not only does this work show how important a large sample size is, it also modifies the distribution patterns given in Figure 6.7, which specifically excludes the occurrence of Pantellerian obsidian from Sicily in the Neolithic and Copper Ages; a distribution map which included this new data would need to incorporate the percentage of obsidian from each source per site, and provide results for obsidian use in each period. An important consideration is the analysis of a statistically acceptable proportion of obsidian from a site in order to establish within-site compositional variability and to provide the basis for an estimate of the proportion of obsidian used from each source. Naturally, to be confident of establishing a reliable pattern of distribution, it is essential to analyse a sufficiently large amount of obsidian from well-dated archaeological contexts. Some early analytical projects on obsidian suffered from inadequate sampling, though in fairness this must be seen in the context of the more time-consuming and labour-intensive nature of carrying out the chemical analyses at that time.

Figure 6.7 is a conflation of different time period distributions for sub-periods within the Neolithic and Copper Ages (Hallam *et al.* 1976: Figure 4). While the locations of the origins of obsidian plotted in the distribution patterns are well worth working out, it is quite possible that the four sources were exploited at different intensities and for different lengths of time through the period considered, from *c.* 5000 BC to *c.* 2000 BC. Nevertheless, the work by Hallam *et al.* laid important foundations for later work and, as we have seen, these distributions have been modified by subsequent research. What we should aim for in each project should be the analysis of a sufficient number of well-dated obsidian artefacts which can be treated as representative of specific periods rather than of a broad sweep of time. This would lead to fine-tuning of the data and more specific archaeological interpretations. An interesting feature of Figure 6.7 is the Palmarolan zone, which lies within the Liparian interaction zone. Its existence

can probably be explained in technical terms: it may exist because Liparian obsidian occurs in much larger lumps producing longer blades than obsidian from the Palmarolan zone, making it more attractive and saleable over a larger area (Hallam *et al.* 1976: 99). The distribution of obsidian from Lipari actually extends beyond the Palmarolan zone and perhaps this is an example of competitive trading. Renfrew (in Hallam *et al.* 1976) suggests that sea travel would have been avoided. However, Ammerman (1979: 102) has now produced strongly conflicting evidence.

For the southern part of Italy, in Calabria, Ammerman has made a substantial contribution to the archaeological interpretation of chemically characterised obsidian. By carrying out an extensive survey of the Neolithic sites in the area (Figure 6.8) he provided a dense distribution of sites where obsidian has been found. Obsidian was found at over 200 sites dating mainly to the Neolithic and Copper ages, though some was also found in Mesolithic contexts. Ammerman closely studied the *total* lithic assemblage from these sites. Using chemical analysis, he has established that Lipari was the primary source with an alternative at Palmarola on the Pontine island. The lithic material from the sites on the west coast of Italy ranged from about 100 to several hundred pieces, and many assemblages contained over 90% obsidian. On the other hand, on the east coast near the town of Crotone, the proportion of obsidian was less than 40%. When compared to the pattern we saw for the Near East, the rate at which obsidian declines away from the source is much greater. Here it falls by 50% in less than 100 km, yet in the Near East the percentage of obsidian remained at 80% within 300 km of the source. Some sites on the east coast of Calabria contained as little at 10% obsidian in their lithic assemblages, and others lying at about the same distance from Lipari contained more than 30%. This pattern is therefore quite different from the monotonic down-the-line movement of obsidian, the suggested model for obsidian exchange in the Near East.

Possible archaeological interpretations of the pattern (Ammerman 1979; Ammerman and Andrefsky 1982) seen on the east coast of Italy are: (1) some sites take a greater part in the long distance exchange

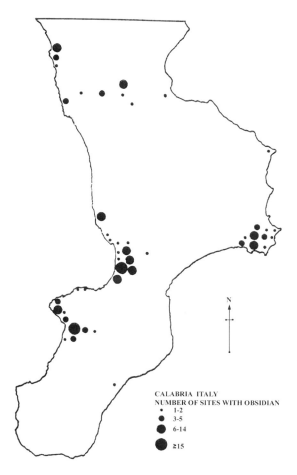

Figure 6.8 The result of a survey of Neolithic sites in Calabria, Italy showing the number of sites on which obsidian has been found.

obsidian by sea from Lipari, and that we do not need to invoke a down-the-line mechanism for its distribution. It also seems probable that obsidian reached the east coast of Calabria over land and, as we have noted, there are probably several local factors which might have caused its uneven distribution. The working assumption had been that all sites participated to the same extent and in the same way in the exchange networks. If this had been the case the same pattern of lithic utilisation would be observed at sites which were of equal distance from the source. Ammerman (1979) has shown this *not* to be the case and that the proportions of different sizes of obsidian artefact sizes and by-products are important (Ammerman and Andrefsky 1982). Greater proportions of obsidian, including more pieces in a reduced form, occurred at sites closer to the coast. The research by Ammerman and Francaviglia shows how important large-scale analytical projects are; both have extensively modified the distribution patterns from individual obsidian sources built up by earlier work in the area.

In the study of Neolithic obsidian from Gaione in the Po plain, northern Italy Ammerman *et al.* (1990) have suggested that obsidian which reached the site deriving from different sources was possibly treated as having a different value according to its origin. The highly translucent blades of Liparian obsidian may have been valued more as special prestige items (they show few signs of edge damage) rather than as utilitarian objects. The Sardinian obsidian circulating as cores was probably regarded as much more utilitarian.

Another (complementary) approach to obsidian studies has been taken by Tykot (1997a). By focusing on the Sardinian source of obsidian in the Monte Arci volcanic complex he has shown, by using electron microprobe and ICP-MS, that there were nine chemically distinct sources; other workers focusing on archaeological obsidian had already detected three of these (Hallam *et al.* 1976). Tykot (1992) had already shown that five distinct sources were to be found from the chemical analyses of archaeological artefacts. He identified nine distinct geological sources by first carrying out a comprehensive field survey of potential obsidian sources of which, five

networks of obsidian; or (2) the patterns result from local differences in the availability of chert; or (3) we are seeing the results of multiple local exchange systems which cannot as yet be disentangled. If movement of obsidian had taken place across the land avoiding sea transport, as Hallam *et al.* (1976) suggest for this area, then we should expect that, as the supply of obsidian moved up the west coast of Calabria, the amount available would decrease, due to loss or deposition among the sites. However, Ammerman's work has indicated that obsidian is present up the west coast of Calabria in uniform proportions. He suggests a radial distribution of had been used for making prehistoric tools. It is interesting to note that the quantity and quality of the obsidian at each site varies (Tykot 1997a: 468–72). Clearly an investigation of any correlation between the quality of the obsidian and the function it was put to is the next step. Tykot (1997b) does, however, underline the variation in intensity of use of each Monte Arci sources and also that the obsidian was used on different sites at different times during the Neolithic in the western Mediterranean. Both Francaviglia (1986) and Tykot (1997a) show that the major Mediterranean sources – Sardinia (A, B and C), Lipari, Pantelleria, Palmarola, Melos and Giali can be distinguished on the basis of their major elemental compositions.

Other recent work has shown that other sources of obsidian were exploited at Szöllöske and Malá Toroňa in the Carpathians in southeastern Slovakia. Carpathian obsidian was found to have been used in eleven out of twelve samples from late Neolithic and Bronze Age contexts at Mandalo, Macedonia, tested by Kilikoglou et al. (1996) using neutron activation analysis; the twelfth sample was found to have derived from the 'anticipated' source of the Greek island of Melos. One of the important archaeological inferences from this work is that there was interaction between Macedonia, central Europe and the Aegean in the late Neolithic. Two other occurrences of Carpathian obsidian, each single pieces, were found in north-eastern Italy. The first was at a Neolithic cave site, Grotta Tartaruga, but in this case one of the 'expected' more local sources of obsidian had been used predominantly, that of Lipari (Williams-Thorpe et al. 1984). The second was at an early Neolithic site of Sammardenchia (Randle et al. 1993). In both cases the obsidian was from a distant source even though there were nearer, local, sources, raising the question of why it was selected for use – perhaps its fracture characteristics or its colour created the demand for it.

The Greek islands also form part of a volcanic zone in which obsidian has been found. The island of Melos, in particular, has been the focus of an analytical study. It has been found that Melos formed the source for most obsidian found in Neolithic and early Bronze Age Aegean contexts (Renfrew et al. 1965); Renfrew and Aspinall (1990) detected its use in Upper Palaeolithic and Mesolithic contexts at Franchthi Cave in the Argolid. Renfrew (1972: 442–3) has suggested that a direct access model is appropriate for the exploitation of Melian obsidian. In this model consumers travelled directly to the source to procure their obsidian; no movement of obsidian to intermediate locations or the involvement of middlemen needs to be invoked. Torrence (1986: 105) has suggested that this form of access may have continued into the Bronze Age and included specialist knappers seeking out suitable nodules of obsidian on Melos.

However, in considering the distribution of Greek Neolithic obsidian Perlès (1992: 119) urges that consideration of a full range of materials is necessary in order to interpret fully systems of exchange and organisation. It is clear for example, that 'prestige goods' and utilitarian goods are likely to be exchanged/traded using different systems – though at the same time possibly relying on the same initial contacts. For obsidian, a complex picture emerges. During the early and middle Neolithic preformed cores were imported to village sites and blades made there. While prismatic cores were produced at Melos for export during the late and final Neolithic, they were also produced at sites like Saliagos, where a probable workshop for their manufacture has been found. Furthermore, Perlès (ibid.: 128) suggests that the same core may have been used for blade production on more than one site, though this must be difficult to prove absolutely. This does, however, remind us that such core reductions may have occurred in a rather more complex sequence than may at first be assumed. In considering the distribution of stone use in the Greek Neolithic, Perlès (1992) has included andesite, emery and honey-coloured flint, and she also considered the type of site involved in stone procurement. This approach, though painstaking, is clearly one of the ways forward for this area of research, since it also involves the difficult concept of value.

Before leaving discussion of obsidian it is worth briefly pointing out the potentially different archaeological interpretations provided by use of trace element analysis and major element analysis. Figure

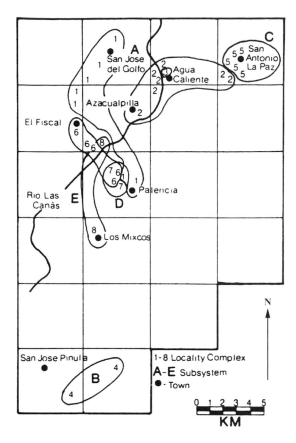

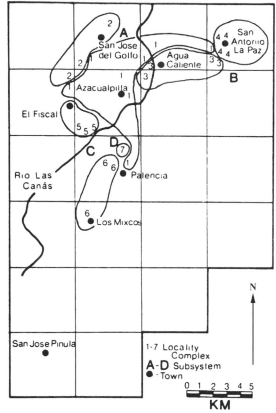

Figure 6.9 The distribution of obsidian for the El Chayal source, Guatemala based on trace element analysis. Each sub-system is labelled with a letter; each locality complex affiliation with a number.

Figure 6.10 The distribution of obsidian for the El Chayal source, Guatemala based on major element analysis. Each sub-system is labelled with a letter; each locality complex affiliation with a number as defined in Figure 6.9.

6.9 is a map of what we have called obsidian interaction zones in the El Chayel area of Guatemala built up from trace element analysis (Michels 1982): some rather confused overlapping zones are produced. If major elements are used for obsidian characterisation instead, the zones become discrete and geographically definable (Figure 6.10). This pattern can now be used for the interpretation of other features of the archaeological system. These results underline the importance of initially determining a wide range of chemical elements in obsidian analysis. It might be argued that the selection of major elements to provide a 'true' characterisation, and the rejection of a trace elemental fingerprint on archae-

ological grounds removes the objectivity from the process of characterisation and that one is in danger of getting involved in a circular argument (i.e. if the type of characterisation of the obsidian agrees with other archaeological features that particular characterisation is correct). However, it must be realised that successful chemical fingerprinting of obsidian using trace elements in the Mediterranean area does not *necessarily* mean that such a means of characterisation would also be valid for other areas of the world, given different geochemical environments. The study of obsidian compositions in the North Mexico basin (Findow and Bolognese 1982) provides a further example of useful archaeological results.

6.7 The origins and transportation of the bluestones of Stonehenge

Stonehenge on Salisbury Plain in Wiltshire, southern England is one of the most famous prehistoric sites in Europe. The first written description of Stonehenge was as early as the twelfth century, in the chronicle of Henry of Huntingdon (Chippindale 1983). Today the site consists of an imposing outer circle of giant stone uprights which originally held crosspieces and which were built using silicified sedimentary quartz rocks, called sarsens (silicretes). The use of prepared stone joints, including mortice and tenon and tongue and groove, have apparently been borrowed from woodworking technology. This outer circle enclosed a horseshoe of smaller bluestones of largely basaltic origins (basaltic 'spotted' dolerite). Scientific investigation of the stones has experienced a long history, mainly because the site of Stonehenge has an enduring fascination in European prehistoric studies. Stonehenge consists of a series of constructional phases dating to the third and early second millennia BC. The three principal ones (Cleal *et al.* 1995) consist of:

(I)   A typical henge with a bank and ditch; a series of 56 Aubrey holes which held timber posts (Lawson 1997) formed a circle within the bank and ditch. None of the large stones were present yet; the sediments at the bottom of the Aubrey holes contained no debris from stoneworking. This first phase probably dates to the later Neolithic around the end of the fourth and into the third millenia BC (Bayliss *et al.* 1997)

(II) The second phase saw the silting of the ditch; cremation burials were cut into Aubrey holes. A number of timber structures were built. Atkinson's excavations (1979) revealed holes which had apparently been only partially dug in the north-western quarter. This phase started in the late third millennium and is therefore of early Bronze Age date (Bayliss *et al.* 1997).

(III) In the third phase the stone settings were constructed. It would originally have consisted of 85 stones, of which 51 dressed stones remain today. Both the outer circle of pairs and the inner horseshoe were surmounted by stone lintels. At the entrance to the embanked area two further stones were erected; one, 'the Slaughter Stone', survives. An oval arrangement of stones was constructed within the horseshoe arrangement; the stone holes which provide the evidence for this suggest 18 uprights were involved. The largest stones were used in the central pair of uprights in the horseshoe, the surviving one standing to 6.7 m in height and with 2.4 m below ground it weighs around 50 tonnes. The Sarsen Circle was in place by 2620–2480 cal BC; the remodelling of the bluestones into the circle and horseshoe occurred by 2280–2030 cal BC and 2270–1930 cal BC (Bayliss *et al.* 1997: 56).

A later sub-phase of building involved a further configuration of bluestones, with a horseshoe being constructed within the sarsen horseshoe and a circle between the sarsen horseshoe and the sarsen circle. Later still a circle of (Y and Z) holes was dug outside the sarsen circle and it is clear that they were not used for stone uprights. The remains that can be visited today date to *c.* 1800 BC.

A lot has been written about the origins of the stones at Stonehenge and there are many arguments about their geological origins. There is no argument about the sources of the sarsens found there. They are widely encountered in southern England and are considered to have been the result of silicification affecting sand in the Lower Tertiary formations (Summerfield and Goudie 1980). Green (1997: 5–6) argues convincingly that sarsens *of sufficient size* are unlikely to have been deposited by glacial action of Salisbury Plain and that they would have derived from the Marlborough Downs more than 20 km to the north.

The source of the bluestones, a spotted dolerite, has been established with almost complete confidence to the Preseli mountains in south-west Wales. Petrological investigations started as early as 1878 (Maskelyne 1878). The means by which the stones arrived at Stonehenge, however, has provided meat for a long string of research papers and the use of an intriguing range of scientific techniques. The stones were either deposited in the area of Stonehenge on Salisbury Plain by glacial action, although this area today is virtually devoid of such stones, or they were transported from south Wales by prehistoric man. If the latter interpretation is accepted, then clearly the implications for the organisation of labour are enormous; Colin Renfrew has suggested that 30 million man-hours would have been needed to construct the site.

Recent analytical research by Williams-Thorpe and Thorpe (1992) has involved a detailed investigation of the sources of the bluestones. By chemically analysing 15 Stonehenge monoliths and 22 excavated volcanic bluestone fragments from Stonehenge, they have shown that 30 are basaltic dolerite, something that had been known for a while (Thomas 1923), but that, in addition, 5 are rhyolite, 5 are other volcanic materials and 3 are sandstone. They also investigated the possible sources of the bluestones. Eleven of the dolerites that they tested were found to have derived from *at least* 3 different *loci* in the Preseli Hills; the spotted and unspotted dolerites derived from an area within a radius of 1.75 km, or possibly 0.5 km (Green 1997: 7). On the other hand the rhyolites came from 4 other sources which were fairly close to the Preseli Hills, 1 about 8 km from the edge of the dolerite distribution, 2 in northern Pembrokeshire and a fourth more generally in Pembrokeshire. Twenty-two volcanic bluestone fragments (9 dolerites and 13 rhyolites) which had been excavated from Stonehenge were also chemically analysed. All except one of these could be sourced to the same area as most monolith samples, in the eastern Preseli Hills. The remaining one, a rhyolite sample, derived from a *locus* about 2 km away in north Pembrokeshire. This research clearly revealed incontrovertible evidence for the exploitation of stones from the same general area, but that within that area, stone from a number of sites was used.

One particular question therefore needs to be addressed: if the stones were deliberately quarried and transported by man why did they not stick to one source? *For the stones that have been tested* the majority did derive from a small number of sources which were relatively close to each other. If most of the stones had derived from a range of widely spaced

locations the inference would be that the stones were probably transported by glacial action long before Stonehenge was constructed.

However, there is only equivocal evidence that the Anglian glaciation of 400,000 years ago deposited material on or near Salisbury Plain (Green 1997: 8–9). A more likely interpretation is that its route from the Irish Sea, and perhaps from as far as Scotland stopped at the Bristol Channel. Williams-Thorpe and Thorpe suggest, nevertheless, that the bluestones were glacial erratics dropped by an ice-sheet close to Salisbury Plain. The available evidence for the use of stone to build other British and Continental prehistoric megalithic structures indicates that stones were generally only moved over distances of 5 km or less (Thorpe and Williams-Thorpe 1991). However, Green (1997: 8) raises the point that if the ice sheet had traversed a range of durable rock types why was it that rocks from a relatively limited geographical area were deposited on Salisbury Plain. Green's own investigation of terrace sediments of rivers draining Salisbury Plain (1973) including 50,000 pebbles, where bluestone erratics would be expected to turn up, has drawn a blank. An early reference by De Luc (1811) to volcanic rocks being strewn across Salisbury Plain has been used as evidence that they were available in the early nineteenth century, so would also have been available in prehistory. However, this reference has now been discounted (Green 1997: 8) because it refers to deposits in the Midlands.

Up to this point, the balance of argument would appear to be in favour of the transport of stones from south Wales by humans, not by glacial action. The results of yet another scientific technique, chlorine-36, can now be brought into play. The principles of this technique are that the chlorine-36 atoms start to decay as soon as the rock face is exposed and that the ratio of chlorine-36 and its stable form can provide an estimate of the period for which the rock was exposed. Early results from the analysis of a fragment of bluestone excavated by Richard Atkinson (Bowen 1995) suggest that it was first exposed towards the end of the last glaciation. This might indicate that it could not have been transported by glacial action – unless, that is, it was transported by earlier glacial action. Another possible (likely) scenario could result from the bluestones being worked at the site of Stonehenge, whether they had been transported there by man or by glacial action, producing the same result. Clearly when chlorine-36 determinations are carried out on a much larger number of samples, a more balanced result will be obtained (Green 1997a: 305).

6.8 Stone axe studies

Moving on to other studies, the examination of British Neolithic stone axes by thin-section petrology has led to the identification of several sources of stone for the axes. While the mineralogical and geological description of many stone axes has been carried out, only a small proportion of the possible natural sources have been similarly characterised. Two such sources and associated distribution zones are axes of group VII, an augite-granophyre outcrop at Graig Lwyd, Gwynedd, Wales (Keiller *et al.* 1941), and group XX (Shotton 1959), an epidotised ashy grit which probably has its source in the Charnwood Forest area of Leicestershire in England. Though the exact source in Charnwood Forest is unlocated, fragments apparently also occur in Iron Age and early medieval pottery (see sections 4.4.2 and 4.5.2.2) (Cummins and Moore 1973; Cummins 1979; see also Clough and Cummins 1988: maps 7 and 17). Cummins (1979) produced a cumulative axe frequency graph which is the inverse of the decay function used by Renfrew for obsidian. It is evident that the number of axes in the distribution zone starts tailing off markedly after about 300 km from the source. The reasons why the distribution of axes extends so far from the source *may* be related to their essential use in forest clearance in the Neolithic, or alternatively their function as prestigious items. Careful measurement and statistical and contextual analysis of the axe groupings by Hodder and Lane (1984) indicates that group VII, and group XX axes get sharper with distance from source, and that for group VII in particular the length and cutting edge of the axes changes in a regular way. Both group VII and group XX axes decrease in length with distance from source, the axes being sharpened or broken down and re-used for what may have been utilitarian functions. Also, certain larger axes found close to the

sources apparently show fewer signs of use; a possible prestige non-utilitarian function can be suggested for them.

Darvill (1989) published a discussion of the circulation of stone and flint axes. Although his data agree with Hodder and Lane's (1982) data in showing that the overall length of group VII axes decreases from source and also that the greatest density occurs around the source, he points out (as Ammerman does with obsidian) that unless stone, flint axes and other stone types are studied together as a complete assemblage, the relative contributions of specific sources to the axe population of a given area will be false and the interpretation of national distribution patterns misleading. There may however be difficulties in making direct comparisons between the distributions of different materials since, when broken, flint may be more easily re-used than a stone axe, and flint is rather more difficult to chemically characterise (see Section 6.5 above; see also Matiskainen *et al.* 1979). Darvill also tentatively identified three main types of distribution patterns: regional, local and waterborne, the last being a distinctively coastal/riverine variation of the regional distribution pattern. He has suggested gift exchange, seasonal migrations and pastoral communication as distribution mechanisms, though exchange between cultivators and herdsmen cannot be ruled out. The use of the term 'trade' as an explanatory term for axe distributions by Cummins (1974) seems inappropriate; the actual social and economic contexts in which Neolithic stone axes changed hands are difficult to prove, though the distribution patterns are nonetheless worth attempting to explain.

Work on group VI axes of the Great Langdale/ Scafell Pike area of Cumbria, originally designated group VI on the basis of its petrology (Keiller *et al.* 1941), has advanced through a comprehensive survey (Quartermaine and Claris 1986; Bradley and Edmunds 1988; 1993), with the result that mineralogical and textural definitions of the sites where axes were made are now much better than those made in the original study. The tuff was found to have various new mineralogical characteristics (epidote and scapolite) which enabled Claris *et al.* (1989) to localise the origin of the stone used. This has helped to characterise and locate the sources of the stone in a way which had not been possible before. McVicar (1982) interpreted the gradual decrease in axe length from the source among communities in the Western Isles as indicating that access to the supply was relatively easy and reasonably direct. The distribution showed a marked fall-off towards more distant communities; as in the previous example, the axes were probably being kept longer because damaged specimens were resharpened before being finally discarded. Access to stone may have been reasonably easy close to the source, but not as the distance from the source increased.

Bradley (1984) has interpreted several other characteristics of stone axe distributions. His recognition of clusters of 'foreign' axes at the outer limits of axe distributions (e.g. group VII axes from north Wales) may constitute evidence for some form of 'directional trade' under political control and increasingly specialised treatment afforded to stone axes (e.g. conversion to mace heads) once they have left their areas of origin may turn out to be a significant factor (Bradley 1990: 303). In general, there is little evidence for a strong 'political' direction from axe production at quarries, and although henge monuments can be sited close to major lithic sources, with little apparent evidence for influencing the 'axe trade', there is some evidence for specialised deposits of artefacts in and around ceremonial centres (Bradley and Edmonds 1988: 183). As a means of examining the functionality of stone axes Bradley *et al.* (1992) have investigated the tensile strength of various stone sources used to make axes. For example, they have found that the Langdale and Graig Lwyd axes had a higher tensile strength than porcellanites from North Antrim, Northern Ireland (see below). Sheridan (1986: 20) has pointed out that the distribution of group IX porcellanite axes extended well into Britain, and this is in spite of their lower tensile strength. On the other hand group VI Langdale axes with greater tensile strength rarely occur in Ireland (Jope and Preston 1953). There are several ways of interpreting this result. It is possible that the difference in tensile strength was not sufficiently great to affect the use to which they were put. Alternatively if the 'use' was purely ritual then other characteristics such as colour and texture might have been considered to have had greater importance and determined the axe distribution.

Indeed, consideration of the tensile strength of stone axes in Great Langdale, Cumbria and other areas by Bradley *et al.* (1992) has provided an important means of assessing whether the use of stone with a particular strength played an important part in determining the kind of rock used or whether other explanations need to be put forward. The tensile strengths determined for Great Langdale rocks ranged between 34.2±3.2 MPa and 42.0±2.1 MPa which are higher values than most major rocks types from Britain. They showed that although on a local level in Cumbria (especially in Great Langdale) there was some evidence for the use of stone with greater tensile strength to make axes, the evidence also showed that better quality rock was not worked on a larger scale than the lower quality rock. In general, the situation they discovered was far from simple. Loft Crag, for example, which was easy to reach and which had rock with the second highest tensile strength out of eight quarry locations tested (Bradley *et al.*: 1992, Table 1), was only used to a limited extent. Sites where rocks with some of the lowest tensile strength had been extracted and worked covered about the same area as sites where rocks with the highest tensile strength had been extracted and worked. One suggestion is that production of axes in different locations in Great Langdale may have been controlled by particular individuals or communities (Bradley and Suthren 1990) and that access to some outcrops was restricted for some reason. It was clear from this research that utilitarian considerations were just one of a range of reasons why particular stone sources were exploited and that they certainly did not determine the form of Neolithic 'axe trade'. The work with northern Irish porcellanite also serves to underline this finding in a powerful way.

A major source of stone used for the manufacture of Neolithic axes was porcellanite, a hard contact metamorphic rock which formed from the contrasting primary lithologies of highly weathered basalt and Jurassic clay. Knowles (1903; 1906) and Mallory (1990) have clearly recognised the evidence for the working of porcellanite into axes at Tievebulliagh near Cushendall and at Brockley on Rathlin Island, Co. Antrim, Northern Ireland. Keiller *et al.* (1941) allocated this to group IX. At Tievebulliagh, Mallory (1990) showed that scree materials appeared to have been used for making axes, whereas for the second source, at Brockley, fire setting was almost certainly used in the mining operations.

Meighan *et al.* (1993) have determined trace element levels in porcellanites from North Antrim using wavelength-dispersive X-ray fluorescence analysis and determined their mineralogical compositions using X-ray diffraction. In addition they used strontium isotope determinations to attempt to determine provenances. The trace element analyses showed that they could distinguish between porcellanites from first Portrush and second Tievebulliagh, and Brockley on Rathlin Island. Their formation by contact metamorphism of Jurassic clay and Tertiary basalt respectively led to these geochemical differences. Although formed under similar conditions, Tievebulliagh and Brockley are 26.5 km apart and on opposite sides of a major Tertiary 'divide', the Tow Valley Fault, so for them to have exactly the same major/trace element and isotopic signatures would be exceptional. Meighan *et al.* (1993: 27, Figure 2a) have demonstrated, although with rather small numbers, that a plot of the relative levels of strontium and calcium does discriminate not only (as expected) between Portrush and Tievebulliagh, but also between Brockley and the other two. Strontium isotope analysis also distinguishes between the three sources (ibid.: Figure 2b).

In comparison with the Great Langdale, Cumbria, source many more examples of porcellanite axes have been found: some 6,400 compared to 1,612 (Clough 1988: 4). Martyn Jope (1952) carried out early work on the occurrence of porcellanite, with the number of examples being increased by Sheridan (1986) and by Cooney *et al.* (1994). Given that porcellanites were used so extensively in the Neolithic, if the characterisation by Meighan *et al.* (1993) holds up for samples which derive from securely dated archaeolgical contexts, then it will be possible to examine the form of distribution patterns associated with *each* of the three porcellanite sources: whether they display boundedness, whether there is a chronological distinction in the use of the three sources and whether they occur on particular site types.

Over and above the work with stone axes the results of these research projects are a good example of how easy it might be to make false assumptions about the use of raw materials in the past based solely on their material properties and to ignore aspects of human behaviour which determine their use and which are unconnected to positivism. Ethnographic studies of stone axe production make this clear (Burton 1987), even though some workers ignore completely the results of research which shows that approaches based purely on features found in capitalist societies (Steinberg and Pletka 1997) are inappropriate.

References

Allan, R.O., Luckenbach, A.H. and Holland, C.G. (1975) 'The application of instrumental neutron activation analysis to a study of prehistoric steatite artefacts and source materials', *Archaeometry* 17, 1: 69–83.

Ammerman, A.J. (1979) 'A study of obsidian exchange networks in Calabria', *World Archaeology* 11: 95–110.

— and Andrefsky, W. (1982) 'Reduction sequences and the exchange of obsidian in Neolithic Calabria', in J.E. Ericson and T. Earle (eds), *Contexts for Prehistoric Exchange*, New York: Academic Press, pp. 149–72.

——, Cesana, A., Polglase, C. and Terrani, M. (1990) 'Neutron activation analysis of obsidian from two Neolithic sites in Italy', *Journal of Archaeological Science* 17: 209–20.

Aspinall, A. and Feather, S.W. (1972) 'Neutron activation analysis of prehistoric flint mine products', *Archaeometry* 14, 1: 41–54.

——, —— and Phillips, A.P. (1975) 'Preliminary analyses of French flint samples', in F.H.C. Engelen (ed.), *Proceedings of the Second International Symposium on Flint*, Maastricht, Netherlands, 8–11 May 1975, Nederlandse Geol. Vereniging, Maastricht (Staringia no. 3), pp. 42–6.

Atkinson, R.J.C. (1979) *Stonehenge: Archaeology and Interpretation*, Harmondsworth: Penguin.

Bayliss, A., Bronk Ramsey, C. and McCormac, F.G. (1997) 'Dating Stonehenge', in B. Cunliffe and C. Renfrew (eds) *Science and Stonehenge*, Proceedings of the British Academy 92 Oxford: Oxford University Press, pp. 39–60.

Blackman, M.J. (1984) 'Provenance studies of Middle Eastern obsidian from sites in Highland Iran', in J.B. Lambert (ed.), *Archaeological Chemistry II*, American Ceramic Society, Advances in Chemistry Series no. 205, Columbus, Ohio: American Ceramic Society, pp. 19–50.

Bowen, D.Q. (1995) 'Late Cenozoic Wales and south-west England', *Proceedings of the Ussher Society* 8: 208–13.

Bowman, H.R., Asaro, F. and Perlman, I. (1973) 'Composition variations in obsidian sources and the archaeological implications', *Archaeometry* 15: 123–7.

Bradley, R. (1984) *The Social Foundations of Prehistoric Britain*, London: Longman.

—— (1990) 'Perforated stone axe-heads in the British Neolithic: their distribution and significance', *Oxford Journal of Archaeology* 9, 3: 299–304.

—— and Edmonds, M. (1988) 'Fieldwork at Great Langdale, Cumbria 1985–1987: preliminary report', *The Antiquaries Journal* 68: 181–209.

—— and —— (1993) *Interpreting the Axe Trade. Production and Exchange in Neolithic Britain*, Cambridge: Cambridge University Press.

——, Meredith, P., Smith, J. and Edmonds, M. (1992) 'Rock physics and the Neolithic axe trade in Britain', *Archaeometry* 34, 2: 223–33.

—— and Suthren, R. (1990) 'Petrographic analysis of hammerstones from the Neolithic quarries at Great Langdale', *Proceedings of the Prehistoric Society* 56: 117–22.

Burton, J. (1987) 'Exchange pathways at a stone axe factory in Papua New Guinea', in *The Human Uses of Flint and Chert*, in G. de G. Sieveking and M.H. Newcomer (eds), Proceedings of the Fourth International Flint Symposium, Brighton Polytechnic, 10–15 April 1983, Cambridge: Cambridge University Press, pp. 183–91.

Cackler, P.R., Glascock, M.D., Neff, H., Iceland, H., Pyburn, K.A., Hudler, D., Hester, T.R. and Chiarulli, B.M. (1999) 'Chipped stone artefacts, source areas, and provenance studies of the Northern Belize chert-bearing zone', *Journal of Archaeological Science* 26, 4: 389–97.

Cann, J.R. and Renfrew, C. (1964) 'The characterization of obsidian and its application to the Mediterranean region', *Proceedings of the Prehistoric Society* 30: 111–33.

Chippindale, C.C. (1983) *Stonehenge Complete*, London: Thames and Hudson.

Claris, P. and Quartermaine, J. (1989) 'The Neolithic quarries and axe factory sites of Great Langdale and Scafell Pike: a new field survey', *Proceedings of the Prehistoric Society* 55: 1–26.

Cleal, M.J., Walker, K.E. and Montague, R. (1995) *Stonehenge in its Landscape*, London: English Heritage.

Clough, T.H. McK. (1988) 'Introduction to the regional reports: prehistoric stone implements in the British Isles', in T.H. McK. Clough and W.A. Cummins (eds), *Stone Axe Studies, The petrology of prehistoric stone implements from the British Isles* vol. II, Council for British Archaeology Research Report no. 67, London: Council for British Archaeology, pp. 1–11.

—— and Cummins, W.A. (eds) (1988) *Stone Axe Studies, The petrology of prehistoric stone implements from the British Isles* vol. II, Council for British Archaeology Research Report no. 67, London: Council for British Archaeology.

—— and —— (1988a) 'The petrological identification of stone implements from the east Midlands: third report', in T.H. McK. Clough and W.A. Cummins (eds), *Stone Axe Studies, The petrology of prehistoric stone implements from the British Isles* vol. II, Council for British Archaeology Research Report no. 67, London: Council for British Archaeology, pp. 41–4.

Consigny, S. (1992) *Méthode géochimique et origine des silex archéologiques*, Memoire de Maîtrise de Préhistoire de l'Université de Paris I.

—— and Walter, P. (1997) 'Flint origin and ion beam analysis: archaeological results in the Paris basin, France', in R. Schild and Z. Sulgostowska (eds), *Man and Flint*, Proceedings of the VIIth International Flint Symposium, September 1995, Institute of Archaeology and Ethnology, Warszawa: Polish Academy of Sciences, pp. 337–42.

Cooney, G., Mandal, S. and O'Carroll, F. (1994) 'Review of the Work of the Irish Stone Axe Project 1991–1993', unpublished report, Dublin.

Cowell, M.R. (1979) 'The archaeological and geochemical implications of trace element distributions in some English, Dutch and Belgian flints', in F.H.C. Engelen (ed.), *Proceedings of the Third International Symposium on Flint*, Maastricht, Netherlands, Nederlandse Geol. Vereniging, Maastricht (Staringia no. 6), pp. 81–4.

——, Ferguson, J. and Hughes, M.J. (1980) 'Geochemical variations in East Anglian flint with particular reference to Grimes Graves flint mines', in E.A. Slater and J.O. Tate (eds), *Proceedings of the 16th International Symposium on Archaeometry and Archaeological Prospection*, Edinburgh 1976, Edinburgh: National Museums of Antiquaries of Scotland, pp. 80–9.

Craddock, P.T., Cowell, M.R., Leese, M.N. and Hughes, M.J. (1983) 'The trace element composition of polished flint axes as an indicator of source', *Archaeometry* 25, 2: 135–64.

Cummins, W.A. (1974) 'The Neolithic stone axe trade in Britain', *Antiquity* 48: 201–5.

—— (1979) 'Neolithic stone axes: distribution and trade in England and Wales', in T.H. McK. Clough and W.A. Cummins (eds), *Stone Axe Studies*, Council for British Archaeology Research Report 23, London: Council for British Archaeology, pp. 5–12.

—— and Moore, C.N. (1973) 'Petrological identification of stone implements from Lincolnshire, Nottinghamshire and Rutland', *Proceedings of the Prehistoric Society* 39: 219–55.

Darvill, T. (1989) 'The circulation of neolithic stone and flint axes: a case study from Wales and the mid-west of England', *Proceedings of the Prehistoric Society* 55: 27–44.

De Bruin, M., Korthoven, P.J.M., Bakels, C.C. and Groen, F.C.A. (1972) 'The use of non-destructive activation analysis and pattern recognition in the study of flint artefacts', *Archaeometry* 14, 1: 55–63.

De Luc, J.A. (1811) *Geological Travels. Volume III. Travels in England*, London: F.C. and J. Rivington.

Doran, J.E. and Hodson, F.R. (1975) *Mathematics and Computers in Archaeology*, Edinburgh: Edinburgh University Press.

Ericson, J.E. (1988) 'Obsidian hydration rate development', in E.V. Sayre, P. Vandiver, J. Druzik and C. Stevenson (eds), *Materials Issues in Art and Archaeology*, Proceedings of the Materials Research Society, vol. 123, Reno, Nevada 1988, Materials Research Society, Pittsburgh, pp. 215–24.

Findow, F.J. and Bolognese, M. (1982) 'Regional modeling of obsidian procurement in the American Southwest', in J.E. Ericson and T.K. Earle (eds), *Contexts for Prehistoric Exchange*, New York: Academic Press, Chapter 3.

Francaviglia, V. (1988) 'Ancient obsidian sources on Pantelleria (Italy)', *Journal of Archaeological Science* 15: 109–22.

Gordus, A.A., Wright, G.A. and Griffin, J.B. (1968) 'Obsidian sources characterized by Neutron Activation Analysis', *Science* 161: 382–4.

Gowlett, J. and Henderson, J. (forthcoming) 'Scientific analysis and sourcing of obsidian from East Africa'.

Gratuze, B. (1999) 'Obsidian characterization by laser ablation ICP-MS and its application to prehistoric trade in the Mediterranean and the Near East: sources and distribution of obsidian within the Aegean and Anatolia', in J. Henderson, H. Neff and T. Rehren (eds), Proceedings of the International Symposium on Archaeometry, University of Illinois at Urbana-Champaign (UIUC), Urbana, Illinois, 20–4 May 1996, *Journal of Archaeological Science* 26, 8: 869–82.

Green, C.P. (1973) 'Pleistocene gravels and the Stonehenge problem', *Nature* 243: 214–16.

—— (1997) 'Stonehenge: geology and prehistory', *Proceedings of the Geologists' Association* 108, 1: 1–10.

—— (1997a) 'The provenance of rocks used in the construction of Stonehenge', in B. Cunliffe and C. Renfrew (eds) *Science and Stonehenge*, Proceedings of the British Academy 92, Oxford: Oxford University Press, pp. 257–70.

Hallam, B.R., Warren, S.E. and Renfrew, A.C. (1976) 'Obsidian in the western Mediterranean: characterization by neutron activation analysis and optical emission spectroscopy', *Proceedings of the Prehistoric Society* 42: 85–110.

Heyworth, M.P., Hunter, J.R., Warren, S.E. and Walsh, J.N. (1988) 'The analysis of archaeological materials using inductively-coupled plasma spectrometry', in E.A. Slater and J.O. Tate (eds), *Science and Archaeology, Glasgow 1987*, British Archaeological Reports series 196, Oxford: British Archaeological Reports, pp. 27–40.

Hoard, R.J., Bozell, J.R., Holen, S.R., Glascock, M.D., Neff, H. and Elam, J.M. (1993) 'Source determination of White river group silicates from two archaeological sites in the Great Plains', *American Antiquity* 58, 4: 698–710.

——, Holen, S.R., Glascock, M.D., Neff, H. and Elam, M.J. (1992) 'Neutron activation analysis of stone from the chadron formation and a Clovis site on the Great Plains', *Journal of Archaeological Science* 19: 655–65.

Hodder, I. and Lane, P. (1982) 'A contextual examination of Neolithic stone axe distribution in Britain', in J.E. Ericson and T.K. Earle (eds), *Contexts for Prehistoric Exchange*, New York: Academic Press, Chapter 10, pp. 213–35.

Holmes, L.L. and Harbottle G. (1994) 'Compositional characterization of French limestone: a new tool for art historians', *Archaeometry* 36, 1: 25–39.

Hudler, D., Iceland, H., Cackler, P.R. and Glascock, M.D. (1996) 'A sourcing study of preceramic constricted unifaces in northern Belize', a paper presented at the 1st Annual Meeting of the Society of American Archaeology, 10–14 April 1996, New Orleans.

Hughes, R.E. (1994) 'Intrasource chemical variability of artefact-quality obsidians from the Casa Diablo area, California', *Journal of Archaeological Science* 21: 263–71.

Jack, R.N. (1976) 'Prehistoric obsidian in California I. Geochemical aspects', in Taylor, R.E (ed.), *Advances in Obsidian Glass Studies*, Park Ridge, New Jersey: Noyes Press, pp. 183–217.

Jope, E.M. (1952) 'Porcellanite axes from factories in north-east Ireland: Tievebulliagh and Rathlin. Part I. Archaeological Survey', *Ulster Journal of Archaeology* 15: 31–55.

—— (1989) 'Preface', in J. Henderson (ed.), *Scientific Analysis in Archaeology and its interpretation*, Oxford Committee on Archaeology, Monograph no. 19 and UCLA Institute of Archaeology, Archaeological Research Tools 5, Oxford: Oxford University Committee on Archaeology, pp. xi–xv.

—— and Preston, J. (1953) 'An axe of stone from Great Langdale, Lake District, found in County Antrim', *Ulster Journal of Archaeology* 49: 19–32.

Keiller, A., Piggott, S. and Wallis, F.S. (1941) 'First report of the Sub-Committee of the South-Western Group of Museums and Art Galleries on the petrological identification of stone axes', *Proceedings of the Prehistoric Society* 7: 50–72.

Kilikoglou, V., Bassiakos, Y., Grimanis, A.P. and Souvatzis, K. (1996) 'Carpathian obsidian in Macedonia, Greece', *Journal of Archaeological Science* 23: 343–9.

Knowles, W.J. (1903) 'Stone axe factories near Cushendall', *Journal of the Royal Anthropological Institute* 33: 360–6.

—— (1906) 'Stone axe factories near Cushendall', *Journal of the Royal Society of Antiquaries of Ireland* 36: 383–94.

Kohl, P.L., Harbottle, G. and Sayre, E.V. (1979) 'Physical and chemical analyses of soft stone vessels from Southwest Asia', *Archaeometry* 21, 1: 131–59.

Lawson, A.J. (1997) 'The Structural History of Stonehenge', in B. Cunliffe and C. Renfrew (eds) *Science and Stonehenge*, Proceedings of the British Academy 92, Oxford: Oxford University Press, pp. 15–38.

Luetke (1978) 'Chert sources and trace-element analysis', *American Antiquity* 43, 3: 413–23.

Luedtke, B.E. (1979) 'The identification of sources of chert artefacts', *American Antiquity* 44, 4: 744–57.

Mallory, J.P. (1990) 'Trial excavations at Tievebulliagh, Co. Antrim', *Ulster Journal of Archaeology* 53: 15–28.

Maskelyne, N.S. (1878) 'Stonehenge: the petrology of its stones', *Wiltshire Archaeological and Natural History Magazine* 17: 147–60.

Matiskainen, H., Vuorinen, A. and Burman, O. (1979) 'The provenance of prehistoric flint in Finland', in Y. Maniatis (ed.), *Archaeometry*, Proceedings of the 20th International Symposium, Athens, Greece, Oxford: Elsevier.

McDonald, R., Smith, R.L. and Thomas, J.E. (1992) *Chemistry of the Subalkalic Silicic Obsidians*, US Geological Survey Professional Paper 1523, Washington: The US Geological Survey.

McVicar, J.B. (1982) 'The spatial analysis of axe size and the Scottish axe distribution', *Archaeological Reviews from Cambridge* 1, 2: 30–45.

Meighan, I.C., Jamison, D.D., Logue, P.J.C., Mallory, J.P., Simpson, D.D.A., Rogers, G., Mandal, S. and Cooney, G. (1993) 'Trace element and isotopic provenancing of north Antrim porcellanites: Portrush – Tievebulliagh – Brockley (Rathlin Island)', *Ulster Journal of Archaeology* 56: 25–30.

Merrick, H.V. and Brown, F.H. (1984) 'Rapid chemical characterization of obsidian artefacts by electron microprobe analysis', *Archaeometry* 26: 230–6.

Michels, J.W. (1982) 'Bulk element composition versus trace element composition in the reconstruction of an obsidian source system', *Journal of Archaeological Science* 9: 113–23.

—— , Tsong, I.S.T. and Nelson, C.M. (1983) 'Obsidian dating and East African Archaeology', *Science* 219: 361–6.

Moorey, P.R.S. (1994) *Ancient Mesopotamian Materials and Industries*, Oxford: Clarendon Press.

Peacock, D.P.S. and Maxfield, V.A. (1997) *Survey and Excavation at Mons Claudianus, volume 1 Topography and Quarries*, Le Claire: Institut Français d'archéologie orientale.

Perlès, C. (1987) *Les Industries Lithiques Taillées de Franchthi (Argolide, Grèce), Tome I, Présentation générale et industries paléolithiques, Excavations at Franchthi, Greece*, Fascicule 3, Bloomington and Indianapolis: Indiana University Press.

—— (1992) 'Systems of exchange and organisation of production in Neolithic Greece', *Journal of Mediterranean Archaeology* 5: 115–64.

Pigeot, N. (1987) *Magdaléniens d'Etiolles, économie de débitage et organisation sociale unité d'habitation*, 25e supplément à Gallia-Préhistoire.

Pollard, A.M. and Heron, C. (1996) *Archaeological Chemistry*, London: Royal Society of Chemistry.

Quartermaine, J. and Claris, P. (1986) 'The Langdale axe factories', *Current Archaeology* 102: 212–13.

Randle, K., Barfield, L.H. and Bagolini, B. (1993) 'Recent Italian obsidian analyses', *Journal of Archaeological Science* 20: 503–9.

Renfrew, C. (1972) *The Emergence of Civilisation*, London: Methuen.

—— (1975) 'Trade and action at a distance: questions of integration and communication', in J. Sabloff and C.C. Lamberg-Karlovsky (eds), *Ancient Civilization and Trade*, Albuquerque: University of New Mexico Press, pp. 3–59.

—— (1977) 'Alternative models for exchange and spatial distribution', in T. Earle and J.E. Ericson (eds), *Exchange Systems in Prehistory*, New York: Academic Press, pp. 71–90.

—— and Aspinall, A. (1990) 'Aegean obsidian and Franchthi Cave', in C. Pèrles (ed.), *Les Industries Lithiques de Franchthi (Argolide, Grèce), Tome II: Les Industries du Mésolithique et du Néolithique Initial, Fasicule 5*, Bloomington and Indianapolis: Indiana University Press, pp. 258–70.

—— , Cann, J.R. and Dixon, J.E. (1965) 'Obsidian in the Aegean', *Annals of the British School of Athens* 60: 225–47.

—— , Dixon, J.E. and Cann, J.R. (1966) 'Obsidian and early cultural context in the Near East', *Proceedings of the Prehistoric Society* 32: 30–72.

—— , —— and —— (1968) 'Further analysis of Near Eastern obsidians', *Proceedings of the Prehistoric Society* 30: 319–31.

Sheridan, J.A. (1986) 'Porcellanite artifacts: a new survey', *Ulster Journal of Archaeology* 49: 19–32.

Shotton, F.W. (1959) 'New petrological groups based on axes from the West Midlands', *Proceedings of the Prehistoric Society* 25: 135–43.

Sieveking, G. de G., Craddock, P.T., Hughes, M.J., Bush, P. and Ferguson, J. (1970) 'Characterization of flint mine products', *Nature* 228: 251–4.

Steinberg, J.M. and Pletka, B.J. (1997) 'The value of flint in Thy, Denmark', in R. Schild and Z. Sulgostowska (eds), *Man and Flint*, Proceedings of the VIIth International Flint Symposium, September 1995, Warszawa: Institute of Archaeology and Ethnology, Polish Academy of Sciences, pp. 337–42.

Summerfield, M.A. and Goudie, A.S. (1980) 'The sarsens of southern England: their palaeoenvironmental interpretation with reference to other silicretes', in D.K.C. Jones (ed.), *The Shaping of Southern England*, London: Academic Press.

Thomas, H.H. (1923) 'The source of the stones of Stonehenge', *Antiquaries Journal* 3: 239–60.

Thompson, M., Bush, P.R. and Ferguson, J. (1986) 'The analysis of flint by inductively coupled plasma atomic emission spectroscopy, as a method of source determination', in G. de G. Sieveking and M.B. Hart (eds),

The Scientific Study of Flint and Chert, Proceedings of the Fourth International Flint Symposium held at Brighton Polytechnic, 10–15 April 1983, Cambridge: Cambridge University Press, pp. 243–7.

Thorpe, R.S. and Williams-Thorpe, O.W. (1991) 'The myth of long-distance megalithic transport', *Antiquity* 65: 64–73.

Torrence, R. (1986) *Production and Exchange of Stone Tools*, Cambridge: Cambridge University Press.

Tykot, R.H. (1992) 'The sources and distribution of Sardinian obsidian', in R.H. Tykot and T.K. Andrews (eds), *Sardinia in the Mediterranean: A Footprint in the Sea. Studies in Sardinian Archaeology Presented to Miriam S. Balmuth*, Sheffield: Sheffield Academic Press, pp. 57–70.

—— (1997a) 'Characterization of the Monte Arci (Sardinia) obsidian sources', *Journal of Archaeological Science* 24: 467–79.

—— (1997b) 'Mediterranean islands and multiple flows: the sources and exploitation of Sardinian obsidian', in M.S. Shackley (ed.), *Method and Theory in Archaeological Volcanic Glass Studies*, Advances in Archaeological and Museum Science Series, New York: Plenum Press.

Weisgerber, G. (1987) 'The ancient chert mines at Wadi el-Sheikh (Egypt)', in G. de G. Sieveking and M.H. Newcomer (eds), *The Human Uses of Flint and Chert*, Proceedings of the Fourth International Flint Symposium held at Brighton Polytechnic, 10–15 April 1983, Cambridge: Cambridge University Press, pp. 165–72.

Williams-Thorpe O.W., Warren, S.E. and Courtin, J. (1984) 'The distribution and sources of archaeological obsidian from southern France', *Journal of Archaeological Science* 11: 135–46.

——, and Thorpe, R. (1992) 'Geochemistry, sources and transport of the Stonehenge Bluestones', in A.M. Pollard (ed.), *New Developments in Archaeological Science, Proceedings of the British Academy* 77, Oxford: Oxford University Press, pp. 133–61.

——, Warren, S.E. and Nandris, J.G. (1984) 'The distribution and provenance of archaeological obsidian in central and eastern Europe', *Journal of Archaeological Science* 11: 183–212.

Wright, G.A. (1969) *Obsidian Analyses and Prehistoric Near Eastern Trade: 7500 to 3500 B.C.*, Anthropological papers of the Museum of Anthropology, University of Michigan no. 37, Ann Arbor: University of Michigan.

Yellin, J. (1995) 'Trace element characteristics of Central Anatolian obsidian flows and their relevance to pre history', *Israel Journal of Chemistry* 35: 175–90.

7

ARCHAEOLOGICAL SCIENCE
AND THE WAY FORWARD

Before discussing the way forward for the study of (inorganic and organic) archaeological materials, it is first crucial to identify phases in which archaeological science (of which the study of archaeological materials forms a part) has developed.

Archaeology sits at the centre of an enormous web with links to other disciplines, including not just the biological and physical sciences, but also a wide range of disciplines in the humanities. Clearly scientific archaeology can be approached from a variety of viewpoints. The earliest work in archaeological science included the investigation of ancient technology. A paper published by Humphrey Davy in 1815 involved the investigation of a synthetic pigment made from copper, silica and natron, later known as Egyptian Blue. Another early publication, which was to set an unfortunate trend, although it appeared in Schliemann's excavation report on Mycenae, was the appended chemical analysis of gold, copper and bronze from the site. These investigations in archaeological science are what might be discerned as phase I in the development of archaeological science: 'early stirrings'. At the time when they were carried out, these investigations revealed unexpectedly sophisticated aspects of ancient technologies, but these findings were not fully integrated with archaeology. Such investigations were, in a sense, 'stabs in the dark'.

If we move forward in time to another discernible phase in the development of scientific archaeology, we find that, while, as in the past, analytical techniques were borrowed from disciplines like biology, physics and chemistry, new techniques were emerging which

were designed specifically for the investigation of archaeological objects or materials. One such was the so-called milliprobe, the description of which was published in 1973 by Hall, Schweitzer and Toller. This device focused a beam of X-rays on inorganic materials. The development of the milliprobe was symbolic of the way in which the discipline advanced. Another advance in technique and instrumentation was also made in Oxford: the invention of thermoluminescence as a means of dating pottery, a useful technique which at the time was seen as a supplement to what was perceived as the principal technique, carbon-14 (Aitken 1974; 1990). With these new techniques coming on stream, and with the enormous potential which they offered archaeology, it is clear that this was an exciting growth phase, which we can label phase II: 'the phase of invention'.

Modifications of existing techniques and the use of new techniques in archaeology, such as the introduction of accelerator mass spectrometry for dating minute samples, have both occurred subsequently, but nothing has occurred which is comparable to the phase of what can only be described as *invention*. Another advance (phase III), which can be labelled a 'primary phase of archaeological science research' (as opposed to a phase of purely scientific invention or the determination of certain technological characteristics) was exemplified by Colin Renfrew and his co-workers.

Here a substance (obsidian) which lent itself to chemical characterisation – partly due to the fact that man had *not* modified it at high temperatures – was analysed (see Section 6.6). For the first time, this work by Renfrew provided an example of where optical emission spectrometry produced a series of numbers which could be linked directly to distribution of the material. The use of this first technique was followed by a range of others – neutron activation analysis, X-ray fluorescence spectrometry and electron probe microanalysis. These analyses contributed in a new way. The research into obsidian from the Middle East and southern Europe clearly converted the measurement of the natural characteristics of a material into a reconstruction of man's past behavioural patterns, coming to fruition in the 1970s. This was very different from either the investigation of a small number of archaeological samples to determine certain technological characteristics (phase I) or from the invention of new techniques (phase II).

This point about the interplay between science and archaeology and the ways in which science contributes to archaeology and archaeology to science will be returned to. Suffice to say, that when techniques of scientific analysis are used as investigative tools, the researcher must keep a clear head in defining precisely what it is that he or she is investigating archaeologically. In this case, the fact that obsidian could, in some cases, be sourced to the specific volcano vent which produced it meant that distribution patterns could be assembled around the origin of the obsidian. If one adds to this a consideration of the proportion of other lithics from the sites studied, the kinds of archaeological sites on which the obsidian was found (e.g. whether obsidian was processed there) and the 'significance' of the material to the society involved, a very powerful set of links between chemical analysis, society and technology is produced. It is these *archaeological considerations* which can make the difference between a complex interplay between science and archaeology and what can be a simple statement of scientific facts which sit at the fringe of archaeological endeavour. It is also clear that some research in archaeological science can be technique-driven and some driven by archaeology.

Subsequent scientific characterisation of obsidian use and distribution in Calabria by Ammerman has clearly shown that a solid archaeological framework – starting with a full survey of the archaeological sites in the region on which obsidian was found, consideration of the proportions of lithic material including obsidian on each site, distance from the source and the topography of the region involved – have clearly led to firmly-based models of obsidian use and distribution (see Section 6.6.2).

This phase, in which the archaeological significance of the materials played an important part, continued to strengthen and refine the links between archaeology and science. This surely is the essence of the full interplay between the best science and archaeology. Having emphasised how important the archaeological research framework must be, one should not lose sight for a minute of the critical importance of first-rate science. The conditions in which chemical analysis and dating (for example) are carried out must be monitored very closely – there is absolutely no room for a 'black box' mentality, or one would be accused of pursuing the rubbish in – rubbish out approach to science, based on only a partial understanding of the technique or poor conditions of sample preparation.

In reviewing *Old World Archaeometallurgy* edited by Andreas Hauptmann, Ernst Pernicka and Günther A. Wagner which was published in 1989, Roger Moorey (1991: 118) made the following comments:

Archaeologists have tended to expect miracles of materials science. Conclusions have consequently been drawn too fast from initial, necessarily narrow, databases. The due caution of the specialist has often been lost in cultural conclusions loosely based on their research. Powerful new scientific techniques from time to time open up exciting new horizons to archaeologists, who do not always fully appreciate how treacherously deceptive the results may be unless critically assessed over a period of time as much in geological and metallurgical as in cultural terms.

These comments underline clearly the tension that exists between the different groups of people who regard themselves as archaeological scientists – those with minimal understanding of the science, those with minimal understanding of cultural features and a spectrum of people in between. But it is surely what would be expected in such a multidisciplinary area of research and a relatively new one at that.

An excellent example of where a refined approach to the application of a technique to answering very specific archaeological questions is the use of accelerator mass spectrometry to investigate the re-colonisation of Europe after the last glacial maximum. Housely *et al.* have shown that by examining closely the contexts from which objects were derived and re-dating samples which appeared to be aberrant, a model for the re-colonisation of Europe involving clustered dates was produced, showing, even this far back in time, between 20K and 12K BP that they could identify expansions from refugia and work out the rates at which the expansions in a northerly and a westerly direction from southern and central Europe took place. The broad and important philosophical approach here was to attempt to date the *event*, not simply produce a series of independent dated points. So there is no doubt that such a carefully constructed research project based on clear-headed science with clear objectives, incorporating an environmental component and a careful consideration of other aspects of archaeological context must form the basis for future research in scientific archaeology. I would regard this project as an example of a new phase of research – phase IV: 'holistic archaeological science'.

By reviewing some of the developmental phases of scientific archaeology from early stirrings, through phases of invention, a primary phase of archaeological science research to holistic archaeological science research it is possible to see how the interaction of otherwise discrete disciplines have led to the significant enrichment of archaeology. Funding of archaeological science research will always present a challenge, but there is no harm in striving for a bright future. The careful integration of the application of science to answering archaeological questions in a *holistic* approach to this area of discourse can produce by far the most powerful results with the greatest contribution to mainstream archaeology.

The case studies presented in this book mainly fall into this last kind of archaeological science research – holistic archaeological science – in which a range of approaches to the scientific investigation of ancient materials are brought together so that a clear and meaningful integration with archaeology occurs. The integration relies on successful communication between those involved, especially if they fall at opposite ends of the archaeological science spectrum. The way forward must be a further refinement of the interplay between science and archaeology.

References

Aitken, M.J. (1974) *Physics and Archaeology*, Oxford: Oxford University Press.
—— (1990) *Science-based Dating in Archaeology*, London: Longman.
Davy, H. (1815) 'Some experiments and observations on the colours used in painting by the ancients', *Philosophical Transactions of the Royal Society of London*, 105: 97–124.
Hall, E.T., Schweitzer, F. and Toller, P.A. (1973) 'X-ray fluorescence analysis of museum objects: a new instrument', *Archaeometry* 15: 53–78.
Housley, R.A., Gamble, C.S., Street, M. and Pettitt, P. (1997) 'Radiocarbon evidence for the late glacial human recolonisation of northern Europe', *Proceedings of the Prehistoric Society* 63: 25–54.
Moorey, P.R.S. (1991) 'Review of *Old World Archaeometallurgy*' (eds A. Hauptmann, E. Pernicka and G.A. Wagner, *Der Anschnitt*, Beiheft 7, Deutsches Bergbau-Museum, 1989), *Archaeomaterials* 5, 1: 117–19.

INDEX